THE POEMS OF
PATRICK BRANWELL BRONTË

GARLAND REFERENCE LIBRARY OF THE HUMANITIES
(VOL. 1050)

THE POEMS OF
PATRICK BRANWELL BRONTË
A New Text and Commentary

VICTOR A. NEUFELDT

GARLAND PUBLISHING, INC. • NEW YORK & LONDON
1990

Library of Congress Cataloging-in-Publication Data

Brontë, Patrick Branwell, 1817–1848.
  [Poems. Selections]
  The poems of Patrick Branwell Brontë : a new text and commentary /
[edited by] Victor A. Neufeldt.
      p.   cm. — (Garland reference library of the humanities ; vol.
  1050)
  Includes bibliographical references and index.
  ISBN 0–8240–4590–4 (alk. paper)
  I. Neufeldt, Victor A. II. Title. III. Series.
PR4174.B23A6   1990
821'.8—dc20   90-38464
                                                                    CIP

Printed on acid-free, 250-year-life paper
Manufactured in the United States of America

For Geoffrey, Keith and Karin

CONTENTS

Acknowledgements

It is with pleasure that I acknowledge the cooperation and assistance of the many persons and agencies without whose generous help this work could not have been undertaken.

For their generous financial assistance in the form of various research grants I wish to thank the Social Sciences and Humanities Research Council of Canada and the Office of Research Administration of the University of Victoria, and for its generous secretarial assistance, the Department of English, University of Victoria.

For their permission to reproduce the texts of manuscripts, transcriptions, and letters held by them it is my pleasure to acknowledge the following libraries and individuals: the family of the late C. K. Shorter; the Council of the Brontë Society; Miss Agnes Hatfield; the Brotherton Collection, the Brotherton Library, University of Leeds; the British Library, Department of Manuscripts; the National Library of Scotland, Department of Manuscripts; the Robert H. Taylor Collection, Princeton University Library, the Henry W. and Albert A. Berg Collection, the New York Public Library, Astor, Lenox and Tilden Foundations; the Pierpont Morgan Library; the Houghton Library, Harvard University; the Harry Ransom Humanities Research Center, University of Texas at Austin; Special Collections Division, University of British Columbia; Roger W. Barrett; William Self.

For their assistance in locating and making available materials and answering my numerous queries, I wish to acknowledge the generous assistance of the following individuals: Juliet R. V. Barker, Librarian/Curator, Sally E. Johnson and Kathryn White, Assistant Librarians, Margery Raistrick, Brontë Parsonage Museum; Christopher D. W. Sheppard and staff, Brotherton Collection, University of Leeds; the Keeper and staff, Department of Manuscripts, British Library; the late Thomas I. Rae and staff, National Library of Scotland; Brian Wilks, Everard Flintoff, University of Leeds; Mark R. Farrell, Alexander D. Wainwright, Ann Van Arsdale, Princeton University Library; Bonita Craft Grant, Rutgers University Library; Lola L. Szladits and staff, Berg Collection; Kurt W. Hettler, Herbert Cahoon and staff, Pierpont Morgan Library; Rodney G. Dennis, Emily C. Walhout, Vicki Denby and staff, Houghton Library; Cathy Henderson and staff, Harry Ransom Humanities Research Center; Joan Selby and staff, University of British Columbia Library; Roger W. Barrett; William Self; staff of the McPherson Library, University of Victoria; and colleagues Peter Smith, Keith Bradley, David Campbell, Barry Beardsmore, Johannis Maczewski, Patrick Grant, Anthony Jenkins, Lionel Adey.

Finally for their help in preparing the manuscript I wish to thank Colleen Donnelly for her patient and meticulous work on the word-processor, and my wife, Audrey, the unpaid assistant editor for this work.

List of Abbreviations

Notebook A: 9" x 7 1/2". Originally 24 pages, but with the first four pages missing, a fair copy in Branwell's small ordinary handwriting, the manuscript book contained five poems dated from May 1832 to September 1834, with a date of November 10, 1834 at the end of the table of contents. Although the notebook is listed in 1927 BSC, Mildred Christian's catalogue of objects in the BPM (1956-58) makes no mention of it, and the Parsonage Librarians have been unable to discover any trace of it. However, Shorter, in **Charlotte Brontë and Her Circle,** 1896, p. 434, lists the volume as "Ode to the Polar Star, and Other Poems," and both J. A. Symington and C. W. Hatfield transcribed poems from the volume, noting the missing four pages. Both transcribed Branwell's table of contents at the end of the notebook as follows:

The Fate of Regina		
[see No. **39**] May 1832		430 lines
Third Ode for the African Games		
[see No. **40**] June 1832		177 lines
Ode to the Polar Star		
[see No. **41**] June 1832		87 lines
The Pass of Thermopylae		
[see No. **80**] March 1834		56 lines
An Hours Musings		
[see No. **79**] September 1834		295 lines
	Total	1045 lines

P. B. Brontë Nov 10
1834

Notebook B: 6 1/4" x 3 3/4". Lined paper. Originally at least 60 pages, it is dismembered and scattered amongst the BPM, PML, NYPL, and HRC. It contained fair copies of eight poems (though some are unfinished) dated December 1835 to May 1838:

"How fast that courser fleeted by" (pp. 2-8).
    [**Misery,** Scene I, No. **54**]
"Wide I hear the wild wind singing" (pp. 9-17).
    [**Misery,** Scene II]
"Still and bright in twilight shining"
    (pp. 18-24). [No. **60**]

"Behold the waste of waving sea" (pp. 25-28).
   [No. **62**]
"Sleep, mourner, sleep! I cannot sleep"
   (pp. 29, 30). [No. **133**]
"Well! I will lift my eyes once more" (pp. 31-36).
   [No. **66**]
"Alone she paced her ancient Hall"
   (pp. 37-41). [No. **67**]
"How Eden like seem Palace Halls" (pp. 42-52).
   [No. **95**]
"At dead of midnight, drearily" (pp. 53-60).
   [No. **103**]

Notebook C: 9 1/2" x 7 3/4". Stiff brown covers. Originally at least 72 pages. At the BPM. Between 9
March 1837 and 12 May 1838, Branwell entered the
following:

(a) 9 March to 30 May 1837, revisions of
    twenty-five earlier poems (plus the first
    twelve lines of a twenty-sixth--see No.
    92);
(b) 16 June 1837 to 23 January 1838, fair copies
    of six new poems;
(c) January to May 1838, translations of six
    Odes of Horace (including the five he sent
    to De Quincey in April 1840).

He provided the following table of contents:

The Vision of Velino.....
   W H Warner........Decr 1833........52 lines
The 137th Psalm.....
   A Percy...........Spring 1834.......45
Song. I saw her in the Crowded Hall.....
   Marseilles........June 1834.........26
The Rover.....
   A Percy...........May 1834..........62
Augusta.....
   A Percy...........Spring 1834.......56
Song. Sound the Loud Trumpet.....
   H Hastings........Spring 1834.......40
The Angrian Hymn.....
   W H Warner........Spring 1834.......36
The Angrian Welcome.....
   H Hastings........Octr 1834.........48
Northangerlands Name.....
   H Hastings........Novr 1834.........40
Morning.....
   H Hastings........Decr 1834.........40

```
[A translation of Ode XIV]          24
[A translation of Ode XV]           52
                                  ─────
                                  2145
```

*Addition does not seem to have been Branwell's forte; the figure 886 at the bottom of the first page of the table should be 618.
**This is admittedly conjecture: these pages have been removed from the Notebook and have disappeared; however nothing else among Branwell's verse totals 143 lines.

In 1842 Branwell added two more items-- **Azrael** (No. 125) and the second draft of **The Triumph of mind over body** (No. 127).

Notebook D: 6" x 4". Red cover. 28 pages. The Luddenden Foot Notebook, which is divided between the BPM and the BCL. It contains twelve poems mainly composed while Branwell was station-master at Luddenden Foot (the earliest is dated August 1841), but in use up to March 1843 (see Nos. **106, 108, 109, 110, 111, 112, 113, 115, 116, 117, 127, 128**).

Alexander — **A Bibliography of the Manuscripts of Charlotte Brontë**, by Christine Alexander, The Brontë Society in association with Meckler Publishing, 1982.

Alexander CB — **An Edition of the Early Writings of Charlotte Brontë**, vol. 1, ed., Christine Alexander, Oxford: Basil Blackwell, 1987.

Alexander EW — **The Early Writings of Charlotte Brontë**, Oxford: Basil Blackwell, 1983.

BC 1932 — **Catalogue of the Bonnell Collection in the Brontë Parsonage Museum**, Haworth, 1932.

BCL — Brotherton Collection, University of Leeds.

BH — **Bradford Herald.**

BPM	The Brontë Parsonage Museum Library.
BSC 1927	**Catalogue of the Brontë Parsonage Museum,** Haworth, 1927.
BST	**Brontë Society Transactions,** 1895-1989.
Butterfield	**Brother in the Shadow,** by Mary Butterfield and R. J. Duckett, Bradford: Bradford Libraries and Information Service, 1988.
Dembleby	**The Confessions of Charlotte Brontë,** by John Malham-Dembleby, Bradford: Privately published, 1954.
De Quincey	**The De Quincey Memorials,** 2 vols., by Alexander H. Japp, London: William Heineman, 1891.
Du Maurier	**The Infernal World of Branwell Brontë,** by Daphne du Maurier, New York: Doubleday & Co., 1961.
Flintoff	"Some Unpublished Poems of Branwell Brontë," by Everard Flintoff, **Durham University Journal,** LXXXI (June 1989) 241-252.
Gaskell CB	**The Life of Charlotte Brontë,** by Elizabeth C. Gaskell, London: Smith, Elder & Co., 1857.
Gérin BB	**Branwell Brontë,** by Winifred Gérin, London: Hutchinson & Co., 1972.
Gérin CB	**Charlotte Brontë. The Evolution of Genius,** by Winifred Gérin, Oxford: Oxford University Press, 1967.
Grundy	**Pictures of the Past,** by F. H. Grundy, London: Griffith and Farrar, 1879.
HG	**Halifax Guardian.**

Hatfield Papers	The papers of the late C. W. Hatfield at the BPM, containing notes, transcriptions, and correspondence.
HRC	Harry Ransom Humanities Research Center, University of Texas.
Leyland	**The Brontë Family, with Special Reference to Patrick Branwell Brontë**, by Francis Leyland, 2 vols., London: Hurst and Blackett, 1886.
Leyland Letters	**A Complete Transcript of the Leyland Manuscripts Showing the Unpublished Portions From the Original Manuscripts**, by J. Alex. Symington and C. W. Hatfield, Privately printed, 1925.
Neufeldt PCB	**The Poems of Charlotte Brontë**, by Victor A. Neufeldt, New York: Garland Publishing Inc., 1985.
NYPL	New York Public Library, Berg Collection.
Oliphant	**Annals of a Publishing House; William Blackwood and His Sons, Their Magazine and Friends**, by Mrs. Oliphant, 2 vols., Edinburgh: William Blackwood and Sons, 1897.
PML	Pierpont Morgan Library.
Ratchford Papers	The papers of the late Fannie E. Ratchford at Harry Ransom Humanities Center, University of Texas, containing notes, transcriptions, and correspondence.
Ratchford Web	**The Brontës' Web of Childhood**, by Fannie E. Ratchford, New York: Columbia University Press, 1941.
SHB C and B	**The Poems of Charlotte and Patrick Branwell Brontë** (The Shakespeare Head edition), ed., Thomas J. Wise and Alexander Symington, Oxford: Basil Blackwell, 1934.

SHB LL	**The Brontës: Their Lives, Friendships, and Correspondence** (The Shakespeare Head edition), ed., Thomas J. Wise and John Alexander Symington, 4 vols., Oxford: Basil Blackwell, 1932.
SHB Misc	**The Miscellaneous and Unpublished Writings of Charlotte and Patrick Branwell Brontë** (The Shakespeare Head edition), ed., Thomas J. Wise and John Alexander Symington, 2 vols., Oxford: Basil Blackwell, 1936 and 1938.
Shorter 1923	**The Complete Poems of Charlotte Brontë**, ed., Clement Shorter, with assistance of C. W. Hatfield, London: Hodder and Stoughton, 1923.
Shorter EJB 1910	**The Complete Works of Emily Jane Brontë**, 2 vols., ed., Clement Shorter, London: Hodder and Stoughton, 1910.
Symington Papers (BPM)	Correspondence, news clippings and other materials, mainly concerned with the publication of the SHB.
Winnifrith PBB	**The Poems of Patrick Branwell Brontë**, ed., Tom Winnifrith, Oxford: Basil Blackwell, 1983.
Winnifrith PCB	**The Poems of Charlotte Brontë**, ed., Tom Winnifrith, Oxford: Basil Blackwell, 1984.
Wise Bibliog 1917	**A Bibliography of the Writings in Prose and Verse of the Members of the Brontë Family**, by Thomas J. Wise, London: Privately printed, 1917.
Wise Collection	The Stockett-Thomas J. Wise Collection, Special Collections Division, Library of the University of British Columbia, containing, along with works by and about Wise, Hatfield's proof copy of Shorter 1923, and correspondence concerning the Brontës by Hatfield, Davidson Cook, Alice Law, and J. A. Symington.

Wise Orphans 1917   **The Orphans and Other Poems, by Charlotte, Emily, and Branwell Brontë,** ed., Thomas J. Wise, London: Privately printed, 1917.

List of Manuscript Locations

A   The Houghton Library, Harvard University

B   (1) Brontë Parsonage Museum: Bonnell Collection
     (2) Brontë Parsonage Museum: Brontë Society's
     Collection
     (3) Brontë Parsonage Museum: Seton Gordon
     Collection

C   Library of William Self, Los Angeles, California

D   (1) The British Library: Ashley Collection
     (2) The British Library: Additional Manuscripts

E   Brotherton Library, University of Leeds: Brotherton
    Collection

F   Harry Ransom Humanities Research Center, University
    of Texas at Austin

G   New York Public Library: Berg Collection

H   National Library of Scotland

I   Pierpont Morgan Library, New York: Bonnell
    Collection

J   Library of Roger W. Barrett, Chicago, Illinois

K   Princeton University Library: Robert H. Taylor
    Collection

In addition there are the manuscripts held by the descendants
of Sir Alfred Law, and transcriptions of manuscripts made by
Davidson Cook, J. A. Symington and C. W. Hatfield in the
Ratchford Papers, the Hatfield Papers, and the Symington
Papers.

Publications Containing Previously Unpublished Poems by Branwell Brontë

The following publications, listed in chronological order, contained previously unpublished verse by Branwell Brontë. Where a poem has first been partially, then completely published, both publications are included.

Halifax Guardian, June 5, 1841.

Halifax Guardian, August 14, 1841.

Bradford Herald, April 28, 1842.

Bradford Herald, May 5, 1842.

Leeds Intelligencer, May 7, 1842.

Bradford Herald, May 12, 1842.

Bradford Herald, June 2, 1842.

Bradford Herald, June 9, 1842.

Bradford Herald, July 7, 1842.

Bradford Herald, July 12, 1842.

Bradford Herald, August 25, 1842.

Halifax Guardian, November 8, 1845.

Halifax Guardian, December 20, 1845.

Halifax Guardian, April 18, 1846.

Halifax Guardian, June 5, 1847.

The Life of Charlotte Brontë, Elizabeth C. Gaskell, London: Smith, Elder & Co., 1857.

Pictures of the Past, F. H. Grundy, London: Griffith and Farrar, 1879.

The Brontë Family, with Special Reference to Patrick Branwell Brontë, Francis Leyland, 2 vols., London: Hurst and Blackett, 1886.

The De Quincey Memorials, Alexander H. Japp, 2 vols., London: William Heineman, 1891.

Annals of a Publishing House; William Blackwood and His
Sons, Their Magazine and Friends, Mrs. Oliphant, 2
vols., Edinburgh: William Blackwood and Sons, 1897.

The Complete Works of Emily Jane Brontë, ed., Clement
Shorter, 2 vols., London: Hodder and Stoughton, 1910.

A Bibliography of the Writings in Prose and Verse of the
Members of the Brontë Family, Thomas J. Wise,
London: Privately printed, 1917.

The Orphans and Other Poems by Charlotte, Emily, and Branwell
Brontë, ed., Thomas J. Wise, London: Privately
printed, 1917.

BST (1919) 5:29.

BST (1920) 6:30.

The Odes of Horace, Book I, Translated by Branwell Brontë,
John Drinkwater, London: Privately printed, 1923.

The Complete Poems of Charlotte Brontë, Clement Shorter
and C. W. Hatfield, London: Hodder and Stoughton,
1923.

The Bookman (December 1926).

Catalogue of the Brontë Society Museum, Haworth, 1927.

BST (1927) 7:37.

Catalogue of the Bonnell Collection in the Brontë Parsonage Museum, Haworth, 1932.

BST (1933) 8:43.

The Poems of Charlotte Brontë and Patrick Branwell
Brontë (The Shakespeare Head ed.) Thomas J. Wise and
John Alexander Symington, Oxford: Basil Blackwell,
1934.

BST (1934) 8:44.

The Miscellaneous and Unpublished Writings of Charlotte and
Patrick Branwell Brontë (The Shakespeare Head ed.)
Thomas J. Wise and John Alexander Symington, 2 vols.,
Oxford: Basil Blackwell, 1936 and 1938.

The Brontës' Web of Childhood, Fannie E. Ratchford, New
York: Columbia University Press, 1941.

The Confessions of Charlotte Brontë, John Malham-Dembleby, Bradford: Privately published, 1954.

The Infernal World of Branwell Brontë, Daphne du Maurier, New York: Doubleday & Co., 1961.

The Poems of Patrick Branwell Brontë, Tom Winnifrith, Oxford: Basil Blackwell, 1983.

The Poems of Charlotte Brontë, Tom Winnifrith, Oxford: Basil Blackwell, 1984.

The Poems of Charlotte Brontë, Victor A. Neufeldt, New York: Garland Publishing Inc., 1985.

Brother in The Shadow, Mary Butterfield and R. J. Duckett, Bradford: Bradford Libraries and Information Service, 1988.

"Some Unpublished Poems of Branwell Brontë," Everard Flintoff, Durham University Journal, LXXXI (June 1989).

INTRODUCTION

On October 2, 1848, the day after Branwell's funeral, Charlotte wrote to W. S. Williams:

> My unhappy brother never knew what his sisters had done in literature--he was not aware that they had ever published a line. We could not tell him of our efforts for fear of causing him too deep a pang of remorse for his own time misspent, and talents misapplied (SHB LL, II, 262).

Ironically, nothing in Charlotte's letters suggests that she or any other member of the family was aware that Branwell had published at least fifteen poems between 1841 and 1847--fourteen of them before the appearance of **Poems By Currer, Ellis, and Acton Bell,** May 1846. It seems that he in turn had kept his "efforts" secret from them. As a result, Charlotte was never to know that Branwell had achieved his life-long ambition to become a published author almost five years before she accomplished hers.

Charlotte's lack of knowledge and consequent underestimation of her brother's achievement has remained characteristic of Branwell Brontë scholarship to this day. The documentation of his publications is a good example. Winifred Gérin's 1961 biography notes that between August 1841 and July 1842 six of his poems appeared in the **Halifax Guardian;** but identifies only four (BB, pp. 186, 209-10). In fact he published ten during that time. Similarly, in the most recent edition of Branwell's poems (1983), Tom Winnifrith identifies only six publications (PBB, pp. xxxii-xxxvi, 287, 291, 297). Not surprisingly, therefore, previous editions have provided a very incomplete picture of Branwell's poetic achievement. The main text and **Appendix A** in this volume contain 11,582 lines. In comparison, the two other major editions of Branwell's poems--the SHB and Winnifrith PBB--contain 8779 (spread over three volumes with some in facsimile only) and 8359 (of which over 500 are trial lines and early drafts) respectively. Of the 155 poems/verse fragments in this edition, 34 (not including trial lines and variant drafts in the **Commentary**) appear in print wholly or substantially for the first time. An additional 34 items have appeared in print for the first time in whole or in part within the last ten years--twenty in Winnifrith PBB, seven in Neufeldt PCB, six in Flintoff, and one in Butterfield.

Yet, as Christine Alexander has rightly pointed out, in quantity the body of Branwell's early work is approximately equal to Charlotte's (EW, p. 6); unfortunately, large portions of it remain unedited, and the text of much of what has been published is notoriously unreliable.[1]   Branwell's 11,582 lines total more than Emily's and Anne's combined, and only 1600 less than the 13,204 in my edition of Charlotte's poems. Alexander has summarized nicely the inaccuracies and distortions in biographies of Charlotte that have resulted from "inadequate knowledge of original materials, reliance on inaccurate and fragmented publication, and . . . a tendency to study individual stories and poems in isolation" (EW, pp. 4-5). In the case of Branwell these problems are, clearly, even more serious. The lack of reliable information and texts, combined with an over-emphasis on the more sensational aspects of his life, has perpetuated Charlotte's misguided view of her brother's lack of literary achievement,[2] and illustrates why the reader must approach existing biographies of Branwell with caution. While this volume makes possible the fuller assessment that Branwell's poetic achievement deserves, only when all of his work has been properly edited will the true picture of his success or failure as a literary artist emerge.

THE TEXT

    Charlotte's sense of "the emptiness of [Branwell's] whole existence" (SHB LL, II, 261) is perpetuated in the dismissive neglect that has characterized the handling and publication of his manuscripts from the beginning. When C. K. Shorter was negotiating the 1895 purchase of Brontë manuscripts from Arthur Bell Nicholls, the latter wrote on June 18, "There are a large number of Branwell's manuscripts, but I don't suppose you care to have them" (Nicholls-Shorter Correspondence, BCL). On July 3 he wrote that he would be sending Branwell's manuscripts in a day or two, yet he obviously did not send them all, for Sotheby's sales of the second Mrs. Nicholls' effects in 1907, 1914 and 1916 contained at least eighteen of Branwell's manuscripts, including the whole of Notebook C and all the items last known to have been in the possession of Mrs. C. B. Branwell.[3] This early disparagement of Branwell's manuscripts is nicely demonstrated in Mrs. Chadwick's comments on the sale in London in 1912 of six autograph fragments of the children's early work: "A curious feature of the sale was the high price obtained for the two manuscripts by Branwell Brontë, who has been discarded, and considered unfit to be associated with his sisters, either as an author or a brother. There was, however, quite as keen a competition for his manuscripts as for others."[4]

    Although in this instance the competition may have been as keen, such was not always the case, nor did it mean the manuscripts were handled with care and respect. Both Shorter and T. J. Wise (on whose behalf Shorter had purchased the manuscripts from Nicholls) passed Branwell's manuscripts off as Charlotte's or Emily's when it was advantageous to do so. On 6 June 1895, Nicholls wrote to Shorter, "I send a number of manuscripts of Emily and Anne Brontë"; underneath the comment Shorter penciled, "they turned out to be Branwell's." Yet in Shorter's 1910 edition of Emily's works, twenty-five poems and verse fragments are, in fact, Branwell's. Of these, thirteen are facsimile reproductions--nine duplicating printed items; of the printed items, several are fragments from the same poem, and one item consists of lines from two different poems. However Shorter's volume also contains facsimile reproductions of Emily's verse manuscripts, and the difference in the two hands is readily apparent. Thus, despite Shorter's assertions that "seventy-one new poems are taken from original manuscripts that have passed through my hands," and that "the new poems . . . have been carefully collated by me, and these are unquestionably Emily's work as she left it in the rough manuscript" (EJB 1910, II, vii), it seems likely that he had simply accepted T. J. Wise's attributions, for he also comments that the facsimiles were "reproduced from the Original Manuscripts in the possession of Mr. Thomas J. Wise and Mr. Walter Slater" (EJB 1910, II, 417). I have discussed elsewhere some of Wise's attempts to pass off Branwell's manuscripts as Emily's or Charlotte's (Neufeldt PCB, pp. xxv-xxvii), but it is worth noting here that there exist today four volumes of manuscript fragments bound and labeled as Emily's by Rivière for Wise, which contain eighteen items belonging to Branwell, including one removed from Notebook B (No. 133). Since all of these appear as Emily's in Shorter's edition, it is clear that Wise had put together these random collections of manuscript leaves before 1910.

While Wise mistreated the manuscripts of all the Brontës, his treatment of Branwell's suggests a particular lack of interest, based presumably on his belief that they had less commercial value than those of his sisters. At the 1907 Sotheby's sale of Mrs. Nicholls' effects, Wise bought nine miniature booklets--six belonging to Charlotte, three to Branwell--which he subsequently gave to Amy Lowell. It seems, however, that he originally intended to sell them, for the booklets (in the Lowell Collection, Harvard University) are accompanied by a printed advertisement which describes Charlotte's booklets individually, but covers Branwell's with the single statement: "The three written by Patrick Branwell Brontë form part of 'Branwell's Blackwoods Magazine,' with poems, letters, advertisements, and illustrations." Also included is a sheet of notes in Wise's autograph with page references to Gaskell CB and Shorter's 1896 biography for each Charlotte item, but no references to either for the

Branwell items because neither provides any information on
these Branwell manuscripts, and Wise, obviously, had made
little effort to discover for himself what they actually contained, nor had he had them transcribed. Another advertisement in the Lowell Collection, also prepared by Wise, again
illustrates his low regard for Branwell's manuscripts. It
contains a facsimile reproduction of the first page of Branwell's **The Life of Feild Marshal the Right Honourable
Alexander Percy**, but is accompanied by the following
announcement which makes clear what he thought was
marketable:

> Bronte (Charlotte) the highly important Series of 51
> HOLOGRAPH LETTERS, addressed principally to her most
> intimate friend, Ellen Nussey. Other letters are to her
> father, her brother (P. Branwell Bronte) and Messrs.
> Smith and Elder (her publishers). The majority of these
> letters are of considerable length, and of the most
> private nature. In addition to the letters there is a
> manuscript of Emily Bronte (who died when young), and
> three manuscripts of P. Branwell Bronte. This Corres-
> pondence exhibits seven different signatures of
> Charlotte Bronte, and really constitutes a most valuable
> Manuscript Bibliography of Charlotte and the Bronte
> family. The whole inlaid to a uniform size, folio, and
> bound in brown morocco extra, gilt leaves.
>
> PROBABLY THE FINEST BRONTE COLLECTION IN EXISTENCE
> FULL PARTICULARS ON APPLICATION

I have detailed elsewhere (Neufeldt PCB, pp. xxv-xxvi) how
Wise "prepared" manuscripts for sale, and how he used unbound
leaves for exchanges or gifts. Materials he felt were too
insignificant for the major sales or to be used as gifts, he
disposed of through minor London booksellers, among them
Herbert Gorfin. In 1899, four years after Wise had acquired
them, Gorfin sold twenty-one Branwell manuscripts to the
Brontë Society for £5.50, including Notebook D, suggesting that it was Wise who removed the seven leaves now in the
BCL.[5]

Wise's negative attitude toward Branwell's manuscripts
remained consistent to the end. While C. W. Hatfield was
assisting Wise in the preparation of the 1929 Brontë
Bibliography, he wrote three times (17 May, 22 May, 2 June--
Symington Papers, BPM), warning him that "The Wanderer" was
not Emily's, but an early draft of **Sir Henry Tunstall**,
and pointing out that large portions of the poem had been
printed as Branwell's in De Quincey. Yet the Bibliography
appeared with the poem ascribed to Emily, with a note acknowledging that it was an early draft of the poem in De

Quincey, but suggesting that Branwell had either pinched the work from Emily or that she had transcribed it for him.[6]

Half a century later not much has changed. Branwell was not, for example, included in the **Index of English Literary Manuscripts** (1982), and to date no complete and accurate index of his manuscripts has been produced, nothing that provides the scholar with any reasonably accurate sense of the extent of Branwell's literary activity.

Ironically, the consequences of this dismissive attitude have been positive as well as negative. On the one hand, Branwell's manuscripts are not as widely scattered as those of Charlotte: twelve locations for the poems as opposed to nineteen. Also, because of their lack of interest, Shorter and Wise did not produce a series of textually inaccurate private editions of his works during the first two decades of this century, as they did of Charlotte's. On the other hand, Branwell's manuscripts, especially from 1836 on, have been much more mutilated and dismembered than those of his sisters. For example, he left behind at least six notebooks,[7] two of which have disappeared, and the other four have all been dismembered and scattered to some degree. Parts of the manuscripts of the copy texts for at least three poems are at different locations, for at least twenty-seven poems variant drafts exist at different locations--in some cases more than one--and in at least thirty-eight cases, a manuscript for at least one version of a poem is missing. Similarly, in at least twenty-one cases the main text or an earlier draft is in a bound volume made up of leaves from various manuscripts,[8] and at least sixteen items in the main text have been attributed to Emily or Charlotte at one time or another. Some of this dismemberment seems to have resulted from the scattered condition in which Branwell left his manuscripts; according to Hatfield, he frequently did not stitch his manuscripts together, as Charlotte did (letter to Davidson Cook, 14 June 1926--Wise Collection), and at least twenty of the missing manuscripts are ones he sent to Joseph Leyland, which were subsequently published in the newspapers and/or in Leyland. Nevertheless, as I have described above, T. J. Wise also bears a considerable responsibility for the condition of Branwell's manuscripts (see also Neufeldt PCB, pp. xxv-xxvii). When one adds the difficulty of reading Branwell's minute script--the most difficult of the Brontë miniature scripts--it becomes clear why even those editors who set out to give Branwell his due lost heart, and why the commentary in this edition may reflect certain hesitancies in making attributions, in dating items, and in defining contexts and interrelationships.

The publication history of Branwell's poems suggests a similar history of neglect and sporadic, unsuccessful attempts to redress that neglect. Although Branwell published fifteen poems in three newspapers--the **Leeds Intelligencer**, the **Halifax Guardian**, and the **Bradford Herald**--between 1841 and 1847, his publications seem to have attracted even less attention than the volume of poems his sisters published in 1846, in part, at least, because he insisted on publishing under a pseudonym (see pp. xlvi-xlvii below). Just how he did place his poems in the newspapers is not entirely clear. Gérin's comment that he did so through the Leyland family's connection with the **Halifax Guardian** (BB, p. 186) needs to be qualified, because Roberts Leyland, the father of Francis and Joseph, resigned as publisher/printer of the **Guardian** in 1837 to devote himself to his printing firm. As a major printer, however, he and his sons would have known James Uriah Walker, the publisher/printer during the years that Branwell's poems were published. Since Walker, a close friend of Edwin Augustus Taylor, publisher of the **Bradford Herald**, also printed it during its brief life (January-October 1842), it seems likely he sent on to Taylor the poems that appeared in the **Herald**. We also know that Branwell began sending poems to Joseph Leyland for criticism as early as 1838 (see p. xliv below), and that he sent poems to him for publication in the **Guardian** (Leyland Letters, p. 23). Yet neither Francis Leyland in his 1886 biography or Mary Leyland in her 1954 monograph on the Leyland family provides any indication that the family had a hand in getting Branwell's work published, or that they were aware of how much he had published: Francis mentions only the one publication in the **Leeds Intelligencer** and Mary none at all.

But, did Branwell submit poems for publication only through Joseph Leyland? If so, as the inclusion of 14 of the 15 published poems in the 1886 biography seems to suggest, why does No. **107** not appear in it? And why were certain poems sent to Joseph, obviously intended for publication--see, for example, Nos. **104, 126, 127, 131, 132, 134, 144, 150**--not published? Did Joseph keep manuscripts or make copies once he received them? The evidence suggests he did, for Joseph died in 1851, thirty-five years before Francis printed what presumably had been left in his brother's papers. But because the manuscripts submitted to the newspaper are no longer extant, we do not know how much the texts were edited by Joseph and/or the newspapers--for there are significant differences between the versions in the newspapers and those that appear in Francis Leyland's biography--nor do we know if Branwell approved the text as published. Unfortunately, any attempt to answer these questions is hampered by the fact that so few of Branwell's letters to Joseph Leyland remain extant. For example, of only four before 1845, only one makes any reference to literary matters, yet Branwell published eleven poems in 1841-42.

After Branwell's death, part of No. **60** appeared in Gaskell CB, 1857; No. **114** in Grundy, 1879; and twenty-seven items in Francis Leyland's two-volume biography (1886), written to counteract what he felt was an overly negative portrayal of Branwell by Mrs. Gaskell (see p. 1 n. 2). Unfortunately, in assessing Branwell's literary achievement, Leyland was limited to the manuscripts his brother had accumulated; the rest were with Nicholls in Ireland. In 1891, No. **126** appeared in De Quincey and in 1897, parts of No. **54** in Oliphant. However, for the reasons noted above (p. xxvi), the Shorter/Wise 1895 purchase of Brontë manuscripts did not lead to the flurry of publications that appeared for Branwell's sisters between 1896 and 1923. Wise published only four poems: three in his 1917 Brontë Bibliography (Nos. **47, 71,** and **72**) and part of one (No. **95**) in Orphans 1917. Shorter's contribution was equally characteristic: twenty-five items (nine duplicates) as Emily's in his 1910 edition of her works and three as Charlotte's in his 1923 edition of her poems. In the same year, however, John Drinkwater produced a privately printed edition of Branwell's translations of the Odes of Horace to demonstrate his considerable ability as a translator, and in 1927 C. W. Hatfield reproduced the Luddenden Foot Notebook (Notebook C) in the BST. Additional items appeared in the BST in 1919, 1920, 1927, and 1933; in **The Bookman,** 1926; and in catalogues in 1927 and 1932.

Other editions containing Branwell's poems, such as A. C. Benson's 1915 edition of the poetry of the Brontës, merely reprinted items already published. In doing even that Benson felt he was breaking new ground; he comments in his Introduction: "It has been customary to omit all mention of Branwell's work. The catastrophe of his life was so deplorable, and the wreck of a charming and attractive nature, through self-indulgence and morbidity, so tragical, that he has been hurried out of sight."[9] Ten years later, C. W. Hatfield, in a letter to Davidson Cook (9 January 1926, Wise Collection) reiterated the continuing lack of interest in Branwell's work:

> I was two or three years in preparing a book of his poems which I completed a short time ago, and I am hoping that Hodder and Stoughton will issue it towards the end of this year . . . . But Branwell Brontë, unlike his sisters, has no literary reputation to back him up, and although the quality of his poetry is higher

than that of Charlotte's or Anne's I doubt whether the
publishers will consider it of a high enough standard to
justify them in incurring the expense of producing the
volume.

In the end, Hatfield never published his edition. He sent
the manuscript to C. K. Shorter for submission to Hodder and
Stoughton, with whom Shorter had close connections, but
Shorter fell ill, and Hatfield wrote to Cook, 29 October 1916
(Wise Collection): "It has never been sent to the publishers
and if I do not succeed in getting it back again there will
be two years wasted . . . . I feel annoyed when I think of
it, for Mr. Shorter lost my first typescript volume of the
poems of Charlotte Brontë. What became of that volume I
never learnt, and in order to get the poems published I had
to prepare another volume for the printers." His manuscript
was finally returned in December by Mrs. Shorter after her
husband's death, but by that time Hatfield had become involved in other Brontë projects, and he never got around to
doing the revisions he felt the volume needed before it could
be published.

Not surprisingly, therefore, J. A. Symington saw the
proposed Shakespeare Head edition as a means of redressing
the neglect of Branwell. He wrote to T. J. Wise, 23 March
1931, "The distinctive feature will, of course, be the Branwell section"; to Basil Blackwell on 26 June 1931, "I think
we shall cause a little sensation when we publish the remaining volumes of the edition by being able to prove that many
of the works attributed to Charlotte by Shorter, are none
other than the writings of Branwell, and that Branwell will
come into the full share of his credit" (Symington Papers,
BPM). His optimism reached its zenith in an interview in the
Yorkshire Evening News, February 3, 1932, announcing the
publication of the Shakespeare Head edition:

> BROTHER OF THE BRONTËS
> VINDICATED IN NEW WORKS
>
> An authoritative vindication of Branwell Brontë, so
> generally regarded as the irresponsible and philandering
> brother of the famous Brontë sisters, will be one of
> the features of a new edition of the Brontë works,
> part of which is to be published this week . . . . The
> aim of the edition is to achieve finality[10] on the
> subject, for probably all the existing material of value
> has been accumulated after 10 years of research by the
> editors . . . . 'The results may well prove,' said Mr.
> Symington to a representative of the "Yorkshire Evening
> News" today, 'that the great esteem in which Branwell
> was held by his family was justified and that, indeed,

he was the dominant factor in the early literary life of the sisters.'
Branwell will be revealed not as the 'bad lad of the family,' but as a well-read and scholarly young man. 'Actually, he was tutor in a clergy-man's family for nearly three years, which proves,' said Mr. Symington, 'that he had some attainments worthy of his job.'
It will be shown that it was not till after he had done his best work, and in the last year or two of his life, that he really gave way and weakened, but that was due to love affairs.

Unfortunately, these high expectations were at best only partially realized because, as Symington's later letters reveal, once he actually confronted Branwell's unpublished manuscripts, he found himself "getting into a maze trying to ferret out some key to their construction" (5 December 1932). Manuscripts were incomplete and confused; existing transcriptions suspect (for the reasons, see Neufeldt PCB, pp. xxvii-viii); the whereabouts of manuscripts needed to check them against unknown; and the task of reading the minute script daunting. In the introduction to the 1934 volume of Charlotte's and Branwell's poems, Symington hinted at the difficulties he was beginning to encounter, difficulties that were already dampening the enthusiasm he had expressed two years earlier. In the end, he resorted to facsimile reproduction of many pages of manuscript in the two volumes of Miscellaneous and Unpublished Works (1936 and 38), and expressed his reservations about the reliability of the edition in his "Conclusion" to the 1938 volume (see Neufeldt PCB, pp. xxx-xxxii). Even so, there were some inexplicable omissions: most of Notebook C, an easily readable fair copy text in the BPM; the early version of No. **80** in Notebook A, which Symington had transcribed; six items from Leyland; four items from Notebook D, published in BST 1927.

In the end, the three volumes containing material by Branwell included 65 poems and verse fragments of which only 23 were wholly new. Since then 71 items have been added to the Branwell canon, 68 of these since 1983 (see p. xxv). Ironically and entirely in keeping with the publication history I have described, in 1954 John Malham-Dembleby added parts of three new items to the Branwell canon in his attempt to prove that Charlotte had written most of the work ascribed to Branwell, Emily and Anne.

Though not "complete," (see **Appendix B**), this edition seeks to provide a reliable text for all of Branwell's available verse, and thus to provide the "comprehensive edition," "accurate, available and readable" Tom Winnifrith admits his 1983 edition is not (p. xiv). Because of the unreliability of existing texts, this edition is based on my own transcriptions of all available manuscripts. In addition to the lost manuscripts noted in **Appendix B,** there are no manuscripts extant for sixteen items (excluding variant versions in the **Commentary**). For six of these I have used the printed text in Leyland and Grundy, to whom Branwell had sent the manuscripts; for nine items I have relied on transcriptions made by C. W. Hatfield and Davidson Cook, and for one on a photograph of the manuscript. For the fifteen poems Branwell published in newspapers I have reproduced the printed text, although because the manuscripts sent to the newspapers are lost, there is no way of knowing how much they were edited before publication, and if Branwell approved the changes (see pp. xxx-xxxi for a fuller discussion). As was the case with my edition of Charlotte's poems, this edition is heavily indebted to the work of previous Brontë scholars. In particular, I wish to acknowledge my indebtedness to C. W. Hatfield, Tom Winnifrith, Christine Alexander, and Everard Flintoff.

THE LAYOUT OF THE TEXT

   As noted above, for the fifteen poems published by Branwell the primary text provided is the printed text. In all other cases, where the manuscript is available, the text follows the manuscript as closely as possible. Branwell's spelling, punctuation, and verse format are reproduced, but canceled words, lines, stanzas, etc., are omitted. In cases where Branwell asterisks a word or line and provides an alternative reading at the bottom of the page, the first reading is considered canceled, and is not reproduced as an alternative reading. Where uncanceled variant readings occur, the primary text gives the latest reading, with earlier variants noted at the end of the poem. Similarly, where more than one draft exists, the primary text provides the latest; the earlier drafts appear in the commentary. Only titles provided by Branwell are included, except in the case where the text has been taken from Leyland or from transcriptions by Hatfield or Cook, in which case their titles, if any, are included. Editorial insertions appear in [ ], uncertain readings in < >.

   The poems are arranged in chronological order, and Branwell's signature and date are reproduced where they exist. Where the date appears in square brackets, either the poem is undated but part of a dated manuscript, or the manuscript is undated. In the first case, the date and signature on the manuscript are provided in the commentary; in the second case, the reasons for the placement of the poem are provided in the commentary.

In the notes at the end of each poem the reader will find:

(a) The coded location of the manuscript(s) (for the key see p. xvii). Where more than one location is listed, either the manuscript has been dismembered and scattered, or more than one version is extant. In the latter case, the locations appear in chronological order and the primary text is the last one noted.

(b) The first publication of the poem keyed to the List of Abbreviations, pp. xi-xviii.

(c) Variant readings and other textual matters.

In addition to information about dating and variant drafts, the commentary includes other relevant information about the manuscripts, information about the context of the poems, and some glossing of literary and Biblical references and sources. For Glass Town/Angrian references, see **Appendix D**.

BRANWELL'S POETIC CAREER

Rebecca Fraser's comment that from the age of eleven Branwell thought he would be a great poet[11] is only partly true. In fact, from the time he produced the first issue of **BRANWELL'S BLACKWOOD'S MAGAZINE** in January 1829, he saw himself not only as poet (though perhaps pre-eminently so), but also as critic, dramatist, historian, conversationalist, editor and publisher--in short as the great Man of Letters he saw exemplified by Christopher North and James Hogg in **Blackwoods**, particularly in the "Noctes Ambrosianae." Seven years after he "published"[12] his first little magazine, he wrote to the editor of **Blackwoods** (December 7, 1835):

it is not from affected hypocrisy that I commence my letter with the name of James Hogg; for the writings of that man in your numbers, his speeches in your Noctes, when I was a child laid a hold on my mind which succeeding years have consecrated into a most sacred feeling. I cannot express, though you can understand, the heavenliness of associations connected with such articles as Proffesor Wilsons; read and reread while a little child with all their poetry of Language and divine flights into that visionary region of imagination which one very young would beleive reality and which one entering manhood would look back on as a glorious dream. I speak so

Sir because while a child Blackwood formed my cheif delight, and I feel certain that no child before enjoyed
reading as I did, because none ever had such works as
"The Noctes" "Christmas Dreams" "Christopher in his
shooting Jacket" to read . . . . One of those who
roused those feelings is dead [Hogg], and neither from
himself or yourself shall I hear him speak again.   I
greive for his death because to me he was a portion of
feelings which I suppose nothing can arouse hereafter:--
Because to you he was a Contributor of stirling originality, and, in the Noctes, a subject for your
uneaqualled writing.   He and others like him gave your
Magazine the peculiar character which made it famous:--
As these man die it will decay, unless their places be
supplied by others like them.   Now Sir, to you I appear
writing with conceited assurance,--but I <u>am</u> not--for I
know myself so far as to beleive in my own originality;
and on that ground I desire of you admittance into your
ranks; And do not wonder that I apply so determinedly,
for the remembrances I spoke of, have fixed you and your
Magazine in such a manner upon my mind that the Idea of
striving to aid another periodical is <u>horribly
repulsive</u>.   My resolution is to devote my ability to
you, and for Gods sake, till you see wether or not I can
serve you do not so coldly refuse my aid.   All, Sir,
that I desire of you is that you would in answer to this
letter request a specimen or specimen's of my writing
and I even wish that you would name the subject of which
you would wish me to write . . . .[13]

Like Charlotte (see Neufeldt PCB, pp. xxxiii-iv), he believed
that he had been called to a life of literature, though
clearly not with the modest aspirations and expectations she
expresses in **The Violet.**   Although he later tried painting as a vocation, the creation and production of literature,
especially poetry, remained his first love.   Most of his
early manuscripts up to the end of 1835 are "published"
works; by the end of 1837 he had produced three "collected
volumes" of poems (Notebooks A, B and C), and, after major
disasters/crises, such as the Royal Academy failure, the
Bradford failure, Luddenden Foot, and Thorp Green, he tried
to redeem himself with feverish efforts to get his work
(mainly poetry) published.   Unlike Charlotte, who ceased to
write poetry with the publication of the 1846 volume of poems
because from 1838 on she had sensed that prose fiction rather
than poetry was her real metier (see Neufeldt PCB, pp.
xxxix-xli), Branwell never relinquished his belief that his
first calling was that of poet.   In 1845 he began a never
completed three volume novel--**And The Weary Are At
Rest**--because, he wrote to Leyland, "in the present state

of the publishing and reading world a Novel is the most sale-able article, so that where ten pounds would be offered for a work the production of which would require the utmost stretch of a man's intellect--two hundred pounds would be a refused offer for three volumes whose composition would require the smoking of a cigar and the humming of a tune" (Leyland Letters, p. 19). Yet his last published work was a poem (**The End of All**) in the **Halifax Guardian** June 5, 1847, just four months before the publication of **Jane Eyre.**

Branwell's literary activities in 1829, at the age of eleven/twelve, can only be described as a kind of volcanic eruption with all the sense of undisciplined exuberance the image suggests. He had already written a few prose pieces in 1827-28, including a six-page **HISTORY OF THE REBELLION OF MY FELLOWS.** But with his appearance as editor/publisher of **BRANWELLS BLACKWOODS MAGAZINE** in January 1829, he pro-duced over the next twelve months, in addition to at least four and probably seven issues of his magazine, a two-volume travel book,[14] at least thirty-four poems or verse frag-ments (including an attempt at Latin verse), and a verse drama, totalling approximately 1300 lines. Of the poems, fourteen, totalling 433 lines, were written in collaboration with Charlotte; twenty, totalling 564 lines, were by Branwell alone.[15] Seventeen poems were included in the ten known issues of the little magazine he and Charlotte produced in 1829; eleven in a "published" volume of poems, and the verse drama was a separately "published" volume. There are no uncanceled variants, and all but the three fragments at the end of **Laussane,** (Nos. **32, 33, 34**) are complete fair copies.

The poems are short, ranging in length from 6 to 104 lines with only three more than fifty lines long. But where all but two of Charlotte's poems in 1829 were in quatrains and very regular metre (the two exceptions were in blank verse), and she did not begin to experiment with verse form and metrics until 1830 (Neufeldt PCB, p. xxxv), Branwell was much more venturesome from the outset. Of the fourteen poems on which he collaborated with Charlotte, thirteen are in quatrains, one is in blank verse. Of the nineteen extant that are his own, eleven are in quatrains, but employ three different rhyme patterns (sometimes two in one poem) and very irregular metrical patterns in which he varies not only the number of feet per line, but also combines different types in one line, principally iambs and anapests. In addition, he also produced a five-line stanza, with the fifth line a re-peated refrain, blank verse, a carefully constructed ode (reflecting, along with the attempt at Latin verse, his schooling under his father in the classics), and a blank

verse drama, something Charlotte was not to attempt for
another year. Similarly we can see him experimenting with
mood and tone. While most of the poems in Young Soult's two
volumes are of the noisy Byronic/apocalyptic variety, No.
23 shows him to be capable not only of a quieter, more
meditative strain, but also of adopting at age twelve an
adult's retrospective point of view. Clearly, some of Branwell's irregularities result from inexperience and lack of
discipline,[16] but it is also evident from Chateaubriand's
comments (pp. 21, 25, 368-69) that the experimentation with
verse and meter was deliberate, and not always to Charlotte's
taste. She commented on Young Soult's two volumes: "His
poems exhibit a fine imagination, but his versification is
not good. The ideas and the language are beautiful, but they
are not arranged so as to run along smoothly, and for this
reason I think he should succeed best in blank verse. Indeed
I understand that he is about to publish a poem in that metre
which is expected to be his best" (Alexander CB I, 127).
Presumably she was referring to the blank verse drama, **The
Revenge**, begun the day after her comment.

In fact this experimentation with irregular forms was
part of an image of himself as poet and Man of Letters that
Branwell was consciously propagating at the time, an image
with some contradictory features. On the one hand, we have
the sober and scholarly Sergeant Bud, who after receiving a
copy of Ossian's Poems from Chief Genius Taly, writes to the
editor of Branwell's magazine: "upon an attentive perusal of
the above said works I found they were most sublime and
exelent I am engaged in publishing an edition of them in
Quarto--3 vols--with notes commentarys &c I am fully con-
vinced that it is the work of Ossian who lived a 1000 years
ago--and--of no other there is a most intense anxiety prevailing amongst literary men to know its contents in a short
time they shall be gratified for it will be published on the
first of July, 1829" (June magazine).[17] The proposed
edition is to have "29 vols Folio" with the same elaborate
apparatus of the actual volume of Ossian's poems the Brontë
children read.[18] The same scholarly persona reappears in
the guise of Chateaubriand, who provides not only the elaborate learned commentaries on Young Soult's poems, but also
censures the poet's excesses and irregularities. On the
other hand, we have the rebellious and undisciplined Young
Soult the Rhymer, whose romantic posturing is the subject of
a number of satirical comments by Charlotte (see Neufeldt
PCB, p. 397 and Alexander CB I, 127, 180ff, 309; EW, pp.
64-66). Soult's rebelliousness is evident not only in his
experimentation, his bohemian appearance and behaviour, but
also in his derivation--he is the son of one of Wellington's
major adversaries--in his praise of and sympathy for Napoleon
and France, and in his opposition to the Genii, whom he

describes as tyrants, but who are, after all, the ruling establishment.[19]

Although Branwell continued his prodigious output over the next two years, his interest for a time shifted to drama and prose.[20] The two verse dramas (Nos. **35, 36**), totalling 661 lines, are again in blank verse, although each has a song, one in quatrains with a regular rhyme scheme and metric pattern, the second very irregular. Though the second drama is unfinished, both are "published" works and in both it is Young Soult who now dons the mantle of serious scholar, citing Captain Bud on the aims of dramatic poetry, explaining his sources, and dismissing his sister's criticisms of his work in **The Liar Unmasked.** "They are . . . remarkable," suggests Alexander, "for the seriousness and pretension with which the thirteen-year-old boy sets about his task of producing 'great' literature" (EW, p. 65). In 1831, his verse consisted of only two short poems, both irregular Odes included in the **Letters From An Englishman.** While the "serious" Young Soult may well have lacked a sense of humor as Alexander suggests (EW, p. 64), the first of these two poems indicates that Branwell was quite capable of laughing at his own poetic posturings.

Eighteen thirty-two, however, marked a renewed interest in writing poetry, and over the next four years, until his abortive trip to become a student at the Royal Academy, Branwell produced 25 poems (including variant drafts but excluding the two lost poems noted in **Appendix B**) totalling approximately 2000 lines. Of these, all but two are fair copies; seventeen are part of larger narrative manuscripts, and five comprised the now lost Notebook A (his, as opposed to Young Soult's, first collected volume of poems). The classical influence reflected in the two Odes of 1831 continues with the creation of two Odes in 1832, one (No. **41**) with a very complicated rhyme scheme, in the epic devices used in **The Fate of Regina,** and in four poems/fragments on the subject of Thermopylae.

The renewed interest in poetry accompanied a change in Branwell's conception of himself. Up to the end of 1831 he thought of himself as Young Soult, poet of Glass Town, published in Glass Town. After 1831, however, Young Soult rapidly disappears[21] and a new dual self-conception begins to emerge. On the one hand, Branwell continues as the chronicler of Glass Town/Angria in the persons of John Flower (Viscount Richton), Captain Bud, Henry Hastings and Charles Wentworth, although only Hastings, as the poet of Angria, writes poems; the others merely record poems by various Angrian personages, mainly Warner and Percy.[22] And even Hastings is no posturing pseudo-Byronic figure; rather he is an inexperienced but enthusiastic army officer whom Charlotte treats much more gently than she did Young Soult (see Alexander EW, p. 149), and who reflects on the nature of poetic composition (see comment for No. **77**). On the other hand, Branwell is also P. B. Brontë producing poems in his own right. That these are in ordinary handwriting, five in a separate notebook now lost (Notebook A), the sixth (No. **48**) possibly intended as a much longer work, suggests that Branwell by now had an eye toward publication in the real world. While the separation from Angria is obviously not complete, the image projected in these poems is of a classical philosophical bent; even Percy, Branwell's Angrian hero, is retrospective and reflective in most of his poems during this time, discussing the nature of human existence and the transitoriness of happiness (see, for example, Nos. **78, 79**). This change in Branwell's perception of himself coincides interestingly with Charlotte's return from Roe Head in May 1832, for after her return Branwell demonstrates some of the same growth in sophistication in the handling of verse form and meter, and in the variety of verse forms used, that we see in Charlotte's work in 1833-34 (Neufeldt PCB, p. xxxvi). However, where her most complex and sophisticated poems result from her almost exclusive concentration on the Glass Town/Angria saga, Branwell's do not. In her famous caricature of Branwell as "Patrick Benjamin Wiggens" (October 1834), it is precisely this inability to act with undivided purpose that she sees as potentially dangerous. As Gérin points out, "She sees how his emotions are too strong and too easily aroused; how the very range of his tastes and talents is too extended ever to allow of concentration upon one object; how his ambitions are too inordinate ever to be satisfied with moderate achievement" (BB, p. 69). Not only was Branwell's perception of his role as poet fragmented; that role also had to compete with his interest in music and painting.

Ironically, about the time Charlotte wrote her description of Wiggens, the family decided that Branwell would make portraiture his profession, and he began to take lessons from William Robinson in Bradford. In the summer of 1835, it was decided that Branwell would go to London to try to gain admission as a student to the Royal Academy. Although the exact date of his disastrous trip to London has never been established, it must have taken place during the latter half of September.[23] His response to the London fiasco was not only an immediate return to writing, but also a feverish attempt, until May 1838 when he went to Bradford to set up as a portrait painter, to gain literary employment and to get himself published. On December 7, 1835 Branwell sent his now famous letter to **Blackwoods,** offering himself as a replacement for the late James Hogg (see pp. xxxv-xxxvi above).

However, according to this letter he had already written twice before, presumably in the same vein, though the letters are no longer extant. On April 8, 1836, he sent **Blackwoods** the manuscript of **Misery** (No. 54) offering both poetry and prose in the future (see p. 384). On January 4, 1837 he wrote again:

Now, Sir,

When I first wrote to you, it was with the intention of knowing what I was, and finding what I could do. I told you that I wrote,-- that no one had seen what I wrote,--that I knew you to be a man such as this world has seldom beheld,--and therefore I requested you to judge whether or not I was a worthless person, sending you a specimen for inspection, and offering you the use of my services in return for your Judgement.

Apparently refusing this offer, you then returned me no answer and--although I wrote again and more earnestly--you were silent still--.--But could you not see that I was determined not to be deterred from my endeavour? And if I was so then, I am so now-- Therefore Sir when I find fruitless all my past attempts to write your attention, I will make one last attempt,-- I will at last and most earnestly ask of you a personal Interview,--and I will tell you why I ask it.

In a former letter, I hinted, that I was in possession of something the design of which, whatever might be its execution, would be superior to that of any series of articles which has yet appeared in Blackwood's Magazine---But, being prose, of course, and of great length, as well as peculiar in character, a description of it by letter would be impracticable.--So surely a Journey of 300 miles should not deter me from a knowledge of myself and a hope of enterance into the open world.

Now, Sir, all I ask of you is----To permit this interview; and, in answer to this letter, to say that you will see me, were it only for half an hour--the fault be mine should you have reason to repent your permission.

Now, is the trouble of writing a single line, to outweigh the certainty of doing good to a fellow Creature and the possibility of doing good to yourself?-- Will you still so wearisomly refuse me a word, when you can neither know what you refuse or whom you are refusing?--Do you think your Magazine so perfect that no addition to its power would be either possible or desirable?--Is it pride which actuates you--or Custom-- or prejudice?--Be a Man Sir! and think no more of these things! Write to me--Tell me that you will receive a visit--And rejoicingly will I take upon myself the

labour, which, if it suceed, will be an Advantage both
to you and me,--and, if it fail, will still be an advantage, because I shall then be assured of the impossi-
bility of succeeding.

> with this request and <u>Hope</u>
> I remain, Sir, your obdt Ser^t;
> P. B. Brontë.

In the same month he also wrote to Wordsworth, enclosing a
version of No. **60** ("Still and bright in twilight shining") and stating that having "arrived at an age wherein I
must do something for myself . . . . My aim, Sir, is to push
out into the open world, and for this I trust not poetry
alone; that might launch the vessel, but could not bear her
on.   Sensible and scientific prose . . . would give further
title to the notice of the world; and then again poetry ought
to brighten and crown that name with glory" (for a complete
text see the comment for No. **60**).   Throughout these
letters, Branwell clearly still aspires to be the Man of
Letters, with poetry as his first love.

Unfortunately to none of these letters did he receive a
reply, and so continued to create and revise poems for publication, unchecked and unguided.   He prepared, for example,
two manuscript volumes of poems (Notebooks B and C).   The
first, begun in December 1835 and continued until May 1838
when he left for Bradford, contained eight poems, on sixty
pages, totalling 2630 lines.   Except for an additional eight
trial lines on the first page, the poems are fair copies,
although three are unfinished and three were revised once
more.   In the second notebook Branwell entered

> (a) between 9 March and 30 May, 1837, revisions of
> twenty-six (last one only partial) earlier poems,
> composed between December 1833 and July 1836, total-
> ling 1117 lines.   However, the first drafts of thir-
> teen of these poems, totalling 563 lines, were com-
> posed after the return from London;

> (b) between June 1837 and January 1838, six new poems
> totalling 554 lines;

> (c) between January and May 1838, translations of six
> Odes of Horace, totalling 167 lines.

All but two of the poems in the two notebooks are related to
Angria, but in most cases so vaguely that they could easily
be adapted for publication--as his sisters were to do for
their poems in 1846--indeed four (one only partially) were

later published, and he sent **Misery** (No. **54**) to
Blackwoods, using for the first time the signature
"Northangerland" that he was to use for all but one of the
poems he published. In addition to the two notebooks, he
composed 19 other poems (15 Angrian; 4 non-Angrian) totalling
832 lines (one--the first draft of **Sir Henry Tunstall**
(No. **126**)--was composed in Bradford immediately after his
arrival). Of these, two (one only partially) were later
published. In all, then, Branwell composed 49 new poems,
totalling approximately 4500 lines, excluding trial lines and
revisions. With all this activity, of course, the number of
variant drafts, fragments, and trial lines begins to
proliferate.

Even more significant than the fervor of poetic activity, however, is Branwell's gradual resolution of his dual
conception of himself as poet. Richton, Wentworth and Hastings continue to pour out page after page of narrative concerning Angria, especially its politics and wars. At the
same time, it is P. B. Brontë who reaffirms his dedication
to poetry in **The Spirit of Poetry** (No. **86**), one of
the two poems in Notebook C not composed by an Angrian per-
sonage. The other poems, though related to Angria, are not
embedded in a prose narrative, or are being lifted out of and
divorced from their original narrative context, and whoever
their original "Angrian author," the poems in Notebook C are
all "corrected," "enlarged" and "transcribed" by "P. B.
Brontë." Closely related to this change is the move
toward long narrative poems, with a strong retrospective/
reflective cast, continuing the trend noted on pp. xxxix-xl
above. All of this activity coincides with what I have
described as Charlotte's "third and last period of intensive
poetic composition" (Neufeldt PCB, pp. xxxviii-ix) with some
interesting parallels, but also at least one significant
difference. It was during this period (1836) that Charlotte
wrote to Wordsworth and Southey about her possibilities of
earning a living by writing, and that the boundary in her
poems between the personal/autobiographical and Angrian
gradually became more and more blurred. But if, as I have
suggested, Charlotte became aware of a waning poetic impulse
by 1838, the opposite is true of Branwell. Although he was
to make one more attempt to earn a living by painting, his
desire and drive to become a poet was strengthening. From
the time he left for Bradford, although he did produce a few
more prose narratives, Branwell essentially abandoned Angria
and turned more and more to writing long poems, complete in
themselves: public pieces meant for publication, meant to
establish him, suggest Barbara and Gareth Evans, as "the
James Hogg of Yorkshire."[24]

That aspiration obviously received encouragement from the friendship he developed with Joseph and Francis Leyland, especially when it became clear that his career as portrait painter was going nowhere. Mary Leyland describes Joseph, a sculptor and poet, who became Branwell's closest friend and confidant, as

> self opinionated, sarcastic, and unreliable, scornful of religion and of anyone who disagreed with him, only working when the spirit moved him, and spending the intervals in conviviality with William Dearden, Branwell Bronte, John Nicholson, the Airedale poet, and other kindred spirits of art and literature who had their headquarters at the George Hotel in Market St, Bradford, though they also met at the Black Bull at Haworth; Cross Roads, near Keighley; Anchor and Shuttle, Luddenden Foot; the Lord Nelson, Luddenden; and the Broad Tree, Union Cross, Talbot, and Old Cock in Halifax. At these meetings the literary members read the manuscripts of their latest books or poems for criticism by the other members.[25]

Branwell must have begun the practise of passing manuscripts on to Leyland (presumably for criticism) while he was still in Bradford, for two items dated January and May 1838 (see Nos. **98, 105**) for which the manuscripts have disappeared, appeared in Leyland in 1886. However, except for the first draft of **Sir Henry Tunstall**, Branwell seems not to have composed any significant poetry while he was in Bradford, nor after his return to Haworth in May 1839, when he began a study of the classics with his father, presumably, since painting was not to be his profession, to prepare him to take up teaching (Gérin, BB, p. 149).

This plan of study seems to have again revived Branwell's literary ambitions, for while he was a tutor for the Postlethwaites at Broughton-in-Furness, January–June 1840, he attempted once more to establish a literary career, this time as poet and translator. On April 15, he sent De Quincey a revised draft of **Sir Henry Tunstall** along with his translations of five Odes of Horace (see comment for **Appendix A**). On April 20, he sent Hartley Coleridge a revised draft of the last poem in Notebook B (No. **103**) and translations of two Odes of Horace, "two out of many" he claims in the accompanying letter (SHB LL, I, 205). He goes on to say that he is "about to enter active life" and needs to ascertain "whether by periodical or other writing, I could please myself with writing, and make it subservient to living," and if it would "be possible to obtain remuneration for translations for such as these from that or any other classic author?" The similarities of wording in this letter and the one he

sent to Wordsworth three years earlier (see comment for No.
60) seem to suggest that Branwell is dismissing his
painting and teaching in the interim as irrelevancies that
have distracted him from his true vocation. Coleridge must
have responded positively, for Branwell spent the first of
May with him, and encouraged by him (SHB LL, I, 210), continued work on the translations, sending Coleridge Book I of
Horace on June 27 (see comment for **Appendix A**), after he
had been dismissed from his position as tutor. However
further literary activity was curtailed by his appointment as
Assistant Clerk at Sowerby Bridge Railway Station on 31
August, and not until he became Clerk in charge of the station at Luddenden Foot, April 1, 1841, did Branwell once more
find the time and energy for literary composition.

Contrary to the traditional view that Branwell's days at
Luddenden Foot consisted of little more than lack of attention to his duties, idleness, and drunken debauchery (see,
for example, Gérin BB, pp. 186, 193, 197-201) which turned
him into a "mental and physical wreck" (Gérin, BB, p. 201),
the move from Sowerby Bridge provided new impetus to Branwell's literary aspirations. Just over a month after the
move--5 June 1841--he achieved his life-long ambition when
one of his poems (No. **105**) appeared in the **Halifax
Guardian** under the pseudonym Northangerland. In August he
not only published a second poem in the **Guardian** (No.
107), this time a political satire under his own initials, but he also began to enter drafts of poems into a
small, twenty-page notebook (Notebook D). Most of these
poems are related to a very ambitious project he seems to
have envisaged: a series of poems about a group of prominent
historical figures (see comment for Nos. **108-13**) who had
achieved human greatness in the face of human adversity, a
theme well summed up by the title he eventually gave to "Lord
Nelson," the third and longest poem in the notebook--**The
Triumph of mind over body** (see also No. **112**, ll. 29-
42).[26] Significantly, most of the figures are men of
letters. If not in real life, then in imagination, Nos.
111 and **112** make clear, he felt himself closely
allied to his heroes, and in chronicling their achievements
would in a small way experience the same triumph. In No.
114, addressed to his friend Grundy, and written about
the same time, though not in the notebook, Branwell, in a
similar vein, condemns those who would dismiss others on the
basis of station or appearance; the mind can triumph over
such disadvantages, especially the mind devoted to
literature. As Juliet Barker has pointed out, the ambition,
energy, optimism, and quality reflected in these poems belie
the usual description of Branwell's existence at Luddenden
Foot, and show instead that he "still believed he had a
future as a poet and that his present comparatively humble

station   in   life   was   no   impediment   to   future
greatness."[27]

Consistent with the pattern already noted, Branwell's
dismissal at Luddenden Foot at the end of March 1842 did not
dampen his literary activity; instead it seems to have
spurred him on to even greater efforts to establish himself
as a poet, perhaps again as a means of compensating for his
failure. Between April 1842 and January 1843, when he left
Haworth to become tutor at Thorp Green, he published nine
poems in three newspapers, six of which were revisions of
earlier poems; three (Nos. **119, 124, 125(b)**) were new.
In addition, he wrote No. **125(a)**; prepared the third
draft of No. **126**, and the second and third drafts of No.
127. All three were also intended for publication; in
fact he sent No. **125(a)** to Leyland and No. **126** to
Blackwoods in September (see **Commentary**); No. **127**
is a fair copy signed, as is **126**, "Northangerland," "consciously written on a high-minded theme with an eye to publication. Nelson was a national hero, as well as being a
family hero of the Brontë's."[28] The significance of
Branwell's eleven published poems between June 1841 and
August 1842 must not be underestimated, for it placed him in
the company of poets with established reputations. As Leyland points out, in those days there was scarcely a locality
in West Yorkshire without its poet, "and that poet, too, a
man of no mean powers" (Leyland I, 187), and their poems
appeared in the Yorkshire newspapers. However those newspapers included not only the work of such local worthies as
Thomas Crossley, Robert Storey, James Montgomery, Alaric
Watts and John Nicholson, the Airedale poet, but also poems
by Wordsworth, Tennyson, Shelley, Southey, Hood, Leigh Hunt,
Thomas Campbell, and Longfellow among others. And indeed
Branwell seems to have made some effort to draw attention to
his poems. In a letter to Grundy, 9 June 1842, he notes that
"Mr. James Montgomery, and another literary Gentleman, who
have lately seen something of my 'head work,' wish me to turn
some attention to literature; sending me, along with their
advice, plenty of puff and praise" (SHB LL, I, 265)[29]; in
his letter to **Blackwoods** noted above, he states that "the
kind advice and encouragement of Mrs. Southey has alone emboldened me to make this offering"; and in a letter to
Grundy, 25 October 1842, he states, "I had meant not only to
have written to you, but to the Rev. James Martineau, gratefully and sincerely acknowledging the receipt of his most
kindly and truthful criticism" (SHB LL I, 273). Grundy indicates that he, at Branwell's request, sent **The Triumph of
mind over body** to "Leigh Hunt, Miss Martineau, and others.
All spoke in high terms of it" (p. 79). Also in 1842, according to Francis Leyland, Joseph Leyland advised Branwell
to publish his poems "with his name appended, rather than the

pseudonym of 'Northangerland'" (Leyland II, 25). Perhaps unfortunately, Branwell seems to have lacked the confidence to
take that step. He replied in a letter of 12 July 1842:
"Northangerland has so long wrought on in secret and silence
that he dare not take your kind encouragement in the light in
which vanity would prompt him to do" (Leyland Letters, p.
15).[30]

However, such publication and notice as Branwell did
achieve did not provide any income, and so from January 1843
to July 1845 he was employed as tutor at Thorp Green. During
this time he produced only six short poems, but desire to
publish did not disappear, for the last two (Nos. **131** and
132) were signed "Northangerland" and sent to Joseph Leyland, though perhaps not until after Branwell's dismissal,
for there is no evidence of correspondence between Branwell
and Leyland while the former was at Thorp Green. Why they
were not published is not apparent.

Despite his distraught condition, his physical and
mental turmoil, after his dismissal from Thorp Green Branwell
once more turned his energies to literary composition and
publication, embarking on several ambitious projects during
1845 and 46. However, as 1846 wore on, more and more work
was left unfinished. Immediately after his dismissal, he
began revisions of three earlier poems (Nos. **133-35**), the
second of which was to be the first canto of a long poem.
However, the first two remained unfinished (though No.
134 was sent to Leyland), and the third was part of his
unfinished novel, **And the Weary are at Rest**, begun in the
summer of 1845, with the first volume completed, says Branwell, in September (Leyland Letters, p. 19). In the same
letter, he notes that he had earlier sent Leyland some verse
(possibly Nos. **134** and/or **136**), and that his proposed
novel is a diversion dictated by the need to earn some money
(see pp. xxxvi-xxxvii). Before the end of 1845, he completed
four more poems, two of which (Nos. **136** and **138**) were
published in the **Halifax Guardian**, thereby at least
partially negating his comment to Grundy (October 1845) that
"at the kind request of Mr. Macaulay and Mr. Baines [editor
of the **Leeds Mercury**], I have striven to arouse my mind
by writing something worthy of being read, but I really
cannot do so" (SHB LL, II, 68).

His professed inability to write anything worthwhile
notwithstanding, Branwell began 1846 with one published poem
(No. **141**), another obviously intended for publication
(No. **140**), and a scheme to write an epic in several
cantos about Morley Hall (see comment for No. **147**). In
his letter of 28 April, requesting information about Morley,
Branwell complains to Leyland about the "hopelessness of

bursting through the barriers of literary circles, and getting a hearing among publishers . . . . Otherwise I have the materials for a respectably sized volume, and if I were in London personally I might try Henry Moxon,--a patronizer of the sons of rhyme . . . . As I know that while here, I might send a manuscript to London, and say good bye to it I feel it folly to feed the flames of a printer's fire" (Leyland Letters, p. 26--italics added). Although the death of Mr. Robinson in June and its attendant consequences upset and distracted Branwell greatly, by October he was back at work on **Morley Hall**, writing optimistically to Leyland about progress on the poem (see comment for No. **147**), and Nos. **148** and **149** seem to have been begun in late 1846 or early 1847. In all, then, he produced ten poems in 1846, not including item **(d)** in **Appendix B.** Contrary to common belief, therefore, the result of the Robinson affair was not immediate total collapse.

In 1847 it becomes apparent, however, that whatever his intentions might be, Branwell's will and ability to write are fading rapidly. He produced only two poems and six fragments, and of these, five were reworkings of earlier Angrian material, yet he published No. **154** and sent No. **150** to Leyland, asking if "it would be worth sending to some respectable periodical like Blackwood's Magazine" (Leyland Letters, p. 42). Even now the Blackwood's dream had not died completely, nor had his dreams of publishing, for in January 1848, only eight months before his death, he wrote to Leyland, "When you return me the manuscript volume which I placed in your hands [presumably in the previous week] will you (if you can easily lay your hands on it) enclose that manuscript called 'Caroline' [No. **134**]--left with you many months since" (Leyland Letters, p. 46). Clearly, Branwell's dream of becoming a man of letters and a poet remained with him to the end.

This brief sketch of Branwell's poetic career establishes, I believe, that he came much closer to realizing that dream than any of his biographers have been willing to acknowledge. There are those who have argued that potentially, at least, Branwell was Emily's equivalent as a poet. As early as 1915, E. F. Benson wrote:

I believe he had a higher instinct for poetry than either Charlotte or Anne . . . . He had the same untamed, imprisoned sense that Emily had, the same passionate rebellion against the discipline of life. And there is a real originality of phrase and even of thought about his best work, a relentless fidelity which is more akin to art than the deliberate and misapplied toil which characterizes the weaker work of Charlotte

and Anne . . . . Unlike Emily he was deeply ambitious,
and like Charlotte, he would have found success sustaining (pp. xviii-ix).

C. W. Hatfield, in his introduction to **And the Weary are at
Rest** in 1924, offered a similar assessment of Branwell's
status as a poet, and lamented that "Only a few of his poems
have been printed" (p. x), implying that until the full cor-
pus of Branwell's work was available such assertions could
neither be substantiated or discredited. With this edition,
it will be possible to make that informed assessment of the
quality of Branwell's poetic achievement.

Notes

1 Speaking of the early writing of Charlotte and Branwell, Barbara and Gareth Evans note:

> There is no one complete and accurate edition of all these MSS . . . . Some have been transcribed and editions published, but by no means all of them, particularly in the case of Branwell's writing. Moreover, what has been published is not always easily accessible. Some volumes are either out of print or so large and expensive that they are beyond the pocket of the ordinary book-buyer. Some that have been reissued or republished are, sadly, not updated in the light of more recent knowledge and are often unreliable, with material omitted, misdated or misread. There are also references to some manuscripts, by title, that seem no longer to exist at all--or are being held back, wittingly or unwittingly, their location and/or history of their acquisition shrouded in mystery. As there is, therefore, no single complete and accurate source for the scholar or the interested amateur to go to and browse through, it has not yet been possible to feel the full impact of the vast amount of writing that Charlotte and Branwell accomplished during their early childhood and teenage years.--**Everyman's Companion to the Brontës** (London: J. M. Dent and Sons, 1982), p. 154.

While Alexander CB, when completed, will produce such a source for Charlotte, the foregoing comment still remains an accurate assessment of the state of Branwell's works.

2 One early exception is Leyland, who felt that Branwell had been badly misrepresented by Mrs. Gaskell and that "his life should be treated independently of the theories and necessities of his sisters' biographers, and in a spirit not unfriendly to him" (I, 162).

3 See Nos. **129, 137, 140, 142, 143, 152.** For reasons never explained, Nicholls not only gave away bits of manuscript by Branwell, Charlotte and Anne to his relatives, he also retained sizable quantities of manuscript by both Charlotte and Branwell which were later sold at the Sotheby's sales of his wife's effects (see Neufeldt PCB, p. xxiv). Clearly, Nicholls deceived Shorter and Wise about the amount of manuscript material he had, and led them to believe that they had cornered far more of the market than they actually had.

4 **In the Footsteps of the Brontës** (London: Sir Isaac Pitman and Sons, 1914), pp. 85-86.

5 See notes for items 35 and 36 in the catalogue for **Sixty Treasures,** the Diamond Jubilee exhibition at the Brontë Parsonage Museum in 1988-89, prepared by Juliet R. V. Barker.

6 At the same time, Hatfield also wrote to Wise to point out that the manuscript volume he had bound and titled **A New Year Story** (Ashley 187), and described as a single work, signed and dated at the beginning and end, in fact consisted of fragments from several manuscripts "not even arranged in chronological order" (Symington Papers, BPM). He provided Wise with the correct chronological order on the proof sheets; the information was ignored.

7 In addition to Notebooks A, B, C and D (see pp. xixiv), the poems last known to have been in the possession of Mrs. C. B. Branwell (note 3 above) all seem originally to have been part of one notebook (see Flintoff, p. 241), and the leaves containing No. **155** and the other items noted in **Appendix B (e)** are from a larger notebook.

8 On 17 November 1926, C. W. Hatfield wrote to Davidson Cook, "I now learn from him [H. H. Bonnell], and am not at all surprised, that his Branwell Brontë manuscripts, which are beautifully bound and which he thought to be complete, are really made up of odd sheets from various manuscripts." On 24 December 1926, Hatfield wrote, "He [Bonnell] bought a lot of Branwell's poems as Emily's but both the dealers and he were deceived in these instances by Shorter's Complete Works of E. B. printed in 1910 and 1911" (Wise Collection).

9 **Brontë Poems** (London: Smith Elder and Co., 1915), p. xviii.

10 Ironically, the call for "finality" was first issued by T. J. Wise. Initially Symington and Blackwell considered omitting poetry entirely from the proposed edition. Wise responded in a letter to Symington (6 April 1931--Symington Papers, BPM):

> I cannot understand your suggestion to omit the Poems.
> To do so would in the first place be to render your edition incomplete, and thus deprive it of one of its chief attractions, and one of its greatest claims. Your warcry should surely be "The Final, and only Complete Edition of the Writings of the Brontë Family." If you fail in this, sooner or later, probably sooner than later, some other publisher will take the wind out of your sails. With all the new stuff you can add, you are in a position to bring out an absolutely definite and final edition; under such circumstances every copy is

bound to sell; it is only a question of time, for the Brontës are classic, and no competition could by any means be introduced into the market" (Symington Papers, BPM).

Despite being named Co-editor and offering "to assist the great undertaking in any way I can," Wise contributed very little to the preparation of the edition, constantly pleading illness of one kind or another in his subsequent letters of 1932-34. Although he supplied Symington with some transcriptions, he was at times unable to find manuscripts and/or transcriptions that were supposed to be in his library.

11 **Charlotte Brontë** (London: Methuen, 1988), p. 57.

12 Like Charlotte's (see Neufeldt PCB, p. xxxiv), most of Branwell's early manuscripts were "published" works in Glass Town, with title page and full bibliographical information.

13 Perhaps the fact that from June 1827 on, Christopher North had, in the "Noctes," a Newfoundland dog named Bronte, who became a character in his own right, and who, when poisoned, was replaced with another Newfoundland named O'Bronte, also played a part in Branwell's childhood fondness for **Blackwoods.**

14 See **Appendix B** on the number of issues of Branwell's magazine. In August, Charlotte took over the editorship, renaming the magazine **Blackwoods Young Mens Magazine,** but Branwell continued to contribute until the end of the year. The travel book, the manuscript of which has disappeared, has the following title-page according to Dembleby, p. 31, who saw the manuscript while it was in the possession of the London bookseller, Walter T. Spencer:

The TRAVLES of ROLANDO SEGUR
Comprising his Adventures throughout the
voyage, and in America, Europe, South Pole, etc, etc
By
PATRICK Branwell
BRONTE--
Author of Townslaw Book   Journey to Leeds
Young Men's magazine -- Tragical Book,
Newspaper, &c, &c, &c -- Volumn I -- Begun
April The fifteenth -- Ended May Twenty sevmth
1829

15 There is no information on the length of the poem in the missing May issue of the magazine noted in **Appendix B.**

16 Note, for example, the lapse from blank verse into rhyme beginning at Act II, l. 39 of **Laussane.**

17 See also No. **28.** For Charlotte's less generous view of Sergeant Bud, see No. **29** and Alexander CB, I, 56, and 128.

18 The edition read by the children (at the BPM) contains as introductory material "A Preliminary Discourse" (with extensive notes), pp. vii-xxxvi; a "Preface," pp. 1-6; "A Dissertation Concerning The Aera of Ossian," pp. 7-18; "A Dissertation Concerning the Poems of Ossian," pp. 19-46; "A Critical Dissertation on the Poems of Ossian," pp. 47-137. According to the review of Bud's 29-volume commentary in the July magazine, "The preface occupied l. vol. folio. Introduction l vol folio. Introductory dissertation 3 vols folio--Ossian with Commentarys--23 vols folio & Appendix Index &c l vol folio." The review then offers two samples of Bud's commentary, each occupying a tiny page: the first consists of nine lines of verse, followed by 38 half-lines of commentary in two columns (as in Young Soult's poems), the second of two lines of verse, followed by 58 half-lines of commentary. Perhaps with some justice, the reviewer (P B B) concludes: "This is one of the most long winded Books that have ever been printed we must now conclude for we are dreadfully tired." As Fannie Ratchford notes, twelve-year- old Branwell "joins astonishing bibliographic technique to childish conceptions" (p. 31).

19 Charlotte's poems are much more supportive of the Genii, as are the poems she and Branwell collaborated on. See also Alexander EW, pp. 31 and 37.

20 For reasons yet to be determined, there are no known manuscripts of Branwell's for the first five months of 1830.

21 See Nos. **37** and **42.** He does, however, reappear as the Marquis of Marseilles, composer of No. **70.**

22 Nos. **88** and **89** by Richton and Wentworth are exceptions. In general, Branwell separated his poetic persona from his prose persona with different pseudonyms--for example Young Soult/Sergeant and Captain Bud; Hastings/Flower and Wentworth, although in Hastings the two functions merge.

23 On 7 September, Patrick Brontë wrote to William Robinson, "If all be well, Branwell hopes to be with you on

Friday next, in order to finish his course of lessons" (SHB LL, I, 132). However, the final section of the so-called Battle of Loango manuscript (see Alexander EW, pp. 277 n. 14; 278 n. 17; 279 n. 1) at the PML is dated 3 October 1835, and is followed by a steady stream of manuscripts through the rest of 1835.

24 **Everyman's Companion to the Brontës**, p. 179.

25 "The Leyland Family," **Transactions of the Halifax Antiquarian Society**, 1954, p. 37.

26 Having begun this poem in late August/early September, Branwell worked at it intermittently until early December, with Nos. **110** and **111** interspersed among the first 297 lines, then seems to have abandoned it until after he returned home from Luddenden Foot, for ll. 238-68 appear after No. **116** dated April 25, 1842.

27 **Sixty Treasures**, comment for item 36. See also Juliet Barker, **The Brontës: Selected Poems** (London: M. J. Dent & Sons, 1985), pp. 116-17. The list of names-- Tasso, Galileo, Milton, Otway, Johnson, Cowper, Burns--that occurs in conjunction with No. **112** is partially written over an unfinished, caricatured self-portrait.

28 Barker, **Brontë Poems**, p. 118. Mr. Brontë, whose surname was originally Brunty, changed his name to Brontë while he was at Cambridge, taking the name from Nelson's Sicilian title, Duke of Brontë.

29 Note, however, that the SHB LL quotes the letter inaccurately.

30 Branwell persisted in using the pseudonym to the end. He used it not only for 14 of his 15 published poems, but also for Nos. **54, 126, 127, 131,** (likely **132**), **133** and **144,** all of which were also intended for publication.

THE POEMS

1   Oh may America
           Yeild to our Monarchs sway--,
           And No more contend &
           May they their interest see
           With England to agree   5
           And from oppression frre--
           All that amend

                        [January 1829]

MS: A
First Publication: Ratchford Web
Text: l. 6: "free" obviously intended

2   DIRGE OF THE GENii--*

           THUS I begin my song--
           The Genii all are gone--
           Theyre gone gone gone--
           Gone for ever gone--

           The sky is blackning--   5
           +Its rain pours down--
           Its tears for the Genii--
           while we are dancing rond

           while we are dancing rond
           wile the merry bagpips sound   10
           answer to our triping feet
           above below around--

           So hurra O ye Genii--
           Ye have got your maches now
           Alas once to your Feiry eye   15
           all all the earth did bow--

           but now O ye Genii--
           ye are laid in your graves
           & above below around you
           do dance the merry knaves   20

           thus I do end my song--
           the Genii all are gone--
           there gone gone gone--
           gone for ever gone--
           _____

                        3

          +should be The sky it is <bl--->
          The clouds porus down

                                        [June 1829]

MS: A
First Publication: Ratchford Web, in facsimile
Text: ll. 9 and 10 are badly blotted

* For a glossary of Glass Town/Angrian person and place
names, see **Appendix D**

3   the bill it [h]as past
           at last at last--
           it has past like the sun in his glory
           in my mind I cast
           that it would not have past   5
           or else two[u]ld have pased gory

                                        [June 1829]

MS: A
Not previously published

4   If you live by the sunny Fountain--
           if you live in the streets of a town
           if you live on the top of a mountain
           or if you wear a crown--
                       --The Genii meddle with you   5

           Think not that in your graves
           you will be quiet there--
           For Genii come with spades
           To dig you up they dare
                       Genii will meddle with you   10

           even if in your palaces--
           among your courteir[s] there
           The genii meddle with you--
           For mischief is there care--
                       Genii must meddle with you   15

           Come Britons then arise--
           and let your swords be bare
           of wich the geniis blood--

                          4

```
        let them be covered fair--
                --They shall not meddle with you 20

                              [June 1829]

MS:  A
First Publication:  Ratchford Web, partial



5        One day I went out awalking
         and I saw a sheet of fire
         hovering oere the mountian
         kindled was my are

         It blazed upon the mountain                    5
         and upon the castle wall--
         It blazed upon the Ocean--
         & the distant coast of Gall--

         then suddenly it flew afar
         over Africs desart sand                       10
         till it seemed like the even star
         I saw it streech its wand--

         upon a caravan of Arabs--
         I saw him streech his hand
         so that they every one did die                15
         by the stroke of his great wand

         I saw it was a Genius now
         so that I ran away--
         For fear that he should let me know
         if this was my last day--                     20

                              [July 1829]

MS:  A
First Publication:  Ratchford Web, partial
Text: 1. 4:  "are"--"ire" probably intended



6        High minded Frenchmen love not the ghost
         who rides on the clouds of war
         with the eye of an eagle he views your hosts
         and grins with delight from far
                  ----------------
```

For the time in his powerful mind he sees   5
when like a slave before him led
the kingdom of France shall bow at his knees
& gloryfy him as its head

Though at this time his brow ma<y> not lour
he looks to the future with Joy   10
when from his high embattled tower
in his terrible might he shall cry

Kingdom of France I bid thee beware
at the storm which is drawing nigh
Look at the troubled & darkening air   15
Look at the wrath in mine eye

                    Young Soult July 17 1829

MS: B(1)
First Publication: Winnifrith PCB

7   O when shall our brave land be free
               when shall our castles rise
               in pure & glorious liberty
               before our joyful eyes

               How long shall tyrants ride in state   5
               upon the thundercloud
               the arbiters of Englands fate
               and of her nobles proud

               Thou sun of liberty arise--
               upon our beauteous land   10
               terrible vengeance rend the skys
               let tyrants feel they hand

               let tyrants feel thy hand we cry
               & let them see thy gaze
               for they will shrink beneath thy eye   15
               & we will sing thy praise

               the song of vengeance shall arise
               before the morning sun
               illuminates the arched skys
               or its high course doth run   20

6

the song of vengeance shall not cease
when midnight cometh on
when the silver moon shines out in peace
to light the traveler lone

July the 24   U T

MS: A
First Publication: Neufeldt PCB

8   what is more glorious in nature or art
       than a bottle of Brandy clear
       there's nothing I like so well for my part
       it rids you of evry fear

       it raises your spirits on stillest night   5
       it carries you lightly along
       it wings you away from this pitiful sight
       & disposes your min[d] for a song

       for a song like mine it makes you wish
       & it keeps your eyes from a doze   10
       unless you are dull as a kettle of fish
       then't sends you of to repose

       I hope high Duke that you like my song
       which for your pleasure I chant
       as it is beautiful & not long   15
       your approbation grant

                        [July/August 1829]

MS: A
First Publication: Neufeldt PCB

9   **Interior of A Pothouse By Young Soult**

       the cheerful fire is blazing bright
       & cast[s] a ruddy glare
       on beams & rafters all in sight
       & on the sanded floor

the scoured pewter on the shelf
glitters like silver pure
& all the ware of stony delf
doth like to Gold allure

and where this fire so magical
doth spread its light around
sure many scenes most magical
are acted on that ground

about that oaken table
in the middle of the floor
are sat those who are able
to play one card or more

and now behold the stakes are set
now watch the anxious faces
of all who have laid down a bet
scarce can they keep their places

but see the teller holds the card
above the silent crowd
look at his meagre visage hard
& list' his accents loud

he says the card is number one
look at that fellow there
I think he has his buisness done
Behold his ghastly stare

now he has drawn his sword
and plunged it in his side
look at his dying struggle
while <r>ushes forth the tide

of red & streaming blood
the current of his life
pouring a crimson flood
while all within the strife

of racking pain of body
& torturing pain of mind
doth rend his heart in peices
& will no freind mos[t] king

wipe from his brow the calmy swet
& cheer his dying hour
promise to aid his orphans dear
with all within his power

5

10

15

20

25

30

35

40

```
            no there they'll alway let him lay              45
            & pass unheeding by
            unless the[y] find him in their way
            when theyll kick him all awry

            or tearing up a flag
            in the neatly sanded floor                      50
            theyll throw him in & leave <him> there
            & think of him no more

            & now I've done my verses
            you may read them if you choose
            or throw them in the fire                       55
            as Ive nought to gain or lose

                              Young Soult
                              August the 21 1829
```

MS: B(3)
First Publication: Neufeldt PCB
Text: ll. 40-41: "kind" and "clammy" obviously intended

10   **The Glass Town by U T**
              the Glass Town

                          1
```
            tis sunset & the golden orb
            has sunk behind the mountains far
            & rises now the silver moon
            & sparkles bright the evening star
```

                          2
```
            but in the west an crimson light                5
            above the horizon glows
            tinting all nature with the bright
            gay colours of the rose
```

                          3
```
            and over all the eastern sky
            the robe of twilight gray                        10
            is heaving up the heavens nigh
            while the pale milky way
```

                          4
```
            goes clearer still & clearer
            as vanishes the light
```

till it arches all the firmament   15
like a rainbow of the night

but the sound of murmuring waters
from distance far I hear
like the rushing of a cataract
it fall[s] upon my ear   20

tis the roaring of the multitude
within those mighty walls
whose noise is like to rageing
or rushing waterfalls

tis that great & glorious city   25
whose high ruler doth defy
the might[i]est of the a[r]mies
who their strength against her try

O may he ever reign in glory
may his glittering sword be dyed   30
in the life blood of his enemies
though on the clouds they ride

O may he bring them to the <earth>
with fearful scorn and shame
may they bow their heads before him   35
& dread his mighty name

but now the roaring sound has ceased
the city is sunk to sleep
& oer the world nights curtain falls
mid silence still & deep   40

but yet the silver moon shine[s] out
& the brilliant sparkling stars
are wheeling down the firmament
their shining pearly <cars>

no sound doth break the silence   45
save the merry nightingale
as it pours its sweet warbling
dow[n] the still & lonely vale

                    U T August the 25 1829

MS: B(3)
First Publication: Neufeldt PCB

10

11   on seeing A beautiful statue
            & a rich golden vase full of wine lying beside
            it in the desert of Sahara

see that golden goblet shine
decked with gems so starry bright
crowned with the most sparkling wine
casting forth a ruby light

Emerald leaves its brim encircle   5
with their brilliant green
and rich grapes of saphire purple
twined with these are seen

near a majestic statue
of purest marble stands   10
rising like a spirit
from the wilderness of sand's

but heark unto that trumpet swell
which soundeth long and loud
rivalling the music   15
of the darkest thundercloud

tis the signal that from hence
we both of us must go
so come my brother dear
let it be even so   20

           U T Sep^t 2 1829

MS: A
First Publication: Neufeldt PCB
Text: A canceled stanza following stanza three reads:
      but see a flash of lightning
      has darted from that cloud
      now listen to that thunder peal
      so crashing long and loud

12   THE SONG of THE ANCIENT
                  BRITON'S
        ON LEAVING THE GENILAND by U T

Farewell O thou pleasant land
rich are thy feild's and fair

thy mighty forest's they are grand
but freedom dwells not there

thy rugged mountains rise sublime   5
from the barren desert wild
and thou wouldst be a pleasant land
if freedom on thee smiled

Our hearts are sad as we turn from thee
and thy pleasant smiling shore   10
to think that not again shall we
Behold thee ever more

ere many day's are passed away
the sea will between us lie
and when in freedoms land we dewll   15
for thee we'll heave a sigh

because that oer thee triumph
those tyrant's of the air
who dwell in halls of thunder
& robes of lightning wear   20

but now we're bound afar off
to our fathers land we go
swift foaming billows roll us
and winds of heaven blow

there rises freedoms palace   25
like a tower of burning gold
around it roars the ocean
with its world of waters rolled

up to the glorious castle
where mighty freedom dewells   30
while round her like a tempest
sea music sweetly swells
                          U T
                          Sep^t 7 1829

But now were bound afar [off]
to our father's land we go
swif[t] foaming billows roll us   35
and winds of heaven blow

                          U T
                          Sep^t 7 1829

MS: A
First Publication: Neufeldt PCB

ON seeing the Garden of
A Genius by U T

How pleasant is the world
where mighty Geni dwell
like a vision is the beauty
of wild forest stream & fell

their palaces arise   5
from the green and flowry ground
while strains of sweetest music
are floating all around

their castles of bright adamant
all mortal strength defy   10
encircled round with geni
towering like rocks on high

& now behold that verdant plain
spa[n]gled with star like flowers
watered by purest silver lakes   15
& crowned with emerald bowers

in the midst appear[s] a palace
of yellow topaz bright
from which streams forth a glory
of sunny golden light   20

O if the dwellers in this land
heeded their dreadful name
how all the mortal world would sing
that bright & quenchless Fame

But now the eye of hatred   25
follows whereere they go
in the sea or in the firmament
it trys to work them woe

they may robe themselves in darkness
themselves with lightning crown   30
they may weild the sword of vengeance
but to them we'll not bow down

they may frame in the dark ocean
high palaces of pearl
mid the silver orbs of heaven   35
their dragon wings unfurl

& throned on the star's of night
while thunder rolls around

may bid the earth to wait on them
but vain shall be the sound   40

                        U T
                   Sep^t 9 1829

how pleasant is the world
where mighty geni dwell
like a vision is the beauty
of wild forest stream & fell &c &c

MS: A
First Publication: Neufeldt PCB

14   **THE AMMON TREE**
                 Cutter a poem by young Soult
                        the Ryhmer
                 ==============================

O Miserable man
who to the injury of thyself
and others leadest a wretched life
of pain and sorrow not one drop of joy
O think how many thou hast made lamen[t]   5
even untill their last and worst day
I tell thee think and leave thy wret[c]hed life
Or die by the Remor[s]eless hand of Law
wich spareth not nor knoweth how to spare
those wretches who to Dare it do pretend   10
Think when thou hearst the sentence of the jud[ge]
thou wretch thou art by law condemd to die
then Bound then Manacled thou art led
  unto the yawning bloody guilotine

Ammon Cutter- - - - -	or make stools of
or Ammon skinner	their bones- - - - - - -
these are a most dang	O vile amon tree cutter
erous class of men--	thee I will slay
Inhabitants of Paris	and fling thee in the gutter
and its enviorns they	that thou may rot away
go out in the Nights--	O vile Ammon tree cutter
and cutt down all the	thee I do hate
Ammon Trees and- - -	and some day wen. I see. thee
burn all the vineyards	Ill dash thy dismal pate
of those against whom	Culvin<gton>
they have a spite. and	vol 3.325
If they can catch the	Guilotine- - - - - - -
owners they flay them	A instrument used in--
allive--and then tie--	France instead of the--

14

them to a tree with	Gallows- - - - -
their skin as an--	
umbrella	

O leave thy wicked life when thou dost hear   15
what I am going to say tis for thy good
in Paris in that most famous city
though it is oft convulsed by horrid wars
their lived a Man by nature feirce & high--
also proud and disdainful. rich he was.   20
but with low villains meetin[g] they did strip
him of his riches and did leave him poor--
Desolate and fo[r]lorn he wrung his hands--
he stamped he raved he tore his hair--
but all for nought for they s[t]ood looking on   25
with the utmost composure hah thou poor
Deluded man. he could not brook all this
but forth with out he ran and for long time
nothing of him was heard- - -
End of the First Book
PBB.   Sept 1.
1829

In Paris that most & c	abodes of misery wide
PARIS a city and- - -	spacious streets little
capital of Frenchyland	dirty narrow lanes- - -
situate on the River--	Travles. vol 2
Siene. 50 miles of the	p. 355
open sea it is a glassto	with low villains- - - -
wn. and very large it is	this alludes to a Tavern
thus de[s]cribed by Capt	the most horrid
Tree- - - - - - - - - -	places imaginable for
O Paris I approach thee	an accurate
thou world in minature	discription of one see
full of Wickedness.	Discription of a Tavern
Rioting Idleness &	Branwells Magazine
Grandeur thou hast	March 1829- - - - - -
Tembles* reaching	by M Chateubriand
to the skys the abode	
of Grandeaur holes	
in the groung* the	

* "Temples" and "ground" obviously intended

The Ammon tree cutter
BOOK 2

One moonlight stary Night along the side
Of the clear lake which semed another sky--
I slowly walkt. thinking upon those times

when europe was involved in dreadful war
and wild dest[r]u[c]tion raised her standard high   5
I saw a shining light burst from the Trees
calld Ammon which their heads did statly rear--
and O that light did shine so briliantly
that it seemd like the sun on Oceans wave
Into the grove I walked to see that light   10
which did shine with such splendour on the lake
that it did serve ins[t]ead of the pale moon
which then enwraped in clouds did hide itself
I went and Oh wat met my aching sight
The very man of whom I spoke before--   15
his face was haggard and his sleeve tuckt up--
a knife which reekd with blood was in his hand

When Europe was &c	fruit called Almonds
the time of the late	like the sun on oceans &c
French Revolution--	this passage may seem
in which all the	obscure at first but after
Nations of--	a little reflection people
that qua[r]ter of the	will see that it is a just
globe acted and took	simile for the sun set
the part	ing on the sea causes a
Amonn. tree- - - - -	long Train of light
of Almond tree is a	to shine over the sea--
tall and sta[te]ly tree	this may well be compa
which produces the	red to the rays darting
	from some <su[r]fess after>
	bright light <streams>

He trampled upon a victim skinnd
Who writhd about in dying agonies
Onward I rushed on the Murderer.   20
I seized him by his throat & cried forbear
forbear thou Wretch from slaugthe[r]ing this man
He stared at me then with a fearful cry
Away he dashd leaving part of his flesh
with me such was the fearful wrench he gave   25
I He[s]itated to pursue for he--
did run like leopard bounding oer the plain
And now the morning came with swiftest wings
The sun arisen brightend all the feilds--
and gladned Natuere sung her song of joy   30
as on to <Paris> I did bend my way
                Eend of the Second Book
PBB.   Sept 6
                                            1829.

16

What do I hear--
Is it the sou[n]d of multituds--
Or the mighty cataracts roar--
Yes tis a Roaring Rushing multitude--
that Horrid Instrument the guilotine   5
which doth before them gapind* bloody stand

A victim skinned	of the Amon trees**
alluding to the mann	see <Note> page 1--
er in which they	the < >
treat the masters	see <Note> page 1--

* "gaping" obviously intended
** these two notes are heavily blotted and virtually
unreadable

before the judge whose is seated on high
their stands a wretch in whom I recognise
that very murderer who flayed alive
that man in the dark grove of Ammon tre[es]   10
handcutted and bound and pale he was
and haggard was his cheek deep sunk his eye
but still a sterne and frowning look had he
<Taws>* he who once was rich who Now was poor
Sternly he eyed the Judge who thus began--   15
Villain thoust dared the Mighty Empreurs laws
In killing his great Marshall Peirre Marmont
Thy punishment is Death by th[e] guillotine
The villain raised a Horrid wailing cry
Ha Ha you vile partial Judge Murat- - -   20
I am then doomed to die the Dismal death
Yes but before I do Revenge is Mine
Revenge Revenge Revenge so saying he flew
on the Judge Murat and like a madman
  Tore him in peices saying Revenge Revenge   25

The Mighty Empreur	Judge Murat
Napoleon Bonaparte	Napoleons Brother in
Empreure of the--	Law a savage man--
French	who would not care
great Peirre Marmont	for the death of his
the famous Marmont	own son more than
or Marma. as he is--	that of a Rabbit--his
sometimes calld he	Name at full lenght
is a mortal enemy	is Jean Joachim- - -
to young soults--	Murat. Mayor
Fathrer Marshall	of the City of Paris
Alexander Soult--	Chateaubriand.

```
the soldiers and police did now rush on--
like to the waves driving against a rock
to take him from the dead Jean Joachim
who was torn peicemeal in a thousand bits--
and lay in his last agoneis on t. floor--                    30
Stern the villain stood his sword was lifted high
and the first that came up his skull in tow** was
     clef[t]
another and anothe[r] followd him--
but at the last the Murderer was took
they flayed him then coated him with salt                    35
then laid him on a gridiron to roast alive
and Oh the Horrid yells that burst from him
was like the roaring of the wind mid trees
and rocks and mountains in a misty Isle
untill at last they slowly died away                         40
unto a low hoarse mourmur then were gone
and nought was heard but dripping of the fat
into the raging fires which blazd around
THE multitude movd of and left him there

* "Twas" probably intended
** "two" obviously intended
```

```
                    concluding observations on the
                    Poem of the Ammon
                    Tree Cutter.
```

```
The Ammon tree cutter is certanly one of the best
of young Soults productions and also one of th[e]
longest it is said the reason why he wrote
it was one of them had been spoiling his
Fathers trees.  in this poem he evidently
makes fun of Murat as any person will
see who reads it.  some will wonder
why he speaks of persons living after
they are skinned alive and it to them
(especialy those living in England)
seem[s] impropable* and erroneous--
but it is neither for it is known how
Hard Frenchmen are to kill some--
cant be killed for a day others for 2
days and Pigtail. cannot be killed--
for 3-days!!!  certainly these
cases are not often but a vast--
Number will live 12 hours afte[r]
they are skinned alive or their--
Hearts cut out.  but No Frenchman
```

or Englishman or any other man--
can remain alive after their Heads are
cut of
    Frenchmen can live while their heads are on
    Frenchmen can live when their Hearts are gone
    Frenchmen cant live when their heads are of
    & Frenchmen cant endure a scoff
                  Tree. vol 2 p11
this saying of Captain Trees is very jus[t]
For Frenchmen can never endure a- - -
Scoff. or Taunt or Bitter joke they--
either will fly out into an ingovernab
le--feury or go and hang or poison--
themselvs without more ado- - - - - -

                CHATEAUBRIAND

* "improbable" obviously intended

                      [September 1829]

MS: B(2)
First Publication: Ratchford Web, partial

15   **Visit to the ruins--ColdaiDuh--**

        ———————————————————————

    THE golden sun had long gone down
had sank beneath the azure sky
when I from Vina journ[i]ed on
    To see the ruins of coldaiai

Along I travlld many a mile--   5
    over the bleak and dseart plain
    wher nought was seen but high mondile
And the far distant stormy main

I travlld till the Moon arose--
    I travlld till the Night was gone   10
    I travlld till the Midnights close
I travlld till the Morning sun

In his high splendour did arise
    to drive the clouds afar away
    to reedn all the arched skys   15
    To promise a fine Harvest day

When before me what did their stand
but the ruins of great coldaiduh
still stood his eastern tower grand
but of its other ruins few--   20

coldaiduh	Vina
a misterious castle	a town near the desar[t]
on the Genii Desart	Mondile
built by the Anceints	a Mountian on its--
	border

Now still remain to show what was
    The glory once of the whole world
    For by the mighty cheif Dalcos
it from its powre was buried

I sat me down upon a stone   25
    and thought of the days gone by
    but the sudden screech of Farras throne
And the blackning cloudy sky

And the moaning wind which blew arou[nd]
were warnings of a mighty strom   30
    and soon there was a Dreadful sound
    of trumpets and a heideus form

Appeared striding upon a cloud
red lightning flashing from his eye
what dost thou here he asked proud   35
what dost thou here for thou mus[t] fly

Fly or red lightning from a cloud
Shall thee prusue away I went
and was far from this Genius proud
Ere he his dreadful lightning sent   40

Dalcos	Farras throne
a famous British or	a misterious build[ing]
Gaulic Prince who	or tower whenev[er]*
fought agains[t] the	it screeches <there>
Prince of Coldai &	is shure <to be a>
overthrew him &	storm
burnt his palace &	This poem < >
city the ruins of	red in < >
which I now went	Branwell < >
to see- - - -	

* The rest of this note has been largely obliterated
  by a piece of paper glued over to repair a tear in
  the manuscript

                                        [September 1829]

                        20

MS: B(2)
Not previously published
Text: 1. 6: "desart" obviously intended
       1. 30: "storm" obviously intended
       1. 38: "pursue" obviously intended

16   **Ode to the cheif Genius**
                        BANY
                _____

              O thou mighty Genius
              Thou ruler of the world
              Take care lest from thy power
              Thou shouldest soon be hurled

              Thou ridest on the Thunder cloud   5
              above all here below
              Take care lest from thy hight so proud
              Thou art humbled low

              O look at the planets
              look at the bloody moon   10
              and then thou wilt see
              that thy time will come soon

              O look at the storm clouds
              hear thunder rumbling slow
              O look at the Dreadful   15
              starry Archers bow

              O thou mighty Genius
              Thou Ruler of the world
              Take care lest from thy Power
              Thou shouldest soon be hurld   20

Starry Archers--	This poem is
One of the 12.	short & irregular
signs called	it is an address to
Sagitories	Bany cheif Genius

                    [September 1829]

MS: B(2)
First Publication: Ratchford Web, partial

17

ON seeing the ruins of
The tower of Babylon---

Ah what is that peeping above the hill
Towering to the sky
it is reflected in this rill
which far from it doth lie--

whichever way I turn my eyes   5
No mortal can I see
For in this Mighty Desart
There is No one but me

To gaze upon this tower--
Raised by the hand of Man   10
which Defieth the Geniis power
For down with it who can

it is reflected in the rill	Tower of Babylon
which far from it doth lie	or Babel a tower founded in the
This may seem un meaning to many	earlyest ages of the world and after
but it is not so for anything which is	wards repaired by-- Nebuchadnassar
at a great distance must be emensly	King of Babylon it is now in ruins--
high to be reflect ed in a rivulet	the dwelling place of all manner of- - -
20 miles distance from it- - - - -	monsters &c &c
Chatueab	

Thy name great Tower is Babylon
Once the abode of kings
Ah now the Vulture doth not deign   15
In thee to spread her wings

Thou risest in lone grandeur
Above the Desart Plain
thou seest the sun roll oer thee
but no king thee doth claim   20

But now to other scens I turn
And leave thee desolate
My heart doth for my country burn
And for her pending fate

The Desart Plain	fo[r] lorn
The Tower of- - -	O Babylon thou that
Babylon is situate	once was the abode
in a plain which	of kings now liest
though once fert	humbled
ile is now Desert	in the dust thy
ed save a few- - -	sun [h]as sunk
wretched villiages	thy glory is forever
of mud hovels--	gone- - - - - - - -
belonging to the--	Luciens speech
Arabs- - - - - -	or oration on the ret
Buds Travels vol 2.13	urn of the men sent
But no king thee doth	to explore Babylon
claim	My heart doth for my
Alluding to Babylon	country burn
once being the abode	Alluding to the faction
of kings but now	Du Mange and the
she is Deserted	troubles caused by it

[September 1829]

MS: B(2)
Not previously published

18 ## Ode to Napoleon----

O great Napoleon son of storms--
Whose Heart in Dreadful Battle warm
        Mild in peace
        Just when War
Raises her Death shout from afar   5
        To thee I raise
        my tuneful lays
Ruond me play the glorys of thy star

how many victorys thou hast won
My mind cannot take nor yet my pen   10
        Thy star flew
        through the span
Of the blue arches to meet the man
        who is the one
        that thee has Done   15
Because all of thy followers ran

round me play the glorys	To meet the man
of thy star	This means the Duke

Bonaparte believs
that their is a ruling
star to direct him for
he is very supers
titious
_____
my mind cannot take
nor yet my pen
This is not right for
it should be- - - -
my mind cannot th
ink. nor yet my tou
nge--
think tounge

of Wellington and the
whole verse alludes to
the Battle of Waterloo
at which the General
is sore Displeased and
when he first read
it he said- - - - -
   This is Hatred under
   the mask of freind
   ship & if this fellow--
   writes any more such
   <trash he> shall be
   guilotined

At Austerlitz bright laurels bound
thy head and round thy Temples
            Swords were Red
                victims hair   20
was dyed with blood by sabers bare
            and the wild cries
            from soldiers rise
that Victry Victry crowns our Emprair

Russia Russia was the cry--   25
and to it all thy Liegones fly--
            but the Ice
            made them cold
And they sore mangled left their hold
            but Empruair   30
            you did stare
and of you ran through Poland old

Then to Elba Frances Eagle flew
And Ah Napoleon if thou knew
            thy dire fate   35
            thou would not fly
to waterloo whereon to Dye--
            the feild with blood
            Thy soldeirs stood
    strong gainst th[e] opposing Eneimy--   40
_____
At Austerlitz--
the battle of Aust
erlitz- - - - - -
_____
Russia Russia was the cry
the war with Russia

Then to Elba--
Bonaparte was sent--
an exile to Elba a little
before the battle of
Waterloo- - - - - -

but thou wast beaten and thou did fly
to under Africas burning sky

24

```
                   Helena--
                 was the Isle
    where prisoned thou wast to live awhile          45
                 Thou ran away
                 from hellena
    and of to France thou sailed full a 1000
           mile away


    but now Napoleoon I have done
    my story which of the[e] makes fun            50
                 I hope that
                 Thoult pardon me
    for all I uttered was in a spree
                 I have finishd
                 and have diminishd
         Thy most splendid height and grate glory    55
```

| For all I uttered was in a spree spree is a low cant-- term for fun. vide Boyers Dict. p. 322 | passion for the Emp reur had decided against him in some-- cause or other- - - - |
| THIS poem is an ex cedingly rambling and irregular meter and contain s--a great many things for which he ought to be punish ed Yong Soult-- <I> wrote it while-- drunk and under the influence of | but however young-- Soult was tried and sentenced to be fined <1100 !!!!> which he in 3 weeks time- - - paid but he promisis es that he will- - - not write anymore against the Empreuer- - - - - - - S//Chateaub.^d |

[September 1829]

MS: B(2)
First Publication: Ratchford Web, partial

19   **THE PROPHECY--**
              By young Soult TR

    I saw a flame which shot along the sky
    And then I heard a peal of thunder loud
    The rain came down in torrent I did fly
    for there did stand a genius on a cloud

In his right hand he held a flaming sword   5
and in the other a trump whose dreadful blast
made the earth shake he loud as thunder roared
O faction Du Mange thy glory is past
thou art gone thou art gone like morning Dew--
before the glorious rising sun- - -   10
thy insolence thou shalt forever rue
For now in th[e] scale of parties thou art gone--

Soon as the genius had said those words
A peal of Dreadful thunder <underground>
I fell upon my face when it I heard   15
but in the pale blue sky the Genius had <gone>

I saw a flame- - -	bill for suppressing
This means a flash	the faction Du Ma
of Lightning- - -	nge in the chamber
thourt gone thou art	of Deputies- - - -
gone like morning Dew	Make your enemies
Before the glorius	Die away like Mist on
rising sun	the hill before the
This passage is very	Glorious rising sun
similar to one used	It appears to be so
by Rarras in the	similar that I think <it>
2 reading of the	is took from it- - -
	Chateaub^d

[September 1829]

MS: B(2)
Not previously published

20   **[Adress to the Genius &c]**

Onward thou rushest in glory and might
Onward thou rushest all men to affright
Onward thou rushest black clouds are lowering
Onward thou rushest lightning is pouring

and far of stands that mighty tower   5
Over whose top the cloud doth lower
lightning streams upon its side
which but for it the storm would hide

Thou ridest on terrific clouds
and beneath thee are firghtend crowds   10
fleeing like sheep arcross the plain
but ah thoult soon upon them gain

26

And far of stands that
mighty tower
the Tower of ALL
NATIONS which is
a Immensely high
tower built on the plan
of the tower of Babyl
on it is situate in the
Cheif Glass Town- - -
Belongs to the Cheif
Genii & is the highest
in all the Glass town

which but for It the
storm would hide
meaning. The storm
would hide the side of
if it was not that the
Lightning darting up
on it enlightens it- - -
and beneath the[e] are fri
ghtend crowds
alluding to the crowds
of people fleeing away
from under the Genius

Onward thou rushest a flood & a storm
Onward thou rushest a Terrible form
while low at thy feet hunderds do lie--   15
Or else afar from thee the cowards do fly

Onward thou rushest Destruction thy name
Onward thou rushest companion of fame
Onward thou rushest ally of war
Onward thou rushest of famine the star   20

while low at thy feet
hunderds do lie
In the painting there
are represented many
people are liying beneath
the cloud on which the
Genius is riding- - - -
Destruction thy name
alluding to the name
of the painting which
is The Flight of the
Genius of Destruction
over the glass town
companion of fame
meaning that Destru
cton being closely all
ied to war and war
being akin to fame
Destruction
must be the- - - -

companion of- - -
fame- - - - - - -
of famine the star
alluding to war all
wa[y]s occasion a drea
dful famine in the
cou[n]try which [h]as lat
ley been its seat--
This poem was com
posed after soult
had seen the paint
ing from which the
engraving of the--
Flight of the Geniu
s of Destruction
over the glass town
published in the Acts
of the Genii (engra
vings) by PBB & CB

[September 1829]

MS: B(2)
First Publication: Ratchford Web, partial

21   **[The shipwrecked mans complaint]**

We ride upon the rageing sea
And soon from our veiw fair land
Thoult Die
we go to make all nations free
Over the stormy waves we fly

Soon will the world in Darkness be   5
For the glorious sun is going Down
his gold rays glimmer oer the sea
and on thy palaces O town--

On our vessell a flood of light
comes beaming from the sky   10
tis a sign that we shall conquer
and make the rebels fly

well emulate those heroes
who for their country died
over the billowy ocean   15
well like an arrow glide

O now the trump is sounding
Of glory & renown--
Over the sea were bounding
Far from our Native town   20

fair land thoult Die	on thy palaces O town
or thoult vanish	the glass town

[September 1829]

MS: B(2)
Not previously published

22   **[Song 1]**

W[h]ose that who ridest on the storm
Swiftly oer the sky he glides
it is a genius hideos form
but in his hideousness he prides

See now he strides upon a cloud   5
and blows his trumpet strong
Ah tis the dreadful note of war
Tis loud impetuos--long--

He says ye Nations listen
A war is coming on--   10
Already Deaths bright met[e]ors glisten
and dance the sky along--

See there they are in clusters
dancing around the sky
See there they are their bright green forms   15
are leaping shooting high

Around around me meteors
Around around me fly
My name is wars dread messenger
I am a genius high--   20

When the Genius had said these word[s]
He flew into the air
And I bid you O Nations--
For a dread war to prepare

                              [September 1829]

MS: B(2)
First Publication: Ratchford Web, partial

23   **[Song 2]**

O those Days wich are long gone by
Which have fled like a morning beam
O those glorious days whe[n] I
Did hear the Falcon scre[a]m

Did climb up those rocks towering grand   5
to take the Hawks nest which stood there
And when I in my own Native land
Did rouse the Moor cock from his lair

And when when the storms blew around
And loud thunder rolld through the air   10
homeward oer the Heath I did bound
As gaily as if [i]t. had been fair

Those days of my childhood are past
They are fled forever away
Ah now on a shore I am cast   15
where Despair must end my day

                    29

Im cast on a land where th[e] keen
and Pitiless winter winds blow
where the gay summer never is seen
& where nought but the Iceicles grow   20
O those days they have long gone by
They are fled like a morning beam
Those glorious days when I
lived by brawling carrils stream

[September 1829]

MS: B(2)
First Publication: Butterfield, partial

24   **[Address to the Genius of War]**

Roll Roll o ye Thunders
And you ye Lightnings fly
Rush on Rush on ye black cloud[s]
And Deluge the sky

while on the Bleak Mountain   5
I am sitting fo[r]lorn
looking on this Tempest
with deris[i]on & scorn

in the glens & plains below m[e]
There hunderds do lie   10
benumbed & chilld with horror
unable to fly--

while the rolling Darting rushing
Thunder lightning rain
Are around me around me   15
but to me they give no pain

Rocks & mountains are tumbling
From the Tempest riven Sky
And the people wild are screaming
At the wrack which is on high   20

Roll Roll O ye Thunders
And you ye lightnings fly
Rush on Rush on ye torrents
And Deluge the sky

[September 1829]

30

MS: B(2)
Not previously published

25   **Found in the Inn belonging to you**

Thou art a sweet & lovely flower
planted in a fairy's bower
cherished by a bright sunbeam
watered by a silver stream

Thou art a palm tree green & fair   5
rising from the desert plain
thou art a ray of silver light
streaming o'er the stormy main

When the mighty billows mix
with the hanging cloud   10
when the light[n]ings flashes
& the thunder roaring loud

Then when some pale star sends out
a gentle pearly ray
the mariners all hail it   15
as the herald of the day

When the sun shall rise in splendour
ting[e]ing the coursing foam
with the colours of that gorgeous bow
Which arches heavens dome   20

When the rocking ship shall rest
on the glassy ocean calm
its red flag stirred by the gale
whose breath is sweetest balm

Blowing from Britan's shore's   25
& her roses red and white
O'er Scotia's thistle wild
and Erin's emerald bright

While the music of the harp
and the music of the song   30
are borne upon the passing wind
in solemn strains along.

U T
Sep^t 28. 1829

31

MS: C
First Publication: SHB C and B

26   **Addressed to 'the tower of all nations[']**

O thou great thou mighty tower
rising so solemnly
o'er all this splendid glorious city
this city of the sea

thou seeme'st as silently I gaze   5
a pillar of the sky
so lofty is thy structure
so massive & so high

the dome of heaven is oer thee
hung with it's silver star's   10
the earth is round about the[e]
with it's eternal bars.

& such a charming dogge[re]l
as this was never wrote
not even by the mighty   15
& high Sir Walter Scott

                    U T   October 7 1829

MS: C
First Publication: BST 1920

27   **On the great Bay of the glass Town**

1   tis pleasant on some evning fair
    after a sumers day
    when still the breeze & calm the air
    & seawaves gently play

2   to veiw the bay o'er whose still breast   5
    white sails do softly glide
    how peacefully its waters rest
    like to a sleeping child

3 when the blue concave of the sky
   is clear without a stain   10
   & the bright arch of heaven on high
   imparts to the wide main

4 its beautiful & saphire glow
   while the suns golden light
   makes all the western sky to flow   15
   with fair streams like ruby bright

5 then like fair piles of burnished gold
   those marble pillars stand
   palaces of imortal mould
   & castles towring grand   20

6 while mur'm'ring sounds of pomp & mirth
   rise from the mighty walls
   & wildly mingleing sweep forth
   like thund'ring waterfalls

7 till softened lute echo's tone   25
   on the calm sea they die
   or rising with the <drearest> moan
   on winds of heaven fly

8 to play with them amid the strings
   of harps whose magic voice   30
   in the lone dark'ned forest sings
   while fairies round rejoice

9 as through tall trees the wild winds moan
   & silver moonbeams glance
   the harp peals forth with triumphs tone   35
   & spirits mirthful dance

                        U T November 2
                             1829

MS: B(2)
First Publication: BST 1919
Text: "bay town" is written above "Bay" in the title
       1. 27 is badly blotted and partially illegible

33

28   **lines spoken by a lawyer** on the occasion of the
transfer of this magazine

All soberness is past & gone
the reign of gravity is done
frivolity comes in its place
light smiling sits on every face

gone is that grave & gorgeous light   5
which every page illumind bright
a flimsy torch glare in the stead
of a bright golden sun now fled

Foolish romances now employ
each silly senseless girly & boy   10
O for the strong hand of the law
to stop it with its powerful claw

at night I lay my weary head
upon my sofa or my bed
in the dark watches of the night   15
does flash upon my inward sight

visions of times now pass'd away
when dullness did the sceptre sway
then to my troubled mind comes peace
Would those bright dreams did never cease   20

thus sang a lawyer in his cell
when suddenly the midnight bell
rang out a peal both loud & deep
which told it was the hour of sleep

W T   Nov 20   1829

MS: B(2)
First Publication: BST 1919

29   **lines by one who was tired of dullness**
upon the same occasion

Sweep the sounding harp string
all ye winds that blow
let it loudly swelling
make sweet music flow

let the thundring drum roll   5
gladness fly around
merry bells peal & toll
ringing trumpets sound

let the mighty organ
play & peal & swell   10
roll its floods of sound on
till echos every dell

sweetly sweetly breath[e] flute
pour thy gentle strains
let thy music rise lute   15
no more Dullness reigns

sweep the sounding harp string
all yee winds that blow
let it loudly swell & ring
make sweet music flow   20

in your splendid cloud halls
princely Geni dance
till from the vapour walls
bloody lightnings glance

your music is black thunder   25
therefore let it sound
tear the earth asunder
shake the sky around

fair[i]es of the greenwood
Sing amid the trees   30
pour of joy a bright flood
dance upon the breeze

drink from the bright flower
crowned with crystal dew
<burnish> with the green bower   35
buds of snowy hue

no longer hid your name is
ye spirits of the air
for now your mighty fame is
set forth in coulours fair   40

35

```
        sweep the sounding harp string
        all ye winds that blow
        let it loudly swelling
        make sweet music flow

                        U T
                        Nov 21 1829

MS:  B(2)
First Publication:  BST 1919



30              HARVEST IN SPAIN


    Now all is joy & gladness, the ripe fruits
    Of autum hang on every orchard bough
    The living gold of harvest waves around
    The festooned vine empurpled with the grape
    Weighed to the ground by clusters rich & bright      5
    As precious amethyst, gives promise fair
    Of future plenty.  While the almond tree
    Springs gracefully from out the verd[ant] earth
    Crowned with its em'rald leaves its pleasant fruit
    and waveing in the gentle Fragrant breeze            10
    which sweeps o'er orange groves mid myrtle bowers
    & plays in Olive woods drinking the dew
    which falls like crystal on their tufted leaves
    hid by luxuriant foliage from the beam
    of the great glorious sun which shines on high       15
    In bright & burning strength casting its rays
    to the far corners of the mighty land
    enlightning & illuminating all
    making it glow with beauty and with joy
    & raising songs of gladness and of praise            20
    To God the Father & the king of all

            December 9   [C. Bronte deleted]   UT 1829

MS:  D(1)
First Publication:  The Bookman, December 1926
```

[LAUSSANE]
A DRAMATIC POEM BY
--YOUNG SOULT
IN THREE ACTS   AD 1829
--PROLOGUE

The scene is laid in France in the year 1423. ALBERT
Count of Laussain in France ofends another count named
John of Liliard Count Liliard attacks him in his castle
drives him out of it and the count of lausainne is
obliged to fly to Spain and while siting on the sumit of
a Hill near Toledo says and does as follows

ACT FIRST
Scene Ist

Laussainne

My Native Land, no more shall I Behold.
Thy hills, with Castles crowned; thy fruitful plains
No more the splendid scene arrests my gaze
Of Trampling Horses & the gorgeous Train
Of livered servants. To my high command   5
Obiedient. At my sight no more shall bow
Atennding vassals. but why am I scornd?
scouted. & weeded from my rightful Land?
By low born rascals? I will rise & go
Will fling the firebrand of avenging war   10
Upon the Monsters head! Oil on my soul
Is poured to kindle up the <sa[c]red> flame
Wich soon shall rise; upon his haughty towers
The Beacon blaze; of my returning fame!
But whose yon stranger?   15
                    A Hermit--
                    startled at seeing a man
                    in arms

          HERMIT

Art thou a Traveller?

          Laussane

Be not afraid I am but who art thou?

          HERMIT

I am a Hermit who where younder light

From mongst those trees doth gleam lives
       far retire[d]   20
From noisy haunts of men where only pain
And vice; and folly. hold their dreadful reing.*

    Laussaine

Thourt right. & I have felt their Iorn rod.
Hast thou?

   HERMIT

If thoult go to my Hut then thou shalt hear   25
The story of my pleasures & my woes
For num'rous as the stars that sparkle high
In the blue firmament. or as the Leaves
wich clothe the tree in springs heart glading time
both pleasures & my woes have been   30
But now they both are few as sunny days
when winter wraps his sonwy* robe around
all th[e] wide creation wilt thou go or stay?

    Laussaine

I will & tell thee mine for both had I

They Depart to the hermitage

* "reign" and "snowy" obviously intended

     SCENE 2

They both having arrived at the Hermitage--sit
down & the Hermit begins his story

  PBB
Dec 18 1829   HERMIT   evening sunset

How changeful are all sublunary things!
One day the sun shines bright all Nature smiles
Another & the sky is wrackd with storms
The Thunder rolls the vivid lightning flys
rending the Hardest rocks   5
                  One time you stand
On the high sumitt of th[e] abode of joy
Another & youve falln in the pit of woe
In me you see a lonly Hermit who
In woods doth live from Humankind retir'd   10
I was not always so 3 winters now
Oer me have rolld since I was Blythe & gay

As th[e] merry streamlet wich with jocund Din
Doth gaily rush through meadow & through grove
Dashing its spray upon the sun gilt stones   15
Under Count Lilliard I served--

     Laussane

Under Count Liliard, ah ah thou Villain!
may fire & vengeance on thy gui[l]ty head
Fall like the cataract! & crush thee down
To the vile Dust from whence thou like a mist   20
or pestilential fog arose to slaughter
But thou shalt perish! with thy Tale go on

     Hermit--

What means that storm of passion which has <burst>
From thee? & what these words so vehement?

     Laussaine

I soon will tell thee but go on. go on   25

     HERMIT

Under Count Liliard I serv'd, & laburd
To serve him single hearted, but alas!
Capricious man! his anger on me fell
With thunder & with lightning crashing loud
Just at some fellow servants envious tale   30
He then not hearing as in justice bound
Defence or prayer for pardon. hurld his lightnings
At me. and Drove me far from his domains:
Though I one day had saved his life in hunting,
Had been his trusty steward many a year.   35
Waiting for my reward. he left me now
Like some old oak wich stands alone & Blasted
By stormy winds. where once it rose on high
the pride of all the smaller throng of Bushes
And of the other trees. how diff'rent now!   40
long time I laboured with the pelting storm.
Untill at last. resolved to lead a lonely
And quiet life knowing that amongst all mortals
There is No Happiness I have retired
Now the account of all my woes & sorrows   45
I've finish'd, tell me thine.

     LAUSSANNE

And dost thou not remembe[r] Count Laussaine?

HERMIT

I Do.   I Do.   remember him with pleasure,
For he one time seeing me lying frozen
In the cold night in Dark Decembers time   50
Orderd his servants to recover me.

          LAUSSANE

Well I am He

          HERMIT

And art thou He can I believe my senses!
And how art thou reduced to this low ebb?

          LAUSSANE

This base. vile. envious man the Count of Liliard   55
Seeing that I was powerful as himself
Forg'd letters to th[e] intent that I my sovreing*
Intended to Dethrone & showd them to him
Who to to credulous believ'd the wretch
And frowning on me blasted all my fire   60
Forcing me from my native land to fly,
here I now wander like the frighting* hare
Startled at evry wind that Blows--

          HERMIT

Thou Trat'rous villain! now thy deeds unfold
Their Bloody leaves to keen inqur'y's sun!   65
Whose Beams shoot through them bringing to the world
Thy foul thy Base thy cruel slaug[h]trous deeds!

          LAUSSANE   after some silence

I have a project

          HERMIT

What Ist?

          LAUSSANE

To morrow thou shalt know   70

          HERMIT

Thou mayst want food?

                                    goes & gets some
                                    they sit down and
                                    eat after wich
                                    they both retire
                                    to rest

* "sovereign" and "frightened" obviously intended

PBB   SCENE
Dec 21 1829.   THIRD.   Morning-sunrise

          LAUSSANE.

I will Die!
rather than that Count Liliard should go on.
                              What sayest thou?

          HERMIT

the same:
Why should he send his lightnings & destroy   5
Why should he roll his torrents & oerwhelm
                         Whoere he pleases?

               LAUSSANE

Then let us to his castle go with minds
Low'ring & Bloody
                         Bent T'e'nwrap in flame   10
His castle, & that castles inmates, too.
Ill see my native hills again. but I
Will Die them with the bloods of slaughterd men
Liliard thy aincent house is falling down.
Tumbling to ruins. Thy last hour hath come   15
Swift as the mornings beam. or swifter still.

          HERMIT

Ill join thee at the peril of my life   lets go

They Both Depart for the Count of liliards castle--a
distance of 200 miles

                    ACT SECOND
PBBronte   Scene First   Dec 21 1829.

          -- INTRODUCTION --

The Count of Laussane and the Hermit having arrived at

                          41

the domains of Count Liliard lodge in a deserted
building in a tolerable state of repair. this scene is
laid in that building at 5 oclock in the morning the
Hermit alone the Count of Laussane having gone out to
procure persons to enter into the conspiracy against
Liliard The Hermit soliloquises thus

HERMIT

Liliard thy star doth sink in tears
Behind th[e] Horizon. & thy years
Are fast approaching to their end.
And down that pathway thou must wend
Where the black mists enwrap thine eyes   5
Which from thee hide the world its sighs
Its joys its sorrows & its fame
And more than earthly tongue can name
O when thou seest that gateway wide
Through which dim ghosts & shadows glide   10
I fancy I can hear the crys
Which thou will give when to thee flys
A skinny form besmeard with gore
With scythes & arrows coverd oer
Round thee I see him wrap his scaly form   15
And roar with joy like some wild northern storm
Then through the gloomy gate he drags thee on
And thou for ever from this world art gone

                          Enter Laussane with 10 more
men the chief of whom are John De valence Richard De
raymont Albert Fresnoy &c &c &c

        Laussane   with a bitter smile

I fancy that we have got our helpmates here
to crush the haughty Liliard who this day   20
Shall grovling bloody in the splashy mire
Whith his last breath groan out how am I falln

        Fresnoy

Een the degraded gibbet were too good
For him so black so dark his caracter

        VALENCE

Enough of him how shall our deed be done   25

        LAUSSANE

You have appointed me. I must command

42

Silence therefore!

                        They now sit down to eat wich
 is done in silence after they have finished Count
Laussane rises & says

          LAUSSANE

My friends you see that golden Orb wich oer
Yon hill doth rise rejoicing in his strenght
Determined to fulfill his Task. like him   30
What you have thought of do & do it well
Like him go on in glory & in joy
Like him shower good around you & like him
By men be reverencd, But now my friends
We must proceed to overthrow the towers   35
And all the pride of Liliards bloody count
Now let us go like bloody lions or
like yon bright glorious sun WILL YOU <DINE>

          Omnes   with a loud shout

We will we will Now Liliard is your hour

They all depart for liliards castle

                    SCENE THE
                    SECOND =
PBB Dec 21 1829   The Afternoon--

Count Liliard seated in a Hall in his palace surrounded
by his retinue of knights squires &c &c an Attendant
enters announ[c]ing that 10 men wish to speak with him

          LILIARD

Order them in

                        Laussane the Hermit
and their followers enter disguised as Italians

          LILIRD

What want ye fellows

          LAUSSANE

Most Noble Count we are your humble slaves
The Land of Italy's' our native home
By sad Disasters from that home were forc'd.   5

                        43

like a dark thunder cloud. wich oer the plains
A while doth hover & then on them bursts
with forked lightnings scattering ruin round
So Count Laussan
   whom you for ever banished from yo[u]r
     sight   10
Came on us drunk with Black & foul Revenge
He burnt our dwelling & in bloody spite
& ourselves would have destroyd if we had not
Fled blasted exiles from our Native land
And he prusues* us like the scorching wind   15
Which rages in Arapias* desart land
To thee most Noble count weve come with pray'res
That thou would have compassion

   LILIARD coldly

Whithout a cause I never steer through whirlpools

   HERMIT

Most Noble Count we are your slaves & this   20
Is your Estate therefore--

   LILIARD

How! my Estate? Then may my anger fall
On Count Laussane before the Iinquisition
As Heritic he shall be branded and
Fire round him like a snake shall coil   25
Till all his bones do hiss his muscles crack
And down he falls a worthless blackned coal

   HERBERT VALOISE one of Liliards Knights

Ev'n as our count hath said
So shall it be

   RAYMONT

This moment is the Traitor within sight   30
of these High tow'rs

   LILIARD

Treason! arm arm yourselves my gallant
Knights

   LILIARDS Knights starting up
            in great anger

We will!   we will!

LAUSSANE   drawing his sword his
             followers do the same

Monster   I stand before you   35
I am Laussane

LILIARD

My Knights go to Deluge this Hall with Blood
blood of these traitors

                    Liliards Knights
attack Laussanes followers who also attack them
                    Laussane rushes
upon Liliard throws him down and says

LAUSSANE

Foul monster!   thou art overthrown
Now bloody mayst thou loudly groan   40
O were I humble & obscure
O that my Heart & mind were pure
Then should I have escapd this flash
Which now it[s] might doth on me <lash>
O then with heart as free as wind.   45
Id leave these wiked senes behind
leave me O leave me just one hour
I would not were it in my power
howere thou groan howere thous sigh
If tears of blood stream from thy eye   50
I would not spare thee die then die!!!

        prepares to stab him

LILIARD

My life ebbs out apace & I must die
but O Laussane if pity dwells in thee
have pity oh have pity on my child
To him be has a father & a friend   55

LAUSSANE

My heart relents I cannot strike the blow
liliard wilt thou amend?

LILIARD

I will I will Lassane

45

Laussane

Then I relese thee

Liliard

my bright & glorious blessing   60
<beam> on thee
henceforth Ill walk amid
the pleasant paths
of pure & shining virtue
I give thee back thy lands   65
and all that thou desir[e]st

                    They all desist from fighting

        Liliard

I order I proclaim a sumtous feast
for you Lassane & you his followers
Till such time as your castles ready

        THE CURTAIN FALLS

PB Bronte begun
December 1^t ended Dec
ember 23 A D 1829

        Young Soult TR

* "pursues" and "Arabias" obviously intended

MS: B(1)
First Publication: Dembleby, partial

32   One eve as through a Darksome lane
        I lonely walked mid scenes of pain
        Before my eyes thick as a wood
        A herd of lean parisians stood
        And in the middle of this throng   5
        There stood a youth lank pale and long
        A Ballad in his hand held
        Which when he read full soon dispelld
        All sorrow and in joy they yelled
        While on his seat he sung and dirld   10
        As if that day hed' gained the world
        Thus oft within his wiry cage
        The Ape doth chat and spit and rage

[December 1829]

MS: B(1)
Not previously published

33   But now the night with dusky wings
          Flys on the world & darknes brings   15

[December 1829]

MS: B(1)
First Publication: Dembleby

34   _ ˘   Donavit Me, Tullius Moriens
Hujus Teserae, Ait. "Ō Silviŭs
Hujus Donavit me, Tullius moriens
Portia Tesserae, Dicens, "O Silvius!
Tu pater Memoriam hic in Reserva   5
Dum habes crescam que candidus agris
- - - - - Tu quam flos floris
vos in cruenti
O Romanos ruite Bellum O splendidus Tonitrus
velox quam Fulgor Nubem Jubarque   10
Terribilis qam Dii qui Regunt in <Caeli>
Laelux quam illic Sul in Caelum <Ca   s>
Ei quam stellae quae ardeant in Noctibus
Multis
Sic Ruite vos que   15
luceamini   Aut Expirate
vincite
O vos Romanos ruite in cruenti bellum
Velox quam fulgor Nubes

Ruite bellum in cruenti O vos Romanos   20
In cruenti O vos Romanos ruite bellum
    Volitate quam tonitrus Fulgor splendidus <unbe>
tonitrus quam Nube
Regunt quam dei terribilis in celi sublime
Cealum in ardens <   re> sol illic quam Italus   25
Et stella quam Ardeant quae noctibus multis
Vinicte que ruite sic vos aut expirate

Ruite in bellum Romanos O vos cruenti nos

[December 1829]

MS: B(1)
Not previously published
Text: ll. 11-12: The final words are badly blotted

35

[CARACTACUS]
ACT, FIRST.
P B Bronte June 26.
AD 1830. AD.
SCENE
I

The palace of Cartismandua. the queen seated on her
throne Caractacus Brigantes and Carausias k[n]eeling
before her. The Druids &c standing round

CARACTACUS

O Queen a humble suppliant kneels before you
Caractacus my Name once high in power
But late there came to desolate my land
The Romans keen in war and eagle eyed
They Drove us from our homes and native forests   5
They burnt our towns and ravaged all our lands
Long I withstood but fortune on them shone
And we were worn with famine plagues & care
Like billows rushing onward to the shore
Even so they came in thousands after thousands   10
T'oppose were vain. So slowly we withdrew
And wandered Exiles. till amid the woods
We saw to cheer our souls these rising towers
And now O queen I kneel before your throne
A suppliant not for my life but my country's   15

CARTISMANDUA

Arise Caractacus I know your deeds
Your Wars your exploits fame round all the earth
Has blown them In my Palace rest your selves
Till from these clouds the smiling beams of fortune
Burst forth And show the way to glorious victory   20

CARACTACUS

O Queen your name for this in after times
Shall brightly shine "the Helper up of Britain"

48

MUMIUS   a Druid

Will th[e] Romans give rewards to those who take you?

CARACTACUS

Yes! For my head they offer crowns and kingdoms
And heaps of gold   25

CARTISMANDUA

                    Proclaim a splendid feast
To receive a king with Honour worthy of Him
Go now Caractacus you needs must want
Sweet rest for 'tis the Balm of every pain
28*

                    CARACTACUS and his followers
                    depart leaving the queen alone
                    with her Druids and a cheif
                    named Icenus. Druid MUMIUS cheif ICENUS

        MUMIUS

Queen herest thou what he said? Crowns kingdoms
        gold   30
are offered for him Ill would it beseem
One so renowned for wisdom not to seize
That way to power shown to thee by the Romans.

        CARTISMANDUA

What say you! Shall I act so base a part
As to deliver up a stranger, one who fled   35
To me for shelter? rather would I die!

        MUMIUS

Stop Queen! The gods require not such a strict
Performance of the rights of Hospitality
They offer to thee riches glories Honour
Why should thou slight these offers?   40

        CARTISMANDUA

                    Slight them! yes!
They are no gods who offer these to me.
To yeild a stranger to the mercilless fury
of the ferocious and cool blooded Romans!

49

```
T'were not the act of Human creatures rather          45
Of the most savage & the wildest beasts

                    MUMIUS

No one shall know the deed thou needst but tell
The Roman General thou hast seized Caractacus
In He will enter like a noisless River
And seize the wretch among his silent waters.          50
Icenus what sayest thou?

                    ICENUS.

                            Nought but what thou sayest
For what else should I say?   seize him O Queen!
Or else thou wilt repent when in the dungeon
Thou liftest up thy eyes and sees him seated            55
High on thy throne thy scepter in his hand
King of thy country having seized thy power
Who to securly trusted him.

                    CARTISMANDUA

I waver. shall I!   no the--

                    MUMIUS

                            away the thought!          60
The rights of Hospitality! away! away!
Icenus go thou to the Roman general
He's not far distant

                    ICENUS

                        Yes and quickly to!

                                            Departs

                    CARTISMANDUA

Stop O Icenus Stop--what can I do                       65
T' avert the storm wich hangs upon thy head
Caractacus. Mumius I am a queen
Remember that.   how dare you--

                    MUMIUS

                        Kill me Queen
But if thou dost the vengeance of the gods              70
Shall fall upon the[e] like some dreadful Tempest
Wich rushes on the plain with Horrid noise
```

Sweeping away whole woods and villiages
Into Eternal everlasting ruin.

                                        All depart

* Branwell's numbering

                        SCENE. 2D.

    Night a Hall in Cartismandua's palace. CARACTACUS.
and his companions in misfortune CARAUSIUS and BRIGANTES
seated together conversing

            BRIGANTES

What unexpected changes oft the Gods
Give to us It is like a lowring sky
Black clouds and Tempests overcast its surface
While we despair of all but storms and waters
But Lo the clouds Break up a Beam of sunshine   5
Shoots through the Hazy mist to cheer our souls
The flowers lift their heads the wild birds sing
And all is joy and lightness so our state
Lately the Romans with a bloody fury
Oerwhelmed us drove us from our native soil   10
But now we find releif and joyous comfort
Protected by this queen

            CARACTACUS

                        Tis so my friend
But Hope not thou to higlly* damp forbodings
Now chill my soul I feel a surety   15
We have not yet passed through our hardest journey
Sawst thou that Druid hoary white with age
Who stood beside the throne sawst thou his frown
His eye which <smoot>** upon us with a Radiance
Which showd that Death was brooding in his heart   20
For though I fear him not. yet still Ill heed him

* "highly" obviously intended
** "smote" probably intended

            CARAUSIUS

Fear him! no!

                            Enter
                            Ostorius Roman general

                            51

                                        Mumius the Druid
                                        with soldiers

            MUMIUS

Now we have caught the lion in the coils!

            CARACTACUS

Stand back! what want you here?

            MUMIUS

                                    Come soldiers bind him   25

            CARACTACUS

Stand back or die!   What you O Roman here?
Think on my power on the well fought feild
Of Cambria when the rivers red with blood
Ran rolling to the main Think on my power
When with my sword I forced your men to yeild   30
And made my way through lanes of slaughtered foes!

            OSTORIUS

I know you Briton then you conquerd me
But now your turn is come or yeild or perish!

            BRIGANTES

100*
What! yeild to you foul Roman?   no I would not
Even though I stood with thousand enimies   35
On all sides round me with uplifted swords

            MUMIUS

Rush on them soldiers bind them with these chains
Kill those who dare oppose you

            CARACTACUS

Old Man what say you
Die first thyself!   40
                                    rushes on MUMIUS
                                    who flies off

            CARAUSIUS

O Brave and valiant man!

                                        The Roman[s] rush
                                        on & seize
                                        all but Caractacus
                                        who stands still
                                        menacing them with
                                        his drawn sword

          CARACTACUS

Come on ye Romans is a wall before me?
What hinders you from rushing on me? Come!
How ist that you before whose conqring Eagles
Whole kingdoms t[r]emble kneeling to adore you,   45
How ist that you are held at bay by one?
One only man and he a wandring exile!

          Ostorius

Give thyself up

          CARACTACUS

               Take me I stand before you

          Ostorius

Rush Soldiers bind him fast with Iron chains   50

          ROMANS

we dare not!

          CARACTACUS

as a rock I stand around
Whose base the billows dash and loudly murmur
Striving to shake it but amid the clouds
It soars unmindful of their din   55

                                        MUMIUS again enters
                                        surrounded by guards
                                        and trembling--

          MUMIUS

               Gold Romans
Gold will I give you this shall be your pay

                                        holds out a purse of
                                        gold--

                              53

CARACTACUS advancing towards them

I now myself surrender. Keep thy gold
Old man for all the world is not like thee
All prize not gold as the cheif human god   60
                              They take him

                    MUMIUS

Now burn him on the Altars of our gods

                    OSTORIUS

Thy gods old man. But know the Romans care not
For god[s] like thine. Caractacus thou goest
To Rome Imperail Ceasar their shall judge thee

                              Him & his companions
                              are led of--

* Branwell's numbering

                    SCENE, 3D.

A another room in the palace of Cartismandua. MUMIUS
and Cartismandua herself. with Bards.

                    MUMIUS

Well I have executed half my purpose
I've set my face against the least compassion
Like some vast Rock its stony front opposing
To all the rage of warring elements
But still tis not accomplished yet the villain   5
Must go to ROME th' eternal city there
To meet the scorn and the reproach of thousands
For having braved so long their choicest armies

                    CARTISMANDUA

To meet the scorn and the reproach of thousands!
O Mumius could they scorn the man who waged   10
A war of Nine long years against all their force
The force of ROME?

                    MUMIUS (aside)

                         Ah! does the queen still thwart me
But she shall suffer.

54

                                        Enter Icenus--
                                        with the reward
                                        given them by the
                                        Roman general

        ICENUS

                        Here is the reward.   15
Of all our Bloody deeds I now repent
What have we done!   the thought like peircing
        lightning
Strikes me we have betrayed a confiding stranger

        MUMIUS   eagerly snatching
                                        at the money

What now Icenus?   Why so womanish
Call up your spirits like the new fledged Eagle   20
Lo here is gold enough to buy a kingdom
Half's for my self & take the rest to thee
And to the queen for I--I have worked the hardest

        CARTISMANDUA

No Mumius and Icenus take your gains
I will have none I wash my hands of all   25
Your foul and murdrous and base conspiracies.

                        (She departs)

        MUMIUS

Icenus! how she thwarts us let us kill her
For she'll not let us rest till in the tomb
She lies

        ICENUS   starting back

Ha!   Villain!   Murdrer!   base conspirator!   30
What having kill[ed] thy guest at least nigh
        killed him
to kill thy Queen!

        MUMIUS

                        Soft softly speak Icenus
Or else the Bards will here our plots and darkness
Icenus now I feel an Inward dampness   35
A horror in my soul tis guilt guilt guilt!
Sing Bards It may divert my Melancholy

1　UNTO our fathers in the sky
　　　This joyful song we raise
　　Round the whole earth their fame shall fly　　40
　　　Born by our tuneful lays

2　If, on the Billowy ocean
　　　Like misty clouds they sail
　　Or on the Tempest howling loud
　　　Or on the <rageing> gale　　45

3　Or if in distant kingdoms
　　　They pour the storms of war
　　Upon on the cursed Inhabitants
　　　In civil hate and jar

4　Or if in Desert Halls they　　50
　　　Sit like giants hoar
　　Our gladdning and our tunful songs
　　　Into their ears well pour

5　Like sweetly murmring waters
　　　Which through the meadows flow　　55
　　Or like the loud and passing wind
　　　Which mid the forests blow

6　And when thou diest O Mumius
　　　Thy fame shall swiftly run
　　From the rising to the setting of　　60
　　　The chariot of the sun

7　Unto our fathers in the sky
　　　Our joyful songs we'll raise
　　Round the whole world their fame shall fly
　　　Born by our tuneful lays　　65

End of the
FIRST ACT P B B
June 26 1830

ACT, THE, SECOND
SCENE FIRST

CARACTACUS having been conveyed to the City of Rome is
seen seated in a dismal Dungeon Lighted by a glimmering
lamp and the moonbeams which stream through the small
grated window.

CARACTACUS

Fortune how ficle and how vain thou Art
One hour thou smilst upon th' unhappy wretch
Who is deluded by thy tempting offers
The next struck by thy withring frown he falls
Into the Black abbyss of hop[e]less woe   5
Just so the sky unspotted by a cloud
Fortelleth not the dark and coming Tempest
All is serene but lo above the brow
Of yon high mountain thick and gloomily
It comes oershadowing all the wide stretched plains   10
Feirce lightning flashes from its sides and Thunder
Mixed with the Rain rolls round the darkned world
And where so late was calm and joyous sunshine   200*
Now stretches wide a bleak and stormy region
For thus O Fortune hast thou been to me   15
Who late in Britain braved Romes choicest legions
But thou and fell Adversity conspired
To throw me from mine eminence, Adversity!
Who enters in the Roofs of king and peasant
All men are subject to its visits all men   20
Have seen its haggard features, feirce as Lightning
It hurls the monarch from his throne the proud man
I[t] makes to bite the dust in wild despair.
Exepting Hope naught can allay its terrors
HOPE which een in the Dungeon lights the eye   25
Of the poor criminal and bears him up
When tossed upon lifes wide and stormy ocean
And the Huge billows of Adversity break oer him
And now while in this damp and darksome cell
O HOPE I cast my lingring eyes upon thee   30
Thou art my Lamp whose bright but glimmering rays
Do light me on my way when oer Adversitys
Thorny and darksome wilderness I travel.
Nor wilt thou leave my footsteps till I gain
That Broad and stormy torrent which no man   35
Has eer oercome. "DEATHS loud and billowy waters--"

    Enter MUMIUS the British Druid who whis[h]ing to see
    Caractacuses death has come to Rome to see it. and
    also Gaurds. to take him before the Empror Claudius

        MUMIUS

Rise up thou wretch and make obeisance to me
Is not thy spirit broken yet?

CARACTACUS

                    No Mumius
Nor ever will be tis a Giant Oak   40
Which winds and storms do not oerthrow but strenghten

     MUMIUS

Wretch Villain know that like a criminal
Thourt to be dragged before the Roman Empror
And there to die amid the shouts of thousands
Look here is my reward for taking thee
          Holds out his gold   45
Do you not Envy me my riches villain?

     CARACTACUS

No Mumius I do not but here this
Not all the gold and wealth of Rome would tempt me
To do the like to thee or such another
Would I betray. A wandring exiled stranger   50
Who trusted I wold save him from the fury
Of the merciless Romans!   never Mumius never!!!

     CAPT'N of the GUARD.

CARACTACUS come to await the judgement
Of Romes Imprial monarch, as to you
Old Briton know we Romans do not Revrence you   55
So scoff not at th[e] oppressed & Desolate
Though He must die yet not a better fate
Awaits you, Rascal.

     MUMIUS

O Valiant Roman if youll get me pardoned
This gold is yours.   60

     CAPTAIN

Ah! Ah! vain man, nor gold nor all thy tresure
Could get thee pardoned if it were decreed
That you should die but t'is not yet commanded

     MUMIUS

O Valiant Roman much I thank you for
Your generosity to me your slave.   65

                         gladly puts up his purse
                         All depart.

SCENE. 2.

The Ampitheatre. Claudius the Empror seated on his
throne surroundy by his attendants &c Ostorius his
general with several others on his right hand
The British Cheifs Brigantes and Carausius. with other
minor Britons Before him. and Immense crowd of Romans &c
looking on--

      CARAUSIUS.   kneeling

Spare us great Empror spare us yet a little
We do Implore thee O august and mighty
Claudius before whose golden Eagles fly
Whole kingdoms and before whose awful frown
Their Monarchs fall we in the Dust for pardon   5
Repentant beg, And never more against thee
Will we uplift our vain and feeble arms

      BRITONS

O King we echoe these our cheittlans prayrs

      CLAUDIUS

Where is your King CARACTACUS go Soldiers
Go bring him hither   10

      SOLDIERS

              Yes but lo! he comes

                      CARACTACUS
                      Enters surrounded by
                      soldiers with
                      Mumius who very
                      officiously has come
                      with them

      CLAUDIUS

Art thou the king of these ferocious Britons
Who hast for nine long years braved all our Legions?

      CARACTACUS   Advancing forward
                      And standing intrepidly
                      before the Emprour

Yes I am he. I glory in my deeds
And if I had the power this glorious city   15
Should soon be one wide waste of tossing flames!

And you O King should perish by these arms!
What did I do? defend my Native country
From desolation from the Merciless fury
Of you O greedy and destructive Romans!   20
Ah! how is it that you O mighty Romans
Possesed of such Magnificence. these Temples
Whose glittring domes shine like th' meridian sun
This wide spreads city and whole hills of gold.
Whose glory fame has spread round all the world!   25
How is it possible that you should envy
Me a Barbarian in my Native forests
A peacful cottage and unharming people!
But such you are--can never rest content
Without the world lies prostrate at you[r] feet   30
But King your victorys resound as much
Unto your honour as to my disgrace
For had I given up the war as hop[e]less
When first it shed its lurid beams upon us
Then neither my dishonour nour your glory   35
Would eer have drawn the thunders of applause
Which now I hear from these your Mighty subjects
Not then would all this hight of Human granduer
This pomp these golden Eagles and these chariots
And high Triumphal Arches had been planned   40
But softly stealing waters of oblivion
Had flowed on you Ostorius and on me
But Roman now I stand allone before you
Not with my armies and the storms of war
But a poor pris'ner bound with Iron chains   45
I'm at your mercy if my life be spared
I shall remain an everlasting monument
Of Roman clemency and moderation

          CLAUDIUS

Caractacus thou now hast shewn thyself   300*
An Enimy worthy of the Roman arms   50
Thy Air thy stature and thy kingly dignity
Do give thee title to complete forgivness.
SOLDIERS RELEASE THERE BONDS.

          Roman people

                    Long live the Empror!

          Britons

We thank they with our hearts most mighty Claudius   55

          MUMIUS   throwing himself
                                    before the Empror

                    60

Hear me O Empror hear me of thy clemency
This villain whom thou now hast rashly pardoned
Thinks to dethrone thee nay he has already
Planned his design. Then let the executioner
Send him a victim to the shades below!   60

          CLADIUS

Old man! who art thou!

          CARACTACUS

                    Great Empror this his he
Who has betrayed me to your conqring legions
With such a malice has might well befitt
One whom I'd persecuted and destroyed   65
His House and all his wealth with wasting flames

          CLAUDIUS

Hence with him give the wretch that recompense
His guilt demands go soldiers go behead him

          MUMIUS

Mercy O Empror! Spare me yet a little!
Grant me a day of Life and all my gold   70
My choicest treasurs I will yeild to thee
For but a hour one only hour of Life
I cannot die!

          CLADIUS

                    Wretch thinks thou that thy gold
Can buy thee Life no! to the scaffold with him   75

          MUMIUS

Then must I die! O Life fly swift away!
I Hate the sun! I sicken at the sight
But yet I dare not no I will not die!
Despair now seizes me I feel the flames
O guilt of opened guilt CARACTACUS   80
I have betrayed the[e] and now thou'st conquerd
Little did I expect this thunder bolt
This peir[c]ing arrow this unmoveable sentence!

    He is hurried of to excectution by the soldiers
    and followed by the shouts of the Romans & Britons.

               330 lines

                   61

CURTAIN FALLS

Young Soult.

Begun June 26, Ended. June 28. A D 1830 Therefore I
have finished it in 2 days Sunday wich happened between
being left out

                                            P B BRONTE

* Branwell's numbering

MS: E
First Publication: SHB Misc II

36   **[THE REVENGE]**
                         ACT THE I,
                        SCENE the I

    John a prince of Germany in the 14th century having
alienated his subjects from him by ecsessive tyrany a
conspiracy is formed against him having Count ALBERT
THURA at their head This scene represents Albert alone in
a dark room of an old building or watch tower now
deserted waiting for the rest of the conspirators who had
promised to meet him there.
P B Brontë Nov 23. AD 1830.

        ALBERT

ALBERT   Tyrant thy course is stopt no longer now
         Shalt thou relentless desolate the earth
         All things devouring in thy rapid vortex
         Thousands have falln before thy bloody throne
         And yet vain hope thou thinkst that thousands
                   more   5
         Shall shortly bite the dust beneath thy
                   footstool
         And roll in agonies before thy eyes
         Fond man thou little thinkest what a tempest
         Shall shortly burst on thy accursed head
         Thy Honours all are blasted ravving Fortune   10
         Vails her bright countenance in clouds and
                   tempests
         Soon shall this strong right arm and faithful
                   sword
         Destroy thee King or thou destroyest me
         Yet as the sun has set and the pale moon

62

Rolls up the vault of Heaven her silver car   15
Ill wile away the eve with songs of vengeance
And tune my harpstrings Tyrant to thy downfall

        He sings

    O ye departed spirits fallen
    By the tyrants bloody hand
Oer him fulminate your thunders   20
        Desolate his land
    Though now he sit upon a throne
    Though kingdoms now beneath him groan
    Though he be robed in kingly state
    Though daily flatterers round him wait   25
    Yet see the cloud of vengeance nigh
    It shades his land it blots his sky
        It darkens round his throne
    His kingdom glories power and fame
    What are they but an empty name   30
        His Honours all are gone
    I had a son but slain by thee
He now lies lonely in his watery grave
And oer him loudly roars Old Norways wave
        From earthly sorrows free   35
Never Ah never to return
        Then shall a Father cease to mourn
        T'vow for vengeance on the slain
        And dye his sword in blood again
    Yes I will rise though age benumbs my arm   40
        Though not now as of yore
    Runs through my veins the lifeblood red and warm
        Yet I will rise and steep my sword in gore
        Prepare now tyrant for thy doom
        Thy sun has set in deepest gloom   45
Soon mangled and deserted shalt thou lie
Exposed to chilling blasts and winters stormy sky
        Not one shalt shed a tear
Oer the[e] laid silent on some desart moor
Where Ghosts and wolves shall round the[e] moan and
    roar   50
        Unwept neglected there

                        a loud noise
                        of men entr
                        ing is heard

Hark! now they come! Tyrant thy fate is sealed!
This days the last which thou shalt have to live

            A band of Robbers enter to deposite their
            booty They discover Albert

                        63

CAPTAN of the Robbers

What! ho! whose this? seize him companions seize him.

ALBERT

Come at your peril seize me and you die   55
Back villains!

CAPTAIN

Why delib'rate rush upon him
Bind him with chains convey him to our cavern
There to abide my judgment and his fate

They rush on
and seize him.
All depart

SCENE, II.

The Robbers cavern Albert standing bound before the captain
Robbers armed and ranged round the sides and entrance

CAPTAIN

Now pris'ner tell thy name thy rank thy fortune
What brought thee to that ruin? Why so lonely
In the dark hour of night? Thou seemest not
If I from thy appearance may conjecture
A humble sheperd or some way worn traveller   5
Wandring among these wilds and cloudy mountains

ALBERT

Cease ye these vain conjectures and intreateis
I am count Albert Thura and a subject
Of John our Tyrant for no better name
Methinks that man deserves who slew my son   10
And me he would have slain but feared to do it
He sent him exiled to old Norways shores
And there twas said he fell destroyed in secret
While I his Father since that fatal day
Have cherished up my vengeance, Like the miner   15
Who digging secret saps the strongest wall
Ra[i]sed from its deep foundations even thus
I silent sapped his throne the fatal hour
has come when with a band of strong conspirators
Men injured like myself we had appointed   20
To give him his reward for all his deeds.

64

CAPTAIN

                    kneeling before
                    him (i.e Albert)

Father I am thy son!

        ALBERT

                        What do I hear!
Art thou indeed that son for whom I greived?
And thought for ever snatched from these old eyes?   25
And comst thou now to cheer thy Fathers spirit,
And waken all my fainting energies   the captain
Into-new life? arise! my son arise!   a[rises]
Little-thought I this morn when stung with sorrow   30
With sorrow for thy loss little I thought
That fortune ere should crown my aged head
Whith Joy like this with such allcheering beams!
Yet she bright Godess showers on us her favours
When least expected and when most desired   35
Yet now the transports oer relate O Werner
Thy dangers since that dark that fatal day
Had snatched thee from my sight I am Impatient
To know how thou could scape from his red fangs

        WERNER The late captain of Robbers
                    and Alberts son

Wer Thou knowest O Father how on false conviction   40
    Of Traitrous designs against his throne
    False as the Tyrants heart He had condemned me
    To exile on Old Norways desart shores
    Swift from the port the Gallant vessel darted
    Which should convey me with afflictions burdened   45
    To the far distant land when lo the Heavens
    With murky clouds surcharged muttered dull thunder
    Big drops descended from the reddning sky
    The air was still as death and the green billows
    Rolled dull and hevily on the dark sea   50
    Silence reigned through the ship the saddend sailors
    Raised hurried glances to the gloomy Heavens
    Then fixed them on the labouring waves below
    Yet for myself I felt no fright or terror
    Reckless willing to die not caring how   55
    When soon a broad red flash shot from the heavens
    And the big thunders rattled through the air
    Loud roared the winds and with inconstant blast
    Swelled the dull waves to vast and raging billows
    The sea was one continued roar with heads   60
    Hoary and white the waters rushed upon us
    The huge ship heaved and groaned the cables cracked

The sails were rent The tall masts broke asunder
While the dread Genius of the gloomy tempest
Rode on a thunder cloud and from his urn   65
Poured down his blasts his fires his rushing torrents
Man after man was by the billows snatched
From the rent ship. and tossed on the dark Ocean
Found there his executioner and grave
But now the maddning billows bore us on   70
To certain death for frowning oer our heads
Towered a huge rock blackned with fires and tempests
Now seeing certain death before my eyes
I frantic plunged in the dark world of waters
And the storm bore me on the shaking strand   75
And there O Horrid sight I saw our ship
Sturggling in vain to brave the ravenous ocean
When lo a billow swifter than the lightning
Relentless dashed her on the frowning rock
One cry I heard one loud despairing cry   80
Which echoed in the Heavens Then all was oer
And the white waters curled above their grave
All Night the thunders through the aerial hall
Continual rolled while tempests shook the heavens
And Ocean raged inccessant oer his prey   85
While I fo[r]lorn upon this dreary shore
Heard the shrill seamews voice and cormorants cry
But lo when morn with wing of rosy hue
Suffused the Heavens with light the storm departed
And left the azure vault cloudless and calm   90
Whith the suns golden beams all Nature smiled
And ocean slumbring seemed another sky
But I nor smiled nor cast a gladdened eye
Upon the rosy east. no, worn with sorrow
I cast myself upon the sea beat shore   95
There all the live long day I lay bewailing
My adverse fate. torn from my native country
By a relentless Tyrant and surviving
My lost companions drowned in the waves
But to perish by a more dreadful fate   100
But when the second Night rolled oer the heaven
And covered all with tenebrific gloom
Twas then frantic with sorrow cold and hunger
I called on frowning fortune with these words
"O thou soul withring power call down thy vengeance 105
"This moment strike me to the stygian gloom
"Hurl your black cliff upon my sorrowing head
"And bury me at once in blank oblivion
"Ending at once my hope and my despair
"Or roll the clouds from of thy shining throne   110
"O burst upon me with renewed splendour
"Give me ah fond vain hope! to see my country
"And all I once held dear let me oh let me

"Hurl the dark Tyrant from his bloodstained throne
"And satisfy my thirst with his hearts gore"   115
When I had ended this vain Imprecation
I cast my eyes around the swelling sea
And lo! all dim upon the far Horizon
Oh Happy sight I saw a small white sail
Bending its course full to the fated rock   120
On wich I stood what joy then filled my heart
Joy mixed with thoughts of vengeance till the morn
I stayed Impatiently straining my sight
To see if twas a flase* Inconstant vapoure
But no It held Its rapide course till Heaven   125
Glowed with the rising sun then full before me
The ship like lightning passed I called I shouted
For help for succour did the[y] hear my voice?
did they regard me? breathlessly I waited
THEY DID! the pilot turning round the helm   130
Full to my sight displayed a mighty vessel
Glowing majestic to the rising sun
Soon they received [me] on their welcome deck
And swift we sailed to the German coast
And after many perils many dangers   135
We landed on my countrys wished for shores
Where bent on vengeance on the Tyrants head
Gathered a band of strong and bold assasins
Him to destroy the rest you Father know

* "false" obviously intended

        ALBERT

I do my son. but now my freinds are waiting   140
For me to join and to assault our King
Now with thy followers join thy own Avengers
And me thy Father to destroy thy Thyrant
Let us begone. yet how my strenghts renewed!
High beats my heart elestic bounds my step   145
My youth returns at sight of thee returned

        WERNER

Yes Father I will go Id go alone
This only Arm should make his lifes blood flow
If You commanded come my follower[s] come!

                           Albert and
                           his recovered
                           Son Werner
    ACT, I,I: depart with
    SCENE, I.   the Robbers--
                           followers of Wer

67

An Apartment in the palace
of John the Tyrant--His
Knights and Retainers
conversing

ner to meet--
the rebels at
the old ruin

RAYNER, a Knight.

Lodbrog knowst thou the reson why our prince
With such a company of men prepares
To visit Albert Thura's castle?

LODBROG. a knight and the favourite of John.

Rayner!
Why askest thou to know our princes secrets?   5
But wilt thou promise never to reveal
What I shall tell thee?

RAYNER.

Yes I will, go on!

LODBROG.

Hark Rayner then! Twas me and not our prince
Who exiled Alberts son the brave young Werner!   10
For seeing his large possesions waving woods
Fit haunts for regal deer his golden Harvests
And wide spread medows and his towring castle
I saw and envied and resolved to have them
Therefore I forged a paper in the name   15
Of Werner Alberts son its purport was
Our sovreign to dethrone and also murder
And give the kingdom to Count Alberts hands
This to our prince I showed and he beleived
Grey headed Fool and Dotard as he is!   20
Aught wich I tell him he'll directly credit
He me empowered to send young Werner exiled
To Norways shore and there tis thought he died
This gained I had removed the strongest barrier
Twixt Alberts lands and me twas no hard task   25
Farther t' unbend our sovereigns doting mind
I showed to him how powerful Albert Thura
Was now becoming and that fame had spread
Some some darkling hints that he and other Nobles
Were leagued to kill him and usurp his Kingdom   30
This struck the final blow our prince was feared
For life his sceptre and his crown he appointed
This day to visit Alberts lordly castle
With a strong retinue of knights and vassals
And under the pretence of hunting there   35

To seize the count and here to murder him
And best of all to grant me his estates!

        RAYNER. in great Anger.

Foul villain!   Cursed art thou!   cursed John our
      sovreign!
Neer shall my hands be stained with such a deed!

        LODBROG. dissembling his anger at Rayner.

Nay hush thee Rayner!   For our King is coming!   40

      JOHN.   Enter John--
                        the King follo
Now knights prepare to visit   wed by many
    Alberts castle   vassals
Come and let us begone!

        LODBROG.   kneeling before John

           My lord my sovereign
How can I go? seeing we have among us
A faithless Traitor! one who cursed his king!   45
And me thy knight He cursed

       JOHN

           Who!   Where!   Which is he?
Bind him in chains!   behead him!

       LODBROG

           This is he
This is the Traitor Rayner is his name   50
The dark the Bloody monster Take him Guards
Bind him and when our sovreign doth return
Triumphant laden with his just renown
Then lead him out behead him throw his carcaso
To the feirce wolves and to the keen eyed Ravens   55
To whom shall his estates be giv'n?

       JOHN.

           To thee,

       LODBROG.

I thank thee prince thy humblest vassal thanks thee!

       RAYNER.

Unjust! tyrannical! O! Lodbrog! Lodbrog!
Heaven shall reward thee for--   60

        LODBROG Hastily

                  Of with him Of!
Why wait to hear the babbling wretch of with Him!

                Guard c[arries]
                off Rayn[er]
                Enter An Attenda[nt]

        ATTENDANT

My lord a man wrapt in a sable robe
Desires to speak with thee in private

        JOHN   Exit Atte[ndant]
                     Enter an [Ast]
        Order him   rologer--   65
To enter.   He bows to [the]
                     King

        ASTROLOGER

          King before thee I appear
And from the Fates this message I declare
A storm there comes from Norways billowy shore
Even now I hear the distant thunders roar   70
On high sits death a black and gory form
On thee O king he wreaks the avenging storm
Eere yet again the sun enrobed in gloom
Silent descends the Fates have fixed thy doom
But cheifly Lodbrog thou are doomed to feel   75
The peircing vengeance of the shining steel
Now to this Hour the course of live thoust run
But here thy journey stops the Fates decrree tis done
Full many a flower blighted by thee now lies
Exposed to winters blasts and stormy skys   80
From many a heart thoust wrung the bitter groan
And now thy life must for thy crimes atone
Perhaps my head is do[o]med your rage to feel
Perhaps through my heart youll drive the shining
      steel
I heed you not my message I declare   85
Fate wings its way towards you prepare O King prepare

           Lod-brog and the king stand confou
           nded and unable to speak. at length
           Lodbrog hurridly exclames

LODBROG

Villain! what now how what meanst thou by this
Thou dampst my (recovers himself) But whith wine my
    heart is flushed
I know not what Im saying hence thou vagrant
Guards take him bind him bind him in the dungeon   90
And if we come not by to morrows dawn
Release him if we do then drag him forth
To see the end of all his false predictions
And die himself

ASTROLOGER

            Freely I give myself   95
Into your hands knowing my life is certain
                    Exit
                    Astrologer
                    to the prison

JOHN

Come knights let not this vain Astrologer
Oercast your mind with such a gloomy cloud
Bring wine to cheer our souls let us be merry
And drown all gloomy thoughts in songs and feasting 100
Then let us go to haughty Alberts castle.
                            Exeunt
            297 300 lines   Omnes

MS: B(2)
First Publication: Dembleby, partial

37   O Mars who shakest thy Fiery hair
           Portending desolation blood and arms
           Thee I address O lord of war
           Who wakest the world to glorys charms
           Oft on some mountains lofty steep   5
           When all creation's laid asleep
               I thoughtful stand alone
           And see the lightnings round me sweep
           And hear the thunders loud & deep
               Roll over heavens high dome   10
           While mid the dark tempestous night
           Thou shinest flickering red and bright
               The Genius of the Storm
           Nor can the clouds thy brightness hide
           Which hurry oer heavens concave wide   15

71

Nor thee beddim those fires which glide
Athwart the gloom filling thee minds of men--
With dire alarm

[March 16, 1831]

MS: E
First Publication: SHB Misc I

38   ODE IN PRA[I]SE OF
                  The Twelves
            Sung at the Olympian games

       O Fathers of our glorious land
       Who oft avert the Geniis dreadful hand
       And when they leaning from the storm[y] sky
       Oer us extend their flaming swords on high
       Do sheild onweariedly thy chosen band   5
         Ye w[ho] have raised those mighty towers
         Over who[se] heads the flying hours
             have past unnoticed by
         while moveless as yon mountains vast
         Which oer us frown bleak drear & waste   10
             They seek their kindred sky
         ye who long woes and toils have born
         And from your home and country torn
             have fought mid fields of gore
         Who now have seen your glorious name   15
         Born on the eagle wings of Fame
             To every clime and shore
       We now repentant kneel before your throne
       And all our crimes and our tran[s]gressions own
         What though by angers whirlwind born   20
         We have ourselves relentless torn
       Though we in ruins have our city laid
       And have destroyed the works ourselves have made
         Yet oh withdraw these gloomy clouds
         Which now from us your glory sh[r]ouds   25
             And shed your brightest rays
           Shine on us as in times of yore
           and sheild us with your mighty power
             Through all succeding days

[March 23. AD 1831]

MS: E
First Publication: SHB Misc I

72

39

[The Fate of Regina]
[Book 1st.]
[330 lines]

While round the battlements and round the plain   167
The swift scouts note O'Connor's coming train
The din tumultuous ever rattles round
And the proud coursers snort and the loud trumpets
    sound.   170
But here I stop to tell each leader's name
And show their actions and their souls to fame.
First rises Arthur who in days of yore
Through every land the English banners bore
Before his look his stricken foes would fly   175
Stern is his mind and eagle-like his eye.
Next to him stood Alexander bold and wise
No art of war was hidden from his eyes.
Edward and John in the last order stand
Brothers in arms and valiant hand to hand   180
All these had fought in the same fields of yore
And had together swept the seas and shore
And now to crown their honours and their fame
The sons were worthy of their fathers name.
    Meanwhile, O'Connor, down the mountain's brow   185
Pours his fierce warriors on the plains below
Whose far off bugles with a solemn wail
Fortell Regina's fate, a melancholy tale.
Mixed with the clash of arms whose sudden light
Breaks o'er the hills and blazes on the sight.   190
And hark yon shout through all the city sounding
And from its mighty vales and towers rebounding
They come! They come! All seize their glittering
    arms
And each bold soul for death and danger warms
Determined thousands at the Eastern gate   195
With burning hearts O'Connor's warriors wait
Whose brazen bugles near and nearer blown
Strike on the ear with sad foreboding tone
With iron throats the black Artillery lower
On every battlement and every tower   200
Battery ranged high o'er battery, gun o'er gun
Doomed soon to shake the heavens and shade the sun.
    But now the first deep roar with crashing sound
And burst of thunder rapid rattles round
Thick wreaths of smoke blot out the rising sun   205
And black and dense declare the battle is begun.
Now crash on crash and roar succeeding roar
Shakes the vast heavens and echoes round the shore
Above the smoke mounts heavy to the pole
Beneath, bright lances gleam and cannons roll   210

While all around the shouts of conflict rise
And the loud tumult mounts and thickens in the
    skies.
At every gate the storm increasing roars
While o'er the rout Mars wrapt in terror soars
He shakes his lance and bids the mighty fall   215
Gashed o'er with wounds round the contested wall.
    But chief the Eastern Gate withstood the shock
Of Connor's warriors like some mighty rock
Which, towering high above the stormy main,
Defies the waves which round it rage in vain   220
Still frowning o'er the deep with ages grey
While boiling round its base the white foam breaks
    to spray.
Thus stood the Gate amid the mortal jar
Thus backward rolled the fiery tide of war
There Arthur firm amid the tumult stands   225
And hurls his thunders 'gainst the rebel bands
High on his foam-white charger forward flying
Victorious trampling o'er the dead and dying
Though oft a mighty weight of steel-clad foes
Bursts furious on and round his warriors close   230
Yet when his glittering sword he waves on high
Scared by the flash they start recede and fly
On bursts he then his white plume waving far
Now seen now hidden as 'mid clouds a star
Not less O'Connor towers amid the fight   235
Fierce in his mein his eye in vengeance bright
With savage Gordon on he mows his way
Like a fierce tiger thirsting for his prey
Thus all the day the storm of battle roared
While on each side red death the slaughter poured   240
Rank ranged 'gainst rank they fight and fall and
    slay
While clouds of smoke and dust obscured the fatal
    day.
Thick the red flames around the city stream
And through the streets with baneful lustre gleam
The cannons thunder and the towers around   245
With hundred echoes rattle back the sound
Thus hours on hours unnoticed rolled away
Till on the horizon hung the setting day
And yet though evening's shades fast close o'er all
The battle rages round the blood-bathed wall   250
    Still at the gates are heaped the mangled slain
And still the gory torrent stains the plain
But yet Regina's Kings refuse to yield
Though their dead warrior's strew in heaps the
    field
Though Gordon's troops impetuous on them pour   255
Though 'gainst the wall fast beats the iron shower

Though bands on bands fresh pouring round them
        close
Yet still they keep their gates and stand the
        charging FOES.
But Mars no more will brook this long delay
He bids the fates to clear the doubtful day   260
They with new force the rebels hearts inspire
And with the hope of conquest sets their souls on
        fire.
But chief O'Connor at the Eastern Gate
Ranged his black cannons marking it for fate
Loud roared the guns, forth shot the jets of flame   265
And the loud crash the postern's fall proclaim
'Mid clouds of dust the mighty portals fell
And seemed to ring Regina's funeral knell
With shouts of joy which drowned the cannons roar
On through the breach the furious rebels pour   270
On like a cataract man by man impelled
One mingled blaze of arms rolled swiftly through the
        field.
Still to the gate they rush a yelling throng
While shouts of "Victory!" break from every tongue.
But, lo! all stop amid their full career   275
And stand with look aghast and straining ear
For while the shades of night fast veil the sky
High o'er the crowd they hear a mighty cry
First burst it forth in shrill heart-freezing tide
Then wailed o'er heaven's vast arch and in the
        distance died.   280
Now, not till now, despair the Monarchs' know
Frozen is each heart, cold sweat stands on each brow
For with that yell and in that dreadful hour
Despairing fled Regina's guardian power
But Gordon's troops emboldened by the sound   285
Make heaven's high arches to their shouts rebound.
Still furious onward through the breach they fly
While rent on either side the walls wide yawning lie
Their foes before them thon in thousands fall
And block their passage with another wall   290
High o'er the rest amid the shock of war
Their mighty leaders every danger dare
Here savage Gordon spreads destruction round
And heaps with arms and slain the groaning ground.
There furious Connor to his warriors cries   295
To bring the fires, and bids the flames arise
Then first a blazing beam the chieftain took
And high in air the giant torch he shook.
His soldiers now with his example vie
And soon the flashing fires glare through the
        reddening sky   300
Oh! who can paint the horrors of that night

When bloody terror ruled with wild affright?
Where'er the wretched fugitive can fly
Death in some form is present to his eye.
If here, the fires mount aye with bloody light;   305
If there, the battle glitters to his sight.
If hid in night he hopes to escape his doom
The foemen's sword still flashes through the gloom.
Regina's Kings, while arms or strength remain,
Still nobly fight, but fight, alas! in vain   310
But when they heard the sad foreboding cry
Which warned them from their native homes to fly
When they beheld the clouds of smoke and fire
Borne by the wind to heaven's black arch aspire
Their own ancestral mansions wrapt in flame   315
And their high temples but an empty name
Then then hope leaves them sinking on the ground
All heedless of the battle roaring round.
To heaven's tempestuous shriek they raise their eye
And mournful to their guardian genius cry.   320
    "O ye! who brought us to this far-off shore
And gave us glory by your mighty power
Now, now, if ever, o'er us raise your shield
And give us victory in this battle-field."
    They ceased. A voice within them cried "Depart", 325
And rising mournful with despairing heart
Unknown, unnoticed through the war's red tide
They bent their course to Niger's sedgy side
And lay on earth with care and sorrow worn
To wait the rising of another morn.   330

The Fate of Regina.
Book IId.
100 lines.

    Again black night o'er vast Regina falls,
And shades her giant towers and hoary walls.
But oh! how different from the former night
Now rage, revenge, despair and pale affright
Stalk through her streets. No moon shines forth
    on high,   5
But frequent storms traverse the cloudy sky
While the heavens tremble and the deeps resound
To the rough thunder loudly roaring round.
The blast impetuous howls along the plain
And sweeps across the waste in showers of sleety
    rain.   10
Black ocean boils through all her thousand caves

And round the rocks all horrid howl the waves
The trembling stars have hid their beams divine
No light through all the gathering storm can shine
Save yon fast reddening fires which blaze on high   15
And burst in showers of sparks amid the cloudy sky.
How fast the fire-flakes round the city rise
And in their roarings drown the shrieks and cries
Of dying and wounded men, now equal all,
Alike the vanquished and the victors fall   20
There by the unsparing sword or lances die
Those mangled 'neath the o'erwhelming bulwarks lie.
From every opening glares the wasting blaze
Through every street are shed the lurid rays
High o'er the citadel at length they rise   25
And shake one vast white sheet against the troubled
        skies
Its broad walls tottering in the furious blaze
Stand black and huge against the fiery rays
While the high towers with dun smoke circled round
Stand like the guardian genii of the ground   30
Till down they fall impetuous from on high
While to the thundering burst the ruins round reply
But still O'Connor through the city flies
And bids the towers to fall and flames to rise
Still savage Gordon joyed their sights to see   35
Alike slays those who fight and those who flee
Nor fires nor ruins stop his fell career
Nor flying nor fighting foes engage his spear
His warriors follow where their leader flies
And maddening fury fills their hearts and eyes   40
Though scorched with fire and bathed in sweat and
        gore
Though scarce their weight their tottering limbs can
        bear
Yet still through smoke and fire they force their
        way
Nor can the fiercest blaze their headlong passage
        stay.
    But now when towers and halls in ruins lie   45
When scarce one hapless foe remains to die
When sleep the stiller of the human breast
Flies with soft wings to give the passions rest
The bloody swords the rebel warriors stay
And in the royal square wait for returning day.   50
There 'mid the fires which flickering round them
        shine
They warm their wearied souls in feasts and wine
While riot, rout, and revelry, and song
The silent gliding hours of night prolong
                        within a desert cave   55
Between whose rocks the echoing surges rave

77

That the four Kings with wounds and care oppressed
Their country's woes lay rotting in their breast.
Now frantic hope, now dark and deep despair
Breaks on their hearts with never ceasing care.   60
They view their city blazing to the skies
They hear their foemen's shouts, their subjects
        dying cries.
Grief nerves their hearts, they seize their arms of
        war,
And forward rush resolved the worst to dare.
With death before them, and despair behind,   65
On toward the town they rush on wings of wind.
    But when they reached the gates 'twas silence
        all:
No sentries paced around the battered wall,
Nought heard but streams of blood which trickling
        ran
And groans of anguish from some dying man.   70
Onward they marched amid the blazing halls
But saw no foe through all the wide-spread walls
Until they reached where drunk with foaming wine
The rebel warriors lay in sleep supine
Which 'mid their circling warriors there they found   75
Connor and Gordon stretched along the ground.
Now Wellesly with grief and rage oppressed
Plunged his bright sword in Gordon's traitorous
        breast.
Inspired by him next Alexander stood
And drenched his falchion in O'Connor's blood.   80
Then Edward blew his horn. The rebels round
Start, and their Kings amid them standing found,
While at their post all weltering in their gore
Lay their two chiefs, their wars and conquests o'er.
Advancing forward, Alexander cried: 85
"Rebels submit and tame your haughty pride:
Behold your leaders stretched along the plain;
Confess your Kings, and live in peace again."
He ceased. The armies loud applauses rise
And the glad shout re-echoes through the skies.   90
    But now the gloomy night is changed to day,
And the tempestuous clouds are rolled away.
The rising sun illumes the gladdened morn
And the bright dews the opening flowers adorn,
While in the joyous city all unite   95
To bind the wounded of the former fight,
The fires to quench, the ruins to repair,
And Nature breathes at length from those fierce
        storms of war.

                              [May 1832]

MS: Unknown
First Publication: SHB Misc I
Text: The first 166 lines are lost
       Book II, 1. 55--"part line unreadable" Hatfield notes
       in his transcription

40

Ode
on the
Celebration of the Great
AFRICAN GAMES
177 lines

Once again bright Summer now
Shines on Afric's scorched brow;
Once again the vales appear
In the new glories of the year.
Once again! yet once again!   5
Sunlike towering o'er the plain
Rises in light the immense Olympian Hall,
Back casting from its front grey twilight's dusky
       pall.
Then rise, ye thousand Nations, rise!
Lift to the East your joyful eyes.   10
Lo, o'er the desert drear and grim,
Floats, widely sounding, the triumphal hymn.
Its parched and barren sands rejoice
In the sounds of human voice.
Let the heavens and earth and seas   15
       Hail with joy the coming morn;
On the widely wafting breeze
       Let the tidings round be borne.
Let every Nation now rejoice
While mighty Genii with an answering voice   20
       Re-echo back the song;
While you ye woods and mountains grey,
And thou, O everlasting sea!
       The joyful notes prolong.
Come, thou stern monarch, Lord of War!   25
Come from thy chosen land afar,
That land where forests huge and hoar
Stretch their black shadows to the Western shore,
While Gambia's stream with glittering pride
Pours through those vales her winding tide   30
And on her rocky margin sees
Halls, towers and towns of men rise o'er the shady
       trees.
King of the North! arise and come

Down from thy wild and mountain home
Where Caseputh hugh and Dimdim grey   35
Frown beetling o'er the Genii's sea;
Where hills o'er hills rise black and high:
Eternal clouds! they shade the sky,
Their serried peaks by thunder riven
And standing 'gainst the vault of heaven   40
    With an eternal frown;
While from their summits bleak and hoar
O'er craggy rocks the torrents pour,
And onward with unceasing roar
    Rush hoarsely thundering down.   45
Thy freeborn sons, O King! attend thee now
From Morven's snowy heights and Dimdim's cloudy
    brow.

And thou, O smiling plain
    Where Ardrah's stream unfettered glides
    Sloping from vast Nevada's sides   50
Toward the glassy main,
Like Niger's waves your thousands pour
From every hill and every shore;
Haste onward, haste your coming feet
While brightest joy appears your footsteps here to
    greet.   55
As when the sailor on the sea
Tossed by the force of storms away
    Beholds the heavens all hushed in gloom,
While the black ocean stretching round
In long dull waves without a bound   60
With a drear melancholy sound
    Seems destined for his tomb.
Slowly the vessel labours on,
As slow the black waves glide along;
    Her streamers drooping hang on high,   65
    Still sleep the clouds in the iron sky:
Nature seems turned to stone.
When sudden bursts upon their sight
A little Island shining bright
    Girt by the foaming sea;   70
All fair and green and broad it lies,
In mists the blue hills stately rise
Their tall tops piercing through the skies
    With aspect bold and free.
A sudden breeze sweeps o'er the main: 75
Up start the waves to sight again;
From their high tops they shake the spray
And whiten with surf the merry sea.
The stately vessel 'mid sheets of foam
Glides swiftly through her watery home.   80
Shrill scream the winds in her sailyards high,

And her streamers long and gay
Wave proudly in the summer sky
   As she plunges upon her way.
All heaven bursts forth in sight again,   85
Bright shine the clouds and bright the main.
Even thus time silent passed along
   Nor left one flash to mark the circling year,
Nature herself seemed turned to stone
And the great world rolled round, a ruin dark and
   drear.   90
When as if sent from heaven the Olympian Hall
Sudden erects its pillared wall:
It dawned upon the joyous eyes of men
And gave them Light and Life again.
All thought dead Greece restored once more,   95
Afric' seemed the Achaian shore,
'Mid sandy plains and burning skies
A greater Athens seemed to rise.
Again Olympus towered above the plain
But looked not on the sunny Grecian sea   100
Where 'mid a thousand isles the light waves sported
   free.

No; round it roared the immense Atlantic main,
Cradle of tempests and the whirlwind's reign.
Not awful Jove not golden Juno here
With bursting splendour fills the air;   105
Not here does great Athenia shine,
Nor Phoebus spread his beams divine.
No; here dim forms involved in gloom,
Like spectres rising from a midnight tomb
With winds and tempests fill the air.   110
I see, I see appear
   Awful Branii, gloomy giant,
Shaking o'er earth his blazing spear,
Brooding on blood with drear and vengeful soul
He sits enthroned in clouds to hear his thunders
   roll.   115
Dread Tallii next like a dire eagle flies
And on our mortal miseries feasts her bloody eyes.
   Emii and Annii last with boding cry
Famine and war foretell and mortal misery.
All these, the blighters of the varied year,   120
All these, and more than these, before my eyes
   appear.
Yes, more, far more, a horrid train
Rising like clouds above the main
   Meagre and black and thin,
Round their huge jaws the red foam churning,   125
Their souls for blood and battle burning,
And though from conflict still returning

Yet still again impatient to begin.
These--not the golden deities of Greece--
   These are the powers that rule our land;   130
Nor can we hope their fetters to release
   Or quench their scorching brand.
Then where, oh where, must Mortals turn their
   eyes?
Not to the Genii-throning hills or tempest-giving
   skies.

No; to the <u>Twelves</u>. O Fathers of our Fame,   135
O Fathers, founders of our glorious name!
To you we look, our latest hope,
Our great Defenders, and our common prop.
Led on by you we force our way
O'er every land, through every sea;   140
Yes, the vast Atlantic main
Shall oppose her waves in vain
With all the loudest winds of heaven
Full against its surface driven.
Let its billows rage and rave,   145
We will dare the stormiest wave
   If you upon us shine
Let it be our common grave
   If you hide your light divine.
But why thus cloud one glorious day   150
With these sad thoughts? Oh, pass away,
Away ye tempests of the North
Let the sun of hope shine forth
Bursting bright on earth and sea
Gilding the <u>Olympian Hall</u> with splendour gay.   155
And you our Fathers now descending
   Glorious in your chariot's ride
While your children round attending
   Hail in you their country's pride.
Let us onward hasten all   160
To the vast <u>Olympian Hall</u>
Now let the trumpets loud and shrill
Awake the falcon on the rocky hill.
Let the heavens all tremble now
While the majestic Organs blow   165
While your assembled thousands raise
One universal song of praise.
Haste, oh haste your coming feet
Joy appears your steps to greet
Haste upon this day of gladness   170
Drive away the voice of sadness
   And of Grim Despair
To the <u>Olympian Hall</u> arising
Your bewildered eyes surprising

Or all cares of Life despising   175
    Haste, oh haste, rejoicing there.

P.B. BRONTË
June 26th
A D 1832

MS: Unknown
First Publication: SHB Misc I

41   **Ode to the
                     Polar Star**
                    87 lines

LORD of the Northern feilds of Heaven
May light like thine to me be given
    While I thy praises sing
Let sordid flatterers cringe and wait
Before the rich mans open gate   5
And bow beneath the glare of state
    And there their offerings bring
But on some rocks tremendous steep
High hanging oer the hoary deep
    Let me be seated lone   10
And while the tempests round me fly
Howling across a midnight sky
Behold thee shining bright and high
    And silent and alone
Star of the pole amid the sea   15
How many now may look on thee
    And bless thy light divine
How often doth the sailor pray
When tossed by tempests far astray
That thou wouldst guide his wandering way   20
    And on his vessel shine
How often from the abyss of air
Hast thou heard the sailor's prayer
--Lo yon tall vessel lab'ring amid the storm
--But vainly struggling gainst his giant arm   25
With shattered masts with sails all rent & riven
Tossed from the gulphs beneath to the black clouds
        of heaven
    Lo! the night increasing shrouds the sky
    While upward burst the waves on high
    Oer unseen rocks they rage & roar   30
    Whit'ning with surf the shaken shore
    High oer the ships tall bows they break away

And fill the air with showers of spray
Black clouds vast billows drive along
And as they drive she hurries on   35
Now on the secret quicksands dashed
And girdled round with foam
Then from her rocky harbour washed
And hurled upon the main mid its huge waves to roam
Then then how droops the s[a]ilor's soul   40
Hopeless he gazes toward the pole
For tossing on an unknown sea
How may he hope to look to thee
But Lo the clouds all rent and riven
Have to the winds a passage given   45
Forth breaks upon his upward sight
The dark blue concave of the night
Its thousand stars all fixed on high
And twinkling in the silent sky
High throned in heaven he sees thee shine   50
Well know[n] to him thy Light divine
He sees thee and adores
Unheeded now may rage the sea
Secure in thy directing ray
He learns to avoid the rocky way   55
And seeth his native shores
But not alone to him
Who doth a wanderer oer the Ocean roam
Wilt thou bestow thy beam
And guide him toward his home   60
The traveller oer the desert drear
Gazes on thee his heart to cheer
Though waste on waste expand before
Nor can his eye a bound explore
Though far behind his native valley lies   65
Though unknown scenes his wildered sight surprise
Yet as he folds his mantle fast
To guard him from the bitter blast
Swept from the inclement sky
Unmindful of the gathering night   70
Upward to thee he strains his sight
Where he beholds thee shining bright
His Guardian in the sky
Blesser of Mortals! Glorious Guide
Nor turning ever from thy course aside   75
Eternal pilot while Time passes by
While earthly guides decay and die
Thou holdst thy throne
Fixed and alone
In the vast concave of the nightly sky   80
Kingdoms and states may droop & fail
Nor ever still abide
The mighty moon may wax and wane

84

But thou dost silent there remain
      An everlasting guide!   85

                                   P. B. Brontë
                                   June 26th
                                   A D 1832

MS: Unknown
First Publication: SHB C and B

42   **SONG applicable to the present crisis**
              By Young Soult the Ryhmer

                    =======

            A cloud is rolling oer us
              A bloody cloud of war
            Dark looms its shade before us
              Cast forward from afar

            How long hath it been gathering   5
              And wherefore doth it come
            From whither rolls it fold on fold
              With fast increasing gloom

            It comes from kumriis Mountains
              From Hylles misty main   10
            From Nigers infant fountains
              From Gambia's watery plain

            It comes full charged with thunder
              With stormy winds and rain
            It come[s] in desolation   15
              Nor shall destroy in vain

            Red Genii fly around it.
              Before the furies ride
            Mars frowns in vengeance oer it
              With death portending pride   20

            Eeath Earth the rod of chastisement
              Must now upon thee fall
            Long have we slept in quietness
              Within each guardless wall

            Long mindless of the Genii   25
              We have seen our days pass on

                        85

        Careless of future weal or woe
        Of crimes. unvenged done

    But Now in dreadful ordeal
        We must abide the storm   30
    Must sink from our proud pinnacle
        And. seek our kindred worm

                        YOUNG SOULT

        P. B. Brontë.   April. 26. 1833

MS: B(2)
First Publication: SHB Misc I

43   **A SERENADE.**

    The guardian is old and the castle is dreary
        Fair was the Maiden and fond is the swain
    But the tempest is high and the night is uncheery
        And. ne'er may she see her true lover again

    The morn on her marriage must gloomily lighten.   5
        Mid. tempests and torrent and glittering rain.
            And her Guardian has told her
            A Noble must hold her.
    Who owns round his castle hill valley and plain

            Oh to that Maiden fair   10
            Ocean and earth and air
    All seem resolved her destruction to claim
            But love will ne'er cower
            To tempest or shower
    And Natures worst madness its bright beams can tame 15

    The Niger is broad and its waters unruffled.
        Far through broad Afric its waves wind along
    A thousand wide Kingdoms it[s] billows have watered
        In history renowned and immortal in song

    Rage then O Ocean and hurl thy white billows   20
        high oer the rocks of this desolate shore
    Drive shower on shower oer temple and tower
        And down each dark valley thy sleety storm pour

    Plains may be flooded and roads may be broken
        And torrents may burst oer the travellers way   25

                        86

But Never O Never
Can Nigers vast river
Fall. like. a roadbank. or rise like a sea.

There then fair Maiden thy boat lies at anchor
   There the rough sailors recline on the oar   30
There thy true lover beneath thy proud castle
   But waits thy forth-coming to. sail from the
      shore

[August/September 1833]

MS: E
Not previously published

44   Why dost thy pine fair Maiden
      Within thy castle tower.
   Why does the tempest chain thee there.
      Or Oceans driving shower.

   What recks it. if the Night be dark.   5
      Or. roughly roars the sea.
   What. needs it that. a. feeble bark.
      Shall bear thee far away.

   There are gates enow within this wall.
      And posterns. safe an sure.   10
   Then rise. awake. command thy page.
      To unbar the hostile door

   Why need we fly oer Nigers. stream.
      Or wander through the storm.
   When I may enter. quickly here.   15
      And clasp thee in my arm.

[August/September 1833]

MS: E
Not previously published

45   Raise your triumphant songs
      To an immortal tune
   Let the wide earth resound the. deeds
      A saving grace has done.

87

```
            Now sinners dry your tears                    5
            Let. hopeless sorrow cease
      Bow to the. signs of saving grace
            And take--"

                              [September 1833]

MS:  E
Not previously published



46       Faith is the brightest evidence
            Of things beyond our sight
         Breaks through the clouds of flesh and sense
            And dwells in heavenly light
         IT sets times past in present veiw              5
            Brings distant prospects home
         Of things a thousand years ago
            And thousand years to come

                              [September 1833]

MS:  E
Not previously published
```

      An early draft of **The Vision of Velino,**
      December 3, 1833--see No. **68,** p. 143

      An early draft of **Thermopylae,** March 3,
      1834--see No. **80,** pp. 96 and 165

      An early draft of **The CXXXVII**[th] **Psalm,**
      Spring 1834--see No. **69,** p. 145


```
47   Backward I look upon my life.
     And see one waste of storm and strife
     One wrack of sorrows hopes and pain.
```

Vanishing too arise again.
   That life has moved through evening where   5
Continual shadows veild my sphere
From youths horizon upward rolled
To lifes meridian dark, and cold.
The gathering clouds of vengeance. form.
In many a sudden pouring storm.   10
Yet forming in the silence of the tomb.
Save when the sudden lightning flash
Save when the awakning Thunder crash.
Rolled through the desert heart. or glanced across
     its gloom
Yes prides, hates, lightning and ambitions thunder.   15
Alone could rend that Iron heart asunder.
   I would not praise myself or deem.
   Me greater, better, than I seem.
   I know that I am dead and cold.
   My fortunes black my spirit old   20
Yet there are echoes in my heart that well
Can answer to the awakning Bugle's swell.
There is a feeling in me which can warm
In the stern senates strife or ocean storm
Gods wrath mans hatred my own misery   25
A foemans glance a womans smiling eye.
All these may fall may centre all on me
Yet like yon Niger surging to the Sea.
  64 Can only swell the torrent of my soul
128 Can only urge me faster xxxxxxxxxx.   30
  33   x x x x x x x x x x x x x
Northangerland stopped here for an instance and again
commenced scratching the paper seemingly on a new train
of thought.
161 Why do I thus my spirit guage and scan
    Am I then other than a common man
    I am--Volo! an Idiot.--
       x x x x x x x

                     [May/June 1834]

MS: D(1)
First Publication: Wise Bibliog 1917
Text: The numbers in the left margin are Branwell's

An early draft of **The Rover,** May/June 1834--see
No. **71,** p. 147

An early draft of **Sound The Loud Trumpet,**
May/June 1834-- see No. **73,** pp. 97 and 151

An early draft of **The Angrian Hymn,** May/June
1834--see No. **74,** pp. 132 and 153

An early draft of **I saw her in the crowded
Hall,** June 26 1834--see No. **70,** p. 146

48   **Thermopylae, PBB**
                          Book Ist
                  Ten stanzas . . 217 Lines

                            I
                           18
        Now morning rises broad & bright
          Above the Egean sea
        And gives to heaven returning light
        While hill and valley plain & height
        Roll of the iron shroud of night   5
          And welcome in the day
        Awake Egean wake from sleep
          Behold the sunlight dawn
        Come join thy waves in glittering light
          To hail the rising morn   10
        All Grecias shores beneath the sun
          With golden lustre glow
        And heaven reflects a dazzling light
          From thy wild waves below
        High oer the vapours curling off   15
          The Argolic Mountains rise
        And Attica her arid ridge
          Rears far amid the skys

                           II
                           18
        Now all around this smiling sea
        One swelling champaign sweeps away   20
        Shewn in this early morning light
        With streams and trees & temples bright
          Beyond its eastern bound

                           90

Rise the dark hills of Thessaly
Above it beetling awfully   25
As proud its guardian walls to be
    They gird the champaign round
Rise up oh hills still sterner rise!
Still blacker frown against the skys
This morning dawns how fair & gay   30
How shore and ocean seem in play
    To hail returning life
But has not oft and outside fair
A forehead seeming smoothed from care
Striven to conceal a hearts despair   35
    And inward burning strife

III
25

A gnawing worm hath Grecia now
    Though sumer like all round her lie
Beneath Thessalia's frowning brow
    Her soft vales smiling on the sky   40
Behold! far outward round the plain
Yon mighty host of moving men
Slow as they wheel in line on line
Their helms and arms & armour shine
Still pressing on each trodden place   45
Still closing round each vacant space
And still as farther on the sight
Forth flashes up this newborn light
For mile on mile across the plain
Moves on this mighty warrior train   50
Behold them joined, one glittering mass
Thermopylae's tremendous pass
    Above them beetling lone
While neath it, village feild or tree
The eyesight strives in vain to see   55
All calmer scenes of nature flee
    As that huge host rolls on
The sudden shout the long drawn hum
The Trumpets blast the thundring drum
Like smoke oer mountains rolling come   60
    With mixed and mu[r]mering tone

IV
20

Now far & wide the Ensigns fliy
Like thousand flashes mid the sky
Their silken folds all fluttering bright
Make wide heaven quiver with varying light   65
Behold yon broad bright crimson shown
In gold emblazed its gilded sun
Great Mithra[s] with a borrowed glow

Blazes along the closing row
A thousand suns this fated day   70
In Oceans breezes glance & play
And sunny helm and suntipped spear
Above each mountain gorge appear
Greece! let me drop one tear for thee
    Where hath thy light of freedom gone   75
I know thy sons will perish free
Yet what avails a glory flown
And when thy childern all are gone
    Where will that light of Freedom be
Where!--Thou struck, blasted, lying alone,   80
Must feel this huge hosts tread & wither neath
    its throne

V
12
I said a mountains stormy hight
Hung beetling oer that Army bright
Yes! there thou frownst Thermopylae
Stern standard of the brave & free   85
High oer rough Peneus roaring flood
Oer swelling hill & shadowed wood
Thy huge rocks starting to the sky
Swell forth a barrier broad & high
And seems as rent by thunders stroke   90
Between the ribbed and frowning rock
That path which upward from the shore
Winds high above the torrents roar

VI
17
Now all beneath that bulwark high
The whole wide champaign sounds with joy   95
And Oh! in what unnumbered lines
Yon mighty army shades & shines
First breaths the spearlight oer the hill
Then seems its flash the vale to fill
And still oer all that wide expanse   100
One broad bright sunbeam seems to glance
Hark to the roar of revelry!
Hark to the ceaseless shouts of joy!
See! how the rising morning wind
    Swells up each banners glorious fold   105
See! how before around behind
    Flames forth in crimson & in gold!
    Yon long long ranks of war unfold
Lo how they crowd in burnished ring
Around the standard of their King!   110

That King upon his golden throne
High oer the tumult shines alone
Their Xerxes with insatiate eye
Roams oer the hosts which round him lie
Parthians & Medians beneath him stand   115
Glittering in purple a kinglike band
Aye many a Monarch is in yon train
Doomed to the sun his beams to wane
Where far mid the desart the Nile flows on
Egypt hath given her shaven son   120
The sunscorched Arabian stands haughtily there
The Parthian lifts his wandering spear
And glorious Indias climes unknown
Sends her dark hostage round that throne
Aye there they crowd a jewelled throng   125
Loud notes of triumph on each tongue
Yet all in thrice redoubled ring
Prone kneeling neath their lord the King!
He rising, lord of Glory stands
And spreads toward heaven his sceptred hands   130

Ha! Mithra[s] thou in glory now
Mayst shed thy halo round my brow
To thee I vow a sacrifice
Such as hath never to the skys
    Blazed in accepting flame   135
To thee yon Grecian army dies
To thee I vow its obsequies
A Hecatomb, ye favouring skys!
    Accept the whole Grecian name!
Gods have a band of traitorous men   140
Thus braved the lion in his den
Lo twice ten thousand Persians lie
To stiffen neath a Grecian sky
And yet Achaia's evil star
Can shine a[s]cendant through the air   145
Well twice I have seen my warriors fall
Beneath yon heaven erected wall
Twice have my troops in vain assayed
To force yon rocks tremendous shade
But not a third time never more   150
Shall we roll backward on the shore!
    Thou saidst a Goatherds step might find
    A path which up yon dark hills brow
High toward Thermopylae may wind
    To 'oerlook the Traitor host below   155
    Tis well now Persians strike your blow

Mardonius, seize thy trustiest brand
Thou boastedst oft head thou the band
   To storm yon heaven built wall
Let all our choicest troops advance   160
Take Parthian javelin Persian lance
   And heaven for Xe[r]xes call
Vengeance on Greece aye let them know
That what hath stayed the coming blow
Shall only force it on our foe   165
   With heavier dint to fall
The meanest cloud which spots the sky
May hide even Mithras light on high
Yet when again breaks out the day
How those vain vapours fade away   170
   Now thou who hast betrayed to me
      Thy country and thy home
   Tis meet that I should show to thee
      Thy own reward to come
Ha! base Trachinian deemst thou then   175
   Because I seize thy way
That I will weigh three hundred men
   Against thy craven clay
Go slave and know a Persian eye
Though it accept the treachery   180
   The Traitor casts away
Thou hast shown my way to victory
Oer the dead corses of the free
And death base slave I shew to thee

        IX
        8
The Traitor wretch is born away   185
He casts a wild glance round the sea
But dares not face Thermopylae
   On thy betrayed brow
He who to the proud spoilers hand
Hath given the bravest of his land   190
Beneath the glad receivers hand
   Rolls headless breathless now

        X
        25
Just then the sun with sudden light
Burst full on yon far fronting height
And flashing back in golden lines   195
Wide oer the champaign streams and shines
Lo all along yon brazen sea
How flame the bright arms gallantly
See how they spread from side to side
Forth streaming oer the champaign wide   200
And what a cloud of standards stare

Lighten and darken through the air
For Victory for Victory
Roars high above the living sea
Aye ye may shout proud Persians now   205
For all hopes garlands bind your brow
Aye ye shall gain yon mighty height
And fight and conquer in that fight
    Oh, Greece in this dark hour of gloom
When round thee yawns one bloody tomb   210
Think through destructions dreariest day
Freedom can shine with brightest ray
That in the Tyrants mightiest hour
One godgiven sword may shake his power
Now bid thy armed children see   215
On thy huge heights Thermopylae
Three hundred fight gainst millions three

                    August 9th 1834.
                    P B Bronte

MS: B(1)
First Publication: 3IID C and B

An early draft of **An Hour's Musings on the
Atlantic,** September 1834--see No. **79,** p. 158

An early draft of **The Angrian Welcome,**
September/October 1834--see No. **75,** p. 154

An early draft of **Northangerland's Name,**
September/October 1834--see No. **76,** p. 155

An early draft of "We leave our bodies," late
1834/early 1835--see No. **78,** p. 158

An early draft of **Augusta**, late 1834/early
1835--see No. **72**, p. 150

An early draft of **Morning**, December 1834/
January 1835--see No. **77**, p. 157

A possible second early draft of **Thermopylae**,
January 19, 1835--see No. **80**, pp. 88 and 165

49 And is this Greece is this the land I sing
These Mountains hoar and this tempestous land
Yes this is Greece Behold in gathered ring
Beneath yon dreary brow that little band
Helms on each head and lances in each hand   5
The wild waste round them and the flick<ering>
Soft light amid them flashing while they stand
On each <ste[r]n> front while clouds of smoke aspire
Above their crested helms and still ascending higher
Why gathering thus on Pindus stormy <steep>   10
Why <marching> thus in daylights dim <   >
War sounds not in these <gusts> which round you sweep
Greece may be robed in light <or> Wrapt in storm
little avails it <to> her sons <laid> there

[early 1835]

MS: I
Not previously published

50   (a)   Now the sweet Hour of closing day
Draws down from Heaven her latest smile
And Evenings beams have ceased to play
Round Scyros lofty Isle
Thermopylaes commanding height   5
Looks oer the silent march of Night
And wide benea[t]h it Grecia lies
As still and silent as the skies
A moveless shadow dim and blue
Spreads oer her Hills one deathlike hue.   10

96

And wide Thessalis far away
Spreads her deep shadows cold and grey
From far Euboea wild and lone
Why hear I note the shepheards tone
Why do his shrill notes dying afar   15
Cease to soothe the twilight air
Where is the twinkling lamp of night
Which used to flash on Phecias height
And down the Peneus brawling stream
Glint the lone travellers warning beam   20

Where dost thou ask., through smiling Greece
Have fled these signs of life and peace
Where is the youth of the old man gone
Why hath the joy of the Hop[e]less flown
Where is the light in the closing eye   25
Of the wretch in sickness stretched to die
And why have the sweet sounds of Evening time
Sunk into silence through Hellas clime

(b)   Well now All Grecia seems to sleep
        In peaceful twilight dark and deep   30
        Where is the wild red fire of war
        No cries of Anguish fill the air
        No clash of arms no battle cry
        And not one. lightning from the sky
        Can thus a mighty Nation die   35

                                        [early 1835]

MS: B(2)
First Publication: Winnifrith PBB

A second early draft of **Sound The Loud Trumpet**,
early 1835--see No. **73**, pp. 90 and 151

An early draft of "Son of Heaven, in heavenly
musing," October 20, 1835--see No. **81**, p. 167

An early draft of **The Doubters Hymn**,
October/November 1835--see No. **82**, p. 168

                        97

An early draft of "Thou art gone but I am here,"
November 17, 1835--see No. **83**, p. 169

An early draft of "Frozen fast is my heart at
last," November 17, 1835--see No. **84**, p. 169

An early draft of "Now then I am alone," December
17, 1835--see No. **85**, p. 170

An early draft of **The Spirit of Poetry**, late
1835--see No. **86**, p. 171

An early draft of **Misery Part I**, December 18,
1835--see No. **54**, p. 99

51   Welcome Welcome Mighty King
                 Welcome to our hearts and homes
              Hope upon untiring wing
                 To announce thee onward comes

              Welcome Welcome Lord of Glory   5
                 Who on earth is like to thee
              Shines the light of triumph oer thee
                 Beams thy Brow with Victory

                               [December 25, 1835]

MS: K
Not previously published

52   There are Thrones to be shaken
              There is Vengeance to be taken
          Ere this Dark and Dreary Midnight shall give place

to rising Day!
Ere the cloud of the Eclipse shall give place to
    lucid day

                                Verdopolis Dec 28th
                                    A D 1835

MS: K
Not previously published

53   has he in it lain
            Still and stiff and drenched with rain
            Wishing the dawn of morn again
                    Though death should come with day

                                    [February 1836]

MS: B(1)
Not previously published

            An early draft of **An Angrian Battle Song**,
            January 1836--see No. **87**, p. 172

54   **Misery. Scene 1st**

            _____

    How fact that courser fleeted by,
    With arched neck backward tossed on high,
    And snorting nostrils opened wide,
    And foam flecked chest and gory side.
        I saw his riders darkned form   5
    As on they hurried through the storm;
    Forward he pressed, his plume behind
    Flew whistling in the wintery wind,
    But his clenched teeth and angry eye
    Seemed wind and tempest to defy;   10
    And eagerly he bent his sight
    To peirce the darkness of the night;
    And oft he gazed and gazed again
    Through the rough blast and driving rain.
        Look up, and view the midnight heaven,   15

Where, mass oer mass continual driven
The wild black storm clouds fleet and change
Like formless phantom's vast and strange,
That bend their gloomy brows from high,
And pass in midnight darkness by: 20
And still they pass, and still they come,
Without a flash to break the gloom.
I cannot see the foam and spray
Which mark that raging torrents way;
But I can hear the ceaseless roar,   25
Where, swollen and chafed, its waters pour.
There--where yon blackned Oaks on high,
Blend wildly with the midnight sky,
Tossing their bare and groaning boughs
Like some dread fight of giant foes;   30
There--where that glimpse of moonlight shines,
    From the wild wrack of heaven sent down,
And spreads its silver trembling lines
    Amid the darkness, then is gone,--
There stays the Horseman--. wide before,   35
Deep and dark, the waters roar:
But, down the lone vale, far away,
Glances one solitary ray.
The sounds of winds and waters, rise,
And sweeps the sleet shower, oer the skys;   40
While dreariest darkness, all around,
Makes still more drear each sight or sound:
But heeds not such that Cavalier;
Reining his trembling charger there,
He halts upon the rivers brink   45
Where all its wild waves surge and sink,
Shades with his hand, his anxious eye,
And through the night looks eagerly:
Why smiled he, when that far off light
Again broke twinkling on his sight?   50
Why frowned he, when it sunk again
Amid the darksome veil of rain?
Till, brightly flashing forth once more,
It streams and twinkles far before!

"Oh, through the tempests of this life,   55
    However loud they sound,
However wild their storms and strife
    May burst and thunder round,
Though reft and riven each aid and prop,
There may be heaven, there may be hope!   60
I Thought just now, that life or death
    Could never trouble me,
For That I should draw my future breath
    In silent apathy.
That, oer the pathway of my fate   65

Though steady beat the storm,
As I walked alone and desolate,
I'de to that path conform.
Affection should not chain me,
    Or sorrow hold me down,   70
But despair itself sustain me,
    Whom itself had over thrown.
I Thought, that Fame and Glory,
    Were names for shame and woe;
That lifes deceitful story   75
    I had finished long ago:
That all its novelty was gone,
    And that thus to read again
The same dull page in the same sad tone
    Was not even change of pain.   80
Defeat had crushed me into dust,
    But, only laid my head
Where head and heart and spirit must
    Be soon for ever laid.
My fearless followers all were slain;   85
    My power and glory gone;
My followers met the fate of men;
    And power!--I am now alone!
Not so!--I thought it, till that light
    Glanced glittering down the glen,   90
And, on my spirits dreary night
    Flashed brightness back again.
Yes,--I Had thought I stood alone,
That I need sigh or weep for none,
Had quenched my love in apathy,   95
Since none would weep or sigh for me.
Yes!--But that single silver beam
    Which flashes on my eye,
Hath waked me from my dreary dream
    And made the darkness fly!   100
Then, pardon, That the storms of woe
    Have whelmed me in a drifting sea;
With death and dangers struggling so,
    That I--a while,--forgot even thee.
This moment, as I gain the shore,   105
    And clouds begin to dissapear,
Even steadier, brighter, than before,
    Thou shinest--my own, my guardian Star!
O, could I speak the long lost feeling;
The inward joy, its power revealing;   110
The glimpse of something yet to come
Which yet may give a happy home!
Oh, could I speak my thoughts of thee,
Whom, soon again, my eyes shall see:
The Dove that bore the olive leaf,   115
Could never bring such glad relief

To wanderers oer a shoreless main,
As, in my weariness and pain,
   That single light has given to me!
My Gallant Horse, speed swiftly thou,   120
Soon shall a Hand caress thee now,
Grateful that thou hast born me on
Through deadliest deeds and dangers gone;
A Touch, thou mayest be proud to own,
Though thou so oft hast felt my own.   125
O, That fair hand, and faithful heart,
From mine, what power shall ever part!
What power!--Ha, well indeed I know
The very fire which burns me now,
The very energy of soul   130
   Which to thine arms impells me on,
When once I've gained that wished for goal,
   Will--like a comet from the sun,
Hurl me, with power that scorns controul
   Far from thy beams of happiness,   135
   Into the expanse of wild distress
Where passions lightnings burst and Battles
   thunders roll!"

Impetous then that Horseman sprung
Down the steep bank--His Armour rung
   Mid the wild waters roar;   140
And, dashing through the old Oak trees,
His coursers hoofs, upon the breeze
Their reckless rattle swiftly cease,
   In the dark night before.

Who, that hath felt the feeling wild   145
   Which struck upon the excited mind
When, perhaps long since, while yet a child,
   In awful mystery undefined
Old tales, and legends, often told,
   While winter nights fell long and drear,   150
Have made his hearts blood curdle cold
   Their dreary fates to hear.
Of Ancient Halls where Destiny
   Has brooded with its raven wing.
Of castles stern, whose riotry   155
   Hid not the gloomy crimes within.
Of Death Beds, where the sickman lying
   Mid anxious listners standing by,
Ere he had told the secret dying,
   And left a sealed mystery.   160
Of Heirs, who to some fearful doom
   Suceeded with their ancient Hall.
Of Marriage Feasts, where Ghosts would come
   The new made Bride to call.

--He, that hath still in memory   165
   Kept fast those dreams of childhoods hours
Who these far visions yet may see
   Of Castle Halls and Feudal towers,
--To Him I shew this stormy night
That seems to darken on my sight.   170

Far above their forest trees
   Those dreary Turrets rise,
And round their walls, the midnight breeze
   Comes shreiking from the skies.
Scarce can I note the central tower   175
   Amid the impetous storm,
Till, shimmering through the pelting shower
   The moonbeams mark its form.
Far downward to the raving stream
   The woody banks decline,   180
Where waters, flashing in the beam
   Through deepest darkness shine.
Those Giant Oaks their boughs are tossing
   As wild winds wilder moan,
Trunks and leaves confusedly crossing   185
   With a ceaseless groan.
And, over all, the Castle walls
   Rise Blacker than the night,
No sign of man amid their Halls
   Save that lone turret light.   190
The upward path is wild and steep,
   Yet, hear that Horseman come,
Not toiling up with cautious creep,
   But hotly hasting home!
The steed is to the stables led,   195
   But, wheres the Rider gone?
Up that high turret staircase sped
   With gladdened haste alone.
The Ante room looks hushed and still,
   With lattice curtained close,   200
That tempests, sweeping round the Hill,
   Disturb not its repose.
All's soft and calm, a holy balm
   Seems sleeping in the air,
But, what on earth has power to calm   205
   A spirit chafed with care?
The Warrior hastes to seek that power,
   He knows the only one
Whose love can sooth his lonly hour
   Or Hush his rising groan: 210
And, where that soft and solemn light
   Shines through the opened door,
He hastens in with armed tread
   Across the chequered floor

And entering--though a sacred stream   215
    Of radiance round him fell,
It could not with its silent beam
    His eager spirit quell.

"Maria!" But the silence round
    Would give him no reply,   220
And straightway did that single sound
    Without an echo die.
"Where hath my gentle Lady gone
    I do not find her here?"
Lo, on that statly couch, alone   225
    Reclines thy Lady fair.
But--Cold and pale is her marble brow,
    Dishevelled her sunny hair,
Oh! is it in peaceful slumber now
    That she lieth so silent there?   230
"Heaven bless thy dreams!" Lord Albert cried
    But his heart beat impatiently,
And as he hasted to her side
    He scarce had power to see.
All wildly the scenes of his former life   235
    Flashed back upon his eyes,
And at once, a shade of despair and strife
    Before him seemed to arise.
But, as the sailor to his ship
    Clings with more frenzied power,   240
As, louder thundering oer the deep,
    Fresh billows whelm him oer;
So madly, on his only prop
    This war worn man reclined,
He could not, would not, deem his hope   245
    Delivered to the wind.

Yet then, why is this start of wildered fright
    And whence can arise this fear?
Is it not now in the depth of night?
    And sleeps not thy Lady there?   250
And art not thou on thy castle height,
    From wars alarms afar?
See--Is that sleep?
                    --With opened eyes,
Chilly white and cold she lies,   255
Sunk her cheeks, and blanched her lip,
    That trembles as with suffering:
She sleeps not, till the eternal sleep
    Its dreamless rest shall bring!
Heaven had occupied her mind,   260
To onward hasting death resigned,
But, mid those strange uncertainties
    Which crowd their ghastly phantoms round

When all our reasons guiding ties
  Are from the parting soul unbound,   265
She thought, when first she heard that tread,
  That Death himself was hasting near;
The conjured vision of his form
  Obeyed her ready fancies fear,
  And to her dim eyes seemed to appear,   270
  Till--that one word--and all was clear!
Then--sinking reason rose again;
Then--joined the links of memorys chain;
Then--spite of all her dying pain
    She felt, she knew, Her Lord was there! 275
Oh! when, across that dreary sea
The light broke forth so suddenly,
What soul can feel, what tongue express
The burst of raptured happiness,
That from her spirit chased its care,   280
For--She was dying But He was there!

Ah! swiftly, surely, art thou gliding
  Over Deaths unfathomed sea,
Dark and deep the waves dividing
  Thee from earth and earth from thee   285
Life--thy own, thy happy land,
Parted far on either hand,
As the mighty waters widen
  Onward to Eternity.
Shores of Life, Farewell for ever,   290
  Where thy happiness has lain,
Lost for ever, Death must sever
  All thy hopes and joys and pain.
Yet, how blest the sound must be
  Which comes upon thy dying ear,   295
From off the dim departing shore,
  Although its landmarks dissapear,
Still sounding oer the eternal roar,
  The voice of him thou heldst so dear.
  Tis as when the Mariner   300
Just parted from his native home,
  After a night of dread and fear
Whose storms have riven the waves to foam
When nights dark hours have swept away
All, save the sounding of the sea,   305
Morn breaks, where all looks new & strange
But hark, a sweet, a sudden change,
For, on his ear strikes soft from far
  In Sabbath chime--his Native Bells;
He starts--And bursts the joyful tear,   310
For things unutterably dear
  That farewell music tells!

Yet stay!--Why do I wander so
To wile me from this scene of woe?
    There stood the Armed man;   315
The very wildness of Despair
In his red eyeballs stricken glare,
    His cheek so ghastly wan.
And, on her couch his Lady lying,
Still and slow and sur[e]ly dying,   320
Yet, with an enraptured smile
And glistning of her glassy eye,
As her weak arms she would the while
    Have stretched to clasp him standing by,
But, they would not her will obey   325
And motionless beside her lay.
    Then her white lips moved to speak,
But nothing could she say.
This was deaths triumphant hour,
Grasped by his tremendous power   330
    She must pass away!

Speak, Maria! Speak, my love!
    Let me hear thy voice;
Naught on earth, or Heaven above,
    Could make me so rejoice!   335
Speak! O, speak! and say to me,
I am not come too late to thee.
O, tell me, that my arm can save
Thy sinking spirit from the grave!
Maria!--Oh my only love,   340
    Tell me thou wilt not die,
And nought below, and naught above
    Shall feel so blest as I!
Oh, would that I were far away,
Alone upon a stormy sea!   345
Might I awake on yonder plain
Where I have left my soldiers slain;
So I could wake, and rise, and know
    That this was but a fearful dream,
That thou at least wert smiling now   350
    As once in love and beautys beam.
But--Heres the truth which now I know,
My God--My God--I cannot bear thy blow!"

All was vain! She moved not, spoke not,
Speech or sound the silence broke not.   355
But, He flung him oer her lying
As he would catch her spirit flying.
All was vain! That spirit flies
To God who gave it in the skies.
That within his arms which lay   360
Was but a lifeless form of clay;

Naught of feeling in that face,
No return to his embrace;
Not a wish or power to save
Its own cold members from their grave 365
    Go, Lord Albert, go again,
      Drown thought amid a world of storms
    Go--! For thy Despair is vain,
      And thy HOPE lies food for worms

Scene. 2^d

Wild I hear the wild winds sighing
    Oer the hills and far away,
Heaven in clouds before them flying,
    Through the drear December day:
    Dull and dark its evening ray, 5
As, oer the waste, the ceaseless rain
Drives past, is gone, and then again
Sweeps cold and drenching by in showers of sleety
    spray.
    And now, the watery mountains rise
All dimly mingling with the skies, 10
At times, some black brow darkning forth
Bleared by the tempest from the north,
And then, as fast the clouds sail on,
All its crags and heath knolls gone,
The changing veil of sleet drives oer the waste
    alone. 15
    Alone I list to hear the sigh
Of the wild blast passing by,
Hark, far away with mournful moan
It bends the heath on the old grey stone,
Then rising in the Ash trees bough 20
Scatters the withered leaves below;
Blackens the wall with pelting spray,
And wails, and wanders, far away.
Oh when I hear that wintery sound,
    The very voice of a mountain land, 25
A thousand feelings crowding round
    Start up and rise on every hand,
And wake to life, as the wild winds wake,
    And pass with them away,
Sunbeams, that oer the spirit break 30
    Amid the dreariest day.
But, Hush!--And hark that solemn wail;
Tis past!--and yet, tis on my ear;
Shrill piercing through the misty veil,
    Like voice of the departing year. 35
Oh, Hush! Again, and yet again
Bursts forth that loud and longdrawn strain

Soldiers! Attend!--It calls you back
From the pursuers bloody track,
And wildly oer your foemens fall   40
Resounds your evening Bugle call.
The Battle is done, with the setting sun;
The struggle is lost, and the victory won.
Tis over.--No sighs, no anguished cries
From the wild wreck of conflict rise.   45
The sensless corse on earth reclining,
Nor feels defeat, nor knows repining;
And they who survive in their agony
Now stiff and spent and speechless lie,
Their dim eyes wander toward the sky,   50
    Yet seek, and see, no comfort there;
For here, upon this stormy Heath,
The laboured faintness of the breath,
The chill approach of Iron Death,
    Demands a sterner care.   55
And, well I know, that lifes last light
Just bordering on eternal night,
When all these souls shall take their flight,
    Must crush those souls with fear.

Then, There they lie, and wildly oer them   60
    Howls the wind with hollow tone,
While, between its banks, before them
    Hear the torrent chafe and groan;
    Heavily with sullen tone,
    Yet still careering swiftly on.   65
And, torn with shot, a shattered tree
    Shakes its bare arms to the bitter gale,
Oer the blood red eddies that rapidly
    Down the swolln streamlet curling sail.
And the blackened stones of a fallen wall   70
    Dashed down by the Iron hail of war,
With their earthy bank above them thrown,
    Obstructs the torrents passage there;
Till angrily its waters roar,
All white with froth, and red with gore.   75
And--There--a shattered carcase lies
Without the power to look or rise!
Tis He!--The conquered cheiftain--He
Whose look could once give victory;
But sightless now--   80
The shot has torn his eyes away,
And his gashed face is dashed with clay
Cast backward in the eddying flood
That washes off his bursting blood,
The stones across his body thrown   85
That, as he fell, drove following down
Oh! scarce we know the human form

In this cheif victim of the storm!
Yet, though thus crushed and torn he be,
  Though hence, he never more shall rise,   90
Though just as now, till waves shall wash
From the crushed bones the wasting flesh,
  There shall he lie as there he lies;
Yet, still--oh still, look down, and see
How vast may mortal misery be,   95
For, in that bloody battered cell
Still Life and Soul and Memory dwell.
Never, when he was fair and young,
Did feeling thrill more fresh and strong,
Never the hell hounds of despair   100
Had wilder power to worry there.

  "O, could I untormented die,
  Without this gnawing agony
  Which wrings my heart so!--
                      --Heavily and slow   105
The blood ebbs forth,--but, parts not so the soul.
Hither, I came with pain,--Hence must I go
Still, still, in pain!--Is such our changless doom?
God!--Shall such destiny unroll
Its agonies beyond the tomb?   110
    Alls dark without--Alls fire within--!
    Can Hell have mightier hold on sin?
    But yet--through all, my dying mind
    From such a present turns behind
    To what has been,--and then looks oer   115
    The dark dark void of things before;
The land of souls beyond the sable shore!
Oh, how my eyes have stretched to see that land!
How, even when sunk in lifes bewildering roar
  All my strained thoughts have striven to reach
      its strand,   120
  Have striven its mysteries to understand,
Though dark indeed the unreturning sea
That separates what lies beyond from me.
Though those vast waves which bear such thousands
      thither
Have never brought again one spirit hither,   125
  If spirits those who pass may truely be:
Those fearful passengers, Whose sightless eyes
  And blanched lips and tongues which cannot move
May either see the expans which round them lies,
  Or tell the scenes which open where they rove.   130
Oh, might I send across yon sea, that dove
  Which bore the Olive branch; Now might it bear
From hence some token toward me hovering here,
Even though it were the fruit of bitterness,
So I might cease this doubt and fearful-ness   135

                            109

When I embark to sail--I know not where--
I scarce know whence, or how,--But such distress,
Vain is the hope that it will end, and then
How vain the wish to know where lies our pain
        Oh it lies here!--and if my mind   140
        Survives, it will not lag behind!
        And, if indeed, I truely die,
        Lost in the abyss of vacancy,
        Why then--the sum of all will be,
        That I on earth have lived to see   145
        Twice twenty winters beat on me,
        Not one whole day of happiness,
        And year on year of mad distress!

They say, when on the bed of death
        The wasted sickman lingering lies,   150
His breast scarce heaving with his breath,
        And cold his brow and quenched his eyes,
'See!   How resignedly he dies!"
Aye!   What a look of peace and love
That glazed eye casts to heaven above!   155
Even those white lips will scarcly quiver,
Though he must leave this world for ever.
And though his childern round him stand,
Tis not for them--that outstretched hand!
        Angels shall press those clay cold fingers   160
        In the unknown void round which he lingers!
            Ha!   Does the _victim_ reason so,
        Thus, bound beneath that fatal blow?
        No!   There indeed he lies inert,
        For death's cold frost congeals his heart;   165
        Yet, while that dim and dazing eye
        Can wander oer one stander by,
        While those mute lips, that silent tongue,
        Can one short broken gasp prolong,
        While in that whirled and burning brain   170
        Reasons last spark can wax or wane,
        So long, across that parting soul
        Unmixed--unmingled--torments roll.
        He--look on death with smiling eye!
        He--content and peaceful die!   175
        He!   No, like fire, one burning strife
        Convulses each riven string of life,
        And, could those lips be moved to say,
        Could those stiff hands be clasped to pray
        That only voice and prayer would be,   180
        'Oh save me from that fatal sea
        Where Hell and death join agony!'
            I am dying, and what a rayless gloom
        Seems darkning round my dreary tomb
        I know no light, I see no ray   185

To guide me on my heavenly way.
There was a light--But it is gone!
    There was a hope--But all is oer!
And, powerless, sightless, left alone,
I go where Thou hast gone before;   190
And yet, I shall not see thee more!
Ha said I that the dying man
Could only think of present pain?
Oh No! For scenes gone long ago
Make the main torrent of his woe.   195
I meant, he thinks of pain alone,
It skills not wether come or gone:
All dark alike to him and me
What has been, is, or is to be!
And keen I feel such misery now,   200
For where, Maria, where art thou?
Lost--Though--I seem to see thee now,
Thy smiling eyes and shining brow
And sunny cheek and golden hair,
In all thy beauty smiling there.   205
How often has that bright blue eye
    Driven sorrow shrinking from its shine
And banished all my misery
    Before one heavenly look of thine!
    How often has that look divine   210
Roused up this heart from bitterness,
And bowed it in its worst distress
    To kneel before thy shrine!
When troubles hastened, thickning on,
When every hope of rest seemed gone;   215
When, mid the blight of hating eyes
    I stood, bewildered, sick with woe,
What was the star which seemed to rise
    To light me on and guide me through
What was that form so heavenly fair,   220
Untouched by time, unmarked by care,
To whose fond heart I clung to save
My sinking spirit from its grave?
Maria!--hadst thou never been,
    This hour I should not living be,   225
But while I strove with fate, between
    The strife thou camest to set me free,
And wildly did I cling to thee!
    I could not, would not, dared not part,
    Lest Hell again should seize my heart!   230
Can I forget, how toward my eye
    Still ever gazed for guidance thine,
As if I were thy star on high,
    Though well I knew twas thou wert mine
That azure eye, that softened smile,   235
That heavenly voice whose tones to me

111

The weariest wintriest hours could wile,
    And make me think that still might be
    Some years of happiness with thee;
That thou, amid my life to come,   240
Shouldst be my hope my heaven my home
But--we are sundred--thee thy grave,
And me this dreary wild will have.
Whateer the world to come may be
I must never look on thee,   245
If theres no God, no Heaven, no Hell,
Thou within thy grave must dwell,
I here blackning in the storm,
Both a banquet for the worm.
If--there is a Heaven above,   250
    Thou, I know, art shining there
At the Almighty throne of love,
    Angel bright and Angel fair
From heaven thou wanderdst like the Dove
    To the wild world of waters here,   255
But--never made oer it to rove,
    Thou hast left its waves of sin and care
    Back for thine Ark, while I staid where
The rottenest mass of carnage lay,
A Raven resting on his prey.   260

            x x x x x x x x x x x x x

But, Oh why will the parted return to our heart
    When the sods have grown green on their tomb?
Oh, why will the twilight refuse to depart,
    When it only gives depth to the gloom!
Oh why, in the snows and the storms of December,   265
    When branches lie scattered and strewn,
Do we oftest, and clearest, and brightest, remember
    The sunshine and summer of June!
Oh why, mid the hungry and cottagless waste
    Do we dream of the Goblet filled high,   270
Why will our spirits, when famishing, taste
    Of such visionlike revelry!
Moralist speak--Ist in Lifes deepest sorrow
    That these gleams of the past which has vanished
        away
Though misery and mourning await on the morrow   275
    May strenghten to bear through the shades of
        to day?
    Since we have had our sunshine, we must have our
    storm,
If Once with an Angel, Then now with a worm.
Christian speak--sayest thou, Cares and annoy
Are probations on earth to a heavenly joy.   280
Or next, wilt thou point to the desolate sea?

                        112

And shew me the Mariner, drifting away,
Behind him the shores of his vanishing home,
Around him the billows all crested with foam,
Yet he casts not a look upon ocean or shore,   285
But fixes his eyes on his haven before.
Sayest thou, Thus should man smile on his joys
    and his sorrow
And press toward Heaven his haven of to morrow.
  Aye, Man!--on let him press, till that heaven
    shall break
    In lightnings and thunders and tempests and
    gloom,   290
Then, let the spirit, in saf[e]ty, speak,
    Where is the rest beyond the tomb?
    Where are the joys of his heavenly home?
Then, let the moralist seek for his strength,
  And smile on the past in its visionlike form,   295
Then, let the Christian, anchored at length,
  See light in the darkness, a Sun through the
    storm!
    Away with all this false disguise,
    See midnight truth with noonday eyes.
    The past has had a single joy,   300
    But when that past has long gone by,
    When cares have driven cares away,
    When general darkness clouds the day,
    That single star amid the sky
    Will shed a brighter light on high;   305
    And in, the Horizon, only one
    Is yet the All which can be shewn.
    And still, as gloomier frowns that night,
    Brighter it flashes on the sight,
    And still--Oh still--as time flys by,   310
    While other things in shades may die,
    Tis but more present to my eye
    My own sole star of memory!
    Well,--oer me shining let it be,
    That thus one glimmering I may see   315
    Fixed far above to shew my gloom,
    And light my spirit to its Tomb!

    Yet--How I wander! Grasping now
    At the glorious dream of a world to come--
Then, recoiling back, I scarce know how,   320
    Upon that hideous hopeless gloom
    The nothingness within the tomb!
Thinking on Thee, and then again
Shrinking within my present pain.
All wide!--All wandering!--This is Death!   325
    And I would calmly meet him now,
    As stern I'de feel my shortning breath,

```
                 As I have seen my power laid low,
                 But, for the thought--
                                --O whats to come?              330
                 God!--If there be a God--look down,
                   Compassionate my fall!
                 O, clear away thy awful frown,
                   And hearken to my call!
                 Nay--All is lost,--I cannot bear               335
                 In mouldering dust to dissapear,
                 And Heaven will not the gloom dispell,
                 Since, if theres Heaven, my home is--Hell!
                 No hope!--No hope!--And, Oh, farewell
                 The form so long kept treasured here!          340
                 Must thou then ever dissapear?
                 Gone long--But kept in memorys shrine,
                   Now dying again as memory dies,
                 First passed from earth my star divine
                   And now--Tis passing from the skies!         345
                 Then--Thou art gone, and Heaven is gone,
                 And sights, and sounds, and all are gone!
            Oh, what a shade is Life!--I am Dying--
            AND HOW LIKE A DREAM IS EXISTENCE FLYING!"


                 See, through the shadows of the night          350
                   Burst hotly hasting onward here,
                 A wounded Charger vast and white
                   All wildly mad with pain and fear.
                 With hoofs of thunder, on he flies,
                 Shaking his white mane to the skies,           355
                 Till, on his huge knees tumbling down,
                 Across the fallen Cheiftan thrown,
                 With a single plunge of dying force
                 His vast limbs hide Lord Albert's corse.


                                      Northangerland.
                                      [March/April 1836]
```

MS: D(2), B(2), I, H
First Publication: Oliphant, partial; SHB C and B

An early draft of "Before our mighty Makers
throne," May 1836--see No. **135**, pp. 175 and
273

55 May 17   The sunshine of a summer sun
    1836   Oer the proud domes of Elrington
             Glows with a beam divinely bright
             In one unquenched unvaried light
             And high its arched windows rise   5
             As if to invite the smiling skies
             And proud its mighty columns shew
             Between them ranked in haughty row
             And sweet and soft the solemn shade
             By the oerarching portals made   10
                The statly halls of Elrington
             May fitly meet that glorious sun
             For fetes are feasts are given to day
             To Noble Lords and Ladies gay
             And that vast city of the sea   15
             Which round us lies so endlessly
             Has hither poured its proudest train
             To worship mirth and fly from pain
                The sunshine of a summers sun
             Glows oer the groves of Elrington   20
             Where city girt spreads wide around
             The flower and foliage laden ground
             All round the Hot and glaring sky
             Bespeaks a mighty city nigh
             And through each opening in the shade   25
             Palace and temple crown the glade
             So here as an oasis stands
             Mid the wide waste of Egypts sands
             This glorious vision of a grove
             With flowers beneath and fruits above   30
             Lies in that citys human sea
             Whose streets stretch round so ceaslessly
                Oh who could pass unnoticed by
             This scene of Natures royalty
             Instead of Birds to warble there   35
             Etherial music fills the air
             Breathed from these Halls thrown open wide
             To admit the ever changing tide
             Of Earths and Africs hope and pride

MS: B(1)
First Publication: Shorter EJB 1910

56   A Breeze embued with rich perfumes
             Is waving yonder sea of plumes

                                [1836]

                        115

MS: B(1)
First Publication: Shorter EJB 1910

An early draft of **Lucifer,** June 22, 1836--see
No. **89,** p. 176

An early draft of "Now heavily in clouds comes the
day," June 1836--see No. **90,** p. 177

An early draft of **The Battle Eve,** July 9,
1836--see No. **88,** p. 174

57 July   My Ancient ship upon my Ancient sea
    1836   Begins another voyage--Nay thourt gone
           But whither pending? who is gone with thee?
           Since parted from thee I am left alone
           Unknowing what my Rovers fate may be   5
           Into Its native world of tempests thrown
           Lost like a speck from my diverted eye
           Which wilder mightier visions must survey

           Lost and unnoticed--far away the roar
               Of southern waters breaking to the wind   10
           With restless thunder rolling still before
               As the wild gale sweeps wilder on behind
           And every vision of old Afric's shore
           As much forgot and vanished out of mind
           As the wild track though markedst so long ago   15
           From those eternal waves which surge below

           Gone--tis a word which through lifes troubled
                   waste
           Seems always coming and the only one
           Which can be called the PRESENT. Hope is past
           And Hate and strife and love and peace
                   are gone   20
           Before we think them for their rapid haste
           Scarce gives us time for one short smile
                   or groan

116

Ere that thought dies and new ones come
    between
It and our heart with some as fleeting scene

And yet there is or seems at least to be   25
A general hue of thought that colours all
So though each one be different all agree
In the same melancholy shade like pall
Even as the shadows look the same to me
Though cast I know from many a varying wall   30
In this vast city--Hut and Temple sharing
In the same light and the same darkness
    wearing

Not that I deem all life a course of shade
Nor all the world a maze of streets like
    these
From youth to age a mighty change is made   35
As from this city to the Southern Seas
For years through youthful hope our course
    is laid
For years in sloth a sea without a breeze
For years amid the stir of civil jar
For years within some silent sleepless care   40

Changing and still the same yet swiftly
    passing
Tis here tis there tis nowhere oh my soul
Is there no rest from such a fruitless
    chasing
Of the wild dreams that ever round thee roll
Each as it comes the parting thought defacing 45
Yet--all still hurrying to the selfsame goal
Gone ere I catch them but their path alone
Stretching afar toward one for ever gone!

What have I written--nothing for tis over
And seems as nothing in the single cloud   50
That shadows it and long has seemed to Hover
Oer all the crossing thoughts that ever flowd
In this wrecked spirit Oh my ocean Rover
Well mayst thou plough the deep so free and
    proud
Thou bearst the uniting tie of ceasless
    dreams   55
The fount the confluence of a thousand
    streams

    I do not see myself again
A wanderer oer the Atlantic main
I do not Backward turn my eye

```
                    Toward sleepless sea and stormy sky        60
                    Oh no these vanished visions rest
                    In far woodlands of the west
                    And there let Hesperus arise
                    To watch my treasure where it lies
                       The present scenes the present clime    65
   28               Forbid the Dreams of olden time
   28               The present thoughts the present hour
   56               Are rife with Deeds of sterner power
   14               And who shall be my leading star
   70               Amid the howling storm of war.             70
   25
   95
                    Hark Listen to the Distant Gun
                    From the Battle feild of Edwardston
                    It breaks upon the awful roar
                       Which stuns my ears around
                    And oh the shout of Victory                75
                       Strikes with a Hollow sound
                    My struggles all are crowned with power
                    And fortune gives a glorious hour
                    Men who hate me kneel before me
                    Men who kneel are forced to adore me       80
                    My Name is on a million tongues
                    The Million babbles of my wrongs
                    And Twenty years of Tyrant pride
                    Which strove this Modern God to hide
                    At last have vanished in the rays          85
                    Of his unquenched unclouded blaze
                    Oh is not Jesus come again
                    Over his thousand saints to reign
                    To free the world from errors chain
                    While sin and Satan vainly spit            90
                    Their venomed fury <from> the pit
                    Where they may lie for<gotten>
                    Till Heaven descends in <judgment down>
                    Their reign is past their power
                       <oerthrown>
                    For fallen is Mighty Babylon               95
```

MS: B(1)
First Publication: Shorter EJB 1910
Text: ll. 91-4 partially obliterated by an ink-blot. The
       numbers in the left margin are Branwell's.

An early draft of **Percy's Musings Upon the Battle
of Edwardston,** July 22, 1836--see No. **91,** p. 179

58   Memory how thy majic fingers
              With a wild and passing thrill
          Wakes the chord whose spirit lingers
              Sleeping silently and still
          Fast asleep and allmost dying   5
              Through my days of changless pain
          Till I deem those strings are lying
              Never to be waked again
          Winds have blown but all unknown
          Nothing could arouse a tone   10
          In that Heart which like a stone
              Senselessly has lain
          All seemed over freind and Lover
              Strove to waken music there
          Flow the strings their fingers over   15
              Still in silence slept the air

          Memory Memory comes at last
          Memory of feelings past
          And with an Eolian blast
              Strikes the strings resistlessly   20

                  [July/August, 1836]

MS: I, B(1)
First Publication: Shorter EJB 1910

59   Oh all our cares these Noontide airs
              Might seem to drive away
          So glad and bright each sight appears
              Each sound so soft and gay
          And through the shade of yonder glade   5
              Where thick the leaves are dancing
          With jewels rare and flowrets fair
              A hundred plumes are glancing
          For there its palace portals rise
              Beyond the myrtle grove   10
          Catching the whitest brightest dies
              From the deep blue dome above
          But here this little lonely spot
              Retires among its trees
          By all unknown and noticed not   15
              Save sunshine and the breeze

                  [July/August, 1836]

MS: I
First Publication: Shorter EJB 1910

60
PBB

Still and bright in twilight shining   Aug 8th 1836
 Glitters forth the evening star
Closing Rosebuds round me twining
 Shed their fragrance through the air
Slow the river pales its glancing   5
Soft its waters cease their dancing
Calm and cool the shades advancing
 Speak the hours of slumber near!
Why this solemn silence given
 To the close of fading day   10
Feels the earth the hush of heaven
 Can the expanse of nature pray
And when daylights toil is done
Gratful for summer sunshine gone
Can it before the Almighties throne   15
 Its glad obeisance pay?
Such a hush of sacred sadness
 Wide around the weary wild
Oer the whirl of Human madness
 Spreads the slumbers of a child   20
These surrounding sweeps of trees
Swaying to the evening breeze
With a voice like distant seas
 Making music mild
Percy Hall above them lowering   25
 Darker than the darkning sky
With its halls and turrets towering
 Wakes the wind in passing by
Round that scene of wondrous story
In their old ancestral glory   30
All its Oak's so huge and hoary
 Wave their boughs on high

Among these Turrets there is one
The soonest dark when day is done
And when Autumns winds are strongest 35
Moans the most and echoes longest
So--On the steps that lie before
A solitary arched door
In that lone Gable far away
 From sights and sounds of social joy 40
Fronting the expanse so dim and grey
 There sits a lonly boy
One hand is in his curling hair
 To part it from his brow
And that young face so soft and fair   45
 Is lifted heavenward now
On the cold stone he has laid him down
 To watch that silver line
Beneath the power of twilights frown
 In the wide west decline   50

For Heaven still guides his azure eyes
    Toward its expanse so wild
As veiled in darkness their he lies
    A little Angel Child!

Oh who has known or who can tell   55
    The fountain of those feelings high
Which while in this wild world we dwell
    At times will lift us up on high
    In a celestial sympathy
With yon blue vault yon starry dome   60
    As if the spirit deemed the sky
Was even on earth its only home
And while the eye is dim with tears
    The feelings wrapt in dreams sublime
How dead seem earthly hopes and fears   65
    How all forgot the cours of time
And yet the soul can never say
    What are the thoughts which make it glow
We feel they are but what are they?
    Tis this which we must never know   70
While lingering in this world of woe
Yet did Mans Soul descend from heaven
With feelings by its Maker given
All high all glorious all Divine
    And from his hand perfected gone   75
With such a bright reflected shine
    As the full moon bears from the sun
But then--The Soul was clothed in clay
So straight its beauty passed away
And through a whirl of misery driven   80
Earths shadow came 'tween it and heaven
A darkned orb the moon became
Lost all its lustre quenched its flame!
Or entering on this mortal life
The clouds of woe the alarms of strife   85
Continual passing veil it round
With gloomy wreaths of shade profound
So only shining fitfully
A single gleam of light we see
As part the clouds on either hand   90
To shew the clear calm heaven beyond
Yet as one moment soars our soul
    Into these wayward dreams divine
Till back again the darkness roll
    And hide the uncertain shine   95
Yet shall a time come rapid on
When all these clouds that round us frown
From Heavens vast vault all past & gone
Leave the full moon in glory there
To shine for ever bright and fair   100

When this dull clay is cast away
These THOUGHTS shall shine with cloudless ray
And we shall understand what now
But dimly is revealed below

In yon lone childs uplifted eyes   105
    Such dreams can scars[e] be dim
So late upon those mortal skies
    The moon has risen to him
So late his soul has passed from Heaven
    That it can scarce forget   110
The visions bright whose haloed light
    Is round its musings yet
Silent he sits on the darkned stone
    With night around him falling
As if to him that hollow moan   115
    From the old tree tops were calling
He listens to the eerie wind
    Around his Fathers dwelling
Till faster following on his mind
    More glorious thoughts seem swelling   120
For both his little hands were stretched
    In rapture to the sky
When wilder from the wilderness
    Each blast came howling by
Toward clouds all southward resting wide   125
    Above the Atlantic sea
While oer them far the darksome air
    Is haloed lustrously
He gazes as some wondrous sight
    To him were opening soon   130
Till, lo!--that sudden shining light
    "The MOON the glorious MOON!"

Oh soft and sweet is the silver beam
    That floods the turret high
While fairy woodlands round it seem   135
    All glinting gloriously
Each window glitters cold and clear
    Upon the southern tower
And--though the shade is darker made
    Around his lonly bower--   140
Yet oer his face a solemn light
    Comes smiling from the sky
And shows to sight the lustre bright
    Of his uplifted eye
The aimless heedless carelessness   145
    Of happy Infancy
Yet such a solemn tearfulness
    Commingling with his glee
The parted lips the shining hair

```
        Cast backward from his brow                          150
Without a single shade of care
But Bathed amid that moonlight air
    Oh who so blest as thou!
The moon in glory oer the grove
    Majestic marches on                                      155
With all the vault of heaven above
    To canopy her throne
And from her own celestial rest
Upon the dark woods waving crest
    Serenly she looks down                                   160
Yet beaming still as if she smiled
Most brightly on that beauteous child
But what thought he as there he lay
    Beneath the arched door
Amid the ever trembling play                                 165
    Of moonshine through the bower
Gazing with blue eyes dimmed by tears
To that vast vault of shining spheres
    Till its mysterious power
Makes the bright drops unnoticed break                       170
In dewy Lustre oer his cheek


    "Oh how I could wish to fly
Far away through yonder sky
Oer those trees upon the breeze                              175
    To a paradise on high!
Why am I so bound below
That I must not cannot go
Lingering here for year on year
    So long before I die!                                    180
Now how glorious seems to be
Heaven's huge concave stretched oer me
But--Every star is hung so far
    Away from where I lie!
I love to see that Moon arise                                185
It suits so with the silent skies
I love it well, but cannot tell
    Why it should make me cry!
Ist that it brings before me now
Those wondrous times gone long ago                           190
When Angels used from Heaven to come
And make this earth theire happy home?
When Moses brought from Egypts strand
Gods favoured tribes through seas and sand
Victorious to the promised land!                             195
When Salem rose her Judahs pride
Where David lived and Jesus died!
Ist that I know this very moon
Those vanished wonders gazed upon
When Shepherds watched their flocks by night                 200
```

```
                    All seated on the ground
                And Angels of the Lord came down
                    And glory shone around
                Ist that I think upon the sea
                Just now tis beaming beauteously              205
                Where I so oft have longed to be
                    But never yet have been?
                Ist that it shines so far away
                On Lands beyond that oceans spray
                Mong Lonly Scotlands hills of grey           210
                    And ENGLANDS groves of green!
                Or ist that through yon Deep blue dome
                It seems so solemnly to roam
                As if upon some unknown Sea
                    A vessels statly form                    215
                It oer the waves was wandering free
                    Through calm and cloud and storm!
                --I cannot tell but its in heaven
                    And though I view it here
                Till I am mouldring dust to dust             220
                My parted spirit never must
                    Behold its brightness near
                I am crying to think that mighty throng
                Of Glorious Stars to heaven belong
                That they can never never see                225
                A little earthly child like me
                Still rolling on still beaming down
                And I unnoticed and unknown
                Though Jesus once in ages gone
                    Called Childern to his knee              230
                So where He reigns in glory bright
                Above these starry skies of night
                Amid his paradise of light
                    Oh why might I not be!
                Oft when awake on christmas morn             235
                In sleepless twilight laid fo[r]lorn
                Strange thoughts have oer my mind been born
                    How he has died for me
                And oft within my chamber lying
                Have I awaked myself with crying             240
                From dreams where I beheld him dying
                    Upon the accursed tree
                And often has my mother said
                While on her lap I laid my head
                She feared for time I was not made           245
                    But for Eternity!
                So I can read my title clear
                    To mansions in the skies
                And let me bid farewell to fear
                    And wipe my weeping eyes                 250
                Ill lay me down on this marble stone
```

And set the world aside
To see upon its ebon throne
Yon moon in glory ride
Ill strive to peirce that midnight vault   255
Beyond its farthest star
Nor let my spirits wanderings halt
Neath Edens crys[t]al bar
For sure that wind is calling me
To a land beyond the grave   260
And I must not shrink upon the brink
Of Jordans heavenly wave
But Ill fall asleep in its waters deep
And wake on that blest shore
Where I shall neither want or weep   265
Or sigh or sorrow more
Oh Angels come! Oh Angels come!
And Guide me to my Heavenly Home!

Guide thee to Heaven!--Oh lovely Child
Little knowest thou the Tempests wild   270
Now gathering for thy future years
There blighting floods of bitter tears
Little thou knowst how long and dread
Must be thy path ere thou art laid
Within thy dark and narrow bed   275
Or how thou then wilt shrink to be
Launched out upon Eternity
All those celestial visions flown
All Hope of Heaven for ever gone!   280
This passionate desire for Heaven
Is but the beam of brightness given
Around thy spirit at its birth
And not yet quenched in clouds of earth
The inward yearnings of the soul   285
Toward its original sad goal
Before that goal is hid from sight
Amid the gloom of mortal night
To thee just entering into Time
This world is like a stranger clime   290
Where--nothing kindred--nothing known--
Leaves thy young spirit all alone
To spend its hours in thinking on
The Native home whence it has gone
But--Oh at last a time will come   295
When Heaven is lost and earth is Home
Where pleasures glimmering in thy sight
As soon as seen shall sink in night
Whilst thou pursuest them through the gloom
Sinking like meteors to the tomb   300
This light shall change to lightning then
This love of Heaven to Hate of men

So if thou seekest a glorious name
Thy path shall pass through blood and flame
From crime to crime impetous hasting   305
Blasted thyself and others blasting
For that which from on high is thrown
Will always fall most rapid down
And sink the deepest.--So with thee
Thy quick and passionate heart shall be   310
But further plunged in misery
Then those around thee oft may find
Earth and its joys to suit thine mind
For dust to dust the sons of earth
Will love the land that gave them birth   315
Yet never thou or if thou dost
Too quickly thou shalt find it DUST!

He sleeps!--in slumber calm and deep
An Infants blest and balmy sleep
Dreaming of heaven those closed eyes   320
See glorious visions of the skies
And tremblingly their fringes lie
On the yong cheek of Infancy
The softened curls of golden hair
Just moving in the moonlight air   325
But his white brow so sweetly still
So free from every shade of ill!
Shall it be so for ever?--NO!
Who in this world would wish it so
Yon is the Image of a man   330
Destined to lead the formost van
Of coming time and in his land
The future chooses to command
Tis He whose never dying name
Shall set a future world on flame   335
PERCY! awake thee from thy sleep
Awake! to bid thy country weep

P B Bronte
August 13th
1836.

MS: B(1), B(2), I
First Publication: Gaskell CB, partial; Shorter EJB
1910, partial; SHB C & B

61   Forgotten one! I know not when nor how
          Thou diedst--for even thy very tomb is dead
      The stone that covered thee so long ago
          Itself by weeds and grass is overspread

[September 1836]

MS: D(1)
Not previously published
Text: l. 4: "overspread" written after "covered"; neither
      is canceled

Oct 4 1836
PBB

62 Behold the waste of waving sea
      In stormy shadow lying
As vast and shoreless stretched away
      As the clouds above it flying
As rough as restless and as free   5
      As the wild winds oer it sighing
There mingled with the ocean gale
      I hear the sea birds crying
As through the unmeasured Heaven they sail
      Some far off rest descrying   10
And oft their white wings glittering forth
Till lost amid the stormy North
And still from out the Atlantic surge
      The heavey vapours rise
Whence darkly gathering they diverge   15
      Around the dusty skies
And ist the Heaven to Ocean speaks
      Or Ocean back replies
That such a mournful music breaks
      And swells and falls and dies   20
For as the wild winds wilder sound
More hoarse the surges murmur round
Till they are rolling oer the deep
      With such a thundering roar
As might arouse from fastest sleep   25
      The Dwellers on the shore
And waken many in anxious start
      For those who never more
To some yet warm and yearning heart
      Such tempests shall restore   30
Each Gust still calling it to mourn
For one who never can return
Look How the tumbling ridges swell
      And roll in restless agony

The very burning lake of Hell   35
   Could scarce more rough and raging be!
Black billows ever rising round
And hurried on toward oceans bound
Till if a blast more strongly sweeps
It tears the waters from the deeps   40
Whose boiling crests of tortured spray
Are torn and shivered oer the sea
While that white foam eternally
   Brewed in the tempests feircest wrath
   As on the bit steeds champ their froth   45
Mounts on the broken blast and scatters to the sky
   Yet--what is that--which mid the spray
   Scuds like a mist wreath oer the sea
   Now bending downward through the surge
   Then as its dripping sides emerge   50
Cast back upon the waves or forward born away

A Ship! A Ship! She bends her side
   Rejoicing to the seas
Beneath a cloud of canvass wide
   That stretches in the breeze   55

The bristled poles which rise above
   Are glancing through the rain
And bow beneath the tempests breath
   With many a sudden strain

So wild the blast so dense the press   60
   Of canvass oer her prow
That on her decks the tempest breaks
   Like flying clouds of snow

And yet--as if her desperate crew
   Had maddened in the gale--   65
Though driving past as whirlwinds fast
   Swells forth another sail!

And yet another!--Till she bends
   The boiling deeps below
Where every dash the water sends   70
   In flashes from her bow

One moment stopping on her course
   As doubtful what to obey
& Then with unresisted force
   Born forward oer the sea   75

Her crew with dark locks oer their brows
   Amid the tempest streaming

To each wild eye a spirit rouse
    That fires its fitful gleaming

And breif words mixed with breifer smiles   80
    Are passed from man to man
As for a moment from their toils
    The[y] pause their cheif to scan

He stands upon the rocking prow
To see the surges boil below   85
And mark his vessel plough her path
Through Heavens and Oceans feircest wrath
And then he lifts his wild blue eye
To note the changes of the sky
Then through the storm a glance he flings   90
As if to search for unseen things
Since--failing even that eagle gaze
To peirce the ever varying maze--
His seamen start to hear him hail
"All Hands aloft and crowd all sail"   95
    Tis grand to view his Noble brow
Confront the breezes while they blow
Aside his curls of Auburn Hair
That forehead leaving free and fair
To change with the resistless light   100
    Which flashes from his Azure eye
Now softened like the calm moonlight
    Now troubled as that stormy sky
    Now feircly daring to defy
The deepest gulph those waves could form   105
The loudest piping of that storm
And loud that storm does pipe and vast
The foam white waves are roaring past
And stands he on his streaming deck
    As chiding even the flying gale   110
Till Lo! the restless vapours break
    A wild wide waste of waves to unveil
    There forward fleets a distant sail
Tossed in distress--And eagerly
That storm lost ship these sailors eye   115
With such a shout as through the sky
    Oer powers the tempests wail
"Hurrah! she heaves in sight again!
Now merrily haste we oer the main
        Though from us she flew   120
        Like the fleet sea mew
As like lightning we follow her speed were in vain!"
"Heave ho--my Hearts" the Boatswain cries
"Now draw your lots and chuse your prize!"
And back an Ancient Mariner   125
His Answer shouts with ruthless sneer

"Lets leave 'em their sails their shroud to be
Their ship their coffin their grave the sea"

That Sailor was a hoary man
Tottering on lifes remotest span   130
But still his step was on the seas
And still his grey locks faced the breeze
Not one of all that desperate crew
With eye more quick or hand more true
Not one with oaths more terrible   135
Could speak the mother tongue of Hell
His ragged garments scarce might warm
His blighted carcase in the storm
Yet those mean limbs had forced a way
Where thousands trembling stood at bay   140
And though so rough his cursing tongue
His oaths had mid a palace rung
Tutor and Oracle in crime
To Serf or Lord who wished to climb
    And blithly now his Wolfish eyes   145
Stretchs to behold the promised prize
While cool between his toothless jaws
A Glittering knife he grimly draws
Feels its keen edge and laughs to mind
The deeds it did in times behind   150
And to his comrade watching nigh
Slowly he turns his tyger eye
    That comrade was of statlier form
As yet scarce battered by the storm
Youth still oer him her beams had flung   155
If not in sins in seasons young
Wild rose the locks above his brow
And brown his cheek's unfading glow
His eye rolled ever feirce and free
As fits a spoiler of the sea   160
His pirate vest was dashed aside
For that wild breast would scorn to hide
The beating of its lawless pride
And loud and carelessly he sung
As reckless in the shrouds he hung   165
Riot in peace and spoil in war
Were all O Connors hope or care
    But standing by a silent gun
Behold another darker one
A man of crime whose eyes had neer   170
Been clouded with a single tear
Hard were those eyes and black the brow
That shadowed oer their tiger glow
Though scathed by storms an Age might pass
With all its winters oer his face   175
Yet never clear away the frown

Which called revenge in bloodshed down
Nor might his Cheiftan brook that scowl
But that he trusted Gordons soul
However black the path he trod   180
Would never bid him leave the road
                                       [unfinished]

MS: (B2)
First Publication: SHB Misc II

63 Thus lived thus died she never more on her
        Shall sorrow light or shame she was not made
    Through years on years the inner weight to bear
        Which colder hearts endure till they are laid
    By age in earth her days and pleasures were   5
        Breif but delightful such as had not staid
    Long with her destiny But she sleeps well
    In that wide land wherein she loved to dwell
                            PD Bronte
                      Nov 11   1836
                         Haworth

MS: J
Not previously published

            An early draft of **Queen Mary's Grave**, dated
            December 10, 1836--see No. **92**, p. 182

64 Sing Hoy for Cock Robin in regular verse
    How he harnessed Old Dobbin one day to the hearse
    For a marvel had happened that could not be holpen
    His wifes mouth was shut! and the graves mouth was
            open

    To the Grave they went gravely with groaning and
            sighs   5
    And Bob headed them bravely with tears in his eyes
    The Mourners in black and the Parson in white
    Were he couldnt help thinking a mighty fine sight

    A Lady was there and her face looked so fair
    That each look he cast on her dried up a tear   10

Lord he said if its greivous a old wife to bury
Why sure the best cure is a new one to marry

If I lost my Old Horse say shouldnt I try
A new one of course directly to buy
And isnt a woman as good as old Dobbin?   15
Sing Ho and Hievo for my Jolly Cock Robbin!

Cock Robin is kneeling devout at the Altar
To furnish his thrapple again with a Halter
'For richer for poorer for better for worse'
Odd he thinks is it this way Ide buy me a Horse?   20

Then he says to the preist If a man take a wife
Is he bound with that one to remain all his life?--
'Yes certainly Brother"--And if he dont marry
He's not bound at all--"No"--then by the Lord Harry!

Since I see when a mans wed he's wedded to one   25
And that he may wed twenty if he will wed none
Ill bid for the twenty the folly's too great
When the world has such plenty to stick too one mate
And wed without trying and rue it too late!

I tried all his paces ere I bought Old Dobbin   30
Sing Ho and Hievo for my Jolly Cock Robin!

                                    [December 1836]

MS: D(1)
First Publication: SHB Misc II, in facsimile

65   Then climbed the fugitive an airy height
            And resting, back oer Eden cast his sight;

            Far on the Left to Man for ever closed
            That Mount of Paradise in clouds reposed

                                    [December 1836]

MS: K
Not previously published

            A second early draft of **The Angrian Hymn,**
            December 1836--see No. **74,** pp. 90 and 153

An early draft of "Poor Mourner Sleep,--I Cannot
sleep," dated January 13, 1837--see No. **133**,
p. 264

P B B---te
Feb 9 1837

66   "Well! I will lift my eyes once more
That Western Heaven to wander oer
Though I had thought them closed for ever--
Had thought that last long look should sever
My Thoughts from all this upper air!   5
But--Who can still the Spirits care
Or hush the Greifs contending there?

What! Shining still! Oh Thou canst shine
    With light and heat unchangeably
Even though descends Thine Orb divine   10
    On this wild world of misery!
Bright journeyer on a path like mine
Companion of my dark decline
    Thus let me welcome Thee!
And Oh behind my native West   15
While Thou descendest to thy rest,
To that far Land I love the best
    Might I but, following, flee!--
My Noble West! My Native Home!
How all my feelings round thee roam   20
    Since not even death can kill
The thoughts which from my Infancy
Have twined thee round my memory
But I can feel thy majesty
        And, Dying, I'll Love thee still!   25

Glorious in Heaven That Sun goes down
    Lost in his own unclouded blaze
And glorious is the splendour thrown
        Round his declining rays!
Glorious where cheif, his central light   30
    Crowns those dim hills so far away
Till all their summits float from sight
        Amid a sunbright sea!
Though Life with me is waning low
I feel my Heart expanding now   35
And tears are trembling in my eyes
While gazing on those Glorious Skies
This dreadful Death forgot awhile
These Lips can frame one farewell smile
        Alls fleeting and alls mingling now   40

133

In-to a strange celestial glow
The Summer clouds the Sunlit Trees
The Blackbirds song the Evening breeze
The raptured thoughts that fill my brain
Even this my Bed of fevered pain   45
All float in wildered maze around me
All confounded All confound me!
Nature I know smiles fresh and fair
And bright the Heavens and still the air
But basking in those dreamlike skies   50
Afar a sea of glory lies
With all its Isles of Paradise
        Revealed before my sight
And kissed by Evenings Westering Blaze
And melting in its golden haze   55
They wanderi weakening on my gaze
        In strange unsteady light!
Oh why is such a dreamy feeling
Over my dying spirit stealing?
Is this the dyzzying whirl of death?   60
Does memory with my parting breath
        Yeild up her trust to him?
Oh God Oh God! and must I go?
Is This the Voice that warns me to
        Awaken from my dream?   65
I know not the reality
Which when awake these eyes must see
        To look upon for ever
But I do know the thrilling ties
Which bind my spirit to those skies   70
And which my dying agonies
    In vain may strive to sever
I cannot wake! My spirit seems
As if amid unearthly dreams
        Its course were born away   75
From out this Ark of Wretchedness
Oer blighting waves of bitterness
For some green olive branch of peace
        A Weary flight to stray
Lost Bird! upon yon stormy sea   80
        I seem to see thee hovering
Where buried Nature's sepulchre
        The waste of waves is covering
And thy white wings are glistening there
        As thou for rest wert yearning   85
But there's no hope in that dark air
        To sooth thee back returning
Submerged thy Native forests lie
        With leafless branches torn
So homeward through that wintery sky   90
        Return Lost Bird Return!"

So that sweet sufferer spoke--Her mind
 Seemed passing fast from earth
In forms and fancies undefined
 To give its feelings birth   95
In glimpses of a spirit shore
The strength of eyesight to restore
 Which coming Death denied
That while the world was lost to her
Her soul might rove a wanderer   100
 Through visional wonders wide

And strange it is how oft in death
 When Reason leaves the brain
What sudden power the fancy hath
 To seize the falling rein   105
It cannot hold a firm controll
But it can guide the parting soul
 Half leading and half led
Through dreams whose startling imagery
Hide with their feigned reality   110
 The tossed and fevered bed

It seems as to the bleeding Heart
 With dying torments riven
A quickened Life in every part
 By fancys force was given   115
And all those dim disjointed dreams
Wherewith the railing memory teems
 Are but the bright reflection
Flashed upward from the scattered glass
Of mirror broken on the grass   120
Which shapeless figures on each peice
 Reveals without connection

And is her mirror broke at last
 Who motionless is laid
To await her hour approaching fast   125
 Upon her dying bed
Are her wild dreams of western skies
The shattered wrecks of memories
 That glitter through the gloom
Cast oer them in the cold decay   130
Which signs the sickening soul away
 To meet its early tomb

What pleasant Airs upon her face
 With freshening coolness play
As they would kiss each transient grace   135
 Before it fades away
And backward rolled each deep red fold
Begirt with tasselled cords of gold

```
            The Open Arch displays
Oer towers and trees that Orb divine                    140
His own unclouded light decline
            Before her glistning gaze

On pillows raised her drooping head
            Confronts his glorious beam
And all her tresses backward strayed                    145
            Look golden in the gleam
But her wan lips and sunken cheek
And full eyes eloquently speak
            Of sorrows gathering near
Till those dark orbs oerflowing fast                    150
Are shadowed by her hand at last
            To hide the streaming tear

Oh say not that her vivid dreams
            Are but the shattered glass
Which but because more broken gleams                    155
            More brightly on the grass
Her spirit is the unfathomed lake
Whose face the sudden tempests break
            To one tormented roar
But as the wild winds sink in peace                     160
All those distorted waves decrease
Till each far down reflection is
            As Lifelike as before

She thought when that confusion crossed
            Upon her dying mind                         165
Twas sense and soul and memory lost
            Though feeling burned behind
But that bright Heaven has touched a chord.
And that wide west has waked a word
            Can still the spirits storm                 170
Till all the greifs that brought her here
Each gushing with a bitterer tear
Round her returning sight appear
            In more tremendous form

"Land of the West!   Thy glorious skies                 175
            Their dreamy depths of azure blue
Their sunset Isles of paradise
            That float in golden glory through
Those depths of azure oer my sight
            This musing moment seem to expand           180
Revealing all their radiance bright
            In Cloud Land Gorgeous Land!
Land of the West--Thine Evening Sun
            Brings thousand voiceless thoughts to mind
Of what I've said and seen and done                     185
```

In years by time long left behind
And forms and faces lost for ever
    Seem arising round me now
As if to bid farewell for ever
    Before my spirit go   190
Oh! how they gush upon my heart
    And overflow my eyes
I must not keep I cannot part
    With such wild sympathies
I know its called a sin and shame   195
    To mourn oer what I mourn
I know twill blacken oer my name
    And desecrate my urn
I know that I must soon decay
    Without a single tear   200
My freindships buried with my clay
    And love forgotten there
I know that I must meet my God
    Before an hour has flown
To seek my sentence from his word   205
    For all the deeds I've done
I know!--But Oh!   Thou Western Sky
    Take all my thoughts with thee!
And fly my Spirit fleetly fly
    Across that Western Sea!   210
And Raise my head that when the Shade
    Of Death comes darkning oer me
The mighty king may find me laid
    With my Sweet West before me
Yet still my Heart How wild thou art   215
    That throbbst so anxiously
Where with the whole world though I part
    I cannot part with thee
And though the thoughts which ought to stay
    Will fastest farthest flee   220
The thoughts I ought to keep away
    The closest cling to me!
And comes the vision back again
    Which I should strive to quell
With all its wildly welcome pain   225
    In might Invincible
And I must wake these tears for Him
    Whose heart is parted far
The worship of my fevered dream
    My Lifes bright.--Western Star!   230
'And must the dart that shed thy blood
    Be consecrate by thee?'
Say--Shall all Lethe's dreary flood
    Wash out His memory?
My God has left me--But my Heart   235

Through life to death is THINE
Nor can Eternal Torments part
Thy Memory from Mine!

MS: G, F, I, B(2)
First Publication: Shorter EJB 1910, partial; BSC 1927,
                    partial; SHB C and B

                                              PBB
67 Alone She paced her ancient Hall   March 1st
          While Night around hung dark and drear   1837
    And silent--even her footsteps fall
          Mocked echoless the aching ear
            That ever watched but nought could hear   5
    And through the windows arched on high
          Alone looked forth the opening where
    Their mullions mingled with the sky
    In midnights cheerless vacancy
            Each lingering moment winged with fear   10
    And filling her with dread unknown
    Till scarce she dared to stop alone
    Although she felt she could not go
    That aimless dread had chilled her so!
    And motionless with clasped hands there   15
    Against an unseen pillar leaning
          She gave her spirit to the hour
          Gazing the unfathomed darkness oer
    As if for signs of ghostly meaning
    And oh--one wild wish crossed her brain   20
          Might she but look on future years
    She felt she'd courage to sustain
    All their array of phantom pain
            So it should end her doubts and fears
    For fast despair and hope combined   25
    Were bringing all the past to mind
    And--whispered Hope--the scene before
    <u>Might</u> shew more bright than sorrows oer
    And nought <u>can come</u>--chimed in Despair
    More darksome than those sorrows were   30
    And thus at every sound her soul
          Woke in those eyes that gazed to see
    Phantoms amid the gloom unroll
            Her future History

    There is a time--when earthly aid   35
          Glides from the sinking soul away
    Wherein twill desperate call instead

                        138

On brain born gods of empty sway
And then unmoored with anchor lost
Oer years of lifes wide ocean tost   40
Twill make a land of clouds and find
A Home in phantoms of the mind
And so it was with Her who there
Waited for help from forms of air
She would have smiled in happier years   45
        To think of such a vain releif
        But little knew she then how greif
Can move the soul to hopes and fears
Far far away from Reasons road
Wide wandering from the throne of God!   50

Against the pillar leaned her cheek
        Even colder than that marble stone
And fast she felt the tear drops break
From her strained eyes that wandered wide
Reft like her heart of aim or guide   55
        For something they might rest upon
They wandered till they ached and then
Closed heavily with wearied pain
And pressed one hand her burning brow
        And one dropped coldly by her side   60
And gathering fast her voiceless woe
        Began to dim all thought beside
Till faded in her deep distress
Even the eerie consciousness
Of where she stood--That lonly room   65
And midnight hour and phantom gloom
All mingling in a strange decay
All subsiding far away!
        It was as if the world to her
        Was sinking in a vast profound   70
        With clouds and darkness whirling round
And thunders bursting on her ear
But if her sudden start brought back
Her senses to their former track
Twas lost as soon and wrapt again   75
She seemed above a dreary main
With tired wing wandering and beneath
The deep unfathomed waves of death
Herself the only living thing
Oer that wide water hovering   80
And seemed as though she lighted on
A floating form to her unknown
Some wretched relic of the sea
Unnoticed festering to decay
Its uncurled hair with seaweed tangled   85
Its bleaching cheek by seabirds mangled

And grave worms nestling in the eyes
Turned sightless to the unpitying skies
From whence upon the dreary dream
Came sudden down a single beam   90
Enough for her--that beam revealed
All that the kinder clouds concealed
The face the form--one moment shewn
All death despoiled--but ALL HIS OWN!
Her Hope Her Heaven lay there!--Tis gone   95
All gone that Lonly Lingering light
Gone--drowned in one unchanging night
Whose deep dead clouds of darkness lie
Around their grim and lowring sky
With bitter blasts whose moaning scream   100
Aroused her from the dreary dream
And hardly roused her for twas vain
To wake the wearied sense again
And though she knew twas phantasy
Whose fancied visions mock the eye   105
She could not combat with it--still
That dreary dream deemed visible
And even her struggles to get free
From such unreal imagery
Her painful chasing from the soul   110
Thoughts far beyond its lost control
Her frightful doubts lest reasons reign
Was passing from her wildered brain
All but increased the weight of care
And fixed the visions firmer there   115
    Twas dead of night and yet the sun
        Seemed strongly struggling through the gloom
Twas that old Hall and yet he shone
On some far mansion not her own
        And in an unremembered room   120
    The antechamber to her tomb
For life around her seemed to swim
Like phantoms in a fever dream
Mingled with wild realities
That struck upon her dizzied eyes   125
As sudden strikes the racking pain
That wakes the sleeping wretch again
Till half she saw each curtained fold
    Gathered above the bed of death
And half the being might behold   130
    That came to stop her fleeting breath
He stood between her and the sun
    All things in dizzy whirl save him
A shadowy something dark and dun
    Who back to the declining beam   135

Pointed with warning hand, to show
That as it sunk, so she must go
Nor hope of respite there--subsided
Evenings beam to night--and glided
Her soul into forgetfullness   140
Of every pleasure or distress
Till each cold member turned to clay
And each faint feeling passed away
Till fluttered forth her latest breath
And all seemed everlasting death   145
    She slept and not even death could bring
A more unbroken slumbering
No!--not even NOW.--within that grave
    Whose marble floors yon Minster aisle
Can she a rest more peaceful have   150
    From worldly wrongs and tears and toil!

Oer these cold bones so lowely laid
    In that far tomb forgotten now
Be slow thy step and soft thy tread
    And long thy lingering look below!   155
There sleeps the soul that knew no sleep
    There throbs no more the burning brow
There eyes of greif have ceased to weep
    There passions storms are silent now!
Those walls have heard the Guns whose roar   160
Broke the Enchanters mightiest spell
Those Towers have seen the strife that bore
    Down from his throne the Invincible
    That Roof has echoed back the knell
Of buried Hopes and pride and power   165
When burst the storm on Parthas shore
That quenched Rebellions torch in gore
    But THEE--not even that Thunders swell
Aroused from darkness!--Though afar
Fell stricken Afric's Morning Star   170
    No--not though thine own PERCY fell!
Could that dread voice awake thee--Thou
    Slept mouldering on amid the yell
Of thousands trampled neath the foe
Whose sudden shouts of victory won   175
Left thee alone to slumber on!

But--whence this dreamy wandering?--Back
Through vanished years retrace our track.
From darkness into such a gloom
As might befit the darkest tomb!   180
No--Hours have passed, and as they fly
Time brings his changes ceaselessly
Tis the first dawn of summer morn

And looms the light oer Alnwicks hill
In one long gleam that seems to stream   185
        Through darkness visible!
And hover round this lordly Room
Realities half hid in gloom
That makes them visions--But they eye
Seeks for one fair reality   190
Now long a vision!--There she lies!
In silence closed her weary eyes
But nought can hide the loveliness
Of her fair form of youthful grace
Whose soft curls shade the marble cheek   195
    Yet dewy with the undried tear
Whose one fair hand her eyelids hide
And one drops moveless by her side
All still as she no more might wake
        To mornings freshning air!   200

    Brightens at last that summer morn
And sudden on its breezes born
Out gushes oer the rustling grove
The skylarks happy song of love
Like Hopes that soaring up on high   205
Look brighter near their kindred sky
And next about its fragrant bough
Even close that windows arch below
All round the echoing walls prolong
An answer to the Blackbirds song   210
    Who--when the earliest sounds they hear
Are tones so soft and sweet and clear--
Oh who would think this world a den
Of warring weeping wretched men!--
But soft!--Her Ears have caught the strain   215
That calls her back to life again

Oh! that it called to hope--her eyes
Like sunshine smiling out through rain
Gaze strangly on that daylight air
Un recognizing aught around   220
For something in that thrilling sound
Awoke her--not pertaining there
    Something that spoke of far off skies
And vanished years--a passing glance
    Toward a long lost paradise   225
Cast back across this worlds expanse
Soon hid by clouds and only leaving
For what is past a fruitless greiving!
So her that Blackbirds happy voice
Recalled to thoughts of perished joys   230
That lightning like before her flew

142

And lost as soon in darkness too!
   She rises--proudly calm and cold
Nay even the shadow of a smile
Bespeaks her out ward looks controuled   235
   All prying gazers to beguile
Scarce marked her bouyant footsteps fall
While passing through that Lordly Hall
Scarce seen the tear drop in her eye
That greets the morn so carelessly   240

MS: B(2)
First Publication: SHB C and B

68   **THE Vision of Velino**
Composed by W. H. Warner on the night of battle
December 3^{d}. 1833.
Corrected March. 9th. 1837.

═════════

I see through Heaven with raven wings
   A Funeral Angel fly,
The Trumpet in his dusky hands
   Wails wild and mournfully.

Beside him on her midnight path   5
   The Moon glides through the sky,
And far beneath her chilly face
   The silent waters lie.

Around me--not the accustomed sight
   Of Hill and vale I view,   10
With meadows bathed in cheerless light
   And woods in midnight hue:

No! All these Moors around me here
   Seem one wide waste of graves,
And round each trench, so dark and drear,   15
   The black earth stands like waves.

These are not common graves of men
   With Yew Trees waving by,
Where when their life's short hour is gone
   They slumber peacefully.   20

These seem, as if a torrents force
    Had rent its sudden way,
And they the channels of its course,
    Towards some tremendous sea.

These are the graves of Armies where;   25
    Together must consume,
Foeman and freind and sword and spear,
    Within their bloody tomb.

Oh God!   And what shall this betide?
    Why does that Angel fly?   30
Why does that Moon so solemn glide
    Across that stormy sky?

Why does my spirit cold and chill,
    Though winter roars around,
In visioned wonders linger still   35
    On this mysterious ground?

Behold upon the midnight Heath
    A mighty Army lie,
In slumber hushed each warrior's breath
    And closed each eagle eye.   40

The Moon from heaven upon each face
    With saddest lustre shines,
And glitters on the untrampled grass
    Between the longdrawn lines.

Are They the Tenants of the Tomb?   45
    And did those trenches yawn
To hide them in eternal gloom
    Before to-morrow's dawn?

Avert my God the avenging sword,
    And turn thy wrath away;   50
Or if battle come with midnight gloom
    Let Victory come with day!

P. B. B---te.
                        Transcribed
                        March 9th 1837.   52 lines

MS: A, B(2)
First Publication: Winnifrith PBB

144

The CXXXVIIth Psalm

Composed by Alexander Percy as word's to his--
Celebrated Motet "The Captivity"
Written by PBB--in 1834
Transcribed Mar. 9. 1837.

========

By the still streams of Babylon
We sat in sorrowing sadness down,
All weeping when we thought upon
    Our Zion's holy dome;
There hung our Harps, unheeded now,   5
From the dark willows bending bough,
Where mourning o'er the waves below
    They cast their evening gloom.

There round us stood that Iron band,
    Who tore us from our home;   10
And in their far off stranger land,
    Compelled our feet to roam.
They turned them to our native west,
    And laughed with victor tongue;
Now sing--they said in stern behest--   15
    Your Zions holiest song!--

How can we name Jehovah's name
So far away from Jordans stream!

Jerusalem! Jerusalem!
    May hand and heart decay   20
If I forget thy diadem
    And sceptre passed away!
If mid my brightest smiles of joy
    I do not think of thee,
Or cease one hour my thoughts to employ   25
    On Salem's slavery,
Let this false tongue forget to speak
And this torn heart with anguish break!

Remember, God! how Edom's sons
    In Zions darkest day,   30
Rejoiced above her prostrate wall,
    Like Lions o'er their prey:
How ruthlessly they shouted then
    As dark they gathered round,
"Down with it! Yea Down with it   35
    Even to the very ground!"

Daughter of Babel! worn with woe
    And struck with misery,
As thou God's people didst destroy
    Shall thy destruction be!   40
And in thine own dark hour of death
    When foemen gather round,
Happy be they who on thy stones
Of ruin, take thy little ones
    And dash them to the ground!   45

        P. B. B.---te
            Transcribed
                March 9th 1837. 45 lines

MS: Unknown, B(2)
First Publication: Winnifrith PBB

70   **SONG:**
          I saw her in the crowded Hall
           Composed by Marseilles
             June 26th 1834
       Transcribed and amended Mar. 9th. 1837

                =========

I saw Her in the Crowded hall
    When plumes were waving there
But mid the mases of the Ball
    Seemed none like her so fair!

I saw the circlet round her brow   5
    The diamonds in her hair
But her hazel eyes with angel glow
    Out shone their borrowed glare!

Yet call her from that glittering crowd
    For Fate oer shades her brow   10
And the neck which sorrow never bowed
    Must bend to anguish now!

Oh Loftiest of the Lofty
    And fairest of the fair
Must the spectres shade pass oer thee   15
    Must <u>thou</u> shake hands with Care!

Then where in Heaven or where in Earth
Can our eyes find tearless mirth

Alike the man of stormy life
Unwed to battle blood and strife   20
Alike that beauteous queen of May
        Their perished hopes must mourn
In a single glimpse of gladness gone
        Never to return!

Then cease my Lyre thy wailing cease   25
Lingering quivering die in peace!

            P. B. B---tē
                corrected
            March 9th 1837. 26 lines

MS: D(1), B(2)
First Publication: Wise Bibliog 1917

71   **The Rover**
            Composed by the Earl of--
            Northangerland May--1834
            Transcribed and corrected March
                9th 1837.

            ═══════════

Sail fast sail fast my gallant ship Thy Ocean
        thunders round thee
At Length thourt in thy paradise thy own wide
        heaven around thee
The morning flashes up in light and strikes its
        beams before
Where those wide streaks of lustre bright lie
        like a fairy shore
The day presages storm and strife But what need
        Percy care   5
The deck that braved the blast of Heaven can brave
        the fires of war
The thundering winds are swelling up and whistle
        through thy shrouds
Though over head in the Iron sky sleep sullenly the
        clouds
Lo that first blast hath swept the seas and covered
        them with foam
Yet it shall bear thee oer the deep whereere thou
        mayest roam   10
Though the rich but puny Mearchant ship may quiver
        in this gale

For it toward such a destined prey shall speed thy
    swelling sail
  When Night and tempest gather up to shroud the
      stormy sky
The timid sheep will look to heaven with an
    imploring eye
But while they flock with frightened haste and
    crowd the narrow way   15
What cares the Lordly Lion then who pounces on his
    prey
The storm has but his reaper been to gather in his
    grain
And thus to thee my ship shall be this hoarse
    resounding main
Oh look beneath those thick black clouds on yon
    dark line of water
A home returning merchant fleet just gathered for
    the slaughter   20
See how their spread sails glimmer white as
    scudding far before
They steering in unsteady line oerpass the watery
    roar
  Now rouse ye then my Gallant Men rouse up with
      hearty cheer
Quick clear your deck and crowd your sail and
    bring your guns to bear
Ha Connor! Gordon!--Steer ye right the winds
    confuse them now   25
And as mid the swans an Eagles flight so mid them
    drive my prow
I stand upon my steady deck around me flies the foam
And my Rover skims before the blast across her
    ocean home
The Merchant Convoy still before with furled or
    shivered sail
Like helpless geese together crowd and tremble in
    the gale   30
Now Light Your Matches!--From that smoke burst up
    one crash of thunder
Rebellowing from the clouds above and from the
    surges under
They know that voice they hear my call but dred
    hath paled each brow
So canvass furl and Grapples cast for were upon
    them now
And fastened by our trusty hooks one proud Galleon
    lies   35
Whose hesitating broadside burst uncertain to the
    skies
We heed it not And I'm the first upon her shaking
    deck

While all my band of gallant heart[s] have followed
     at my back
Now mid the thickning smoke and sleet one mighty
     tumult reigns
And sparkles flash before our eyes and blood boils
     through our veins   40
Men dashed on men in trampled blood strew thick
     each groaning plank
And all unseen the Sabres clash amid each gory rank
Where am I--?   dashed into the hold upon a dying foe
All stir and smoke and shouts above--that writhing
     wretch below
He dies--I rise and grasp a Rope--am on the deck
     once more   45
And Percy's arm and Percy's sword bath all that
     deck with gore
An hour of tempest passes by the Galleon blazes now
And smoke and slaughter crowd her deck and heap her
     bending prow
Our swords are grown into our hands our eyes glance
     fiery light
As faint we stagger oer the wrecks of that impetous
     fight   50
Ye have done your work most gallantly that precious
     merchandise
Convey upon our Rovers deck--to be our well earned
     prize
Then fire the ship and follow me to our own deck
     again
To chase the coward wanderers across the stormy
     main
   The evening sinks in sullen gloom behind the
       heaving sea   55
And sees the Rover oer its waves plough on her
     gallant way
While far behind across the surge a blaze of blood
     red light
Drifts on to wind ward shrouding round the relics
     of that fight
I see afar the blackened masts stand gainst the
     flaring flame
While high in heaven the heavy smoke curls oer its
     blazing frame   60
Whose fires discharge its cannonry with sullen
     sounding boom
Till like a blood red moon it sets behind its
     watery tomb.

                    PBB--March 10th.   62 lines

MS: D(1), B(2)
First Publication: Wise Bibliog 1917

72   **Augusta.**
                written by Alexander Percy in 1812.
                     At the Philosopers Isle
                     But by PBB. in Spring 1834

                     ═══════

            Augusta! though I'm far away
               Across the dark blue sea
            Still eve and morn and night and day
               Will I remember thee!

            And though I cannot see thee nigh   5
               Or hear thee speak to me
            Thy look and voice and memory
               Shall not forgotten be

            I stand upon this Island shore
               A single hour alone   10
            And see the Atlantic swell before
               With sullen surging tone

            While high in heaven the full Moon glides
               Above the breezy deep
            Unmoved by waves or winds or tides   15
               That far beneath her sweep

            She marches through this midnight air
               So silent and divine
            With not a wreath of vapour there
               To dim her silver shine   20

            For every cloud through ether driven
               Has settled far below
            And round the u[n]measured skirts of heaven
               Their whitened fleeces glow

            They join and part and pass away   25
               Beyond the heaving sea
            So mutable and restless they
               So still and changless she

            Those clouds have melted into air
               Those waves have sunk to sleep   30

                          150

But clouds renewed are rising there
And fresh waves crowd the deep

How like the chaos of my soul
    Where visions ever rise
And thoughts and passions ceasless roll   35
    And tumult never dies

Each fancy but the formers grave
    And germ of that to come
While all are fleeting as the wave
    That chafes itself to foam   40

I said that full Moon glides on high
    Howere the world repines
And in its own untroubled sky
    For ever smiles and shines

So darkning oer my anxious brow   45
    Thou[gh] thicken cares and pain
Within my Heart Augusta Thou
    For ever shalt remain

And Thou art not that wintry moon
    With its melancholy ray   50
But where thou shinest is summer noon
    And bright and perfect day

The Moon sinks down as sinks the night
    But Thou beamst brightly on
She only shines with borrowed light   55
    But Thine is All Thine own!

        P, B, B---te.
            Transcribed March 10th 1837   56 lines

MS: E, B(2)
First Publication: Winnifrith PBB

73   **Sound the Loud Trumpet**
            The National Song of Angria
            Composed by H Hastings.
    For the Coronation of Adrian Augustus Wellesly
                First King of Angria
                Spring ====== 1834

Sound the loud Trumpet oer Africs bright sea

                        151

Zamorna has triumphed the Angrians are free
Sound that Loud Trump and let winds waft its story
Sound! For our Day Star hath risen in its glory
   Sing! For the Sunbeams have burst forth to
      brighten   5
      A Reign such as never through age or in clime
The pages of History has deigned to enlighten
      Alone in its glory and proud in its prime
      Never to darken and never decline
Tempests may threaten and storms may assail us   10
Freinds may forsake us and Fortune may fail us
Yet with Zamorna alone to avail us
      Angria thy full sun unshadowed shall shine!

Sing for the power of our Foemen has flown
Quenched in the Sunbeams that smile round thy throne 15
Raise higher and louder your voices to sing
Angria our Country and Adrian our King!
   River! whose waves through the wide desert
      winding
      Hurry their floods toward the home of thy
         pride
      Each weary waste of our glory reminding   20
         Rise and spread round thee thy life giving
         tide!
All ye proud mountains that shadowing afar
Crown your blue brows with the wandering star
Tell you each summit and valley and plain
Adrian has triumped oer Angria to reign   25
   Tell ye the North with its tempests and snow
   Tell ye the South where the oceans gales blow
   Tell ye the West where the suns ever glow
      Angria and Arthur are shining again!
      Midnight and tempest may darken in vain   30
      Foes may arise and Fate may suprise--
Dust on the mountains and drops in the main!

Sing for the Sun has arisen on Creation
   Sound ye the Trumpet to herald his dawn
Rise Man and Monarch and City and Nation   35
   Away with your Midnight and hail to your morn
Sound the Loud Trumpet oer land and oer sea
   Join Hearts and voices rejoicing to sing
Afric arising hath sworn to be free
   And Glory to Angria and God save our King!   40

              Transcribed P B Bronte
                March 10th 1837 40 lines

MS: E, B(2)
First Publication: SHB Misc I

The Angrian Hymn

composed by W H Warner Esqr M.P.
on the coronation of Adrian the 1st
Spring. 1834.
greatly altered and enlarged by P B B---te
March 11th--1837

========

Shine on us God of Angria shine
And round us shed thy light divine
For sailing oer a stormy sea
Through life to death we trust in Thee!

Do thou with thine almighty power   5
Sheild us in Battles darkest hour
If dying, take our souls to thee
If living, grant us victory!

And Oh should Foemen threaten round
Let not amid our ranks be found   10
One Traitor Craven who would fly
His countrys Flag of Liberty!

And ever may that Flag remain
As we received it--Free from stain
And never may its watch word shine   15
In feilds unblessed by beams of thine

Yet may it wave through years afar
Oer glorious feilds of conquering war
To free the world from Errors chain
And bring thy kingdom back again   20

May future ages thus proclaim
Our noble Adrians deathless name
Look back on what his arm has done
And press with him to conquest on

And may he long as life to him   25
Shall spare his sun bright diadem
Think on the brow its glories shade
As not for kin but kingdom made

Oh let not care that circlet hide
Nor crime nor sorrow stain its pride   30
And when in Death he lays it down
Give him an Everlasting Crown

And when his subjects meet their doom
following their Monarch to the Tomb
Be theirs an endless paradise   35
When the Last Trumpet sounds ARISE!

        P B B---te
                Altered and enlarged
                March 11th 1837.
                                ____ 36 lines

MS: E, B(2)
First Publication: SHB Misc I

75   **The Angrian Welcome**
                        composed by Hastings
                            October 1834
                    Transcribed by P B B March 11th
                                1837

                            ====

        Welcome Heroes to the war
            Welcome to your glory
        Will you seize your swords and dare
            To be renowned in story
        What though Fame be distant far   5
        Flashing from her upper air?
        Though the path which leads you there
            Be long and rough and gory
        Still that path is straight and wide
        Open to receive the tide   10
        Youths First Flush and manhoods pride
            Age all stiff and hoary
        Sire and son may enter in
        Son and sire alike may win
        So rouse ye then and all begin   15
            To seek the glory oer ye

        Angrians! when your morning rose
            Before your monarch's eye
        He swore that ere its evenings close
            All your Foes should fly   20
        He knew that Adrians very name
            Would force those foes to fly
        He saw the brightest star of fame
            Was flashing forth on high
        So down from Heaven ZAMORNA came   25

                            154

```
            To guide you to the sky
      And shook his sword of quenchless flame
            And shouted Victory!

      Angrians! if your Noble King
            Rides foremost in the fight                    30
      Up in glorious gathering
            Around that Helmet bright

      Angrians! if you weild your sword
            Every stroke shall be
      Fixed as one undying word                            35
            In Afric's History

      Angrians! if in fight you die
            The clouds that oer you rise
      Shall waft your spirits to a sky
            Of everlasting joys                            40

      Angrians! when that fight is oer
            Heaven and earth and sea
      Shall echo in the cannons roar
            Your shouts of victory

      So now if all your bosoms beat                       45
            To reach your native star
      Shake the shackles from your feet
            And Welcome to the War!

            P B B---te
               corrected March 11th 1837.   48 lines
```

MS: E, B(2)
First Publication: Shorter 1923

76   **Northangerlands Name**
                  Composed by Hastings
                  Novr--1834

                  ════

```
History sat by her pillar of fame
   With a shade on her brow and a tear in her eye
And Oh! must she blot her Northangerlands name
   From its own glorious chapter of victory!
```

She held oer that chapter the pencil of fate 5
    But her white arm drew back from the page as it
        lay
So in sorrow and silence she mournfully sat
    Oppressed with the shades of her Heros decay

She raised her dark eye and she gazed on the sea
    Where all its black billows were whitened with
        foam 10
And she thought of the "Rover" unconquered and free
    Her noble Northangerlands Empire and Home

"Oh for the hours of that ocean to come!
    When shall I write of such sunshine and storm
When shall a pirate so gallantly roam 15
    As unconquered in heart and as glorious in form!"

She looked to the south and she looked to the north
    And she looked to the East where the twilights
        decline
Had melted from morning who joyously forth
    Was rising in glory oer Angria to shine 20

She thought of that Empire so bright and divine
    She thought of the Monarch its ruler in war
And "Angria" she cried then "Two leaders like thine
    Has Fate then denied to one empires share?

And must He whose bidding has roused up a land 25
    From midnight to morning to life from the tomb
Oh must his great name now be traced by my hand
    In pages of darkness and letters of gloom!"

She paused and she pondered but Freedom drew nigh
With pride in her port and with fire in her eye 30
She looked to the shore and she looked to the sea
And she vowed that eternal his memory should be
"From all my wide empire through ages to come
From palace to cottage from cradle to Tomb
Shall the name of my Saviour through ages endure 35
Vast as that Ocean and firm as this shore!"
    So History seizes her pencil of light
And again with rejoicing she bends to indite
While high on the top of her column of Fame
She blends with ZAMORNA'S, NORTHANGERLAND'S name! 40

    P B B---tē
        Transcribed March 11th 1837. 40 lines

MS: E, B(2)
First Publication: SHB Misc I

Morning.

written at Gazemba by Hastings
Dec 6th 1834

Morn comes and with it all the stir of morn
New light new life upon its sunbeams born
The Majic dreams of midnight fade away
And Iron labour rouses with the day
   He who has seen before his sleeping eye   5
The times and smiles of childhood wandering by
The memory of years gone long ago
And sunk and vanished now in clouds of woe
He who, still young, in dreams of days to come
Has lost all memory of his native home   10
Whose untracked future opening far before
Shews him a smiling heaven and happy shore
While things that are frown dark and drearily
And sunshine only beams on things to be
To such as these night is not all a night   15
For one in eve beholds his morning bright
The other basking in his earliest morn
Feels manhoods noontide oer his spirit dawn
   But that worn wretch who tosses night away
And counts each moment to returning day   20
Whose only hope is dull and dreamless sleep
Whose only choice to wake and watch and weep
Whose present pains of body and of mind
Shut out all glimpse of happiness behind
Whose present darkness hides the faintest light   25
Which yet <u>might</u> struggle through a milder night
And He like me whom present cares engage
Whithout the glare of youth or gloom of age
Who must not sleep upon his idle oar
Lest lifes wild Tempests dash him to the shore   30
Whome high Ambition calls aloud to awake
Glory his goal and death or life his stake
And long and rugged his rough race to run
Ere he can stop to enjoy his Laurels won
To these the night is weariness and pain   35
And blest the hour when day shall rise again!
Mid visions of the Future or the past
Others may wish the shades of night to last
Round these alone the <u>present</u> ever lies
And these will first awake when morning calls Arise! 40

      P B B---tē
        Transcribed March 11th 1837. 40 lines

MS: F, B(2)
First Publication: Winnifrith PBB

78   **Lines**
                    composed by Percy and adapted
                         by him to music

                    ═══════════

            We leave our bodies in the Tomb
               Like dust to moulder and decay
            But while they waste in coffined gloom
               Our parted spirits where are they?
               In endless night or endless day?   5
            Buried as our bodies are
            Beyond all earthly hope or fear
            like them no more to reappear
               But festering fast away
            For future's but the shadow thrown   10
            From present and the substance gone
               Its shadow cannot stay!

                    P B B---tē
                              Transcribed and corrected
                              March 11th 1837. 12 lines

MS: E, B(2)
First Publication: Winnifrith PBB

79   **An Hours Musings**
                       on the Atlantic
                    Composed off Norway--by
                        Alexander Percy
                           1818.

                    ═══════════

            Blow ye wild winds wilder blow
            Flow ye waters faster flow
            Spread around my weary eye
            One wide waving sea and sky!

Aloft the breezes fill my sail
And bend its canvass to the gale
In its own etherial dwelling
Oer the Ocean proudly swelling
   See the billows round me now
Dash against my cleaving prow
Far and wide they sweep away
Oer the rough and roaring sea
By heaven! my heart beats high to day
Lord of such a realm to be
Monarch of the feirce and free!

But I'll turn my eyes toward the skies
   And view the prospect there
Where broad and bright the noonday light
   Shed's glory through the air
I'll gaze upon that dome of heaven
   With its deep cerulean hue
The white clouds oer its concave driven
   Till lost amid the blue
Then I'll turn my forehead to the blast
   And gaze upon the sea
That chainless boundless restless waste
   Which shines so gloriously
That only Lethe for the past
   Or Freedom for the free!

The winds are whistling in my hair
   As I gaze upon the main
And view the Atlantic from his lair
   Aroused to rage again
And view the horizon stretched afar
Wide around that ambient air
One weary water weltring there
   Where I seek for rest in vain!

   Well! Here I am and Afric's shore
Has sunk beneath the Atlantic roar
Yet seems to me as but even now
Had set Leone's glittering brow
That <u>hardly.</u> yet that azure line
Conceals fair Gambias shores divine!
Not so!--a thousand miles away
I ride upon this raging sea
And long long Leagues of ocean roar
Between me and my native shore
   Oh all the scenes of a lifetime past
   Far Far behind me lie
   And tossing on this stormy waste
   Oh who so lone as I!
I Heard that wind It sighed to me

5

10

15

20

25

30

35

40

45

50

Like memory of feelings gone
Bleak Blast! my heart responds to thee
   With mourning bitterer than thine own!   55
  And my own voice with stronger tone
Now strikes upon my startled ear
   It seems mid these wild waves unknown
      A Thing I should not hear
Tis the voice of my morning fresh and free   60
The very voice of my Infancy
But what has that voice to do with me
     A wearied wanderer here!

Oh Afric Afric' where art thou!
Even I can sorrow oer thee now   65
Though ere I left thy smiling shore
I knew my joy in life was oer
Yes! I had seen my evening sun
   Sink in a sullen sea of tears
Had seen his race of daylight run   70
   Gone lights and shadows hopes and fears!
Yes I had seen my day decline
Never again to rise and shine
And it was not pleasure blighted
   It was not hope destroyed   75
Nor love nor freindship slighted
   That made the dreary void
And yet my pleasures all had flown
All my hopes were dashed and gone
And though none scorned the love I gave   80
Yet--THOU! The loved wert in thy grave
Twas that despair of heart which can
Nor joy nor sorrow yeild to man
Twas that decay of spirit when
Twill neither wake to joy or pain   85
When heard no more Ambitions call
Can while the Soul to rise or fall
When seen no longer beauty's beam
Can wrap it in an Eden dream
When not even rage can rouse the mind   90
To leave its apathy behind
   Ah power and place were lost to me
And beauty brought satiety
And who would quarrel with a worm
Because it writhed in human form?   95
   I could not love when all the charms
I clasped so madly in my arms
Where sure that day to pass away
From sudden death to dark decay
I would not hear Ambitions voice   100
Delude me to its visioned joys
When while I stood the cheif mong men

I paid for peace and purchased pain
Why should I hate an enemy
When firmest freinds had turned on me   105
Why think on lover foe or freind
When all so soon in death must end!
   Nor this the worst--For ever gone
The mind had lost its native tone
Here is the ocean--but to me   110
Its mighty waste has ceased to be!
There is the Heaven but now no more
My eyes its glorious paths explore
Im only yearning for the tomb
And that last refuge will not come*   115

Oh! when I was a little child
    Upon my mothers knee
With what a burst of pleasure wild
    I gazed upon the sea
I stretched my arms toward its face   120
And wept to meet its proud embrace!
   And when amid youths earliest day
    I paced the foam white shore
   I smiled to see the wild waves play
    And joyed to hear them roar   125
And now where am I?--On that sea
Where I so often longed to be
But it is like all human joys
One single touch their bloom destroys
The waves around my vessel sweep   130
    And cover her with foam
Yet though they shake the shattered ship
    They still shall bear her home
The sleep which shuts the watchers eye
    Mid dangers threatening near   135
Though helplessly the sleeper lie
    Still quiets all his care
The night that darkens oer the earth
    Mid daylights deep decline
Shall give a glorious morrow birth   140
    In morning's light divine
But thou stern midnight of my soul
    With thy dread darkness closing round
Ye storms of strife which oer me roll
    Where have ye hope or rest or bound?   145
Well roll ye waves of ocean roll!
And close ye sorrows oer my soul
I care not though your fatal blight
Should cloud this mind with lasting night
But while one streak of daylight lies   150
Behind the far off twilight skies
Permit the wanderers weary gaze

To fix upon its fading rays
The wretch whom nought from death can save
Still grasps the grass around his grave   155
The Lion in the Hunters toils
Glares madness from his eye
And nets and dogs and Lances foils
    Though Lost to Liberty
The prisoner bound with iron chains   160
His wearied Load of life sustains
By gazing on the vanished days
That beamed like heaven with freedoms rays
And strange it is when we look back
We still see sunshine on our track   165
For false they speak who say we spy
Nothing but joys before our eye
No! all the future path to me
Seems beat by storms of misery
And scenes alone long past away   170
Can glimmer through lifes dark decay
For through his short and narrow span
Pleasure can only follow man
And yet when wearily he dies
He dreams before him in the skies   175
He sees its happy paradise!
     x x x x x x x x x x x
     x x x x x x x x x x x

What is MAN? A wretched being
      Tossed upon the tide of time
All its rocks and whirlpools seeing
Yet denied the power of fleeing   180
      Waves and gulphs of woe and crime
Foredoomed from lifes first bitter breath
To launch upon a sea of death
Without a hope without a stay
To guide him on his weary way   185

See that wrecked and shattered bark
      Drifting through the storm
Oer the ocean drear and dark
      Sweeps its shattered form
Where those sails which late on high   190
Swelled amid the smiling sky
Where those masts which braved the gale
Towering oer the swelling sail
Where the glasslike deck below
Where the gilt and glorious prow?   195
    Where are they? sunk beneath the sea
Or shattered tossing far away
Where are they? sawst the shreiking gale
Tear from the arms the swelling sail?

162

Sawst thou the mast beneath the storm   200
Bend to the surge its statly form
And Hark that Crash!--as foam and spray
Force oer the deck a boiling sea
So there--! its gallant glories gone
There the wild Tempests drive it on!   205
And now as round the shivered mast
As shrinking from the screaming blast
How do the hop[e]less sailors brave
The Heaven and ocean, wind and wave!
    Aye how have all the hopes of life   210
Stood gainst its fears and storms and strife
And what thinks MAN, when--danger oer--
Stranded he lies on Deaths dark shore?
Oh view him, sickened, palsied, lone,
Where is his strength his beauty gone!   215

I am a MAN. Yes I have seen
Each change upon lifes changing scene
And I am on the track which thou
And thine and mine are following now!
Well when I first launched from Eternity   220
Upon this undiscovered sea
Hope shone forth with glorious ray
Blazing round my dawning day
Expectations eager gale
Swelled and sounded in my sail   225
Ambitions world impelling power
Urged me on in mornings hour
And Love thy wide and welcome light
Beamed and brightened on my sight
Beauty strength and youth divine   230
With all the heaven of Mind were mine
And when I saw the expanse before me
When I knew the glory oer me
Oh how little did I dream
Heaven and Glory all a dream!   235
Life alone with its midnight sea
The Terrible Reality!

    Sleeper awake! Thy dream is flown
And thou'rt on Ocean all alone!

    I am awake and round the sky   240
Wild I cast my wandering eye
Where is the love and hope and light?
Vanished for ever from thy sight!
And now I am on the wild wide sea
Without a hope to shine on me   245
The winds arise and the stormy skies
Snatch my daylight from my eyes

Ambitions sails that bore me on
Shiver in the blast they seemed to have won
And Glory!--Aye thou welcome wave   250
Dash that illusion to its grave!
but spare, wild ocean, spare me Love!
That only power that can above
Like one mild star from out the sky
Beam comfort on my misery!   255
Oh! Life, though all its oceans roll
Thee neer shall sunder from my soul
for thou within this heart shalt lie
With this heart alone to die!
Well be it so!--The peeling blast   260
Howls wilder round the quivering mast!
With what a sweep the surge and spray
Thunder above the whitening sea
A gloomier tempest darkens down
Love survives--but the LOVED is gone!   265
Gone! and one unfathomed ocean
Oer me bears its vast commotion
Sails and masts and cordage gone
All unaided! all ALONE!

Oh MARY! when I closed thy eye   270
When I beheld thee slowly die
When thou before me silent lay
A loveless lifeless form of clay
When I saw thy coffined form
Decked out to feast the gnawing worm   275
When the dull sod oer thee thrown
    Hid thee from my tearless eye
When they laid the marble stone
    Above where Thou must ever lie
Twas then my Mary then alone   280
        I felt what twas to Die!

Oh! Long Long years may lie before me
A thousand woes may darken oer me
And ere I lay me down to die
Old age may dim this anguished eye   285
Yet through that wide wide waste of years
That channelled gulph of burning tears
Aye if I live till Earths decay
Is crumbling to its latest day
If thousand winters winteriest snow   290
fall withering on my blighted brow
Still through that vast Eternity
I know that Thou Hast ceased to be!
Lost! for ever Lost to me!
That all thy woes and joys are oer   295

```
That thou art dead!--gone long before!
That I shall never never see thee more!

         P. B. Brontē.
            Transcribed and
               Corrected.
                  May 2ᵈ 1837.
                     297. lines.

            ═══════

         Haworth Yorkshire.
```

MS: Unknown, B(2)
First Publication: SHB Misc II
Text: l. 115: Branwell's note at the bottom of the page:
                "This whole passage if as I fear it--
                contradicts in one or two places the rest of
                the poem ought at some time to be either
                cancelled or amended"

80   **Thermopylae.**

                    ═══

```
      Thermopylae's tremendous Height
   Has lost the evenings latest light
   And each huge mountain girdling round
   Stands blackning in the shade profound
   Alike wild waste and ocean wild                    5
   Dark as those clouds above them pil'd
   Lie gloomy as they neer had worn
   The sunshine of a summer's morn
   Above the moonbeans fitful light
   Breaks shivering through the darksome night    10
   And as the stormy wrack sweeps by
   Fades--lost amid the troubled sky
      At times that moonlight sadly shines
   Where yon vast hill its steep declines
   Where bloody grass and trampled heath           15
   lie soaked beneath their loads of death.
   Where scattered rocks with mossy head
   Form many a warriors dying bed.
   Where many a dim and darkning eye
   Up gazes toward that stormy sky!                 20
      Tis o'er!--No sighs no anguished cries
   from the wild wreck of battle rise
   The senseless corpse on earth reclining
```

Nor feels defeat nor knows repining
No murmered moan of misery   25
No sudden shout of victory
For death has stretched his dreary wing
Oer that wide waste of suffering
   Sleep Noble Soldiers, sleep alone!
The whistling winds your burial moan   30
The bloody rocks your bed of death
Your shrouds grey grass and trampled heath
While that vast rock Thermopylae
Your monument and grave mave be!
   O Glorious Dead unconqured lie   35
Your very death your victory
By you your country saved from chains
Still free unconqured Greece remains
And not a drop of all that blood
Which curdles now in Peneus flood   40
No, not one drop is spent in vain
For every drop dissolves a chain!
And each cold hand and nerveless arm
Which never more that blood shall warm
Have while they struck their meanest foe   45
Given Susa's domes a fatal blow
and though long past the flight of time
In distant age and different clime
Still may your memory wake a flame
Which, once aroused, no power can tame   50
Still when infuriate factions rise
Their native Land to sacrifice
Not like the Mede a foreign band
But fighting gainst their father land
Still to oppose their impious war   55
Their pride to crush their power to dare
May once again Thermopylae
Rise oer the storms of Albions sea!
Still may <u>Three Hundred</u> once again*
Gainst that <u>mad march</u> their fight maintain   60
And while they stay the troubled tide
From its dire deluge wild and wide
Another mightier Marathon
Complete the victory thus begun!
And if, two thousand years ago   65
Gainst Greece a Monarch struck the blow
And Freedom saved her from the foe
Here through this Island of the Free
Our Foemen shout for Liberty
Our <u>Throne</u> is our Thermopylae!

    P B. Bronte. written Jany 19. 1835 --
       Transcribed May 14th 1837 <u>68 lines</u>

MS: Unknown, B(2)
First Publication: Winnifrith PBB
Text: 1. 34: "may" obviously intended
      1. 59: Branwell's note at the bottom of the page:
             "The conservative party in the Commons being
             300 in number--"

81   **Song**
                    written by Percy in 1813.

                    ════════

          Son of Heaven, in heavenly musing
             Gaze beyond the clouds of time,
          Future glory rather choosing
             Than a present world of crime.

          Thou, whose heart, that world caressing   5
             Bows, its bubbles to adore,
          On and hunt each fleeting blessing,
             Still in sight but still before!

          Christian, World[l]ing, Hence and leave me
             Here with thee my love alone;   10
          Things to come shall neer deceive me
             While I hold Thee now my own!
          Earth of bliss shall neer bereave me
             While we two continue one!

                    P B Bronte written Oct 20th. 1835
                         Transcribed May 14. 1837.
                                      14 lines

MS: E, B(2)
First Publication: BST 1934

The Doubters Hymn
composed by
Alex^r Per[c]y.   1813

═══════

Life is a passing sleep
    Its deeds a troubled dream
And death the dread awakening
    To daylights dawning beam

We sleep without a thought   5
    Of what is past and oer
Without a glimpse of consciousness
    Of ought that lies before

We dream and on our sight
    A thousand visions rise   10
Some dark as Hell some heavenly bright
    But all are phantasies

We wake and, Oh! how fast
    These mortal visions fly!
Forgot amid the wonders vast   15
    Of immortality!

And Oh! when we arise
    With wildered gaze to see
The aspect of those morning skies
    Where will that waking be?   20

How will that Future seem?
    What is Eternity?
Is Death the Sleep?--Is Heaven the Dream?
    Life the reality?

─────────

P B Brontë
        Written Nov^r--1835
        Transcribed May 14. 1837.   <u>24 lines</u>

MS: E, B(2)
First Publication: Winnifrith PBB

83   **Song**
                  written by Percy in 1814
                  =================

          Thou art gone but I am here
             Left behind and mourning on
          Doomed in Dreams to deem thee near
             But to awake and find thee gone!
          Ever parted! Broken hearted!   5
             Weary wandering all alone!

          Looks and smiles that once were thine
             Rise before me night and day
          Telling me that Thou wert mine
             But art dead and past away   10
          Beauty banished--Feelings vanished
             From thy dark and dull decay
          No returning! Nought but mourning
          Oer thy cold and coffined clay!

                  P B Bronte
                          written Nov 17. 1835
                          Transcribed May 14. 1837
                          14 lines

MS: E, B(2)
First Publication: Winnifrith PBB

84   **Song.**
                     written by Percy
                           1814.

                     =========

        Frozen fast is my heart at last
           And unmoved by thy beams divine
        For wild oer the waste the wintery blast
           Has withered and weakened thy shine

        The pulse that once beat to each look each word,   5
           Is congealed by the frosts of care
        And thine eyes are ungazed on thy voice is unheard
           For love ever flies from despair

                          169

Farewell then farewell then for parted for ever
   The blooming and blighted should be   10
So soon shall the ocean eternally sever
   My Heart from my country and thee

     P B Brontē
         written Nov 17th 1835
         transcribed May 14. 1837.
               12 lines

MS: E, B(2)
First Publication: Winnifrith PBB

85   **Lines**
          written by Percy on his
          Departure from Africa. 1818.

                ══════════

Now then I am alone
   And theres none to trouble me
So I will hasten on
   From present scenes to flee

The Land where I have lived   5
   The Hall where I was born
Whatever hath survived
   Through my wild life unworn

The outline of those Mountains
   Which still have towered the same   10
The brooks whose rushing fountains
   Can still supply their stream

Each token and each trace
   Of a life time passed away
Ill from my spirit chase   15
   Through every future day

The waters of the Ocean
   Shall drown that life gone by
Shall give a lethean potion
   To banish memory   20

      P B Bronte
        written Dec 17th 1835
        Transcribed May 14th 1837. 20 lines

MS: Unknown, B(2)
First Publication: Winnifrith PBB

86   **The Spir[i]t of Poetry**
═══════════

List to the sound that swells alone
Shrilly and sweet with trembling tone!
Why should such music strike my ear
In thoughtful silence seated here?

The sky is ebon black to night   5
But the stars are fixed on high
Each glorious planet twinkling bright
Or smiling silently
Dreary and dark the mountains rise
All underneath those starlit skies   10

And far beyond the gloomy moor
Hear how the Lochs low waters roar
While wearied with his wanderings wide
The Goodman by his ingle side
Stirs up the fire that glows afar   15
In yonder reddened mountain star

The midnight hills are passing by
And gone the black and starlight sky
That music thrills in the rising morn
Upon the blasts of ocean born   20
It mixes its notes with the rising gale
And sounds in the cords of the flowing sail
It rises and falls as the waters flow
Oh why does that music haunt me so!

It is not the night on the Highland moor   25
It is not the cot on Loch Maris shore
It is not the Ocean so boundless and drear
That wakens around me the notes that I hear
For gone is the cot and the moor and the main
Yet I here those wild notes and the're rising again   30
Vanished those visions of skies unknown
But present that changing Eolian tone!

Tis a chord of the Heart Tis the music of mind
From Eearth and its cares for a moment refined

Tis a sound caught by it as it soars toward the sky   35
Wafted down from the Heaven of bright <u>Poetry</u>!

        P B Bronte
                written (I beleive) in 1835
                altered & amended May 16 1837
                        36 lines.

MS: Unknown, B(2)
First Publication: Winnifrith PBB

87   An Angrian Battle Song
                  composed by H Hastings

=======

Storms are waking to inspire us
   Storms upon our morning sky
Wildly wailing Tempests fire us
   With their loud and God given cry
Winds our trumpets howling come   5
Thundering waves our deeper drum
   Wild woods oer us
   Swell the chorus
Bursting through the stormy gloom
Whats their Omen?   whence its doom?   10

Loud those voices stern their pealing
   Yet what ist those voices say?
Well we feel, when, God revealing,
   All his wrath their powers display
   Trembles every child of clay   15
      Still we know
      That blow on blow
   Oer us bursting day by day
   Shews that wrath as well as they

But tis not a common call   20
   That wakes such mighty melody
Crowns and kingdoms rise or fall
   Man and nation's chained or free
   Living death or liberty
   Such their terrible decree   25
      And yonder skies
      Whose voices rise
   In that unearthly harmony
      Through Angria round

```
                Shall wake a sound                          30
        A voice of victory
        A thundering oer the sea
                Whose swelling waves
                And howling caves
        Shall hear the prophecy                             35

                Storms are waking
                Earth is shaking
        Banners wave and bugles wail
            While beneath the tempest breaking
        Some must quench and some must quail               40
        Hark the artillery's iron hail
        Rattles through the ranks of war
            Who beneath its force shall fail
            Must the Sun of Angria pale
                Upon the Calabar?                           45
                Or yonder bloody star
                    Oer Afric's main
                    With fiery train
                That wanders from afar

        No O God! our Sun its brightness                    50
            Draws from thine eternal throne
        And come what will through good or ill
            We know that thou wilt guard thine own!
            Tis not gainst us that thunders tone
                But, risen from hell                        55
                With radiance fell
        Tis the wanderer of the west whose power shall be
            oerthrown!

        Tempest blow thy mightiest blast
            Wildwind wail thy wildest strain
                From Gods right hand                         60
                Oer his chosen land
            Your music shall waken its fires again
        And over the earth now and over the ocean
            Where ever shall shadow these storm covered skies
        The louder through battle may burst your commotion  65
            Twill only sound stronger O Angria Arise!
                        ─────
```

        P B Brontē.

                    Written January--1836--
                    Transcribed May 26. 1837.
                        67 lines

                ═══════════

        Haworth.   Yorkshire.

MS: D(1), B(2)
First Publication: SHB Misc II

88   **The Battle Eve.**
           composed by Lord Richton

           ========

     Alone upon Zamorna's plain
          With twilight oer me falling
     And once again the bugles strain
          To troubled slumber calling

     Alone with thousands round me laid   5
          In dizzy torments dying
     All, stretched upon their bloody bed
          In sleep eternal lying

     So not alone yet all alone
          For these sad wrecks of slaughter   10
     Are senseless thrown as forms of stone
          Or dead to all but torture

     I stand, and see the silent Moon
          Drive wildly through the sky
     Mong clouds that, gathering up since noon   15
          Commence their march on high

     It is not night--it is not day
          So she can hardly shine
     And dull and dead and cold and grey
          Behold the eve decline   20

     A Battle Eve, a victory,
          A day of deathless fame
     For which the Muse of history
          Must seek a noble name

     A Monarch's and a Nation's fall   25
          The Grave of Glories cherished
     That Hope proclaimed with trumpet call
          Now silent sunk and perished

     A Day of far extended power
          Which changes smiles to tears   30
     And from this lonley twilight hour
          Oer looks a hundred year's!

                        174

That casts its shadows oer the things
   Which latly seemed to shine
As night to gloom and darkness brings   35
   The evening skies divine

Oh soon again this natural night
   In happy morn shall rise
But, Never more returning light
   May gladden Adrian's eyes   40

That Sun of Angria rose in red
   To chase the clouds away
That sun has sunk his light has fled
   His power has passed for aye

How like a Star from upper air   45
   I see Zamorna fall
Archangel once and throned so far
   Above this earthly ball

But vast thine hopes and high thy pride
   Thou man of shining crime   50
Till pride has perished Hope has died
   All withering ere their time

Come. listen to the distant gun
   That thunders on the wind
The awful voice of Victory won   55
That seems to say Thy race is run
   And vanished out of mind

Better for thee that thou hadst died
Than thus to see thy newborn pride
In this wild warfare scattered wide   60
And Thou a wretched Captive left alone behind!

        P B Brontë
            written July 9th 1836
            Transcribed May 26 1837
                  61 lines.

———

MS: Unknown, B(2)
First Publication: Winnifrith PBB

A second early draft of "Before our Mighty Makers
throne," entitled **Ashworth's Hymn,** "written May
4th 1836/Transcribed May 26 1837"--see No. **135,**
pp. **114** and **273**

175

Lucifer.
composed by Charles Wentworth
<u>1836</u>

Star of the west whose beams arise
 To brighten up oer Africs shore
While coming clouds and changing skies
 Bring on the shades of twilights hour

Who as our day sinks fast away   5
 While flowers of pleasure close their bloom
Sendst down from Heaven thy flashing ray
 And shinest to dazzle--not to illume

Who as upon our sunken sun
 The storm clouds gather from the sea   10
So far above goest wandering on
 As if our hopes were nought to thee

And gathering glory while the night
 Comes deeper darker drearier down
And shining still with brighter light   15
 When every beam save thine is gone

Star of the west we see thee shine
 We know thy glory from afar
But we have seen our sun decline
 As if it sunk for thee to appear   20

We have seen our sun of happiness
 Mid coming clouds of conflict fall
Nor can thy lustre beam in place
 Of that which blessed and brightened all

We know that in our time of pride   25
 Mid summer suns and noonday skies
Though Heaven were cloudless calm and wide
 Such lights as thine dared never rise

We know Thou art an Orb divine
 Within thine own celestial sphere   30
But still a storm portending sign
 To us who gaze in wonder here

Star of the West. though storm and night
 Gave birth and beauty to thy blaze
Still that which kindled up thy light   35
 May in a moment quench its rays

As darker grow the clouds of woe
  As day declines as empires fall
Brighter and brighter burst's thy glow
  Till thou seemst soaring lord of all   40

But westward clouds are rolling on
  And louder thunders swell the wind
The tempest comes and thou art gone
  Past like the sunshine out of mind

Percy--amid the coming hour   45
  When peace and pleasures dissapear
Those storms and strife's which gave thee power
  May darken Afric's 'Western Star'!

            P B Bronte
                  Written June 22^{d} 1836
                  Transcribed May 27 1837.
                          48 lines.

MS: F, B(2)
First Publication: Winnifrith PBB

90   **Lines.**
              composed at day break before the
            Revolution of June 26. 1836 by Percy.

                  ═══════════

Now heavily in clouds comes on the day
      The great the important day
That gathering all its gloom shall roll our foes away

Come life come death or conquest or defeat
I who am called my Judgement here must meet   5
With my own arm must carve my road to power
With my own deeds must fill my fated hour
With my own lips proclaim what is to be
And then in my own self meet my own destiny
      Tis man must struggle--man must fight   10
And stigmatise his wrong and name his right
But fate or chance the question will decide
His hopes and fears and plans all scattering far
      and wide

      Here I will crown a life of war
With power which long has lured me from afar   15

With vengeance taken on my slaughtered foes
Contempt repaid with hate and hatred soothed with
    blows
Kings crowns and armies fallen and all to be
A bloody footsto[o]l of ascent for me
The wings of conquest folded oer my head   20
Supporters kneeling on opponents dead
What I hate lowest & next what I despise
So who dare speak to me of miseries
Chance will--or fate, with still small voice it
    cries
"Man though thou hast <u>seized</u> the lamp its <u>light</u> is
    gone   25
And blindly still thy steps must wander on!
She is gone!   The last bright link which bound thy
    mind
To years of paradise left long behind
Treasure of hopes stored up in happier years
To feed thy famine in this vale of tears!   30
And she is gone whom in thy worst distress
Thou foundst, a fountain in the wilderness!
And He is gone who glorious used to shine
With radiance steadier brighter far than thine
Yet such as shewed on earth their still might be   35
Communion with a soul so like to thee.
All these are gone whom thou hast left to gain
A flying hope--a meteor light and vain!
Thy sun has sunk and left the darkening air
To seek inlightning from that wandering star   40
Thy flower deprived of warmth will withering die
Thy store is squandered and thy well run dry
While <u>HE</u> whose glory chased the clouds of woe
Thy Dearest Freind thou'st made thy Deadliest Foe!"

                P B Bronte

                    Written in June 1836.
                    Transcribed May 27. 1837.
                         <u>44 lines</u>
            Haworth Yorkshire

            _____

MS: Unknown, F, B(2)
First Publication: Winnifrith PBB
Text: l. 33: "glories" obviously intended

Percy's Musing's
upon the Battle of Edwardston
June 1836.

Through the hoarse howlings of the storm
   I saw--but did I truely see
One glimpse of that unearthly form
   Whose very name was--VICTORY
Twas but a glimpse--and all seems past   5
   For cares like clouds again return
And I'll forget him till the blast
   For ever from my soul has born
That vision of a Mighty Man
   Crushed into dust!--   10

Forget him!--Lo the cannon's smoke
   How dense it thickens till on high
By the wild stormblast roughly broke
   It parts in volumes through the sky
   With dying thunder drifting by   15
Till the dread burst breaks forth once more
   And loud and louder peals the cry
Sent up with that tremendous roar
Where--as it lightens broad before
   The thick of battle rends in twain   20
With roughened ranks of bristling steel
   Flashing afar while armed men
In mighty masses bend and reel
   Like the wild waters of the main
   Lashed into foam!--Where, there again   25
Behold him! as with sudden wheel
At bay against a thousand foes
He turns upon their serried rows
All heedless round him though they close
      With such a bloodhound glare   30
That eye with inward fires so bright
Peirces the tempest of the fight
And lightens with the Joyless light
      Of terrible despair!
He sees his soldiers round him falling   35
In vain to heaven for vengeance calling
He sees those noble freinds whom he
   Had called from happy--happy Home
For a vain prise of victory
   Over the eastern world to roam   40
He sees them lie with glaring eye
   Turned up to him that wandering star
Who led them still from good to ill

179

In hopes of power to meet with war
And fall from noontide dreams of glory   45
To this strange rest so grim and gory!--.
When rolling on those freinds oer thrown
War's wildest wrack breaks thundering down
Zamorna's pale and ghastly brow
Darkens with anguish--all in vain   50
To stem the tide of battle now
    For every rood of that wide plain
Is heaped with thousands of his dead
Or shakes beneath the approaching tread
    Of foes who conquer oer the slain   55
    No! never must he hope again
Though still abroad that bannor stream's
On whose proud folds the Sun of glory beams
   Though still, unslaughtered, round their lord
His chosen cheifs may grasp the unvanquished sword   60
Still, all is Hopeless!--and he knows it so
Else would not anguish cloud his brow
Else would not such a withering smile
Break oer his hueless face--the while
Some freind of years falls hopelessly   65
And yet upon that Eagle eye
Gazing with dying extacy!
That Eagle eye! the beacon light
Through all the changes of the fight
Whose gloryous glance spoke victory   70
And fired his men to do or die
On the red roar of battle bent
As if it[s] own wild element
And glancing oer each thundering gun
As he were wars unconquered Son   75
That Eye! Oh I Have seen it shine
   Mid scenes that differed far from these
As Gambias woods and skies divine
    From Greenlands icy seas
I've seen its lustre bent on me   80
    In old adventure gone
With beam as bright and glance as free
    As His own Angria's sun
When oer those mighty wastes of Heath
    Around Elymbos' brow   85
As side by side we used to ride
    I smiled to mark its glow
I smiled to see him how he threw
    His feelings into mine
Till my cold spirit almost grew   90
    Like his a thing divine
I saw him in his beauty's pride
    With manhood on his brow
The Falcon eyed with heart of pride

```
                 And spirit stern as now                    95
     Almost as stern--for many a shade
          Had crossed his youthful way
     And clouds of care began to mar
               The dawning of his day
     I knew him and I marked him then               100
               For one remote as far
     From Earths surrounding crowds of men
               As Heaven's remotest star
     I saw him in the battles hour
               And conqured by his side            105
     I was with him in his height of power
               And triumph of his pride


     Tis past!--but I am with him now
          Where he spurs feircly through the fight
     His pride and power and crown laid low         110
          His glorious future wrapt from sight
     Mid clouds like those which frown on high
          Over the plains in purpled gloom
     With rain and thunder driving by
          To shroud a nations bloody tomb           115
          And in the cannons ceaseless boom
     The Toll which wafts the parting soul
          While Heavens bright flashes serve to illume
     Like torches its funeral stole
     Its Horrid funeral--Far and wide               120
          I see them--falling in the storm
     Mid ranks of Horse that wildly ride
          Above each gashed and trampled form
     His charger shot Zamorna down
     Mid foes and freinds alike oerthrown!          125
     Yet never may that desperate soul
     Betray the thoughts which oer it roll
     Teeth clenched cheeks blenched and eyes that dart
     A Lion feirceness from his heart.
     As all the world were nought beside            130
     The saving of his iron pride
     For every one on earth might die
     And not a tear should stain that eye
     Or force a single sob or sigh
               From him who cannot yeild            135
     Yet stay--one moment--tis but one
     A Single glance to heaven is thrown
     One frenzied burst of greif--!--Tis gone
               Again that Heart is steeled!
     That was a burst of anguish--there             140
     Blazed all the feirceness of despair
     It said--Oh all is lost for ever!
          All he loves to him is dead
          All his hopes of glory fled


                          181
```

                All the past is vanished   145
                    Save what nought can sever
                Ever living memories
                That shall haunt him till he dies
                With what he can realise
                    Never Never Never!   150

            I said I saw his anguished glance
                Say did it fall on me?
            Incendiary of rebel France
                Parrot of Liberty!
            The wretched Traitor who let in   155
                On Africs opened Land
            Deceit and craft and hate and sin
                In an united band
            Who raised the Standard of Reform
                And shouted Earth be free   160
            To whelm his country neath the storm
                Of rebel Tyranny
            Who called himself the good right hand
                And Father of our King
            Only on his adopted Land   165
                A Double curse to bring
            Aye it was I and only I
                That hurled Zamorna down
            From power and glory placed on high
                This day to be oerthrown   170
            I barbed the arrow which has sped
                To peirce my sovereigns breast
            And only on my guilty head
                May all his sufferings rest!

                    P B Bronte
                        written June 22^d 1836.
                        Transcribed May 30th 1837.
                                175 lines.

MS: B(1), E, B(2)
First Publication: Shorter EJB 1910, partial; SHB Misc II

92   **QUEEN MARYS GRAVE.**

        I stand beside Queen Mary's grave neath Alnwick's
            holy dome
        With sacred silence resting on the marble of her
            Tomb

                            182

The Organs thunders hushed to sleep the Mourners
    past away
All left to her the sepulchre the coffin and the
    clay
The Vault is closed the stone is placed the
    inscription only tells   5
Within that dark and narrow house whose corpse
    corrupting dwells
lest one with those who passed from earth forgotten
    years ago
from their's around by sight or sound her tombstone
    none might know
So I will stand to think awhile on things for ever
    gone
And drop a tear to memory dear above her Funeral
    stone.   10
    What seek my eyes--they rest not on the columns
        arching oer me
Nor the storied window's shimmering round or
    sculptures piled before me
They are watching through its prisoning tomb the
    cold corrupting clay
They are wandering oer the eternal gloom of deaths
    unfathomed sea
Not the wintery winds which moan without in such a
    mourning tone   15
Have so wild a path or so far a flight as the[y]
    gaze on a spirit gone
    How strange seems now that vanished Past
        reflected to my eye
That pride of rank that pomp of power that blaze of
    Royalty
Collecting all their brightest beams around a single
    brow
Yet paling all their borrowed light neath Beautys
    native glow   20
    How strange to know that she to whom I bent my
        willing knee
Among a thousand round her throne who joyed to kneel
    with me
Is now so near me--All alone! with arms clasped oer
    her breast
Lying clothed with white in an endless Night of
    everlasting rest
Her lovely limbs stretched stiff and still her
    ey[e]lids closed for ever   25
And her white lips in silence pressed no more on
    earth to sever
And her pale brow surrounded now with wild flowers
    withering

Like her to a long long winter snatched from a short
    and sudden spring
My mind retraces back the path of this quenched and
    fallen star
To that bright morn when first its light shone oer
    the Calabar   30
Companion of our Country's Sun in his refulgent rise
The chosen and the only one beside him in the skies
And farther back upon her track to the hour
    remembered well
When Loves first word upon her heart like whispered
    thunder fell
Her fathers Palace roof above its glorious Halls
    around   35
When her cheek first flushed and her bosom beat to
    hear that awful sound
War settled to triumphant peace and DOURO home
    returned
Crowned with the crest of victory that oer its love
    burned
But brighter in unborrowed beams that form
    magnificent
Above the chosen of his pride its kingly stature
    bent   40
What darkning curls oer hung the brow whose
    smoothness seemed to be
Like the oerpowering stillness of a deep but
    treacherous sea
The imperious eyes half closed to hide the lurking
    feind within
The proud lips curled in a witching smile of decked
    and gilded sin
For not in garb more Angel like to Eve appeared the
    Devil   45
Nor the winged Dragons gilded mail hid thoughts of
    deadlier evil
Nor the words that changed our Earth to Hell like
    sweeter thunder rolled
Than that deep voice whose Organ tones his love in
    music told
Oh shook not younder gorgeous Hall when words so
    eloquent
Delivered oer one beauteous Bride to lonely
    Banishment   50
And gave another one short flash of loved celestial
    light
To and in such a frightful change of deaths eternal
    night
    He says he had grasped her fathers hand their
        freindship sworn to share

184

And that each summoned by his band of conquerors
    fresh from war
With all the youth of Afric round could dare a
    thousand dangers   55
Their hands creators of their power their arms their
    own avengers
He opens up a dazzling dream where parting clouds of
    glory
Disclose a land of paradise unknown to former story
His own white finger points the place of realms that
    are to rise
And his own deep voice prophetic speaks of coming
    victories   60
Till she surveys that glorious brow whose crown had
    just been won
And knows in its refulgent glow Creations rising sun
Her heart is in her eyes and they with burning tears
    run over
For who unmoved could hear the voice of such a
    glorious Lover
Not that bright form of beauteous youth whose
    thoughts unutterable   65
Thrill wild through veins of Percyian blood with
    feelings none can tell
Oh none but one who had been like her a child of
    Poetry
If round him youths romantic dreams arose--reality!
And he had heart and soul to thrill with joys so
    wonderous wild
Oh none but such could know the thoughts of Percys
    lovely child   70
And when he speaks again and says of all the world
    that she
Alone is meet Zamorna's bride and Angrias Queen to be
Even if his looks of light at once had changed to
    Satans frown
The eloquence of her mute reply must seal her for
    his own
The Auburn curls from her kindled brow in
    inspiration flung   75
The whole heart and spirit in that vow which
    trembles on her tongue
But straight his own curls bent oer hers are
    mingling with their tresses
And his royal lip with a burning Kiss the cheek of
    beauty presses
And his Statly limbs on the cushions thrown are
    straight her own beside
That to her ear more sweetly false his poisoned
    words may glide   80

MS: J, B(2)
First Publication: Winnifrith PBB, partial

An early draft in Notebook B of "Calm and clear the
day declining," dated June 16, 1837--see No. **134,**
p. 265

93   **Mary's Prayer.**

                           ====

        Remember Me when Deaths dark wing
                Has born me far from Thee;
        When, freed from all this suffering
                My Grave shall cover me.

        Remember me, and, if I die   5
                To perish utterly
        Yet shrined within thy memory
                Thy Heart my Heaven shall be!

        'Twas all I wished when first I gave
                This hand unstained and free   10
        That I from thence might ever have
                A place my Lord with thee

        So if from off my dying bed
                Thou'dst banish misery
        O say that when I'm cold and dead   15
                Thou wilt Remember Me!

                P B B.   June 16 1837.   16 lines

MS: B(2)
First Publication: Winnifrith PBB

$$\frac{\begin{array}{r}79\\4\end{array}}{316}$$

94   Now--But one moment, let me stay:
          One moment, ere I go
    To join the ranks whose Bugles play
          On Eveshams woody brow

    One calm hour on the brink of life   5
    Before I dash amid the strife
          That so[u]nds upon my ear
    That sullen sound whose far off roll
    Bursts over many a parting soul:
          That deep mouthed voice of War!   10

    Here am I, standing lonely neath
          The shade of quiet trees
    That scarce can catch a single breath
          Of this sweet evening breeze
    And nothing in the twilight sky   15
    Except its veil of clouds on high
          All sleeping calm and grey
    And nothing on the summer gale
    But the sweet trumpets solemn wail
          Slow sounding far away   20

    That, and the strange uncertain sound
          Scarce heard though heard by all
    A trembling through the summer ground
          A murmering round the wall

========================

[Summer 1837]

MS: B(1)
First Publication: Shorter EJB 1910
Text: The numbers in the left margin are Branwell's

PBB.
Aug 27.
1837.

95   How Eden like seem Palace Halls
          Where Youth and Beauty join
    To waken up their lighted walls
          With looks and smiles divine
    How free from care the perfumed air   5
          About them seems to play

How glad and bright appears each sight
    Each sound how soft and gay!

Tis like the Heaven, which parting days
    In summers pride imbue
With beams of such imperial blaze
    And yet so Tender too
But, parting day, however bright
    It still is--parting day!
The Herald of descending night,
    The Beacon of decay!

So when my mind recalls to me
    The Hour in years gone by
When such a scene of majesty
    First met my wondering eye
I think--within that Lordly Dome
    How soon its glory fell
And woe and darkness made their home
    Where joy was wont to dwell

I think--till oer the unknown main
    Departed spirits glide
And bring before my eyes again
    That Warning night of pride
So turn from yon bright clouds that spread
    Those sunset skies behind
And look with me and thou shalt see
    The sunset of the mind!

A Hundred Lustres light the Hall
    Where power and pleasure reign
And gilded Roof and mirrored wall
    Reflect their rays again
And, entering from the starless night
So dazzling seems this blaze of light
    That scarce the eye may know
Who form the proud patrician throng
Whose glittering mazes pour along
    With such imperial show
Till, slowly on the senses stealing,
Saloons and Galleries seem revealing
Columns clad in many a fold
Of costly crimson ribbed with gold
Ancient Arches ranked between
And long drawn lighted Halls within
Where mid the ever varying Dance
Visions of Loveliness advance
Beheld one moment, but an age
    Wipes not such sights away, and when
    Long years of Lifes corroding pain

10

15

20

25

30

35

40

45

50

188

Has hardened every feeling, still
The vision shall have power to asswage   55
    The troubled heart, and warm the chill
        Of Life's most Northern stage

There is in such a majic Hour
Something of so divine a power
That the full heart and thrilling eye   60
Oerflow with sudden tears of joy
For we feel at once there lingers still
Like Evening sunshine oer a Hill
A glory round Lifes pinnacle
And, though our fortunes lie below   65
The splendour of that sunny brow
Still will Ambition beckon on
To IT, a Height which may be won
And Hope still whispers in the ear
'Others haven been, Thou mayst be there"   70
But scape the shade of humble birth
And something of Heaven is thine on Earth!'

Amid this Royal Bower of Love
    One Vision seems to glow
Of a resounding Dome above   75
    And a gathered crowd below
Whose glancing plumes and curling hair
    Beneath the lights on high
Wave gladly to each perfumed air
    That sighs so sweetly by   80
But all assembled in a ring
As still as they were worshipping
Beneath the eye of Heaven divine
At some blest Martyrs Holy shrine
And whither wafts the sacred sound   85
Which makes this tranced quiet round
And lures these stealing footsteps on
    Before its Heavenborn breathings die
Till peals from its ascending tone
        Tumultous Melody!--   90
        Whose is the Minstrelsy?
Sounding in chords abrupt and loud
Or in the Bosom of the crowd
        Subsiding Mournfully?

    The Minstrel sits begirt by eyes   95
That gaze on him with mute suprise
But away with that last quivering note
His own wrapt spirit seems to float
For silent droops his curling head
Oer which the Lights a Halo shed   100
And on the keys that neath them lie

189

His eyes are fixing vacantly
Unheard by him the sounds that come
Of Resounding from the lighted Dome
Of Of distant dance and laughter gay   105
For his bent brow and looks of gloom
    Show feelings wandering far away
But there is something in his face
Beyond its outward form of grace
A forehead dark with frowns of ire   110
An eye of feirce unholy fire
A Lip of scorn--but all oerspread
With the chill whiteness of the dead
And noble though the features be
They are marked with hidden treachery   115
And sickness left from hours gone by
Of riot and Debauchery

A sudden welcome wakes his ear
In tones that sound familiar
So from his dreams he starts to know   120
The faces of the princly Row
Forgotten--though they round him stand
And though so bright the Beauteous Band
Whose soft approving glances swim
With tears of rapture roused by him   125
And whose red lips so softly parting
Smile upon his sudden starting.--
Then, He knows his power, revealed
In Them, though from themselves concealed
His power upon each Beauty's soul   130
That bows to feelings soft controul
Unconscious that her real shrine
Is, that high front and face divine!

    Tall and Erect the minstrel rises
With placid calmness that disguises   135
Each Treacherous hope within his breast
For there to greet their Noble Guest
The Lord and Lady of the Hall
Are both arrived at music's call
He--a man severe to sight   140
Of mighty bone and manly height
With restless eyes and Raven hair
Dashed from his forehead broad and bare.
She, Oh! could I paint her form--
A sunbeam wedded to the storm!   145
With such a look of freindship shining
    Through her bright and dewy eye
That not the silken lash declining
    Could oershade its brilliancy
No not even the shadows passing   150

Through her heart and oer her brow
Could avail in wholly chasing
    Thence, its soft and sunny glow
Strange that she thus formed to be
The Banisher of misery   155
Should have one cloud of care or sadness
To overcast her smiles of gladness
But--where feeling most appears
There springs the fullest fount of tears
Since on this earth the seeking eye   160
Meets more of sorrow than of joy
And Lady! thus the youthful bloom
    From thy soft cheek so soon declined
    And thus so oft thy inward mind
Seemed looking forward to the tomb!   165
For early hopes, in thee so strong
With early scenes and times were gone
And--wedded to an Iron Breast
    Whose feelings neer replied to thine
For thy far forests of the west   170
    Long days of summer saw thee pine
And Halls in statliest grandeur drest
    Could neer thy sorrowing soul resign
To cold content when those far skies
Hold all thy spirits sympathies!   175

But let us to that night return--
    And mid that noble company
    Beside the minstrel standing--why
Did her fair cheek with blushes burn?
Oh what awoke the sudden red   180
That oer its sorrowing paleness spread
And when her lips a greeting tried
    What broke their quick and trembling tone
And oh when His to her replied
    Why--through their tears--her dark eyes
       shone?   185
    He said--"I thought you'd scarce have known
A face and form so changed as mine
    But through the shade that years have thrown
It seems that still the past can shine!
Yet time has marked us both with care   190
And are our freindships what they were?
My old regards except from me
As wracks of many a stormy sea
And I'll forgive if you've forgot
For ships In harboured rest will rot   195
Sooner than those whose tattered sails
Have braved wild waves and wracking gales----"
    With wandering look the Lady stood
        As if his voice she hardly heard--

As if Her inmost thoughts would brood   200
     On thoughts more deep than spoken word
And then she said--still tremblingly
"Percy!--We Heard that you were far
Across the stormy northern sea
     Still sailing--but we knew not where   205
Though every wind that swept the sky
Recalled you to my memory
     And every hour reminded me
Of Happier skies and brighter weather
When we used to walk together   210
I--unconscious as a child
How years of winds and waters wild
Should separate--
            Oh Sir forgive
The weakness of this womans tear
For--as we stand together here   215
     Old Times and Memorys will revive!--"
    So Harriet with her Heart alive
To other hours of vanished bliss
But dead to all the pomp of this
Stood by her Noble freind whose eye   220
Lit with a look of double meaning
As if some thought of darkness screening
     With a strange smile of treachery--
And yet--to Hers replying for His
Was not the Heart which could unmoved   225
Behold the mind of one he loved
So changed--so saddened--
           There she stood
Leaning against his Instrument
    And the unbidden flush of blood   230
Dying from off her cheek that bent
    To hide in vain the sudden flood
Of sorrows long suppressed till now!--
--But what a shadow crossed his brow
Whose eyes upon her beauty fell   235
With a reflected light of Hell
That woke in every gazers mind
A fear of something undefined
And Percy knew it so to chase
    The dampness oer that circle lying   240
He called the demon from his face
And with an air of winning grace
    Over the keys his fingers trying
He struck a chord of sudden sound
That gathered quick his listners round   245

"Harriet--" He said--"Shall hear a song--
    Oer many a wave has swelled its strain!--
    And often it has brought again

The hours when she and I were young!--"
    He smiled and straight his fingers woke   250
A solemn change of swelling tone
    That with an aimless seeming broke
        As if at Random round him thrown
Such music as the Atlantic gale
Had often sounded in his sail   255
Till all its chords began to join
With his deep voice in melody divine.

                Song..
        Air Auld Lang Syne
              Varied

        SONG BY PERCY.
                —————

Should Old Aquaintance be forgot
    As Time leaves years behind?--
Should Lifes for ever changing Lot   260
    Work changes on the mind?

Should Space that severs Heart from Heart
    The Hearts first Love destroy?--
Should Time that bids the youth depart
    Bid youthful memories die?   265

Oh! say not that these coming years
    Can fresh Affections bring
For freindships Hopes and freindships fears
    From deeper fountains spring

Their feelings to the Heart belong   270
    Their token--glistening Eyes
While later freindship on the tongue
    Arises lives and dies!

And passing crowds may smiles awake
    The passing hour to cheer   275
But--only Old Aquaintance' sake
    Can ever wake a Tear!

                ——————————

So the statly Minstrel sung
Turning as that last note rung
To mark the impression of his song   280
Upon the mute surrounding throng

                    193

And, when he turned his eyes were brightning
   With a fervour so divine
That many a soft heart felt like lightning
   The thrill of their poetic shine   285
While thrilled indeed that Ladys hand
   By his a single moment pressed
   As softly smiling He addressed
   His Old Aquaintance and his best
      And last and only freind!   290
Oh how that voice seemed music's own
As yet again with winning tone
He said--"Our spirits vainly strive
To keep old freindships still alive
If happy Hearts and pleasant hours   295
Our path-way strew with countless flowers
For such a constant joy destroys
The former memory of former joys.--
Tis care and sorrow round us strewn
That give us back the pleasures gone   300
As darksome nights not sunny days
Awake the far of Beacon Blaze
And minds content, from Happy home
May never find a cause to roam
While hearts fair Lady such as mine   305
   Continual tossed from storm to storm
The vanished Hopes the parted form
   Will still remember--still repine!
And these thoughts--deeming you were true--
Have lit the fire which warmed me through   310
Many a dark day of maddened slaughter
And many a night of stormy water
So, though declares my altered brow
That as I was I am not now
If your fair eyes my Heart could see   315
That is as it was wont to be!"--

So burst in such impassioned tide
   Those words breathed from a burning mind
   That little cared for Ill designed
If but the Hour was gratified   320
With conquering passion hate or pride
And Harriet dared not--could not think
Her yeilding Heart on ruins brink
When every look and word from him
Awoke some sweet reme[m]bered dream   325
   Of Auld Lang Syne--of Happy youth
   Of Summer Skies and sunny smiles
   When after Treacheries and wiles
Stained not the Souls unsullied truth
Tis true she saw the shade severe   330
Impressed by many a stormy year

Collected on His forehead high
And oer his deep unquiet eye
But in its glance of dissolute joy
That truely sparkled to destroy   335
Her fond heart traced with answering thrill
The Old impassioned feeling still.
So she replied with solemn sweetness
     Such as thrilled the listners ear--
Sorrow she was used to witness   340
     And had shaken hands with Care!
But oer that Deluge of Distress
     Oh should she dream that Hope would bear
One welcome Olive branch of Peace
     To save Her future from Despair!--   345
Twas sweet to join the broken chain
     Of Old associations gone
By such a meeting once again
     To the long future coming on!

But--!   350
     There she stopped for trusted not
Her Heart to speak of him who stood
Apart in black and brooding mood
The Gloomy Partner of that Lot
Which he embittered with a life   355
Of wild debauchery and strife
And serpent like revenge--
                         Oh well
     To Percys heart was Hector known!
     His comrade dear in riot gone   360
And now his foe implacable
For He--while Percy, far away
Was tossing over Norways sea,
For his broad Lands found ample grace
Before Her freinds and fathers face   365
So she was sacrificed to be
The Bride of wrath and Treachery
However much hor sunny soul
Might shrink beneath his harsh controul
However Hate neglect or pride   370
Should cast her dreams of comfort wide!
     "And now"--thought Percy, Home returned--
          With spirit practised to destroy--
While every nerve for vengeance burned
          "If I my thoughts on ought employ   375
Save how to wake the ancient flame
Till headlong passion end in shame
To him who dared my prize to take--
May I no more have power to wake
     A look of love from Womans eye!--"   380
Yes--Percy saw and Percys soul

```
        Felt all the flame he wished to inspire
Till doubly spurning all controul
        He plunged in that destroying fire
And gave his fiery Heart the rein              385
Heedless of punishment or pain!

But--turn we to that majic ground
Where wheeled th[e] Dance on music round
        Mid merry laughter through the room
        While echoed back the regal Dome        390
That busy Hum of social sound
And mirrors gave in mimic nature
Many a fairy form and feature
And lustres gloriously supplied
The light by midnight hours denied:            395
While--There They Two together stood
        No one near them--all alone
        In a bright world of their own
Whose sunny light no cloud subdued
With worldlike shadow--Heard by them           400
        The whirl of pleasure round them flying
        On their enraptured ear fell dying
Like an Incoherent Dream!
But Recollections crowding came
To reawake the smouldering flame               405
And as on each refulgent Head
A glorious glow those Lustres shed
How glanced in Harriets eyes a shine
That made their tearful looks divine
Beneath those golden locks that shaded         410
The Angel brow their curls invaded
While mutely mild her soft lips smiled
        To note the change on Percy made
By long long years of waters wild
        Whose storms she thought had given that
                shade                          415
Of passing sternness oer his face
        Though never yet in womans eye
        Did marks of woes and wars gone by
A Noble countenance deface
His voice too had a deeper tone                420
Than that her earlier years had known
While Her Blue eyes more sadly shone
        Than in departed days
But both indeed seemed passing fair
In rapt communion standing there              425
And oer them lingered many a gaze
From forth the giddy passing maze
And many a Heart of Rank and power
Did Homage to that lovely flower
```

Whose very whiteness far outshone   430
The Redder Roses round her strewn!

But--wherefore will Times warning finger
    Sign these Happy Hours away?
Cares and sorrows always linger--
    Cannot these a moment stay?   435
Yet Great Destroyer whose will is dooming
    All the world to be thy prey
Know thine own last hour is coming
    Faster still with our decay!
For since that fateful night had birth   440
A score of years have past from earth
And thou whose Avarice nought will leave
Art so much nearer to thy grave!

Now slowly through that mighty Hall
    The sound of mirth and music dies   445
And softly signs of parting fall
    From lips and hands and eyes
Corridors receive the tide
Underneath their Arches wide
And many a chariots wheels are heard   450
    Departing through the starless night
And many a whispered farwell word
Shall long through memory glisten bright
And many oh many a Heart sinks down
    From forced smiles vainly kept so long   455
    Amid the mazes of the throng
To growing care or sullen frown
Till now, at last the Lustres bright
Gleam on a floor of lonely light!
And all alone fair Harriet stands   460
    Beneath their beams all dimly waning
    Of that proud crowd the last remaining
With wandering eyes and clasping hands
Entranced--as if all livings things
    Were but the shadows of a dream   465
    Till oer her blue eyes humid gleam
The oerwrought gush of feeling springs!
An outburst of the souls suprise
When buried Hopes so sudden rise
And then so soon depart--He is gone!   470
    That glorious face that Noble form
    Returning from so many a storm
To bring her back a lifetime flown
And then to leave her thus alone!--
She had not spoken the farewell word   475
She scarce his own farewell had heard
But in her hearing something rung
As if he had said--"Oh wait not long

197

```
         For spite of fate--if I am thine
         Thou art thou wilt--Thou Shalt be mine!"        480
```

                    ═══════════

```
                    P.B. Bronte.
                 Haworth Novʳ. 9ᵗʰ.
                      1837.
```

MS: B(1), B(2)
First Publication: HG, partial; Shorter EJB 1910, partial;
                    Wise Orphans 1917, partial; SHB C and B
Text: l. 57: originally read, "Of sad and stoic Age";
               neither reading is canceled

96   "Lets drink and be merry
                    In port or in sherry
                Or Coqniac or Nantz or Jamaica
                    But if you cant carry
                    Your three bottles fairly   5
                I wish that the D--l may take ye!"

                                      [October 1837]

MS: B(1)
First Publication: Not previously published

97   "Round about round about round about Jolly Boys
              Fill up your glasses and swig off your wine
          Truth and Religion are d--nable folly Boys
              Tis th[e] only Bottle makes human Divine!

                                      [October 1837]

MS: B(1)
First Publication: Not previously published

          An early draft of **ON PEACEFUL DEATH AND PAINFUL
          LIFE,** dated October 1837--see No. **120,** p. 225

An early draft of **AN EPICUREAN'S SONG**, dated
December 11, 1837--see No. **123**, p. 227

An early draft of **On the callousness produced by
cares**, dated December 13, 1837--see No. **118**,
p. 222

An early draft of **The End Of All**, dated
December 15, 1837--see No. **154**, p. 296

An early draft of **HEAVEN AND EARTH**, dated
January 23, 1838--see No. **105**, p. 210.

An early draft of "At dead of midnight---
drearily---" dated May 14th, 1838--see No.
103, p. 202

98   DEATH TRIUMPHANT
                        May, 1838.

'Oh! on this bright Mayday morn,
    That seems to change our earth to Heaven,
May my own bitter thoughts be borne,
    With the wild winter it has driven!
Like this earth, may my mind be made   5
    To feel the freshness round me spreading,
    No other aid to rouse it needing
Than thy glad light, so long delayed.
    Sweet woodland sunshine!--none but thee
    Can wake the joys of memory,   10
Which seemed decaying, as all decayed.

'O! may they bud, as thou dost now,
    With promise of a summer near!
Nay--let me feel my weary brow--

Where are the ringlets wreathing there?   15
Why does the hand that shades it tremble?
    Why do these limbs, so languid, shun
    Their walk beneath the morning sun?
Ah, mortal Self! couldst thou dissemble
    Like Sister-Soul! But forms refuse   20
    The real and unreal to confuse.
But, with caprice of fancy, She
Joins things long past with things to be,
Till even I doubt if I have told
    My tale of woes and wonders o'er,   25
Or think Her magic can unfold
    A phantom path of joys before--
Or, laid beneath this Mayday blaze--
Ask, "Live I o'er departed days?"
Am I the child by Gambia's side,   30
Beneath its woodlands waving wide?
Have I the footsteps bounding free,
The happy laugh of infancy?

MS: Unknown
First Publication: Leyland I

An early draft of **Sir Henry Tunstall,** dated
July 31, 1838--see No. **126,** pp. 202 and 240

99   "Drink to me only with thine Eyes
                And I will pledge in wine!--
            For Angels know of no such joys
                As in this hour are mine!--
            O Glorious Glass! that givest to me   5
                The sights that make my heaven
            Such forms as theirs could never be
                By real mirror given!

                                    [February 1839]

MS: I
First Publication: Winnifrith PBB

200

100   From the Thunder of the Battle
           That has laid a thousand low
        From the cannons conquering rattle
           That has stilled the sternest foe

        From Etrei's far off water   5
           That has died with blood the sea
        From Leyden's feild of slaughter
           Thou hast risen to rule the free

        Again thy country meets Thee
           Who broke the Captives chain   10
        Again thy Kingdom greets Thee
           A Conquering King again!

        Thou hast given them peace that love thee
           And they shall give thee praise
        They shall pray to Heaven above thee   15
           For a lengthened round of days

        For a Brow unmarked by furrow
           For a hand unstained by crime
         For a joy unchecked by sorrow
           Beyond the Bounds of Time   20

        For Laurels oer thee, sleeping,
           Whose leaves shall ever bloom
        For a Land like children weeping
           Oer a Kings like a fathers tomb!

                    [February 1839]

MS: I
First Publication: Winnifrith PBB

101   "Twas ever thus -- since childhoods hour
           Ive seen my fondest hopes decay
        I never loved a tree or flower
           But twas the first to fade away!"

                    [February 1839]

MS: I
Not previously published

102   "Happy sinks a summer day
    From the twilight air
Gazing ere it fades away
    On the evening star!

Happy sleeps the sickmans mind   5
    If before he dies
Ere his being is resigned
    Friendship close his eyes!

Happier still my worried heart
    Ere its memory fade   10
Takes a last look where thou art
    Lightner of its shade!

Be the star to smile afar
    At my evening glow
Be the freind to cheer my end   15
    Ere my spirit go!--"

[February 1839]

MS: I
Not previously published

A second draft of **Sir Henry Tunstall**, April 15,
1840--see No. **126**, pp. 200 and 240

103 At dead of midnight---drearily---
I heard a voice of horror say,---
    "Oh God!--I am lost for ever!"
And then the bed of slumber shook
As if its troubled sleeper woke   5
    With an affrighted shiver,
While--in her waking--burst a sigh
    Repressed by sudden fear,
As she gasped faintly--"Where am I?--
    "Oh help!--Is no one here?--"   10

No one was there--and, through the dark,
Only a single trembling spark
Left from a Taper's dying light
With red gleam specked the void of night;
And which--scarce waken'd from her dreaming,   15
    She thought was this receding world

From whence her spirit's flight seemed hurled,
In hopeless distance dimly gleaming.
    Quick came that thought--and, quickly gone,--
She found herself laid all alone,   20
While burst unbid the choking sob
As that dread truth with wildering throb
Almost stopped the fleeting breath
Of her who woke to wait for death.
There--both her hands, as cold as clay   25
Pressed her Forehead, while she lay
Motionless, beneath the power
That weighs upon life's latest hour.
    Short--short had been her fevered slumber,
        And filled with dreams of that dread shore   30
    Where she must meet her Judge--before
Another hour that night might number!
And fails my pen to paint the room--
Veiled, like her hopes, in utter gloom--
Where she, unseen, unwatched, unknown,   35
And thought and feeling almost gone,
Gasped, breathless, neath the mighty Foe,
And watched each moment for his blow!
    "Oh God!"--she murmured forth again,
        While scarce her scattered senses knew   40
        What darkness shrouded from her view---
"Oh! take from me this weight of pain!
That frightful dream--if 'twas a dream--
        Has only wakened me to die,
But death and life confounded seem   45
        To inward thought and outward eye!
Tis not this agony of death
That chills my breast and chokes my breath---
Tis not this flush of fevered pain
That dizzies so my burning brain---   50
That makes me shudder to implore Thee
When my soul should bow before Thee---
I shrink not from the eternal gloom
That waits my body in the tomb---
Oh no!--Tis something far more dread   55
That palsies heart and hand and head----
        I have lost--long lost my trust in thee--
            I cannot hope that thou wilt hear
            The unrepentant sinner's prayer,
So whither must my spirit flee   60
For succor from eternity
Beside me yawns its awful void,
And, of the joys I once enjoyed,
Not one remains my soul to cheer
When I am launched unaided there!   65

"Eternity--Oh, were there none!--
      Could I believe what some believe,
      Soon might my spirit cease to greive
At the cold grave and church yard stone!
But--God--to appear before thy face   70
In all a sinner's nakedness,
Without a single hour to spare
To make that sinner's sins more fair,
      Without the slightest power to shun
      Thine eye, whose anger looks upon   75
      All things I've thought--all deeds I've done--
Repentance past--and, useless prayer!
      How can thy spirit live to stand
      That look, and hear that dread command
Which even Archangels shrink to hear---   80
That voice, whose terrors none can tell--
'Depart, lost Spirit, into Hell!'

      "Oh Christ! when Thou wert crucified
Thou heardst the felon at thy side,
And in his bitterest agony   85
Thou gavest him a heaven with Thee.
But--He repented and confessed
Ere Thou would give his anguish rest,
And--Oh, in my last hour--do I--
Thus wretchedly afraid to die?--   90
Dare I repent---can I repent,
When with my very life are blent
The feelings that have made me sin?---
Who have scorned Thy name to adore my crime?--
Repent!--No, No! The sands of time   95
      Fleet far too swiftly to begin!

Can I repent---Can I forget
The face, the form, scarce vanished yet--
The only vision that has proved
There's aught in this world worth being loved!   100
Can I forget the noble name
For which I lost my earthly fame--
Can I forget--when, darkly, round
Parents and friends and kindred frowned--
When home was made a Hell of strife   105
By those who gave and shared my life--
When far had fled the inward peace
That gives the troubled spirit ease--
When--Heaven's and earth's affections reft--
Nor present hope, nor Future, left--   110
Can I forget the glorious star
That cheered me through the weary war!
The long long hours of wrapt communion
      Mid the quiet moonlight grave,

204

The wild hopes of future union   115
    Gilding oer my guilty love:
Even the bursts of maddened mourning
    When I saw his happy bride,
Lost--amid the joys returning
    If again He sought my side!   120
  "Oh! I led a life of sinning
    At His beck whose soul was sin,
Yet my spirit ceased rapining
    If a look from him 'twould win.

Bright the beams with hellish glory   125
    That around His spirit shone,
Dark His heart whose influence oer me
    Led me in and lured me on!
All His mirth I knew was hollow--
    Gain and guilt his path and aim--   130
Yet I cared not what might follow--
    Deaf to warning dead to shame!
What to me if Percy Hall
Held all Hell within its wall,
So I might in His embrace   135
Drown remembrance of disgrace.

    "God!--Thou knowest, my inward thought,
        Through many a dreary after day
        When to another sold away,
Could never with my hand be bought.   140
Or, if a moment's madness gave
My heart, to throb, a Tyrant's slave,
Still--still--how often--true to one
Whom still I thought for ever gone,
I'de sadly sit and silent weep   145
While all the wide world seemed asleep,
Thinking upon the surging sea
That bore His vessel far from me.

    "It was Thy curse--when sneers and scorn
From a stern jesting feind, had worn   150
My Soul, so long disquieted
And chafed between disgust and dread,
It was Thy curse--yon fatal night--
That once more brought him to my sight,
When all the room went whirling round   155
As first I heard his music sound--
When all my veins ran living flame,
As first--for years--he named my name
As first I pledged my broken faith
To fly with him to---friendless death.   160
    I'de spent my life in search of pleasure,
I thought that hour I'de found the treasure,

All else I lost to gain that one,
And--when I gained it---all was gone!
    Then Honour left me--peace of mind   165
    Fled with it, and conscience came
    To gnaw my heart with quenchless pain,
And wither what remained behind;
    Yet for a while, a little while---
If I could gain a single smile   170
From him, my bane, my happiness--
I ceased to think about distress.
            'Twas when the dreadful death blow came,
'Twas when he left me to my shame,
That, sudden, ceased my star to shine---   175
That happy hopes--that joys divine,
As they were centred, past with him,
And---I awakened from my dream!

"Sure--never bore a human frame
            Unmaddened--agonies, like me,   180
Who have lived as if hell's hottest flame
            Was kindled by that agony;
Till day and night has oer me flown,
Alike, unnumbered, and unknown,
Tossing on my tearless pillow   185
As if it were hell's burning billow--
Straining eyes that wept no longer--
Weakening down, while woe waxed stronger.

    "Where--in such an hour of pain--
Where were friends and flatters then?   190
Where were hearts that would have died
So they perished at my side?
Where were knees that joyed to kneel
Waiting on my slightest will?
Where were tongues that seemed to be   195
Only framed to flatter me?
        Ah--the wide world held them still!
            All was whirling round the same--
            The same feigned words and fancied flame
But--waiting on another's will.   200
Then, and now, as once they shone,
Thousand lights were beaming down
And dizzy dance and thrilling song
Gather many a noble throng.
        There was but a single change--   205
            One was lost--and no one heeded,
For along the glittering range
            No one felt that one was needed.
Faces blushed to name her name--
Silence hushed the Adulterer's shame--   210
Little cared they how she greived

```
          Oer her monstrous wickedness--
Hardly knew they if she lived
          Through her desolate distress--
Three short words would speak her lot--                    215
F A L L E N--F O R S A K E N--and F O R G O T!"


     There she stopped, far spent and broken,
The last deep accents she had spoken
Fell, as if no more could come
From lips with utter anguish dumb,                         220
          There she stopped--but even the bed
Trembled with her dying dread,
And for a while she moaning lay
As if she'd weep her heart away,
While now and then a broken word                          225
Amid her sobbing, might be heard--
Some name, perhaps, that childhood knew
And yet to fleeting memory true---
Some thought, perhaps, of far off time,
Before these hours of grief and crime                     230
Had changed that voice of music mild
Into a Key so sadly wild.


     Could He have bent above her head--
          Even He whose guilt had laid her there
One burning drop he must have shed                         235
     Those old yet altered tones to [hear]
     Like west winds breathing [on his ear]
          The memory of climes [afar]
     She thought herself old scenes
Where recollection, lingering, hung                        240
In life's last hour, to take farewell
Of what her heart had loved so well.
          Me thought she called on C a r o l i n e !
          As long ago she used to cry
When--laid at rest in eve's decline--                      245
          Till Caroline all tenderly
Would bend above her golden head,
          And sing to sleep the guileless child
Ah! had she known this change so dread
          Fair Caroline had never smiled                   250
To see her sister's blue eyes close,
And kiss her sweet lips to repose!


     But let us haste to present woe,
From pleasures perished long ago---
     As Harriet lay--the spark of red                      255
In her spent Taper vanished,
So, turning toward the wall, her head,
She murmured---
               "Ah! so all depart
```

From blasted hopes and broken heart!--- 260
I thought IT might have seen my end,
But not a sinner will attend
To the dark flood---They're gone!--all gone!--

        Where's P E R C Y ?---"
             with that word, again, 265
Like bowstring loosened from its strain,
Her wandering spirit sprung!--<u>That</u> tone
Called voice and vigour back--
               "Whose gone?--
Oh Percy! Percy!--where art Thou! 270
   I've sacrificed my god for thee,
   And yet thou wilt not come to me!--
How thy strong arm might save me now!
My heart should chase away despair,
I'de hope--Ide live if Thou wert there! 275
Percy--where art Thou?--tell me--where?
   He's far away--He minds no more
Than winds or waters mind the shore
   [His own] "loved [Harriet"--] Halls of light
   [And] beauteous for¯s with beaming eyes, 280
   [Echo and look] this very night
[To] his rich floods of harmonies.
He smiles and laughs--among the throng
None smile so much or laugh so long.
Ah Lady! fly that witchery, 285
Or Thou wilt soon be fallen as I!
Ah fair and frail--and must his tale
Over thee--like me--prevail?--
And wilt thou kneel to such a god?
And canst thou bear his iron rod? 290
   What though thy stately dome contain
As bright a sene, as fair a train,---
---But---my own head whirls dizzily,
For these are visions that I see--
Save me!--I'm falling--<u>was that him</u> 295
Me thought I saw a sudden beam
Of passing brightness through the room
Like lightning vanish---Percy! come!
Leave me not in the dark---'tis cold,
   And something stands beside my bed-- 300
Oh! lose me from its icy hold
   That presses on me---raise my head--
   I cannot breathe!--"
              She'd scarcely said
That word, when, sudden, oer her frame 305
Again, a chilling trembling came,
And died upon her palsied tongue
The charmed word, adored so long,
And--all relaxed--her hands unclasped,

And faint--and feebler still, she gasped--   310
---Why fell that silence?--Hush! I hear
    A wing like winnowing--'Tis the wind
In the Cathedral Towers afar,
    But it came strangely on my mind
Like one departing------   315

            x   x   x   x   x   x   x

                         [April 1840]

                 P. B. Brontë

            Broughton in Furness

                 Lancashire.

MS: B(2), Unknown: last known to have been in the
     possession of Sir Alfred Law
First Publication: SHB C and B
Text: ll. 236-38; 279-82: the manuscript is torn; the
     completions in square brackets are taken from the 1838
     version.

104   BLACK COMB.

'Far off, and half revealed, 'mid shade and light,
Black Comb half smiles, half frowns; his mighty
        form
Scarce bending into peace--more formed to fight
    A thousand years of struggles with a storm
    Than bask one hour, subdued by sunshine warm,   5
To bright and breezeless rest; yet even his height
Towers not o'er this world's sympathies, he
        smiles--
While many a human heart to pleasure's wiles
    Can bear to bend, and still forget to rise--
As though he, huge and heath-clad, on our sight,   10
    Again rejoices in his stormy skies.
    Man loses vigour in unstable joys.
Thus tempests find Black Comb invincible,
While we are lost, who should know life so well!

                              [1840]

MS: Unknown
First Publication: Leyland I

Of Earth beneath, a little space
    Our eyes at once descry;
But Heaven above us meets our gaze
    Like an Infinity.
On <u>Earth</u> we see our own abode,   5
A smoky town, a dusty road,
    A neighbouring hill, or grove;
In <u>Heaven</u> a thousand worlds of light
Revolving through the gloom of night
    O'er endless pathways rove.   10

While daylight shews this little Earth
    It hides the mighty Heaven,
And, but by night, a visible birth
    To all its stars is given;
And, fast as fades departing day,   15
When silent marsh or moorland grey
    Mid evening's mist declines,
Then, slowly stealing, star on star,
As night sweeps forward, from afar,
    More clear and countless shines.   20

I know how oft-times clouds obscure them,
    But, FROM earth ascend
All such vapours drawn before them,
    As TO earth they tend;
And when the storm has hastened by,   25
Upon the earth their ruins lie
    Subsided down again,
While Heaven unstained, more glorious glows,
And every star more star-like shews,
    "Clear shining after rain."   30

So thus we view, in mortal life,
    As circumscribed a scene,
When worthless joys and petty strife
    Alone are heard or seen;
But when beyond this life's wild maze,   35
We let our minds a moment gaze,
    How vast the prospects seem!
Not worlds of everlasting light,
But joys on joys celestial bright
    In Heaven unbounded gleam.   40

'Tis day—the day of pomp and power,
    Which hides that Heaven divine,
And few will heed in such an hour
    How bright its glories shine;

But when declines youth's summer sun,   45
When life's last vanities are gone,
    Our thoughts from <u>Earth</u> are driven;
And, as the shades of Death descend,
How truly seems it's night our friend,
    Because--<u>it shews us Heaven</u>.   50

There's many a grief to shade this scene
    And hide those starry skies,
But all such clouds that intervene
    From this world will arise;
And, may I smile, O God! to see   55
Their storms of sorrow beat on me,
    When I so surely know
That <u>Thou</u> the while art shining on;
That <u>I</u>, at last, when they are gone,
Shall see the glories of thy throne   60
    Beam brighter far than now'

               NORTHANGERLAND.
               [June 5, 1841]

MS: B(2), Unknown
First Publication: HG

An early draft of **On Landseer's painting**,
August 1841--see No. **117**, p. **222**

106   Oh Thou whose beams were most
                  withdrawn
PBB   When should have risen my morning
Brearley Hill   Sun
Aug 0   Who, frowning most at earliest dawn
1841   Foretold the storms through which
                  t'would run

           Great God! when hour on hour has past   5
             In an unsmiling storm away,
           No sound but bleak Decembers blast--
             No sight but tempests, through my
                day--

           At length, in twilights dark decline
             Roll back the clouds that mark Thy
                frown   10

Give but a single Silver line
    One Sunblink as that day goes down

My prayer is earnest for my breast
    No more can buffet with these storms
I must have one short space of rest   15
    Ere I go home to dust and worms

I must a single gleam of light
    Amid increasing darkness see
Ere I resigned to churchyard night
    Bid day farewell eternally!   20

My body is oppressed with pain
    My mind is prostrate neath despair
Nor mind nor body may again
    Do more than call thy wrath to spare

Both void of power to fight or flee   25
    To bear or to avert thy eye
With sunken heart with suppliant knee
    Implore a peaceful hour to die!

When I look back on former life
    I scarcly know what I have been   30
So swift the change from strife to
        strife
    That passes oer the wildering scene

I only feel that every power--
    And thou hadst given much to me
Was spent upon the present hour   35
    Was never turned My God to thee

That what I did to make me blest
    Sooner or later changed to pain
That still I laughed at peace and rest
    So neither must behold again   40

MS: E
First Publication: BST 1927

An early draft of **The Triumph of mind over
body**, Autumn 1841--see No. **127**, pp. 228 and
253

107

ON THE MELBOURNE MINISTRY.

Men call us worthless, though our deeds,
    Since our long reign had birth--
(If any proof our country needs,)
    Show <u>even</u> <u>We</u> have worth.

Though 'going out,' like dying lamps,
    And smelling like them too,
You'll find us good "Adhesive Stamps;"
    Or first rate calf-skin glue.

                    P. B. B.
            [August 14, 1841]

MS: Unknown
First Publication: HG

108

PBB

Sept 3rd

1841

Man thinks too often that his earth-
        born cares
    Bind chains on mind and can overcome
            its sway
That faint and feeble proves the soul which
        wars
        Against its storm struck prison house
            of clay
        But henceforth know that on its dreary
            way   5
    Whateer of Ills with all its race it shares
        Though pain and poverty becloud its day
And want begins and sadness ends its years
Soul still can brighten through its mortal
        gloom
    As THINE did JOHNSON Englands true born
            son   10
Who in thy Garret or a lordlings room
        Calmly let hunger creep or pride strut on
        Intent on manly thoughts and honours won
    Mid hours as darksome as thy dreaded Tomb

MS: B(2)
First Publication: BST 1927
Text: l. 11:   "lordlings" written above "lordly"; neither is
                canceled
        l. 14:   "Mid" written above "From"; neither is
                canceled

109   Far up in heaven I view the brightest star
That ever blazed amid the storms of war
The star that blazed oer Persias burning vale
When battle crushed the rose and scared the
      Nightingale

[Sept 1841]

MS: B(2)
First Publication: BST 1927
Text: l. 2: "storms" written above "clouds"; neither is
      canceled

110   Amid the worlds wide din around
      I hear from far a solemn sound
PBB   That says "Remember Me!"
Sept 11 "And though thy lot be widely cast
1841   From that thou picturedst in the past   5
      Still deem me dear to thee
"Since to thy soul my light was given
To give thy earth some glow of heaven
And, if my beams from thee be driven
      Dark! Dark! thy night will be!"   10

What was that sound? Twas not a voice
      From Ruby lips and Sapphire eyes
Nor echoed back from sensual joys
      Nor a forsaken fair ones sighs
I when I heard it sat amid   15
      The bustle of a town like room
Neath skies, with smoke stain'd vapours hid,
      By windows, made to show their gloom.
The desk that held my Ledger book
Beneath the thundering rattle shook   20
      Of Engines passing by
The bustle of the approaching train
Was all I hoped to rouse the brain
      Or startle apathy

And yet as on the billow[s] swell   25
A Highland Exiles last farwell
      Is born oer Scotlands sea
And solemn as a funeral knell
I heard that soft voice known so well
      Cry--"Oh Remember me!"   30

      Why did it bring such scenes to mind
As Time has left so long behind?

Those summer afternoons when I
Laid basking neath a glorious sky
Some noble page beneath me spread   35
Some bright cloud floating over head
And sweet winds whispering in the tree
Of wondrous prospects meant for me!
        Why did it bring my eyes before
The hours spent wandering on the moor   40
Beneath a grey and Iron Sky
        With nothing but the waters still
To break the stern monotony
        Of withered heath and windy hill
While fancy to the heedless child   45
Revealed a world of wonders wild
Adventures bold and scenes divine
Beyond the Horizons gloomy line
Untill I thought my footsteps trod
The pathless plains round Volgas flood   50
Or paced the shores of Grecias sea
Or climbed the steep of Calvary

        Why did I think I stood once more
At night beside my fathers door
And while far up in heaven the moon   55
        Through clear and cloud was driving on
A moment dark but bursting soon
        Upon the heaven she made her own
I often times would think that she
Was some bold vessel oer a sea   60
        Mid unknown regions gliding
Perhaps with Parry in the north
On stra[n]ge discovery venturing forth
        On stormy waters riding
Perhaps with Sindbad mid those Isles   65
Where Genii haunt and sunshine smiles.
Perhaps--and nobler still than these
With Vincent guarding England[s] seas
        From might of foreign war
Or bearing Nelson oer the wave   70
To find a glorious Hero's grave
        On Deathless Trafalgar!

MS: B(2)
First Publication: BST 1927
Text: l. 25: "billow[s]" written above "soft winds";
                neither is canceled
       l. 38: "Of" written above "A"; "prospects" written
                above "future"; none are canceled
       l. 42: "with" written above "and"; neither is
                canceled

215

l. 44: "withered" written above "darksome"; "windy"
written above "windless"; none are canceled

l. 48: "gloomy" written above "swelling"; neither is
canceled

l. 49: "I" written above "He"; "my" written above
"his"; none are canceled

l. 57: "but" written above "then"; neither is
canceled

111   **ROBERT BURNS**

He little knows--whose life has smoothly passed
    Unharmed by storm or strife, undimmed by care
Who--clad in purple laughs at every blast
    Wrapped up contented in the joys that are
    He little knows the long and truceless war   5
Of one on povertys rough waters cast
    With eyes fixed forward on the glorious star
    That from fames temple beams--alas! how far
Till backward buffetted oer oceans waste

                                              [1841]

MS: B(2)
First Publication: BST 1927

112   The desolate earth--the wintry sky--
               The ceasless rain showers driving by--
PBB   The farewell of the year--
Decr 15th   Though drear the sight and sad the sound
1841   While bitter winds are wailing round   5
               Nor hopes depress nor thoughts confound
                    Nor waken sigh or tear

               For as it moans Decembers wind
               Brings many varied thoughts to mind
                    Upon its storm drenched wing   10
               Of words not said mid sunshine gay
               Of deeds not done in summers day
               Yet which when joy has passed away
                    Will strength to sorrow bring

               For--when the leaves are glittering bright   15
               And green hills lie in noonday night

                        216

```
        The present only lives
But when within my chimnies roar
The chidings of the stormy shower
The feeble present loses power                    20
        The mighty past survives

I cannot think--as roses blow
        And streams sound gently in their flow
And clouds shine bright above
Of aught but childhoods happiness                 25
Or joys unshadowed by distress
Or voices tuned the ear to bless
        Or faces made to love

But when these winter evenings fall
Like dying natures funeral pall                   30
        The Soul gains strength to say
That--not aghast at stormy skies
That--not bow[e]d down by miseries
Its thoughts have will & power to rise
        Above the present day                     35

So winds amid yon leafless Ash
        And yon swollen streamlets angry dash
And yon wet howling sky
Recall the victory of mind
Oer bitter heavens and stormy wind                40
And all the wars of human kind--
        Mans mightiest victory!

The darkness of a dungeons gloom
So oft ere death the spirits tomb
        Could not becloud those eyes              45
Which first revealed to mortal sight
A thousand unknown worlds of light
And that one grave shines best by night
        Where Galileo lies

But--into drearier dungeons thrown                50
With bodies bound whose minds were gone
        Tassos immortal strain
Despite the tyrant's stern decree
Mezentius like--rose fresh & free
And sang of Salems liberty                        55
        Forgetful of HIS chain

And thou great rival of his song
Whose Seraph wings so swift & strong
        Left this world far behind
Though poor neglected blind and old               60
The clouds round paradise unrolled
```

And in immortal accents told
    Misery must bow to mind

See--in a garret bare and low
While mighty London roars below   65
    One poor man seated lone
No favorite child of Fortune he
But owned as hers by poverty
His rugged brow his stooping knee
    Speak woe and want alone   70

Now who would guess that yonder form
Scarce worth being beaten by lifes storm
    Could ere be known to fame
Yet Englands love and Englands tongue
And Englands heart shall reverence long   75
The wisdom deep the courage strong
    of English Johnsons name

Like Him--fordoomed through life to bear
The anguish of the hearts despair
    That peirces spirit through   80
Sweet Cowper mid his weary years
led through a rayless vale of tears
poured gentle wisdom on our ears
    And his was English too

But Scotlands desolate hills can shew   85
How mind may triumph over woe
    For many a cottage there
Where ceaseless toil from day to day
Scarce keeps grim want one hour away
Could shew if known how great the sway   90
    Of spirit over despair

And he whose natural music fills
Each wind that sweeps her heathy hills
    Bore up with manliest brow
Gainst greifs that ever filled his breast   95
Gainst Toils that never gave him rest
So though grim fate Burns life oppressed
    His soul it could not bow

MS: B(2)
First Publication: BST 1927
Text: l. 15: "For" written above "Yet"; neither is
                canceled
      l. 28: "made" written above "framed"; neither is
                canceled
      l. 63: originally read "The conquering might of
                mind"; neither version is canceled; in the

revised line "bows" is written above "must
bow"; neither is canceled

l. 83:   "wisdom" written above "music"; neither is
canceled

l. 84:   "his" written above "he"; neither is canceled

l. 91:   "despair" written above "care"; neither is
canceled

l. 92:   "natural music" written above "Harp of
nature"; neither is canceled

113   Dec/19 1841   **at Luddenden Church**   PBB

———————————————

O God! while I in pleasures wiles
    Count hours and years as one
And deem that wrapt in pleasures smil[e]s
    My joys can neer be done

Give me the stern sustaining power   5
    To look into the past
And see the darkly shadowed hour
    Which I must meet at last

The hour when I must stretch this hand
    To give a last adieu   10
To those sad freinds that round me stand
    Whom I no more must view

For false though bright the hours that lead
    My present passage on
And when I join the silent dead   15
    Their light will all be gone

Then I must cease to seek the light
    Which fires the evening heaven
Since to direct through deaths dark night
    Some other must be given   20

MS: B(2)
First Publication: BST 1927

114   The man who will not know another,
Whose heart can never sympathize,
Who loves not comrade, friend, or brother,
   Unhonoured lives--unnoticed dies:
His frozen eye, his bloodless heart,   5
Nature, repugnant, bids depart.

O Grundy, born for nobler aim,
Be thine the task to shun such shame;
And henceforth never think that he
Who gives his hand in courtesy   10
To one who kindly feels to him
His gentle birth or name can dim.

However mean a man may be,
Know man is man as well as thee;
However high thy gentle line,   15
Know he who writes can rank with thine;
And though his frame be worn and dead,
Some light still glitters round his head.

Yes! though his tottering limbs seem old,
His heart and blood are not yet cold.   20
Ah, Grundy! shun his evil ways,
His restless nights, his troubled days;

But never slight his mind, which flies,
Instinct with noble sympathies,
Afar from spleen and treachery,   25
To thought, to kindness, and to thee.

         [1841]

MS: B(1), Unknown
First Publication: Grundy

115   When first old Time with me shook hands
   And pointed out my way
I little knew the unknown lands
   Through which life's journey lay

         [1842]

MS: E
First Publication: BST 1927

220

116

PBB
April 25th
1842

When side by side at twilight sitting
   All our household group we see
The shade and firelight oer them flitting
   The smiles and converse circling free

Though winds within the chimney thunder   5
   And rain showers shake each window pane
With perhaps one glance of awe or wonder
   Song or tale begins again

Even when our house seems hushed and lonly
   Save whispers round a sick ones bed   10
We find a pleasure were it only
   To sooth and still the throbbing head

And though our eyes seem moist with weeping
   Hope is still our guest the while
Our hearts feel soothed if pain be sleeping   15
   Satisfied if sickness smile

Even--though far be such a sorrow!
   Death takes back his 'clay to clay'
Though that face shall see no morrow
   Which the coffin hides to day   20

Still a holy calm comes oer us
   All have loved though one has died
As round our hearth shall death restore us
   Neath one gravestone--side by side

But Oh! when eye to eye replying   25
   Glistens with the unbidden tear
As the storm th[r]ough heaven is flying
   As each dreary gust we hear

Of the well loved wanderer thinking
   Tempest tossed and torn from home   30
At his unknown perils shrinking
   Doomed for years so far to roam

Still his fate the mind is painting
   As we see his vacant chair
Perhaps mid wilds in famine fainting   35
   Breathing for us some feeble prayer

And when we know that all is over
   That he has died on foreign shores
Neer may our hearth its joys recover
   Toil may stun but rest deplores   40

MS: B(2)
First Publication: BST 1927
Text: 1. 8: "begins" written above "drives on"; neither is
            canceled
      1. 28: "th[r]ough" written above "oer"; neither is
            canceled

117   **SONNET I.**
On Landseer's painting--"The Shepherd's Chief Mourner"
A dog keeping watch at twilight over its master's
grave.

The beams of fame dry up affection's tears;
    And those who rise forget from whom they spring;
    Wealth's golden glories--pleasure's glittering
        wing--
All that we follow through our chase of years--
All that our hope seeks--all our caution fears,   5
    Dim, or destroy those holy thoughts, which cling
    Round where the forms we loved lie slumbering;
But--not with thee--our slave--whose joys and cares
We deem so grovelling--power nor pride are thine,
    Nor our pursuits nor ties, yet, o'er this grave   10
    Where lately crowds the form of mourning gave,
I only hear thy low heartbroken whine;
I only see thee left, long hours to pine
    For him whom thou--if love had power--would'st
        save!

                            NORTHANGERLAND.
                            [April 28, 1842]

MS: E, B(2), Unknown
First Publication: BH

118   **SONNET II.**
            On the callousness produced by cares.

Why hold young eyes the fullest fount of tears;
    And why do youthful breasts the oftenest sigh,
    When fancied friends forsake, or lovers fly,
Or fancied woes and dangers wake their fears?
Ah! he who asks has seen but spring tide years;   5

Or Time's rough voice had long since told him
    why!
Increase of days increases misery,
And misery brings selfishness, which sears
The hearts first feelings: 'mid the battle's roar
    In death's dread grasp the soldier's eyes are
        blind   10
To comrades dying, and he whose hopes are oer
    Turns coldest from the sufferings of mankind:
A bleeding spirit oft delights in gore;
    A tortured heart oft makes a tyrant mind.

                         NORTHANGERLAND.
                      [May 5 & 7, 1842]

MS: B(2), F, Unknown
First Publication: BH and HG

119   **THE AFFGHAN WAR**

Winds within our chimney thunder,
    Rain showers shake each window pane;
Still--if nought our household sunder--
    We can smile at wind and rain.
Sickness shades a loved one's chamber; ·   5
    Steps glide gently, to and fro;
Still--'mid woe, our hearts remember
    We are there to soothe that woe.

Comes at last the hour of mourning;--
    Solemn tolls the funeral bell;--   10
And we feel, that no returning
    Fate allows to such farewell;
Still, a holy hope shines o'er us,
    We wept by the one who died;
And, 'neath earth, shall death restore us--   15
    As round hearthstone--side by side.

But--when all at eve, together
    Circle round the flickering light,
While December's howling weather
    Ushers in a stormy night;   20
When each ear, scarce conscious, listens
    To the outside winter's war,
When each trembling eye-lash glistens
    As each thinks of one afar--

Men to chilly silence dying,   25
    Ceases story, song, and smile;
Thought asks--Is the loved one lying
    Cold, upon some storm-beat isle?"
And, with death--when doubtings vanish,
    When despair stills hopes and fears;   30
Though our anguish toil may banish,
    Rest brings unavailing tears.

So, Old England--when the warning
    Of thy funeral bells I hear,
Though thy dead a host are mourning,   35
    Friends and kindred watch each bier.
But, alas! Atlantic waters
    Bear another sound from far!
Unknown woes--uncounted slaughters--
    Unwept deaths--inglorious war!   40

Breasts and banners crushed and gory,
    That seemed once invincible;
England's children--England's glory,
    Moslem sabres smite and quell.
Far away their bones are wasting,   45
    But I hear their spirits call--
Is our Mighty Mother hasting
    To avenge her children's fall?

England rise! thine ancient thunder
    Humbled mightier foes than these;   50
Broke a whole world's bonds asunder;
    Gave thee empire o'er the seas.
And while yet one rose may blossom,
    Emblem of thy former bloom,
Let not age invade thy bosom;   55
    Brightest shine in darkest gloom.

While one oak thy homes shall shadow,
    Stand like it as thou hast stood;
While a spring greets grove and meadow,
    Let not winter freeze thy blood.   60
'Till this hour St George's standard
    Led the advancing march of time.
England! keep it streaming vanward;
    Conqueror over age and clime.

                        NORTHERANGERLAND.
                        [May 7, 1842]

MS: Unknown
First Publication: Leeds Intelligencer

120
SONNET III.
ON PEACEFUL DEATH AND PAINFUL LIFE.

Why dost thou sorrow for the happy dead?
   For if their life be lost their toils are o'er,
   And woe and want can trouble them no more;
Nor ever slept they in an earthly bed
So sound as now they sleep, while dreamless laid   5
   In the dark chambers of the unknown shore,
   Where Night and Silence guard each sealed door.
So--turn from such as these thy drooping head
And mourn the dead alive, whose spirit flies,
   Whose life departs, before his death has come;   10
Who knows no Heaven beyond his gloomy skies;
   Who sees no Hope to brighten up that gloom:
'Tis he who feels the worm that never dies,
   The real death and darkness of a tomb!

                    NORTHANGERLAND.
                  [May 12 & 14, 1842]

MS: B(1), B(2), Unknown
First Publication: BH and HG

121
CAROLINE'S PRAYER.
ON THE CHANGE FROM CHILDHOOD TO WOMANHOOD

My Father, and my childhood's guide,
   If oft I've wandered far from thee;
Even though thine only son has died
   To save from death a child like me.

O! still--to thee when turns my heart,   5
   In hours of sadness--frequent now--
Be thou the God that once thou wert;
   And calm my breast, and clear my brow,

I'm now no more a little child
   Oer'shadowed by thine angel wing,   10
My very dreams seem far more wild
   Than those my slumbers used to bring.

I farther see--I deeper feel--
   With hope more warm, but heart less mild,
And former things new shapes reveal,   15
   All strangely brightened or despoiled.

I am entering on Life's open tide;
   So--Farewell, childhood's shores divine!
And, Oh my Father, deign to guide
   Through these wide waters, Caroline!   20

NORTHANGERLAND
[June 2 & 4, 1842]

MS: D(1), A, H, Unknown
First Publication: BH and HG

122   **SONG.**

Should Life's first feelings be forgot,
   As Time leaves years behind?
Should Man's for ever changing lot
   Work changes on his mind?

Should space, that severs heart from heart,   5
   The heart's best thoughts destroy?
Should years, that bid our youth depart,
   Bid youthful memories die?

Oh! say not that these coming years
   Will warmer friendships bring;   10
For friendship's joys and hopes and fears
   From deeper fountains spring.

Its feelings to the <u>heart</u> belong;
   Its sign--the glistening eye;
While new affections, on the <u>tongue</u>   15
   Arise, and live, and die.

So, passing crowds may <u>smiles</u> awake,
   The passing hour to <u>cheer</u>;
But--only old acquaintance' sake
   Can ever wake a <u>tear</u>.   20

NORTHANGERLAND.
[June 9 & 11, 1842]

MS: B(1), B(2), Unknown
First Publication: BH and HG

The visits of sorrow,
    Say, why should we mourn?
Since the sun of to-morrow
    May shine on its urn;
        And all that we think such pain   5
        Will have departed--then
Bear for a moment what cannot return:

For past time has taken
    Each hour that it gave,
And they never waken   10
    From yesterday's grave,
        So surely we may defy
        Shadows, like memory,
Feeble and fleeting as midsummer wave.

From the depths where they're falling,   15
    Nor pleasure, nor pain,
Despite our recalling,
    Can reach us again:
        Though we brood over them,
        Nought can recover them;   20
Where they are laid they must ever remain.

So seize we the present,
    And gather its flowers;
For--mournful or pleasant--
    Tis all that is ours.   25
        While daylight we're wasting,
        The evening is hasting,
And night follows fast on the vanishing hours.

Yes--and we, when that night comes--
    Whatever betide,   30
Must die as our fate dooms, And sleep by their
        side;
        For change is the only thing
        Always continuing;
And it sweeps creation away with its tide!   35

                      NORTHANGERLAND
                    [July 7 & 9, 1842]

MS: B(2), Unknown
First Publication: BH and HG

The light of thy ancestral hall,
   Thy Caroline, no longer smiles:
She has changed her palace for a pall;
   Her garden walks for Minster aisles.
Eternal sleep has stilled the breast   5
   Which peace and pleasure made their shrine;
The golden head has sunk to rest,
   Which used to beam with rays divine.

To thee, while watching o'er the bed
   Where mute, and motionless she lay,   10
How slow the midnight moments sped!
   How void of sunlight broke the day!
Nor oped her eyes to morning's beam,
   Though all around thee woke but her;
Nor oped thy raven pinioned dream   15
   Of coffin, shroud, and sepulchre.

Why beats thy breast when hers is still?
   Why lingerest thou when she is gone?
Hopest thou to light on good in ill?
   To find companionship, alone?   20
   Perhaps thou think'st the church-yard stone
Will hide past smiles, and bury sighs;
   That memory, with her soul, has flown;
That thou can'st leave her where she lies?

No! joy _itself_ is but a shade,   25
   So well may its _remembrance_ die;
But cares--life's _conquerors_--never fade,
   So strong is their reality!
Thou mayest forget the day which gave
   That child of beauty to thy side,   30
But, not the moment when her grave
   Took back again thy borrowed bride!

               NORTHANGERLAND
            [July 12 & 14, 1842]

MS: Unknown
First Publication: BH and HG

A second draft of **The Triumph of mind over
body,** Summer 1842--see No. **127,** pp. 212 and
253

Azrael.
or
The Eve of Destruction
part Ist
Rough Draught.

"Brothers and Men--One moment stay
    Beside your latest patriarchs grave--
While God's just vengeance yet delay--
    While Mercy yet have power to save!--
Now will you force my Tongue to say   5
    That, underneath this nameless sod
Your hands and mine have laid Today
    The last on Earth who walked with God!

Shall this pale Corpse whose hoary hairs
    Are just surrendered to decay   10
Dissolve the chain that bound our years
    To hurndred ages past away?--
Shall six score years of warnings dread
    Die like a whisper in the wind?--
Shall that dark doom which hangs oer head   15
    Its blinded victims darker find?--
Shall storms from Heaven without the world
    Find wilder storms from Hell within?--
Shall long stored late come wrath be hurled?--
    Or, will You--can You, turn from Sin?--   20
Have patience, if too plain I speak
    For time, My Sons, is hastning by!
Forgive me, if my accents break--
    Shall I be saved--and Nature die?--

Forgive that pause!--One look to Heaven   25
    To plainly tells me He is gone
Who long with me had vainly striven
    For Earth beneath its Makers throne.
He is gone!--My Father, full of days
    From life that left no joys for him;   30
Born, in Creations earliest blaze
    Dying--himself its latest beam!

But--He is gone!--and, Oh behold,
    Shewn in his death Gods latest sign
Than which, more plainly never told   35
    An Angels prescence his design.--
By it--the Evening beam withdrawn
    Before a starless night descend--
By it--the last blest spirit born
    From this beginning of an End,--   40
By all the coming strife of war

That brews above yon fated Town--
By all the Hearts worst passions there
That call so loud for Vengeance down--
By that vast wall of Cloudy gloom   45
Surrounding all Heavens firmament--
By all its presages of doom--
Childern of Men!--Repent! Repent!"

The patriarch ceased and rung his voice
Like knell of iron from the skies   50
But echo, none, the earth returned
Whose blinded sons with anger burned
As silent swayed their mighty tide
Around the grave from side to side
All eyes were bent with threatning gloom   55
On Him who prophesied their doom
And One arose--upon whose face
Passions and crimes had left their trace
Contending with a tameless pride
That Man and God alike defied   60

    "Be Thine"--He cried with trumpet voice
        While hoarse applauses rolled--
                        "Be Thine
The task to embitter human joys
    To raise to cherish them be Mine!--   65
Die with the Head that now has died
    The miseries of a time gone by
Descend with him the Tyrants pride
    Rise from his ashes, Liberty!
Take him--the Type of old things past--   70
His death--Our chain, dissolved at last--
I grant it--Take that cloudy gloom
For omen of the storm to come--
Take all thy Types--, but, know thy age
Looks blindly on lifes lettered page   75
Dim eyes see darkness even in day
And wrinkled brows scare smiles away
Age always thinks the past was bright
And--like itself--deems present, night.
    Is't fit that he whose memory fails   80
Save when repeating old world tales--
That he who scarce the present knows
Should prophesy of future woes?
    Oh Human Heart! how waywardly
From Truth to error thou wilt flee!   85
We say this world was made by One
Who's seen or heard or known by none
We say that He, the Almighty God
That framed Creation with a nod
His wondrous work so well fullfilled   90

                        230

That--in an hour--it All rebelled!--
That though he loves our race so well
He hurls our spirits into Hell--
That though He bids us turn from sin
He hedges us, with tempters, in--   95
That though he says the world shall stand
Eternal--perfect--from his hand
He is just about to whelm it oer
With utter ruin--evermore!--
And all for deeds that we have done   100
Though he has made us every one--
Yes WE--the image of his form!--
We!--the dust to feed the worm!
        Away with all such phantasies!--
Just trust your reason and your eyes!--   105
Beleive that God exists when I
Who, here--this hour--His name deny
Shall bear a harder punishment
Than those whose knees to him have bent.
Beleive that He can rule above   110
    When you shall see him rule below
Beleive that he's the God of love
    When he shall end his childern's woe
Beleive that this firm earth we tread
And that vast canopy oerhead--   115
Beleive that they have stood for ever
And that they shall for ever stand--
Till something really strive to sever
    The earth from Heaven--the sea from land
Beleive that hoary descending hairs   120
Are far more sage than youthful years
When rotting planks shall prove to be
More fruitful than a forest tree
Old Man!--a truce to dotard dreams
    And turn from heaven thy hazy eyes   125
A Thought for Earth far more beseems
    Than childish gazing at the skies
    Tis Earth--not Heaven--shall shortly rise
Tis Man--not God--shall soon avenge
    And if there be a paradise   130
We'll bring it in the coming change!--
    To Morrow morn--my country men
        We meet within that City's wall--
Let us our Liberty regain
Be that the "Breaking of our chain--   135
Then if all Heaven its terrors rain
    We'll smile upon them all!--".

As Azrael ceased, throughout the throng
Uprose a tumult loud and long
That howled about the Man of God   140

And laughed his sorrowing looks to scorn
Nor could he speak one warning word
   Away by surging thousands born.
One look he cast--one withering look
   At Azrael, whose triumphant eye   145
Could scarce withstand its mute rebuke
   Even in his hour of Victory
Then swayed the tide on either side
And each apart were sundered wide
But oer the thousands Azrael's form   150
Shone like a Beacon through a storm
And oer the tumult Azrael's voice
Swelled like a trumpet through the skies
   On toward the wall he bade them tend
      And fast the concourse hurried on   155
      Forgot Methuselahs burial stone
      Where only Noah mourned alone
Above his Father and his freind!

Why walks within his palace Hall
   Lord Azrael, silent and alone   160
   While back its roof of marble stone
Returns his footstep's measured fall?--
Why gathers in his restless eye
   A shadow of such troubled meaning--
   Why--sometimes, at the window leaning   165
So anxious looks he on the sky?--
Why comes so sad the evening down?--
Why sleeps so dark the Mighty town?--
And why <u>does</u> every palace dome
<u>Seeming</u> mourning mid the misty gloom   170
While the wind whistles wild and low
<u>About</u> each pillared portico?--
   Twas but an hour since thousands roared
      For Azrael, oer Methuselahs grave,
Then why is He so late adored   175
      Untended by a single Slave?--
His ears yet ring with uproar loud,
The Applauses of a maddened crowd,
He has left the streets choked up with men
Whose shouts might call him back again   180
Alone He has left them but his eye
Shews that his mind has company,
And, pacing oer the darkning floor
On mighty thoughts he seemes to pore
At length the solemn silence breaking   185
As if a Spirit heard him speaking
So clenched his hands so fixed his look
So earnest every word he spoke.

Azrael solus loquitur

"There is no God--I know theres none!   190
Neither of spirit nor of stone;
No Holy Hill nor Idol Shrine
Has ever held a power divine,
Nor Heaven above nor Hell below
Can minister to weal or woe!--   195
    I feel that, when the Body dies
        Its memories and feelings die
That they from earth shall never rise
        As it in earth shall ever lie:
I know that Mortal eyes incline   200
        Whenever aught remains unseen
With phantoms dreadful or divine
        To people the mysterious scene,
That Human life revolts to think
It ever stands on nothing's brink,   205
That Human pride recoils to see
The Heap of dust tis doomed to be!--
    I know that if I staid till night
        Alone in this unlighted Hall
My mind would fill with many a sight   210
        The vacuum of the midnight wall,
But when the Morning light should rise
The real would banish phantasies.
    So when the shadow of TO COME
Surrounds the Heart with boding gloom   215
Nature abhorrs to look at naught
And frames for ease a world of thought.--
So--when the sickman lies to die
He gasps for Hope in Agony
And as the Earth yeilds none to save   220
He makes a Hope beyond the grave!--
    Thus Heaven is but an Earthly dream,
Tis Man makes God--not God makes him!--

    "But why should I of others speak
As if all minds but mine were weak?--   225
We are all the same and each one tries
To cheat his sense with phantasies--
Weak as the weakest--now, even now
When Conquest almost crowns my brow,
When with a word I cheer or check   230
The crowd that follows at my beck,
When those I hated fear my name
And those I feared are bowed with shame,
When--though I tread on Hostile laws
Am welcomed with the worlds applause--   235
Yet, all avails not!--There is still
A sickening sense of future ill
Of what I love, about to be
A part of what has ceased to be!--

                    233

For I may rise to sovereign sway   240
But--MARAH must descend to clay
To morrow night must bring me power
But--this may bring her dying hour
To me a Throne--To her a Tomb--
Fleeting light--And fixed gloom!   245
   Well, so arise through each one's life
From laughter tears--from feasting strife
And earth is not--as some have said
From Chaos but to Chaos made
   Sometimes I think this inward pain   250
Is but the ferment of the brain
Which on this eve of mighty things
While all is doubt, vain phantoms brings
To fill the void--But comes anon
Death the real phantom striding on   255
Which if with wine I drive away
From merry night comes mournful day
At night I drive the tumult on
Pledging healths to lose my own
Or bask in light from beauties eyes   260
Which I enjoy--and then despise!
At morn I rise with head confused
To work neglected, food refused
Untill my mind reverts on schemes
To realise a traitors dreams   265
Untill the day brings forth again
The evil thoughts of restless men
Who me their Leader hurry on
Towards the deed that must be done
And while their minds my own employ   270
My heart can feel a troubled joy
But if my thoughts a moment roam
Towards what should be my happy home
Then, Oh! My Marah! comes the shade
Of hopes beclouded--joys decayed!   275
Then I feel that I must be
Soon--how soon! deprived of Thee!"

   There Azrael stopped with bated breath
As if he saw the face of death
But while he stood there--on his sight   280
   Between him and the darkened wall
Behold! a Lady clothed in white
   With frighted haste swept through the hall
Her face and lips were pale as death--
   Her glassy eyes were fixed on him--   285
She strove to speak but gasped for breath
   Like one oppressed with goblin dream
But Azrael cryed--"Good God! Is't Thou?--
Marah my love! what ails thee now?--"

She answered--but he scarce might hear   290
    Her words, so faint and chilled they were
She said--"I've risen, who never thought to rise--
Death has unclasped--a little space
The strictness of his cold embrace
That I may warn thee ere this body dies--   295
    Ive seen--Oh Azrael!--"
                    There her gaze
    Went wildly round while Azrael caught
    Her almost falling in the maze
        Of some strange scene or stunning thought   300
        And back his clasp her senses brought
    For once more wildly gazing round
    She said, with awed and solemn sound
"I've seen God rise from His eternal throne
And say--'Bring Mercy back--be Vengeance done!' 305
Then every Angel stooped his golden wing
        Before that voice divine
That utter darkness seemed to bring
    Even over Heavens unutterable shine!
Azrael--I lay alone in bed   310
    Composing--in my silent room--
My mind to meet its coming doom
    When lo! a Holy Angel came
    And opened on my dimming sight
        That scene terrifically bright--   315
All Heaven--revealed like a wide world of flame
    Oh!   Then I heard that dread command,
    Which bowed with awe that shining band
While wide the Angel of destruction spread
His midnight wings and from the prescence sped 320
Bent on the deed of doom--
                    All, all is oer!
And this wide world will never brighten more
        Nor joy be seen again!
A thousand Storms are waiting for the word   325
And when its deep commencing peal is heard
    Over this heedless Earth they'll spread a
        shoreless main!
My mourning Angel told me I must go
    Before begins the march of woe
    Called where the blest in glory reign   330
The last on earth who may to heaven attain!
    So I must bid farewell to Thee
Doomed to so dread--
                    Oh God!   I cannot speak!
    This miserable heart will break   335
        For--NONE will hear!"

She sickened in his arms--
    On his broad breast declined her head

                    235

And strayed her hair
All sense of feeling fled   340
And blighted all her charms!
   "She raves" Lord Azrael said "Her brain
Is dizzied with her dying pain--"
   So on a couch her form he laid
And called her servants--all dismayed   345
To find their Lady--when, so nigh
All knew the hour when she should die--
Arisen unhelped and lying there,
They knew not how--but whispers fraught with fear
Passed as they bore her to the bed   350
Where decked for death she erst had laid

   They left Lord Azrael wrapt in thought--
His restless schemes for once forgot
For once declined his haughty brow
His haughty hopes for once laid low   355
For though he strove to scoff away
All he had just heard Marah say
It would not go--Methuselahs tomb
   And Aged Noah's warning cry
And that strange night of utter gloom   360
   Those gathering clouds that boding sky
   That mournful wind bewailing by
All fell upon him in that hour
With Nightmare-weight and stunning power

   But while in _sorrows_ lost, his mind   365
Was wandering into years behind
A hand was placed upon his arm
And he turned round with vague alarm
Of some new ill--but at his back
   Lo Moloch!--with a treacherous eye   370
Glinting with false hilarity
   Beneath his eyebrows broad and black
Ah Tyger heart! that jesting mein
Hides nought but bitterness and sin
   Then each of Hell a worthy brother--   375
Azrael and Moloch face each other.
"Ha Azrael! Sure that dotards preaching
   Has waked at last thy erring heart
And softened by his heavenly teaching
   Thou hast taen the better part   380
Nonsense! leave your saintly sighs
Fill that goblet--and be wise!"
   "But--Marahs dying!--"
                        "Tell me not so
When crowns and thrones are waiting on her   385
   A crown will cheat both death and woe
And women best love pomp and honour

But what _is_ sighing--what is death
Why too much or too little breath!
I laugh to think what fools we are   390
To pull unmeasured jaws at care
When just a simple glass of wine   14
    Will drive the demon power of evil   20
        To his and our good lord the Devil! 00
Come drain this draught and--feel
        divine!"--   28   395
    Lord Azrael at his _feinds_ command   280
The goblet seized with shaking hand
And while at heart the tempter laughed
Deep and devotedly he quaffed
And with more flushed but brighter brow   400
Said grimly--"To our _buisiness_ now!
To morrow night must pleasure gay
From all but us drive care away
But oh! _with us_ to morrow night
Come counsel black and genius bright   405
Then let our statliest beauties bloom
Like roses round an open tomb
Then let our Monarch think his power
Stands firmest in its latest hour
Let Midnight end his dream!--"   410
                    "Let night bring morn
To us brave hearts! from darkness born!
Remember--That, to morrow night
    Our Hate, our Tyrant means to join
With _Thy_ dear SARA'S looks of light   415
    His Faltering form and soul supine
Remember--All his Noble's eyes
Will gaze upon the sacrifice
When she must say with voice divine
To that old Dotard "I am thine"!   420
Remember--To the Royal Court
His sycophants will all resort
While Cain and Haman mean to vie
Neath their proud roofs with majesty
And all the citizens prepare   425
To feast beneath the midnight air
But--the dark lanes--the alleys vile--
On what will _they_ be bent the while?
Will their grim brows shine bright with joy?
Yes--with the longing to destroy!   430
Yes--they _will_ join the festival!
Yes--they _will_ visit each proud hall!
Heres to their health! Soon may I see
    Their naked arms and matted hair
Tossing aside festivity--   435
    Frighting the rose from faces fair--

237

+unning the music laden air;
And--where they gather--We'll be there!"

He ceased--Each drained another draught
And Moloch smiled and Azrael laughed   440
For laughter waits at troubles side
    And shouts through cities taen by storm--
So--when Lord Azrael saw the wide
    Commencing waste assume its form
Grim gladness buoyed his heart. He took   445
    His comrades hand and pledged him well
And spoke a word and gave a look
    That seemed of blood to tell
They ran oer many a haughty name
    Marked who should scape and who should fall 450

[July/August 1842]

MS: B(2), Unknown
First Publication: BH, partial; BST 1933
Text: l. 85: originally read: From truth to error still
                thou'lt flee; neither is canceled; the figures
                in the right margin are Branwell's

125 (b) NOAH'S WARNING OVER METHUSELAH'S GRAVE.
(FROM AN UNPUBLISHED POEM.)

Brothers and men! one moment stay
    Beside your latest patriarch's grave,
While God's just vengeance yet delay--
    While God's blest mercy yet can save.

Will you compel my tongue to say   5
    That, underneath this nameless sod,
Your hands, with mine, have laid to-day
    The last on earth who walked with God?

Shall his pale corpse, whose hoary hairs
    Are just surrendered to decay,   10
Dissolve the chain which bound our years
    To hundred ages passed away?

Shall six score years of warnings dread
    Die like a whisper on the wind?
Shall the dark doom above your head   15
    Its blinded victims darker find?

238

Shall storms from heaven, <u>without</u> the world,
   Find wilder storms from <u>hell, within</u>?
Shall long stored--late come wrath be hurled;
   Or--will you--can you turn from sin?   20

Have patience if too plain I speak,
   For time, my sons, is hastening by:
Forgive me, if my accents break;
   Shall <u>I</u> be saved and <u>Nature</u> die?

Forgive that pause:--One look to heaven   25
   Too plainly tells me He is gone
Who, long, with me in vain had striven
   For earth, beneath its Maker's throne.

He is gone!--My Father!--full of days--
   From life which left no joys for him;   30
Born in creation's earliest blaze;
   Dying--himself its latest beam.

But he is gone! and, oh, behold,
   Shewn in his death, God's latest sign!
Than which more plainly never told   35
   An angel's presence, his design.

By it, the evening beam withdrawn
   Before a starless night descend;
By it, the last blest spirit born
   From this beginning of an end!   40

By all the strife of civil war
   That brews within yon fated town;
By all the heart's worst passions there,
   That call so loud for vengeance down;

By that <u>vast</u> wall of cloudy gloom,   45
   Piled round heaven's boding firmament;
By all its presages of doom,
   Children of men--Repent! Repent!

               NORTHANGERLAND.
               [August 25, 1842]

MS: B(2), Unknown
First Publication: BH

Tis only afternoon--but midnights gloom
Could scarce seem stiller, in the darkest room,
Than does this ancient mansions strange repose,
So long ere common cares of daylight close:
I hear the clock slow ticking in the hall,   5
And--far away--the woodland waterfall:
Sounds, lost, like stars from out the noonday
        skies;
And seldom noticed till those stars arise.
    The parlour group are seated all together,
With long looks turned toward the threatning
        weather;   10
Whose gray clouds, gathering oer the moveless
        trees,
Nor break--nor brighten in the passing breeze.
        Why seems that group attired with such a
                care;
And who's the visitor they watch for there?
The aged Father, on his customed seat,   15
With cushioned stool to prop his crippled feet,
Averting from the rest his forehead high
To hide the drop that quivers in his eye;
And strange the pang which bids that drop to
        start;
For hope and sadness mingle in his heart;   20
A trembling hope for what may come to day--
A sadness sent from what has passed away.
Fast by the window sits his daughter fair;
Who--gazing steadfast on the clouded air--
Clasps close her mothers hand, and paler grows   25
With every leaf that falls or breeze that blows:
Sickened with joy, impatient to be born,
Too bright for her, with long repining worn.
Even those young children, oer the table bent;
And on that map with childish gaze, intent,   30
Are guiding fancied ships through oceans foam;
And wondering--"What he's like"--and--"When
        he'll come".
        Ah! many an hour has seen yon circle pore
Oer that great map of India's far off shore;
And sigh at every name the paper gave,   35
Lest it might mark their well loved warriors
        grave.
Oft have their eyes a burning tear let fall
Oer Ganges mimic tide, or Delhi's wall;
Oft have their hearts left England far away,
To wander oer the wrecks of red Assaye!   40

240

But long that house has lost all trace
        of him;
Whose very form in memory waxes dim.
Long since his boyhoods chosen friends have
        died:
His dog, so faithful to its master's side--
The rooks and doves that hover round the door   45
Are not the same his young hand fed of yore:
The flowers he planted, many seasons past,
Have budded, bloomed, and disappeared at last;
For him, afar, tempestous seas had torn
Before the children round that map were born;   50
And now so many years have past between
The last long look upon that parting scene,
That scarce they saw it then, through gathering
        tears,
So dim as now through intervening years:
"And yet"--said Mary--"Still I think I see   55
Our soldiers plumed helmet bent oer me:
The arm that raised me to a last embrace--
The calmness settled on his youthful face--
Save when I asked, how soon he'd come again?
And all that calm was lost a moment then!   60
Our Father shook his hand, but could not speak;
Our Mother, weeping, kissed her soldiers cheek;
Our sisters spoke not--twas a mute farewell;
And yet no voice could speak it half so well.
We saw our Henry on his charger spring;   65
We heard his swift hoofs on the pavement ring:
There, long we stopped, as if he still were
        there;
Hand clasped in hand and dim eyes fixed on air:
He scarce seemed gone while yet our eyes beheld
The shadowy avenue, and open field;   70
But--when we turned within--when closed the
        door
On that bright heaven, we felt that all was
        oer!
That ne'er those rooms should hear his joyous
        call;
That ne'er his rapid step should cross that
        hall.
We sat together, till the twilight dim;   75
But all the world seemed past away with him;
We gathered close, but could not drive away
The dreary solitude which round us lay;
We felt--when One has left the home fireside,
It matters not though all be there beside;   80
For, still, all hearts have wandered with that
        one;
And gladness stays not when the heart is gone;

241

And where no gladness is a crowd may feel alone!
        Since then, how oft we've sat together
        here,
    With windows opening on the twilight air;   85
    Silently thinking of the climes afar
    Beneath the radiance of that evening star;
    Dear as a friend unto our loneliness,
    Because it seemed to link those lands with us.
    He saw it--perhaps--whom times and oceans tide   90
    So many years had sundered from our side;
    And 'twas the same he used to look upon,
    While all beside so different had grown:
    Our woods, our house, ourselves were not the
        same
    As those that floated through his boyhoods
        dream: 95
    Was He too changed?--Alas! the cannons roar,
    The storms, the summers of that tropic shore
    May have made the last great change!
                      --Too well I know
    Even our calm woods cannot escape that blow!
100 We cannot meet him--if again he come,--   100
    With the same group that formed his ancient
        home:
    The hearts that loved him best are clad in
        clay;
    They are laid in lasting rest--They are far
        away!"

       So Mary spoke--but so she spoke not now;
    Turning so earnestly her pallid brow   105
    On the cold heavens, to which they all were
        turning,
    With looks which could not chase the shade of
        mourning
    Worn far too constantly upon each face
    For that one day of fevered hope to chase:
    That day, determined, from Madeira's shore,   110
    When they their wanderer might behold once
        more;
    Not now the boyish Ensign he had gone,
    But full of honours from his foes oerthrown.
    Time after time fresh tidings of his fame
    Had roused to life his fathers failing frame;   115
    When the old man would raise his gushing eye,
    And lose his sighs of greif in smiles of joy.
    At last, that letter, with "Sir Henry's" crest,
    The tidings of his swift approach expressed,
    A Victor General, to his Englands shore--   120
    At last that sixteen years suspense was oer:

At last the fresh rolled walks, and shaven
      lawn,
That long a look of such suspense had worn--
The rooms so fairly decked--the expectant calm
Oer all things brooding, like a magic charm,   125
Proclaimed, at last, the mighty moment come
When hope and doubt should both give place to
      doom.
      Stay, what was that which broke the hush
         profound?
Like rapid wheels I heard its murmer sound:
Why are the servants footsteps heard within   130
So sudden intermixed with hasty din?
What pales each cheek? What lights each
      swimming eye
Through the close circle of that company?
Advances hastily a strangers tread:
The children shrink behind with sudden dread: 135
All rise together--open flies the door;
And steps that stranger on the parlour floor.

      My pen might paint the start of wild
         suprise;
The tears that flashed in scarce believing
      eyes;
The long embrace--the silence eloquent   140
Of thoughts that ne'er in words might find a
      vent;
The Fathers look, that said--"Thy will be done!
Take me--if fit--since Thou hast given my son!"
The Mothers gaze, too fond to turn above;
Her son beholding with a mothers love;   145
The sisters eyes, that shone in youths oer flow
Of feelings such as age could never know;
150   Through which this world is not the earth it
      seems,
But all surrounded by the light of dreams;
Through which even sorrow takes a heavenly die;   150
Since where it broods hope ever hovers by.
So thus, while, speechless, held in his embrace
She saw--she knew her long lost Henry's face!
She let past times part--hurrying down the
      wind;
And years of vain repining leave her mind.   155
      Not so old age--for sorrow breaks it in;
And--used to harness--it can ill begin
Existence oer again--Dissolved in tears
Of heartfelt gratitude, each head of years
Was bowed before that soldier--but, in vain   160
Each parent sought to shake off sorrows chain:
They saw their first born's golden locks appear,

243

Shining amid the haze of memories dear.
They looked--and, was this war worn warrior
    Him?
Ah! How the golden locks waned, dark and dim!   165
Those golden locks were gone, for India's clime
Had touched them with the iron hoar of time:
Was't him?--They gazed again--a look--a tone
Brought back the past--twas Henry; twas their
    own!
They did not mark his restless glances roam   170
As if he sought, but could not find a home;
They did not mark the sternness of his cheek,
Even if to smiles its muscles chose to break;
They only saw their stately soldiers form
Confirmed, not altered by the battles storm;   175
They only saw the long lost face again,
Darkened by climate, not by crime or pain.
        But what he thought it would be hard to
        tell,
Since worldly life can mask the heart so well;
Can deck with smiles a sorrow eaten cheek;   180
Can bitter thoughts in cheerful accents speak;
Can give to icy minds heart eloquence;
Can 'clothe no-meaning in the garb of sense.'
Words he poured forth, of warm and welcome
    greeting,
For heaven--he said--smiled in this happy
    meeting: 185
By turns he wandered oer each long lost face;
By turns he held them in a strict embrace;
Then--Mary saw--though nought her parents
    knew--
For youthful love has eyes of eagle view--
She saw his features in a moment alter,   190
Their rapture vanish, and their fondness
    falter;
And, in that moment, oh how cold seemed all
The mind that lurked beneath that passions
    pall!
A corse beneath a gilded shrine--the corse
Of him who left them on his battle horse   195
Sixteen long years ago.
                --Sir Henry broke
A sudden pause, where only glances spoke,
With a request for one half hour alone,
To call his spirits to a steadier tone
200   And moderate their swell. He left them then   200
To spend their time in calling back again
The ancient image to their wildered view,
And note the difference 'twixt the old and new.
But, strange--whene'er they strove to realize

The form so lately constant in their eyes--   205
The visioned idol of each vanished year--
How like a vision did it now appear!
They could not bear to see it sink from view
Like a vain dream--but ever came the new
Before the old; thus on a sudden faded,   210
When by life's stern realities invaded.

    Changed, like lifes dreary path from
        youth to years,
And dull as age, the twilight hour appears;
The hour ordained by God for mans repose,
Yet often made by man an hour of woes;   215
A summing up of daylights toils and greif;
Of moody musing; not of mild relief.
    That dull hour darkened in the boding
        sky,
And bore the breeze in mournful murmers by,
With promise of a storm: Within the room   220
No cheerful candle shone to light the gloom;
Or cheerful countenance smiled; for only one
Lone tenant held it; seated still as stone--
Sir Henry Tunstall--with a vacant gaze,
As if his mind was wandering in a maze   225
Of alien thoughts, though on that very bed
Long years ago had lain his youthful head
In sleep unstained by sorrow--Still there
    hung--
Wrecks of a time when all the world looked
    young--
His guns, his rods, with which he'd often trod   230
The breezy hills, or wandered by the flood,
Or breasted mountain winds, and felt, within,
The first bold stirrings of the man begin.
There, pictured as of yore, the self same wall
Shewed Englands victory and her hero's fall   235
On cold Canadian hills--With strange delight
In other days the child would fix his sight
Whene'er he woke, upon that time dimmed view;
And burn within to be a hero too:
Would fill his spirit with the thoughts divine   240
Of the loud cannon, and the charging line,
And Wolfe, departing, mid those mingled cries,
To join immortal spirits in the skies.
Twas that dim print that fixed his destinies,
And led his footsteps over Indian seas;   245
So why--on what was childhoods cheif delight--
Will manhood hardly deign to bend its sight?
The old print remains--but, does the old mind
    remain?

Ah world! why wilt thou break enchantments
    chain!

250   Bending his brows, at last Sir Henry
      said,   250
"Well--now I know that time has <u>really</u> sped
Since last my head has in this chamber lain;
That nothing has my <u>now</u> to do with <u>then</u>.
Yes--I at last have reached my native home,
And those I loved have joyed to see me come;   255
And memory of departed love is nigh
To cast a holier halo round that joy;
I've seen my Father--full of honoured days,
Whom last I left adorned with manhoods grace,
Who has lived, since then, long seasons, but
    to see   260
Once more, his first born, world divided me:
I've seen those eyes rekindle that have mourned
for me--I've seen the grey locks that have
    turned
From raven black for me--I've seen Her too;
The first on earth I loved, the first I knew;   265
She who was wont, above that very bed,
To bend in blessing oer my helpless head--
I've seen my Sister--I have seen them all--
All but <u>Myself</u>--They've lost me past recall,
As I have them; and vainly do I come   270
These Thousand leagues--My home is not my home!
      "But let me recollect myself; for strange
And visionlike appears such utter change.
In what consists it? I am still the same,
In flesh and blood, and lineaments, and name: 275
Still wave the boughs of my ancestral trees;
Still these old gables face the western breeze;
Still hang these relics round this chamber lone;
I still can see--can call them still my own:
    "But--well I used to love the things I
      see;   280
Now--if I lost them 'twould be nought to me;
And once my sires or sisters voice was dear;
Now--if they perished--friends are every where:
Once nought could tear me from my own dear
    home;
Now--every roof's the same where'ere I roam: 285
Once--when I saw that picture, every vein
Beat, fame like that, even with that death to
    gain;
Now--I have looked on many a bloody field;
But, Oh how different are the thoughts they
    yeild!
They bend my brow to calculate their plan;   290

But wake no wishes wild to combat in their van.
        They fancied, when they knew me home
            returning,
   That all my soul to meet with them was
      yearning;
   That every wave I'de bless, which bore me
      hither:
   They thought my spring of life would never
      wither;   295
   That in the dry, the green leaf I could keep;
As pliable as youth to laugh and weep.
They did not think how oft my eye sight turned
Toward the far skies where Indian sunshine
      burned;
300   That I was leaving a companion band;   300
   That I had farewells even for that wild land:
They did not think my head and heart were
      older;
My strength more broken, and my feelings
      colder;
   That spring was fading into Autumn sere--
And leafless trees make lovliest prospects
      drear--   305
   That sixteen years the same ground travel oer
Till each wears out the mark which each has left
   before.
      So, Old Affection is an empty name,
When nothing, loved or loving, keeps the same;
But, while we gaze upon the vapour gay,   310
The light that gave it glory fades away:
And Home affection--where <u>have</u> we a home?
For ever doomed in thoughts or deeds to roam;
To lay our parents in their narrow rest,
Or leave their hearthstone when we love them
      best;   315
Nay--sometimes not to know we love at all
Till oer loves object death has spread his
      pall.
I feel 'tis sad to live without a heart;
But sadder still to feel dart after dart
Rankling within--Tis sad to see the dead,   320
But worse to view the tortured sickmans bed.
      Well--I have talked of change, and, oh!
        how changed
Am I from him who oer those dim hills ranged
With trusty dog--poor Rover! where art thou!
I seem to see thee looking upward now   325
To thy young masters face, with honest eye
Shining all over with no selfish joy.
Ah Rover! wert thou here, and couldst thou
      feel

The utter change this spirit would reveal,
Thou'dst rather keep thy long neglected grave   330
Than lick again the hand that would not have
One welcoming stroke to give--My dog, they say
That when I went thou pinedst fast away
Till death restored thee to thy humble clay;
And ceasedst there, at last, to think of me,   335
Who then, afar, was fast forgetting thee:
Yes--twas forgetting--Memory lingered yet
But lost Affection makes the word forget."

  He paused, with heavy eye, and round the
    room
Looked through the shadows of descending gloom, 340
Like one heart sick, for 'twas a bitter task
The hollowness of spirit to unmask,
And shew the wreck of years--To change his mind,
He took a book lying by, from whence to find
Some other course for thought; and, turning
  oer   345
Its Leaves, he thought he'd seen that book
  before;
On whose first page some hand had lightly
  traced
These lines, by times dim fingers half effaced.

  "My Father, and my childhoods guide,
350   If oft I've wandered far from Thee,   350
  Even though Thine only Son has died
    To save from death a child like me,

  Oh! still, to Thee when turns my heart
    In hours of sadness--frequent now--
  Be Thou the God that once Thou wert;   355
    And calm my breast, and clear my
    brow.

  I am now no more a guileless child,
    Oer shadowed by Thine angel wing:
  My very dreams seem far more wild
    Than those my slumbers used to bring.   360

  I farther see--I deeper feel--
    With hope more warm, but heart less
    mild;
  And former things new shapes reveal,
    All strangly brightned or despoiled:

  I am entering on Lifes open tide;   365
    So--farewell Childhoods shores divine!

And--Oh my Father--deign to guide
          Through these wide waters, CAROLINE!"

        Long on that darkning page Sir Henry
              pondered;
Nor from its timeworn words his eyesight
        wandered;   370
Though scarce he comprehended what they were,
For other words were sounding in his ear
Sent to him from the grave--Far off and dim,
As if from heaven a spirit spoke to him,
And bade the shadows of past times glide by   375
Till present times seemed hidden from his eye
By their strange pictured veil: Scene after
        scene
Sailing around him, of what once had been:
He saw a drawing room, revealed in light
From the red fireside of a winters night;   380
With two fair beings seated side by side,
The one arrayed in all a soldiers pride,
The other sadly pale, with angel eyes
Oer whose fair orbs a gushing gleam would rise
Whenever--tremblingly--she strove to speak,   385
Though not a sound her voiceless calm could
        break,
So silent seemed despair--He took her hand
And told her something of a distant Land
Soon to be won with fame, and, soon again,
Of his return, victorious oer the main.   390
        "Oh no!" at last, she said "I feel too
              well
The hollow vanity of all you tell!
You'll go--you'll join the ranks by Ganges
        flood:
You'll perhaps survive through many a field
        of blood:
You'll perhaps gain fames rewards--but never
        more   395
Those far off climes My Henry shall restore
To Englands hills again!--another mind--
Another heart than what he left behind,
And other hopes, he'll bring--if Hope at all
Can outlive fancy's flight and feelings fall,   400
To flourish on an iron hardened brow--
The soldier may return but never thou!
And, farther--Know, our meeting must not be;
For even thyself will not be changed like me:
I shall be changed, my love, to change no more: 405
I shall be landed on a farther shore
Than Indian isles--a wider sea shall sever
My form from thine--a longer time--For ever!

                    249

Oh! when I'm dead and mouldering in my
     grave,
Of me, at least, some dim rememberance have,   410
Saved from the sunken wrecks of ancient time,
Even if to float oer waves of strife and crime:
Then--on the grave of her who died for thee
Cast one short look, and--Oh, remember Me!"

     "Alas! Lost shade!--Why should I think
          upon   415
The mouldering letters of thy burial stone?
Why should I strive thine image to recall;
And love thy beauty's flower, and weep its fall?
It cannot be--For far too well I know
The narrow house where thou art laid below.   420
I know its lifeless chill; its rayless gloom;
Its voiceless silence; and its changeless doom.
I know that, if from weeds I cleared thy name,
And gazed till memories crowding round me,
     came,
Of all that made the sunshine of my home,   425
'Twould be of no avail--Thou couldst not come:
That I might almost think I saw thee stand
Beside me--almost feel thy fairy hand;
Still would that form be pressed neath earth
     and stones;
And still that hand would rest in dust and
     bones.   430
     No Caroline! The hours are long gone by
When I could call a shade reality;
Or make a world of dreams; or think of one
As present with me, who--I knew--was gone:
No--If the sapling bends to every breeze,   435
Their force will rather break the forest trees;
If infancy will catch at every toy,
Pursuits more solid must the man employ:
He feels what is, and nought can charm away
The rough realities of present day.   440
Thou art dead--I am living--Thy world is not
     mine;
So, keep thy sleep--and--Farewell Caroline!
     Yet--while I think so--while I say
          farewell--
Tis not in words the weariness to tell
Which sweeps across my spirit; for my soul   445
Feels such a midnight oer its musings roll,
At losing--though it be a vapour vain--
What once gave rest to toil and ease to pain.
I knew not, while afar, how utterly
450   These memories of youth were past from me.   450

250

It seemed as if--though business warped my
    mind--
I could assume them if I felt inclined;
That though, like dreams, they fled my waking
    brain,
I--if I liked--could dream them oer again.
I did not think I <u>could</u> be seated here   455
After the lapse of many a toilsome year;
Once more returning to accustomed places,
Amid the smiles of old familiar faces;
Yet--shrinking from them--Hiding in the gloom
Of this dull evening and secluded room,   460
Not to recall the spirit of the boy,
But all my world-worn energies to employ
In pondering oer some artifice to gain
A future power, or present to maintain.
      Well, world--oh world! as I have bowed
        to thee,   465
I must consent to suffer thy decree:
I asked--thou gavest me my destiny.
I asked--when gazing on that pictured wall,--
Like Englands Hero to command or fall;
I asked--when walking over mountains lone--   470
For years of wanderings over lands unknown;
I asked for gain and glory, place and power;
Thou gavest them all; I keep them all this
    hour:
But--I forgot to ask for youthful blood;
The thrill divine of feelings unsubdued;   475
The nerve that quivered at the sound of fame;
The tongue that trembled at a lovers name;
The eye that glistened with delightful tears;
The Hope that gladdened past, and gilded future
    years.
So I have rigid nerves and ready tongue,   480
Fit to command the weak, to obey the strong;
And eyes that look on all things as the same;
And Hope--nay callousness, that thinks all
    things--<u>a name</u>!
      Then--Caroline I'll bid farewell once
        more:
Nor mourn--lost shade! for, though thou'rt gone
    before,   485
Gone is <u>thy</u> Henry too--and didst not thou,
While just departing from a world of woe,
Say, thou no longer wert a guileless child?
That all old things were brightned or
    despoiled?
And--hadst thou lived--thy angel heart--like
    mine--   490

251

Would soon have hardened with thy youths
        decline:
Cold perhaps, to me if beating, as when laid
Beneath its grave stone in the church yard
        shade.
It rests--mine labours--There the difference
        lies;
For mine will change but little when it dies.   495

        I home returned for rest, but feel, to
            day,
    Home is no rest, and long to be away;
    To play lifes game out where my soldiers are,
    Returned from India to a wilder war
500 On blood red fields of Spain: again to ride   500
    Before their bayonets, at Wellesleys side:
    Again to sleep with horses trampling round;
    In watch cloak wrapped, and on a battle ground:
    To waken with the loud commencing gun;
And feed lifes failing flame, and drive the
        moments on.   505
    There is our aim--to that our labours tend--
    Strange--we should strive to hurry on our end!
    Yet so it is, and no where can I speed
    So fast through life as on my battle steed."

        He ceased--Unconsciously declined his
            head;   510
    And stealingly the sense of waking fled;
    Wafting his spirit into weeping Spain;
    Till--starting momently--he gazed again,
    But all looked strange to his beclouded brain:
    And all was strange, for--though the scene was
        known,   515
    The thoughts that should have cherished it
        were gone:
    Gone like the sunlight--and none others came
    To chase the encroaching slumber from his
        frame;
    So--while he lay there, twilight deepened fast,
    And silent, as resistless, hours swept past;   520
    Till chairs and pictures lost themselves in
        gloom,
    And but one window glimmered on the room,
    With its pale star, above the sombre trees,
    Listening from heaven to earths repining
        breeze.
        That Star looked down with cold and quiet
            eye;   525
    While all else darkened, brightning up the sky;

And, though his eye scarce saw it, still, his
    mind--
As half awake and half to dreams resigned--
Could scarce help feeling--in its holy shine--
The solemn eyes of parted Caroline,   530
With mute reproachfulness reminding him
That Faith--that fondness were not all a dream;
That Form--not feeling should be changed by
    clime;
That looks--not love should suffer hurt by
    time;
That, guiding wanderers oer lifes waves afar,   535
And brightning with deaths night, should glitter
536   Memory's Star.

NORTHANGERLAND.
[September 1842]

MS: D(1), A, H
First Publication: BH and HG, partial; De Quincey
Text: The numbers in the left margin are Branwell's.

127   The Triumph of mind over body.

Man thinks too often that the ills of life,
Its ceaseless labour, and its causeless
    strife,
With all its train of want, disease, and care,
Must wage gainst spirit a successful war;
That, when such dark waves round the body
    roll,   5
Feeble and faint will prove the strugging
    soul;
That it can never triumph or feel free,
While pain that body binds, or poverty.
    No words of mine have power to rouse the
    brain
Oppressed with greif--the forehead bowed with
    pain;   10
For none will hear me if I tell how high
Mans soul can soar oer bodys misery:
But, where Orations, eloquent and loud,
Prove weak as air to move the listening crowd,
A single syllable--if timely spoken--   15
That mass inert has roused--its silence broken,

253

And driven it, shouting for revenge or fame,
Trampling on fear or death--led by a single name!
   So now, to him whose worn out soul decays
Neath nights of sleepless pain or toilsome
     days;   20
Who thinks his feeble frame must vainly long
To tread the footsteps of the bold and strong;
Who thinks that--born beneath a lowly star--
He cannot climb those heights he sees from far;
To him I name one name--it needs but one--   25
NELSON--a worlds defence--a Kingdoms noblest son!

   Ah! little child, torn early from thy home
Over a weary waste of waves to roam;
I see thy fair hair streaming in the wind
Wafted from green hills left so far behind;   30
Like one lamb lost upon a gloomy moor,
Like one flower tossed a hundred leagues from
     shore.
Thou hast given thy farewell to thine English
     home,
And tears of parting dim thy views of fame to
     come.
   I seem to see thee, clinging to the mast,   35
Rocked roughly oer the northern oceans waste;
Stern accents only shouted from beneath,
Above, the keen winds bitter biting breath,
While thy young eyes are straining to descry
The Ice blink, gleaming in a Greenland sky.   40
All round the presages of strife and storm
Engirdling thy young heart and feeble form.

   Each change thy frame endured seemed fit
     to be
The total round of common destiny;
For next--upon the Wild Mosquito shore   45
San Juans guns their deadly thunders pour,
Though, deadlier far, that pestilential sky
Whose hot winds only whisper who shall die.
Yet, while--forgotten all their honours won--
Strong frames lay rotting neath a tropic sun,   50
And mighty breasts heaved in deaths agony,
Death only left the storm worn Nelson free.
   Death saw him laid on rocky Tenereiffe,
Where stern eyes sorrowed oer their bleeding
     cheif
Born down by shot and beaten back by fate,   55
Yet keeping front unblenched and soul elate.
   Death saw him, calm, off Copenhagen's shore,
Amid a thousand guns heaven shaking roar,
Triumphant riding oer a fallen foe

50--

With hand prepared to strike, but heart to spare
    the blow.   60
     Death touched, but left him, when a tide
       of blood
Dyed the dark waves of Egypts ancient flood,
As mighty L'Orient fired the midnight sky
And first bedimmed Napoleons destiny;
When in that blaze flashed redly sea and
    shore,   65
When far Aboukir shook beneath its roar,
When fell on all one mighty pause of dread
As if wide heaven were shattered over head,
Then--From the pallet where the hero lay--
His forehead laced with blood and pale as
    clay--   70
He rose--revived by that tremendous call--
Forgot the wound which lately caused his fall,
And bade the affrighted battle hurry on,
Nor thought of pain or rest till victory should
    be won!

     I see him sit--his coffin by his chair--   75
With pain worn cheek and wind dishevelled hair,
A little, shattered wreck, from many a day
Of cares and storms and battles passed away;
Prepared, at any hour God bade, to die,
But not to stop or rest or strike or fly;   80
While--like a burning reed--his spirit's flame
Brightened, as it consumed his mortal frame.
He knew his lightening course must soon be oer,
That death was tapping at his cabin door,
That he should meet the grim yet welcome guest 85
Not on a palace bed of downy rest,
But where the stormy waters rolled below,
And, pealed above, the thunders of his foe;
That no calm sleep should smooth a slow decay
Till scarce the mourners knew life passed away, 90
But stifling agony and gushing gore
Should fill the moments of his parting hour;
He knew--but smiled--for, as that polar star
A thousand years--as then--had shone from far,
While all had changed beneath its changless
    sky--   95
So, what to earth belonged with earth should
    die;
While he--all soul--would take a glorious
    flight,
Like yon--through time--a still and steady
    light;
Like yon, to Englands sailors given to be

100--The guardian of her fleets--the Pole Star of the
      sea!   100

        A Vessel lies in Englands proudest port
    Where venerating thousands oft resort,
    And, though ships round her anchor, bold and
        gay,
    They seek her only, in her grim decay;
    They tread her decks--all tenantless--with
        eyes   105
    Of awe struck musing--not of vague suprise;
    They enter in a cabin, dark and low,
    And oer its time-stained floor with reverence
        bow:
    Yet nought appears but rafters, worn and old,
    No mirrored walls--no cornice bright with
        gold: 110
    Yon packet steaming through its smoky haze
    Seems fitter far to suit the wonderers gaze;
    But--'tis not present time they look at now,
    They look at six and thirty years ago:
    They see where fell the 'Thunderbolt of war'   115
    On the storm swollen waves of TRAFALGAR:
    They read a tale to wake their pain and pride
    In that brass plate, engraved--"HERE NELSON
        DIED!"

        As 'wise Cornelius' from his mirror, bade
    A magic veil of formless clouds to fade,   120
    Till gleamed before the awe struck gazer's
        eye
    Scenes still to come, or passed for ever by;
    So let me, standing in this darksome room,
    Roll back a generations gathered gloom,
    To shew the morn and evening of a sun   125
The memory of whose light still cheers old
        England on.

        Where ceaseless showers obscure the misty
            vale,
    And winter winds through leafless osiers wail,
    Beside a stream with swollen waves rushing
        wild,
    Sits--calm amid the storm--yon fair haired
        child.   130
    He cannot cross, so full the waters flow--
    So bold his little heart, he will not go;
    Patient of hinderances, but deeming still
    Nothing impossible to stedfast will;
    While from the old Rectory, his distant home,   135
    'All hands' to seek their darling truant roam,

                        256

And <u>one</u>--his mother--with instinctive love,
Like that which guides aright the timid dove--
Finds her dear child--his cheeks all rain
        bedewed,
The unconscious victim of those tempests rude, 140
And, panting, asks him why he tarries there?
Does he not dread his fate--his danger fear?
That child replies--all smiling in the storm--
"Mother--what is this Fear?--I never saw its
        form!"
        Ah! oft, since then, he heard the tempests
                sound,   145
Oft saw far mightier waters surging round,
Oft stood unshaken--death and danger near,
Yet saw no more than then the phantom Fear!

        Now wave the wand again--Be Englands shore
150--   Sunk far behind the horizon's billowy roar;   150
And Lo! again, this cabin dark and grim,
Beheld through smoke wreaths, indistinct and
        dim!
"Where is my child" methinks the mother cries:
No! far away that mothers tombstone lies!
Where is her child? He is not surely here,   155
Where reign, undoubted sovereigns, Death and
        Fear?
        A prostrate form lies, neath a double shade
By stifling smoke and blackened timber made,
With head that backward rolls, wheneer it
        tries
From its hard, thunder shaken bed to rise.   160
Methought I saw a brightness on its breast,
As if in royal orders decked and dressed;
But its wan face, its grey locks crimson died,
Have surely nought to do with power or pride;
For death his mandate writes on its white
        brow--   165
"Thine earthly course is run--come with me
        now!"
Stern faces oer this figure weeping bend
As they had lost a father and a friend,
While, all unanswered, burst yon conquering
        cheer,
Since He--their glorious cheif is dying here.   170
<u>They</u> heed it not--but, with rekindled eye,
As He, even Death would conquer ere he die,
<u>He</u> asks--"Where was't?--What deed had England
        done?
What ships had struck?--Was victory nobly won?
Did Collingwood--did Trowbridge face the foe?   175

Whose ship was first in fight--who dealt the
    sternest blow?"
      I could not hear the answer--lost and
        drowned
In that tremendous crash of earthquake sound,
But, I could see the dying Hero smile,
As pain and sickness, vanquished--bowed,
    awhile,   180
To <u>soul</u>, that soared--prophetic--oer their
    sway,
And saw, beyond deaths night Fames glorious
    day;
That deemed no bed so easy as a tomb
Neath old Westminster's hero sheltering gloom;
That knew the laurel round his dying brow   185
Should bloom for ever as it flourished now;
That felt, this pain once oer, to him was
    given
Honour on earth and happiness in heaven:
That was a smile as sweet as ever shone
Oer his wan face in childhoods sunshine gone;   190
A smile which asked as plainly--"What is
    fear?" As then unnoticed, though as then,
    so near.

    Now faint and fainter rolled the cannons
      sound
On his dull ear--each object, wavering round,
Mocked his dim eye--nor face, nor form seemed
    known;   195
He only felt that his great work was done,
That one brave heart was yearning at his side,
So, murmering "Kiss me Hardy"--NELSON smiling
    died!

    Oh! When <u>I</u> think upon that awful day
200--   When all I know or love must fade away--   200
When, after weeks or months of agony,
Without one earthly hope to succor me,
I must lie back, and close my eyes upon
The farewell beams of the descending sun;
Must feel the warmth I never more may know   205
Mock my fast freezing frame of pain and woe,
Must feel a light is brightening up the sky
As shining clouds and summer airs pass by;
While I--a shrouded corpse, my bed must leave
To lie forgotten in my narrow grave,   210
The world all smiles above my covering clay;
I silent--senseless--festering fast away:
And, if my children, mid the churchyard stones,

Years hence, shall see a few brown mouldering
    bones;
Perhaps a scull, that seems, with hideous
    grin,   215
To mock at all this world takes pleasure in,
They'll only from the unsightly relics turn,
Or into ranker grass the fragments spurn;
Nor know that these are the remains of him
Whom they'll remember, like a faded dream,   220
As one who danced them on a fathers knee
In long departed hours of happy infancy.

Then--then I ask--with humble--earnest
    prayer--
O Mighty Being! give my strength to dare
The certain fate, the dreadful hour to bear,   225
As thou didst, NELSON! mid the battles roar
Lying, pale with mortal sickness--choked with
    gore,
Yet, thinking of thine England--saved, that
    hour,
From her great foemans empire crushing power;
Of thy poor frame so gladly given, to free   230
Her thousand happy homes from slavery;
Of stainless name for her--of endless fame for
    thee.
    Give me--Great God!--give all who own thy
        sway
Soul to command, and body to obey:
When dangers frown--a heart to beat more
    high;   235
When doubts confuse--a more observant eye;
When fortunes change--a power to bear their
    blight;
When Death arrives--to life, a calm 'good
    night'.
We are Thy likeness--Give us on to go
Through Lifes long march of restlessness and
    woe,   240
Resolved thy Image shall be sanctified
By holy confidence--not human pride.
We have our task set--Let us do it well;
Nor barter ease on earth with pain in Hell.
We have our Talents, from thy treasury
    given--   245
Let us return Thee good account in heaven.
    I know this world,--this age is marching
        on;
Each year more wonderous than its parent gone;
And shall I lag behind it, sad and slow?
With wish to rise but void of power to go?   250

250--   Forbid it God! Who hast made me what I am;
         Nor, framed to honour, let me sink in shame;
         But, as yon Moon, which <u>seems</u> mid clouds to
             glide,
         Whose dark breasts ever strive her beams to
             hide,
         Shines, <u>really</u>, heedless of their earth born
             sway,   255
         In her own heaven of glory, far away;
         So may my soul which seems, to eyes below,
         Involved in lifes thick mists of care and woe,
         Far--far remote--from holy calm look down
         On clouds of fleecy shine or stormy frown;   260
         And while mankind its beams so shaded see,
         Gaze steadfast on this lifes inconstancy,
     And find itself--like her--at home in heaven
             with Thee!

     262 lines
                           NORTHANGERLAND.
                           [Fall 1842]

MS: B(2), B(1)
First Publication: BST 1927
Text: The numbers in the left margin are Branwell's.

128   **THORP GREEN.**

PBB
March 30th I sit this evening far away
1843   From all I used to know
               And nought reminds my soul to day
                   Of happy long ago

               Unwelcome cares unthought of fears   5
                   Around my room arise
               I seek for suns of former years
                   But clouds oercast my skies

               Yes--Memory wherefore does thy voice
                   Bring old times back to view   10
               As Thou wouldst bid me not rejoice
                   In thoughts and prospects new

               Ill thank thee Memory in the hour
                   When troubled thoughts are mine
               For thou like suns in Aprils shower   15
                   On shadowy scenes wilt shine

                           260

Ill thank thee when approaching death
Would quench lifes feeble ember
For thou wouldst even renew my breath
With thy sweet word remember!   20

MS: E
First Publication: BST 1927
Text: ll. 1-8 are canceled in pencil and are followed by two
      crossed-out lines (canceled in ink):
            I seek for what has smiled one hour
            And in the next has flown
      ll. 9-20 are in pencil and may have been added later

129   O'er Grafton Hill the blue heaven smiled
                 serene,
On Grafton Hill the grass waved bright and green,
Round Grafton Hill, Old England's noblest vale
Opened to summer's sun and balmy gale,
Southward three towers crowned England's noblest
          pile   5
At York, that oldest sovereign of our Isle.
Eastward, long wolds formed barriers to a sea
That bursts upon the shores of liberty,
As wave on wave the ocean Queen regains
From shores of war and toil and slaves and chains.   10
Northward, a loftier range, more scarred and riven,
Claimed kindred with a farther, sterner heaven;
And though from "Caledonia, stern and wild",
Remote, proclaimed it Caledonia's child.
Westward, blue Whernside, o'er the source of Nidd,   15
Still mightier brothers with his forehead hid;
And Romillies Moor, with far extended length,
O'erlooked the fountains of our county's strength.
      Still nearer Grafton, Ripon's holy fane,
Like York's, drew heaven toward our earth again: 20
And, girt by Studley's woods, the walls that now
Like sunbeams shining upon winter snow
Mock, with their ruin, splendours long since gone,
And say one fate awaits on flesh and stone.

                                        [1843-45]

MS: Unknown; last known to have been in the possession of
     Mrs. C. B. Branwell
First Publication: Flintoff
Text: l. 6: Hatfield changed "And" to "At," with a question
       mark in the left-hand margin.

130   I saw a picture yesterday
           Of him who died for me
    Which vainly struggled to display
           His mortal agony.
    And, though the painters name was old   5
           And high his meed of fame
    I scarce could guess the tale he told
           Or deem him worth acclaim.

    To-day I saw a picture too
           With lighter pencil drawn   10
    Which to its subject not more true
           Gave midnight hues to morn;
    And, if I blame Pietro's skill
           In painting features gone
    I must, believe her feebler, still   15
           Who could not paint her own!

    Her effort shews a picture made
           To contradict its meaning.
    Where should be sunshine painting shade
           And smiles with sadness screening   20
    Where God has given a cheerful view
           A gloomy vista showing
    Where heart and face, are fair and true
           A shade of doubt bestowing

    Ah Lady if to me you give   25
           The power your sketch to adorn
    How little of it shall I leave
           Save smiles that shine like morn
    Ide keep the hue of happy light
           That shines from summer skies   30
    Ide drive the shades from smiles so bright
           And dry such shining eyes

    Ide give a calm to one whose heart
           has banished calm from mine
    Ide brighten up Gods work of art   35
           Where thou hast dimmed its shine
    And as the wages I should ask
           For such a happy toil
    Ill name them--far beyond my task--
           THY PRESENCE AND THY SMILE

                     [1844/45]

MS: E
First Publication: SHB C and B
Text: 1. 5: "Was" has been changed to "were," but the hand
             is not Branwell's

l. 14: "In painting" canceled but no alternative
provided

131   The Emigrant.

                      ===========

When sink from sight the landmarks of our Home
    And--all the bitterness of farewells oer--
We yield our spirit unto Ocean's foam,
    And in the newborn life which lies before,
    On far Columbian or Australian shore   5
Strive to exchange time past for time to come;
    How melancholy then--if morn restore
[Less welcome than the nights forgetful gloom]
    Old England's blue hills to our sight again,
While we, our thoughts seemed weaning from her sky-- 10
    The Pang--that wakes an almost silenced pain.
Thus, when the Sickman lies resigned to die,
    A well loved voice, a well remembered strain
Lets Time break harshly on Eternity.

                              Northangerland.
                              May 26th.
                              1845.

MS: B(2)
First Publication: Leyland II
Text: 1. 8: The square brackets are Branwell's.

132 'When, after his long day, consumed in toil,
         'Neath the scarce welcome shade of unknown
                 trees,
     Upturning thanklessly a foreign soil,
         The lonely exile seeks his evening ease,--
         'Tis not those tropic woods his spirit sees;   5
     Nor calms, to him, that heaven, this world's
                 turmoil;
         Nor cools his burning brow that spicy breeze.
     Ah no! the gusty clouds of England's isle
         Bring music wafted on their stormy wind,
     And on its verdant meads, night's shadows lower, 10
         While "Auld Lang Syne" the darkness calls to
                 mind.

                         263

Thus, when the demon Thirst, beneath his power
    The wanderer bows,--to feverish sleep consigned,
He hears the rushing rill, and feels the cooling
    shower.'

MS: Unknown
First Publication: Leyland II

133   "Poor mourner--sleep." "I cannot sleep--
    My mind, though wearied, wanders on"--
"Then, Mourner, weep." "I cannot weep,
    For eyes and tears are turned to stone".

Oh, might my footsteps find some rest;   5
    Oh might my eyes with tears run oer
Oh might my life-thoughts leave my breast
    Could they my life's sweet love restore!

But if I might in silence mourn,
    Apart from canting sympathy;   10
Form man's sour scoff and bitter scorn,
    From woman's heartless flattery,

Then, nothing nearer Paradise
    Need, as a heritage, be mine;
For I've survived unreal joys;   15
    and cannot bear their dreamlike shine.

I have been given oer to grief,
    Nor could I live were sorrow gone;
So all my solace or relief
    Must be, to drop my tears alone.   20

To live in pleasure would be now
    To live forgetful--every thought
Of all that I have known below
    Must be forsaken or forgot--

And, Oh, can I, departed years,   25
    Forget, as though they had not been!
Though, if I <u>must</u> remember, tears
    Will dim the storm and sunshine scene

I have no choice; However bright
    May burst the blaze of July's sun   30

264

T'will only give a far off sight
   Like breaks in clouds, of pleasures gone.

However young and lovely, round,
   Fresh forms may court my frozen eye,
They'll only desecrate the ground   35
   Where fairer far, corrupting lie.

And voices sweet as musics thrill,
   And laughter light as marriage strain
Will only wake a ghostly chill
   As if the buried spoke again.   40

All--all is over--Friend or lover
   Need never seek for refuge here;
Though they may sweep my heart strings over
   No music will awake the air!

I'm dying away in dull decay,   45
   I feel and find the sands are down,
That evening's latest lingering ray
   At last from my wild heaven has flown

I feel and find that I am cast
   From hope and peace and power and pride   50
A withered leaf on autumn's blast--
   A scattered wreck on ocean's tide!

                             Northangerland
               Unfinished.
                              [1845]

MS: B(1), B(2)
First Publication: Shorter EJB 1910
Text: l. 11: "From" obviously intended

134 Calm and clear the day, declining
   Lends its brightness to the air,
With a slanted sunlight shining,
   Mixed with shadows stretching far:
Slow the river pales its glancing,   5
Soft its waters cease their dancing,
As the hush of eve, advancing,
   Tells man's toils that sleep is near.

Why is such a silence given
   To this summer day's decay?   10
Does our earth feel aught of heaven--

Can the voice of nature pray?
And, when daylight's toils are done,
Before its mighty Maker's throne
Can it, for noontide sunshine gone,   15
    I'ts debt, with smiles repay?

Quiet airs of sacred gladness
    Breathing through these woodlands wild,
Oer the whirl of human madness
    Spread the slumbers of a child: 20
Those surrounding sweeps of trees
Swaying to the evening breeze,
With a voice like distant sea's
    Making music mild:

'Woodchurch Hall above them lowering   25
    Dark against the pearly sky,
With its clustered chimneys towering,
    Wakes the wind while passing by:
And in old ancestral glory,
Round that scene of ancient story,   30
All its oak-trees, huge and hoary,
    Wave their boughs on high.

''Mid those gables there is one--
    The soonest dark when day is gone--
Which, when autumn winds are strongest,   35
    Moans the most and echoes longest.
There--with her curls like sunset air,
Like it all balmy, bright, and fair--
Sits Harriet, with her cheek reclined
    On arm as white as mountain snow;   40
While, with a bursting swell, her mind
    Fills with thoughts of "Long Ago."

'As from yon spire a funeral bell,
Wafting through heaven its mourning knell,
Warns man that life's uncertain day   45
Like lifeless Nature's must decay;
And tells her that the warning deep
Speaks where her own forefathers sleep,
And where destruction makes a prey
    Of what was once this world to her,   50
But which--like other gods of clay--
    Has cheated its blind worshipper:
With swelling breast and shining eyes
That seem to chide the thoughtless skies,
She strives in words to find relief   55
For long-pent thoughts of mellowed grief.

266

'"Time's clouds roll back, and memory's light
Bursts suddenly upon my sight;
For thoughts, which words could never tell,
Find utterance in that funeral bell.   60
My heart, this eve, seemed full of feeling,
Yet nothing clear to me revealing;
Sounding in breathings undefined
AEolian music to my mind:
    Then strikes that bell, and all subsides   65
Into a harmony, which glides
As sweet and solemn as the dream
Of a remembered funeral hymn.
    This scene seemed like the magic glass,
Which bore upon its clouded face   70
Strange shadows that deceived the eye
With forms defined uncertainly;
That Bell is old Agrippa's wand,
Which parts the clouds on either hand,
And shows the pictured forms of doom   75
Momently brightening through the gloom:
Yes--shows a scene of bygone years--
Opens a fount of sealed-up tears--
And wakens memory's pensive thought
To visions sleeping--not forgot.   80
It brings me back a summer's day,
Shedding like this its parting ray,
With skies as shining and serene,
And hills as blue, and groves as green.

'"Ah, well I recollect that hour,   85
    When I sat, gazing, just as now,
Toward that ivy-mantled tower
    Among these flowers which wave below!
No--not these flowers--they're long since dead,
    And flowers have budded, bloomed, and gone,   90
Since those were plucked which gird the head
    Laid underneath yon churchyard stone!
I stooped to pluck a rose that grew
    Beside this window, waving then;
But back my little hand withdrew,   95
    From some reproof of inward pain;
For she who loved it was not there
    To check me with her dove-like eye,
And something bid my heart forbear
    Her favourite rosebud to destroy.   100
Was it that bell--that funeral bell,
    Sullenly sounding on the wind?
Was it that melancholy knell
    Which first to sorrow woke my mind?
I looked upon my mourning dress   105
    Till my heart beat with childish fear,

And--frightened at my loneliness--
   I watched, some well-known sound to hear.
But all without lay silent in
   The sunny hush of afternoon,   110
And only muffled steps within
   Passed slowly and sedately on.
I well can recollect the awe
   With which I hastened to depart;
   And, as I ran, the instinctive start   115
With which my mother's form I saw,
Arrayed in black, with pallid face,
   And cheeks and 'kerchief wet with tears,
As down she stooped to kiss my face
   And quiet my uncertain fears.   120

'"She led me, in her mourning hood,
   Through voiceless galleries, to a room,
'Neath whose black hangings crowded stood,
   With downcast eyes and brows of gloom,
My known relations; while--with head   125
Declining o'er my sister's bed--
My father's stern eye dropt a tear
Upon the coffin resting there.
My mother lifted me to see
What might within that coffin be;   130
And, to this moment, I can feel
The voiceless gasp--the sickening chill--
With which I hid my whitened face
In the dear folds of her embrace;
For hardly dared I turn my head   135
Lest its wet eyes should view that bed.
   'But, Harriet,' said my mother mild,
'Look at your sister and my child
One moment, ere her form be hid
For ever 'neath its coffin lid!'   140
   I heard the appeal, and answered too;
For down I bent to bid adieu;
But, as I looked, forgot affright
In mild and magical delight.

'"There lay she then, as now she lies--   145
   For not a limb has moved since then--
In dreamless slumber closed, those eyes
   That never more might wake again.
She lay, as I had seen her lie
   On many a happy night before,   150
When I was humbly kneeling by--
   Whom she was teaching to adore:
Oh, just as when by her I prayed,
   And she to heaven sent up my prayer,
She lay with flowers about her head--   155

Though formal grave-clothes hid her hair!
Still did her lips the smile retain
    Which parted them when hope was high,
Still seemed her brow as smoothed from pain
    As when all thought she could not die.   160
And, though her bed looked cramped and strange,
    Her too bright cheek all faded now,
My young eyes scarcely saw a change
    From hours when moonlight paled her brow.
And yet I felt--and scarce could speak--   165
    A chilly face, a faltering breath,
When my hand touched the marble cheek
    Which lay so passively beneath.
In fright I gasped, 'Speak, Caroline!'
    And bade my sister to arise;   170
But answered not her voice to mine,
    Nor ope'd her sleeping eyes.
I turned toward my mother then
    And prayed on her to call;
But, though she strove to hide her pain,   175
    It forced her tears to fall.
She pressed me to her aching breast
    As if her heart would break,
And bent in silence o'er the rest
    Of one she could not wake: 180
The rest of one, whose vanished years
    Her soul had watched in vain;
The end of mother's hopes and fears,
    And happiness and pain.

'"They came--they pressed the coffin lid   185
    Above my Caroline,
And then, I felt, for ever hid
    My sister's face from mine!
There was one moment's wildered start--
    One pang remembered well--   190
When first from my unhardened heart
    The tears of anguish fell:
That swell of thought which seemed to fill
    The bursting heart, the gushing eye,
While fades all present good or ill   195
    Before the shades of things gone by.
All else seems blank--the mourning march,
    The proud parade of woe,
The passage 'neath the churchyard arch,
    The crowd that met the show.   200
My place or thoughts amid the train
I strive to recollect, in vain--
    I could not think or see:
I cared not whither I was borne:

And only felt that death had torn   205
    My Caroline from me.

'"Slowly and sadly, o'er her grave,
The organ peals its passing stave,
And, to its last dark dwelling-place,
    The corpse attending mourners bear,   210
While, o'er it bending, many a face
    'Mongst young companions shows a tear.
I think I glanced toward the crowd
    That stood in musing silence by,
And even now I hear the sound   215
    Of some one's voice amongst them cry--
'I am the Resurrection and the Life--
    He who believes in me shall never die!'

'"Long years have never worn away
The unnatural strangeness of that day,   220
When I beheld--upon the plate
Of grim death's mockery of state--
That well-known word, that long-loved name,
Now but remembered like the dream
Of half-forgotten hymns divine,   225
My sister's name--my Caroline!
    Down, down, they lowered her, sad and slow,
Into her narrow house below:
And deep, indeed, appeared to be
That one glimpse of eternity,   230
Where, cut from life, corruption lay,
Where beauty soon should turn to clay!
Though scarcely conscious, hotly fell
The drops that spoke my last farewell;
And wild my sob, when hollow rung   235
The first cold clod above her flung,
When glitter was to turn to rust,
'Ashes to ashes, dust to dust!'

'"How bitter seemed that moment when,
    Earth's ceremonies o'er,   240
We from the filled grave turned again
    To leave her evermore;
And, when emerging from the cold
    Of damp, sepulchral air,
As I turned, listless to behold   245
    The evening fresh and fair,
How sadly seemed to smile the face
    Of the descending sun!
How seemed as if his latest race
    Were with that evening run!   250
There sank his orb behind the grove
    Of my ancestral home,

With heaven's unbounded vault above
    To canopy his tomb.
Yet lingering sadly and serene,   255
    As for his last farewell,
To shine upon those wild woods green
    O'er which he'd loved to dwell.

'"I lost him, and the silent room,
    Where soon at rest I lay,   260
Began to darken, 'neath the gloom
    Of twilight's dull decay;
So, sobbing as my heart would break,
    And blind with gushing eyes,
Hours seemed whole nights to me awake,   265
    And day as 'twould not rise.
I almost prayed that I might die--
    But then the thought would come
That, if I did, my corpse must lie
    In yonder dismal tomb;   270
Until, methought, I saw its stone,
    By moonshine glistening clear,
While Caroline's bright form alone
    Kept silent watching there:
All white with angel's wings she seemed,   275
    And indistinct to see;
But when the unclouded moonlight beamed
    I saw her beckon me,
And fade, thus beckoning, while the wind
    Around that midnight wall,   280
To me--now lingering years behind--
    Seemed then my sister's call!

'"And thus it brought me back the hours
    When we, at rest together,
Used to lie listening to the showers   285
    Of wild December weather;
Which, when, as oft, they woke in her
    The chords of inward thought,
Would fill with pictures that wild air,
    From far-off memories brought;   290
So, while I lay, I heard again
    Her silver-sounding tongue,
Rehearsing some remembered strain
    Of old times long agone!
And, flashed across my spirit's sight,   295
    What she had often told me--
When, laid awake on Christmas night,
    Her sheltering arms would fold me--
About that midnight-seeming day,
    Whose gloom o'er Calvary thrown,   300
Showed trembling Nature's deep dismay

At what her sons had done:
When sacred Salem's murky air
    Was riven with the cry,
Which told the world how mortals dare   305
    The Immortal crucify;
When those who, sorrowing, sat afar,
    With aching heart and eye,
Beheld their great Redeemer there,
    'Mid sneers and scoffings die;   310
When all His earthly vigour fled,
When thirsty faintness bowed His head,
When His pale limbs were moistened o'er
With deathly dews and dripping gore,
When quivered all His worn-out frame,   315
As Death, triumphant, quenched life's flame,
When upward gazed His glazing eyes
To those tremendous-seeming skies,
When burst His cry of agony--
'My God!--my God!--hast Thou forsaken me!'   320
    My youthful feelings startled then,
As if the temple, rent in twain,
Horribly pealing on my ear
With its deep thunder note of fear,
Wrapping the world in general gloom,   325
As if her God's were Nature's tomb;
While sheeted ghosts before my gaze
Passed, flitting 'mid the dreary maze,
As if rejoicing at the day
When death--their king--o'er Heaven had sway.   330
    In glistening charnel damps arrayed,
They seemed to gibber round my head,
Through night's drear void directing me
Toward still and solemn Calvary,
Where gleamed that cross with steady shine   335
Around the thorn-crowned head divine--
A flaming cross--a beacon light
To this world's universal night!
It seemed to shine with such a glow,
And through my spirit piercing so,   340
That, pantingly, I strove to cry
For her, whom I thought slumbered by,
And hide me from that awful shine
In the embrace of Caroline!
    I wakened in the attempt--'twas day;   345
The troubled dream had fled away;
'Twas day--and I, alone, was laid
In that great room and stately bed;
No Caroline beside me! Wide
And unrelenting swept the tide   350
Of death 'twixt her and me!"

```
                        There paused
        Sweet Harriet's voice, for such thoughts caused--'
              .      .      .      .      .      .      .
```

                                              [1845]

MS: B(2), Unknown
First Publication: Leyland I

135   Before Our mighty Makers throne
               Let us submissive kneel in prayer,
           And strive for scarlet sins to' atone
               For we must pray that He may hear.

           Deep--Mighty Lord--be our despair--   5
               Distinct our consciousness of sin--
           Lest from thine eyes our outside fair
               Should strive to hide our crimes within.

           We know that we are formed for crime,
               That through our lifetime crimes we form,   10
           Believing, madly, all the time
               That mercy sheilds us from the storm;

           Or, as long since, in Shinars plain,
               Rebellious men their Tower of pride
           Raised up, in hopes, by labour vain   15
               That thus thy power might be defied,

           So we, by impious moral code
               Or ever changing creeds of faith,
           Think we may climb the narrow road,
               Elude thy arm, and cheat our death.   20

           But, Oh when we have gained Heaven's gate,
               The eternal crown intent to win,
           Long must we knock and, lingering, wait
               Ere watching angels let us in!

           "Hast thou repented of thy sin?"   25
               What Soul--my God can answer then?
           "Go back--Thy path again begin,
               And weep and watch and wait again!"

           But if returning be denied
               By Deaths grim gateway, closed behind,   30
           Where flies our heaven, our hope, our pride?
               They fly like chaff before the wind!

                              273

Lord, let us know our treacherous mind
    Even though that knowledge bring despair;
For, wandering thus, accursed and blind,   35
    We dare not hope that Thou wilt hear!"

[Summer 1845]

MS: D(1), B(2), K
First Publication: Shorter 1923

136   **REAL REST.**

    I see a corpse upon the waters lie,
With eyes turned, swelled and sightless, to the
        sky,
And arms outstretched, to move as wave on wave
Upbears it in its boundless billowy grave.
Not Time, but Ocean thins its flowing hair;   5
Decay, not sorrow, lays its forehead bare;
Its members move, but not in thankless toil,
For seas are milder than this world's turmoil;
Corruption robs its lips and cheeks of red,
But wounded vanity grieves not the dead;   10
And, though those members hasten to decay,
No pang of suffering takes their strength away;
With untormented eye, and heart, and brain,
Through calm and storm it floats across the main:
Though love and joy have perished long ago,   15
Its bosom suffers not one pang of woe;
Though weeds and worms its cherished beauty hide,
It feels not wounded vanity or pride;
Though journeying towards some far off shore,
It needs no care or purse to float it o'er;   20
Though launched in voyage for Eternity
It need not think upon what is to be;
Though naked, helpless, and companionless,
It feels not poverty or knows distress.
    Oh corpse! If thou could'st tell my aching mind   25
What scenes of sorrow thou hast left behind;
How sad the life which, breathing, thou hast led,
How free from strife thy sojourn with the dead;
I could assume thy place--could long to be
A world-wide wanderer oer the waves with thee!   30
    I have a misery where thou hast none;
My heart beats bursting while thine lies like
        stone;
My veins throb wild while thine are dead and dry;

274

And woes, not waters, dim thy restless eye:
Thou longest not with one well loved to be,   35
And absence does not break a chain with thee:
No sudden agonies dart through thy breast;
Thou hast what all men covet, REAL REST.
   I have an outward frame unlike to thine,
Warm with young life--not cold in death's decline;   40
An eye that sees the sunny light of heaven--
A heart by pleasure thrilled--by anguish riven--
But in exchange for thy untroubled calm,
Thy gift of cold oblivions healing balm,
I'd give my youth--my health--my life to come,   45
And share thy slumbers in thy ocean tomb.

                              NORTHANGERLAND.
                              [November 8, 1845]

MS: Unknown
First Publication: HG

137   **Lydia Gisborne**

              "Cannot my soul depart--
                    Where will it fly?"
              Asks my tormented heart,
                    Willing to die.
              When will this restlessness,   5
              Tossing in sleeplessness--
              Stranger to happiness--
                    Slumbering lie?

              Cannot I chase away
                    Life in my tomb,   10
              Rather than pass away
                    Lifetime in gloom,
              With sorrows employing
              Their arts in destroying
              The power of enjoying   15
                    The comforts of home?

              Home, it is not with me
                    Bright as of yore
              Joys are forgot with me
                    Taught to deplore.   20
              My home has ta'en its rest
              In an afflicted breast

                              275

That I have often pressed
But--may no more.

[late 1845]

MS: Unknown; last known to have been in the possession of
     Mrs. C. B. Branwell
First Publication: Flintoff

138   PENMAENMAWR.

These winds, these clouds, this chill November
        storm
Bring back again thy tempest-beaten form
To eyes that look upon yon dreary sky
As, late, they looked on thy sublimity,
When I, more troubled than thy restless sea,   5
Found, on its waves, companionship with thee.
'Mid mists thou frownedst over Arvon's shore--
'Mid tears I watched thee over ocean's roar--
And thy blue front, by thousand storms laid bare,
Claimed kindred with a heart worn down by care.   10
No smile hadst thou, o'er smiling fields aspiring,
And none had I, from smiling scenes retiring;
Blackness, 'mid sunlight, tinged thy slaty brow,
I, 'mid sweet music, looked as dark as thou;
Old Scotland's song, o'er murmuring surges born,   15
Of "times departed--never to return,"
Was echoed back in mournful tones from thee,
And found an echo, quite as sad, in me:
Waves, clouds and shadows moved in restless change
Around, above, and on thy rocky range,   20
But seldom saw that sovereign front of thine
Changes more quick than those which passed o'er
        mine!
And as wild winds and human hands, at length
Have turned to scattered stones the mighty strength
Of that old fort, whose belt of boulders grey,   25
Roman or Saxon legions held at bay,
So had, methought, the young unshaken nerve
That, when WILL wished, no doubt could cause to
        swerve,
That on its vigour ever placed reliance--
That to its sorrows sometimes bade defiance,   30
Now left my spirit, like thyself, old hill,
With head defenceless against human ill;
And, as thou long hast looked upon the wave

276

That takes, but gives not, like a churchyard grave,
I, like life's course, through either's weary range, 35
Never know rest from ceaseless strife and change.
    But, PENMAENMAWR, a better fate was thine
Through all its shades, than that which darkened
    mine.
No quick thoughts thrilled through thy gigantic
    mass
Of woe for what might be, or is, or was: 40
Thou had'st no memory of the glorious hour
When Britain rested on thy giant power:
Thou had'st no feeling for the verdant slope
That leant on thee as man's heart leans on hope:
The pastures, chequered o'er with cot and tree, 45
Though thou wert Guardian, got no smile from thee;
Old Ocean's wrath their charm might overwhelm,
But thou could'st still keep thy unshaken realm--
While I felt flashes of an inward feeling,
As fierce as those thy craggy form revealing 50
In nights when blinding gleams and deafening roar
Hurls back thy echo to old Mona's shore.
I knew a flower whose leaves were meant to bloom
Till Death should snatch it to adorn the tomb,
Now, blanching 'neath the blight of hopeless grief 55
With never blooming and yet living leaf;
A flower on which my mind would wish to shine,
If but one beam could break from mind like mine:
I had an ear which could on accents dwell
That might as well say "perish" as "farewell"-- 60
An eye which saw, far off, a tender form
Beaten, unsheltered, by affliction's storm--
An arm--a lip--that trembled to embrace
My Angel's gentle breast and sorrowing face--
A mind that clung to Ouse's fertile side 65
While tossing--objectless--on Menai's tide!
    Oh soul! that draw'st yon mighty hill and me
Into communion of vague unity,
Tell me, can I obtain thy stony brow
That fronts the storm, as much unbroken now 70
As when it once upheld the fortress proud,
Now gone, like its own morning cap of cloud?
Its breast is stone. Can I have one of steel,
T'endure--inflict--defend--yet never feel?
It stood as firm when haughty Edward's word 75
Gave hill and dale to England's fire and sword,
As when white sails and steam-smoke tracked the
    sea,
And all the world breathed peace, but waves and me.
    Let me, like it, arise o'er mortal care;
All evils bear, yet never know despair; 80
Unshrinking face the griefs I now deplore,

And stand, through storm and shine, like moveless
    PENMAENMAWR.

                                    NORTHANGERLAND.
                                    [December 20, 1845]

MS: Unknown
First Publication: HG

139   While fabled scenes and fancied forms
           And leanings upon thoughts laid by
       With visionary calms or storms
           May strive to cheat my memory
           Still--still before my inward eye   5
       Thou my lifes sunbeam shinest afar
           And mid a drear December sky
       Givs't comfort to thy wanderer

       Yet hardly <u>comfort</u> for that word
           Speaks too much of security   10
       And peace--two names too long unheard
           To own aquaintanceship with me
           They would be mine were I with thee
       But while dissevered I'm resigned
           If thy far light can let me see   15
       One glimpse where life would keep me blind

                              [late 1845/early 1846]

MS: E
First Publication: SHB C and B

140   <u>An echo from Indian Cannon</u>

       Mans heart feels manly sorrow
           And mankind's birthright pain,
       But Hope still says tomorrow
           May yet avenge the slain
       Whose bloodied breasts are lying   5
           Where Scindes wild waters roam
       Whose last sad pangs in dying
           Are echoed back from home.

We mourn the brave who perished
 We grieve that SALE has died   10
But whom alive we cherished
 When dead can be our pride
And ALBUERA'S story
 Sir Henry's hoary hair
Shall not have gilt with glory   15
 More bright than Indian war.

Long since that bold heart breasted
 The iron hail of fight,
When that strong arm arrested
 The panic spread of flight   20
And ages cold December
 Chill not the pent up glow
The Hero's veins remember
 The pulse of "Long ago".

So once again uniting   25
 The riven ranks of war
His sinews nerved for fighting
 Call victory from despair.
Then rise our pride the higher
 When we our Hardinge name   30
To feel, a hero's fire
 Nor wounds nor years need tame!

       [March 1846]

MS: Unknown; last known to have been in the possession of
   Mrs. C. B. Branwell
First Publication: Flintoff
Text: Following the second stanza, at the bottom of the
   manuscript page, Branwell notes "Air by Baron Gluck
   Adapted to English words/ by P. B. Brontë (Air 'Non
   vi turbate no' or Mater divinae gloriae"

   After l. 4 appear the following heavily amended and
   seemingly canceled lines:
     And now when years of quiet (crossed out)
      slumber
     Have slept on former fields (the whole line is
   crossed out and replaced with)
     Have silenced storms of yore
   Fresh heaps of carnage cumber
     A far remoter shore

From Earth,--whose life-reviving April showers
Hide winter's withered grass 'neath springtide
     flowers,
And give, in each soft wind that drives the rain,
Promise of fields and forests green again--
I write to thee, the aspect of whose face   5
Can never change with change of time or place;
Whose eyes could look on India's wildest wars
More calmly than the hardiest son of Mars;
Whose lips, more firm than Stoic's long ago,
Would neither smile with joy nor blanch with woe;   10
Whose limbs could sufferings far more firmly bear
Than could heroic sinews strung for war;
Whose frame desires no good, nor shrinks from ill,
Nor feels distraction's throb nor pleasure's
     thrill.
     I write words to thee which thou wilt not read,   15
For thou wilt slumber on howe'er may bleed
The heart, which many think a worthless stone,
But which oft aches for its beloved one;
Nor, if God's life mysterious, from on high
Gave, once again, expression to thine eye,   20
Would'st thou thy father know, or feel that he
Gave life, and lineaments, and thoughts to thee,
For, when thou diedst, thy day was in its dawn,
And night still struggled with life's opening morn;
The twilight star of childhood, thy young days   25
Alone illumined, with its twinkling rays,
So sweet, yet feeble; given from those dusky skies,
Whose kindling, future noontide prophesies,
But tells us not that brightest noon may shroud
Our sunshine with a sudden veil of cloud.   30
     If, when thou gavest back the life which ne'er
To thee had given either hope or fear,
But peacefully had passed, nor asked if joy
Should cheer thy future path, or grief annoy--
If, then, thoud'st seen, upon a summer sea   35
One, once in features, as in blood like thee
On skies of azure blue and waters green
Commingled in the mist of summer's sheen,
Hopelessly gazing--ever hesitating
'Twixt miseries, e ery hour fresh fears creating   40
And joys--whate'er they cost--still doubly dear--
Those "troubled pleasures soon chastised by fear"--
If thou hadst seen him thou wouldst ne'er believe
That thou hadst yet known what it was to live.

Thy eyes could only see thy mother's breast,   45
Thy feelings only wish on that to rest;
It was thy world;--Thy food and sleep it gave,
And slight the change 'twixt it and childhood's
          grave.
Thou view'dst this world like one who, prone,
          reposes
Upon a plain and in a bed of roses   50
With nought to see save marbled skies above,
Nor hear, except the breezes in the grove:
I--thy life's source--was like a wanderer breasting
Keen mountain winds, and on a summit resting,
Whose rough rocks rose above the grassy mead   55
With sleet and north winds howling over head,
And nature, like a map, beneath him spread:
Far winding river, tree, and tower, and town,
Shadow and sunlight, 'neath his gaze mark'd down
By that mysterious hand which graves the plan   60
Of that drear country called the life of man.
    If seen, men's eyes would, loathing, shrink
          from thee,
And turn, perchance, with no disgust from me;
Yet thou had'st beauty, innocence, and smiles,
And now hast rest from this world's woes and wiles,   65
While I have restlessness and worrying care,
So, sure thy lot is brighter--happier--far!
    So may it prove--and, though thy ears may never
Hear these words sound beyond Death's darksome
          river
Not vainly, from the confines of despair   70
May rise a voice of joy that THOU art freed from
          care!

                              NORTHANGERLAND.
                              [April 18, 1846]

MS: Unknown
First Publication: HG

142 Tell me what is the most important page
     That, while with life our souls' rough war must
          wage,
     Should first attract, and last detain our eye,
     And live, till death, in our hearts' memory?
     Its face is blank, it holds no lettered word   5
     That our own eyes could see or hands record;
     Yet no engrossment from a lawyer's hand
     That funded millions, or a county's land,

Could grant to me, would such an interest give
As that blank page, unfilled while I shall live.   10
That page is stone or marble, and when I,
Life's fever over, lay me down to die,
Though my eyes close will to some sorrowing friend
Ope his to my beginning and my end.
'Twill only say that some man lived and died,   15
As I might say I saw, on ocean's tide,
A dim blue peak I never saw before,
Nor, since I lost it when the watery roar
Hid it from sight, shall ever see again.
Yet its small rock amid a howling main   20
Holds joys and sorrows, though such sorrowing
And joys, might shelter 'neath a sea-gull's wing.
So I, unknown, unthought of, may decline,
And no one care to think why I repine;
Or fancy that 'twixt "this year he was born"   25
And "this year to the dust we him return".
No long drear agony, no inward sorrow--
Joys of the past day--terrors for to-morrow--
Had intervened since he who's "clad in clay"
Was filled with hope as sunlight fills the day;   30
And now lies, conquered by abhorrent worms,
Though once unshaken by an hundred storms.

[Spring 1846]

MS: Unknown; last known to have been in the possession of
     Mrs. C. B. Branwell
First Publication: Flintoff

143   **LYDIA GISBORNE**

On Ouse's grassy banks, last Whitsuntide,
    I sat, with fears and pleasures in my soul
    Commingled, as "it roamed, without controul",
O'er present hours and through a future wide
Where love, methought, should keep my heart beside   5
    Her, whose own prison home I looked upon:
    But, as I looked, descended summer's sun:
And did not its descent my hopes deride?
The sky though blue was soon to change to grey--
    I, on that day next year, must own no smile--   10
And as those waves, to Humber far away,
    Were gliding--so, though that hour might beguile
        My Hopes, they too, to woe's far deeper sea,

282

Rolled past the shores of Joy's now dim and distant
    isle.

[June 1, 1846]

MS: Unknown; last known to have been in the possession of
     Mrs. C. B. Branwell
First Publication: Flintoff

144   **SONNET.**

When all our cheerful hours seem gone for ever--
    All lost that caused the body or the mind
    To nourish love or friendship for our Kind,
And Charons boat prepares, oer Lethe's river
Our souls to waft, and all our thoughts to sever   5
    From what was once lifes light, still there may
        be
    Some well loved bosom to whose pillow we
Could heartily our utter self deliver;
And if, toward her grave, Death's dreary road
    Our Darling's feet should walk--each step by her   10
Would draw our own steps to the same abode,
    And make a festival of sepulture;
For what gave joy, and joy to us has owed
Should Death affright us from when he would her
    restore?

                              Northangerland.
                              [Autumn 1846]

MS: E, F
First Publication: Leyland II

145   Think not that life is happiness,
                But deem it _duty_ joined with _care_.
            Implore for _Hope_ in your distress,
                And for your answers get _Despair_.
            Yet travel on, for Life's rough road   5
            May end, at last, in rest with GOD.

                              Northangerland.
                              [Autumn 1846]

MS: F
First Publication: Leyland II

146
            "Thy soul is flown,
             And clay alone
        Has nought to do with joy or care;
             So, if the light of life be gone
             There come no sorrows crowding on,   5
        And powerless lies DESPAIR!"

                                              [1846]

MS: E
First Publication: Leyland II

147   **Morley Hall.**
                      Leigh--Lancashire.
                      ─────────────

        When lifes youth, overcast by gathering
                clouds
    Of cares, that come like funeral-following crowds,
    Weary of that which is, and cannot see
    A sunbeam burst upon futurity,
    It tries to cast away the woes that are   5
    And borrow brighter joys from times afar.
    For, what our feet tread may have been a road
    By horse's hoofs pressed, neath a camels load,
    But, what we ran accross, in childhoods hours
    Were fields, presenting June with Mayday flowers   10
    So what was done, and born, if long ago,
    Will satisfy our heart though stained by tears of
            woe.
        When present sorrows every thought employ
    Our father's woes may take the garb of joy,
    And, knowing what our sires have undergone,   15
    Ourselves can smile, though weary, wandering on.
    For, if, our youth a thundercloud oershadows,
    Changing to barren swamps, lifes flowering meadows,
    We know that fiery flash and bursting peal
    Others, like us, were forcd to hear and feel,   20
    And while they moulder in a quiet grave,
    Robbed of all havings--worthless all they have--

                        284

We still with face erect behold the sun--
Have bright examples in what has been done
By head or hand--and in the times to come   25
May tread bright pathways to our gate of doom.
    So, if we gaze from our snug villa's door
By vines or honeysuckles covered oer,
Though we have saddening thoughts, we still can
        smile
In thinking our hut supersedes the pile   30
Whose turrets totter mid the woods before us,
And whose proud owners used to trample oer us;
All now by weeds and ivy overgrown
And touched by Time that hurls down stone from
        stone--
We gaze with scorn on what is worn away,   35
And never dream about our own decay.
    Thus while this Mayday cheers each flower and
        tree
Enlivening earth, and almost cheering me;
I half forget the mouldering moats of Leigh--
    Wide Lancashire has changed its babyhood,   40
As time makes saplings spring to timber wood,
But as grown men their childhood still remember
And think of summer in their dark December
So Manchester and Liverpool may wonder
And bow, to old Halls over which they ponder   45
Unknowing that mans spirit yearns to all
Which--once lost--prayers can never more recall:
The storied piles of mortar brick and stone
Where trade bids noise and gain to struggle on
Competing for the prize that Mammon gives--   50
Youth killed by toil and profits bought with
        lives--
Will not prevent the quiet thinking mind
From looking back to years when summer wind
Sang, not oer mills, but round ancestral Halls,
And, 'stead of engines steam gave dews from
        waterfalls.   55
    He who by brick built houses closely pent
That shew nought beautiful to sight or scent
Pines for green fields will cherish in his room
Some pining plant bereft of natural bloom
And, like the crowds which yonder factories hold,   60
Withering mid warmth and in its springtide old.
So Lancashire may fondly look upon
Her wrecks fast vanishing of ages gone
And while encroaching railroad street or mill
On every sided the smoky prospect fill   65
She yet may smile to see some tottering wall
Bring old times back like ancient Morley Hall
But towers that Leyland saw in times of yore

Are now like Leyland's works almost no more--
The Antiquarian's pages cobweb bound--   70
The antique mansion levelled with the ground.

       When all is gone that once gave food to pride
Man little cares for what time leaves beside,
And when an orchard and a moat half dry
Remain, sole relics of a power past by,   75
Should we not think of what ourselves shall be
And view our coffins in the stones of Leigh.
For what--within yon space was once the abode
Of peace or war to man, and fear of God
Is now the daily sport of shower or wind   80
And no aquaintance holds with human kind.
So we who can be loved, and love can give,
While brain thinks, pulses beat, and bodies live,
Must, in death's helplessness, lie down with those
Who find like us the grave their last repose   85
When Death draws down the veil, and night bids
       evening close.
     King Charles, who, fortune falling, would not
       fall,
Might glance with saddened eyes on Morley Hall
And while his own corse--glides into the grave--
Remember Tyldesly died his throne to save.   90

                                        [1846/47]

MS: B(2)
First Publication: Leyland II
Text: the number in the right margin is Branwell's

148 By Babel's waters Israel, long ago,
         Wept 'neath the willows, oer the overthrow
         Of Sacred Zion's hill, and oer the dead
         Whose brave breasts fronted those by whom they bled
         When fighting neath their Salem's holy Fane   5
         For Victory--but contented to be slain
         If they could see, with death's deep sunken eye
         Safety to His earth's home who rules on high
             The Lord of Israel in his agony
         When laughed at, dying on the accursed tree   10
         Cried "Why, My God hast thou forsaken me?"
             Stern Marius, gazing on the sullen flood
         Which rolled where mighty Carthage once had stood
         Felt bitterly amid that lonely scene
         That he was laid as low as it had been.   15
             Our Falkland, on the field of fatal fight

286

That dashed to earth King Charle's hard held might
Told of his grief for times his death ere night.
   Anson, whom day on day the blast barred still
From shores that could have saved whom waves would
     kill   20
Felt like his sailor on the Cape Horn wave
Who fought for life till Ocean dug his grave.
   Napoleon, when the Danubes flood he crossed
And murmured "Oh, World--World" as all seemed lost
Mid Aspern's clouds of smoke and streams of blood   25
Felt that lifes joys on frail foundations stood.
And when within a little town in France
He felt Despair's huge gun had checked the advance
Of earthly Hopes, he knew in spirit then
That Happiness could not live long with men.   30
   I scarce dare speak of HIM whose heartfelt
       strain
Raised his own Scotland from her dust again,
Who died to prove the boldest, manliest breast
Can neither conquer woe or fix on rest.
BURNS has his graves and Life has had his tears   35
But his bright soul is given to future years.
   And must I mention him whose glorious brow
In Hucknall Thorkard's vault is mouldering now
Sleeping from griefs that dimmed his living eye
Waking in souls that will not let him die   40
For those whose blood and brain have power to feel
Joy's bright but fleeting flame, Woe's stabbing
     steel
Our Byrons spirit can dissect and tell
Why 'twas his spirit bade this world farewell.
With them he dies not though his faithful hound
     (Boatswain)   45
Were his loved masters wasted relics found
And he himself could break deaths well wrought
     chain--
With cold eyes only would behold again,
Wrecks of that vessel which like Cookes begirt the
     main.

                              [1846/47]

MS: B(1)
First Publication: Winnifrith PBB

A lonely speck in oceans waste
   Fernandez' rocks our Anson saw
Yet English parks by beauty graced
   Could ne'er so much his eyesight draw
Or steal from that old heroes eyes   5
The gleam with which he viewed it rise.
For him 'twas hope of rest to come
To worn out men who knew their doom--
If separate from it--must be
A burial neath a boiling sea.   10
To him 'twas hope that Fortune still
   On valours head would deign to smile--
That Fame their greeting cup would fill--
   Worn out with tracing league and mile.
His seamen, while the hand of Death   15
   Composed each shrunk and fevered limb
Felt in each gale Hope's whispers breathe
   And Paradise before them swim
So sweet a wind blew off that shore
The bitterness of death seemed oer.   20

But Oh, as whatsoeer we do
What joy through life we fondest woo
   Will though it seems like happiness
   Unnoticed--drift us toward Despair
   And prove the bane of our distress   25
      And not the balm of our despair

That very gale they loved so well
   Blows from--not to Fernandez' groves
And every flowered and leafy dell
   Which sends them scents the sailor loves   30
Still but the farther oer the foam
Removes them from a happy home.
The salt wind from the prisoning main
Had given them all they longed t'obtain
The sweet wind from the healing shore   35
Denies them what would health restore.
   Oh for the melancholy blast
      That howled round desolate cape Horn
When comrade barks were parting fast
   Through rain and wind and thunder born   40
While nought could close the ocean tomb
Though they had given their hecatomb.
It would have born them howsoeer
Through whitened breakers fraught with fear--
It would have born them to that sand,   45

Whose grains, to them worth more than gold,
Had power to nerve each helpless hand
    Each parting spirit to uphold.

No Fate that loves mans griefs defied them--
The wished for haven of hope denied them--   50
And hour by hour and day by day
As Manhood childlike sunk away
    The sunshine from those thunder-hills
      That frowned oer Chili's hostile shore
Gilt, fairy like the thousand rills   55
      In salt waves lost--those eyes before--
Whom from deaths films they might restore
Again to gaze on Spanish war
    Unblinkingly as Eagles eye--
Again to do--again to dare   60
    And not at least so meanly die
Like aged hound in corner lying
Weak, sore, and unatteneded dying.

    Their cheif had bade his fancy wake
To thoughts--how world surrounding Drake,--   65
And Raleigh--day star of the sea--
The last bright beam of chivalry--
Might greet him when from battle's plain
    War's clouds should bear him up to heaven
    And that green crown he wished to gain   70
    Should by their English hands be given.
But Now a north west wind must doom
To him forgetfulness--to his a tomb.

    Oh When we feel that high emprize
    In melancholy weakness fades   75
      That pulse beats faint and vigour dies
As woe our every thought invades
We can perchance the sorrow feel
    Of that brave heart who, oer the wave
    But led his sailors to their grave   80
When with red fire and flashing steel
He thought to have made his foemen reel
New realms to explore and shew his world
The portrait of herself unfurled
    Now every hour the white wave roared   85
For victims still to be devoured
And still those sweet scents filled the air,
Fernandez' forests still waved there--

    And when we see our Anson reach
    At last yon tantalizing shore   90
What lands he on the welcome beach?
    The wretched wreck of those no more!

How like ourselves whose years of toil
    Are spent lifes hour of ease to gain
And yet when reached through long turmoil   95
To the rich feast of gathered spoil
    No guests can sit but aches and pain
Instead of some beloved bride
Disease and Death are placed beside
    The table where our feast is spread   100
    And "to the memory of the dead"--
Must be our toast mid, all, our pride.

Anson--upon the sea of life
    The worn and wasted soul like thee
Mid winds and waves of care and strife   105
    A rest like Juan's Isle may see--
    May to its woodlands wish to roam
    Forgetting in that happy home
The rough Cape Horn of agony.

    I'de long been tossed like withered leaf   110
        That eddying blasts whirl round and round
And born through many a gust of grief
        While to the port of pleasure bound
I saw at last Fernandez Isle--
    I saw a heart that beat for me   115
A look that gave not friendships smile
    Or kindness of affinity
    The intercourse 'twixt man and man,
    The kindnessess by kindred shewn
Though not extinguished were outshone   120
    When Natures deeper power began
To point the mental sight afar
To loves own sun from friendships star

Sunlike my own Fernandez shines
While early eve oer me declines   125
laid like a log with--deep beneath
The scarce unwelcome gulphs of Death
Tossed overboard my perished crew
    Of Hopes and joys sink one by one
    To where their fellow thoughts have gone   130
When past gales breathed or tempests blew
Each last fond look ere sight declines
To toward where my own Fernandez shines
Without one hope that they may 'eer
Storm worn--recline in sunshine there   135

[1846/47]

MS: B(1)
First Publication: SHB C and B

'The westering sunbeams smiled on Percy Hall,
And green leaves glittered o'er the ancient wall
Where Mary sat, to feel the summer breeze,
And hear its music mingling 'mid the trees.
There she had rested in her quiet bower   5
Through June's long afternoon, while hour on hour
Stole, sweetly shining past her, till the shades,
Scarce noticed, lengthened o'er the grassy glades;
But yet she sat, as if she knew not how
Her time wore on, with Heaven-directed brow,   10
And eyes that only seemed awake, whene'er
Her face was fanned by summer evening's air.
All day her limbs a weariness would feel,
As if a slumber o'er her frame would steal;
Nor could she wake her drowsy thoughts to care   15
For day, or hour, or what she was, or where:
Thus--lost in dreams, although debarred from sleep,
While through her limbs a feverish heat would creep,
A weariness, a listlessness, that hung
About her vigour, and Life's powers unstrung--   20
She did not feel the iron gripe of pain,
But thought felt irksome to her heated brain;
Sometimes the stately woods would float before her,
Commingled with the cloud-piles brightening o'er
     her,
Then change to scenes for ever lost to view,   25
Or mock with phantoms which she never knew:
Sometimes her soul seemed brooding on to-day,
And then it wildly wandered far away,
Snatching short glimpses of her infancy,
Or lost in day-dreams of what yet might be.   30

'Yes--through the labyrinth-like course of
     thought--
Whate'er might be remembered or forgot,
Howe'er diseased the dream might be, or dim,
Still seemed the Future through each change to
     swim,
All indefinable, but pointing on   35
To what should welcome her when Life was gone;
She felt as if--to all she knew so well--
Its voice was whispering her to say "farewell;"
Was bidding her forget her happy home;
Was farther fleeting still--still beckoning her
     to come.   40

'She felt as one might feel who, laid at rest,
With cold hands folded on a panting breast,

Has just received a husband's last embrace,
Has kissed a child, and turned a pallid face
From this world--with its feelings all laid by--   45
To one unknown, yet hovering--oh! how nigh!

'And yet--unlike that image of decay--
There hovered round her, as she silent lay,
A holy sunlight, an angelic bloom,
That brightened up the terrors of the tomb,   50
And, as it showed Heaven's glorious world beyond,
Forbade her heart to throb, her spirit to despond.

'But, who steps forward, o'er the glowing green,
With silent tread, these stately groves between?
To watch his fragile flower, who sees him not,   55
Yet keeps his image blended with each thought,
Since but for _him_ stole down that single tear
From her blue _eyes_, to think how very near
Their farewell hour might be!

                             'With silent tread   60
Percy bent o'er his wife his golden head;
And, while he smiled to see how calm she slept,
A gentle feeling o'er his spirit crept,
Which made him turn toward the shining sky
With heart expanding to its majesty,   65
While he bethought him how more blest _its_ glow
Than _that_ he left one single hour ago,
Where proud rooms, heated by a feverish light,
Forced vice and villainy upon his sight;
Where snared himself, or snaring into crime,   70
His soul had drowned its hour, and lost its count
        of time.

'The syren-sighs and smiles were banished now,
The cares of "play" had vanished from his brow;
He took his Mary's hot hand in his own,
She raised her eyes, and--oh, how soft they shone!   75
Kindling to fondness through their mist of tears,
Wakening afresh the light of fading years!--
He knew not why she turned those shining eyes
With such a mute submission to the skies;
He knew not why her arm embraced him so,   80
As if she _must_ depart, yet _could_ _not_ let him go!

'With death-like voice, but angel-smile, she said,
"My love, they need not care, when I am dead,
To deck with flowers my capped and coffined head;
For all the flowers which I should love to see   85
Are blooming now, and will have died with me:
The same sun bids us all revive to-day,

                    292

And the same winds will bid us to decay;
When Winter comes we all shall be no more--
Departed into dust--next, covered o'er   90
By Spring's reviving green. See, Percy, now
How red my cheek--how red my roses blow!
But come again when blasts of Autumn come;
Then mark their changing leaves, their blighted
       bloom;
Then come to my bedside, then look at me,   95
How changed in all--except my love for thee!"

'She spoke, and laid her hot hand on his own;
But he nought answered, save a heart-wrung groan;
For oh! too sure, her voice prophetic sounded
Too clear the proofs that in her face abounded   100
Of swift Consumption's power! Although each day
He'd seen her airy lightness fail away,
And gleams unnatural glisten in her eye;
He had not dared to dream that she could die,
But only fancied his a causeless fear   105
Of losing something which he held so dear;
Yet--now--when, startled at her prophet-cries,
To hers he turned his stricken, stone-like eyes,
And o'er her cheek declined his blighted head.
He saw Death write on it the fatal red--   110
He saw, and straightway sank his spirit's light
Into the sunless twilight of the starless night!

'While he sat, shaken by his sudden shock,
Again--and with an earnestness--she spoke,
As if the world of her Creator shone   115
Through all the cloudy shadows of her own:
"Come grieve not--darling--o'er my early doom;
'Tis well that Death no drearier shape assume
Than this he comes in--well that widowed age
Will not extend my friendless pilgrimage   120
Through Life's dim vale of tears--'tis well that
       Pain
Wields not its lash nor binds its burning chain,
But leaves my death-bed to a mild decline,
Soothed and supported by a love like thine!"

                                            [1847]

MS: B(1), Unknown
First Publication: Leyland II

151   As if heart sick at scenes of death, the day
From Albuera's hills has passed away
Not with its customed gift of farewell light
To feed our hopes through the dark paths of night
But mingling battle smoke with driving rain   5
And howling blasts with shrieks of mortal pain
    Was that the moon--Methought I saw her shine
As hurrying clouds disclosed one beam divine
But her mild face befits not such an hour
So intervened the increasing sleet and shower   10
And heaven above again looked charged with woe
And darkness veiled the scenes on earth below

[1847]

MS: B(1)
First Publication: SHB C and B
Text: l. 7: "that" is canceled, but no alternative
             provided

152   (a) Might rough rocks find neath calmest sea.

        Percy at length drew near to ask
           If she were old enough to find,
    Like him, that pleasure was a task;
           And years, in lifes race, left behind   5
           The feet of girlhoods morning mind?
"When you--Amelia feel, like me,
The dullness of satiety
You will not smile as now you smile,
With lips that can even <u>me</u> beguile--   10

    (b) Who smiled as only those can smile
Who've served full 'prenticeship to guile,
And think the world is but a den
Where devils don the masks of men.

        If thirsting on the streamlets brink   15
           Its crystal draught we fain would sip
    Yet backward shuddering we would shrink
        If drowning Hornet bit our lip
And yet--the hurtful fly removed--
Nature would make us try the flood,   20
        So when Amelia saw the look
           That triumph lit in Percys eye
    As laughing to his friend he spoke
           Her spirit shrank she knew not why

(c) He said "I scarce know why we have   25
 Our few years freedom from our grave;
 But never, while allowed, refuse
 Our short reprieve from death to use
 So that our dying tongue may say
 I have known sunlight gild my day!   30
 I'm looking on thee--and sincere
 Would be the unwished, unwelcome tear
 If I could think that--unillumed
 To rayless cloud and tempest doomed--
 Thy life's sad evening should descend 35
 Without a hope, without a friend;
 Without, what friendship cannot give,
  The closer clasp, the brighter eye,
 When Love declares, "With thee I'll live,
  And thine shall be my destiny!"   40
 Amelia, once before I've felt
  To one, once mistress of this Hall,
 A strong soul bend, a hard soul melt,
  A proud soul in devotion fall.
 And now again that hour arises,   45
  The extinguished fires burst up again,
 And light again the night surprises
  That shadowed o'er the inward pain.
  With thee, dear girl, the powers remain
 To recreate my happy morn--   50
 To make that light a real dawn.

         [1847]

MS: E, Unknown
First Publication: Du Maurier, partial; Flintoff, partial

153 Our hopes on earth seem wholly gone;
   Each minute hastens thy decline;
  Yet; oh my Mary, thou alone
   Shall still through life, seem only mine!
  The burial of a darling wife   5
   May not kill men so stern as me;
  But only this worlds storm and strife
   Can aid my bosom's agony.

         [1847]

MS: B(1)
First Publication: BC 1932

In that unpitying winter's night,
When my own wife--my Mary--died,
I, by my fire's declining light,
   Sat comfortless, and silent sighed,
   While burst unchecked grief's bitter tide,   5
As I, methought, when she was gone,
   Not hours, but years like this must bide,
And wake, and weep, and watch alone.

All earthly hope had passed away,
   And each clock stroke brought death more nigh   10
To the still chamber where she lay,
   With soul and body calmed to die:
   But mine was not her heavenward eye
When hot tears scorch'd me, as her doom
   Made my sick heart throb heavily   15
To give impatient anguish room.

"Oh now," methought, "a little while
   And this great house will hold no more
Her whose fond love the gloom could wile
   Of many a long night gone before!   20
   Oh! all those happy hours were o'er,
When, seated by our own fire-side,
   I'd smile to hear the wild winds roar,
And turn to clasp my beauteous bride."

I could not bear the thoughts which rose,   25
   Of what had been, and what must be,
And still the dark night would disclose
   Its sorrow-pictured prophecy;
   Still saw I--miserable me,
Long--long nights else--in lonely gloom,   30
   With time-bleached locks and trembling knee,
Walk aidless--hopeless--to my tomb.

Still, still that tomb's eternal shade
   Oppressed my heart with sickening fear,
When I could see its shadow spread   35
   Over each dreary future year,
   Whose vale of tears woke such despair
That, with the sweat-drops on my brow,
   I wildly raised my hands in prayer
That death would come and take me now: 40

Then stopped to hear an answer given--
   So much had madness warped my mind--
When--sudden--through the midnight heaven--

With long howl woke the winter's wind;
    And roused in me--though undefined--   45
A gushing thought of tumbling seas
    Whose wild waves wandering unconfined,
And, far off surging, whispered "Peace."

I cannot speak the feeling; strange,
    Which shewed that vast December sea,   50
Nor tell whence came that sudden change
    From aidless, hopeless misery;
    But, somehow, it revealed to me
A life--when things I loved were gone--
    Whose solitary liberty   55
Might suit me, wandering, tombward on:

'Twas not that I forgot my love
    That night departing evermore--
'Twas hopeless grief for her that drove
    My soul from all it prized before,   60
    Till that blast called it to explore
A new-born life, whose stony joy
    Might calm the pangs of sorrow o'er,--
Might shrine their memory, not destroy.

I rose and drew the curtains back   65
    To gaze upon the starless waste,
And image on that midnight wrack,
    The path on which I longed to haste,
    From storm to storm continual cast,
And not one moment given to view   70
    O'er minds wild winds the memories, past
Of hearts I loved--of scenes I knew.

My mind anticipated all
    The things my eyes have seen since then--
I heard the trumpet's battle-call--   75
    I rode o'er ranks of bleeding men--
    I swept the waves of Norway's main--
I tracked the sands of Syria's shore--
    I felt that such strange strife and pain
Might me from living death restore.   80

Ambition, I could make my bride,
    And joy to see her robed in red,
For none through blood so wildly ride
    As those whose hearts before have bled;
    Yes--even though THOU shouldst long have laid   85
Pressed coldly down by churchyard clay,
    And though I knew thee, thus decayed,
I might smile grimly, when away--

Might give an opiate to my breast--
    Might dream:--but oh! that heart-wrung groan,   90
Forced from me, with the thought confessed
    That all would go if SHE were gone:
    I turned, and wept, and wandered on
All restlessly--from room to room--
    To that still chamber, where, alone,   95
A sick-light glimmered through the gloom:

There, all unnoticed time flew o'er me
    While my breast bent above her bed,
And that drear life which loomed before me
    Choked up my voice--bowed down my head--   100
    Sweet holy words to me she said,
Of that bright heaven which shone so near,
    And oft and fervently she prayed
That I might, sometime, meet her there;

But, soon enough, all words were over   105
    When this world passed, and paradise,
Through deathly darkness, seemed to hover
    O'er her halfdull--half brightening eyes--
    One last dear glance she gives her lover,
One last embrace before she dies,   110
    And then, while he seems bowed above her
His MARY sees him from the skies.

                              NORTHANGERLAND.
                              [June 5, 1847]

MS: B(2), Unknown
First Publication: HG

155   While holy Wheelhouse far above
        In heavens unclouded light of love
        Looks down with a benignant smile
        That Heaven and Hell might reconcile
        And shouts to Satan Thourt a funny un   5
        Give him sauce as well as onion
        You bloody bugger ram him jam him
        And with a forty horse pow[er] Damn him
        Or if your work you dont do well
        By God I'll take your seat in Hell   10

                    ========

Say Dr Wheelhouse is a Jewel
Or you and I must fight a duel--
Say that his skin is white as snow
Or down direct to Hell you go--
Say that his skin is rosy red   5
Or redder stains shall die your head--
Say that his eyes seem formed of fat,
I'll make yours blacker than my hat--
Say that his mouth seems sensual
I'll make yours seem no mouth at all--   10
Say that his neck wants drawing out
And soon I'll twist your own about--
Say that his belly is his God
And soon youll feel Gods chastening rod--
Say that his guts are all his riches   15
And I shall call you sons of bitches--
Say that his legs are walking sticks
And Ill walk into you like bricks--
Say that his temper is the devil
And with the floor your back is level--   20
Say the first word he learnt was damn it
And down your throat--that word I'll cram it--
Say that he's not nor's been a maid
And your guts get my clasp knife's blade--
Say that he longed like me for woman   25
And I and all will call you no man
Say that he isnt Heavens holiest son
Or by the Lord your work is done
      For, listen to Lord Peters prayer
Who never knew what twas to swear--   30
If any man who says the womb
Must be first home, as last the tomb
Or lives by bread or breaths by air
Or knows he walks lifes path of care
Believes not that God never sent   35
A form and soul more innocent
More meek more passionless more calm
More bright with all that heart can charm
Than him whose name begins with Wheel
and ends with House--Oh may he feel   40
His addled brains like molten lead
Anthonys fire blaze in his head
St Vitus dance distort each limb
His ears be deaf his eyes be dim
His tongue but move to curse his fate   45

                    [1847]

MS: E
First Publication: Du Maurier, partial; Winnifrith PBB,
partial; Butterfield

                    299

The Odes of Quintus Horatius Flaccus
Book First,
Ode I.
To Maecenas

Maecenas, sprung of kingly line,
My guardian and my guide divine;
Many there are whose pleasure lies
In striving for the victors prize,
Whom dust clouds, drifting oer the throng   5
As whirls the Olympic car along,
And kindling wheels, and close shunned goal
Amid the highest gods enroll.
    One man perhaps his pleasure draws
From the inconstant crowd's applause;   10
Another seeks more solid gain
From granaries of Lybian grain;
The peaceful Farmer labours oer
The land his fathers ploughed before;
Nor these, from forum or from farm,   15
The wealth of Attalus could charm
To leave their homes, and seek a grave
Beneath the deep AEgean wave.
    The Merchant, when 'at home at ease'
May shudder at tempestous seas,   20
And, scarce escaped from oceans roar,
May praise the pleasures of the shore;
Yet--shuddering too at poverty,
Again he seeks that very sea.
    The son of pleasure, careless laid   25
Beside a fountain, neath the shade,
Will sometimes wish to wile away
With mellowed wine, a summer day;
Though others mother-hated war
With fife's and trumpet's mingled jar   30
To camps and combats calls afar.
    The Hunter, neath a freezing sky,
Can banish from his memory
The tender wife he left at home,
Oer pathless wilds at will to roam;   35
If but his fleet hounds chase the deer;
Or Marsian boar his toils uptear.
    But, Ivy garlands me adorn,
By them to heavenly honours born;

Yes, me swift nymphs and satyrs bear   40
To woods, apart from worldly care;
If but Euterpe yeild to me
Her thrilling pipe of melody;
If Polyhymnia but inspire
My spirit with her Lesbian lyre.   45
    Oh! give thy freind a poets name,
And heaven shall hardly bound his fame!

                        47 lines

Ode II.
To Augustus Caesar.

Oh now enough of hail and snow
The Sire of heaven on men below
        Has sent, in sign of doom;   50
Has scattered from his red right hand
Enough of vengeance 'oer our land;
        And stricken dread through Rome;

And forced a guilty world to fear
Lest Phyrrha's times should reappear,   55
        When Proteus led his flock
Oer mountain tops his path to follow,
And sport in every shady hollow,
        And bask on every rock;

When fishes glided through the groves   60
Where nestled erst the turtle doves
        Amid their native trees;
When oer those woods the trembling deer
Swam, vainly struggling in their fear
        With over-whelming seas.   65

We saw the Tyber spread its reign
Oer Numa's walls and Vesta's fane,
        Rolled from the Etruscan shore;
As, roused by sorrowing Ilia's wrong,
It broke in billows broad and strong,   70
        With hoarse avenging roar.

The youth their fathers crimes have spared,
Will long rememember to have heard
        The civil strife that rose
When Rome itself unsheathed 'gainst Rome   75
Those swords, that should have given that doom
        To their proud Persian foes.

                        301

What God can stay with sacred hand
The fortunes of a falling land?
      With how sincere a prayer,   80
To Vesta's fane shall Virgins go,
Whose songs were silenced long ago
      Amid the howl of war?

Say--whom, around his throne sublime,
With power to appease his wrath for crime   85
      Will angry Jove endow?
O! brightest of his phalanx bright!
With shining shoulders veiled from sight,
      Descend, Apollo Thou!

Or Thou, the fairest of the sky,   90
Round whom thy loves and graces fly,
      My celestial smiling Venus come:
Or, Mars, our father, from thy throne
Thy outcast children look upon,
      And call thy terrors home!   95

Thou joyest in the battles roar,
The gleaming arms, the gushing gore,
      The soldiers iron frame;
But thou hast seen the savage foe,
And made us bear his bitterest blow,   100
      Till wearied of the Game.

Or, Maias son of heavenly birth,
Descending like a child of earth,
      Incline thy gracious head;
Recoil not from our sinking state,   105
Thou, whose strong arm has deigned so late
      To avenge the mighty dead.

Long mayst thou hold a happy throne
Oer lands that trust in thee alone,
      And late mayst thou return;   110
Nor, wearied with the crimes of men,
To thine own heaven from us again
      By rapid winds be born:

But here, where triumphs wait on thee,
As prince and father, love to be   115
      By thousand sons adored;
Nor let the Median dare to ride
Triumphant, oer a land defied,
      While <u>Caesar</u> is our lord!

          72 lines

Ode IIIᵈ
To the Ship that bore Virgil to Athens

───────────────

Safe may Cyprian Venus guide thee;   120
    Clear may Oceans twin stars glow;
Nor may AEolus provide thee
    Aught but winds that eastward blow,
So, O Ship! my Virgil dear,
Thou to Greece unharmed mayest bear.   125

Oak or brass, with triple lining
    Surely fenced his fearless mind,
Who, to sea a bark consigning,
    First 'mongst men dared face the wind;
Heedless of the Southern breeze,   130
Or the rainy Hyades,

Or of Notus' mad commotion,
    Howsoe'er its wrath might grow;
And, oer Adria's changeful ocean,
    Not a wind can wilder blow,   135
Wakener of the wrecking wave,
Maker of the sailors grave!

What approach of death could daunt him,
    Who, with steady eyes, could see
All around, huge monsters haunt him   140
    In his passage through the sea;
Waves his vessel surging under;
Stern Epirus' hills of thunder.

All in vain has God divided
    Solid earth from shifting main;   145
Seas between their shores have glided
    Deep and treacherous, all in vain,
If, with canvass spreading wide,
Ships can cross the unfathomed tide.

Heedless, though the voice of heaven   150
    Call their daring steps away,
Mortal men have ever striven
    Those commands to disobey.
Twas with such an impious soul,
Fire from heaven Prometheus stole,   155

Whence disease round mortals thickened
    All its troops, in ghastly shew;
Whence grim death his footsteps quickened;
    Now so swift, though once so slow.

Thus did wings to man ungiven   160
Waft bold Daedalus through heaven;

Thus did stern Alcides venture
    Hells dark depths to wander through;
Thus we Heaven itself would enter,
    Nought too mad for man to do!   .   165
Nor can God, so much we sin,
Call his angry lightnings in.

                        48 lines

                    _____

                    Ode IVth.
                    To Sestius

    Rough winter melts beneath the breeze of spring,
        Nor shun refitted ships the silenced sea,
    Nor men nor beasts to folds or firesides cling,   170
        Nor hoar frosts whiten over feild and tree;
        But rising moons each balmy evening, see
    Fair Venus with her nymphs and Graces join,
        In merry dances tripping oer the lea;
    While Vulcan makes his roaring furnace shine,   175
And bids his Cyclops arms in sinewy strength
        combine

    Now let us, cheerful, crown our heads with
        flowers,
        Spring's first fruits, offered to the newborn
            year,
    And sacrifice beneath the budding bowers,
        A lamb, or kid as Faunus may perfer: 180
        But--pallid Death, an equal visitor,
    Knocks at the poor mans hut, the monarch's
        tower;
        And the few years we have to linger here
    Forbid vain dreams of happiness and power,
Beyond what man can crowd into lifes fleeting
        hour.   185

    Soon shall the night that knows no morning come,
        And the dim shades that haunt the eternal
            shore;
    And Pluto's shadowy kingdom of the tomb,
        Where Thee the well thrown dice may never
            more
        Make monarch, while thy freinds the wine cup
            pour;   190
    Where never thou mayest woo fair Lycidas,

                        304

Whose loveliness our ardent youth adore;
Whose faultless limbs all other forms surpass,
And, lost amid whose beams, unseen all others pass.

27 lines

Ode Vth . . .
To Pyrrha.

Tell me Pyrrha, who is he   195
    That, with scented locks,
In thy rose bower kisses thee
    Neath the shady rocks?
For whom is bound thy golden hair
Sweetly wreathing, void of care?   200

Oft, alas! shall he deplore
    Vows unkept by thee;
Oft, the Gods he would adore
    Frowning, he shall see;
Oft, astonished, see the main   205
All afoam with wind and rain,

Who beleives thoul't constant prove,
    With thy beauty blind;
Heedless, while he lives in love,
    Of the faithless wind!   210
Ah how wretched, all on whom
Unaware, thy beauties bloom!

As for me, experienced well,
    Rescued from the main,
And mindful of the tempests swell,   215
    I'll hang in Neptunes fane
A picture of that stormy sea,
And garments drenched in ocean spray.

24 lines

Ode VIth
To Agrippa.

On Homer's wing let Varius sing
    Agrippa, good and brave;   220
With what his warriors, conquering,

Have done by land or wave:
But nor to strains like these aspire
Our warblings, nor Pelides ire
    Can we sublimly tell,   225
Nor how across old oceans roar
His course the wise Ulysses bore,
Nor how, defiled with kindred gore,
    The house of Pelops fell;

Nor may our Muse, unwarlike, mar   230
    With coldly creeping line
The praise of Caesar famed so far,
    Or, Great Agrippa, thine!
And who can sing the God of war
With bright arms blazing from afar;   235
    Or Merion famed in fight,
With blackened front and bloody blade;
Or Diomede, by Pallas' aid
    Equal to Gods in might?

No, feasts and frolics be our theme,   240
    And brimming bowls of wine,
And pleasures laugh, and beauty's beam,
    And dance and song divine:
We'll sing of virgins wanton wiles,
Who fight with rage disclosed in smiles,   245
    And tempt the foe to try;
Ourself, as wont, of careless frame,
Whether we feel the general flame,
    Or coldly smile it by.

                                  31 lines

                    _____

                   Ode VIIth
                To Munatius Plancus.

Let others Rhodes or Mytilene praise,   250
Or Corinth built between contending seas,
Or Ephesus, or Thebes, by Bacchus' name,
Or Delphi, by Apollo known to fame,
Or Tempe's shady vale.--There are who sing
The City virgin Pallas worshipping,   255
And think her olive garlands fame can bring;
Others whose harps would white armed Juno praise,
Sing Argos famed for steeds of noble race,
Or rich Mycenae--But nor Sparta, me--
Nor Low Larissa, wakes to poesy   260

                        306

Like the far fount whence loud Albuna roves,
Or Anio's headlong leap, or Tybur's groves,
Or the moist orchards through whose meads he moves.

As south winds sometimes clear a threatning sky,
Nor always sweep in storms and darkness by,   265
So thou, my Plancus, with a manly mind
Sometimes leave melancholy thoughts behind;
And whether arms and ensigns round thee shine,
Or forest's shade, lifes labours drown in wine.
So Teucer, when from Salamis he fled,   270
With poplar crowned his wine besprinkled head,
And his sad freinds addressed--
                              --"Come let us go
Where fortune, kinder than my Sire, shall shew!
Never despair whatever may betide,   275
While Teucer lives, your guardian and your guide!
And Phoebus tells me, that, beyond the main
Another Salamis shall rise again;
So you, who sterner scenes have born with me,
To day in wine forget your misery,   280
To morrow rise to cross once more the mighty sea!"

                                   31 lines

Ode VIIIth
To Lydia.

Why, by Heaven, my Lydia, tell--
    Wilt thou labour to destroy
Even with love--he loves so well--
    Sybaris, thy favourite boy?   285

Wherefore does he hate the plain--
    Careless once of dust or sun?
Wherefore not his charger rein,
    Mid his warriors dashing on?

Wherefore dread the Tyber's flood?   290
    Wherefore hate the wrestlers oil
Worse than venomed viper's blood,
    While his strength can bear the toil?

Wherefore shun his front to shew
    Marked with no ignoble wounds,   295
When with Discus, dart, or bow
    Victor, he might pass the bounds?

Thus did sea born Thetis' son,
    Ere the stormy scenes of Troy
Had their mournful march begun,
    Lurk like this bewildered boy;   300

Shrinking from the call to fight,
    Lest the manly garb again
Should impell him on the flight
    Of the trembling Lycian train.   305

24 lines

Ode IXth
To Thaliarchus

    See'st thou not amid the skies,
White with snow, Soracte rise?
While the forests on the plain
Scarce their hoary weight sustain,
And congealed the waters stand   310
Neath the frost's arresting hand.
    Drive away the winter wild;
On the hearth be fuel piled;
And, from out its inmost cell
Kept in Sabine vase so well,   315
Generous, bring thy four years wine;
Brightest source of song divine!
    Wisely leave the rest to heaven,
Who, when warring winds have striven
With the forests or the main,   320
Bids their ragings rest again.
    Be not ever pondering
Over what the morn may bring;
Whether it be joy or pain
Wisely count it all as gain;   325
And, while age forbears to shed
Snows, or sorrows oer thy head,
Do not scorn the dancers feet,
Nor thy lovers dear retreat.
Hasten to the plain or square;   330
List the voice that whispers where,
While the calm night rules above,
Thou may'st meet thy constant love;
While the laugh round corner sly
May instruct thee where to spy;   335
While the Wantons feigned retreating
Still may leave some pledge of meeting;

Perhaps a ring or bracelet bright
Snatched from arm or finger white.

34 lines

Ode Xth
To Mercury.

Merry God of Atlas' strain,   340
Whose eloquence taught mortal men
    In times remotest age,
To lay their savage wildness by,
And but in freindly rivalry
    Their skill or strength to engage;   345

Hail, Herald of thy heavenly Sire!
Hail, parent of the crooked lyre!
    To praise thee be my pride;
Thou God endowed, with matchless skill
Whate'er, in wanton jest, at will   350
    Thy hand may steal--to hide!

For, long ago, when, young and gay
From him whose glory guides the day
    His cattle thou didst wile,
Although the theif he frowned upon,   355
Yet, when his quiver too was gone
    He could not choose but smile.

Twas Thou that led rich Priam on
When, to redeem his slaughtered son,
    He left sad Troy behind,   360
And safe escaped Atrides ire,
And foemen, round each Argive fire
    Against that Troy combined.

Tis Thou that guidest good men home;
Our spirits urging to the tomb   365
    Before thy golden rod;
Grateful alike to him who reigns
Oer Hell[s] dim, desolate domains,
    And to heavens highest God.

30 lines

309

Ode XIth
To Leuconoe.

Leuconoe, strive no more   370
By impious arts to explore
How long a life our God has given to thee or me;
If we've winters yet in store,
Or if this whose tempests roar
Across the Tyrrhene deep, is the last that we
  shall see.   375

Be cheerful wisdom thine;
Thy Goblet fill with wine,
And shape thy hopes to suit the hour that hastes
  away;
For, while we speak, that hour
Is past beyond our power,   380
So do not trust to morrow but seize upon to day.

           12 lines

Ode XIIth
To Augustus.

Clio, what man or what Hero to sing,
 Wilt thou tune thy shrill pipe or awaken thy
  string?
Or what God?--while afar from thy mountains
  rebounding
  Echo an answer may give to his name; 385
Haemus and Pindus and Helicon sounding
  Vocal at once to the voice of his fame;
For on Haemus it was that the forests, obeying
  The might of the Thracian, bowed down to his
   skill,
Who, with art like his mothers, even torrents
  delaying,   390
And winds on the mountains in mid career staying,
  Made the deep rooted Oak forests dance at his
   will.

First let us honour the Father of heaven
  Who governs the fortunes of gods and of men,
Who each change of the seasons has graciously
  given,   395
  Winter and summer returning again,
  Born at his bidding oer mountain and main;
First and alone in the power of his pride,

While Pallas, his daughter, sits next at his side.
Nor of thee be we silent, who dauntlessly warrest,   400
Bacchus the father of life giving wine;
Nor of thee, Virgin huntress, the dread of the
    forest;
Nor of thee the far shooting God--Phoebus divine!
Alcides we'll sing, and the Brothers twin born,
      Strong on the stadium or swift with the
          steed;   405
Whose stars when they rise on the storm darkened
    skies
      Seamen can save in the hour of their need;
From the wave beaten rock can whirl backward the
    spray,
The loud wind can hush, and the storm drive away,
And calm as they will it the billowy sea.   410

    Next after these, tell me, whom shall we praise?
      Romulus founder and Father of Rome?
Or Numa's unwarlike but prosperous days?
      Or the fasces of Tarquin, the ensigns of doom?
    Or, Cato the last of our citizens, Thee,   415
Who fought for our freedom, and died to be free!

    Say, shall we sing in a loftier strain,
      The Scaurii, or Regulus true to his word?
Or Paulus who died where the war shaken plain
With his country's best heartsblood was drenched
    as with rain   420
      Neath Annibal's conquering sword
Or Fabricius, and Curius with locks wildly waving;
      And Noble Camillus whom poverty nurst;
The hunger and toil of obscurity braving
      Till they rose over millions--the noblest and
          first   425
    Or thy glory, Marcellus, that, secretly growing,
      Like a tree shall shoot forth into branches
          afar,
While bright as the moon mid heavens lesser lights
    glowing
      Shall shine upon mortals the Julian star!
      Sire of Creation! Thine be the care   430
Of Caesar our sovereign--assigned Thee by fate;
      While Thou rulest highest, Caesar the nighest
Under Thy guidance shall govern our state:
And whether the Parthian who threatened so late
      Bow to the power of his conquering throne,   435
Or whether his hand the doom shall command
      Of China, or India, or Kingdoms unknown,
      May he submit to Thy glory alone;

And place neath none other our Sovereigns
     throne.
While shaking Olympus, and darkening the sky,   440
Thy heavy wheeled chariot rolls thundering by,
While over earths temples dishonoured so long,
Thou wreakest thy lightnings in vengeance for wrong.

                                        62 lines

Text: ll. 419-21 originally read (neither version is
        canceled):
             Or Paulus, who yeilded his hearts blood like
                  water
             Where Rome, for one hour, bowed down neath the
                  slaughter
             Of Annibals conquering sword?

Ode XIIIth
To Lydia

When thy youthful lovers charms,
His rosy neck--his waxen arms   445
I so often hear thee praise,
How thy words my passions raise!
Swells my liver--dies my heart;
Calmness--colour, both depart;
While my tearful cheeks proclaim   450
Swift and sure the inward flame.
     How I burn when, drunkenly--
He disports himself with thee--
Stains with wine thy shoulders white--
Hurts thy lip with boisterous bite.   455
     Oh! if thou wilt listen to me,
Let not such a lover woo thee!
Neer will love keep ever warm
That can lips so lovely, harm!
Lips that Venus doth embue   460
With her own nectarian dew!
     Thrice happy those--whose mutual mind
Lasting links of love can bind!
Love unbroke by fear or fray--
Lasting till lifes latest day!   465

                                22 lines

312

Ode XIVth
To the State of Rome

O Ship what waves shall bear thee now?
What course--what waters wilt thou plough?
Haste to thy haven, from the tide,
For, see'st thou not thy oarless side--
Thy shattered mast--thy shivered sail--   470
The wrecks of many a stormy gale!
And hardly may a vessel brave
With broken ropes, the winter wave:
Thou hast not one untattered sail,
Nor God to trust when man shall fail!   475
  Oh! Though thou claim'st a race divine
As fashioned from the Pontic Pine,
The noblest daughter of the wood!
The statliest floater on the flood!
All vain thy boasting--sailors now   480
Trust nothing to a painted prow.
Beware!--unless thou long'st to be
To the wild winds a mockery!
And though, within my mind thy name
Has only wakened fear and shame   485
Yet--when thy danger draws so near--
My fond heart tells me--still thou'rt dear!
So shun--oh! shun those treacherous seas
Among the shining Cyclades!

              24 lines

Ode XVth
The Prophecy of Nereus.

———————————

Twas when the treacherous shepherd bore   490
    His royal prize away
In Phrygian ship--from Spartan shore,
    Across the AEgean sea,

That Nereus raised his auful brow,
    And hushed each favouring breeze,   495
Till not a ship its path could plough
    Across the slumbering seas;

And thus did that old Seagod sing
    His prophecy of doom--
"Vain man! Ill omened dost thou bring   500
    Thy Helen to thy home,

Whom Greece shall seek, with mighty host
    Conjured to overwhelm
Thy pleasure bought at such a cost,
    And thy ancestral realm.   505

Alas! what strife, round Xanthus' wave,
    Thy treachery shall bring!
What fiery funerals oer the grave
    Of Ilion and her King!

See! Pallas lays her olive by,   510
    And grasps her sheild and spear,
And mounts her chariot in the sky,
    And wakes her rage for war.

In vain thy guardian Godess' care
    Thy spirits may inspire;   515
In vain thou combst thy curling hair,
    Or wakest thy wanton lyre;

In vain the shouts--the lances thrust--
    Or Ajax, thou may'st fly;
For, with thy long locks trailed in dust,   520
    Adulterer! Thou shalt die!

Ulysses see--and Nestor grave--
    Thy hapless peoples scourge--
And Sthenelus, and Teucer brave
    Thy flying footsteps urge: 525

Tis Sthenelus the reins can guide,
    While noble Diomede
Greater than Tydeus, at his side,
    Hunts for the Adulterers head,

Whom thou shalt fly, as flys the hind   530
    In vale or woodland lone
From the deep deathbark, heard behind,
    Of wild wolf hasting on,

With beating heart, and bated breath
    Oer mountain and through grove: 535
Was this the glory--this the death--
    Thou promisedst thy love?

Pelides ships--Pelides arm
    Oer Phrygias fated shore,
For these thy deeds, the avenging storm   540
    Resistlessly shall pour;

And, after years of weary wars,
    Shall wrap in funeral flame--
Unquenched by all her blood and tears,
    Thy Ilions very name!   545

56 lines

Ode XVIth.

O Lovely Girl, whose bloom outshines
    Thy lovely Mothers fame,
To ocean give my angry lines,
    Or cast them in the the flame;

But know, that neither wrapt Apollo,   550
    Nor He who rules the bowl,
Nor Ceres preists with tymbals hollow,
    Like Wrath can shake the soul;

Whose direful might, nor sword can fright,
    Nor floods, nor fires, nor Jove   555
Descending on our blasted sight
    In Thunder from above.

When man Prometheus made from clay,
    In fashioning each part,
The Lions rage he stole away   560
    And fixed it in his heart.

'Twas wrath that hurled Thyestes down
    With heavy overthrow;
'Tis wrath, oer many a mighty town,
    That drives the foeman's plough;   565

And me, while young, that wrath beguiled
    In furious rhymes to range,
But Satires wild to songs more mild
    My melting muse shall change;

While Thou--thy passion laid aside   570
    With vows of amity--
Shall hush the urgings of thy pride,
    And back return to me!

28 lines

Ode XVIIth
To Tyndaris.

Faunus from Lucretile
Often shifts, to visit me,   575
And when my goats to shelter run
Sheilds them from the showers or sun.
'Neath his guidance, through the grove
They may, safe, at random rove;
Browzing, mid the summer scene,   580
On the herbage fresh and green;
Fearing not a wolf to meet,
Or rouse the serpent neath their feet,
While they hear his shrill pipe play
Through the valleys far away,   585
And polished rocks of Ustica.
   Heaven my head from harm defends;
Heaven my life and lyre commends;
And to thee my farm shall yeild
All the riches of his feild;   590
Here thou mayest, in long drawn vale,
Fly the sun and court the gale;
Here with old Anacreons string,
Faith or frailty thou mayst sing:
Here beneath the shade recline,   595
Quaffing cups of sober wine;
Far from scenes where furious Mars
With the jovial wine god wars;
Nor suspicious Cyrus fear,
Lest his boisterous passion tear   600
From thy head the festal crown,
And rend thy unoffending gown.

29 lines

Ode XVIIIth
To Quintilius Varus.

Round Catilus or Tibur's walls--O be the duty thine
Before all other trees, My Freind, to plant the
      sacred vine;
Since God unto abstemious men the cares of life
      has given   605
Nor can those cares from heart and home by aught
      but wine be driven:
Who, oer his wine cup, dreads the toil of war or
      poverty?

Nor rather seeks Thee--Joyous God! or, Lovely
  Venus--Thee!
But, lest the glass to oft thou pass--Oh ever keep
  in mind
That oer a bowl the Centaurs 'gainst the Lapithae
    combined;   610
That oer a bowl the Thracian's soul, while bent on
    wanton pleasure
Twixt good and evil sees no bound, in riot knows
    no measure.
    Yet--Honest God, I would not dare thy
        mysteries to explore,
So Thou wouldst hush thy Phrygian horn and drums
    discordant roar,
Whose savage sounds blind self esteem in mazy
    dances lead;   615
And Vanity that over all exalts its empty head,
And Faith that makes each secret known committed
    to its care,
Its inmost thoughts as clear as glass, its promise
    light as air.

                                           16 lines

Ode XIXth
On Glycera.

The mother of Love, and the Father of wine,
    And passion, resuming its throne,   620
Backward command me my mind to incline,
    And kindle the flame that was gone;
        For Glycera warms
        My heart with her charms,
    Whiter than Parian Stone.   625

Her artfulness fires me; Her countenance beams
    Too bright to be gazed upon;
Till Venus, forsaking her Cyprus, seems
    To rush upon me alone;
        And no longer my verse   630
        The deeds can rehearse
    By Scythian or Parthian done.

Raise me an Altar of living sod,
    And crown it with flowers, and bear
Wine without mixture--fit for a god,   635
    That Glycera, hearing my prayer,
        May know I adore,

And be cruel no more,
But an answering passion declare.

                         21 lines

Ode XXth
To Maecenas

Plain Sabine wine, a beverage poor--   640
    If Thou, my freind, my table grace,
    I'll draw from out its Grecian vase;
Stored up since Father Tyber's shore,
    And yonder hill's tower crested face
Re echoed back the applauding roar   645
    That bade the Gods Maecenas bless.
Simple caecubian shalt thou pour,
    Or juice of the Calenan press;
For offers not a poets store
The noble Formian or Falernian glass.   650

                         11 lines

Ode XXIst.
To Apollo and Diana

Virgins, sing the Virgin Huntress;
    Youths, the youthful Phoebus, sing;
Sing Latona, she who bore them
    Dearest to the eternal King:
Sing the heavenly maid who roves   655
Joyous, through the mountain groves;
She who winding waters loves;
    Let her haunts her praises ring!

Sing the vale of Peneus' river;
    Sing the Delian deity;   660
The shoulder glorious with its quiver;
    And the Lyre of Mercury.
From our country, at our prayer--
Famine, plague, and tearful war
These, benign, shall drive afar   665
    To Persias plains or Britains sea.

                         16 lines

318

Ode XXII
To Aristius Fuscus

The man, My Freind, of fearless brow,
    And life of honest deeds,
Nor Moorish dart, nor martial bow,
    Nor poisoned arrow needs: 670

Whether he walk through burning sands;
    Or Scythia's savage shores;
Or, where its waves through unknown lands
    The famed Hydaspes pours:

For while a pathway, through the grove   675
    My careless footsteps led,
As, far from home, I sang my love,
    A Wolf, that saw me, fled:

Sure, such a beast Apulia's wood
    Had never nursed before;   680
Nor,--famous for its Lion brood--
    Wild Afric's burning shore.

But, place me mid a sterile wild
    Where tree could never grow;
Where stormy clouds are ever piled,   685
    And tempests ever blow;

Or place me mid the burning heat
    Of far unpeopled isles;
I still will sing Lalage--sweet,
    Whene'er she speaks or smiles!   690

                24 lines

Ode XXIII^d
To Chloe

   Why, whenever she can spy me,
Like a fawn will Chloe fly me?
Like a fawn, its mother seeking
Oer the hills, through brambles breaking;
Frightened if the breezes move   695
But a leaflet in the grove;
Or a branch the Zephyr tosses;
Or its path a Lizard crosses;
Nothing can its fear dissemble--
Heart and knees together tremble.   700

Stop my love; Thou needst not fear me,
For I follow not to tear thee
Like the Lion, prowling oer
Far Letulia's savage shore:
Stop--Thy budding charms discover   705
Tis thy time to choose a lover.

                              16 lines

Ode XXIVth
On the death of Quintilius Varus

Oh! what shall check our sorrowing
      Above the grave of one so dear?
Melpomene! descend, and bring
Thy Godgiven lyre, whose solemn string   710
      Alone, 'tis meet for us to hear.

Why does the eternal sleep of death
      Compose Quintilius in its reign?
And Truth, and modesty, and faith
Unstained by taint of earthly breath--   715
      When shall they see his like again!

With tears his ashes good men mourn,
      And none--my Virgil more than Thee!
Who weariest heaven for their return
From the dread darkness of their urn;   720
      A joy--alas! Forbidden to be!

Though Thou couldest move a Thracian wood
      With song more sweet than Orpheus strain,
Thou couldst not bid the frozen blood
Through the cold veins to pour its flood;   725
      Or call the buried back again:

For Mercury, in a shadowy train
      Impells them downward--deaf to prayer:
Tis hard--but know, when we complain--
That, which to strive against were vain,   730
      Patience will make us bear!

                              25 lines

320

Ode XXVth
To Lydia

Seldom now the drunken rake
Lydia, will thy windows shake.
To its lintel clings thy door;
So, unnoticed, sleep and snore.   735
   Less and less thou hearest the cry--
"Oh my Lydia! here am I
Ceasless sighing--almost dying,
While in slumber thou art lying!"
   In thy turn, decayed and old,   740
Thou shalt lurk in alleys cold,
While across the moonless sky
Winter winds are wailing by;
And the scoff, shalt weeping, hear,
Of the proud Adulterer;   745
Yet infuriate--in despair
With such lust as fires a Mare:
Mourning that thou canst not move
In our youth, their former love;
Mourning that they rather wear   750
Ivy garlands in their hair,
Than the Myrtle's funeral wreath;
Like thyself the sign of death;
Unto Hebrus such, devoting,
Down his stream they send them floating.   755

             24 lines

Ode XXVIth
In Praise of Aelius Lamia

To the wave and the wind, while the muses are kind,
   My cares and my sorrows I'll fling;
Nor e'er with the question will trouble my mind
   Of the snow covered north, who is King:
Or what is the dread, oer the Parthian's head--   760
   That the shades of misfortune may bring.

O, Godess divine, the first of the Nine,
   Who lovest the fountain clear,
A garland of springs sweetest offerings twine
   For the brows of my Lamia dear;   765
Since oh! without Thee honour to me
   Nor pleasure nor profit can bear!

Thou and thy sisters, his praises to sing,
Once more awaken the lesbian string!

14 lines

Ode XXVIIth
To his Friends.

My friends, across the joyous bowl   770
     'Tis barbarous to fight;
Expel such customs from the soul,
     Nor shame with such a sight
Of mutual brawling blows and blood,
The prescence of the modest God.   775

The flashing cup and lighted hall
     With arms but ill agree;
So cease at once that impious brawl,
     And sit content with me.
Say—would you have me drain to night   780
The heady cup that shines so bright?

And let Megilla's brother tell
     From whence the arrow flew,
And struck by whose bright eyes he fell,
     Come, let him tell me true: 785
Does he from such confession shrink?—
Nay—on no other terms I'll drink.

Whatever heart thine own inspire,—
     Thou needst not blush to me—
I know thou ownst a noble fire,   790
     And lovest generously:
So what thou feelest—Hopes, or Fears,
Disclose them all to faithful ears.

Ah! hapless youth! I feel thy state;
     If there thy passions rove;   795
Ah, worthy of a happier fate—
     A more requited love!
In what a wild Charybdis tossed
Blindly loving! early lost!

What skillful witch can free thine heart   800
     From deadlier witchery?
What Wizard with Thessalian art—
     What God can rescue thee?

322

For thee scarce Pegasus could bear
From such a dire Chimera's snare.   805

36 lines

Ode XXVIIIth
The Ghost of Archytas to the Sailor

Archytas, Thou, whose spirit, Sea and Land
    With unbeclouded gaze hast wandered oer,
Liest, mouldering neath a scanty heap of sand
    In unknown burial, on Apulia's shore.

Nor aught avails it now that thou couldst trace   810
    With master mind the mansions of the sky;
Nor that thy thoughts explored all natures face,
    Since--fashioned mortal--thou wert doomed
        to die.

So fell the man who shared the feasts of heaven;
    So passed Tithonus from our world below;   815
So perished Minos, unto whom twas given
    The secret counsels of heavens king to
        know;

So deeps of Tartarus Euphorbus, hold,
    Though teaching nought but body bows to
        death
By the famed sheild, that, Trojan warfare told,   820
    Yet He himself twice oer resigned his
        breath:

No mean explorer--He, of moral lore,
    Nor lightly learned in the ways of God:
But--One dread midnight looms our sight before;
    One path of death must once by all be
        trod.   825

Some shed their life blood on the battle plain;
    Some sleep, unwaking, neath the ocean
        swell;
Thickens, of old and young, the funeral train;
    No head can scape the cruel queen of hell.

Me, too, tempestous winds that oversweep   830
    Illyrias waters, whelmed beneath the main;
So Sailor, Stop! a little sand to heap
    Oer my poor relics, beat by wind and rain:

323

That so may heaven, whenever storms oerblow
    Venusia's forests, or Hesperia's sea,   835
Preserve, and bid unbounded riches flow
    By Jove, and guardian Neptune showered
        on thee

But if, neglectingly, thou'lt pass me by,
    Thy guiltless children for thy guilt shall
        pay,
Nor all the pomp of future piety   840
    Avail to wash their fathers fault away:
    I would not stay thee--I would only pray
That thrice, a little sand thou'dst scatter o'er
    my clay.

                  38 lines

Ode XXIXth
To Iccius

Iccius, shall Arabian treasures
    Tempt thee with their charms?   845
Wilt thou fly from peaceful pleasures,
    And arouse to arms?
Chains and slavery wilt thou bring
To the Easts unconquered King;
Or the Mede whom, combating,   850
    Danger only warms?

Who's the Maid thou'lt snatch, lamenting
    Oer her lover gone;
Soft relenting--soon consenting
    To be thine alone?   855
Who shall be the bright haired boy
Waiting with thy cup of joy,
And, like his father, skilled to employ
    The arms to China known?

Who'll deny that torrents, rushing,   860
    To their fountains flow;
Tyber's waters upward gushing
    From the plains below,
When--designed for nobler pride,--
Thou thy learning layest aside,   865
Books exchanging, to provide
    War's untutored shew?

           24 lines

Ode xxxth
To Venus.

    Queen divine
    Of Paphian shrine,
Leave those lovely haunts of thine: 870
    Come away
    Where Glycera
Calls Thee to her temple gay.

    Bring with Thee
    Loves deity: 875
The blooming Nymphs, the Graces three;
    The God endued
    With merry mood;
And Youth, without thee wild and rude.

          12 lines

Ode xxxist
To Apollo.

For what does the poet to Phoebus pray--   880
    New wine from his goblet flowing--?
Not for the flocks oer Calabria that stray;
    Nor the corn in Sardinia growing;

Neither for ivory, nor gold, nor land
    Which the Liris, gently gliding,   885
Would crumble away into fugitive sand
    Down its quiet waters sliding:

Let him gather the grape who has planted the vine;
    Let the Merchant, whom Jupiter favours,
His Syrian treasures exchange for wine   890
    Which a golden goblet flavours,

Thrice in a season oerpassing the sea,
    Nor by waters or winds prevented;
But olives and mallows shall satisfy me;
    With the goods fortune gives me, contented. 895

Son of Latona! grant health to taste
    The food Thou hast placed before me;
And a mind undimmed; and an age undisgraced;
    And a Harp, with whose strains to adore thee.

          20 lines

Ode XXXII[d].
To his Lyre

    If, resting neath the shade   900
    With thee I've ever played
Such strains as those who hear shall treasure
    long--
    Sweet Harp! The while I sing--
    Attune the silver string,
    That, once awakening,   905
        Swelled old Alcaeus' Song;

    Who, warlike, mid the sound
    Of battle thundering round;
Or, his tossed vessel anchoring from the tide;
    Still sang the God of wine;   910
    Or Venus--Queen divine;
    Or his beloved Nine,
        With Cupid, at her side;

    Or Lycus, blooming bright,
    With eyes as dark as night,   915
While darker still his long locks seemed to fall:
    Hail! Harp to Phoebus dear!
    My charm from every fear;
    My comforter in care;
        Attend thy poet's call!   920

            21 lines

Ode XXXIII[d]
To Albius Tibullus

Come--Dear Tibullus, and no more
    Of Glycera complain,
But sorrow breathing songs give oer,
    For vows adjured in vain.

For Cyrus' love burns Lycoris   925
    Of forehead fair and free,
While Cyrus wastes each careless kiss
    On haughty Pholoë;

But sooner shall the timid goat
    With rabid wolves combine,   930
Than Pholoë her soul devote
    To lecherous fires, like Thine!

So Venus, who our hearts controuls,
    Will oft, with wicked joke,
Join differing forms and differing souls   935
    Beneath one brazen yoke.

Myself, who higher should have aimed,
    A low born maid have ta'en,
Whose haughty temper might have shamed
    Calabria's stormy main.   940

          20 lines

Ode XXXIVth

My God, each hour, less turned to Thee,
    My mind mans wisdom led astray;
But back across that treacherous sea
    My wandering vessel tracks its way:

For, thundering through an angry heaven   945
    While, rent with lightening, blazed the sky,
Thou, Thy swift car hast lately driven
    With windborn coursers whirling by;

The Heavens Atlantean pillars shaking,
    And solid earth, and fleeting sea;   950
And Hells tremendous confines quaking
    When, in that moment, moved by Thee.

Thou God canst hurl the lofty down,
    And lift the lowly head on high;
While Fortune shifts the glittering crown,   955
    With changing choice, and clamourous cry.

          16 lines

Ode XXXV.[th]
To Fortune.

Goddess of Antium, mighty to raise
The lowly aloft, or the high to abase;
Mighty the pomp of a Triumph to turn
To the darkness and dust of the funeral urn;   960
Mighty to govern the land or the sea;
Alike the poor husbandman prays unto thee,

And the Sailor, whose vessel afar from home,
Drives through the dangers of ocean's foam:
The Dacian and Scythian, the city and plain,   965
Rome the victorious, and Monarchs who reign
Oer hordes of barbarians--and Tyrants of pride,
To thee would do reverence--with thee would abide!
The column still standing--Oh! do not oerwhelm;
Nor waken to war with a weary realm   970
The nations, whose swords are scarce cold in their
     sheath,
Lest they threaten our Empire with danger and
     death.
     Before Thee stalks Fate to obey thy command,
With the engines of death in her brazen hand--
Wedges and hooks for torments dread,   975
And the iron spike, and the molten lead.
Hope and faith, rarely seen, clothed in white,
     hover near thee
And cheerfully follow, and steadfast revere thee,
When, altered in aspect, thou hastest away
From the Halls of the great, to the haunts of
     decay: 980
But the perjured wanton, and faithless crowd
Fly from the freindship they recently vowed;
And the freinds, when the gold and the goblet are
     gone,
Leave the dregs to their host, from his poverty
     flown.
     Fortune! be watchful in Britain, afar,   985
Over Caesar, departed again to war;
And shine on our soldiers, a terrible band
To the far off east, and the Red sea strand.
     Alas how disgraceful! when brother 'gainst
          brother
Deals blows that his arm should have dealt on
     another!   990
What crimes have we shunned in this iron time?
Forborne from what Sacrilege? fled from what crime?
From what blood, for what God did our people
     refrain?
Or shrink from polluting what altar or fane?
     Great Godess! our blunted swords sharpen once
          more   995
Not in our own but our Foemen's gore!

                                        40 lines

                        328

Ode XXXVIth
Numida's return

Incense hither bring,
And tune the joyful string,
And with offerings please the powers who Numida
defend,
For his safe return again   1000
From western wilds of Spain,
To greet and to be greeted by each long dissevered
freind

And he'll none more gladly see
Than, dearest Lamia! thee!
Whose life with his--together taught--from infancy
did twine: 1005
So mark this day with white;
And whirl in dances light;
Nor a brimming glass forget to pass of soul awakening
wine!

Nor let jovial Bassus yeild
To Damalis, the feild,   1010
Though seasoned well and skilled the Thracian cup to
drain;
Nor let the lily fair,
Or the rose, be wanting there;
With long lived parsley blooming above the festal
train:

While wanders every eye   1015
In hot idolatry
On Damalis, all else in beauty conquering;
But whom nothing can remove
From her new awakened love;
Fixed faster than the ivy boughs that round the Oak
Trees cling.   1020

                                    24 lines

Ode XXXVIIth
On the death of Cleopatra

Now, Companions, now's the hour
Generous bowls of wine to pour!
Shake the earth with dances gay;
Let the feast be spread to day,

Neath each Temple's dome divine,   1025
Rich enough for preists to dine!
 Till this hour it seemed a sin
To tap the wine in hidden bin,
While Egypt's Queen decreed a dreadful doom
  Of overwhelming fall,   1030
  And bloody funeral,
To our high Capitol and haughty Rome:
 Surrounded by a filthy crowd
 Of pampered flatterers, boasting loud,
 And drunk with fortunes favours given;   1035
 But down to ruin madly driven:
For, scarcely 'scaping fire and foes,
 A single vessel bore her home;
And, drunk with hope though her ambition rose,
 Great Caesar, breasting oceans foam   1040
From Italy, with swift oars cut the tide,
And brought forgotten fears to crush her new born
 pride.
 Like the wild Hawk that, from above
 Pounces upon the trembling dove,
 Or as the Hunter on the plains   1045
  Of wintery Thrace, pursues the hare,
So would he give to captives chains
That prodigy so fatal though so fair;
 Whose proud heart, panting to be gone,
  Nor, like a woman, feared to feel   1050
  The terrors of unsparing steel,
Nor with swift ship to seek some shore unknown;
 But with calm brow beheld her realm
 Victorious vengeance overwhelm;
 And smiled to see the serpents teeth   1055
 Chill her veins and choke her breath;
 Feirce in such determined death;
 Nor could a heart so noble bear
 Her head to bend, and chains to wear
Like some poor slave, a Captive in the shew   1060
Of Caesar's haughty host triumphing oer her woe.

        41 lines

Ode XXXVIIIth
To his servant

 This ode I have no heart to attempt, after having
heard Mr H Coleridges translation, on May day, at
Ambleside.

P. B. Brontë
Haworth n^r
Bradford. Yorks
June 27
1840

MS: B (2), A, E
First Publication: De Quincey, partial; **The Odes of
Horace, Book I, Translated by Branwell Brontë**, ed.,
John Drinkwater, Privately printed, 1923.

Appendix B

Missing Poems

Based on information from various sources, one can establish the possible existence of at least five poems for which the manuscripts have disappeared and which seem never to have been transcribed.

(a) In Scene 3 of **The Nights** (**BRANWELLS BLACKWOODS MAGAZINE**, July 1829), Young Soult says, "Why the one [Magazine] for May had two or three peices of poetry in it," and Tree replies, "one by you." We know that the May issue actually existed because it contained part I of Charlotte's **The Enfant**, continued in the June issue which is extant. In addition, one of the notes in **THE AMMON TREE Cutter** refers to a "Discription of a Tavern Branwells Magazine March 1829." Unfortunately there is no way of telling if the reference is real or fictitious and if the work is poetry or prose. If Branwell did produce magazines for February, March and April, they likely contained poetry, but if they existed, the magazines seem no longer to be extant.

(b) The manuscript for **Thermopylae** (No. **48**) ends on the recto of the final page; the verso, which is so badly rubbed as to be virtually undecipherable, seems to contain five four-line stanzas in pencil, having to do with Angria (a reference to "Ardsley").

(c) On the last page of **REAL LIFE IN VERDOPOLIS**, dated September 22, 1833, in "Books published this Season by Seargent Tree," Branwell records as the third item of six "The Fate of Coomassie, a poem by Young Soult. I Vol Quarto 2-0-0." Since the other five items are authentic, one has to assume this one is also, but no other evidence of the poem's existence has surfaced to date.

(d) Sotheby's catalogue for the 1914 sale of Mrs. Nicholls' property contains among others the following entry:

180 Bronte (P. B.) Auto. Poem, 1 1/4 pp. 4to, 36 lines, beginning "My heart, pent up in a narrowed cage," etc.

Hatfield confirms the existence of the poem in his transcriptions at the BPM, but seems not to have transcribed it. An unidentified catalogue entry in the Symington Papers at the BPM gives the concluding lines of the poem as:

Ere old Euphrates' willowed waters
Bring to his mind lost Zion's daughters,
Or Nilus rolls its tepid wave
Or Jordan covers Sodom's grave.
And so we think not till we find
That cares like clouds must shade the mind,
That each false Laugh is Tower-stamped gold--
That smiles can ne'er be bought or sold.

(e) The notebook containing No. **155** has two additional pages (8 & 9) of penciled verse so badly rubbed as to be largely undecipherable; they seem to contain two items: a poem of 10 four-line stanzas, signed "Northangerland," and thirteen lines in couplets that may be a continuation of the lines on Dr. Wheelhouse.

Finally, in his letter of 27 June 1840 to Hartley Coleridge, accompanying his translations of thirty-seven Odes from Book I of Horace, Branwell writes: "I have . . . striven to translate 2 books, the first of which I have presumed to send to you," and in a letter to Davidson Cook, 9 January 1926 (Wise Collection), Hatfield notes, "He translated some of the odes in the Second Book, but I have not traced these." To date, no translations from Book II have been found; but see comment for **Appendix A** for additional evidence that he may have been working on them.

Appendix C

Items of Disputed Authorship

a　　　　　　　　**To the horse black Eagle which I
　　　　　　　　Rode at the battle of Zamorna**

　　　Swart steed of night, thou hast charged thy last
　　　O'er the red war-trampled plain
　　　Now fallen asleep is the battle blast
　　　It is stilled above the slain

　　　Now hushed is the clang of armour bright　　　　　　5
　　　Thou willt never bear me more
　　　To the deadliest press of the gathering fight
　　　Through seas of noble gore

　　　And the cold eyes of midnight skies
　　　Shall not pour their light on thee　　　　　　　　10
　　　When the wearied host of the conqueror lies
　　　On a field of victory

　　　Rest now in thy glory noble steed
　　　Rest all thy wars are done
　　　True is the love & high the meed　　　　　　　　15
　　　Thou from thy lord hast won

　　　In daisied lawns sleep peacefully
　　　Dwell by the quiet wave
　　　Till death shall sound his signal cry
　　　And call thee to thy grave.　　　　　　　　　　20

　　　　　　　　　　　　　　　　　　　[1835]

These lines, on an undated and unsigned scrap in the Berg
Collection (NYPL), have been attributed to Emily, Charlotte,
and Branwell.　Though first published as Emily's (Shorter EJB
1910), there is no evidence that Emily was ever involved with
Angria.　The content and language seem to be Branwell's
rather than Charlotte's, but the handwriting is likely hers.

b　　　Not thus, but with the fiery speed all rent
　　　Shrieks round upon that sharp jag-toothed wheel
　　　The father of the cloud-conceived brood.　　　　20
　　　There Pentheus writhes, and tears with teeth and
　　　　　nails
　　　The solid ground, to creep and hide his head
　　　Even in the very heart of pain and night,
　　　So sorely sham'd remembrance vexes him

334

Of that dim evening on Cithaeron's height   25
Where 'mid the lowering glooms and hanging rocks
He couched, to scoff the secrecy of heaven,
And Bacchus flashing thro' the mazy dance
With torches glanced, and loose curls wreath'd
      with grapes;
But him swift vengeance rent and the blind hand   30
Of wild Agave and the hideous glades
Dew'd with his showering blood and entrails torn.
All these and more, the towering livid air
Of that unmeasur'd cave in earth's dim womb
Half show'd, half by concealment direr made,   35
As hideous things half seen loom'd from afar.
Here wail'd the Giants, hidden and abased,
Not wholly crush'd, before that second fall
More dreadful, as from height more glorious, when
Crushed into black eternal sleep they lay,   40
And earth moan'd, taking back her mightiest sons.
      As the sea-blasted pines, bent bleak and rough,
On some lone shore clouded by screaming mews,
Wail in the wind that tears the desolate heath,
So thro' the prostrate ranks unanimous ran   45
A trembling moan, that shudder'd into air
And died; and they lay low in silence pale,
Shadows amid a shadowy world, until
Slow heaving his broad bulk, unbent as yet
With weight of stars incumbent, Atlas rose   50
Painfully, unlike the rapid joyous strength
That mov'd him glorying thro' the exultant
      heavens;
And with sad words and mourning broke the night.
      O fall'n shapes of primeval deity,
Dead, crushèd tombs of pale divinity,   55
Sepulchring your old glories! what is here
For us, so glorious once, but ceaseless wail
And clamour of woe, and chains and night and
      pain?
Lost as we are, and reft of the sweet light,
The joyous balminess of starry dews,   60
That pearl the wan face of maternal night,
The sun, that from his cloudy-skirted shrine
Lures all the unstarred sky with circling wheels,
The sweet moon, and the silence hallowed calm
Of night ambrosial, and the air and seas--   65
These, reft from us, our lowest offspring, man,
As glorified by shame, unworthy war
At hands immortal, and eternal loss,
Enjoy   ; these have we lost; nor these
Alone, but anguished here soothe the dim night   70
That swathes us round, with moans, and wail, as
      now,

Cowering; unworthy of these ancient seats,
Those calm shrines over the far-sphered world
Where crown'd we sat on immemorial thrones!
Ah me, that we enslav'd should grovel so,   75
Forgetful how to strive, inglorious, base,
Worthless redemption of our godheads lost!
My soul is bare of counsel; only this
I know, that I am weary of this yoke,
This sharp corrosive shame of fall and death,   80
And would arouse ye back to Heavenly thoughts,
Worthy your ancient glories; let one speak
Wiser than I, whom following we may reign.
He spoke; and calm amid the breathless hush
Grey Saturn rising spake with dreamy looks,   85
Where dim Philosophy slept vision'd faint.
    Gods, that have died so long in deepening
            swoon
Thro' this wild season of dejection,
Swooning from fall to fall, blind and abased,
Thro' cloud on cloud of sorrow and restless
        thought   90
Unfathomable, alive to only woe;
Pale sorrows, wrestling with a stronger doom,
Listen, and draw a solemn consolation
From Truth, severe and sad, yet strong and calm.
    Thro' all the circling universe of life   95
One inmost Power, unwearied, never sleeps
But circles ever thro' the lifeless deep
Life warm and radiant; hence, when bright-eyed
        Spring
Makes the green buds flush to their sunny core,
The green life gushes thro' earth's parched
        veins,   100
And leaps out glorious into light, and fills
The music-tranced air and thick-leaved boughs
With sudden melody full-throated; nor
Fails the smooth arching field of calmest blue,
Which men call heaven, to rain from airy womb   105
Sweet effluences and radiant; all the clouds
Drop honey and balm-breathed dews from their
        fleeced skirts,
On the fat earth that laughs with flowers of
        light;
And the world smiles out in existence new.
In the red-bolted thunder roars and rends   110
This circulating power of self-born life,
And smiles along the smooth, unfurrow'd deep,
Shrieks down the whirlwind, mutters in the storm,
Grows with the growth of sunny-bosomed woods;
Thrills the huge void with immortality   115
And whirls for ever changing life with life,

336

Round the vast orb of being. Herein we lived,
Throned in the unseen sky, or thundered out
In glorious darkness, o'er the trembling world.
Herein, and thrust by this vast hand of that   120
Which men call Time, or Fate, or Chance, or God.
Nameless and unresisted, tho' unknown,
We fell and newer glories took the place
Of our Supreme. Think ye no inward will,
Self-strong and self-created, wheels along   125
Existence on its void and fathomless way?
Fools are we, this not knowing, that the same
Is Life and Destiny, nor without one
Exists the other regent of itself.
More fools indeed would we now wrestle it down,   130
But yielding in our inward power made strong,
And smiling down the restless rule of Change,
We shall be kings indeed and supreme gods,
Sitting upon calm thrones of Knowledge, strong
In perfect reason and matured peace,   135
Regal, unmoved, shall we for ever reign,
And triumph in our being's perfectness.
    So having said, back to his cloudy dreams
Musing he dropt, and ceasing, husht the air,
That trembled yet melodious by and full   140
With the calm awful music of his words,
To whom Oceanus, with musing brow
Thought-furrowed, rose, and thus with measur'd
        voice:
    Well-framed and hallowed by serenest thought,
As fits our Highest, hath the speech appear'd   145
Of mightiest Saturn; nor to be by us
Unheeded, nor unfruitfully and vain
To moulder in oblivion's rust, but ye
Or must resolve at once to lay down all
Ye have call'd glories, and to build new thrones   150
Of thought in secret places of the heart,
Kings to yourselves, and sever'd from the world;
Or frame deep counsel for recover'd rule,
Or blindly dash and break against high fate,
Grasping at power; these seem your only helps,   155
If helps so hazardous may weak such name.
Yet see I yet a higher and wiser way,
To free ourselves, and crown with glories old.
Strike not against the rocky-based fate,
Dream not beneath it, nurs'd in fancy alone   160
And mystic thought; reign we apart indeed,
Contented with what glory rounds us yet,
To live superior, and divine repose
Quaff, undisturb'd, yet kings where we may rule,
Unscath'd, unperill'd by devouring Time,   165
Or envious change with fettering serpent twine,

He spoke; and calm with quiet lips and eyes
Scornful of pain or blind contention,
Sank back the grey god-sophist of the sea,
With serene look of wisdom satisfied,   170
Serene and mute in godlike changelessness.
But   , rising like a shatter'd rock,
With swift and fierce contempt and eyes that
      gleam'd
Red light and hideous thro' the livid air,
Sprang up and shouted, with loud voice and hoarse 175
As winds that wrestle with the storm-chafed sea:
Fair speech and measur'd craft, most worthy gods!
Crush'd as we are, fallen, mockt images
Of spurn'd divinity, the fragments lost
And shatter'd idols of an older world!   180
Are we cast down beyond all scorn? does Fate
With not a thunder-frown of rousèd wrath
But curvèd smile contemptuous, tread us down,
And pass on careless? Rise, ye ancient gods!
I boast no power of wreathing wily words   185
In serpentine and mazy folds, and winding
A cloudy veil of dull philosophy
About existing woe; are we yet kings?
Gods, thronèd in the deep serene of rule?
No, but fallen shadows in a world of scorn.   190
What loud hymns of our worship hear we ring
Up thro' the rich-curled smoke of incenst shrines?
Who bows and trembles at our awful shrine
With shuddering prayer and adoration prone?
Rise, rise and seize again your ancient rule!   195
Or would ye die, and in the blind night swathed
Lie cold in senseless immortality,
Not by annihilation wholly crush'd
But dying, as far as gods can die? now choose,
Fallen powers, for no other choice is left.   200
      He ended; and a sudden clangour yell'd
From all the host, harsh braying, as the roar
Of charging trumpets on the battle's verge,
When shrieks the air with shafts, and clashes
      round
With clarions; nor less terror shook their foes;   205
As when old earth with windy wrestlings torn
Cleaves, and the deep void opens on the day,
Shakes cities down, and from her womb hurls out
Huge fragments hurtling in the noisy air;
No less a shudder thro' Olympus ran   210
Sudden, convulsing all the deities
With trembling and sick fear; Poseidon quak'd
Pavilion'd with the green vault of his seas,
That kept moan round him for their elder lord;
In the sweet depth of Cyprus' sunniest glades   215

338

Haunted by woodland voices and gleaming shapes,
The fear took Cytherea, where she lay,
Covering the heavy folds of lucent gold
That in thick tresses on the ivory droopt
Of her veil'd shoulders; not more terror quail'd   220
Her deity, when by the sea-built wall
She fronted Diomedes, and became
With the tread of a whirlwind on her   , and
          shook
Ilion; not less amaz'd she rose and fled,
Scattering her nymphs, and as she mounted fell   225
Flowers, all the children of the sunny earth,
Raining around her thick ambrosial showers,
Till at the feet of Zeus she fell, and hail'd
Her father; he scarce less hereat dismayed;
Hermes, tho' skilfullest in deep-woven wiles,   230
Trembled, and loose in his hand the powerful wand
Slumbrous, lay useless; paler grew the light
Of Artemis' brow, and brighter Phoebus paus'd,
One white hand resting on the golden strings
Of his hush'd lyre, that under it throbbed yet;   235
Stern Mars, dark-smiling, graspt his hilt, and
          frown'd,
Blackening the furrows of his war-wrinkled face;
From Bacchus' bright locks the ivy cluster'd
          fell;
And Pallas only was not pale, but calm
Sat statue-like among the trembling gods;   240
Deep thought lay clear and cloudless on her brow.
    Then Zeus, with high words veiling hidden
          fear,
Spake, and the clouds shook into thunder far.
    There is no fear; are we as men, or fall'n
Unscepter'd gods, unkingdom'd and abased,   245
That fear should thrill our veins? Reign we not
          here
Serene among the sunny clouds of Heaven?
If yet gigantic wrath upon the earth
Writhe impotent, and mutter and toss and threat,
What fear we? are they not by supreme fate   250
Our subjects, and we in our thunder kings?
    He spake threatening, and scorn his proud lip
          curv'd
Kinglike; yet scarce they whisper'd scar'd
          applause.
But queenly Pallas with unruffled look,
As when in Academic groves she met   255
Deep-thoughted Plato, or the reverend head
Of Socrates, or likest when she chid
The wrath of war-vext Mars at Ilion, spake
With slow melodious voice: "It is not well

That thus we talk loud thunder and weak rule,   260
And clothe in lightning our so powerless hands;
For strength is weakness without wisdom, rais'd
By her alone to highest calm of power,
Strong as a mountain's blue cloud-wreathed head
Serene, above the murmuring din of earth,   265
Nor else serene nor mighty. Thou art king,
O Zeus, the thronèd thunder shrines thee round;
Bright brows immortal droop before thy might,
Thy hand is strong with sceptre; men on earth
Mount up to thee their prayers in steaming
          clouds   270
Of incense, and the reek of slaughter'd herds;
But thou, God as thou art, must lean thyself
On wisdom's sceptred hand, to rule indeed,
Nor king nor god else; and alleging Fate
That we unmoved from our awful seats,   275
Will work her work, thou errest; not for us
She works, nor we her dim foundations know
Nor ordinances; seizing the swift time
We rule by wisdom and justice unmoved;
Else what strength of command we bring, jars
          back   280
Upon ourselves, and hurls us headlong down
She ended fearless; but no less a death
Of stony silence spelled the Olympian crew;
As some worn voyager from shores remote,
Where the calm sun sleeps on the western verge   285
Of utmost sea, slumb'ring with level ray
Where in the summer sunset ever dream
His woodland race; landing on some lone beach
Thro' tropic shades of giant verdure wide
And alleys deep, with huge magnolia archt,   290
Odorous, long wanders thro' the perfum'd eve,
Till in the dewy dusk a city gleams,
Her humbler towers and bastioned walls in night,
But on her topmost pinnacles the sun
Sits, turrets that flame back his western rays   295
From towering gold and domes of diamond glare;
With hope amaz'd the inlaid gates he passes
Wide gaping to the twilight landskip dim;
Palace on palace, dome on shining dome,
Rises and arches o'er the dusky streets   300
With bridges of gold and stately statues wrought,
And many a pile of grey magnificence
O'er the broad silent ways, curiously wrought
Cornice and buttress, pillars and architrave;
All stony-silent as the sleeping times   305
Unstirr'd by human breath; he gazes maz'd,
Till him too the cold, petrifying night
Clasps and he stands mute in those dusky streets,

A statue among statues, wrought to life;
Nor ever voice breaks the silent of death.   310
No less dead-silent stood the throng amaz'd,
And Fear first trembled thro' the deep of heaven. 312

BOOK II.

Meanwhile amid their night the Titans cheer'd,
Took counsel and with deep thought wove their way
To light and power renew'd and glories lost.
At length amid the crowd a shape arose,
Huge as some column by convulsive page   5
Flung from its base, that o'ergrown with rank
    weeds,
Lies with its shatter'd blazon; hugest he
Of all the giant race, and strongest of limb,
Porphyrion; on his broad brow pride repos'd
Secure, and in each furrow of his dusky cheek   10
War harbour'd, born with Anger at one birth,
Grim twins, but dearest to that grisly shape
Towering with haughty port; and thus he spake
With voice to quell the thunder, and make shrink
Its bolts inaudible, and hand to hurl   15
The baffled lightning strong, or dash down towers.
Titans, the strongest brood of mighty earth,
Short counsel shall make shortest pain too long;
War, war our subject, war our minister,
Sits dreadfully upon the lowering clouds   20
Glaring reluctant patience, till at length,
With signal given her red hand may launch
Death; rise and war, and dash down fear and fate,
Mighty to act, not suffer, but revenge,
Destiny shall quake before us, giving way   25
To our high-battled storm, and we shall reign
Kings by our might, and crush our vaunting foes,
Our puny children, and this rebel Zeus,
A baby tyrant, nurs'd and bred of us,
Puppet of sovereignty, that has caught up   30
High words of supreme rule, and mimics them
With his mock action, playing the prime king,
Chief minister of fate and sovereign be
Of us, his race ancestral, struts and mouths,
With infant courage and ignoble act,   35
And we before this god of puppets quail!
Back to your thrones in thunder! Titans, back!
Rise, Saturn! war and triumph, godlike war!
And death herald us back unto our thrones.
    So closed his words, hot with the breath of
        war,   40
And measur'd thunder echo'd far applause.

341

But now the sagest of the fallen gods,
Sagest and deepest skill'd in world-wide lore
Ancestral, and benignest in his might,
The son of Themis, else all-nurturing earth,   45
Prometheus rose; for not yet his bold hand
Had thro' the hollow reed to man convey'd,
To blind weak man, the golden light of fire;
Nor had Pandora, blushing perfect grace,
From his wise breast repulst, his brother lur'd   50
Unwiser, by bland arts and heaven-deckt wiles;
Nor he rock-fixt groan'd to the reddening beak
And curvèd claw of Jove's strong bird, whom late
Alcides, mightiest among later men,
Slew and release him fetter'd; but now young   55
Full of deep thought and counsel he stood up
In that grim conclave, and sage speech began
Unfolding slow his universal lore;
Fate and the mighty all distinctive will,
The mystery that lives in all things, power   60
By which earth lives, as Saturn first had shown;
Then sager, Fate permitting, how to rule,
However, not by brutal strength and force
Of limb and muscle or thunder-throated war;
But by deep thought   , and subtlest
    craft   65
Hard to unravel, intellectual might
Strongest of things and best, thence godlike life
And rule primeval; and more subtle and wise,
Deep thro' the folds of nature's secrecy
Piercing swift wisdom, and counsel drawing up   70
Of noble craft: but they, blind shapes of
    strength,
Rude and hard-thoughted, helming to all winds,
But bare of counsel and internal strength,
With storm of scorn and whirlwind ignorance
Stifled his voice, and their tempestuous din   75
Drave him away, whence evil to themselves,
Nor of his noblest wisdom good to him,
So slighted is supreme Philosophy.
Wisdom divine and virtue, but itself
Strong, living to itself for glorious ends.   80
    Next to the warlike throng rose high and
        broad
Of giant bulk and port imperial, one
Not lightning-blasted yet, Rhoetus, of brow
Majestic; more of counsel, tho' but shallow
And scattered by the blowing breath of fight,   85
Sat on his brow, than on the broad smooth
        strength
Of huge Porphyrion's; neither sage, but this
Of warlike counsel best, small praise where war

So impotent; and thus for echoing spake
With deeper voice, but not so hoarse and said: 90
    O Titans, well ye have devis'd, and well
Counsell'd, ignoble sloth and dreaming thought
Driving far from ye, and to glorious war
Worthily inclin'd; but not enough devis'd
For perfect rule and conquest, unfulfill'd;   95
Since those, be sure, who our primeval strength
Have graspt with younger hands, not without power
Establisht, and strong counsel thus sustained,
For who shall say that by ignoble strength
And puny tyranny vanquisht we fell,   100
Primeval gods, and nature's mightiest? no;
Else our own words, both what we speak, or do,
Debases us beyond all scorn, thus sham'd
And grovelling beneath an infant arm.
Power then is theirs; but to contend with power   105
An equal strength requires; whence then to us
This strength, that may renew our glories lost?
This to your judgments would I clearly unfold.
And first, whereas these sophists of deity,
Knitting close words in cloudy mysteries, prate   110
Of Power or Destiny supreme, that folds
The orbed world and whirls along its course,
Working to the end all good, and to its end
Calm-travelling: lo, what shatter'd shapes of woe
Here front our eyes, and darken this dim light!   115
Call ye this Destiny's wide-reaching work!
Fools, what but tyrant power and present rule
Insufferable, such evils works? Behold
Our brethren here, by us in counsel lost
Lie undeliver'd, groaning in their bonds: 120
Typhaeus here, the mightiest Titan, writhes
Upon a bed of thorny pain and fire,
And groans from his deep chest reluctant flame,
Fruitless; here Tityus the fell vulture tears,
Pressing with ponderous bulk the groaning soil;   125
There Tantalus, rackt by devouring thirst
And keen-edged hunger, parches in the stream,
Panting, and views the cool dark wave beneath,
And pendant fruits ambrosial; there another,
Tied on the sharp rim of that jagged wheel   130
That grinds thro' him to the earth, then jarring
        whirls
Mangled aloft; and this by newer gods
Done, while we sleep, or strive in fruitless war;
Is this then happiness? this guiding fate?
The work, rather, of shortliv'd tyranny   135
Convulsed now with the last pang of fear,
To prop its perishing rule; nor knows how
        strength

Hence springs to us against them; loose we these,
Pale victims of a rule so swift to crime,
That in such little space so much hath done   140
Of evil, and for such slight cause alledg'd;
One that he slew his son to feasting gods,
Type of no gentle sway, and sacrifice
Pleasant to our new tyrants, and for this
One anguish by another recompenct.   145
See at their hands his guerdon; the other too,
Accus'd that he, with touch audacious late
Dar'd strive to taint the queen august of heav'n;
Rather their will's lost prey, and hapless wreck
Of this upstarted deity's lips and eyes   150
Libidinous; fair cause for hideous pain,
Shatter'd forever in each mangled joint!
These aiding, who have known their tyrannous
     yoke,
We shall pluck down these upstarts and again
Reign, crown'd by war. Ye have heard my
     sentence, gods.   155
     They heard, and they applauded, Erebus
Shook from its darkest depths and all the night
Shudder'd; back Tartarus with reluctant speed
Trembled and shrunk and cast its inmates out;
A groan of thunder shiver'd thro' the dark: 160
Moan'd all the shades, and all the gloomy vales
Of Hades felt a sudden thrill of pain.
Such power, tho' fall'n, was in those early gods,
Not yet by thunder blasted and the bolts
Of Zeus, nor chain'd, tho' ill they sped in war,   165
Yet 'scaping, free of fetters and the doom
At last pronounct; they rose; and each with step
Not slow, and hand speedy to answer will,
Loos'd all the tortur'd; so the wily words
Of Rhaetus counselling war, and arguments vain,   170
Excusing with false glosses blackest sin
And spreading covert veil of glowing words,
Wrought with them, easily counsell'd to their
     bane,
Leapt all the impious into sudden joy;
Free of this galling yoke and festering pain,   175
They triumphed, and in new delight of strength
And satisfied desire of torturous days,
Exulted, running, springing blithe and light
With tread elastic, and new freedom quafft
Delightful, such the joy of pain releast!   180
Long, long the wither'd throat of Tantalus
With fiery drought inflam'd the waters cold
Of icy Lethe bathed with pleasant draught
Sweeter than Bacchus! bubbling purple e'er
To wearied reveller; nor brought his soul   185

344

Sane pain's oblivion. Pleasure yet remain'd,
And glad revenge; Pentheus and Tityus there
Free of their pain, fresh thoughts of godless
          pride,
Swelling conceive, puft with vainglorious joy.
Ixion, freed now from the resting wheel,   190
Stretches his limbs, now whole and eas'd of pain,
On the hard earth, to him delicious bed,
With rest more sweet than what the broidered
          couch
Of Melibaean purple lends to kings
On downy plumes luxurious; Sisyphus   195
Sleeps, and sweet dreams repay his aching toll,
Since now lies still the ever-rolling stone.
All joy'd, all impious, none repented, none
But freed of pain fresh crime began to weave
Fuller destruction drawing on their heads   200
With lavish hand outpour'd; such the fell power
Of Tartarus; sin-breathing air and foul,
Then war propos'd against the younger gods
Gladly they seiz'd, and with resounding note
The brazen trumpets screamed war to the sky,   205
Standards unfurl'd and dash of bristling arms
Were none; strong in themselves they stood, and
          war
Devis'd, unfearing; then in serried force
Huge shapes towering a rocky fence of war
Against the sun, tho' with their wiser king   210
Reluctant, forth they sallied; swung behind
Hell's gates revolv'd with hideous clanguor
          clos'd.

The text is from a typescript by J. A. Symington in the
Ratchford Papers. At the top of the first page Symington has
written "Branwell," and the HRC lists the poem among its
"Transcriptions, by J. A. Symington, of Patrick Branwell
Bronte poems," but I have been unable to find any additional
evidence to corroborate Branwell's authorship. However the
designation of the first line as l. 19 is Symington's, suggesting he knew something about the beginning of the poem.
The blanks in Book I, ll. 69, 172, 223; Book II, l. 65 are
Symington's. The work is an adaptation of the great conclave
in Hell in **Paradise Lost.**

c   The vale is broad, encircled round
          By hillocks passing green,
      Behind whose tops a lengthened row
          Of silvery peaks is seen.
      That, rising through the silent air,
          Communion seem to hold

With the blue skies that, far above,
  Their starry robes unfold.
The restless wind who, on his path
  No track of footsteps leaves,
Hath turned aside from the broad lake
  Which now no longer heaves.
The tall trees droop their tremulous bows,
  No living sound is near,
Save that a voice from yon small stream
  Assails the list'ning ear.
But 'tis the Nymph who evermore
  Within those waters dwells,
And to the attentive ear
  Her hapless passion tells
        x x x x
What light breaks on the solemn scene
What tumult hours alone

According to both the Sotheby's 1914 Sale Catalogue of Mrs. Nicholls' effects and Hatfield's transcription at the BPM, these lines appeared on the verso of the manuscript leaf containing No. **129.** Hatfield notes that the lines are annotated by Branwell "not mine." On the same page appears the continuation of the minutes begun at the back of Notebook C.

d(i)   Have ye seen the stars at morning
       How they blend with rising day,
       Paling still and still adorning
       All the morn with their decay
                Paling, blinking
                Coyly sinking
       While the gold usurps the gray

       So the fancies of the Heathen
       Brightest stars of Heathen night
       Slowly of their reign <beraven>
       Lose themselves in gospel light
                Stars of warning
                Reft at morning
       End their task and bid Good-night

For the meaning of this see Plutarch in the Cesation of Oracles--or Virgils Pollis.

Marginal Comment:

Much too obscure for a song, and so incorrectly transcribed-- as to be unintelligible to myself. Yet the idea is worth working out.

(ii)   The visitation of a passing beam
       Through the quaint fissure of a dungeon wall
       May tempt the fettered captive to recall
       To hope, the objects of his endless dream
       The rippling and the murmur of the stream
       Which the wild passing wind made musical
       While the small billows each and each and all
       Caught their own portion of the passing gleam
       Flash on his inward eye stir in his ear,
       A little light a little sunny isle
       The sea of dim and brown obscurity
       That joyous shape of light may seem to be
       Yet to the captive tis so precious dear
       He feels it reflex of his loved ones smile

       Is not the soul a prisoner fast confined
       In carnal keep, or custody of sin?
       The soul incarnate and all dark within
       Dreams dozes groans on bed of earth reclined
       But wakes and wishes if a single ray
       Of light intrusive force or win its way
       Through conscious weakness to the captive mind
       Thou, that dost lift the Gospel light on high
       That torch inflamed with true Promethean fire
       Shine where thou canst it boots not to inquire
       If <   > is discipline or destiny,--
       Break in the dungeon vaults the aperture
       That lets in light let but the light be pure
       A genuine of spring of the ethereal sky.

Comment:

Both very unfinished, and abrupt, but worth making something
of.

(iii)   To the Air of "Rouseau's dream"

       Rose and Violet and Pansy
       Each have told a tale of love.
       Various with the freak of fancy
       Apt and bold the fields to love
                    See the Pansy,--
       Seek her not in secret grove.

       Rose of summer, lovely creature
       Who did ever look on thee
       But beheld in every feature
       Which he most was glad to see

```
                    Fairest, dearest
        Whoso'er the dear may be.

        Long ago when I was roaming
        In a shady path I met
        Dim and blue as summer gloaming
        Far apart from all her set
                    Meek and lowly
        Her my own dear violet.
```

Comment:

Pretty enough as she sung it--the second verse particularly--
but the necessity of lengthening a short syllable in violet
should have been avoided in a piece intended for music--
though few writers on settings of songs care for these
things.
Opposite 1. 9 Coleridge suggests "the very feature."

Branwell's letter to Hartley Coleridge (20 April 1840) mentions sending only one poem (No. 103) and translations of
two odes; his letter of 27 June mentions only the completed
translation of Book I of Horace's Odes. However, attached to
Coleridge's unfinished letter to Branwell (see comment for
Appendix A) are these three fragments, with Coleridge's
comments as noted. The hand, however, does not seem to be
Branwell's.

        Finally a number of Branwell's prose manuscripts con-
tain bits of verse; many of these I have been able to identify as quotations (sometimes accurate, sometimes loosely
quoted) from such sources as folksongs, Shakespeare, Jonson,
Milton, Dryden, Goldsmith, Gray, Cowper, Isaac Watts, Burns,
Scott, Hogg, and Byron. There remain bits, however, for
which I have not been able to find a source, but which I
strongly suspect are also quotations:

        (a) departed and left not a wreck behind

From the Introduction to **THE HISTORY OF THE YOUNG MEN From
Their First Settlement To The present time**, dated December
15, 1830.

        (b) Stretched like a golden line along the wavy sea

From chapter II of **THE HISTORY OF THE YOUNG MEN.**

        (c) To the Rendezvous of Nations and queen of the
            Globe

From vol. II, **Letters From An Englishman To His Relative In London**, dated March 16, 1831, these words are spoken by James Bellingham, the author.

    (d) Percies of Raystracke cladde in mail
        Belted and branded and horsed for warre
      Never knew thai fro ye. death to faill
        Readyye to do but loathe to bear

From vol. I of **The Life of Feild Marshall The Right Honourable Alexander Percy, Earl of Northangerland,** undated but likely begun late 1834 or early 1835.

    (e)   Wide oer the warlike world hovers my mind
      But To all its doings dead and cold and blind

From Chapter 4 (dated September 3, 1836) of an untitled, 16-page manuscript detailing Percy's triumph, Zamorna's exile, and Mary's illness (see comment for No. **91**).

    (f) Who on that Isle lay dark and lone
      Amid the oceans everlasting lullaby

From an untitled prose fragment, c. 1836.

    (g) Eating and quaffing
      At past labours laughing
      Better far by half in
        Pleasure than before!

From an untitled manuscript fragment (one leaf) dated January 23, 1837.

Appendix D

Glossary of Glass Town/Angria Person and Placenames

I wish to acknowledge my indebtedness in the preparation of this glossary to notes and glossaries in the following publications: Ratchford Legends; SHB Misc II; **Everyman's Companion to the Brontës,** ed. Barbara and Gareth Lloyd Evans, London: J. M. Dent & Sons Ltd., 1982; and Alexander EW, and CB, I.

Adrian, Emporer: See Wellesley, Arthur Augustus Adrian.

Adrianopolis: Emporer Adrian's city on the banks of the Calabar; capital of Angria; 150 miles from Verdopolis; ravaged by the Ashantees under Quashia during the Revolutionary War.

Alnwick House: The Percy family home in Sneachiesland where Zamorna sends Mary, his wife, when Northangerland, her father, begins the Revolution. Branwell has her die there, but Charlotte rebels against her death; she has Mary wasting away, but transformed at the last moment by a letter from Zamorna, assuring her he is alive.

Ancient Britons: According to tradition, "some thousands of years" before the Twelves arrived in Ashantee (West Africa), twelve men from Britain of gigantic size and twelve from Gaul had come to the area, but after years of continual war, returned to their respective countries.

Angria: Kingdom created in 1834 for Zamorna from African territories he conquered; capital, Adrianopolis; has seven provinces: Zamorna, Angria, Douro, Calabar, Northangerland, Arundel, Etrei. Province of Angria; capital, Angria; Lord Lieutenant, W. H. Warner. Percy is made Prime Minister and leads a rebellion against his son-in-law; in the ensuing war the country is ravaged, Zamorna driven into exile, only to return triumphantly and put an end to Percy's political ambitions.

Ardrah, Arthur Parry, Marquis of: Prince of Parrysland; leader of the Reformers in Verdopolis; "the scoundrelly Scot" who is Commander of the Verdopolitan Navy and opposed to creation of the new kingdom of Angria; his forces invade Angria and defeat Zamorna's, but his government is then overthrown by Northangerland.

Ashantees: Natives of Ashantee (Ashanti on the African Gold Coast) against whom the Twelves fight in setting up the

Glass Town Confederacy. To the east of Ashantee lies the
desert; to the west, the Atlantic; to the south, the Gulf of
Guinea; to the north, the Gibbel Kumri Mountains (the Mountains of the Moon).

Ashworth, Brother: alias Northangerland, who, pretending
to identify with the people, preaches at the Wesleyan Chapel
in Slugg Street.

Badey, Dr. Alexander Hume: One of the Twelves; physician
to the Duke of Wellington.

Bellingham, James: A London banker, who visits Glass
Town (Verdopolis) to supervise his firm's business there, and
is quite smitten by the city. He reports on, among other
things, Rogue's insurrection in 1831 and the rebellion of
1832 in letters to a friend.

Bravey, Sir William: One of the Twelves, co-founder of
Glass Town.

Bravey's Inn: Inn in Glass Town where Wellington, his
sons, and friends meet to gossip and discuss war, politics,
and literature.

Bud, Captain John: An eminent Glass Town political
writer and historian, author of **The History of the Young
Men** and other works, the greatest prose writer of early
Glass Town; a pseudonym of Branwell, and at times also for
Charlotte.

Bud, Sergeant: Son of Captain Bud; "a clever lawyer and
a great liar, a brow-beating counsel and an impudent barrister, a lengthy writer and an able arguer, a crabbed miser
and a vile scoundrel, an unsociable fellow and a proud
wretch, a real rascal and a dusty book-worm," and scrivener
to chief Genius Tally.

Calabar: Province in Angria; capital, Gazemba; a river
in Angria on which Adrianopolis is situated.

Caseputh: A mountain in the North.

Castlereagh, Frederick Stuart: Viscount Lord, later Earl
of Stuartville; contemporary and friend of Zamorna, Lord
Lieutenant of Zamorna; a "noble dashing dandy."

Coomassie: Ashantee capital at the foot of Mt. Aornus,
destroyed by the Twelves.

Dimdim: A mountain near the Lake of the Genii.

Douro: Province; capital, Douro; Lord Lieutenant, Earl of Jordan; also a river in Angria.

Douro, Marquis of: See Wellesley, Arthur Augustus Adrian.

Edwardston: The chief manufacturing town in Angria; Zamorna is defeated there by the Reformist Army.

Ellen, George: Squire of Hallows Hall; a bad influence on Henry Hastings, his goal is "to root out morality from the natures of all his acquaintance."

Elrington: See Percy, Alexander Augustus.

Elrington Hall: The Percy family residence in Verdopolis.

Elymbo: Mountainous region in the north.

Etrei: Province; capital, Dongolo; Lord Lieutenant, Henri Fernando Di Enara.

Evesham: City on the Cirhala; fortified by Revolutionary troops; taken by General Thornton in the last major battle in Zamorna's return to power.

Fidena: John Augustus Sneaky, Marquis of Rosendale and Duke of Fidena, who helps his father, Alexander Sneaky, at the Battle of Fidena in 1833.

Fidena: Large city in Sneachiesland, 300 miles from Verdopolis, burned by Rogue in the 1833 rebellion.

Flower, Sir John: Later Baron Flower and Viscount Richton; eminent scholar in Verdopolis and Verdopolitan Ambassador to Angria; one of Branwell's pseudonyms after 1831.

Gambia: River on which Glass Town is situated.

Gazemba: Town and plain on the banks of the Calabar where Zamorna reviews his troops before the battle of Evesham.

Genii: The Chief Genii: Talli--Charlotte, Branni-- Branwell, Emmi-- Emily, Anni--Anne; guardians and protectors of the Twelves, living in a remote mountainous region.

Glass Town: A confederacy of four kingdoms--Wellingtons-land, Sneachiesland, Parrysland, Rossesland--formed by the Young Men in Ashantee. Its capital is the Great Glasstown, later Verdopolis.

Gordon, Captain Julian: One of the "dark-malignant scowling Gordons"; a confederate of Rogue/Percy.

Gravey's Inn: Named after Emily's soldier who was one of the Twelves, King of Parrysland, and later Arch Primate of Verdopolis.

Guadima: River on which Verdopolis is built.

Hastings, Captain Henry: A popular young Angrian soldier and author, who degenerates into a drunken murderer; cashier-ed in 1839 for shooting his superior officer, he joins the Revolutionary forces, and eventually becomes involved in a plot to kill Zamorna. Before his disgrace he is one of Bran-well's pseudonyms.

Hyla (Hyle; Hylle): A vast, stormy lake.

Kumriis: the Gibbel Kumri or Mountains of the Moon; see Ashantees.

Leyden: Scene of Zamorna's most famous victory over Northangerland's forces after his return from exile.

Marseilles: See Young Soult.

Montmorency, Hector Matthias Mirabeau: A Verdopolitan nobleman, banker, and "familiar" of Alexander Percy; marries Harriet O'Connor, sister of Arthur O'Connor. Montmorency's daughter Julia marries Sir William Etty, painter and disowned son of Alexander Percy by his first wife, Maria (Augusta) di Segovia.

Morven: Snowy mountain in the North.

Nevada: Mountain range, source of the Ardrah River.

Niger: River: Forms the border between Angria and the Glass Town Confederacy.

Northangerland: Province of Angria; capital, Pequena; Lord Lieutenant, Earl of Northangerland; see Percy, Alexander Augustus.

O'Connor, Arthur: A profligate associate of Alexander Percy.

O'Connor, Harriet: Sister of Arthur O'Connor, seduced by Percy, she is later unhappily married to Montmorency, elopes with Percy who deserts her, and she dies a sad, lonely death.

Parry, Sir William Edward: Father of Arthur, Marquis of Ardrah; one of the Twelves and King of Parrysland.

Pelfe, Victoria: A wealthy heiress and mistress to Northangerland.

Percy (also Rogue), Alexander Augustus: First wife, Maria (Augusta) di Segovia--son William Etty. In 1814 m. Lady Henrietta Wharton; three sons--Henry, Edward, William, whom he orders S'Death to dispose of, but S'Death saves Edward and William; also one daughter--Mary Henrietta; wife dies of consumption; heartbroken, he leads dissipated life, gambling, drinking, cheating at cards; involved in the 1831 and 1832 rebellions; after the battle of Haslingden, is captured, executed by a firing squad, but brought back to life again in 1833; returns as the handsome Colonel Alexander Augustus Percy; abducts Lady Emily Charlesworth, trying, unsuccessfully, to get rid of her fiance, Lord St Clair, by getting him arraigned for treason; is imprisoned for treachery; released, he elopes with Harriet (O'Connor) Montmorency, later forsaking her; spends sixteen years wandering the world in his boat "The Rover," as bandit, pirate, etc.; seizes Lady Zenobia Ellrington and her father from their ship, abruptly woos and marries her; returns to Verdopolis as Lord Elrington, assists the Marquis of Douro in the War of Encroachment against the French and Ashantee; they now become the Earl of Northangerland and Duke of Zamorna respectively; helps Zamorna become King of Angria (1834); becomes his Prime Minister--an alliance sealed by the marriage of his daughter, Mary Henrietta, to Zamorna; helps lead a Revolution (1836) against Zamorna, who is defeated and captured, but saves his life by sending him into exile to Ascension Isle in "The Rover"; on Zamorna's successful attempt to regain his country, Percy is allowed to live, provided he lives quietly as a private individual; grows more abrasive and irritable the older he gets. Variously known as Rogue, Percy, Elrington, Northangerland; his mistresses include Harriet O'Connor (Montmorency), Lady Georgina Greville, Lady St James, Louisa Dance (Vernon), Miss Pelfe, Madame Lalande.

Percy, Edward: Unpleasant, rejected eldest son of Northangerland; given at birth to S'Death to be destroyed but saved by him; a destitute and wicked childhood; saves the Marquis of Fidena's life; founds Edwardston, where owns a new mill; his factories dominate the main towns; becomes MP, Lord Viscount Percy, rising to post of Secretary of Trade in

Angria; duels with the Marquis of Ardrah; m. Maria Sneachi in June 1834; haughty, handsome, cruel, dishonest, with a coarse mind.

Percy Hall: Percy residence in Wellingtonsland.

Percy, Lady Mary (Maria): See Percy, Alexander Augustus; the soft spirit who had charmed Percy away from his evil genius; after her death Percy becomes a desolate man, his "life and motives utterly perverted."

Percy, Mary Henrietta: Marchioness of Douro, Duchess of Zamorna, Queen of Angria. See Wellesley, Arthur Augustus Adrian.

Pigtail: 7-9 feet high and very ugly; champion of the French; cattle thief; arrested for selling "white bread" (a mould of arsenic and oil of vitriol) and "Prussian butter" (Prussic acid made up to look like butter); picks up stray children to sell to the mills or for torture for public entertainment.

Quashia Quamina: Son of the Ashantee King, Sai Tootoo; adopted by Wellington after Sai Tootoo's death at the Battle of Coomassie and brought up with his children; becomes leader of the Ashantees and incites them to rebellion; allied with Northangerland and Zamorna's enemy, he murders Zamorna's son, Ernest, and sacks Adrianopolis.

Reformers: Attempt to reform the constitution of Verdopolis under the leadership of the Marquis of Ardrah; oppose the creation of Angria and what they see as Zamorna's despotic form of government; gain control of Verdopolis and successfully invade Angria, but are overthrown in turn by Northangerland.

Regina: Site of the major battle during the insurrection led by Rogue in Sneaky's Glass Town (1832) between the rebel forces and those of the four kings of the Glass Town Confederacy.

Richton, Viscount: See Flower, Sir John.

Rogue (Rougue): See Percy, Alexander Augustus.

Ross, Captain John: King of Rossesland; friend of the Marquis of Ardrah.

Rover, The: Northangerland's boat.

S'Death, Robert Patrick: Alias King; Rogue's partner and servant; uncle of Patrick Benjamin Wiggins; saves William and Edward Percy from death; captain of "The Rover."

Segovia, Maria di (later Augusta di Segovia): See Percy, Alexander; plots to kill Percy's father, but is poisoned by her accomplices for withholding payment.

Soult, Alexander (Alphonse) (Young Soult): Marquis of Marseilles, son of the Duke of Dalmatia, "son" of Marshal Soult, leader of the French forces against the Duke of Wellington. As Young Soult the Rhymer, the poet of Glass Town and Branwell's pseudonym, patronized by Zamorna, and later made Angrian Ambassador to Verdopolis. As poet, his apparel is torn, "his shoes often slipshod and his stockings full of holes"; his expression is "wild and haggard, and generally he is eternally twisting his mouth to one side or another"; "devilish but humane and good hearted"; Charlotte recognizes his "beginnings are small" but believes "his end will be great." His friendship with the Marquis of Douro rouses the envy of Lord Charles Wellesley.

Tower of All Nations: Landmark in Glass Town, modeled on the Tower of Babel or Babylon.

Tree, Captain: A Glass Town novelist and rival of Captain Bud and Lord Charles Wellesley; father of Sergeant Tree, Glass Town's chief publisher, printer, bookseller, and an early pseudonym of Charlotte.

Twelves, The: Originally Branwell's toy soldiers; become the discoverers, explorers, and settlers of Ashantee, forming the Glass Town Confederacy; the original Twelves chosen were: Charlotte's--Marcus O'Donell, Ferdinand Cortez (Corky), Felix de Rothesay, Eugene Cameron, Harold FitzGeorge, Henry Clinton, Francis Stewart, Ronald Traquair, Ernest Fortescue, Gustavus Donaley, Frederic Brunswick, Arthur Wellesley; Branwell's--Butter Crashey, age 140; Alexander Cheeky, surgeon, age 20; Arthur Wellesley, trumpeter, age 12; William Edward Parry, trumpeter, age 15; Alexander Sneaky, sailor, age 17; John Ross, lieutenant, age 16; William Bravey, sailor, age 27; Edward Gravey, sailor, age 17; Frederic Guelph, sailor, age 27; Stumps (died May 18, 1770), age 12; Monkey, age 11; Tracky, age 10; Crackney, age 5--these last four were middies. The First Twelves later became the House of Lords of Glass Town; a Second Twelves became the House of Commons; four of them--Arthur Wellesley, Sneaky, Parry and Ross became kings of their countries--Wellingtonsland, Sneachiesland, Parrysland and Rossesland.

Velino: Site of a battle during the War of Encroachment against the Ashantees and the French.

Verdopolis: Capital of the Glass Town Confederacy--first called Glass Town, then Verreopolis, then Verdopolis; on the river Guadima; center for government, "high life," and commerce; "a splendid city rising with such graceful haughtiness from the green realm of Neptune" with walls, battlements, a cathedral, the domed Bravey's hotel, the Great Tower, and many fine streets with fine shops. See also Glass Town.

Vernon, Caroline: Daughter of Northangerland and Louise Vernon (Dance); later Zamorna's ward, then his mistress.

Warner, Warner Howard: Barrister; head of Clan Agars, Howards and Warners; Chancellor of the Exchequer and Home Secretary for Zamorna and his most loyal ally; Lord Lieutenant of Angria; Fellow of St Michael's; MP for the Philosophers' Isle; succeeds Northangerland as Zamorna's Prime Minister; m. Ellen Grenville; residences--Warner Hall, Warner Hotel (Verdopolis), Howard House (Adrianopolis), Woodhouse Cliffe (near Freetown); an honest man whose advice is often rejected by Zamorna; credited with the gift of second sight.

Wellesley, Arthur: Duke of Wellington; father of Arthur Augustus Adrian and Charles Albert Florian; adoptive father of Quashia.

Wellesley, Arthur Augustus Adrian: b. 1812/13; Wellington's eldest son; Marquis of Douro and Alderwood; Earl of Evesham and Baron Leyden; becomes Duke of Zamorna; King of Angria; eventually Emperor Adrian; m. (1) Lady Helen Victorine Gordon, one son, Ernest Edward; (2) Marian Hume, one son, Arthur Julius, Marquis of Almeida; (3) Lady Mary Henrietta (Northangerland's daughter), 6 sons--Archduke Frederic Julius and Alexander (twins), Augustus Stanley, Charles Seymour, Edward Mornington and little Arthur, and a daughter, Ierne; mistresses include Rosamund Wellesley, Mina Laury, Caroline Vernon. Loved by Lady Zenobia Ellrington who tries to prevent his marriage to Marian Hume by trickery and magic. Awarded territory, Angria--taken from parts of the other provinces of the Confederacy--for his fighting on behalf of the Glass Town Confederacy against the Ashantee, Napoleon and the French; there builds his capital, Adrianopolis; marries Mary Percy, Northangerland's daughter and makes Northangerland his Prime Minister; is opposed by Ardrah and his Reformist army from Verdopolis; Northangerland turns against him and joins with Ardrah; sends Mary to Alnwick to die to revenge himself on his father-in-law; is defeated; sent into exile; returns, helped by Warner Howard Warner and

Mina Laury; retakes his kingdom, demoting Northangerland to the status of private individual. See Percy, Alexander.

Wellesley, Lord Charles Albert Florian: Twin brother to Arthur; when presented to the public he leans too far out of the window and falls, seemingly to his death; at first an ugly meddling imp called Charlie (with a drink named after him); later a "lively elegant" man with a "strong and handsome" countenance; as Charles Townshend, the author of several works by Charlotte including **The Green Dwarf, Corner Dishes, The Spell, My Angria and the Angrians.**

Wellesley, Julia: Zamorna's cousin; "a foolish petted little girl"; m. (1) Edward Sydney; (2) General Thornton.

Wentworth, Charles: Another of Branwell's pseudonyms, he is private secretary to Edward Lofty, Earl of Westwood and Arundel.

Wiggins Family: Patrick Benjamin, Charlotte, Emily and Anne; Charlotte's caricatures of the Brontë family--Patrick is a "slightly built man attired in a black coat and raven grey trousers, his hat placed neatly at the back of his head revealing a bush of carroty hair so arranged that at the side it projects like two spread hands, a pair of spectacles placed across a prominent Roman nose, black neckerchief adjusted with no great attention to detail"; the others-- described by Patrick Wiggins (Branwell)--are "miserable creatures not worth talking about"; Charlotte "a broad dumpy thing whose head does not come higher than my elbow"; Emily "lean and scant with a face almost the size of a penny"; Anne "nothing, absolutely nothing."

Wilson, Richard: Alias Henry Hastings; thief and commercial traveler.

Zamorna: Province of Angria; capital, Zamorna, on the Olympia River; Lord Lieutenant, Viscount Castlereagh.

Zamorna, Duke and Duchess of: See Wellesley, Arthur Augustus Adrian.

Commentary on The Poems

1

In January 1829, at the age of eleven, Branwell fashioned the first of the miniature magazines, modeled on **Blackwood's Magazine**, which he edited until Charlotte took over in August. This poem constitutes the "Poetry" section, and reflects Branwell's interest in events in the American colonies, especially slavery and trade with Britain. See also the comment for No. **4** below. At the end of the poem, an adaptation of the British National Anthem, C T (Captain Tree) notes, "this was sung at the young mens ["young mens" canceled] our oratiorio and was much approved." For a glossary of Glass Town/Angrian names, see **Appendix D.**

2, 3 and 4

All three poems appear in **BRANWELLS BLACKWOODS MAGAZINE** for June 1829 (see **Appendix B** about the February-May issues). Although Charlotte is contributing by now and her signature appears at the bottom of the "CONTENTS" page, the magazine is still clearly Branwell's. No. **2**, headed **MAGAZINE. PBB,** is the lead item and reflects Branwell's dislike for the tyranny of the four Chief Genii (see Alexander, CB, I, 39). Nos. **3** and **4** are sung by Young Soult (Branwell's pseudonym) in a little drama entitled **The Nights.** The scene is set in Bravey's Inn, with the Duke of Wellington, Bravey, Badey, Gravy, Captain Parry, Andrew Jackson, Epimanondas Johnson, Cicero Stephenson, Young Soult, Lucien Bonaparte present (the Marquis of Douro, Lord Charles Wellesley, and Sergeant Bud are added in Scene 2). Soult sings No. **3** after Wellington asks Parry whether the "bill for the supression of the Faction Dumange" has passed or not, and, much to the surprise of both the Duke and Lucien Bonaparte, Parry, reading from a newspaper, replies that it has by a majority of 86. The "Faction Dumange" is probably fictional (see Alexander, CB, I, 119), and the song likely a reference to the passage of the Catholic Emancipation Bill in April 1829. Charlotte recorded: "I remember the day when the Intelligence Extraordinary came with Mr Peel's speech in it . . . . With what eagerness Papa tore off the cover, and how we all gathered round him, and with what breathless anxiety we listened . . . . When the paper came which was to decide the question, the anxiety was almost dreadful with which we listened to the whole affair . . . Papa saying that his [Duke of Wellington] words were like precious gold and, lastly, the majority of one to 4 in favour of the bill"

(Alexander, CB, I, 100).   In Scene 2, Soult sings No. **4**
at the request of the group sitting around the supper table
and is applauded by all except the Americans.   Douro then
proposes a toast in which he states "what are you now but the
Slaves of Slavery then you would be freedoms sons--the toast
which I mean is--THE DOWNFALL OF THE GENII."   When Andrew
Jackson proposes a toast to "that cause which raises up so
many ste[a]m engines and such inventions as these--American
Liberty," the group hisses and reviles him.   Branwell likely
took "Epimanondas" and "Cicero" from either J. Lempriere's
Bibliotheca Classica (London,   1797)   or Thomas   Browne's
"Mythological and Historical Appendix of Proper Names" in the
Union Dictionary,   2nd ed.   (London,   1806),   both   of
which Mr. Brontë owned.

5

From   the   July   1829   **BRANWELLS BLACKWOODS MAGAZINE,**   this
song is again sung by Young Soult in Scene 3 of **The Nights**
just after Sergeant Bud and Douro have had a disagreement
over Bud's commentary on "Fingal by Ossian."   In a letter to
the editor (dated June 1, 1829) in the June magazine, Bud
announces that he had received a copy of Ossian's poems on
May 22 from Chief Genius Taly, and is "engaged in publishing
an edition of them in Quarto--3 Vols--with notes commentarys
&c . . . .   there is a most intense anxiety prevailing
amongst literary men to know its contents in a short time
they shall be gratified for it will be published on the first
of July 1829."   In the July magazine, after Bud offers a
sample of his edition with notes to the group (Napoleon Bonaparte, J. Murat, and Alexander Soult have been added to those
listed in the previous note), Douro comments, "that commentary is in many parts very good sound and just but that which
relates to Tura is unjust in the extreme   it says that Tura
is a cave whereas by your account it must be a castle for
Ossian says Cuthullin sat by Turas WALL.--no cave could have
a wall.   A castle could nay must have walls can you answer."
Napoleon at this point asks them not to quarrel, and Old
Soult asks his son for a song.   Given Charlotte's signature
at the end of **The Nights** and the fact that with this
issue Branwell concludes his editorship of the magazine,
Douro's words, though in Branwell's hand, are quite possibly
Charlotte's.   In turning the editorship over to his sister,
Branwell states:

CONCLUDING ADDRESS
To my Readers PB B--te

We have hitherto conducted this Magazine & we hope to
the satisfaction of most.   (No one can please all) but

as we are conducting a Newspaper which requires all the
time and attention we can spare from ot[h]er employi-
ments we have fouund it expedient to relinquish the
editorship of this Magazine but we recomend our readers
to be to the new Editor as they were to me the new one
is the chief Genius Charlotte she will produce it in
Future tho I shall write now and then for it.   ΔΘHᴵ

July 1829   P B Brontë

6

Alexander (item 229) attributes the poem to Charlotte because
it follows 800 words of prose, dated July 13, 1829, and
entitled **THE ENFANT**, a revision of the narrative published in the May and June issues of **BRANWELLS BLACKWOODS
MAGAZINE** (see Alexander, CB, I, 34).   But, we know from
Charlotte's record that she and Branwell had been reading Sir
Walter Scott's **The Life of Napoleon Buonoparte** (Edinburgh, 1827) at this time (see Alexander, CB, I, 28), and
both the subject matter and the signature "Young Soult" suggest that Branwell is the author.   However, on the basis of
other samples of Charlotte's cursive hand at this time, the
fact that her signature appears at the end of the poem,
though lower on the page and separate from the poem's signature, and the marked improvement in poetic quality over the
previous five items in this edition, the poem may well be a
collaborative venture, similar to that suggested in the previous note.   If the poem is a collaboration, then contrary to
the comment on p. 388 of my **The Poems of Charlotte
Brontë**, this is the earliest poem we know Charlotte had a
hand in.   Unfortunately, the leaf containing Charlotte's
prose piece and this poem was bound by T. J. Wise with twelve
other items of poetry and prose in random order, ranging in
date from March 12, 1829 to July 17, 1834.   As a result, we
do not know the original source for the leaf--a good example
of how Wise's activities have made the editing of Brontë
manuscripts so difficult.

7 and 8

The two poems appear in **BLACKWOODS YOUNG MENS MAGAZINE**
for August 1829, the first of the miniature magazines edited
by Charlotte.   No. **7** constitutes the "Poetry" section; in
the magazine's table of contents it is entitled "a song."
The signature "UT" (Us Two) would again suggest a collaborative effort, although Alexander (EW, p. 38 and CB, I, 74)
suggests the initials may refer to the Marquis of Douro and
Lord Charles Wellesley, making the poems signed "UT" or "WT"

Charlotte's. However, though it is not possible to define the extent, we know that Charlotte and Branwell did collaborate (see, for example, Alexander, CB, I, 39), and the thematic similarity of this poem to Branwell's earlier poems is clear. Therefore, I have included all the poems signed "UT" or "WT" in this edition. No. **8** sung by Sir Alexander Hume Badey, is part of **Military Conversations**; after this drunken performance the Duke of Wellington orders that Badey be taken to the triangle. While Alexander again attributes the poem to Charlotte (item 414 and CB, I, 60), the subject matter and the quality of the verse suggest Branwell as author, although it is also possible that Charlotte is lampooning her brother (compare with Nos. **36, 41, 60** in Neufeldt, PCB).

9 and 10

Both poems appear in the September 1829 issue of **BLACKWOODS YOUNG MENS MAGAZINE.** No. **9**'s signature, subject matter and style suggest Branwell as author. However in the magazine's table of contents the poem is listed as "The Pothouse by UT," and in her December "General Index" to the magazines she has edited, Charlotte includes it as by "UT." Note the similarity of the final stanza to those of Nos. **18** and **26.** No. **10**, the final major item in the September issue, is listed in the table of contents as "A Poem by UT." See also Alexander CB, I, 65, n. 6. The first line of the title appears at the bottom of a manuscript page with the blotted initials "CB" before the "UT," followed by a canceled line: "tis evening and the glorious sun." The second line appears at the top of the next manuscript page. Line 36 is followed by ten canceled lines, the canceled signature and date "UT, August 25 1829," suggesting that the poem was originally to end here.

11

From the October 1829 issue of **BLACKWOODS YOUNG MENS MAGAZINE,** the poem is listed as "the statue & goblet in the desert" in the magazine's table of contents.

12 and 13

Both poems appear in the November 1829 issue of **BLACKWOODS YOUNG MENS MAGAZINE.** Between stanzas four and five of No. **13** are two canceled stanzas (followed by "Sep^t 7 1829") which were taken directly from No. **12** (stanzas 7 and 8). There is also a canceled, undecipherable final stanza, with the alternative version added at the bottom of the page, following the table of contents.

14-24

On September 30, 1829, Branwell "published" two tiny hand-stitched volumes (2-1/2" x 2"--the same size as the little magazines) with stiff bluish-grey covers, the first containing six poems; the second, five. The cover for each volume reads **YOUNG:/ SOULTS/ POEMS WITH/ NOTES::/ IN II VOLS QUARTO** followed by **VOL I** and **VOL II** respectively. The title page of each volume (with a few minor variations in spelling and lining and some abbreviations in the second) reads:

A
COLLECTION OF POEMS
by Young Soult
the Ryhmer
ILLUSTRATED WITH
NOTES =
AND COMMENTARYS BY:
MONSEIUR
DE LA CHATEUBRIAND
Author of Travles in Greece the
Holy land &c the state of
France reveiw of the
Empire &c &c &c.
Sept. 30   ——·——   AD. 1829.

PARIS
Published by M D LA Pack
le eleve M De Brunnete &c
Cheif Glass Town.
Seargeant Tree Corporal Bull
Captain legwind &c &c &c &c
Twemys Glass Town Capt leg.
Parrys glass town Col Wind
Rosses glass town Seargt Snow

An "APPENDIX" at the end of volume one reads:

> This volumn of poems was written [by]
> young Soult the Ryhmer with notes
> and commentary by M D Chateaubriand
> The Poems are six in number
> - Namely -
> The Ammon tree cutter--3 books Blank
> verse with 14. notes & a commentary

A visit to the ruins of ColdaiDuh with
6 notes and a commentary (regular
verse.   10 verses- - - - - - - - - -
ADDress to the Cheif Genius Bany- -
with 1. note & a comment[a]ry 5 verses
irregular
On seeing the Ruins of the Tower of Babylon
with 5 notes and a commentary 6 verses
irregular verse
To Napoleon Bonaparte. with 7 notes
and a commentary 7 verses regular
The prophecy--with 1. note & a comm
entary regular verse.   4 verses- - -
            In the whole- -
there are 6 Poems 35 verses and- -
30 notes & commentarys- - - - - - -

                    _____

PS
This is the only compleat edition of an
number of the works of young soult
the Ryhmer excepting the Octavo one
of his Ryhmes--by Cuvier which is
not compleat having no notes wich it
very much needed--(Chateaub.

There is no evidence of an actual volume of Young Soult's
edited by Cuvier; it is probably Branwell's invention,
especially since he is likely referring to Baron Cuvier, the
famous French naturalist. In volume two the poems are not
titled; the titles in brackets are taken from Branwell's
table of contents. This table is followed by "There ar[e] 11
notes P. B Bronte," and a Preface which reads:

    This volumn is/ a continuation of the First--/ It
    contains the productions/ of leisure hours of young/
    Soult every trifle of a great/ genius is worth
    preserving
    signed// Shatuebriand

The "Appendix" reads:

    This volumn was written by
    Young Soult edited by Mr
    De la Chateaubriand --
        = the poems are 5
            = in number

                    _____

The genius of destruction--
5 verses. and 20 lines--
8 notes and a commentary

The shipwercked sailors--
song 6 versees 24 lines

Song. 6 verses 24 lines

Song 5 verses 20 lines
2 Notes - - - -

To the genius of war 6 v^S 24 1^S.

While the volumes are dated September 30, Branwell may have begun work on them as early as July when he relinquished the editorship of the magazine; one of the advertisements in **BRANWELLS BLACKWOODS MAGAZINE** for July 1829 reads: "There is a new work going to be published--it is POEMS by young soult the Ryhmer--with notes and commentarys by <Moses> Chateaubriand--in 1 volumn quarto--it will probably be published on the 1 of October 1829 P B Bronte." Although Branwell invokes Chateaubriand as his model, and Gérin suggests he read the **Travels** in the Ponden House Library (BB, p. 43), the number of notes in the **Travels** is, in fact, very modest and they are either explanatory or indicate historical uncertainty. Branwell's actual model is more likely McPherson's **Ossian** with its copious notes, which Branwell imitates in the "REVIEW OF BUDS Commentary on Ossian" in his July magazine. He was also familiar with the copious notes that sometimes accompanied poems in **Blackwoods Magazine** and the poems of Scott.

I have been unable to find a source for Branwell's almond tree cutter in No. **14**; he is likely taking poetic liberties with several sources. His opening line appears twice as a line of poetry in a review of Robert Southey's **All for Love, or a Sinner Well Saved** in the July 1829 issue of **Blackwoods Magazine**. The description of Paris on the same page resembles that in John Malcolm's "A Trip to Paris," **Tales of Field and Flood** (Edinburgh, 1829, p. 179), a work Charlotte was reading in September 1829 (Alexander, CB, I, 89). The reference to an earlier description of a tavern may be to No. **9**, though if it is, Branwell is mistaken about it being in the March issue (not extant) of his magazine, as the poem is dated August 21. The inclusion of Murat and Marmont suggests his reading of Scott's **Life of Napoleon Buonoparte** (Edinburgh, 1827) which Charlotte refers to in June and September 1829 (Alexander, CB, I, 28 and 90); Murat was Napoleon's brother-in-law and was governor (not Mayor) of Paris in 1804, but Marmont's christian name was not Pierre (rather Auguste Frederic-Louis Viesse de) and neither meets the fate described here. "Culvington" on p. 15 seems to be Branwell's invention, as are ColdaiDuh, Vina, Mondile, Dalcos, Prince of Coldai, and Farras throne in No. 15, all of which possibly refer to the settlement of the "Ancient Britons" in West Africa.

The description of the Tower of Babel in No. 17 may refer to John Martin's painting "The Fall of Babylon" (Alexander, CB, I, 97). See also Nos. 20 and 26. "Lucien" on p. 22 probably refers to Lucien Buonoparte, whom Scott describes as a distinguished orator, "scarce inferior to his brother in ambition and talent." "Boyer's Dict." on p. 25 seems to refer to Abel Boyer's **The Royal Dictionary, French and English, and English and French,** which by 1819 was in its twenty-third edition. However, it contains no such definition. The tone of the last stanza of No. 18 is similar to that of the endings of Nos. 6 and 26. "Rarras" in No. 19 seems again to be Branwell's invention. The Tower of All Nations in No. 20 was based on the biblical Tower of Babel and inspired by John Martin's painting "The Fall of Babylon." However "The Flight of the Genius of Destruction over the glass town" may also refer to Martin's "The Fall of Ninevah," which was reviewed in **Blackwoods,** July 1828. See also Nos. 17 and 26. If the "Acts of the Genii" ever existed, it is no longer extant. "Carrils stream" in No. 23 refers to Carril, Cuthullin's bard in "Fingal" in **Ossian.**

25 and 26

The manuscript text of these poems, on opposite sides of a single leaf bound in green morocco by Sangorski and Sutcliffe, varies considerably from the existing published versions (except for Winnifrith PCB), yet these versions have the same dates as the manuscript. The SHB C and B notes for No. 25 an earlier draft, dated September 18, 1829, but there is no evidence to corroborate the existence of such a draft. Although in previous published versions the title reads "belonging to E," the manuscript clearly reads "belonging to you." No. 26 appears in the BST version with the extra title "THE WALK." In the manuscript the title "THE WALK" (canceled) and two undecipherable lines of canceled verse are part of a third poem (possibly an early draft of Charlotte's **The Evening Walk**). The SHB version of No. 26, except for the deletion of the extra title, follows the BST version. One can only conclude that the two poems were either carelessly mistranscribed or, given the difficulty of reading the microscopic script, liberally "edited."

The size of the manuscript leaf and the subject matter suggest that the poems were intended for **BLACKWOODS YOUNG MENS MAGAZINE,** but were either never included or were part of a lost issue that has been dismembered. For other poems on the same subject as No. **26,** see Nos. **17** and **20.** Note the similarity in tone between the last stanza and the final stanzas of Nos. **9** and **18.**

27, 28 and 29

All three poems appear in the first number of **BLACKWOODS YOUNG MENS MAGAZINE** for December 1829 (the quantity of material necessitated two numbers for December). The signature WT at the end of No. **28** signifies "We Two" (Charlotte's table of contents lists No. **28** as "On the Transfer of this Magazine by UT"). Poems **28** and **29,** in Charlotte's hand though presumably both written in collaboration, point to the differences of interest and emphasis that had arisen between Charlotte and Branwell and mark the end of Branwell's involvement with the magazine, though he obviously regarded the changeover as deleterious. In August 1830, Charlotte launched a new series of the magazine without Branwell's participation. The lawyer referred to in the title of No. **28** is probably Sergeant Bud. Lines 18 in No. **28** and 16 in No. **29** recall Pope's **Dunciad.**

30

From the second number of the magazine for December 1829, the poem is likely more Charlotte's than Branwell's, as indicated by the fact that Charlotte first signed the poem with her own name, then changed to the customary "UT." The change from the quatrain to blank verse quite pos- sibly reflects Charlotte's reading of Milton (see Gérin CB, p. 24).

31

This is the first of three "dramatic poems" Branwell composed in 1829 and 1830 (see also Nos. **35** and **36**) reflecting his reading of Roman and Medieval European history. As in the case of the two volumes of Young Soult's poems (Nos. **14–24**), each of the plays is a "published" volume by Young Soult. The cover for this fourteen-page stitched manuscript (3-3/4" x 2-1/4") reads **LAUSSANE/ A TRAJEDY/ BY/ YOUNG SOULT/ IN I VOL OCTAVO/ PBB::.** Originally the title page began "VALOISE & LAUSANNE," but "VALOISE" is canceled and the page reads:

The figure of Justice appears at the bottom of the page. While the dialogue is in the usual miniature print writing, the stage directions are in long-hand. The last page, however, is almost entirely in long-hand, as if hurriedly tacked on, a possibility also suggested by the rather sentimental ending. The play does not seem to be based on any specific historical or literary incident. Lausanne had been a bishopric well before 1423; thus a Count of Lausanne would not have existed. The English-French mixture "John de Valence" is equally problematical. In fact, Branwell may well have borrowed the names from Charlotte's **The Swiss Artist** begun in 1829; initially set in the south of France, then shifted to Switzerland (see Alexander CB, I, 92-94; 115- 117), it contains among other characters "Jean de Valence" and "Compte de Lausanne." The Brontë family also owned Scott's **Tales of a Grandfather** (Edinburgh, 1827-28), in which Sir Aymer de Valence, chasing Robert the Bruce, comes into Galloway with a large body of men, and Abbe Lenglet Du Fresnoy's **Geography For Youth** (Dublin, 1795). Alexander (EW, p. 21) suggests Byron as a source for Branwell's interest in poetic drama in 1829/30.

32, 33 and **34**

These fragments constitute the last two pages of the manuscript booklet of **Laussane** (No. **31**), appearing after the signature at the end of the verse drama. No. **34** seems to consist of preliminary sketches for a piece of Latin verse composition, a series of attempts, suggests Everard Flintoff of the University of Leeds, to work up a few detached lines that could be read as Latin poetry, explaining why the same words appear over and over and are shuffled about. Despite the obvious problems in grammar and spelling, the heavily Virgilian vocabulary suggests how much Branwell by the age of twelve had already steeped himself in the Virgilian epic. At the beginning are seven canceled lines which read:

> Marcius Moriens Donit Dic Hic
> Reserva Hic in Memoriam tu pater
> Dum Habes tu crescam quam candidus flos Agris
> Marcius Moriens donit Donavit Me
> Partus Hujus Tesserae Ait "O Silvius
> Ego dono tu Hic Tessera
> Dum habes tu crescam quam \<candidusque\>
> Portius   \<Hujus\>

35

The second of Branwell's "published" verse dramas (18 pp., 4" x 5", hand-stitched); the cover reads: **CARACTACUS/ A DRAMATIC/ POEM BY/ YOUNG/ SOULT/ IN/ I/ VOLUMN/ QUARTO.** The title page reads:

CARACTACUS.
A DRAMATIC POEM.
BY PATRICK Branwell
Bronte.
IN
ONE
VOLUMN
QUARTO
B
Y
YOUNG (TR)
SOULT

Cheif Glass Town printed and sold
by
SEARGEANT TREE
DUKE of Wellingtons
Glasstown. S. price & Co
CAPTAIN E PArrys
Glasstown S. Jenvills
CAPTIN J. Ross's
Glasstown & Caleton

"In Dramatic Poetry the passions are the cheif thing and in "Proportion as exelence in the depicting of these is ob

"tained so the writer of the poem takes his class am
"ong Dramatic authors."

C. BUD'S Synopis of Dra
matic writing Vol I. p 130.

JUNE 26. A D 1830.

Following the list of characters (in which Branwell records
not only the number of times each character is mentioned, but
also which of the characters are "fabulous"), is a Preface
which reads

> Of The events recorded in this poem, those which are not
> fictitious are took from the early English History. And
> the truth stands thus "When the Romans under the command
> Ostorius Scapula AD. 51. Invaded Britain Caractacus a
> British King undertook to defend his country and
> therefore put himself at the head of a large army of
> Britons. with these he retired to the Mountains of
> Wales perpetualy harrasing the Romans for Nine years.
> till at last being obliged to come to a descicive
> Enggagement. wherein he was defeated. but however he
> fled to Cartismandua Queen of the Brigantes who basely
> delivered him up to the Romans. he was with other
> prisoners carried to Rome when he was Brought there
> nothing could exceed the curiosity of the people to
> behold a man who for Nine years had braved their
> choicest legions on his part he testified not the least
> sort of dejection and while the other captives were
> meanly beggeing their pardon Caractacus stood before the
> Tribunal with an intrepid air And seemed rather willing
> to accept pardon than meanly sollicitous of sueing it
> And in consequence of his manly and heroic behaviour.
> the Emperor Claudius gave him and them full and
> Immediate LIBERTY.
> This is the true history of Caractacus But whatever
> deviations I have made must be ascribed to the Nature of
> the Poem not Myself. which allows far more Latitud in
> this respect than I have given it, but I now Leave the
> work to my readers let them who are Impartial judge me
> and my work Not the base and snarling critics who having
> no exelence of their own employ themselves in underating
> those of others
>
> Young Soult
>
> Paris June 28
> Anno Dominii 1830.

P B B

Although Lempriere's **Bibliotheca Classica** notes Tacitus'
Annals as the source for Caractacus, it is not the source
for Branwell's Preface. The Preface may well consist of

notes compiled from various sources, including William
Mavor's **Universal History**, 25 vols., London, 1802-04, a
work Charlotte recommended to Ellen Nussey in 1834 (SHB LL,
I, 122). Some similarities with phrasing in vol. VI, pp.
167-77 suggest Branwell had read Mavor, yet the Preface contains details not included in Mavor. Branwell's "deviations"
are, in fact, considerable. The characters he identifies as
"fabulous" (Mumius, Carausius, Icenus, Brigantes) bear no
resemblance to the originals. The Iceni and Brigantes were
tribes defeated by Publius Ostorius. If Branwell took the
names Carausius and Mumius from Lempriere, he changed their
characters completely. Lempriere describes Carausius as "a
tyrant of Britain for 7 years," and Mumius as a Roman consul
who destroyed Corinth, Thebes and Chalcis by order of the
Senate, but "did not enrich himself with the spoils of the
enemy . . . . He was so unaq[u]ainted with the value of the
paintings and works of the most celebrated artists of Greece
. . . that he said to those who conveyed them to Rome, that
if they lost them or injured them, they should make others in
their stead." Thus Mumius' treachery and his conversation
with the Queen in Act I, scene i, as well as the whole of Act
I, scenes ii and iii, Act II, scene i, and the final dialogue
between Mumius and Claudius are Branwell's inventions. The
comments concerning critics are aimed directly at Charlotte,
part of the literary rivalry that had developed between them
(see Alexander EW, pp. 65-6).

36

The third of Branwell's "published" verse dramas (14 pp.,
4.1" x 3.5," hand-stitched); the cover reads: **THE REVENGE/
A/ TRADGEDY/ BY YOUNG SOULT./ II VOLS:/ VOL, I.**

The title-page reads:

> THE REVENGE   204
> A
> TRADGEDY IN :
> 3 Acts by
> : YOUNG SOULT
> IN
> TWO VOLUMNS
> QUARTO
> P B Brontë

In dramatic poetry the cheif thing to be attained
Is an excellence in describing the passions and in
proportion as this excelence is attained so are we
To judge of the merits of the peice

371

GLASS TOWN
Printed and sold by S Tree
PARIS
M De La Pack
December
18th

Between Act II, ll. 44 and 45, upside down and canceled, an earlier draft of Act I, Sc I, ll. 1-15 reads:

Tyrant! thy course is stopt no longer now
Shalt thou relentless desolate the earth
All thing[s] devouring in thy rapid vortex
Thousands have falln before thy bloody throne
And feasting yet thou feasts thy mind with thousands
    more
Which soon thou thinkst shall bite the dust before thee
Rolling in agonies before thy footstool
No now thy torrent stops and favring fortune
Now veile they countenance in clouds and tempests
Ye shades of those who died at thy command
Departed spirits now I do ajure you
Call down your vengeance & fulminate your thunders
On his accursed and <reviled> head
But lo the sun has set and the pale moon
Rolls up the vault of Heaven her silver car

Squeezed in at the bottom of the same manuscript page, following Act II, l. 50, appears the uncanceled trial line "But <cheifly> traitor thou art doomed to feel steel"--see Act II, ll, 75-76.

Although Branwell places the play in fourteenth-century Germany, it does not seem to be based on any readily identifiable historical event or literary source. Indeed, the content is more typical of German/British Gothic than medieval German literature, and suggests a knowledge of Goethe and Schiller. In Act II, l. 79 Branwell echoes l. 55 of Gray's **Elegy Written in a Country Churchyard.** There is no evidence that the second volume was ever completed. In the existing manuscript, the text covers twelve pages, the next two pages have been cut out, and the final two pages are blank.

37

In September 1830 Branwell began a six-volume series of "pub-
lished" **Letters From An Englishman To His Relative
[Freind** from Vol. II on] **In London,** written by James
Bellingham, a London banker visiting Glass Town, to Adam
Scott in London, and edited by Captain John Flower from Vol-
ume II on. Each volume, measuring 2-3/4" x 2-1/4," is hand-
stitched, and has a lettered cover and a title-page. Gérin
(BB, p. 63) suggests Goldsmith's **Citizen of the World** as
Branwell's literary model, and Branwell does quote the **The
Deserted Village** in Letter I, in addition to **The Elegy**
as noted above. However, another possible model is "Letters
From the Peninsula," a series on Wellington's campaigns in
Spain and Portugal in **Blackwoods** from June 1827 to May
1828. This poem appears in Volume II, Letter III, dated
March 16, 1831 (but at the end of Letter IV, dated March 18,
Branwell notes "real date, P B Brontë June 8th
1831"). Bellingham, traveling in a coach with the Marquis of
Douro, Lord Charles Wellesley and Young Soult, and threatened
by the onset of nightfall and a violent storm, reports:

> The Marquis employed himself in lashing on his horses to
> as great a speed as possible I like a true Englishman
> prepared to encounter the tempest by buttoning on a
> ample greatcoat and taking 4 or 5 folds of a silk
> neckcloth round my throat while Young Soult after the
> manner of a hair brained poet sat motionless conversing
> whith the planet Mars which still look[ed] throug[h]
> that gathering tempest in such raphsodies as the
> following
> [poem]
> but he was silenced in the midst of this bombast by a
> loud squall of wind which sweeping full in our faces
> carried of every mans hat into a pool on the road side.

In my edition of Charlotte's poems, I noted her ridicule
of Branwell's melodramatic poetic posturing (see pp. 397-99;
402). Given the parody of himself as poet Branwell offers
here, and the distinctly classical tone and form of his poems
on pp. 72-96, Charlotte's satirical admonitions seem to have
had some effect (see also **Introduction,** pp. xxxviii-
xxxix).

38

This poem appears at the end of a postscript to Letter VI in
the third volume:

Post[s]cript. March 23. 1831.] I have just no[w]
returned from the first day of the celebration of the
Olympic or Great African game[s] where I have witnessed
a scene which I think will serve to expand your Ideas of
the young men (this is only by way of post[s]cript The
assembly in number perhaps 5 or 6 millions being seated.
the orchestra of 10000 performers on the organ harp
trumpet flute and clarionet these being the only
instruments allowed to be used began An Ode to the
praise of the Twelves in a solemn strain of the
sublimest music that ever I heard Handel Mozart and all
those who till now I considered the best musicians in
the universe sunk to notingh before it. it began by a
single flute which was scarcly heard throug[h] the
building but which seemed to float on the air like the
music of a fairy this was in time joined by a trumpet
then 2 or 300 instruments and at last the whole
orchestra of 10000 joined in the chorus To give you an
idea of its sublimity. I will tell you that through the
mysteriou[s] influence of music on the soul not a dry
eye was seen in the whole assembly and rare lads and
poachers present absolutly wept aloud for we--all-ways
see the unsophisticated common people more affected than
the more refined higher orders--not to say that they
were so in this case for the higher orders here are much
less artificial and <u>refined</u> than in England but the
common people shewed it more. To me the delight at last
became to great for pleasure and I felt as if I should
be choked and wept copiously as the majestic music
thrilled and trembled through the arched roof and lofty
walls of this Mighty building The following is the ode
sung on this occasion

Although the Letter is signed "I Remain yours &c/ James
Bellingham/ Glass town March/ the 23. A D 1831," Branwell
notes underneath "P B Brontë June 11th A D 1831."

39

This is the first of the five poems in the lost Notebook A
(see p. xi), transcribed by both Symington and Hatfield. The
text provided is Hatfield's at the BPM, rather than Symington's, used for the SHB version, because in addition to differences in wording, the latter omits six lines. Although
the verse form is reminiscent of Pope's translation of **The
Iliad**, Branwell was clearly also influenced by Milton's
description of the war in heaven; he was reading **Paradise
Lost** at least as early as September 1830, when he quotes
from Book I in the second of the **Letters From An
Englishman.** Also, in the edition of **Ossian** Branwell

and Charlotte were reading in 1829 (see comment for No. 5), following the comment, "The shock of two encountering armies, the noise and the tumult of battle, afford one of the most grand and awful subjects of description; on which all epic poets have exerted their strength. Let us first hear Homer," the text refers the reader to "Iliad IV. 46, and VIII. 60." Underneath, either Charlotte or Branwell added in pencil "Book IX 263/82 129 169 180." Arthur, Alexander, Edward and John are respectively Arthur Wellesley, Alexander Sneaky, William Edward Parry and John Ross, the four kings of the Glass Town Confederacy. Where Regina is located is not clear, but the battle is part of Rogue's insurrection in Sneaky's Glass Town in 1832.

40

According to Hatfield's transcription, used here, which has only minor differences in wording from Symington's transcription used for the SHB, the poem covered pp. 8-12 of Notebook A. Despite Branwell's indication of 177 lines in both the title and the table of contents, both transcriptions have only 175 lines. When Charlotte returned home from Roe Head School for the Christmas vacation in 1831, the four children decided formally to dissolve the imaginary kingdom they had created, and she recorded the dissolution in her poem "The trumpet hath sounded" (Neufeldt PCB, p. 150), but in this poem Branwell seems to be trying to ressurect the four Chief Genii, giving "Awful Branii" pride of place (l. 111ff.), perhaps because the poem is dated on his birthday. His frustration over the failure of his attempt is recorded at the beginning of **The Monthly Intelligencer** (see Alexander EW, pp. 84-5). For additional information on the African Games, see SHB Misc I, 123-4. Morven (l. 47) is from Macpherson's **Ossian.**

Achaian:	Achaea is a district on the northern coast of the Peloponnesus, but in Homer and for the Romans, it referred to Greece generally, as Branwell uses it here.
Olympus:	a mountain in Thessaly, the traditional home of the chief Greek gods.
Jove:	Jupiter, the chief deity of the Romans, the equivalent of Zeus.
Juno:	wife of Jupiter.
Athenia:	Athena, Zeus and Apollo formed a triad which represented the embodiment of all divine power. In Homer she is the goddess of counsel, war, female arts and industries, and the protectoress of Greek cities.
Phoebus:	Apollo, Greek god of the sun.

41

Item three in Notebook A, the text is again based on Hatfield's transcription at the BPM. Here too Branwell seems to have miscounted the number of lines. For the last two poems in the Notebook, see Nos. **79** and **80**.

42

From the first (and only extant) number of **The Monthly Intelligencer**, one of the newspapers of Great Glass Town, created by Branwell between March 27 and April 26, 1833. Although this poem concludes the number as a separate item, it seems to refer to the two preceding articles relating Alexander Rogue's seditious behaviour, one written by the author of **Letters From An Englishman** (see commentary for No. **37**).

43-46

These poems are all from the second volume of a thirty-six page manuscript entitled **Real Life in Verdopolis**, dated August 17-September 21, 1833. No. **43** is sung by Castlereagh, accompanying himself on the lute, to Lady Julia Wellesley beneath her window. After singing his love song, he is about to depart, when another male, hidden in the trees, sings No. **44**. Nos. **45** and **46** are sung by Rogue in chapter V, dated 18 September, as part of his satirical parody of a Dissenting worship service (see also No. **135**).

47

From chapter I of **THE./ WOOL IS RISING./ OR/ THE ANGRIAN ADVENTURE./ A Narrative of the proceedings/ Of/ the Foundation of the/ Kingdom of Angria**, a twenty-four page manuscript at the British Library, begun in May and completed June 26, 1834. Northangerland is reminiscing about his past relationship with Zamorna and the situation he finds himself in. He concludes: "I may then be constantly harrassed with fears of death. a little defeat may enrage me. the advancement of an opponent a rival an enemy a Fidena may half madden me and yet there is enough <earninges> to keep the ship from sinking enough sunshine to warm me in this winter the horrors of actual conflict produce a silent quiet joy the thoughts of future steps gained points accomplished produces a tumultuous excitement--Hah--Faugh!--Hang me. and the world too!

Northangerland dragged a book toward him across the table. opened at a blank leaf and taking a pen began to scribble lines as fast as his practised hand could move." This poem is followed immediately by the early draft of No. 72.

48

In contrast to the miniature print writing of Branwell's previous work, this poem is in copperplate hand, on the same lined paper and page size he used in Notebook B, but it seems to have been bound by him as a separate unit. His use of ordinary hand, rather than the miniature print writing, in Notebook A and this poem may well be related to Charlotte's "public" volume of poems begun in December 1833 (see pp. xxxvi-vii of Neufeldt PCB). The Battle of Thermopylae clearly fascinated Branwell, and "Book 1st" suggests he planned a longer work. Everard Flintoff of Leeds University believes that Branwell originally planned poems covering the morning before the battle, the battle itself, and the battle's aftermath at dusk, a very plausible suggestion in light of Nos. **49, 50,** and **80.**

Thermopylae: the only pass by which an enemy could move from Thessaly into central and southern Greece (Achaia). In 480 B. C. Leonides and 300 Spartans made an heroic defense here against the army of Xerxes, king of Persia, but were defeated when the Persians discovered a path over the mountain, enabling them to attack the Greeks from the rear.

Argolic: the peninsula of Argolis in the district of Argos in the eastern Peloponnesus. The Argives were friendly to Persia and took no part in the war against Xerxes.

Attica: the district around Athens.

Mithras: the ancient Persian god of light and truth, supposed to be the sun or Venus Urania.

Peneus: the chief river of Thessaly.

Parthians and Medians: Iranian tribes, part of the Persian Empire. The Parthians excelled as archers on horseback.

Achaia: Greece--see comment for No. **40.**

Mardonius: one of the chief Persian instigators of the expedition against Greece.

Trachinian: an inhabitant of Trachis in Thessaly who showed the Persians the path over the mountain that enabled them to attack Leonides' troop from behind.

Although both Gérin BB and Winnifrith PBB suggest Branwell read Glover's **Leonides** in the Ponden House Library, all the basic information on the Persian/Greek conflict was also available to him in Mavor's **Universal History** (see comment for No. 35).

49

These faintly penciled lines, undated and unsigned but in Branwell's hand, appear on the endpaper of a Prayer Book in Greek that belonged to Mr. Brontë. The Prayer Book originally belonged to Jane Morgan, and was presented to Mr. Brontë as a memorial of Mrs. Morgan by William Morgan, September 29, 1827. The lines, describing the band surrounding Leonides, seem to be the beginning of a description of the engagement at Thermopylae (see previous comment). The last two lines, however, seem to refer to the battle's aftermath and were likely added later. For the date ascribed to the fragment, see the following comment.

> Pindus: rugged mountain range in northwestern Greece
>   separating Thessaly from Epirus.

50

These lines cover most of the verso of a single manuscript leaf containing an early draft of **Sound The Loud Trumpet** (No. 73) on the recto, and trial lines for **Misery** (No. 54) on both sides, one such set of six lines separating these two passages. This combination of items, and the fact that Branwell seems to have been working on his Thermopylae poems in January 1835 (see No. 80), suggests a date of early 1835 for Nos. 49 and 50.

> Scyros: island off Thessaly where Theseus was slain and
>   buried; sanctuary of Achilles.
> Euboea: largest island of the Greek archipelago where
>   the Greeks won a great naval victory over the
>   Persians in 480 B. C.
> Phechia: Phocus is a district in central Greece con-
>   taining Parnassus and Delphi. During the
>   Persian invasion (480) the Phocians helped
>   oppose the Persians, but their irresolute con-
>   duct at Thermopylae helped lose that position
>   for the Greeks.

51

In an untitled manuscript in the Taylor Collection at Princeton University, Henry Hastings describes how he awakens Christmas morning to the sound of music: "However would I give the sounds of Music in words on paper--What did I hear--Deep and thrilling the Trumpets and Trombones of a great Band with the long warlike rolling of the Drums." Between the two stanzas, he notes, "There was a majestic flood of sounds for ye Then a symphony of Horns and Hark the Blast of the Chorous." The words are sung in honor of Zamorna and Percy who have escaped after having been imprisoned by the Premier, the Marquis of Ardrah.

52

Before these lines at the end of the manuscript noted in No. **51**, Hastings says, "For myself I look forward with Untameable Excitement to the Life which is opening out for me--But let me not speak of it It may be Finished ere tomorrow and under any circumstances let me remember that . . . ." Although Hastings dates his manuscript December 28, 1835, the manuscript is signed below "P B Bronte/ January the/ Seventh/ 1836".

53

Caroline Vernon, speaking these lines to Percy after she has examined Zamorna's cloak, which Percy has brought from the battlefield, wonders what Zamorna was like in his cloak on the battlefield. Three pages further on, the manuscript is dated February 10, 1836.

54

On April 8, 1836, Branwell sent this revised version to the editor of **Blackwood's Magazine** with the following letter:

> **Sir, Read now at least,**
>
>   Abscence from home has for a long time prevented my again addressing you, but that cause being removed I must press forward where as my purpose is earnest I cannot think of laying aside.
>   The affair which accompanies my letter is certainly sent for insertion in Blackwood as a Specimen, which, wether bad or good, I earnestly desire you to look over,

it may be disagreeable--but you will then KNOW wether in
putting it into the fire you--would gain or lose.
    It would now be impudent in me to speak of my
powers since in five minutes you can tell wether or not
they are Fudge and nonsense but this I know that if they
are such I have no intention of stooping under them.
New powers I will get if I can and provided I keep them
you Sir shall see them.
    Yet of this Specimen I must say so much, that if it
possess no incident I know it because I wrote it as a
description of Two Scenes and no more if I wrote my mind
on them with all my earnestness I think I did what I
could. Respecting the fashion of my left handed writing
it is owing to a hurt received by my right hand in
sparring which till now has disabled me from using it.
    Moreover should these Miseries appear in your
periodical a Third shall be indited--a Scene after
Death--the soul followed to its final misery--But dont
think Sir that I write nothing but miseries my day is
far too much in the morning for such continual
shadow--Nor think either (and this I intreat) that I
wish to deluge you with poetry. I send it because it is
soonest read and comes from the heart--If it goes to
yours print it and write to me on the subject of
contribution Then I will send prose--But if what I now
send is worthless what I have said has only been conceit
and folly--Yet CONDEMN NOT UNHEARD
                                --P B Bronte--
                        Haworth near Bradford Yorkshire

An earlier draft of Scene I at the BPM (see p. 98), completed
on December 18, 1835, constituted pages 2-8 of Notebook B.

How fast that courser fleeted by
His arched neck backward tossed on high
His snorting nostrils opened wide
His foam flecked chest and gory side
    I saw his Riders darkned form   5
As on they hurried through the storm
Forward he pressed his plume behind
Flew whistling in the wintery wind
But his clenched teeth and angry eye
Seemed wind and tempest to defy   10
And eagerly he bent his sight
To peirce the darkness of the night
And oft he gazed and gazed again
Through the rough blast and driving rain
    Look up and see the midnight heaven   15
Where mass oer mass continual driven
The wild black storm clouds fleet and change
Like formless phantoms vast and strange

That bend their gloomy brows from high
To pass in midnight darkness by   20
And still they pass and still they come
Without a flash to break the gloom
--I cannot see the foam and spray
That mark that raging torrents way
But well I hear the ceaseless roar   25
Where swollen and chafed its waters pour
There--where yon blackned Oaks on high
Blend wildly with the midnight sky
Tossing their bare and groaning boughs
Like some dread fight of Giant foes   30
There--where that glimpse of Moonlight shines
    From the wild wrack of heaven sent down
And spreads it silver trembling lines
    Amid the darkness then is gone--
--There stays the Horsman--wide before   35
Deep and Dark the waters roar
But down the lone vale far away
Glances one solitary ray
The sound of winds and waters rise
And sweeps the sleet shower oer the skies   40
While dreariest darkness all around
Makes still more drear each sight or sound
But heeds not such that Cavalier
Reining his trembling Charger there
He halts upon the rivers brink   45
Where all its wild waves surge and sink
Shades with his hand his anxious eye
And through the night looks eagerly
--Why smiled he when that far off light
Again broke twinkling on his sight   50
Why frowned he when it sunk again
Mid the rough wrack of stormy rain
Till brightly flashing forth once more
It streams and twinkles far before

"Oh through the tempests of this life   55
    However loud they sound
However wild their storms and strife
    May burst and thunder round
Though reft and riven each aid or prop
There may be Heaven!--There may be Hope!   60
I thought just now that Life or Death
    Could never trouble me
That I should draw my future breath
    In silent apathy
That oer the pathway of my fate   65
    Though steady beat the storm
As I walked alone and desolate
    Ide to that path conform

                        381

Affection should not cherish me
    Or Sorrow hold me down   70
But Despair itself sustain me
    Whom itself had overthrown
I knew that fame and glory
    Were names for shame and woe
That Lifes deceitful story   75
    I had finished long ago
That all its novelty was gone
    And that thus to read again
The same dull page in the same sad tone
    Was not even change of pain   80
Defeat had crushed me into dust
    But only laid my head
Where head and heart and spirit must
    Be soon for ever laid
My fearless followers all were slain   85
    My power and glory gone
My followers met the fate of man
    And Power--! I am NOW alone!
Not so!--I thought it--till that light
    Glanced glittering down the glen   90
And on my spirits dreary night
    Flashed brighter back again
Yes! I had thought I stood alone
That I need sigh or weep for none
Had quenched my love in apathy   95
Since none could sigh or weep for me
Yes! But that single silver beam
    Which flashes in my eye
Hath waked me from my dreary dream
    And bade my darkness fly   100
But pardon that the storms of woe
    Have whelmed me in a drifting sea
With death and dangers struggling so
    That I--a while--forgot even THEE
The moment that I gained the shore   105
    And clouds began to dissapear
Even steadier brighter than before
    THOU shinest my own--my Guardian Star!
    --Oh could I speak the long lost feeling
The inward joy its power revealing   110
The glimpse of something yet to come
Which yet shall give a happy Home!
    Oh should I speak my thoughts of thee
Whom soon again my eyes shall see
--The Dove that bore the Olive leaf   115
Could never bring such glad relief
To wanderers oer the shoreless main
As in my weariness and pain
    That single light hath given to me

My Gallant Horse speed swiftly thou,   120
Soon shall a Hand caress thee now
Gratful that thou hast born me on
Through deadliest deeds and dangers gone
A touch thou mayest be proud to own
Though thou so oft hast felt my own!   125
--Oh that fair hand and faithful heart
From mine what power can ever part?
What Power?--Ha! well indeed I know
The very fire that burns me now
The very energy of soul   130
    That to thine arms impells me on
When once I have gained that heavenly goal
    Will--like a comet from the sun
Hurl me with power that scorns controll
    Far from thy beams of Happiness   135
    Into the Expanse of mad distress
Where passions lightnings burst and battles
    thunders roll!"

    Impetous then that Horseman sprung
Down the deep bank--His Armour rung
    Mid the wild waters roar   140
And Dashing through the Old Oak trees
His Coursers hoofs upon the breeze
Their reckless rattle swiftly cease
    In that Dark night before!

He that hath felt the feeling wild   145
    Which struck upon the excited mind
When perhaps long since--while yet a child
    In awful mystery undefined
Old tales and Legends darkly told,
    While winter nights fell long and drear   150
Have made his hearts blood curdle cold
    Their dreary tales to hear
Of Ancient Halls where Destiny
    Had brooded with its Raven wing
Of castles stern whose riotry   155
    Hid not the gloomy crimes within
Of Death beds, where the sickman lying
    Mid anxious listners standing by
Ere he had told the secret dying
    And left a sealed mystery   160
Of Heirs who to some fearful Doom
    Suceeded with their ancient Hall
Of Marriage Feasts where Ghosts would come
    The new made Bride to call
--He that Hath still in memory
    Kept fast those dreams of childhoods hours   165
Who these far visions yet may see

Of Castle halls and feudal towers
--To Him I show this stormy Night
That seems to darken on my sight!

Far above their forest trees 170
   Those dreary turrets rise
And round their walls the midnight breeze
   Comes shrieking from the skies
Scarce can I note the central tower
   Amid the impetous storm 175
Till shimmering through the pelting shower
   The moonbeams mark its form
Far downward to the raving stream
   The woody banks decline
Where waters flashing in the gleam 180
   Through deepest darkness shine
Those Giant Oaks their boughs are tossing
   As wild winds wilder moan
Trunks and leaves confusdly crossing
   With a ceasless groan 185
And over all the castle walls
   Rise blacker than the night
No sign of man around their Halls
   Save that lone turret light
The upward path is wild and steep 190
   Yet hear that horseman come
Not toiling up with cautious creep
   But hotly hasting home
The steed is to his stables led
   But wheres the Rider gone 195
Up the high turret staircase sped
   With gladdned haste alone
The Ante Room looks hushed and still
   With lattice curtained close
That tempests sweeping round the hill 200
   Disturb not its repose
Alls soft and calm a holy balm
   Seems sleeping in the air
But what on earth has powr to charm
   A spirit chafed by care 205
The Warrior hastes to seek that power
   He knows the only one
Whose love can sooth his lonly hour
   Or hush his rising groan
And where that soft and solemn light 210
   Shines chequreing oer the floor
He hastens in with armed tread
   Toward the opened door
And entering--Though a sacred stream
   Of Radiance round him fell 215
It could not with its silent beam

His eager spirit quell
"Maria!"--But the silence round
    Would give him no reply
And straightway did that single sound   220
    Without an echo die

"Where hath my Gentle Lady gone
    I do not find her here?"
Lo on that statly couch alone
    Reclines thy Lady fair   225
But--cold and pale is her marble brow
    Dishevelled her sunny hair
Oh! is it in peaceful slumber now
    That she lieth so silent there?
"Heaven bless thy Dreams!" Lord Albert cried   230
    But his heart beat impetously
And as he hasted to her side
    He scarce had power to see
All wildly the scenes of his former life
    Flashed back upon his eyes   235
And at once a cloud of Despair and strife
    Before him seems to arise!
But as the sailor to his ship
    Clings with more frenzied power
As louder thundering oer the deep   240
    Fresh billows whelm it oer
So madly on his only prop
    This war worn man reclined
He could not would not deem his hope
    Delivered to the wind!   245

Yet then why is this start of bewildered fright?
    And whence can arise this fear?
Is it not now the depth of night?
    And sleeps not thy Lady there?
And art not thou on thy Castle height   250
    From wars alarms afar?
See--is that sleep?--
                    --With open eyes
Chilly white and cold she lies!
Sunk her cheeks and blanched her lip   255
    That trembles as with suffering--
She sleeps not till the eternal sleep
    Its dreamless rest shall bring!
Heaven had occupied her mind
To onward hasting Death resigned   260
But mid those strange uncertainties
    That crowd their ghastly phantoms round
When all our Reasons guiding ties
    Are from the parting soul unbound
She thought when first she heard that tread   265

385

That Death himself was hasting near
The conjured vision of his form
   Obeyed her ready fancies fear
   And to her dim eyes seemed to appear
    Till--that one word--and all was clear!   270
Then--sinking Reason rose again
Then--joined the links of memorys chain
Then--spite of all her Dying pain
   She felt--she knew her Lord was there!
Oh! when across that dreary sea   275
The light broke forth so suddenly
What soul can feel what tongue express
The burst of raptured Happiness
   That from her spirit chased its care
   For--She was dying! But--He was near!   280

AH! surely swiftly art thou gliding
   Over Deaths unfathomed sea
Dark and Dread the waves dividing
   Thee from earth and earth from thee!
Life thy own thy native land   285
Parting far on either hand
   As the mighty waters widen
     Onward to Eternity!
Shores of life farewell for ever
   Where thy happiness has lain   290
Lost for ever! Death must sever
   All thy Hopes and joys and pain!
Yet how blest that sound must be
   Which strikes upon thy dying ear
From off the dim departing shore   295
   Allthough its landmarks dissapear
Still sounding oer the eternal roar
   The voice of HIM thou holdst so dear!
   Tis as when the Mariner
Just parted from his native home   300
   After a night of dread and fear
Whose storms have riven the waves to foam
When nights dark hours have wrapt away
All save the sounding of the sea
Morn breaks where all looks new and strange   305
But Hark!--a sweet and sudden change
For on his ear strikes soft from far
In Sabbath chime his Native Bells
He starts and bursts the joyful tear
For things unutterably drear   310
   That farewell Music tells!

Yet stay--why do I wander so
To wile me from that scene of woe?
   There stood the Armed man

The very maddness of Despair   315
In his red eyeballs stricken glare
    His cheek so ghastly wan!
And on her couch his Lady lying
Still and slow and surely dying
Yet with an enraptured smile   320
    And glittering of her glassy eye
And her weak arms she would the while
    Have stretched to clasp him standing by
But they would not her will obey
And motionless beside her lay   325
Then her white lips moved to speak
    But nothing could she say!
This was Deaths triumphant hour
Grasped by his tremendous power
    She must pass away!   330

"Speak Maria!--speak, my love!
    Let me hear thy voice
Nought on earth or Heaven above
    Could make me so rejoice!
Speak O speak and say to me   335
I am not come too late to thee!
Oh tell me that my arm can save
Thy spirit from the hideous grave!
Maria! O my only love
    Tell me thou wilt not die,   340
And naught below me or above
    Shall feel so blest as I!
Oh would that I were far away
Alone upon the stormy sea
Might I awake on yonder plain   345
Where I have left my Soldiers slain
So I could wake and rise and know
    That this was but a frightful dream
That thou at least wert living now
    In love and life and beautys beam!   350
But here's the truth which now I know!
My God My God I cannot bear thy blow!'

All was vain! she moved not spoke not
Speech or sound the silence broke not
But he flung him oer her lying   355
As he would catch her spirit dying
All was vain!--That spirit flies
To God Who gave it in the skys!
That within his arms which lay
Was but a lifeless form of clay   360
Nought of feeling in that face
No return to his embrace,
Not a wish or power to save

387

Its own cold members from their grave
  Go Lord Albert go again   365
    Drown thought amid a world of storms
Go--For thy Despair is vain
  And thy Hope lies food for worms!
      Finished Dec. 18th
        1835
      P B Brontē
      Haworth
      Yorks

Text: l. 145: "He" written above "Who"; neither is
               canceled

Page one of Notebook B contains these trial lines:

  He rode across the Moor at night
    When starlight only shone
  But even their dim beams were bright
    Is that woe which weighed His spirit down

  He galloped onward furiously
    But could not fly from ca[re]
  He fearless faced the winter wind
    But could not give His thoughts to air

Charlotte's manuscript **The Scrap Book** in the British
Library contains the following lines on the verso of the
final page of a **Letter to the right honourable Arthur
Marquis of ARDRAH,** dated December 6, 1834, and signed
"Zamorna C Bronte." The lines are, however, in Branwell's
hand.

  How fast that Horse rushed thundering by
  With Arching neck and flashing eye
  So black the Night so loud the Storm
  I scarce could know its fleeting form
  And yet the those flanks all dashed with mire
  Those Nostrils wide which seem to expire
  The hot short breath of agony

An early draft of Scene II in the PML, dated March 2, 1836,
constituted pp. 9-17 of Notebook B.

  Wide I hear the wild winds sighing
    Oer the Hills and far away
  Heaven in clouds before them flying
    Through the drear December day
    Dull and dark its evening ray   5
  As oer the waste the ceaseless rain
  Drives past is gone and then again

Sweeps cold and drenching by, in showers of sleety
    spray
And now the watery mountains rise
All dimly mingling with the skies   10
At times some black brow darkning forth
Cleaved by the tempest from the north
And then as fast the clouds sail on
All its crags and heath knolls gone
The changing vail of sleet drives oer the waste
    alone   15
    Alone I list to hear the sigh
Of the wild Blast passing by
Far away with mournful moan
It bends the Heath on the old grey stone
Then rising in the Ashtrees bough   20
Scatters the withered leaves below
Blackens the wall with pelting spray
And wails and wanders far away
    Oh when I hear that wintery sound
        The very vales of a mountain land   25
A thousand feelings crowding round
    Start up and rise on every hand
And wake to life as the wild winds wake
        And pass with them away
Sunbeams that oer the spirit break   30
        Amid the dreariest day
But Hush!--And hark that solemn wail
    Tis past!--and yet--tis on my ear
Shrill peircing through the misty veil
    Like voice of the departing year!   35
Oh Hush!--Again and yet again
Bursts forth that loud and longdrawn strain
Soldiers! Attend! it calls you back
From the pursuers bloody track
And wildly oer your foemans fall   40
Resounds your Evening Bugle call!

The Battle is done with the setting sun
The struggle is lost and the victory won
Tis over no sighs no anguished cries
From the wild wreck of conflict rise   45
The senseless corse on earth reclining
Nor feels defeat nor knows repining
And they who survive in their agony
Now stiff and spent and speechless lie
With dim eyes wandering toward the sky   50
    Yet seek and see no comfort there
For here upon this storm tost heath
The laboured faintness of the breath
The chill approach of Iron Death
    Demands a sterner care   55

And well I know that lifes last light
Just bordering on Eternal night
When all these souls shall take their flight
   Must crush those souls with fear

There they lie and wildly oer them   60
   Howls the wind with hollow tone
While between its banks before them
   Hear the torrent chafe and groan
   Heavily with sullen tone
   Yet still <careering> swiftly on   65
And torn with shot a shattered tree
   Shakes its bare arms in the bitter gale
Oer the blood red eddys that rapidly
   Down the swollen streamlet curling sail
And the blackned stones of a fallen wall   70
   Dashed down by the Iron hail of war
With their earthy bank above them thrown
   Obstruct the torrents passage there
Till angrily its waters roar
All white with froth and red with gore   75
And--There!--a shattered carcase lies
Without the power to look or rise
Tis He!--the Conquered Cheiftain--he
Whose look could once give victory
But sightless now as   80
The shot has torn his eyes away
And that gashed face is dashed with clay
Cast backward in the eddying Flood
That washes of his bursting blood
The stones across his body thrown   85
Which as he fell drove following down
Oh scarce we know the Human form
In this cheif victim of the storm
   Yet--though thus crushed and torn he be
      Though hence he never more shall rise 90
Though just as now still waves shall wash
      From the crushed bones the wasting flesh
There shall he lie. as there he lies
Yet still! oh still! look down and see
How VAST may mortal misery be   95
For in that bloody battered cell
Still Life and Soul and Memory dwell!
Never when he was fair and young
Did feeling thrill more <fresh> and strong
Never the Hell hounds of Despair   100
Had wilder power to worry there

   "O could I untormented die
Without this gnawing agony
That wrings my hearts so----!

                    Heavily and slow   105
The blood ebbs forth but parts not so the soul
    Hither I came with pain hence must I go
Still Still in pain!--Ts such my changeless doom
    God! shall such destiny unroll
Its agonies Beyond the tomb?   110
    All Dark without All Fire within
    Can Hell have mightier hold on sin
    But yet through all my dying mind
    From such a present turns behind
    To--what has been--and then looks oer   115
    The Dark Dark void of things before
The land of souls beyond the sable shore!
Oh how my eyes have stretched to see that land
How even when sunk in lifes bewildering roar
    All my strained thoughts have striven to
        reach its strand   120
    Have striven its mysteries to understand
Though dark indeed the unreturning sea
That separates what lies beyond from me
Though those vast waves which bear such
        thousands thither
Have never brought again one spirit hither 125
    If spirits those who pass may truely be
Those fearful passengers whose sightless eyes
    And blanched lips and tongues which cannot
        move
May either see the expanse which round them lies
    Or tell the scenes which open where they rove 130
Oh might I send across yon sea that Dove
Which bore the Olive branch Oh might it bear
From hence some token toward me hovering here
Even though it were the fruit of bitterness
So I might cease thiss doubt and fearfulness 135
    While I embark to sail--I know not where
I scarce know whence--or how--but such distress
Vain is the Hope that it will end!--and then
How vain the wish to know where lies my pain!
    Oh it lies here--and if my mind   140
    Survives it will not lag behind
    And if indeed--I truely Die
    Lost--in the abyss of vacancy
    Why THEN the sum of all will be
    That I on earth have lived to see   145
    Twice twenty winters beat on me
    Not one whole day of happiness
    And year on year of mad distress!

"They say when on the bed of death
    The wasted sickman lingering lies   150

                    391

His breast scarce heaving with his breath
   And cold his hand and quenched his eyes
    See!--how resignedly he Dies
Aye what a look of peace and love
That glazed eye casts to heaven above   155
Even those white lips will scarcly quiver
Though he must leave this world for ever
And though his children around him stand
Tis not for them that outstretched hand
Angels shall press those clay cold fingers   160
In the unknown void round which he lingers
    Ha! does the victim reason so
When bound beneath that fatal blow?
No! There indeed he lies inert
For deaths cold frost congeals his heart   165
Yet while that dim and dazing eye
Can wander oer one stander by
While those mute lips that silent tongue
Can one short broken gasp prolong
While in that whirled and burning brain   170
Reasons last spark can wax and wane
So long across that parting soul
Unmixed--unmingled--torments roll!
Ha--look on death with smiling eye
Ha--content and peaceful die   175
Ha--no like fire one burning strife
Convulses each riven string of life
And could those lips be moved to say
Could those stiff hands be clasped to pray
That only voice and prayer would be   180
   'Oh save me from that fatal sea
Where Hell and death join agony!
   I am dying! and what a rayless gloom
Seems darkning round my dreary tomb
I know no hope--I see no ray   185
To light me on my heavenly way
   There was a light--but it is gone
There was a Hope but--all is oer
   And freindless sightless left alone
I go where THOU hast gone before   190
And yet I shall not see thee more
Ha! say not that the dying man
Can only think on present pain
Oh no Oh no it is not so
For where Maria where art THOU!   195
   O do I seem to see thee now
Thy smiling eyes and shining brow
Thy sunny cheek and golden hair
In all thy Beauty Beaming there!
All through the noontide of my years   200
How thou di[d]st enter all my fears

And hopes of joy and smiles and tears
How often has thy bright blue eyes
   Driven sorrow shrinking from its shine
And banished all my misery   205
   Before one heavenly look of thine
   How often has that look divine
Roused up this heart from bitterness
Or bowed it in its worst distress
   To kneel before thy shrine   210
Oh once we thought to pass together
Through stormiest change of wind and weather
And thou wouldst never shrink from me
And I could never part with thee
I clasped within thy arms and thou   215
Lying on my breast thine ivory brow
Unthought uncared for storm or shine
While I was thine and thou wert mine
   When troubles hastned thickening on
When every hope of rest seemed gone   220
When mid the blight of hating eyes
   I stood bewildered sick with woe
What was the star which seemed to rise
   To light me on and guide me through
What was that form so heavenly fair   225
Untouched by time unmarked with care
To whose fond heart I clung to save
My sinking spirit from its grave
Maria! hadst thou never been
   This hour I should not living be   230
But while I strove with fate between
   The strife thou camest to set me free
And wildly did I cling to thee
I could not would not dared not part
Lest hell again should seize my heart   235
   Can I forget how toward thy eye
      Still ever gazed for guidance thine
As if I were thy star on high
   Though well I knew twas thou wert mine
That azure eye that softened smile   240
That heavenly voice whose tones to me
The weariest winteriest hours could wile
   And make me think that still might be
   Some years of happiness with thee
That thou amid my life to come   245
Shouldst be my hope my heaven my home
But--we are sundered--thee thy grave
And me this dreary wild will have
Whateer the world to come may be
I must never look on thee   250
If theres no God no Heaven no Hell
Thou within thy grave must dwell

I here blackning in the storm
Both a Banquet for the worm
If there is a Heaven above   255
    Thou in bliss are shining there
At the wondrous throne of love
    Angel bright and Angel fair!
From Heaven thou wanderedst like the Dove
    To the wild world of waters here   260
But never more oer it to rove
    Thou hast left this site of sin and care
Back to thine Ark while I staid where
The rottenest mass of carnage lay
A Raven resting on the prey   265
And Hell's dread night must close my day!
    Oh God my fear lies there
Without a hope to meet thee then
        But howling in despair!
        *   *   *   *   *
        *   *   *   *   *
Why why will the parted return to our heart   270
    When the sods have grown green on their tomb
Oh why will the twilight be first to depart
    When it only gives depth to the gloom
Oh why in the snow and the storms of December
    When branches lie scattered and strewn   275
Do we oftest and clearest and brightest remember
    The sunshine and summer of June
Oh why mid the hungry and cottagless waste
    Do we dream of the Goblet filled high
Why will our spirits when famishing taste   280
    Such visionlike revelry
Moralist speak!--ist in lifes deepest sorrow
    That these gleams of the past which hath
        vanished away
Though misery and mourning await on the morrow
    May strengthen to bear through the shades of
        today   285
    Since we have had our sunshine we must have
        our storm
    First with an angel and last with the worm
Christian speak--dost thou point to the sea
And shew me the Mariner drifting away
Behind him the shores of his desolate home   290
Around him the billows all crested with foam
Yet he casts not a look upon ocean or shore
But fixes his eyes on his haven before
Sayest thou thus should man smile on his joy
        and his sorrow
And press toward Heaven his Haven of to morrow   295
Aye Man! on let him press till that Heaven shall
        break

394

In lightnings and thunders and tempest and
        gloom
Then let the Spirit in safty speak!
    Where is the rest beyond the tomb
    Where are the joys of his heavenly home   300
Then let the moralist seek for his strength
    And smile on the past in its visionlike form
Then let the Christian anchored at length
    See light in the darkness a sun through the
        storm
            Away with all this false disguise   305
            View midnight truth with noonday eyes
            The past has had a single joy
            But when that past [h]as long gone by
            When cares have driven cares away
            When general darkness coulds the day   310
            That single star amid the sky
            Will shed a brighter light on high
            And in the Horizon only one
            Is yet the ALL that can be shewn
            Well oer me shining let it be   315
            That thus one glimmering I may see
            Fixed far above to shew my gloom
            And light my spirit to its Tomb!

Yet How I wander! grasping now
    At the glorious dream of a world to come   320
Then recoiling back I scarce know how
    Upon that hideous hopeless gloom
The NOTHINGNESS within the tomb
Thinking on THEE and then again
Shrinking within my present pain   325
All wide All wandering--This is Death!
    And I would calmly meet him now
As stern I'de feel my shortning breath
    As I have felt my life blood flow
But for the thought--   330
                Oh whats to come!
God if there be a God look down
    Compassionate my Fall
Oh clear away thine awful frown
    Oh hearken to my call!   335
Nay--all is lost--I cannot bear
In mouldering dust to dissapear
And Heaven will not the gloom dispell
Since were there one my home were Hell
No Hope no Hope--and Oh farewell   340
    The form so long kept treasured here
Must thou then ever dissappear
Gone nay but kept in memorys shrine
    Now dying again as memory dies

First passes from earth my star divine   345
    And now tis passing from the skies
    Thou art alone and Heaven is gone
    And and sights and sounds and all are gone
Oh what a state is life--I am dying
And HOW LIKE A DREAM IS EXISTENCE FLYING   350

See through the shadows of the night
    Burst hotly hasting onward here
A wounded charger vast and white
    All wild with pain and mad with fear
With hoofs of thunder on he flies   355
Shaking his white mane to the skies
Till on his huge knees tumbling down
Across the fallen Cheiftain thrown
With a single plunge of dying force
His vast limbs cover Albert's corse   360

                Finished March 2^d
                     1836
                     P B B

Text: l. 91:   "waves" written above "streams"; neither is
                 canceled
        l. 93:   "there" written above "now"; neither is
                 canceled

Two sets of trial lines in the BPM for ll. 512-24, probably
dating from January 1835, appear on the two sides of a single
manuscript page: (a) in conjunction with an early draft of
Thermopylae (see No. **80**); (b) in conjunction with an
early draft of **Sound The Loud Trumpet** (No. **73**). The
second set appears to be the earlier version.

    (a) When on the thorny bed of Death
        The wasted sick man quivering lies
        His breast scarce heaving with his breath
        And cold his brow and quenched his eyes
        Then when as hopelessly he dies   5
            In that forlorn and dreary hour
        Oh what a host of feelings rise
            To imbitter death with darker power
        Then Death and darkness round him lower
            He sees his children round him stand   10
        And cannot even lift that hand
        Which gave them bread and strength and life
        While they in Anguished hopeless strife
            Pour out the unavailing shewer

    (b) When on the thorny bed of death
            The wasted victim spent with pain
        His breast scarce heaving to his breath

                        396

```
        Still clings to bitter life in vain
    When moveless powerless to complain              5
        All--hope--and voice and eyesight--gone
    And dark and deep the livid stain
        Leaves each frozen member cold as stone
    Then as he turns his sightless eye
    With bitter anguish to the sky                  10
        And strives with hollow tone
    One word--But now the <cleaving> tongue
    But that death rattle can prolong
        It sinks and he is gone
```

On the same manuscript leaf, the following six lines appear between parts (a) and (b) of No. **50**, but seem much more clearly related to part II of **Misery.**

```
    I said that. spent with Iron pain
    The Dying man may not complain
    I said that to the erring sight
    Deaths gleam may seem Hopes beamy light
    A Charnel vapour oft may shine
    As fair as Luna's light divine
```

Who Lord Albert and Maria are is not clear.

55 and 56

Two of six manuscript fragments at the BPM, bound in green morocco for T. J. Wise by Rivière and misattributed to Emily. The other four fragments are trial lines for Nos. **95, 114,** and **94.** The first five fragments must have been composed at roughly the same time as they were written on the back of the draft of Branwell's letter seeking admission to the Royal Academy in the summer of 1835, recorded in SHB LL, I, 128.

57

The first of another set of five items at the BPM, again bound in morocco and misattributed to Emily. The speaker is Percy, Earl of Northangerland, after his victory over Zamorna at Edwardston. Items two and three are trial lines for Nos. **91** and **60;** item four is No. **58** below; item five was removed from Notebook B--see No. **133.**

58

Item four in the volume described in the preceding comment.
Because items two and three are trial lines for Nos. **91**
(July 22, 1836) and **60**, begun August 8, 1836, these lines
seem to have been written in late July or early August.   An
earlier draft in another manuscript volume of five fragments
at the PML, also bound in green morocco and misattributed to
Emily, reads:

> Hours and days my Heart has lain
> Through a scene of changless pain
> As it neer would wake again
> Sad and still and silently
>
> Time has flown but all unknown   5
> Nothing could arouse atone
> Not a single string would moan
> In replying sympathy
>
> Memory memory comes at last
> Memory of feelings past   10
> And with an Eolian blast
> Strikes the strings resistlessly

Opposite these lines Branwell wrote: "I am more terrifically
and infernally and Idiotically and Brutally STUPID--than ever
I was in the whole course of my incarnate existence   The
above prescious lines are the fruits of one hours most agon-
ising labour between 1/2 past 6 and 1/2 past 7 on the evening
of Wednesday, July   1836."

59

From the PML manuscript volume noted in the preceding
comment.   Because of similarities in paper, ink, and hand,
the five items in the volume (one is a prose fragment) seem
to have been composed at roughly the same time--July/August
1836.   The other two verse items are parts of No. **66**.

60

This poem constituted pages 18-24 of Notebook B.   The leaves
have been separated, with five pages, bound by Rivière, in
the Bonnell Collection in the PML, and two pages inserted in
the Notebook B version of "Misery, Part I" at the BPM (see
No. **54**).   After completing this poem, Branwell clearly
felt better about his poetic accomplishments than he did
after the trial lines for No. **58,** noting at the end

"Begun and finished in five days." Despite the August 8 date
at the beginning, we know from surviving drafts that Branwell
began the poem at least as early as January 1836. A manuscript page at the BPM, part of a dismembered and scattered
manuscript volume dated January 7, 1836 at the beginning,
contains the following trial lines for ll. 293-335:

> So spends its hours in thinking on
> The dear loved home whence it has flown
>
> But Oh at last a time will come
> When heaven is lost and earth is home
> When all that fascinates thy sight   5
> The moment seen shall sink in night
> This light shall change to lightning then
> This love of Heaven to hate of men
> For that which from on high is thrown
> Will always fall most quickly down   10
> And sinks the deepest so with thee
> Thy quick and passionate heart shall be
> The further plunged in agony

These spirits round thee oft may find
Earth and its joys to suit their mind   15
For dust to dust the sons of earth
Will love the land that gave them birth
But never thou or if thou dost
Too quickly thou shalt find it DUST

He sleeps in slumber calm and deep   20
And Infants blest and balmy sleep
Dreaming of heaven those closed eyes
See glorious visions of the skies
And tremblingly their fingers lie
On the soft cheek of Infancy   25

The softened curls of golden hair
Just moving with the moonlight air
But his white brow so sweetly still
So free from every shade of ill
Shall it be so for ever NO   30

Who of this world would wish it so
Tis the forehead of a mighty man
Destined on earth to lead the van
Of Onward minds a man whose soul
Nor Death nor Danger shall control   35
One whom no mortal power may tame
One who shall set the world on flame

Part of another dismembered and scattered manuscript at the
BPM contains trial lines for ll. 154-217 and 318-35, with the
two sets of lines separated by a brief prose passage dated
February 10, 1836 between ll. 86 and 87:

> The moon in glory mounts above
> The darkness of the distant grove
> As if the skies were given to be
> The palace of her majesty
> A silver grey is round her throne   5
> And far away the clouds are blown
> With all the lonly mountains dying
> In the pale haze above them lying
>   Now shines she silently and still
> Over the brow of yonder hill   10
> In golden glory gazing down
> On feild and forest tower and town
> But the dense trees that around him rise
> Give lonlier prospects to his eyes
> With far off cypresses whose gloom   15
> In Woodchurch yard oer shade a tomb
> And oer the forests waving crest
> That mild moon in her heavenly rest
>
> The moon in glory oer the grove
>   Majestic marches on   20
> With all the vault of heaven above
>   To canopy her throne
> And from her own celestial rest
> Upon the darkwoods waving crest
>   Serenly she looks down   25
> Yet beaming still as if she smiled
> Most brightly on the beauteous child
>
> But what thought he as there he lay
>   Beneath the arched door
> Amid the ever trembling play   30
>   Of Moonshine through the bower
> That unobstructed enternce made
> <As> the breeze moved foliage shade
>   In an uncertain shower
>
> But what thought he as there he lay   35
>   Beneath the arched door
> Amid the ever trembling play
>   Of Moonshine through the bower
> Gazing with blue eyes dimmed by tears
> To that vast vault of shining spheres   40
>   Till all its heavenly power
> Makes the bright pearl drops trembling break
> To dewy lustre on his cheek

O how I could wish to fly
Far away through yonder sky   45
Oer the trees upon the breeze
    To a paradise on high
Why am I so bound below
That I must not cannot go
Lingering here for year on year   50
    So long before we die
Now how glorious seems to be
Heavens great arch spread wide oer me
But every star is hung so far
    Away from where I lie   55
I love to see that Moon arise
It suits so with these silent skies
I love it well but cannot to tell
    How it should make me cry
Is't that it brings before me now   60
So many things gone long ago
When Angels used from heaven to come
And make this earth their wonderous home
Ist that I think that very moon
Those vanished wonders beamed upon   65
When Shepherds watched their flocks by night
    All seated on the ground
And Angels of the Lord came down
    And glory shone around
Ist that I think upon the sea   70
Just now its beaming beauteously
Where I so oft have longed to be
    But never yet have been
Ist that it shines so far away
On lands beyond that oceans spray   75
Mong lonly Scotlands rocks of grey
    Or Englands groves of green!
Or ist that through yon Deep blue Dome
It seers so solemnly to roam
As if across an Ocean wide   80
Breasting the dark unfathomed tide
    Far far away from home

As if upon some unknown sea
    It were a vessels statly form
Over the waters wandering free   85
    Through calm and cloud and storm

He is but a child so all his dreams
    Are wanderings of the mind
Where all before with glory teems
    And little lies behind   90
Formless as any childs might be
Yet he who looks in them may see

In glowing light defined
The first fond feelings of a soul
Destined a nation to control   95

Text: 1. 14 is written above "To hide <such> prospect from
       his eyes"; neither is canceled
       1. 51: "We" written above "I"; neither is canceled
       1. 54: "But" written above "with"; "hung" written
               above "placed"; "is" written above "all"; none
               are canceled

The bound manuscript volume wrongly attributed to Emily (see
comment for No. 57) contains trial lines for 11. 141-153,
which likely date from July/August 1836:

              Yet oer his face a solemn light
                Comes smiling from the sky
              And shows to sight the lustre bright
                Of his uplifted eye
              The aimless heedless carelessness   5
                Of happy Infancy
              Yet such a solemn tearfulness
                Commingling with his glee
              The parted lips the golden hair
                Cast backward from his brow   10
              Without a single shade of care
              All bathed amid that moonlight air
                Oh who so blest as thou!

Gaskell CB (chapter VIII) quotes 11. 231-54 as the opening
six stanzas--"about a third of the whole"--of the version
Branwell sent to Wordsworth on January 19, 1837, with the
following letter (SHB LL, I, 151):

      SIR,--I most earnestly entreat you to read and pass your
      judgment upon what I have sent you, because from the day
      of my birth to this the nineteenth [twentieth?] year of
      my life I have lived among secluded hills, where I could
      neither know what I was or what I could do. I read for
      the same reason that I ate or drank, because it was a
      real craving of nature. I wrote on the same principle
      as I spoke--out of the impulse and feelings of the mind;
      nor could I help it, for what came, came out, and there
      was the end of it. For as to self-conceit, that could
      not receive food from flattery, since to this hour not
      half-a-dozen people in the world know that I have ever
      penned a line.

      But a change has taken place now, sir; and I am
      arrived at an age wherein I must do something for
      myself; the powers I possess must be exercised to a

                           402

definite end, and as I don't know them myself I must ask of others what they are worth. Yet there is not one here to tell me; and still, if they are worthless, time will henceforth be too precious to be wasted on them.

Do pardon me, sir, that I have ventured to come before one whose works I have most loved in our literature, and who most has been with me a divinity of the mind, laying before him one of my writings, and asking of him a judgment of its contents. I must come before some one from whose sentence there is no appeal; and such a one is he who has developed the theory of poetry as well as its practice, and both in such a way as to claim a place in the memory of a thousand years to come.

My aim, sir, is to push out into the open world, and for this I trust not poetry alone; that might launch the vessel, but could not bear her on. Sensible and scientific prose, bold and vigorous efforts in my walk in life, would give a further title to the notice of the world; and then again poetry ought to brighten and crown that name with glory. But nothing of all this can be ever begun without means, and as I don't possess these I must in every shape strive to gain them. Surely, in this day, when there is not a <u>writing</u> poet worth a sixpence, the field must be open, if a better man can step forward.

What I send you is the Prefatory Scene of a much longer subject, in which I have striven to develop strong passions and weak principles struggling with a high imagination and acute feelings, till, as youth hardens towards age, evil deeds and short enjoyments end in mental misery and bodily ruin. Now, to send you the whole of this would be a mock upon your patience; what you see does not even pretend to be more than the description of an imaginative child. But read it, sir; and, as you would <u>hold</u> a light to one in utter darkness--as you value your own kind-heartedness--<u>return</u> me an <u>answer</u>, if but one word, telling me whether I should <u>write</u> on, or write no more. Forgive undue warmth, because my feelings in this matter cannot be cool; and believe me, sir, with deep respect, your really humble servant,
                                          "
                         P. B. BRONTE.

Lines 247-50 are adapted from the first verse of Isaac Watt's hymn "When I can read my title clear," and there are obvious echoes of Wordsworth's **Intimations of Immortality** Ode and Coleridge's **Kubla Khan.** Branwell reused the first thirty-six lines, slightly altered, at the beginning of No. **134.**

61

These lines appear on the last page of a manuscript fragment at the British Library dated August 31, 1836 at the bottom of the previous page. They are accompanied by four pen and ink portraits, at least one of which is a self-portrait, l. 34 of Book I of **The Iliad** and the words "Thalassa, Thalassa" in Greek, and two trial lines:

> Forgotten one I know not now
> When thou diedst or where or how

Flintoff (p. 242) suggests that Branwell's lines resemble the sort of Greek funerary epigram found in Book VII of the **Greek Anthology** which **Blackwoods** discussed and printed translations from during the 1830's.

62

This is the fourth item in Notebook B (pp. 25-28). The speaker seems to be recalling Percy's days as a pirate, commanding the Rover.

63

The lines conclude a prose manuscript, narrated by Richton, describing the death of Mary Percy, Zamorna's wife, while he is in exile. For Charlotte's reaction, while at Roe Head, to the news from Branwell that he had "killed off" Mary Percy, see Gerin CB, p. 107; Alexander, EW, pp. 153-55; Neufeldt PCB, pp. 421-23. Richton precedes this poem with the comment:

> Reader I cannot do otherwise than drop a last tear to her memory for recollect that I it was whose pen first brought her to your notice who from her rising to her setting <here> so long recorded the different phases of her glory. I wrote on the Brilliant Morning of Angria I described its coronations and its meetings and its short champaign of Victory I told of the troubles as they came till fallen Angria is now lost in falling Africa. So come then this mournful ending is only suited to so Darkened a time and knowing that if I looked around the prospect would <likely> still be graver I am losing no time and forgoing no pleasure in dropping a farewell

tear over this early grave that our parting may be in
tune with our company let it be in the words of the
Noble Poet of and troubled feeling

The poem is followed immediately by the early draft of
Queen Mary's Grave (No. **92**).

64

The lines are sung by a drunken Montmorency after announcing
that he could do anything except marry, toward the end of a
dismembered and scattered manuscript, begun in early November
and completed December 17, 1836.

65

These lines are part of a discussion, in a dismembered and
scattered manuscript dated December 17, 1836 at the
beginning, between Northangerland and Wentworth on the nature
of morality and reputation, centered on the life of Mirabeau.
To Wentworth's "Oh that I might die the death of a Mirabeau
and that my end might be like his . . . . My Lord! What
must I do to be saved?", Northangerland answers, "Why fight
the good fight of faith put on the whole armour of
Righteousness--and win the crown of glory--But an Oracle
shall speak." The four lines follow with the comment "crack
that nut!"

66

Originally pp. 31-36 of Notebook B, the three leaves
containing the poem went to T. J. Wise from A. B. Nicholls in
1892. Wise gave two of the leaves to the Brontë Society;
the third is divided among the NYPL, the PML, and the HRC.
The fragments at the Pierpont Morgan are bound in a
manuscript volume attributed to Emily. The speaker seems to
be Mary Percy, Zamorna's wife, on her deathbed, though
Branwell had recorded her death some months earlier (see
comment for No. **63**).

67

This poem constituted pp. 37-41 of Notebook B. The speaker
is possibly Alexander Percy's wife Mary. Between ll. 176 and
77, Branwell noted "append this to Harriets death"--see No.
103. Note the Miltonic echo in l. 186.

68

The first item in Notebook C, the notebook of fair copies Branwell began in March 1837. The original version (see p. 87), untitled, was part of a manuscript entitled **AN HISTORICAL NARRATIVE of "THE WAR OF ENCROACHMENT"**, begun November 18 and completed December 17, 1833, now in the Houghton Library, Harvard. Sir John Flower, almost asleep at midnight on the heath of Velino before battle the next morning, hears someone recite these lines. At the end he records, "I looked hastily round when this wild and solemn measure ceased my minds was saddened and a superstitious feeling crept over me. a dark figure stood near and I called out 'Who are you' Mr Warner advanced it was him I started up And shaking his hand we both for a moment looked on the dark scene around us."

1 I see through heaven with raven wings
  A funeral Angel fly
  The Trumpet in his dusky hands
  Wails wild and. drearily

2 Beside him on her midnight path   5
  The Moon glides through the sky
  And far beneath her chilly face.
  The silent waters lie.

3 Around me not the acustomed sight
  Of Hill and vale I veiw.   10
  Wide meadows bathed. in cheerless light.
  Dark woods in Midnight hue.

4 No all the earth behind before
  Seems one wide waste of graves
  And round each trench so dark dark and drear. 15
  The black earth stands like waves
  These are not common graves of men
  Where when their lifes short hour is done
  Neath the old. yews trees waving by
  They peacefully and silent lie   20
  These seem as if a torrents force
  Had rent its sudden way.
  They seem as if the channel course
  Of some tremendous sea
  Aye these are graves of armies where   25
  Foeman and Freind and horse and spear
  Bloody and cold together thrust.
  Together must consume
  And. rotting in their native dust.
  Their dark and narrow tomb.   30
  Oh God and what shall this betide

Why does that Funeral Angel fly
Why does yon Moon so solemn ride
Across this dark and stormy sky
Why does my spirit chilled and drear   35
In this dark vision linger here.
Behold upon that midnight heath
A Mighty Army lie
Hushed in deep sleep each warriors breath
Fast closed each lion eye.   40
The Moon from heaven upon each face
With saddest lustre shines
And glitters on the untrampled grass
Between the long drawn lines.
Are ye the tenants of that tomb   45
    Oh ist for you these graves are made
And shall ye in that narrow room.
Be silent laid.
Oh God avert the avenging sword.
    And turn thy wrath away   13   50
Pass of ye hungry yawning toombs   4
    Arise all cheering day.   ——
                                       52

69

The original version (see p. 88) is untraceable. For possible
sources see Cowper's **Psalm CXXXVII**--"To Babylon's proud waters
brought," and Byron's "By the Rivers of Babylon We Sat Down and
Wept" from **Hebrew Melodies.** Branwell may also have seen John
Martin's mezzotint biblical illustration, "By the Waters of Babylon," 1835. I have been unable to find a motet entitled **The
Captivity.** Line 39 originally read "As thou hast served Gods
people--so"; was changed to "As thou destroyest Gods . . ."; and
then altered in pencil to the reading given.

70

The original version (see p. 90), untitled, is part of Chapter VIII
of **The Wool is Rising** (see No. 47). Lady Mavis, wo are
told, "was called upon for one of her own highland airs of mingled
grace and fire and tenderness. She was reluctantly and slow turning with her fair fingers the leaves of. the open Music when
Edward Percy one of the <expecting> listners sternly opened the
page at a noble piece by Purcell. and in cool stern accent said
"Her ladyship will perhaps oblige me with. the one before her."
The song however is Branwell's, not Purcell's.

        I saw her in the crowded Hall
            High plumes were waving there

But mid those statly thousands all
   Were none like her so fair

I saw the Ivory of her brow   5
   The diamonds in her hair
I saw her swanlike neck of snow
   Her bright form shining there.

     Yes wake thee Maiden wake thee
   Thy fate frowns oer thy brow   10
     That neck which sorrow never bent
   Must bend to anguish now
Oh loftiest of the lofty
   Fairest of the fair
Can one dark shade pass oer thee   15
   Hast <u>thou</u>! shaken hands with care.

Oh where in heaven or where in earth
Can I behold a tearless mirth.
Alike the man of stormy life
Long used to battle blood and strife   20
Alike thou Beuteous queen of May
   In woes wild waste must mourn
Must weep your glimpse of gladness gone
   And never to return
Then cease my lyre thy wailings cease   25
Lingering quivering die in peace

71

The original version (see p. 89), untitled, is also part of
The Wool is Rising (Chapter I); it follows immediately
upon No. **47**, also composed by Northangerland.

Sail fast sail fast my gallant ship thy ocean
    thunders round thee
At length thour't in thy paradise thine own wide
    heaven around thee.
The morning flashes up in light and strikes its
    beams before.
Where yon wide streaks of lustre bright lie like a
    fairy shore.
The day presages storm and strife yet what need.
    Percy care.   5
Thy deck hath born him through the storm shall bear
    him through the war
The Thundring winds are swelling up and whistle
    through thy shroud
Yet over head in the iron. sky how sullen sleeps
    each cloud.

Lo! yon feirce blast hath swept the seas and
    covered them with foam
Yet shall it force the[e] on thy way wherever thou
    mayst roam.   10
The rich but feebled Merchant ship may quiver to
    this gale.
For it shall guide thee to thy prey and swell thy
    eager sail
    When Night and tempest gather up. and shroud the
        stormy sky
The timid sheep may look to heaven with an
    imploring eye.
But while they flock. in frightend. haste and.
    crowd the narrow way   15
What cares the Lordly Lion then who pounces on his
    prey.
The storm has but his reaper been to gather in his
    grain.
And thus to thee my ship shall be this hoarse
    resounding main.
Look Look beneath yon thick black cloud. on yon
    dark line of water.
A fair and clustered Argosie just gathered for the
    slaughter   20
See how the spread sails glimmer white. as scudding
    far before.
They steering in one. steady line fly oer the
    watery roar.
    Now rouse ye then my gallant men. rouse up with
        hearty cheer.
Quick clear the deck crowd all your sail your
    cannon bring to bear
My arms my Arms my trusty pike. of quick and bloody
    blow.   25
My pistols black my sabre white.--then onward for
    the foe.
Ha! Connor Gordon steer ye right the winds confuse
    them now.
As mid the geese an Eagle's flight. amid them drive
    my prow
I stand upon my steady deck. around me flies the
    foam
My pirate ship skims in the blast across her ocean
    home   30
The Fleet, the Argosie before. with furled or
    shivered sail.
Like helpless swans together crowd and. tremble to
    the gale
Now light your matches.--from a smoke bursts up one
    crash of thunder

Rebellows from the clouds above and the white
        surges under.
They know us then! They know the Hawk But dread
        hath paled each brow   35
Furl in your sails. your irons cast we are full.
        upon them now.
And fastned by our trusty hooks yon freighted
        galleon lies.
Her hesitating broadside bursts in thunder to the
        skies
We heed it not. I. forward rush upon her. shaking
        deck.
And. all my band of gallant hearts have followed at
        my beck.   40
Now mid the thickning smoke. and sleet one mighty
        tumult reigns
The sparkles flash across each eye. the blood boils
        through the veins
Man dashed on man. in trampled blood. strew thick
        each groaning plank
Unheard unseen the sabres clash amid each gory
        rank.
Where am I. dashed into the hold upon a strangling
        foe.   45
All men and smoke and shouts above. a writhing
        wretch below.
He dies I. rise and grasp a rope--am on the deck
        once more.
And Percys arm and Percys sword still bathe that
        deck with gore.
An hour of tempest passes by the Galleon blazes
        now.
And. smoke and slaughter crowds the deck. and heaps
        the bending prow   50
Our swords seem grown into our hands our eyes
        glance fiery light.
And heaped beneath us scattered lie the wrecks of
        that wild fight
"Ye have done your work most gallantly--that
        precious merchandise.
In haste convey upon our deck, our just and well
        earned prize.
Then fire the ship and follow me to our own deck
        again   55
To chase the coward wanderers across yon stormy
        main."
    The evening sinks in sullen light across the
        heaving sea
And sees the "Rover" oer its waves plough on her
        gallant way.

While far behind across the surge a blaze of blood
    red light.
Drifts on to windward. shrouding round. the relic
    of that fight.   60
I see afar the blackned masts stand gainst the
    flaring flame
And high in heaven the heavey smoke curls oer its
    blazing frame
Those fires discharge its cannonry with sullen
    sounding boom
Till like a blood red Moon it sets behind its
    watery tomb.

72

The original version (see p. 96), untitled, is part of **The
Life of Feild Marshal The Right Honourable Alexander Percy,
Earl of Northangerland,** in the BCL.   Branwell's dating of
"Spring, 1834" is questionable.   The first volume of the
manuscript, which contains the poem, is undated, but the
second volume was not begun until June 3, 1835.   Thus late
1834/early 1835 seems more likely.   The poem concludes a
letter from young Alexander Percy to Augusta di Segovia when
he was a student on the Philosopher's Isle in 1812:   "Well
what is the future to me Augusta or the past. what do I care
for aught but Thee.--When shall I see the again Thou knowest
how   thou   enchanted   me   and   willingly   I   bear   thy
enchantment--"

      Augusta though I am far away
        Across the dark blue sea
      Still eve and morn and night and day
        Will I remember thee

      And though I cannot see thee nigh   5
        Or hear thee speak to me
      Thy look thy voice thy memory
        Shall not forgotten be

      I stand upon this Island shore
        One single hour alone   10
      And view the Atlantic swell before
        With sullen surging tone

      And high in heaven the full moon glides
        Above the breezy deep
      Unmoved by waves or winds or tides   15
        That far beneath her sweep

She marches through the midnight air
  So silent and divine
With not one wreath of vapour there
  To dim her silver shine   20

For every cloud through ether driven
  Has settled far below
And round the mighty skirts of heaven
  Their whitned fleeces glow

They join and part and pass away   25
  Beneath the heaving sea
So mutable and restless they
  So still and changless she

Those clouds have melted into air
  Those waves have sunk to sleep   30
But clouds renewed are rising there
  And new waves rouse the deep

How like the chaos of my soul
  Where visions ever rise
And thoughts and passions ceasless roll   35
  And tumult never dies

Each fancy but the formers grave
  And germ of that to come
While all are fleeting as the wave
  That chafes itself to foam   40

I said yon full moon glides on high
  Howeer the world repines
And in its own untroubled sky
  Forever smiles and shines

So darkning oer my anxious brow   45
  Though thicken cares and pain
Yet in my heart Augusta--thou
  Shalt still for ever reign

And thou art not yon wintry moon
  With its melancholy ray   50
But where thou shinest is summer noon
  And bright and perfect day

The Moon sinks down as sinks the night
  Thou ever beamest on
She only shines with borrowed light   55
  But thine is all thine own!

412

And now Augusta fare thee well
till thou <meetest> Again and roused to strength and energy
thy Alexander Percy.

73

The original version (see p. 90) is part of **The Coronation of Arthur Augustus King of Angria** in the BCL. As Nos. **73** and **74** both precede a June 2 date in the manuscript, May/June seems a likely date of composition. For a possible source, see Moore's "Sound the loud timbrel o'er Egypt's dark sea."

Sound the loud Trumpet oer Africs bright sea
Zamorna hath triumphed the Angrians are free
Sound for our day Star hath risen in glory
Sound that Loud Trumpet uneaqulled in story
Sing for the sunbeams have <burst> forth to brighten 5
   A Reign which hath neare throgh age or throgh
      time
The past page of History burst out to enlighten
   Alone in its glory and proud in its clime
   Never to darken and never decline
Tempests may threaten and storms may assail us   10
Afric may tremble and fortune may fail us
Yet with thee our Zamorna alone to avail us
   Angria thy full sun unshadowed shall shine

Sing for the power of our foemen hath gone
Quenched in the sunbeam that smiles round thy
     throne   15
Raise higher and louder your voices to sing
Angria our Country and Arthur our King
River whose waves through the wide desert winding
   Bearest thy streams toward the Home of thy pride
Each weary waste of thy glory reminding   20
   Rise and spread round thee thy Life giving tide

O All ye proud mountains which high from afar
Crown your blue brows with the wandering star
Tell you each cliff and each vale and each plain
Zamorna hath triumphed oer Angria to reign   25
   Aye tell ye the North with its storm and its
      snow
   Tell ye the South where the Ocean gales blow
   Tell ye the East where the Suns ever glow
     Angria and Arthur are shining again
     Midnight and tempest may darken in vain   30
     Foes may arise

                    And Fate may suprise
                Dust on the Mountain and drops in the main

            Sing for the Sun hath arisen on creation
                Sound ye the Trumpet to herald his dawn   35
            Rise Man and Monarch and City and Nation
                Away with your darkness and hail to your dawn
            Sound the Loud Trumpet oer land and oer sea
                Join tongues hearts and voices rejoicing to sing
            Afric arising hath sworn to be free   40
                Glory to Angria and GOD SAVE OUR KING

There is a later variant of the last twenty-eight lines on
the same manuscript leaf as the January 1835 fragment of
Thermopylae (No. 50) at the BPM.

            Sing for the power of thy foeman hath gone
            Quenched in the sun beam that smiles round thy
                    throne
            Raise higher and louder your voices to sing
            Angria our Country Zamorna our King
            River whose waves through the wide desert winding   5
                Bearest thy streams to the home of our pride
            Each weary waste of thy glory reminding
                Rise and spread round thee thy glittering tide
            O all ye proud Mountains which high from afar
            Crown your blue brows with the wandering star   10
            Tell you your torrents and deep shadowed plain
            Zamorna hath triumphed oer Angria to reign
                Aye tell ye the North with its storms and its
                    snow
                Tell ye the South where the ocean gales blow
                Tell ye the East in its Summer Sun glow   15
                    Angria and Arthur are shining again
                    Mid night and tempest may darken in vain
                        Foes may arise
                        & Fate may suprise
            Dust on a mountain and drops in a main   20
            Sing for the sun hath arisen on creation
                Sound ye the Trumpet to herald its dawn
            Rise Man and Monarch and City and Nation
                Away with your Darkness and hail to your Morn
            Sound the Loud Trumpet oer land and oer sea   25
                Join tongues hearts and v[o]ices rejoicing to
                    sing
                Afric hath risen hath sworn to be free
                Glory to Angria and GOD SAVE OUR KING

74

The original version (see p. 90) is again part of **The Coronation of Arthur Augustus,** and follows No. **73** almost immediately.

Anthem of the Coronation

Shine on us God of Afric Shine
Oh round us shower thy light divine
Sailing across a stormy sea
Mid life and death we trust in thee
That Life and death shall find us free 5
  Thou with all thy mighty power
    Cast our foemen down
  Mid the Battles darkest hour
    Blast them with thy frown
Mid that hour of bloody strife 10
Thou preserve each Angrian life
  Save us if we die
Nerve our arm with iron blow
Lay our foemen cold and low
God and Angria on that foe 15
  Be our battle cry
Death to every enimy
Death to all who yeild us hate
Down to Dust with adverse fate
Angrian vengeance lags not late 20
  Let the Traitors die
  But God save our king
  Joy to him we sing
Tongues and hearts and voices shout
  God save the king 25
Zamorna thou alone
Canst sit on Angrias throne
Swear while thou her sword shall weild
  It shall not be oerthrown
  Then thy fame with untired wing 30
  Still to thee shall laurels bring
Then around the world shall sound
  GOD SAVE OUR KING

Branwell used a variant version of stanza one in a manuscript dated December 17, 1836, at the BCL (see comment for No. **64),** as part of Warner's oration to his troops: "Let us now my freinds praise God for the mercies he has conferred and together intreat for the mercies to come As the one hundreth Psalm."

    Shine on us God of Angria shine
    Oh round us pour thy light divine

For sailing oer a stormy sea
Through life to death we trust in thee!

75

The original version (see. 95) begins an untitled manuscript
in the BCL, describing the opening of the first Angrian
Parliament, composed in September-October 1834.

THE ANGRIAN WELCOME

Welcome Heroes to the war
   Welcome to your glory
Will you seize your swords and dare
   To be renowned in story
What though fame be distant far   5
Flashing from her upper air
Though the path which leads you there
   Be long and rough and gory
Still that path is straight and wide
Opened to receive the tide   10
Youths first flush and manhoods pride
   Age all old and hoary
     Sire and son may enter in
     Son and sire alike may win
     Rouse ye then and all begin   15
   To seek the glory oer ye

Angrians when your morning rose
   Before your Monarchs eye
He swore that ere its evenings close
   All your foes should die   20
He saw the brightest star of fame
   Was flashing forth on high
He knew that Angrias very name
   Should force those foes to fly
And down from heaven ZAMORNA came   25
   To guide you to the sky
He shook his sword of quenchless flame
   And shouted VICTORY!

Angrians if your noble King
   Rides foremost to the fight   30
Up in glorious gathering
   Around that helmet bright

Angrians if you weild your sword
   Every stroke shall be

Fixed as one undying word   35
    In your History

Angrians if in fight you die
    The clouds which oer you rise
Shall waft your spirits to the sky
    Of everlasting joys   40

Angrians when that fight is oer
    Heaven and earth and sea
Shall echo in the Cannons roar
    Your shouts of Victory

And now if all your bosoms beat   45
    To reach your native star
Shake the shackles from your feet
    WELCOME TO THE WAR.

See there the host of Quashia
    Along the Etrei lies   50
Then around the flag of Angria
    ARISE ARISE ARISE

76

The original version (see p. 95), also part of the manuscript
describing the opening of the Angrian Parliament, is a song
offered to the crowd outside Parliament by Henry Hastings,
the poet of Angria, in honour of Northangerland becoming
Premier. Branwell's date of "November" is questionable, as
the manuscript was composed in September/October.

History stood by her pillar of fame
A shade on her brow and a tear in her eye
Oh must I blot my Northangerlands name
From his own glorious chapter of victory
She held oer that chapter the pencil of fate   5
But her white arm drew back from the page as it lay
In sorrow and silence she mournfully sate
And she bitterly thought of Her Angrias decay
She raised her dark eye and she gazed on the sea
Where all its black billows were whitened with foam 10
And she thought of her pirate ship gallant and free
Her Noble Northangerlands empire and home
Oh for the hours of that ocean to come
When shall I write of such sunshine and storm
When will a pirate so gloriously roam   15
As fair and as noble in feature and form
She looked to the south and she looked to the north

And she looked to the west where the twilights
    decline
Had flown from the Morn who exultin[g]ly forth
Was rising in glory oer Angria to shine   20
She thought of that Empire. so bright and divine
She thought of its Monarch its ruler in war.
Angria two Monarchs and rulers like thine
Hath fate then refused to one empires share
And must thou whose bidding has roused up [a] land   25
From midnight to morning to life from the tomb
Oh must thy great name now be traced by my hand
In pages of darkness and letters of gloom.
She paused and she pondered. But Angria is nigh
With pride in her port and with fire in her eye   30
She looks to the shore and she looks to the sea.
And she vowed that eternal his history shall be.
Through all my wide empire. in ages to come
From palace to cottage from cradle to tomb
Shall the name of my Saviour through ages endure   35
Vast as the ocean and firm as the shore
History seizes her pencil of light.
And again in rejoicing she bends to indite
High on the top of her column of fame
She Blends with her Angria Northangerlands name   40

Text: 1. 40: "her Angria" written above "Zamorna"; neither
                is canceled

77

The original version (see p. 96) is part of **A NARRATIVE OF
THE First War. with Quashia undertaken For the purpose of
clearing his Ashantees From the rightful territory of
Angria**, at the HRC begun December 17, 1834 and completed
June 30, 1836. Because the poem occurs between the dates
December 17, 1834 and January 24, 1835 in the manuscript,
Branwell's date, December 6, cannot be accurate. The poem is
composed by Hastings as he listens at night to the joyous
celebrations of Zamorna's victory. He comments, "There
reader is a <strand> of poetry for you as innocent and as
<aimless> of meaning as the mind of a new born babe. I
scribbled it that morning I speak of and it is quite different from what when I began I meant it to be."

    Morn comes and with it all the stir of morn
    New life new light upon its sunbeams born
    The magic dreams of Midnight fade away
    And Iron labour rouses with the day.
       He who has seen before his sleeping eye   5
    The times and smiles of childhood wandering by

The memory of years gone long ago
And sunk and vanished now in clouds of woe
He who still young in dreams of days to come
Has lost all memory of his native home   10
Whose untracked future opening wide before
Shows him a smiling heaven and happy shore
While things that are frown dark and drearily
And sunshine only beams on things to be.
    To such as these night is not all a night   15
For one in eve beholds his morning bright
The other basking in his earliest morn
Feels noontide summer oer his spirit dawn
But that worn wretch who tosses night away
And counts each moment to returning day   20
Whose only hope is dull and dreamless sleep
Whose only choice to wake and watch and weep
Whose present pains of body and of mind
Shut out all glimpse of happiness behind
Whose present darkness hides the faintest light   25
Which yet might struggle through a milder night
And he like me whom <present> cares engage
Without the glare of youth or gloom of age
Who must not sleep upon his idle oar
Lest lifes wild tempests dash him to the shore   30
Whom High Ambition calls aloud to awake
Glory his goal and death or life his stake
And long and rugged his rough race to run
Ere he can rest to enjoy his laurels won
To these the night is weariness and pain   35
And blest the hour when day shall rise again
Mid visions of the future or the past
Others may wish the shades of night to last
Round these alone the present ever lies
And these will first awake when Morning calls Arise! 40

78

The original version (see p. 95) is part of **The Life of Feild Marshal The Right Honourable Alexander Percy** (see comment for No. **72**). The narrator discovers in the studio of Master Percy an organ with a book of music "opened at a 'stabat Mater dolorosa' 'Veni Creator' and 'Dies Irae' and upon the keys a sheet of paper scored over in a childish and unformed hand with a succesion of Breves Semi breves and minims in an Andante movement which the writer was adapting to the words

    We leave our bodies in the tomb
        Like dust to moulder and decay
    Then while they waste in coffined gloom

          Our parted spirits where are they
          In endless night or endless day   5
<inte[r]lined> between the staffs till met by the lines
          Buried as our bodies are
          Beyond all earthly hope or Fear
          Like them no more to reappear

written in an elegant and feminine handwriting A Little
Bible lay open on a music stand with Ecclias V--1--Remember
thy Creator in the days of thy youth. marked in pencil. "I
shall arrange this"--And around the carpet. were scattered
five or six engravings of Battles a whole collection of Hymn
books many odd volumns from a vast variety of <men> odd
little drawings in pencil a little fife Millers jest book and
a much fingered copy of Jewels Sermons." "Miller's jest
book" refers to **Joe Miller's Jests; or the Wits Vademecum,
Being a Collection of the most Brilliant Jests; the Politest
Repartees; the most Elegant Bon-Mots, and the most pleasant
short Stories in the English Language,** edited by John
Mottley in 1739, into its tenth edition by 1759, and reissued
frequently thereafter. According to the **DNB,** "Joe
Miller's name has long been a synonym for a jest or witty
anecdote of ancient flavour." "Jewels Sermons" refers to the
sermons of John Jewel, Bishop of Salisbury, 1582- 1607, whose
most famous work was the **Apologia pro Ecclesia Anglicana,**
1562.

79

Line 103 originally read "I sought but found no pleasure
then," but was later altered in pencil to the reading given.
An earlier version (p. 95) was the final item in the lost
Notebook A, but transcribed by Hatfield (Hatfield Papers) as
follows:

                **An Hour's Musings
              Written by Alexander Percy
                 On the North Atlantic
                    In A D 1818
                    295 lines**

          Blow, ye wild winds, wilder blow;
          Flow, ye waters, faster flow;
          Spread around my weary eye
          One wide waving sea and sky!

          Aloft, the breezes fill my sail,   5
          And bend its canvas to the gale
          'Mid their own ethereal dwelling,
          O'er the ocean proudly swelling.

                        420

      See the billows round me now
Dash against my cleaving prow;   10
Far and wide they sweep away
O'er the rough and roaring sea.
By heaven! my heart beats high to-day,
Lord of such a realm to be,
Monarch of the fierce and free!   15

But I'll turn my eyes toward the skies
    And view the prospect there,
Where broad and bright the noon-day light
    Sheds glory round the air.
I see yon mighty dome of heaven   20
    In deep cerulean hue,
The white clouds o'er its concave driven
    Till lost amid the blue.
Then I'll turn my forehead to the blast
    And think upon the sea: 25
That chainless, boundless, restless waste
    Which shines so gloriously,
Thou only Lethe for the past,
    Sole Freedom for the free!

The winds are whistling in my hair   30
    As I gaze upon the main,
And view the Atlantic from his lair
    Aroused to rage again,
And view the horizon stretched afar
Wise around the ambient air   35
One mightly water weltering there
    Where I gaze and gaze again.

Waves of the Ocean, how nobly ye roll,
Endless and aimless, nor pathway, nor goal;
Proudly ye thunder your white crests on high   40
Shaking their foam to the spray-beaten sky.
Winds of the Ocean, your voices arise,
Shriek in my canvas and storm to the skies.
Ye tell me that life is an ocean of woe
Where the fierce blasts of passion eternally blow.   45
Man's bark may be shattered or ride through the
        storm
To rot on its anchor, a feast for a worm.
Yes, Battle may peal in its glorious thunder
    O'er the young Warrior's closing day,
Yet if he lie the wet sod under   50
    Age must rot by dull decay.

Well, here I am and Afric's shore
Hath sunk beneath Old Ocean's roar.
It seems as if but first even now

Had set Leone's azure brow,   55
That hardly yet yon bounding line
Conceals fair Gambia's shores divine!
Not so—a thousand league's away
I ride upon the raging sea
And long, long leagues of Ocean roar   60
Between me and my native shore.
Oh, all the scenes of a lifetime past
    Far, far behind me lie
There tossing o'er a stormy waste
    Oh, who so lone as I!   65
I heard that wind: it sighed to me
    Like memory of feelings gone.
Black blast! my heart responds to thee
    With mourning bitter as thine own!
    And my own voice, with hoarser tone,   70
Now strikes upon my startled ear,
    It seems 'mid these wild waves unknown
        A think I should not hear.
    'Tis the very voice of my infancy
    The voice of my morning young and free   75
    But what's that voice to do with me,
        A wasted wanderer here!

Oh, Afric', Afric', where art thou?
Even I can sorrow o'er thee now,
Though e're I left thy smiling shore   80
I knew my joy in life was o'er.
Yes, I had seen my evening sun
    Set in a sullen sea of tears,
Had seen his course of daylight gone,
    Gone lights and shadows, hopes and fears.   85
Yes, I had seen my day decline
Never again to rise and shine;
And it was not pleasure blighted,
    It was not hope destroyed,
It was not for love slighted   90
    That made that dreary void.
And yet my pleasures all had flown,
All my hopes were dashed and gone,
And though none scorned the love I gave,
Yet—THOU! the loved wert in thy grave.   95
Yes—yet all these formed but the storm
    Which blackens o'er even morning's sky.
My misery was of darker form,
    Of deadlier, deeper dye.
These were the various streams that flow   100
Into my deep, deep sea of woe,
The shrieking blast, the pelting rain,
May strike the shattered oak in vain.

Storm, can yon scathed trunk yield the victory?
Go, spend thy fury on the young green tree.   105

   Oh, when I was a little child
      Upon my mother's knee,
   With what a burst of pleasure wild
      I gazed upon the sea!
   I stretched my arms toward its face   110
   And wept to meet its proud embrace!
   And when, amid youth's earliest day,
      I paced the foam-white shore,
   I smiled to see the wild waves play,
      And joyed to hear them roar.   115
   But now where am I?--On that sea
   Where I so often longed to be.
   Now!--But away with bitter pain:
   Shall Percy's heart so oft complain?
   The waves around my vessel sweep   120
      And cover her with foam,
   Yet though they shake the shattered ship
      They still shall bear her home.
   The sleep which shuts the watchful eye
      'Mid dangers threatening near,   125
   Though helplessly the sleeper lie,
      Still quiets all his care.
   The night which darkens o'er the earth
      'Mid daylight's deep decline,
   Shall give a glorious morrow birth   130
      In morning's light divine.
   But thou stern midnight of my soul
      With thy dread darkness closing round,
   Ye storms of strike which o'er me roll,
      Where have ye hope or rest or bound?   135
   Well, roll ye waves of ocean, roll;
   Close, clouds of sorrow, o'er my soul;
   I care not if your fatal blight
   Shall shade this mind with lasting night.
   Yet, while one streak of sunshine lies   140
   Behind the far dim twilight skies,
   Permit the wanderer's lingering gaze
   To fix upon its fading rays.
   The wretch whom naught from Death can save
   Still grasps the grass around his grave;   145
   The lion 'mid the hunter's toils
      Glares madness from his eye,
   And nets and dogs and lances foils
      Though lost to liberty.
   Even through life when we look back   150
   We see some sunshine o'er our track.
   They falsely speak who say we spy
   Naught but joys before our eye;

No, all the future path to me
Seems beat by storms of misery;   155
And scenes alone long passed away
Can struggle through with distant ray;
For through his short and hurried span
Pleasure only <u>follows</u> man;
Yet still when weariedly he dies   160
He dreams <u>before</u> him in the skies,
He sees its happy Paradise!
Oh, what is MAN? A wretched being
    Tossed upon the tide of time,
All its rocks and whirlpools seeing,   165
Yet denied the power of fleeing
    Waves and gulfs of woe and crime;
Doomed from life's first bitter breath
To launch upon a sea of death,
Without a hope, without a stay   170
To guide him on his dreary way.

See that wrecked and shattered bark
    Drifting through the storm,
O'er the ocean, drear and dark,
    Drives its shattered form.   175
Where those sails which late on high
Swelled amid the shining sky?
Where those masts which braved the gale
Towering o'er the swelling sail?
Where the glass-like deck below?   180
Where the gilt and glorious prow?
How that vessel lately shone,
Heaven and ocean all its own.
Where are they? Sunk in the surging sea
Shivered and shattered and vanished away.   185
Where are they? Saw'st thou the shrieking gale
Tear from the yard-arms the swelling sail?
Saw'st thou the mast in the strife of the storm
Bend to the billows its stately form?
Hark to that crash as the foam and the spray   190
Force o'er the deck in a boiling sea;
Deep in the waters the curling prow
Bursts on rocks that lurk treacherous below
And there then!--its glory all vanished and gone--
There then it drifts with the tempest alone;   195
And now as they cling to the shivered mast,
As sinking they shrink from the shrill screaming
        blast,
How do the hearts of the mariners brave
The heaven and the ocean, the wind and the wave?
    Aye, how have the hopes and the sunshine of
        life   200

424

Stood 'gainst its darkness and dangers and
    strife?
And what thinks fond MAN when, these dangers
    all o'er,
Stranded he lies on death's desolate shore?
View him thus sickened, palsied, and lone:
Where is his strength and his beauty gone?   205

I am a MAN. Yes, I have seen
Each change upon life's changing scene.
I launched upon life's mighty sea
As free, as fair, as proud as thee;
And I am on the track which thou   210
And thine and mine are drifting now!

Well, when I first launched from Eternity
Upon this undiscovered sea,
Hope shone forth with glorious ray
Blazing round my dawning day.   215
Expectation's eager gale
Swelled and sounded in my sail;
Ambition's ever rousing power
Urged me on in morning's hour;
And Love, thy wide and welcome light,   220
Ever shone before my sight;
Beauty, strength, and youth divine,
With all the heaven of Mind were mine;
And when I saw the expanse before me,
When I saw the glory o'er me,   225
Oh, how little did I deem
Heaven and glory all a dream!
Life alone with its midnight sea
Howled on me in stern reality!

Sleeper, awake! Thy dream hath gone;   230
Now, thou art on ocean all alone.

    I did awake, and round the sky
Wild I cast my frighted eye:
Where is the love and hope and light?
Vanished, vanished from my sight.   235
And now I am on the wild, wild sea;
Not a hope to shine on me.
The winds arise, and the stormy skies
Snatch my daylight from my eyes;
Ambition's sails which bore me on   240
Shiver in the blast they seemed to have won.
And, Glory!--Aye, thou welcome wave,
Dash that illusion to its grave.
But save, O ruthless Ocean, save
Save love alone, that only flower   245

Which can amid this glorious hour,
Like one mild star amid the sky,
Beam comfort on my misery.
No! Life, though all its oceans roll,
Can never part thee from my soul.   250
Thou, quenchless in this heart shalt lie,
With this heart alone to die.
Well, be it so. The pealing blast
Howls wilder 'gainst the quivering mast.
With what a sweep the surge and spray   255
Thunder o'er the billowy sea.
A gloomier tempest darkens down,
Love survives--But THE LOVED is gone!
Gone--one hopeless endless sea
O'er me beats unceasingly.   260
Severed cordage, masts and sail
Drive before the slackening gale;
The storm has passed, but the shattered oak
    Has fallen before the storm,
Trunk and branches cracked and broke,   265
    A black and blasted form.

O Mary! when I closed thy eye,
When I beheld thee slowly die,
When thou before me silent lay
A loveless, lifeless form of clay,   270
When I saw thy coffined form
Decked to feast the gnawing worm;
When the dull sod o'er thee thrown
    Hid thee from my tearless eye;
When they laid the marble stone   275
    Above where thou must ever lie,
'Twas then, my Mary, then alone
    I felt what 'twas to die!

Oh! long, long years may lie before me,
A thousand woes may darken o'er me,   280
And ere I lay me down to die
Old age may dim this anguished eye.
Yet through this wide, wide waste of years,
This channelled gulf of burning tears,
Aye, if I live till Earth's decay   285
Is crumbling in its latest day,
If thousand winters wintriest snow
Fall blighted o'er my stricken brow,
Still through yon vast eternity
I know that thou canst never be!   290
Lost, for ever lost to me!
That all thy woes and joys are o'er,
    That thou art dead, gone long before,
And I shall <u>never</u>, <u>never</u> see thee more!

426

Alexander Percy 1818

P B BRONTE
November 10th 1834
FINIS

80

Although Branwell gives January 19, 1835 as the date for the first version of this poem, it is, in fact, a revision of the fourth item in Notebook A; Branwell either was confused about the date or an intermediate version has been lost (see p. 88). For the larger context for this poem, see the comment for No. **50.** Both C. W. Hatfield (Hatfield Papers) and J. A. Symington (Ratchford Papers) made transcriptions of the Notebook A version, differing only in a few minor matters of punctuation and spelling. Hatfield's text is as follows:

The Pass of Thermopylae
Fifty six lines
P.B. Brontë

Thermopylae's tremendous height
Has lost the evening's fading light,
And each tremendous mountain round
Seems blackening in the shade profound.
Alike wild waste and ocean wild   5
Dark as those hills around them piled
Lie gloomy as they ne'er had worn
The sunshine of a summer morn
Above the moonbeams fitful light
Breaks shivering through the heavy night   10
And as the stormy wrack sweeps by
Fades, lost amid the troubled sky.
    At times that moon so sadly now
Glints on Thermopylae's stern brow
Where bloody grass and trampled heath   15
Lie soaked beneath their loads of death
Where scattered rocks with mossy head
Form many a warrior's dying bed
And many a dim and darkening eye
Now gazes on this stormy sky!   20
Sleep noble soldier, sleep alone
The whistling wind your burial moan,
The bloody rocks your bed of death
Your shrouds grey grass and tangled heath.
The mountain's lofty brow ye have   25
At once your monument and grave.
    O Glorious dead! sleep peacefully:
Your name, your fame, shall never die.

427

By you your country saved from chains,
Still free, unconquered Greece remains,   30
And not one drop of all that blood
Which curdles now in Peneus flood,
No, not one drop is lost in vain,
For every drop dissolves a chain!
And each cold hand and nerveless arm,   35
Which nevermore that blood can warm,
Have while they slew their meanest foe
Given Susa's domes a fatal blow.
There may proud Persia's legions stay
For darkness clouds her future way.   40
Thermopylae, thy conquered dead
Have bent to earth even Xeres head.
Arise, ye Spartan heroes, rise,
Come, seize your sceptres in the skies.
There, from your everlasting throne   45
Behold the wonders you have done.
Not Phecia's mountains dark and hoar
Where all your Grecia's classic shore
Not distant Persia's sorrowing reign
Not Alpine hills or Roman plain   50
Shall limit your great leader's name
Or e'er confine your lasting fame.
Never did trumpet's loudest voice
Rouse the fierce soldiers to rejoice
As now will yon ensanguined pass   55
And that one word, Leonidas!

                              P.B. BRONTE
                              March 3rd
                              A D 1834

Susa's dome: Susa was the capital of the ancient
               Persian Empire and site of the royal
               palace.
Marathon: A plain in the Attic Peninsula where the
            Athenians defeated the Persians in 490 B. C.

81

The original version (see p. 97), in **The Life of Feild
Marshal The Right Honourable Alexander Percy**, dated October
20, 1835, is sung by Augusta to Percy's accompaniment on the
piano; the song is described as "one of his own rich and
melancholy compositions."

        "Son of heaven in heavenly musing
         Gaze beyond the clouds of time

                         428

Future glory rather choosing
   Than the present world of crime

Thou whose heart that world carressing   5
   Bows its Bubbles to adore
On and hunt each fleeting blessing
   Still in sight but still before

Christian, World[l]ing, hence and leave me!
   Here with thee my love alone   10
Things to come shall neer deceive me
   While I hold thee--<u>NOW</u>--my own!
Fate, of bliss can neer bereave me
   While we two continue one!

"And are we not as one now" said Augusta as they concluded with her most winning smile "yet why then that sorrow and that wandering eye?"--"It's the thought of how I am repaying My Mother for her years of affection" he replied "I thought I saw her! What would she think if she knew her son!--O my mother--my Mother!"

82

The original version (see p. 97), in a chapter written between October 22 and November 17, 1835 of **The Life of Feild Marshall the Right Honourable Alexander Percy,** reflects Percy's state of mind as he agonizes over the fate of his soul and his inability to believe in God and traditional Christian doctrine (especially that of an afterlife), following the death of his wife, Lady Augusta, in 1813.

      Life is a passing sleep
         Its Deeds a troubled dream
    And Death the dread awakening
         To Daylights Dawning beam
      We sleep without a thought   5
         Of what is past and oer
  Without one glimpse of consciousness
         Of aught that lies before
      We Dream and on our sight
         A thousand visions rise   10
  Some dark as Hell some heavenly bright
         But all are phantasies
      We wake and o how fast
         Our mortal visions fly
  Forgot amid the wonders vast   15
         Of Immortality
         In visionary joys
         Or dreams of greif and gloom

We start to hear the thunders voice
   Arouse us from the tomb   20
   And o when we arise
   With wildered gaze to see
The aspect of those morning skies
   Where shall that waking be?
   How will that Future seem?   25
   What is Eternity?
Is Death the Sleep?--is Heaven the Dream?
   Life the reality?

Just before the poem, Percy quotes **Childe Harold,** Canto
II, st. 95, ll. 1 and 5 (slightly adapted), and after the
poem, ll. 1-2 of Byron's **Stanzas to Augusta.**

83 and 84

From the same chapter of **The Life of Feild Marshal the
Right Honourable Alexander Percy** (see p. 98), Percy's songs
again reflect his melancholy and despondent state of mind.

Thou art gone but I am here
   Left behind and mourning on
Doomed in dreams to Deem thee near
   But to awake and find thee gone
Ever parted Broken hearted   5
   Weary wandering all alone

Looks and smiles that once were thine
   Rise before me night and day
Telling me that thou wert mine
   But art dead and past away   10
No returning--Naught but mourning
   Oer thy cold and coffined clay
Beauty Banished feelings vanished
   From thy Dark and dull decay

It was but a fragment both in poetry and music yet that music
filled the hearts of all round and their eyes too--He sung
the last word and the chords rung changing upon another key

Frozen fast is my heart at last
   And unmoved by thy beams divine
Wild oer the waste the wintery blast
   Has withered and weakened thy shine

The pulse that once beat to each look and
      each word   5
   Is congealed by the frosts of care
Thine eyes are ungazed on thy voice is unheard
   For Love ever flies from despair

                  Farewell then farewell then for parted
                      forever
                    The blooming and blighted should be   10
                  Soon shall the Ocean eternally sever
                    My Heart from my country and thee

85

Although the original version (see p. 98) is untraceable and
the context unknown, the poem is clearly related to the previous three poems.

86

The original version (see p. 98) is untraceable, the context
unknown, but the lines may well be Branwell's personal expression of his commitment to poetry in late 1835 (see p.
xliii of the **Introduction**).

87

The original version (see p. 99) is contained in a dismembered and scattered manuscript by Henry Hastings, begun January
7, 1836.

                    Storms are waking to inspire us
                        Storms upon our morning sky
                    Wildly wailing Tempests fire us
                        With their loud and Godgiven cry
                    Winds our Trumpets shreiking come   5
                    Thundering waves our deeper Drum
                        Wildwoods oer us
                        Swell the chorus
                    Bursting on the stormy gloom
                    Whats their Omen   whence the doom   10

                    Loud their voices stern their pealing
                        Yet what ist those voices say
                    Well we know when, God revealing
                        All his wrath their powers display
                        Trembles every child of clay   15
                          Still we know
                          That blow on blow
                        Oer us Bursting day by day
                        Shews that wrath as well as they

                    Oh tis not a common call   20
                        That wakes such mighty melody
                    Crowns and Kingdom's rise or fall

                                431

Men and Nations chained or free
Living death or Liberty
Such your terrible decree 25
And yonder skies
Whose voices rise
In such unearthly harmony
Through Angria round
Shall wake a sound 30
A Voice of Victory
A Thundering oer the Sea
Whose swelling waves
And howling caves
Shall hear the prophecy 35

Storms are waking
Earth is shaking
Banners wave and Bugles wail
And beneath the tempest breaking
Some must quiver some must quail 40
Hark the Artillerys Iron hail
Rattles through the ranks of war
Who beneath its force shall fail
Must the Sun of ANGRIA pale
Upon the Calabar 45
Or yonder bloody star
Oer Afric's main
With fiery train
That wanders from afar

No O God Our Sun its brightness 50
Draws from thine Eternal Throne
And come what will
Through good or ill
We know that thou wilt guard thine own
Tis not gainst us that Thunders tone 55
But, risen from Hell
With radiance fell
Tis the Wanderer of the West whose power shall be
oerthrown

Tempest blow thy mightiest blast
Wildwind sound thy wildest strain 60
From Gods right hand
Oer his chosen land
Your music shall waken its fires again
And over the earth now and over the ocean
And wherever shall shadow these storm
covered skies 65
The Louder through Battle may burst your
commotion

'Twill only sound stronger OH ANGRIA ARISE!

Hastings comments: "Those were the sounds which greeted my
ears from our Noble Band of the Royal Guards stationed in the
church yard of Grantley on the Evening of Jan. 6th
1836."

88

The original (see p. 116) is untraceable, but the poem is
related to Zamorna's defeat at the Battle of Edwardston.   In
a note in the Ratchford Papers, Hatfield suggests it was
originally part of a now dismembered manuscript which also
contained "The History of Angria VIII"--SHB Misc II, 197 and
item 145 (1) in the BPM Bonnell Collection.   Line 44 originally read "passed away" and was changed later in pencil to
"for aye."

89

The original version (see p. 116) is part of **A NARRATIVE OF
THE First War. with Quashia For the purpose of clearing his
Ashantees From the rightful territory of Angria** by Henry
Hastings, composed between December 1834 and June 1836 (see
also No. **77**).   Wentworth, in a state of agitation and
excitement over the coming civil war, pens these lines for
relief.   In the untitled manuscript describing the opening of
the first Angrian Parliament (see Nos. **75** and **76**),
Montmorency addresses Percy as "Lucifer, star of the
Morning."

LUCIFER

    Star of the west whose beams arise
        To brighten up oer Afric's shore
    While coming clouds and changing skies
        Bring down the shades of twilights hour

    Who as our day sinks fast away   5
        While flowers of pleasure close their bloom
    Sendst down from heaven thy flashing ray
        And shinest to dazzle--not to illume

    Who as upon our sunken sun
        The storm clouds gather from the sea   10
    So far above goest wandering on
        As if our hopes were nought to thee

And gathering glory while the night
   Comes deeper darker drearier down
And shining still with brighter light   15
   When every beam save thine is gone

Star of the west we see thee shine
   We know thy glory from afar
But we have seen our sun decline
   As if it sunk for thee to appear   20

We have seen our sun of happiness
   Mid coming clouds of conflict fall
Nor can thy lustre stand in place
   Of that which blessed and brightened all

We know that in our time of pride   25
   Mid summer suns and noonday skies
Though heaven were cloudless clear and wide
   Such lights as thine dared never rise

We know thou art an orb divine
   Within thine own celestial sphere   30
But still a storm portending sign
   To us who gaze in wonder here

Star of the West though storm and night
   Gave birth and glory to thy blaze
Still what had kindled up thy light   35
   May in a moment cloud its blaze

As darker grow the clouds of woe
   As day declines As Empires fall
Brighter and brighter burst thy glow
   Till thou soarest onward Lord of all   40

But westward clouds are rolling on
   And louder thunders swell the wind
The tempest comes--and Thou art gone
   Past like the sunshine out of mind

Percy!--amid the coming hour   45
   When peace and pleasures dissapear
Those storms and strifes that gave thee power
   May Darken Africs Western Star!

90

The original (see p. 116) is untraceable, but in a note in
the Ratchford Papers Hatfield links it to "The History of
Angria VII," SHB Misc II, 188, begun June 24, 1836. The last

four lines are also spoken by Percy on the last page of the manuscript noted in No. **89** above. The only difference occurs in the last line: "is now" has replaced "thou'st made."

91

The original version (see p. 118), dated July 22, not June as Branwell suggests, begins a sixteen-page manuscript in the BCL, detailing Percy's triumph, Zamorna's exile, and Mary's illness.

Through the hoarse howlings of the storm   PBB
    I saw--but did I truley see   July 22
A Glimpse of that unearthly form   1836
    Whose name has once been Victory
Twas but a glimpse and all seems past   5
    For cares like clouds again return
And I'll forget him till the blast
    For ever from my soul has torn
That vision of a Mighty Man
    Crushed into Dust!--   10

Forget him!--Lo the Cannon's smoke
    How dense it thickens till on high
By the wild storm blasts roughly broke
    It parts in volumns through the sky
    With dying thunder drifting by   15
Till the dread burst breaks forth once more
And loud and louder peals the cry
Sent up with that tremendous roar
Where as it lightens broad before
    The thick of Battle rends in twain   20
With roughened ranks of bristling steel
    Flashing afar while armed men
In mighty masses bend and reel
    Like the wild waters of the main
Lashed into foam!--where there again   25
Behold Him! as with sudden wheel
At bay against a thousand foes
He turns upon their serried rows
All heedless round him though they close
    With such a bloodhound glare   30
That eye with inward fires so bright
Peirces the tempest of the fight
And lightens with the joyless light
    Of Terrible Despair
He sees his soldiers round him falling   35
In vain to Heaven for vengeance calling
He sees those firmest freinds whom he

435

Had called from happy happy home
And for the prize of victory
   Over the eastern world to roam   40
He sees them lie with glaring eye
   Turned up toward him that wandering star
Who led them still from good to ill
   In hopes of power to meet with war
And fall from noontide dreams of glory   45
To this strange rest so grim and gory
When rolling on those freinds oerthrown
Wars wildest wrack breaks thundering down
Zamorna's pale and ghastly brow
Darkens with anguish--all in vain   50
To stem the tide of battle now
   For every rood of that wide plain
Is Heaped with thousands of his dead
Or shakes beneath the impetous tread
   Of foes who conquer oer the slain   55
   No! never must he hope again
Though still abroad that Banner streams
On whose proud folds the sun of glory gleams
Though still unslaughtered round their Lord
His chosen cheifs may grasped the unvanquished sword   60
   Tis Hopeless! and He knows it so
Else would not anguish cloud his brow
Else would not such a withering smile
Break oer his hueless face the while
Some freind of years falls helplessly   65
Yet still upon that eagle eye
Turning with dying ecstasy!
That Eagle eye the Beacon light
Through all the changes of the fight
Whose glorious glance spoke victory   70
And fired his men to do or die
On the red roar of Battle bent
As if its own wild element
And gazing oer each thundering gun
As he were wars unconquered son   75
That Eye! oh I have seen it shine
   Mid scenes that differed far from these
As Gambias woods and skies divine
   From Greenlands icy sea's
I have seen its lustre bent on me   80
   In old adventure gone
With beam as bright and gaze as free
   As His own Young Angrian Sun!
When oer those mighty wastes of heath
   Around Elymbos' brow   85
As side by side we used to ride
   I smiled to mark its glow
I smiled to see him how he threw

```
          His feelings into mine
Till my cold spirit almost grew                        90
     Like his a thing divine
I saw him in his Beautys pride
     With Manhood in his brow
The Falcon eyed with heart of pride
     And spirit stern as now                            95
Almost as stern--For many a shade
     Had crossed his youthful way
And clouds of care began to mar
     The brightness of his day
I knew him and I marked him then                       100
     For one apart as far
From the surrounding crowds of men
     As Heavens remotest star
I saw him in the Battles hour
     And conquered by his side                          105
I was with him in his height of power
     And triumph of his pride
Tis past--But am I with him now
     Where he spurs feircly through the fight
His pride & power and crown laid low                   110
     And all his future wrapt from sight
Mid clouds like those which frown on high
     Over the plains in purple gloom
With rain and thunder driving by
     To shroud a nations bloody tomb                    115
And in the cannons ceasless boom
     The toll which wafts the parting soul
While heavens bright flashes serve to illume
     Like torches its funereal stole
Its Horrid funeral--far and wide                        120
     I see them falling in the storm
Mid clouds of Horse that wildly ride
     Above each gashed and trampled form
His Charger shot Zamorna down
Mong foes and freinds alike oerthrown!                  125
Yet never may that desperate soul
Betray the thoughts which oer it roll
Teeth clenched cheeks blenched and eyes that dart
A Boar like feircness from his heart
As all the world was nought beside                      130
The saving of his Iron pride
For every one on earth might die
And not a tear should stain that eye
Or force a single sob or sigh
     From him who cannot yeild                          135
Yet stay one moment--tis but one
A single glance to Heaven is thrown
One frenzied burst of greif--Tis gone
     His Heart once more is steeled
```

That was a burst of Anguish--there   140
Blazed all the intensness of Despair
It said "Oh all is Lost for ever!"
All he loves to him is dead
All his hopes of glory fled
All the past is vanished   145
    Save what nought can sever
Ever living memories
That shall haunt him till he dies
With things that he can realise
    Never Never Never   150

I said I saw his anguished glance
    Say did he think on me
Incendiary of Rebel France
    Parrot of Liberty

The wretched Traitor who let in   155
    On Africs opened Land
Deceit and craft and cant and sin
    In one united band

Who raised the Standard of Reform
    And shouted "Earth be free"   160
To whelm his country in the storm
    Of Rebel Tyranny

Who called himself the good right hand
    And Father of his King
Only on his adopted Land   165
    This awful curse to bring

Aye it was I. and only I
    Who hurled Zamorna down
From conquering glory placed on high
    This day to be oerthrown   170

I barbed the Arrow which has sped
    To peirce my sovereigns breast
And Only on my guilty head
    May All his sufferings rest!

                174 lines--

Another version of the first twenty-six lines, dating from
July/August 1836, occurs in a manuscript volume of five items
misattributed to Emily (see No. 57).

            Through the hoarse howling of the storm
                I saw but did I truely see
            One glimpse of that unearthly form

                        438

```
              Whose very name is VICTORY
           Twas but a glance and all seems past          5
              For cares like clouds again return
           And Ill forget him till the blast
              For ever from my soul has torn
           That vision of a mighty man
              Crushed into Dust!--                       10

           Forget him!--Lo the Cannon's smoke
              How dense it thickens till on high
           By the wild storm blasts roughly broke
              It parts in volums through the sky
              That heavily are drifting by              15
           Till the dread burst breaks forth once more
              With whitening clouds which seem to fly
           Affrighted from that ceasless roar
           And there it lightens! dashed with gore
           The thick of battle rends in twain            20
              Whith their rough ranks of bristling steel
           Flashing afar while Armed men
              In mighty masses bend and reel
           Like the wild waters of the main
              Lashed into foam--Where there again       25
      100* Behold him!

         * Branwell's numbering
```

92

On the lower half of the page containing the last eight lines
of No. **91** in Notebook C, Branwell transcribed the first
twelve lines of **Queen Mary's Grave**, but seems to have
given up his revision because the next page was left blank
and the title is not entered in his table of contents.
Therefore 11. 1-12 are the Notebook C text; the rest the
December 10, 1836 text (see p. 131). The differences between
the two versions of the first twelve lines are minor:

l. 3: passed/past
l. 5: Her/The
l. 7: And/Lest
l. 8: That/her
l. 9: may/will; oer/on
l. 10: one/a; this/her
l. 12: nor the/or

93

This poem appears on the lower half of the page containing
the final portion of the early draft of "Calm and clear the
day declining" (No. 134) in Notebook C. Presumably Branwell is still concerned with the death of Queen Mary,
Zamorna's wife. Line 15 originally read "O say that when
my"; the "my" was later changed to "I'm" in pencil.

94

This poem appears on the recto of a single leaf at the BPM;
on the verso are trial lines for No. 95, completed in
August 1837. The figure "316" at the beginning seems to
refer to the early draft of "Calm and clear . . .", dated
June 1837 (No. 134). The leaf is one of fifteen of various sizes bound in morocco by Rivière for Wise and misattributed to Emily. Two leaves were by Charlotte, one by
Branwell. An earlier version also bound in green morocco by
Rivière and misattributed to Emily (see commentary for Nos.
55 and 56), reads:

> Now--But a moment, let me stay:
>   One moment, ere I go
> To join the ranks whose Bugles play
>   On Westwoods waving brow.
>
> One pause upon the brink of life   5
> Before it breaks in headlong strife
>   Upon its downward road
> One insight through the waters clear
> Before their pictures dissapear
>   In the feirce foaming flood   10
>
> Here I am standing--underneath
>   The shade of quiet trees
> Whose leaves can hardly catch the breath
>   Of this sweet evening breeze

95

This poem constituted pp. 42-52 of Notebook B. There are two
sets of trial lines, both bound as Emily's (see comment for
Nos. 94 and 55). The first, for ll. 1-20, reads:

> How Edenlike seem palace walls
>   When Youth and Beauty join
> To waken up their lighted Halls
>   With looks and smiles divine

440

How free from care the perfumed air   5
   About them seems to play
How glad and bright appears each sight
   Each sound how soft and gay

Tis like the heaven which parting days
   In summers pride embue   10
With beams of such imperial blaze
   And yet so tender too

Ah memory brings a scene to mind
   Beneath whose noble dome
Rank beauty worth and power   15
   To light there lordly home

Yet--parting day--however bright
   It still is--parting day!
The herald of approaching night
   The trappings of decay   20

The second, for ll. 58-70, reads:

There is something in this Glorious hour
That fills the soul with heavenly power
And dims our eyes with sudden tears
That center all the joys of years
For we feel at once that there lingers still   5
Like evening sunshine oer a hill
A Glory round lifes pinnacle
And we know though we be yet below
That we may not allways linger so
For still Ambition Beckons on   10
To this a height that may be won
And Hope still whispers in our ear
Others have been--thou mayst be there

A variant of the song beginning at l. 258 was published in
the **Bradford Herald** and the **Halifax Guardian**, 9 and
11 June 1842 (see No. **122**). **Auld Lang Syne** appears
in Branwell's Flute Book at the BPM, dated November 1831.
The poem describes Percy's seduction of Harriet O'Connor, who
loved him in her youth but is now married to Hector
Montmorency.

96 and 97

These bits of verse appear on leaf 8 of 13 leaves of prose
fragments bound in red morocco by Rivière for T. J. Wise.
According to the reconstruction of the correct order for the
13 leaves in BC 1932 (item 149), these verses were written

between October 20 and 31, 1837. The first verse is sung by Hector Montmorency; the second is a response by George Ellen.

98

The manuscript is untraceable; the text provided is Leyland's who states that it is only the beginning of a poem, and "the title is not borne out in the portion I am able to give" (II, 206).

99 and 100

Both poems are part of an untitled manuscript at the PML, signed and dated February 4, 1839. No. 99, based on Ben Jonson's **Song to Celia**, is sung by Richard Wilson, "a desperate Drinker," as part of his pledge "To perish in pleasure." No. 100 is sung by a thousand voices, accompanied by bugles and trumpets, to celebrate the entrance into Verdopolis of Zamorna as King Adrian The First.

101 and 102

Both poems are part of another portion of the same manuscript, signed and dated February 21-23, 1839. No. 101 is murmured by Northangerland after he has asked Lady Charlotte Greville why her daughter Georgiana, who is the Earl's mistress, is not present at the social gathering. No. 102 is sung by Northangerland in flirting with Miss Victoria Pelfe.

103

On April 20 (29 according to Davidson Cook's transcription in the Ratchford Papers), 1840, Branwell sent an eight-page letter containing these lines and his translations of two of Horace's Odes to Hartley Coleridge from Broughton-in-Furness, Lancashire, where he was employed as tutor by Mr. Postlethwaite. He wrote to Coleridge (SHB LL, I, 204):

> SIR,--It is with much reluctance that I venture to request, for the perusal of the following lines, a portion of the time of one upon whom I can have no claim, and should not dare to intrude; but I do not, personally, know a man on whom to rely for an answer to the question I shall put, and I could not resist my

longing to ask a man from whose judgment there would be little hope of appeal.

Since my childhood I have been wont to devote the hours I could spare from other and very different employments to efforts at literary composition, always keeping the results to myself, nor have they in more than two or three instances been seen by any other. But I am about to enter active life, and prudence tells me not to waste the time which must make my independence; yet, sir, I love writing too well to fling aside the practice of it without an effort to ascertain whether I could turn it to account, not in <u>wholly</u> maintaining myself, but in <u>aiding</u> my maintenance, for I do not sigh after fame and am not ignorant of the folly or the fate of those who, without ability, would depend for their lives upon their pens; but I seek to know, and venture, though with shame, to ask from one whose word I must respect: whether, by periodical or other writing, I could please myself with writing, and make it subservient to living.

I would not, with this view, have troubled you with a composition in verse, but any piece I have in prose would too greatly trespass upon your patience, which, I fear, if you look over the verse, will be more than sufficiently tried.

I feel the egotism of my language, but I have none, sir, in my heart, for I feel beyond all encouragement from myself, and I hope for none from you.

Should you give any opinion upon what I send, it will, however condemnatory, be most gratefully received by,--Sir, your most humble servant,

P. B. Brontë.

The first piece is only the sequel of one striving to depict the fall from unguided passion into neglect, despair, and death. It ought to show an hour too near those of pleasure, for repentance, and too near death for hope. The translations are two out of many made from Horace, and given to assist an answer to the question--would it be possible to obtain remuneration for translations for such as these from that or any other classic author?

The text provided is Cook's transcription, made in the Library of Sir Alfred Law in 1925-26, and now in the Ratchford Papers. The first version of the poem (see p. 199) occupied pp. 53-60 of Notebook B:

P.B.B.
May 14th

At dead of Midnight, drearily   1838

I heard a Voice of horror cry
      "O God! I am lost for Ever!--"
And then the bed of slumber shook
As if its troubled sleeper woke
      With an affrighted shiver   5
While in her waking burst a sigh
      Repressed with sudden fear
As she gasped faintly--"Where am I!--
      Oh Help!--Is no one here?--"   10

    No one was there--And, through the dark
Only a last and trembling spark
Left from a dying Taper's light
With red gleam specked the void of night.
Which, scarcly wakened from her dreaming--   15
      She gazed at as this far off world
      From whence her spirits flight seemed hurled
Through Heavens vast void so feebly gleaming!
Quick came that thought, and, quickly gone--
She found herself laid there alone   20
While heard my ear the choking sob
As that dread truth with wildering throb
Seemed as its force would stop the breath
Of Her who woke to wait for death!
There, both her hands as cold as clay   25
Pressed her damp forehead while she lay
All motionless beneath the power
Which weighs upon lifes latest hour
Short short had been her fevered slumber
      And filled with dreams of that dread shore   30
      Where she must wait her Judge before
Another hour that night might number!
And fails my pen to paint the room
So deeply veiled in utter gloom
Where she un-seen, unwatched, unknown,   35
And thought and feeling almost gone
Gasped breathless neath The Mighty Foe
And watched each moment for the blow!

"O God!"--she murmured forth again,
      While scarce her shattered senses knew   40
      What, darkness shrouded from her view--
"Oh, take from me this sickning pain!--
That frightful dream, if twas a dream
      Has only wakened me to die
Yet Death and life confounded seem   45
      To inward thought and outward eye!
Tis not the Agony of death
That chills my breast and chokes my breath
Tis not the flush of fevered pain
That dizzies so my burning brain--   50

444

Which makes me shudder to implore Thee
When my soul should bow before Thee.
I shrink not from the eternal gloom
That waits my body in the tomb--
Oh no!--Tis something far more dread   55
Which haunts me on my dying Bed--!
I have lost--long lost--my Trust in Thee!
     I cannot hope that Thou wilt hear
     The unrepentant Sinners prayer!
So, whither must my Spirit flee   60
For succor through Eternity!--
Beside me yawns that awful void
And, of the Joys I once enjoyed
Not one remains--my Soul to cheer
When I am launched all aidless there!--   65

   Eternity!--Oh, were there none!--
     Could I believe what some beleive
     Soon might my spirit cease to greive
At the cold grave and churchyard stone!
But--God!--To appear before Thy face   70
In all a sinners naked-ness
Without one little hour to spare
To make that sinners sins more fair
     Without the slightest power to shun
     Thine Eye whose lightning looks upon   75
     All things I have thought and deeds I've done
Repentance past and useless prayer--
How can my Spirit live to stand
That look, and hear that Dread Command
     Which even Archangels shrink to hear   80
That voice whose Terrors none can tell
"Depart! Lost Spirit into HELL"!--
Great God! To Night--shall fires infernal
     Hold me down in hideous pains
     With Devils bound in burning chains   85
And fires and pains and chains ETERNAL!--"
     Oh Christ! When Thou wert crucified

Thou heardst the felon at thy side
And in his bitterest agony
Thou promisedst him a Heaven with Thee!--   90
But he repented and confessed
Ere Thou wouldst give his anguish rest
And, Oh!--In my last hour Do I?--
Thus wretchedly afraid to die--
Dare I repent?--Can I repent?--   95
When with my very life are blent
     The feelings that have made me sin
Who have scorned thy name to atone my crime--
Repent!--Ah no! My Sands of Time

```
        Sink far too swiftly to begin!--            100
Can I repent?--Can I forget
The face the form scarce vanished yet!--
The only vision which has proved
Theres aught in this world worth being loved!--
Can I forget the Noble Name                        105
For which I lost my earthly fame--
Can I forget--when harshly round
Parents and freinds and kindred frowned
When Home was made a Hell of strife
By those who gave and shared my life              110
When far had fled the Inward peace
Which gives the troubled spirit ease
When--Heavens, and Earths Affections, reft--
Nor present Hopes, nor future, left--
Can I forget that Glorious Star                    115
That cheered me through the weary war?--
Those long long Hours of wrapt communion
        Mid the quiet Moonlight Grove
Those wild Hopes of future union
        Gilding oer my guilty love!--              120
Even the bursts of maddened mourning
        If I saw his Happy Bride
Lost amid the joys returning
        When once more he sought my side!--

    Oh!  I led a life of sinning                    125
        At HER beck, whose Soul was Sin.
Yet my spirit ceased repining
        If a look from Him twould win!--
Bright that Band with Hellish glory
        Circling round Augusta's Throne            130
Dark those Hearts whose influence oer me
        Led me in and lured me on!--
All their mirth I knew was hollow
        Gain and guilt their path and aim
Yet I cared not what might follow--                135
        Deaf to warning dead to shame
What to me if Jordan Hall
Held all Hell within its wall
So I might in his embrace
Drown the misery of disgrace!                      140

    "God!  Thou knowst, my Inward Thought--
        Through many a dreary after day
        When to Another sold away
Could never with my Hand be bought!
Or--if a moments maddness gave                      145
My Heart to throb--a Tyrants slave
Still--still how often True to one
Whom still I thought for ever gone
```

Ide sadly sit and silent weep
While all the wide world seemed asleep--   150
Thinking upon the surging sea
That tossed his vessel far away!--

Oh wast Thy curse--when sneers and scorn
From a stern jesting feind, had worn
My soul, so long dispirited   155
And chafed between disgust and dread--
Oh wast thy curse--that fatal night--
Which once more brought him to my sight
When all the Room went whirling round
As first I heard his music sound   160
When all my veins ran living flame
As first--for years--he named my name
As first I pledged my broken faith
To fly with him to--freindless death!--
I'de spent my life in search for pleasure   165
I thought that hour I'de found the treasure
All else I lost to gain that one
And--when I gained it--It was gone!--
Then Honour left me!--peace of mind
          Fled with it and conscience came   170
To gnaw my Heart with ceasless flame
          And wither all it left behind
Oh for a while--a little while
While I could gain a single smile
From Him--my Star of Happiness   175
I knew not how to feel distress
Twas when the dreadful death blow came
Twas when he left me to my shame
When sudden ceased my star to shine
That Happy hopes--that joys divine   180
As they were centred past with him
And--I awakened from my dream!--
Sure never bore a Human frame
          Unmaddened--agonies like me
Who have lain as if Hells hottest flame   185
          Was kindled by that Agony
Till day and night has oer me flown
Alike unnumbered and unknown
Tossing on my tearless pillow
As if it were Hells burning billow   190
Straining eyes that wept no longer
Weak[n]ing down while woe waxed stronger!--

Where--in such an hour of pain--
Where were freinds and flatterers then?
Where were Hearts that would have died   195
So they perished by my side?--
Where were knees that joyed to kneel

447

Waiting on my slightest will?--
Tongues and thoughts that seemed to be
Only framed to speak of me!--   200
Ah!--The Wide World holds them still
        All is whirling round the same
        The same feigned words and fancied flame
But waiting on anothers will!
Then and now as once they shone   205
Thousand lights are beaming down
And dizzy dance and thrilling song
Still gather many a Noble throng!--
        There was but a single change
        One was lost--and no one heeded   210
For along the glittering range
        No one felt that ONE was needed
Faces blushed to name her name
Silence hushed the Adulterers shame
Little cared they how she greived   215
        Oer her monstrous wickedness
Hardly knew they if she lived
        Through her desolate distress!
Three short words might speak her Lot--
Fallen Forsaken and Forgot!--   220

        There she stopped, for spent and broken
The last deep accents she had spoken
Fell as if no more could come
From lips with utter Anguish dumb!--
        There she stopped but even the bed   225
Trembled with her dying dread
And for a while she moaning lay
As if she'd weep her heart away
Now and then a broken word
Amid her sobbing might be heard--   230
Some name perhaps that childhood knew
And yet to fleeting memory true
Some thought perhaps of far off time
Before these hours of greif and crime
Had changed that voice of music mild   235
Into a key so sadly wild!

        Could HE have bent above her head,
        Even He whose guilt had laid her there,
One burning drop he must have shed
        Those Old yet altered tones to hear   240
        Like West winds breathing on his ear
        The memory of climes afar!
        She thought herself old scenes among
Where Recollection lingering hung
In lifes last hour to bid farewell   245
To what her heart had loved so well.

Methought she called on 'Caroline!'
        As long ago she used to cry
When laid at rest in eves decline--
        Till Caroline all smilingly   250
Would bend above her golden head
        And sing to sleep the guileless child--
Oh! had she known this change so dread
Fair Caroline had never smiled
To see her sisters blue eyes close   255
And kiss her lips to sweet repose!

    But let us haste to present woe
From pleasures perished long ago.--
    As Harriet lay the spark of red
In her spent Taper vanished   260
So turning toward the wall her head
She murmered--
                "Ah! So all depart
From blasted hopes and broken heart!
I thought It might have seen my end   265
But nought a Sinner will attend
To the dark flood!--They're gone--all gone!--
Where's PERCY?--"
                With that word again
Like bowstring loosened from its strain   270
Her wandering spirit sprung!--that tone
Called voice and vigour back--
                                "Who'se gone?--
O Percy! Percy! where art thou?--
        I've sacrificed my God for thee   275
        And yet thou wilt not come to me!--
How thy strong Arm might save me now!
My heart would chase away despair
I'de hope, I'de live! If thou wert there!
Percy, where art thou!--tell me where!--   280
    He's far away--and minds no more
Than the spent surge of Norways shore
His "Own loved Harriet"--Halls of light
        And beauteous forms and beaming eyes
Echo and look this very night   285
        To his rich floods of harmonies!--
He smiles and laughs!--Amid the throng
None smile so much or laugh so long!
Ah! Lady fly that witchery
Or thou wilt soon be fallen as I!   290
Ah! fair and frail! the tender tale
Must then again oer thee prevail?--
And wilt thou kneel to such a God?--
And darest thou bear his chastning rod?--
What though this mighty Dome contain   295
So bright a scene so fair a train--

                    449

But my own head whirls dizzily
For these are visions that I see!
Save me! I'm falling--!--Was That Him?
Methought I saw a sudden beam   300
Of passing brightness through the room
Like lightning vanish!--Percy! come!--
Leave me not in the dark! tis cold
    And something stands beside my bed--
Oh loos[e] me from its Icy hold   305
      That presses on me!--raise my head--
    I cannot breath[e]!--"
                  She'd scarcly said
That word--when sudden oer her frame
Again the chilly trembling came   310
And died upon her palsying tongue
The charmed word adored so long
And all relaxed her hands unclasped
And faint and fainter still she gasped--
Why fell that silence?--Hush! I hear   315
    A wing like winnowing--Tis the Wind
In the Cathedral Towers afar--
    But it came strangly on my mind
Like one departing----

x x x x x x x x x x x x x x x x x x x

I waited through the waning night   320
Untill the first pale hue of light
    Won wanly oer the gloom
I watched the forms of thing[s] arise
Like midnight spectres to my eyes
While all things showed like mysteries   325
    About the silent Room
I looked intently on the Bed
Where that unhappy Lady laid
    But nought distinct could see
I felt a sense of awful fear   330
Thus to be left so lonely there
I hardly dared to gaze on her
    When seen more plain by me
Oh did she sleep or was she dying?--
The curtain drawn obscured her lying   335
But all distinct each window pane
Was starting in to form again
And longer here I must not stay
For daylight makes me speed away
And yet the task was given to me   340
To watch her through her agony
So back I drew the curtain shade
And startled at the Noise I made
There--then Her gentle cheek declined

                 All white her neck and shoulders gleamed   345
             White as the bed where they reclined
                 As peacful slumbering she seemed
                 As if in Heaven her spirit dreamed
             Till lo! a stronger morning glowed
             And all the solemn vision showed--   350
             Hands clasped--cheeks sunk--
                               --But Oh that Brow
             I saw it and I knew it now!
             I knew it in

Opposite ll. 173-79, Branwell penciled "May 2^{d} 1841", indi-
cating he had the notebook with him at Luddenden Foot.

There is an earlier, heavily amended draft of ll. 1-14;
39-65 on the verso of a manuscript leaf at the BPM; an unrelated prose passage on the recto is dated July 12, 1837.

             At dead of night drearily
             I heard a Voice of Horror cry
                 "Oh God I am lost for ever!"
             And then the Bed of slumber shook
             As if its troubled sleeper awoke   5
                 With chill affrighted shiver!
             And in her waking burst a sigh
                 Sudden and short as checked by fear
             While faint she murmered--"Where am I?"
                 Oh Help!--Is no one here?"   10

             No--nought was there and through the dark
             Only a last and trembling spark
             Left from a dying taper light
             With red gleam specked the void of night

             No one was there--and, through the dark   15
             Only a last and trembling spark
             Left from a dying Taper light
             With red gleam specked the void of night

             "Oh God--" she murmured "take from me
             This awful weight of agony   20
             Twas but a dream--yet such an one
             As weighs my dying spirit down
             Oppressed with horrors chilled with fear
             And lying alone and death so near!
             I feel amid this spectral gloom   25
                 As if my outcast soul was hurled
                 To some void space without the world
             More solitary than the tomb
             There's no one here one word to speak
                 Not one whose heart would <haste> to save   30

The poem describes the death of Harriet (O'Connor) Montmorency after Percy has eloped with her (see No. **95**),
then abandoned her. Caroline would seem to be Harriet's
sister, and the Caroline of Nos. **124** and **134** (see
also Alexander EW, pp. 175 and 284 n. 21).

104

The manuscript is untraceable; the text provided is
Leyland's. Black Comb is the name of a mountain five miles
from Broughton-in-Furness where Branwell was a private tutor
for the first five months of 1840; thus 1840 is a likely date
of composition. He may have been inspired by Wordsworth's
poem on the same subject.

105

The first of 15 poems Branwell published in the **Halifax
Guardian, Bradford Herald** and **Leeds Intelligencer,**
1841-47, all but one under the pseudonym "Northangerland."
The text provided is that in the **Halifax Guardian.** An
earlier version of the first fifty lines (see p. 199) in
Notebook C reads:
> **An Analogy.**
> --composed by Warner H Warner. Esqr

<hr>

Of Earth beneath how small a space
    Our eyes at once descry
But Heaven above us meets our gaze
    like an Infinity
On Earth we see our own abode   5
A smoky town a dusty road
    A neighbouring hill or grove:
But worlds on worlds in ligions bright
Are gliding over paths of light
    Amid yon Heaven above!   10

While daylight shews this narrow earth
    It hides that boundless Heaven
And but by Night a visible birth
    To all its stars is given
Yes fast as fades departing day   15
When silent marsh and moorland grey
    To evening mists decline
So slowly stealing star on star

As midnight hours draw softly near
          More clear and countless shine   20

I know how oft-times clouds obscure them
          But from earth ascend
All such vapours drawn before them
          As to earth they tend
And when the storm has swept them by   25
Upon the earth their ruins lie
          Subsided down again
While Heaven untouched more glorious glows
And every star more star-like shews
          As "shining after rain'   30

Oh! thus, we view in mortal life
          So surcumscribed a scene,
Where petty joys and cares and strife
          Alone are heard or seen;
But when beyond death's darksome tide   35
We let our minds a moment glide,
          How vast the prospect seems!
Not worlds of everlasting light,
But Joy on Joy celestial bright
          O'er Heavens dominion gleams.   40

Tis day--The day of pomp and power,
          That hides the world divine;
And few will heed in such an hour
          How bright its splendours shine.
But when declines youths summer sun,   45
When life's last vanities are gone,
          Our thoughts from earth are driven;
And as the shades of death descend,
How truely seems its night our freind
          Because it shews us Heaven!   50

These lines cover two pages, suggesting that a third page
containing the final eleven lines, and the date and signature
that conclude all other items in the Notebook has been
removed. Leyland printed the last eleven lines, stating that
they originally completed a poem of sixty lines, dated
January 23, 1838.

106

This is the second item in a notebook (Notebook D) Branwell
began to keep while employed as clerk-in-charge of the railway station at Luddenden Foot, April 1, 1841-March 31, 1842.
For the first item, see comment for No. **117**.   Brearley

Hill is near Luddenden Foot. Above the poem are four uncanceled trial lines for stanza one:

> Oh God whose beams were most withdrawn
> When should have risen my morning Sun
> Who, clouded most at earliest dawn
> Foretold the storms through which should run

107

The manuscript is untraceable; the text provided is that in
the **Halifax Guardian.** The poem refers to the Whig Government under Melbourne, defeated in August 1841. The first
adhesive stamps had been introduced with the Penny Post in
1840.

108-113

All from Notebook D, this group of poems reflects Branwell's
preoccupation with great human achievements, often in the
face of adversity. On the page opposite the opening lines of
the first draft of **The Triumph of mind over body** (No.
127, also part of this group), Branwell made the following list: David King of Israel, Alexander of Macedon,
William Shakespeare, Oliver Cromwell, Samuel Johnson, Robert
Burns, Horatio Nelson, Napoleon Buonaparte, Michelangelo,
Sylla of Rome, Julius Caesar, Walter Scott, John Wilson,
Henry Broughton, Danton, Columbus. He may have planned eventually to include all of these figures in his poems, for he
placed an "x" opposite Johnson, Burns, and Nelson, who figure
prominently in these poems. Buonaparte and Michelangelo are
bracketed together with an "x" opposite the bracket-- perhaps
the subjects of a projected comparison? Opposite Alexander
of Macedon, Branwell wrote, "the brightest star that ever
blazed away the night/cloud of war"--see No. **109.**
Johnson appears in both **108** and **112,** Burns in **111**
and **112,** Nelson in the early draft of **127** (begun
immediately after **106)** and **110.** Note also the
similarity of the opening lines of **108** and the early
draft of **127.** No. **109** occurs on the same manuscript
page as **108;** the unfinished fragment on Burns (**111**)
and **110** occur in the midst of the early draft of **127.**
On the page opposite stanzas 5 and 6 of **112,** Branwell
lists Tasso, Galileo, Milton, Otway, Johnson, Cowper, Burns.
No. **113** occurs between the first and second manuscript
pages of **112.** In No. **110,** "Parry" is the Arctic
explorer who was Emily's childhood hero; "Vincent" is Sir
John Jervis, Earl of St. Vincent, who served with Wolfe in
the capture of Canada, was promoted to Admiral after the

capture of Guadeloupe in 1794, defeated the Spanish navy off Cape St. Vincent in 1797 where Nelson distinguished himself, sent Nelson to Aboukir, and in 1801 became first lord of the Admiralty. In No. 112, "Mezentius" is a tyrant expelled by his people in Virgil's **Aeneid**; "Salem's liberty" is a reference to Tasso's poem **Jerusalem Delivered.**

114

The manuscript is untraceable; the text is that published by F. H. Grundy in **Pictures of the Past** (London, 1879). Branwell made Grundy's acquaintance at Luddenden Foot in 1841. Despite Grundy's claim that "On one occasion he [Branwell] thought that I was disposed to treat him distantly at a party, and he retired in great dudgeon. When I arrived at my lodgings the same evening, I found the following, necessarily an impromptu" (p. 78), the poem was not composed for the particular incident. Two earlier versions of stanza one occur in a manuscript volume misattributed to Emily. The first is at the top of the manuscript page containing "The sunshine of a summer sun," dated May 17, 1836 (see No. 55); the second also dates from 1836/37.

> (a) The Heart which cannot know another
> Which owns no lover freind or brother
> In whom those names without reply
> Unechoed and unheeded die

> (b) The heart which cannot know another
> Which will not learn to sympathize
> In whom the voice of freind or brother
> Unheard unechoed sleeps or dies
> Between whom and the world around   5
> Can stretch no life unititing ties

115 and 116

Both poems are from Notebook D, although No. 116 was written at Haworth shortly after Branwell's dismissal from Luddenden Foot, 31 March 1842. Note the repetition of some lines in No. **119.** No. **115** occurs under the words "Blackwoods Magazine."

117

Almost immediately after his dismissal from Luddenden Foot, Branwell revised earlier versions of Nos. **117, 118, 120;** the similarity of the distinctive paper and handwriting suggests that the revisions were carried out at the same time. The revised copies were presumably sent to Joseph Leyland for publication in the **Halifax Guardian,** but this poem appeared in the **Bradford Herald,** and Nos. **118** and **120** in the **Herald** and **Guardian** simultaneously, a result, one has to assume, of their close connection (see **Introduction,** p. xxx). The text provided is that in the **Herald;** Branwell's April/May 1842 manuscript at the BPM reads:

On Landseer's painting--

"The Shepherd's chief mourner"--A Dog keeping watch at twilight, over its master's grave.

The beams of Fame dry up Affection's tears,
    And those who rise forget from whom they
        spring--
Wealth's golden glories--pleasure's glittering
    wing--
Distinction's, pomp and pride, devoid of fears
All that we follow through our chase of years--   5
    Dim or destroy those holy thoughts which cling
    Round where the form we loved lies slumbering;
But not with Thee--our slave--whose joys and cares
    We deem so grovelling--power nor pride are
        thine--
Nor our pursuits or ties yet, oer this grave   10
Where lately crowds the Form of mourning gave,
    I only hear THY low heartbroken whine--
    I only see THEE left, long hours to pine
For him whom thou, if Love had power, wouldst save.

                      Northangerland.

Text: 1. 4 was added later in pencil.

Sir Edwin Landseer, 1802-73, best-known for his paintings of animals, was the most famous artist of his time. The painting referred to was first exhibited in 1837.

An earlier version in Notebook D (see p. 211) reads:

The Shepherds Chief Mourner
vide Landseers Picture

The beams of Fame dry up Affections tears
    And those who rise forget from whom they spring
    Wealths golden glories pleasures glittering wing
All that man chases through his whirl of years

All that his hope seeks all his caution fears   5
    Dazzle or drown those holy thoughts that cling
    Round where the forms he loved lie slumbering
But not so <u>Thou</u>--Mans slave,--whose joys or cares
    Man deems so grovelling--power nor pride are
       thine
Nor Mans pursuits or ties--Yet oer this grave   10
Where lately crowds the <u>form</u> of mourning gave
    I only hear <u>thy</u> low heart broken whine
    I only see <u>Thee</u> left--long hours to pine
For him if love had power thy love could save

    On seeing landseers picture   15
"The Shepherds Cheif Mourner". A Dog
Keeping watch at twilight over its Masters
grave.

118

The text provided is that published jointly in the **Bradford Herald** and the **Halifax Guardian**, 5 & 7 May 1842. Branwell's April/May manuscript at the BPM reads:

The Callousness produced by care.

Why hold young eyes the fullest fount of tears
    And why do youthful breasts the oftenest sigh
When fancied friends forsake, or lovers fly,
    Or fancied woes and dangers waken fears:
    Ah! He who asks has seen but springtide years,   5
Or Times rough voice had long since told him why!
Increase of days increases misery,
    And misery brings selfishness, which sears
The hearts first feelings--mid the battles roar
In Deaths dread grasp the soldiers eyes are blind   10
To other's pains--So he whose hopes are oer
Turns coldly from the sufferings of mankind.
A bleeding spirit will delight in gore--
A tortured heart will make a Tyrant mind.

                      Northangerland.

An earlier version in Notebook C (see p. 199), written in December 1837 reads:

Sonnet.
composed by Northangerland

Why hold young eyes the fullest fount of tears;
    And why will happiest hearts most sadly sigh?
   When fancied freinds forsake or lovers fly
Or Hearts of others throb beneath their cares?
Ah, Questioner! Thou at least art young in years   5
    Or Time's rough voice had long since told
      thee why!
   Increase of days increases misery
And misery brings selfishness which sears
   The Souls best feelings.--Mid the Battles
     roar
In Death's dread grasp the soldier's eyes are blind 10
    To others Dying.--And He whose Hopes are o'er
Smiles sternly at the suffering's of mankind
   A bleeding spirit most delights in gore
A Tortured Heart will make a Tyrant mind.

P B Brontë

       written Decr 13 1837.
          14 lines

In the autumn of 1846, while at the home of Mary Pearson at
Ovenden Cross (see BST, 1986, p. 17), Branwell entered another version into her commonplace book (now at the HRC)
which reads:

SONNET.

Why hold young eyes the fullest fount of tears,
    And why do happiest hearts most sadly sigh
When fancied friends forsake, or lovers die,
Or other's heart-strings crack, oerstrained by
   cares?
Ah! Thou who askest me act young in years   5
    Or Time's rough voice had long since told thee
     why!
   Increase of days increases misery,
And misery brings selfishness, which sears
The soul's best feelings--Mid the battle's roar,
   In Death's grim grasp the soldiers eyes are
     blind   10
To others dying--So he whose hopes are oer
    Smiles sternest at the sufferings of mankind.
A wounded spirit will delight in gore--
    A tortured heart will make a tyrant mind.

              Northangerland.

Beneath the poem, Branwell sketched a bust of Northangerland
labeled "The results of Sorrow."

119

The manuscript is untraceable; the text provided is that in
the **Leeds Intelligencer**, 7 May 1842.   The occasion for
the poem is the disastrous retreat of the British from Kabul
in January 1842, during the first Afghan War.   Note the lines
in stanza one borrowed from No. **116**.

120

The text is the one jointly published in the **Bradford
Herald** and the **Halifax Guardian**, 12 and 14 May 1842.
Branwell's April/May manuscript at the BPM reads:

Peaceful death and happy life

Why dost thou sorrow for the happy dead
   For if their life be lost, their toils are oer
   And woe and want shall trouble them no more,
Nor ever slept they in an earthly bed
So sound as now they sleep while, dreamless, laid   5
   In the dark chambers of that unknown shore
   Where Night and Silence seal each guarded door:
So, turn from such as these thy drooping head
And mourn the "dead alive"--whose spirit flies--
   Whose life departs before his death has come--   10
Who finds no Heaven beyond Life's gloomy skies,
   Who sees no Hope to brighten up that gloom;
Tis HE who feels the worm that never dies--
   The REAL death and darkness of the tomb.

                            Northangerland.

An earlier version (see p. 198) appears in an untitled prose
manuscript at the BPM begun on October 20, 1837.   The prose
fragment is one of seven, on thirteen leaves, bound in red
morocco by Riviere for T. J. Wise.   The ordering of the
leaves in the collection is another good example of Wise's
mischief; to form a continuous narrative, the leaves have to
be read in the following order: 1, 3, 7, 6, 5, 4, 2, 8-13.

PERCYS LAST SONNET.

Cease, Mourner, cease thy sorrowing oer the Dead

For, if their Life be lost its Toils are oer
And Woe and Want shall visit them no more
Nor ever slept they in an earthly bed
Such sleep as that which lulls them dreamless laid   5
   In the lone chambers of the eternal shore
   Where sacred silence seals each guarded door.
Oh! Turn from tears for these thy bended head
   And mourn the Dead Alive whose pleasure flies
And Life departs before their death has come;   10
   Who lose the Earth from their benighted eyes,
Yet see no Heaven gleam through the rayless gloom.
   These only feel the worm that never dies
The Quenchless fire the Horrors of a Tomb!

121

Taken from the second draft of No. **126,** ll. 349-68 (see
p. 200), these lines were published jointly in the **Bradford**
Herald and the **Halifax Guardian,** 2 and 4 June 1842.

122

Taken from No. **95,** ll. 257-77 (see p. 441), these lines
were published jointly in the **Bradford Herald** and the
Halifax Guardian, 9 and 11 June 1842.

123

The text provided is that published jointly in the **Bradford**
Herald and the **Halifax Guardian,** 7 and 9 July 1842.   An
earlier version (see p. 199) in Notebook C reads:

> **Song..**
> **The present days Sorrow.**
> By Henry Hastings
>
> ═══════════
>
> The present day's sorrow
>   Oh why should we mourn
> Since every Tomorrow
>   Must rise oer its Urn
> All that we think such pain   5
> Will have departed then
> Bear for a moment what cannot return
>
> For past Time has taken
>   Each hour that it gave

460

And <u>they</u> do not waken   10
     From yesterday's grave
So surely we may defy
     Shadows like Memory
Feeble and fleeting as midsummer wave

From the depths where they're falling   15
     Both pleasure and pain
Despite its recalling
     Arise not again
Though we weep over them
Nought can recover them   20
There where they lie they shall never remain

Then seize we the present
     And gather its flowers
For, mournful or pleasant
     Tis all that is ours   25
While daylight we're wasting
The Evening is hasting
And night follows fast on the vanishing hours!

Yes and wo when that night comes
     Whatever betide   30
Must die as our fate dooms
     And sleep by their side
For change is the only thing
Always continuing
And it sweeps Creation away with its tide   35

          P. B. Bronte.
               written December 11th. 1837.
               _____ 35 lines

124

The manuscript is untraceable; the text provided is that published jointly in the **Bradford Herald** and the **Halifax
Guardian**, 12 and 14 July 1842.   See comment for No.
103.

125

The manuscript, seemingly incomplete, undated and unsigned,
is part of Notebook C, but was quite probably written in
1842; it is not included in Branwell's table of contents for
the Notebook (see pp. xii-xiv).   Hatfield notes at the end of
his transcription in the BPM, "The remainder of this poem

is missing, several leaves having been torn from the book in which the above text appears." The "part 1st" in the title suggests that Branwell either did or intended to produce a much longer piece. William Dearden, in a letter to the **Halifax Guardian**, June 15, 1867, wrote that "Brontë and I agreed that each should write a drama or a poem, the principal character in which was to have a real or imaginary existence before the Deluge; and that, in a month's time, we should meet at the Cross Roads Inn, which is about half-way between Keighley and Haworth, and produce the result of our lucubrations." Although Branwell did not bring **Azrael** to that meeting in 1842, Dearden states in papers found after his death in 1889 that the poem was written for the Cross Roads Inn meeting (BST 1933). According to Dearden, Branwell intended to publish the poem, and sent it to Joseph Leyland in 1842. The revised version of the first 48 lines, entitled **NOAH'S WARNING OVER METHUSALEH'S GRAVE**, appeared in the **Bradford Herald**, 25 August 1842. Azrael is the Jewish and Islamic angel of death who separates soul from body; Moloch is an Ammonite deity worshipped with human sacrifice—see Amos 5:26.

126

The second draft of **The Triumph of mind over body** (see p. 228) and Nos. **125(a), 126, 127** are all fair copies on the same distinctive paper and in the same distinctive hand, suggesting that Branwell continued his feverish activity to revise and submit work for publication throughout the summer and fall of 1842. The text for No. **126** is the last of three drafts; Branwell submitted it to **Blackwood's** with the accompanying letter dated September 6, 1842:

> Sir,
> I beg most respectfully to offer the accompanying lines, for insertion in Blackwoods Edinburgh Magazine.
> They endeavour—feebly enough, I fear—to describe the harsh contrast between a mind, changed by long absence from home, and the feelings still alive in those who have never wandered; and who vainly expect the absent to return with a heart as warm as when they bade him farewell.
> The kind advice and encouragement of Mrs Southey has alone emboldened me to make this offering; and, if you should cast a favourable eye upon it, I shall remain with more of thankfulness than vanity,
> Your most obd^{t} Servt,
>
> Patrick. B. Brontë.

An early draft of the middle paragraph appears toward the end of Notebook B.

However, Branwell must have begun this second revision at least as early as May, for ll. 349-68 appeared jointly in the **Bradford Herald** and the **Halifax Guardian**, 2 and 4 June (see No. **121**).

The earliest version (bound and misattributed by Wise to Emily--see p. 200) was written while Branwell was living in Bradford in 1838:

Bradford July 31st 1838.

Tis only Afternoon, yet midnights gloom
Could scarce seem stiller in the darkest room
Than does this Ancient Mansion's strange repose
So long ere common cares of daylight close;
I hear the clock slow ticking in the Hall,   5
And, far away, the woodland waterfall--
Sounds, lost, like stars, from out the noonday
      skies,
And only noticed when those stars arise.
    The Parlour Group are seated all together
With long looks turned toward the threatning
      weather   10
Whose grey clouds gather oer the moveless trees,
Nor break nor brighten with a passing breeze.
Why seems that group attired with such a care,
And, who's the visitor they watch for there?--
The Aged Father, on his customed seat,   15
With cushioned stool to prop his crippled feet,
Averting from the rest his forehead high
To hide the Drop that quivers in his eye;
And strange the pang which bids that drop to start
While Hope and Sadness mingle in his Heart,--   20
A sadness sent from what has passed away--
A trembling Hope for what may come to day--!
Fast by the window sits his Daughter fair
Earnestly gazing on the clouded air,
She clasps her Mothers Hand, and paler grows   25
With every leaf that falls or breeze that blows,
So sick, from long Hope, bursting into morn
Too bright for her, with longer pining worn!
Even those young children oer the table bent
And on that Map with childish eyes intent   30
Are guiding fancied ships through oceans foam
And wondering 'what He's like' and 'when He'll
      come.'
    Ah! many an hour has seen yon circle pore
On that great chart of INDIA'S far off shore

And sighing oer every name the paper gave   35
Lest that might mark their far off Wanderer's
        grave!
Oft has the eye a burning tear let fall
Oer Ganges mimic tide or Delhi's wall:
Oft has the heart left England far away
To linger oer the wrecks of Red Assaye!   40

   But--long that House has lost all trace of HIM
Whose very form in memory waxes dim,
Long since his Happy Boyhoods freinds have died
His Dog so faithful to its Masters side--,
The Rooks and Doves that Hover round the door   45
Are not the same his young hand fed of yore
The flowers he planted, many seasons past,
Have bloomed and died and dissappeared at last,
For Him, afar, tempestuous seas had born
Before the children round that map were born   50
And now, so many years had passed between
The last long look upon that farewell scene
That scarce they saw it then through gathering
        tears
So dim, as now, through intervening years
"And yet"--said Mary "still I think I see   55
The Soldiers plumed Helmet bent oer me
The Arm that raised me to a last embrace
The calmness settled oer his youthful face
Save when I asked how soon he'd come again?
And all that calm was lost a moment then!   60
Our Father shook his hand but could not speak
Our weeping Mother kissed his sunny cheek
My Sisters spoke not--twas a mute farewell
And yet--no voice could speak it half so well!
We saw our HENRY to his charger spring--   65
We heard his swift Hoofs oer the pavement ring--
There--long we stopped as if he still were there
Hand clasped in hand and dim eyes fixed on air
He seemed not gone--while yet our eyes beheld
The shadowy woodland and the open feild,   70
But--when we turned within--when closed the door
On that bright Heaven--we felt that ALL was oer!
That neer those rooms should hear his joyous call
That neer his rapid step should cross that Hall
We sat together till the twilight dim   75
But all the world seemed passed away with him
We gathered close yet could not drive away
The dreary solitude that oer us lay
We felt when ONE has left the bright fireside
It matters not though all be there beside   80
For still all Hearts have wandered with that one
And gladness stays not when the Heart is gone

                              464

And, where no gladness is a crowd may feel alone!
Since then--How oft we've sat together here
With windows opening on the twilight Air   85
In silence thinking on the climes afar
Beneath the shining of that Evening star
Dear as a freind unto our loneliness
Because it seemed to link those lands with us
He saw it--perhaps--whom times and oceans tide   90
So many years had sundered from our side
And twas the same he used to look upon
While all beside so different had grown
Our woods our House ourselves were not the same
As those which floated in his bygone Dream   95
Is He too changed?--Alas the cannons roar
The storms and summers of that Torrid shore
May have made the last great change!
                              --Too well I know
Even our calm woods cannot escape that blow   100
We cannot greet him if again he come
With the same group that made his Ancient Home!
The Hearts that loved him best are clad in clay!
They are laid in lasting rest!--They are far away!

    So Mary spoke--but so she spoke not now   105
Turning so earnestly her pallid brow
On the cold Heavens to which they all were turning
With looks which could not clear the shade of
        mourning
Worn far too constantly upon each face
For that one Day of fevered hope to chase--   110
That Day, determined, from Madeira's shore,
When they their Wanderer might behold once more!
Not now the Boyish Ensign, He had gone--
But full of Honours from his foes oerthrown,
Time after time fresh tidings of his fame   115
Had roused to life his Fathers aged frame
When the Old Man would raise his gushing eye
And lose his sighs of greif in smiles of joy
At last that letter with SIR Henry's crest
The tidings of his swift approach expressed   120
A Victor General to His Englands shore--
At last--that sixteen years suspense was oer!--
At last--the fresh rolled walks the shaven lawn
That long a look of such neglect had worn
The Rooms so fairly decked--the expectant calm   125
Oer all things brooding like a magic charm
Proclaimed--at last--the mighty moment come
When Hope and Doubt must both give place to Doom!
Stay--what was that which broke the Hush
        profound?--
Like rapid wheels I heard its murmur sound--   130

465

Why are the servants footsteps heard within
So sudden intermixed with hasty din?--
What pales each cheek? what lights each swimming
    eye
Through the close circle of that company?--
Advances hastily a strangers tread   135
The children shrink behind with sudden dread
All rise together--open flies the door
And steps that stranger on the parlour floor

    My pen might paint the start of wild surprise
The tears that flashed in scarce beleiving eyes   140
The long embrace the silence eloquent
Of thoughts that neer in words could find their
    vent
The Fathers look that said--"Thy will be done!
Take me if fit since Thou hast given my son!--"
The Mothers look too fond to turn above   145
That Son beholding with a Mothers love
The Sisters eyes that shone in Youths oerflow
Of feelings such as age could never know
With whom this world is not the earth it seems
But all surrounded by the light of dreams   150
With whom even Sorrow takes a heavenly die
For where it comes Hope ever hovers by
So thus while speechless held in that embrace
She saw she knew her long lost Henrys face
She let past Times part, hurrying down the wind   155
And years of vain repining leave her mind
    Not so Old Age for sorrow breaks it in
And used to Harness it can ill begin
Existence oer again--Dissolved in tears
Of Heartfelt gratitude the Head of years   160
Was Bowed before that Soldier--but in vain
Each parent strove to shake of Sorrows chain
They saw their first borns golden locks appear
Shining behind the cloud of memories drear
They looked and was this Warworn Warrior Him?--   165
Ah, how the Golden locks waned dark and dim!--
The Golden locks were gone--for Indias clime
Had touched him with the Iron hoar of time
Wast him?--They gazed again--A look, a tone
Brought back the past--Twas Henry! twas their Own!   170
They did not mark his restless glances roam
As if he sought but could not find a home
They did not mark the sternness of his cheek
Even if to smiles its muscles chose to break
They only saw the statly Soldiers form   175
Confirmed not altered by the battles storm
They only saw the long lost face again
Darkened by climate not by crime or pain--.

466

But what He thought it would be hard to tell
Since worldly life can mask the heart so well   180
Can hide with curls a sorrow eaten cheek
Can bitter thoughts in cheerful accents speak
Can give to icy minds heart eloquence
And clothe no meaning in the robes of sense.
Words he poured forth of warm and welcome greeting   185
For Heaven--he said--smiled in this happy meeting
By turns he wandered oer each longlost face
By turns he held them in a fast embrace
Then--Mary saw though nought her parents knew--
For youthful love has eyes of eagle view--   190
She saw his features in a moment alter
Their rapture vanish and their fondness falter
And--in that moment--Oh how cold seemed all
The mind that peeped beneath that passions pall,
A corse beneath a gilded shrine--the corse   195
Of him who left them on his Battle Horse
Sixteen long years ago!--
                         Sir Henry broke
A sudden pause where only glances spoke,
With a request for one half hour alone   200
To call his spirits to a steadier tone
And moderate their swell--He left them then
To spend their time in calling oer again
The ancient image to their wildered view
And mark the difference twixt the old and new.   205
But, strange--wheneer they strove to realize
The form so latly constant to their eyes
The visioned Idol of each vanished year
How dim and distant did it now appear
They could not bear to see it sink from view   210
Like a vain dream--but ever came the new
Before the Old thus on a sudden faded
When by lifes stern realities invaded.
Changed--like lifes dreary path from youth to years
And dull as age--The twilight hour appears--   215
The hour ordained by God for mans repose
Yet often made by Man an hour of woes--
A summing-up ot daylights toils and greif--
Of moody musing--not of mild releif.
     That dull hour darkened in the boding sky   220
And bore the wind in mournful murmurs by
With promise of a storm--Within the Room
No cheerful candle shone to cheat its gloom
Nor cheerful countenance smiled, for only one
Lone tenant held it, seated still as stone,   225
Sir Henry Tunstall, with a vacant gaze
As if his mind was wandering through a maze
Of alien thoughts, though on that very Bed
Long years ago had lain his Infant head

In sleep unstained by sorrow--Still there hung--   230
Wrecks of a time when all the world looked young--
His Guns, His Rods, with which he had often trod
The breezy hills, and wandered by the flood,
And breasted mountain winds, and felt within
The first bold stirrings of the Man begin.   235
There, pictured as of yore, the selfsame wall
Showed Englands victory and Her Heroes fall
On cold Canadian Hills--with strange delight
In other days the child would fix his sight
Wheneer he woke upon that time dimmed view   240
And burn within to be a Hero too
Would fill his spirit with the thoughts divine
Of the loud cannon and the charging line
And Wolfe departing mid the mingled cries
To join Immortal spirits in the skies!   245
Twas that dim print that fixed his destinies
And led his footsteps over Indian Seas
So why--on what was childhoods best delight
Will manhood hardly deign to bend his sight
The old print remains--but, does the old <u>mind</u>
    remain?--   250
Ah World!--why wilt thou break Enchantments chain!

    Bending his brows at last Sir Henry said,
'Well--Now I know that Time has <u>really</u> sped
Since last my head has in this chamber lain--
That Nothing has my NOW to do with THEN!   255
Yes, now, at last Ive reached my Native Home
And all I loved have joyed to see me come
And memory of departed love is nigh
To cast a holier halo round that joy
I have seen my father--full of honoured days   260
Whom last I left adorned with Manhoods grace
Who has lived since then long seasons but to see
Once more his first born, world divided me,--
I have seen those eyes rekindle that have mourned
For me--I have seen the grey locks that have
    turned   265
From Ravenblack for Me--I have seen Her too,
The first on earth I loved, the first I knew
She who was wont above that very bed
To bend with blessings oer my helpless head--
I have seen my Sister--I have seen them all--   270
All but Myself--They have lost Me past recall,
As I have, them,--And vainly do I come
These thousand leagues--my Home is not my Home!
    But let me recollect myself--for strange
And visionlike appears this utter change--   275
In what consists it?--I am still the same
In flesh and blood and lineaments and name

Still wave the boughs of my Ancestral trees
Still my old Gables face the western breeze
Still hang these relics round this chamber lone   280
I still can see--can call them still my own
    But well I used to love the things I see
Now--if I lost them--twould be nought to me--
And--once my Sires or sisters voice was dear--
Now--if They perished--freinds are everywhere.   285
Once nought could tear me from my own dear home--
Now--every roof's the same whereer I roam.
Once when I saw that picture every vein
Beat fame like that even with that death to gain
Now--I have looked on many a bloody feild   290
But oh how different are the thoughts they yeild
They bend my brow to calculate their plan
But rouse no wishes wild to combat in their van
    They fancied when they knew me home returning
That all my soul to meet with them was yearning--   295
That every wave I'd bless which bore me hither--
They thought my spring of life would never wither
That in the dry the green leaf I could keep
As pliable as youth to laugh or weep.
They did not think how oft my eyesight turned   300
Toward the far skies where Indian sunshine burned
That I was leaving a companion band
That I had farewells even for that wild land
They did not think my head and heart were older
My strength more shaken and my feelings colder   305
That spring was hastening into Autumn sere
And leafless trees make loveliest prospects drear
That sixteen years the same ground travel oer
Till each wears out the marks which each has left
    before
So--Old Affection!--is an empty name   310
When nothing that we love remains the same
But while we gaze upon the vapour gay
The light that gave it glory fades away
And Home Affection!--where have we a Home
For ever doomed in thoughts or deeds to roam   315
To lay our parents in their narrow rest
Or leave our Hearthstone when we love them best
Nay sometimes not to know we love at all
Till oer loves object death has spread his pall!
I feel tis sad to live without a heart   320
But sadder still to feel dart after dart
Rankling within--tis sad to see the dead
But worse to view the tortured sickmans bed.
    Well--I have talked of change--But Oh! how
        changed
Am I from him who oer those dim hills ranged   325
With trusty dog--

                    Poor Rover! where art Thou?--
I seem to see thee looking upward now
To thy young Masters face with honest eye
Shining all over with no selfish joy   330
Ah Rover!--wert thou here and couldst thou feel
The utter change this Spirit would reveal
Thou'dst rather keep thy long neglected grave
Than lick again the hand which would not have
One welcoming stroke to give--My Dog--They say   335
That when I went thou pinedst fast away
Till death restored thee to thy humble clay
And have thou ceased, at last, to think of me
Who then afar was fast forgetting thee
Yes--twas forgetting--Memory lingered yet,   340
But Lost Affection, makes the word--forget!"

    He paused with heavy eye and round the room
Looked through the shadows of descending gloom
Like one heart sick for twas a bitter task
The hollowness of spirit to unmask   345
And shew the wreck of years--To change his mind
He took a Book lying by from which to find
Some other course for thought, and turning oer
Its leaves, he thought he'd known that book before
And on one page some hand had lightly traced   350
These lines--by time's dim finger half defaced.

    "My Father, and my childhoods Guide,
        If oft I've wandered far from Thee
    Even though Thine only Son has died
        To save from death a child like me   355

    Oh! still, to Thee when turns my heart
        In hours of sadness--Frequent now!
    Be still the God that once Thou wert
        And calm my breast and clear my brow

    I am now no more a guileless child   360
        Oershadowed by Thine Angel wing
    For even my dreams are far more wild
        Than those my slumbers used to bring

    I farther see--I deeper feel
        With hopes more warm but heart less mild   365
    And ancient things new forms reveal
        All strangly brightened or despoiled

    I am entering on Lifes open Tide
        So--fare ye well! Lost times divine!
    And, Oh my Father--deign to guide   370
        Through its wild waters--CAROLINE!"

                        470

Long on that darkening page Sir Henry pondered
Nor from its time worn words his eyesight wandered
Yet scarce he comprehended what they were
For other words were sounding in his ear   375
Sent to him from the Grave--far off and dim
As if from Heaven a spirit spoke to him
And bade the shadows of past time glide by
Till present Times were hidden from his eye
By their strange pictured vail, scene after scene   380
Sailing around him of what once had been.
He saw a Drawing room revealed in light
From the Red fireside of a winters night
With two fair beings seated side by side
The one arrayed in all a Soldiers pride   385
The other sadly pale with Angel eyes
Oer whose fair orbs a gushing gleam would rise
Whenever, tremblingly, she strove to speak
Though not a sound her voiceless calm could break
So silent seemed despair--He took her hand   390
And told her something of a distant Land
Soon to be won with fame, and soon again
Of his <His> return in victory oer the main
"Oh no!" at last she said--"I feel too well
The hollow vanity of all you tell   395
You'll go--you'll join the ranks by Ganges flood
Youll perhaps survive through many a feild of blood
You'll perhaps gain fame's rewards but, never more
Those far off climes <u>my</u> Henry shall restore
To Englands Hills again!--Another mind   400
Another Heart than that he left behind
And other hopes he'll bring--if hope at all
Can outlive fancy's flight and feelings fall
To flourish on an Iron hardened brow--
The Soldier may return--But, never THOU!--   405
And further--know our meeting must not be
For even thyself will not be changed like me.
I shall be changed my Love, to change no more
I shall be landed on a farther shore
Than Indian Isles, a wider sea shall sever   410
My form from thine, a longer time--FOR EVER!
    "Oh! when I'm dead and mouldering in my grave
Of me, at least some dim remembrance have
Saved from the sunken wrecks of ancient time
Even if to float oer waves of strife and crime.   415
Then--on the Grave of Her who died for thee
414 Cast one short look, And--oh! <u>Remember Me!</u>"

    "Alas Lost Shade!--why should I look upon
The mouldering letters of thy Burial stone?--
Why should I strive thine Image to recall   420
And love thy beauty's flower and weep its fall?--

                        471

It cannot be--for far too well I know
The Narrow house where thou art laid below
I know its lifeless chill its rayless gloom
Its voiceless silence and its changeless doom   425
I know that if from weeds I cleared thy name
And gazed till memories crowding round me came
Of all that made the sunshine of my Home,
Twould be of no avail--Thou couldst not come!
That I might almost think I saw thee stand   430
Beside me--almost feel thy fairy hand
Still would that form be pressed neath earth and
          stones
And still that hand would rest in dust and bones
     No Caroline--the hours are long gone by
When I could call a shade reality   435
Or make a world of dreams--or think that one
Was present with me who, I knew, was gone
No--if the sapling bends to every breeze
Their force shall rather break the forest trees
If Infancy will catch at every toy   440
Pursuits more solid must the Man employ
He feels what is and nought can charm away
The plain realities of present day--
Thou art dead--I am living--my world is not thine--
So keep thy sleep and, Farewell, Caroline!   445
     Yet--while I think so--while I speak farewell
Tis not in words the dreariness to tell
Which sweeps across my spirit for my soul
Feels such a midnight oer its musings roll
At losing--though it be a vapour vain   450
What once was rest to toil and ease to pain.
I knew not, while afar, how utterly
These memories of youth were past from me
It seemed as if, though buisiness warped my mind
I could assume them when I felt inclined   455
That though like dreams they fled my waking brain
I, if I liked, could dream them oer again.
I did not think I could be seated here
After the lapse of many a toilsome year
Once more returning to accustomed places   460
Amid the smiles of Old familiar faces
Yet--shrinking from them--hiding in the gloom
Of this dim evening and secluded room
Not to recall the spirit of the Boy
But--all my world worn energies to employ   465
In pondering oer some artifice to gain
A future power or present to maintain
     Well, world, Oh world! as I have bowed to thee
I must consent to suffer thy decree
I asked thou'st given me my destiny   470
I asked, when gazing on that pictured wall

472

Like England's Hero to command or fall
I asked when walking over mountains lone
Some day to wander over Lands unknown
I asked for gain and glory place and power   475
Thou gavest them all--I keep them all, this hour
But--I forgot to ask for youthful blood
The thrill divine of feelings unsubdued
The nerve that quivered to the sound of fame
The tongue that trembled oer a lovers name   480
The eye that glistened with delightful tears
The Hope that gladdened past and gilded future years!
So--I have rigid nerves and ready tongue
Fit to command the weak to obey the strong
And eyes that look on all things as the same   485
And Hope--nay, callousness that thinks all things a
     Name!--
So--Caroline!--I'll bid farewell once more
Nor mourn lost shade, for though thou'rt gone
     before
Gone is thy Henry too--and didst not thou
While just departing from this world of woe   490
Say thou no longer wert a guileless child
That all old things were altered or despoiled--
And hadst thou lived thy Angel heart like mine
Would soon have darkened with thy youths decline
Cold, perhaps, to me, if beating, as when laid   495
Beneath its gravestone neath the churchyard shade.
It rests mine labours, there the difference lies
For mine will change but little when it dies.

     I Home returned for rest--but feel to day
Home is no rest and long to be away   500
To play lifes game out where my soldiers are
Returned from India to a wilder war
Our blood red feilds of Spain--again to ride
Before their Bayonets at Wellesleys side
Again to sleep with Horses trampling round   505
Wrapped in a watch-cloak on a Battle ground
To waken with the loud commencing gun
And feed lifes failing fame and drive the moments
     on
There is our aim--to that our labours tend
Strange! we should love to hurry on our end   510
But so it is and nowhere can I speed
So fast through life as on my Battle steed!"

Text: 1. 209: "dim and distant" written over "like a
       vision"; neither is canceled
       1. 417: Branwell uses the phrase "oh! Remember Me!"
       again in No. 109.

Branwell revised the poem in Spring 1840, while a tutor at Broughton, using the name Tunstall for the first time (see p. 202). Carus Wilson was Vicar of the Tunstall Church, which Charlotte and her fellow pupils at Cowan Bridge School attended. It was this version which Branwell sent to Thomas De Quincey in April 1840, and which appeared in De Quincey in 1891.

Sir Henry Tunstall

Tis only afternoon--but midnight's gloom
Could scarce seem stiller, in the darkest room,
Than does this ancient mansions strange repose,
So long ere common cares of daylight close.
I hear the clock slow ticking in the Hall;   5
And--far away--the woodland waterfall;
Sounds, lost, like stars from out the noon day
    skies--
And seldom heard untill those stars arise.
  The parlour group are seated all together,
With long looks turned toward the threatning
    weather,   10
Whose grey clouds, gathering oer the moveless
    trees,
Nor break, nor brighten with the passing breeze.
  Why seems that group attired with such a care?
And who's the visitor they watch for there?
The aged Father, on his customed seat,   15
With cushioned stool to prop his crippled feet,
Averting from the rest his forehead high
To hide the drop that quivers in his eye;
And strange the pang which bids that drop to start;
For hope and sadness mingle in his heart;   20
A trembling hope for what may come to day--
A sadness sent from what has passed away!
Fast by the window sits his daughter fair;
Who, gazing earnest on the clouded air,
Clasps close her mothers hand, and paler grows   25
With every leaf that falls, or breeze that blows:
Sickened with long hope bursting into morn
Too bright for her, with longer pining worn!
Even those young children oer the table bent;
And on that map with childish eyes intent,   30
Are guiding fancied ships through oceans foam;
And wondering--'what he's like'--and 'when he'll
    come'.
  'Ah! many an hour has seen yon circle pore
Over that map of India's far off shore;
And sigh at every name the paper gave   35
Lest it might mark their wanderer's far off grave.

Oft have those eyes a burning tear let fall
Oer Ganges mimic tide, and Delhi's Wall.
Oft have those hearts left England far away
To wander oer the wrecks of red Assaye.   40

   But long that house has lost all trace of him;
Who's very form in memory waxes dim.
Long since his childhoods chosen freinds have died;
The shaggy pony he was wont to ride--
The Dog--so faithful to its Masters side--   45
The Rooks and Doves that hover round the door
Are not the same his young hand fed of yore;
The flowers he planted many seasons past
Have drooped and died and dissapeared at last;
For him afar, tempestous seas had torn,   50
Before the childern round that map were born:
And, since, so many years have passed between
The voiceless farewells of that parting scene,
That scarce they saw it then through gathering
    tears
So dim as now through intervening years.   55
"But still"--said Mary--"still I think I see
The Soldiers plumed helmet bent oer me,
The Arm that raised me to a last embrace,
The calmness settled oer his youthful face,
Save when I asked "how soon he'd come again"--   60
And--all that calm was lost a moment then!--
Our Father shook his hand, but could not speak,
Our weeping Mother kissed his sunny cheek,
Our Sisters spoke not--twas a mute farewell
And yet no voice could speak it half so well--   65
We saw our <u>Henry</u> on his charger spring,
We heard his swift hoofs oer the pavement ring,
There--long we stopped--as if he still was there--
Hand clasped in hand and full eyes fixed on air:
He scarce seemed gone so long as we beheld   70
The checquered sunshine and the open feild,
But--when we turned within--when closed the door
On that bright Heaven--we felt that <u>all</u> was oer;
That never more those rooms should hear his call,
That never more his step should cross that Hall.   75
We sat together till the twilight dim,
But all the world to us seemed gone with him.
We gathered close but could not drive away
The dreary solitude that oer us lay.
We felt when <u>one</u> has left the home fireside   80
It matters not though all be there beside,
For still all hearts will wander with that one,
And gladness stays not when the heart is gone,
And--where no gladness is a crowd may feel alone.

Since then--how oft we've sat together here   85
With windows opening on the twilight air,
Silently thinking of the climes afar
Beneath the shining of that evening star,
Dear as a freind unto our loneliness
Because it seemed to link those lands with us.   90
He saw it, perhaps, whom time's and ocean's tide
So many years had sundered from our side,
And twas the same he used to look upon
While all beside so different had grown.
Our woods our House ourselves were not the same   95
As those that floated through his boyhoods dream--
Is he too changed?--Alas! the cannons roar,
The storms and summers of that burning shore,
May have made the last great change!--Too well I
     know
Even our calm woods cannot escape that blow!   100
We cannot greet him if again he come
With the same group that made his ancient home--
The Heart that he loved best is clad in clay--
She is laid in lasting rest--She is far away!--"

     So Mary spoke--but, she said nothing now,   105
Turning so earnestly her pallid brow
On the dull Heavens to which they all were turning
With looks that could not clear the shade of
     mourning
Worn far too constantly upon each face
For that one day of feverish hope to chase;   110
That day, determined from Madeira's shore,
When they their wanderer might behold once more,
Not now the boyish Ensign he had gone
But full of honours from his foes oerthrown.
Time after time fresh tidings of his fame   115
Had roused to life his aged Father's frame,
When the old Man would raise his gushing eye
And lose his sighs of greif in smiles of joy.
     At last, that letter with Sir Henry's crest
The tidings of his swift approach expressed,   120
A Victor General to his England's shore--
At last--that sixteen years suspense seemed oer,
At last--the fresh rolled walks, the shaven lawn
That long a look of such neglect had worn,
The rooms so fairly decked--the expectant calm   125
Oer all things brooding like a magic charm
At last, proclaimed the mighty moment come
When hope and doubt should both give place to doom.
     Stay--what was that which broke the hush
          profound?--
Like rapid wheels I heard its murmur sound--   130
Why are the Servants footsteps heard within

So sudden intermixed with hasty din?
What pales each cheek--what lights each swimming
    eye
Through the close circle of that company?
  Advances hastily a Strangers tread--   135
The children shrink behind with sudden dread--
All rise together--open flies the door
And steps that stranger on the parlour floor!

    I cannot paint the start of mute su[r]prise,
The tears that flashed in scarce beleiving eyes,   140
The long embrace--the silence eloquent
Of more than language ever could give vent,
The Fathers face that said--Thy will be done--
Take me if fit since thou hast given my Son;
The Mothers look, too fond to turn above   145
Her Son beholding with a mothers love;
The Sisters eyes that shone in youths oerflow
Of feeings such as Age could never know,
With whom this world was not the earth it seems
But all surrounded by the light of dreams,   150
With whom even Sorrow took a heavenly die
Since where it darkened Hope seemed shining by;
So thus--while, speechless, held in his embrace
She saw, she knew, her long lost Henrys face,
She let past times part--hurrying down the wind   155
And years of vain repinings leave her mind.
  Not so Old Age--for Sorrow breaks it in,
And--used to harness--it can ill begin
Existence oer again--Dissolved in tears
Of heartfelt gratitude the head of years   160
Was bowed before that Soldier--but in vain
Each parent strove to shake off Sorrows chain,
Their eyes were dim to present joy's--yet still
Past joys to them were far more visible.
They saw their firstborn's golden locks appear   165
Shining behind the cloud of memories dear;
They looked--and was this war worn warrior Him?--
Ah! how the golden locks waned dark and dim!
Their innocence destroyed--for Indias climo
Had touched him with the Iron hoar of time;   170
Wast him?--They gazed again--a look, a tone
Can sometimes bring the past--twas Henry--twas
    their own!

They did not mark his restless glances roam
As if he sought but could not find his home,
They did not mark the sternness of his cheek   175
Even if to smiles its muscles chose to break,
They only saw the stately Soldiers form
Confirmed, not altered by the battle's storm;

                        477

They only saw the long lost face again
Darkened by climate not by crime or pain.   180
   But what he thought it would be hard to tell,
Since worldly life can mask the heart so well,
Can hide with smiles a sorrow eaten cheek,
Can bitter thoughts in cheerful accents speak,
Can give to icy minds heart-eloquence,   185
And "clothe no meaning in the words of sense"--
Words he poured forth of warm and welcome greeting
For--"Heaven" he said "Smiled in this happy
        meeting"--
By turns he wandered oer each long lost face--
By turns he held them in a fast embrace--   190
Then--Mary saw--though nought her parents knew--
For youthful love has eyes of eagle view--
She saw his features in a moment alter,
Their rapture vanish and their fondness falter;
And--in that moment--Oh how cold seemed all   195
The mind that lurked beneath that passions pall!
A corse beneath a gilded shroud--The corse
Of him who left them on his battle horse
Sixteen long years ago!--
                        --Sir Henry broke   200
A sudden pause where only glances spoke,
With a request for one half hour alone
To call his spirits to a steadier tone
And moderate their swell--He left them then
To spend that time in calling back again   205
The ancient image to their wildered view,
To mark the difference twixt the old and new:
But--strange--wheneer they strove to realise
The form erewhile enshrined in their eyes,
The visioned Idol of each vanished year--   210
How like a vision did it now appear!
They could not bear to see it shrink from view
Like a vain dream--but never came the new
Before the old--thus on a sudden faded
When by life's stern realities invaded.   215
   Changed--like life's dreary path from youth to
        years,
And dull as age--The twilight hour appears,
The hour ordained by God for mans repose
Yet often made by man an hour of woes,
A Summing-up of daylight's toils and greif,   220
Of moody musing, not of mild releif.
   That dull hour darkened in the boding sky
And bore the breeze in mournful murmurs by
With promise of a Storm--within the Room
No cheerful candle shone to cheat its gloom,   225
Nor cheerful countenance smiled--for only one
Lone Tenant held it, seated still as stone--

Sir Henry Tunstall--with a vacant gaze
As if his mind were wandering through a maze
Of alien thoughts, though on that very bed   230
Long years ago had lain his infant head
In sleep unstained by Sorrow--still there hung--
Wrecks of a time when all the world looked young--
His guns--his rods--wherewith he'd often trod
The breezy hills or wandered by the flood,   235
And breasted Mountain winds, and felt within
The first bold stirrings of the Man begin.
There--pictured as of yore, the selfsame wall
Shewed Englands Victory and her Hero's fall
On Cold Canadian hills--with strange delight,   240
In other days the child would fix his sight
Wheneer he wakened--on that time dimmed view
And inly burn to be a Hero too;
Would fill his spirit with the thought's divine
Of the loud Cannon, and the charging line,   245
And Wolfe, departing mid commingling cries
To join immortal spirits in the skies!
Twas that dim print that--over Indian seas
First led his feet and fixed his destinies--
So why--on what was childhoods cheif delight   250
Will Manhood hardly deign to bend his sight?
The old print remains--But--does the old mind
          remain?
Ah World!--why wilt thou break enchantments
          chain!--

          Bending his brows, at last Sir Henry said--
"Well--now I know that Time has really sped   255
Since last my head has in that chamber lain--
That nothing has my Now to do with Then!
Yes--Now at last Ive reached my native home,
And all who loved me joy to see me come,
And memory of departed love is nigh   260
To cast a holier halo round their joy.
I have seen My Father full of honoured days,
Whom last i left adorned with manhoods grace,
Who has lived since then long winter's but to see
Once more--his Firstborn--world divided me.   265
I have seen those eyes rekindle, that have mourned
For me--I have seen those gray locks that have
          turned
From raven black--for me--I have seen Her too--
The first I loved on Earth--the first I knew--
She who was wont above that very bed   270
To bend with blessings oer my helpless head;
I have seen my Sister--I have seen them all--
All but myself--They have lost me past recall,
As I have them--And vainly have I come

479

These thousand leagues--my Home is not my Home.   275
     Yet--let me recollect myself--for strange
And visionlike appears this sudden change;
In what consists it?--I am still the same
In flesh and blood and lineaments and name,
Still wave the boughs of my Ancestral trees,   280
Still those old gables front the western breeze,
Still hang these relics round this chamber lone,
I still can see--can call them still my own.
     But well I used to love the things I see,
Now--if I lost them twould be nought to me;   285
And once my Sires or Sisters voice was dear
Now--if they perished Freinds are every where;
Once nought could tear me from my own dear home,
Now--every roof's the same wherere I roam;
Once when I saw that picture, every vein   290
Beat, fame like that, even with that death to gain;
Now--I have looked on many a battle feild
But oh, how different are the thoughts they yeild!
They bend my brow to calculate their plan
But rouse no wishes wild to combat in their van.   295

     They fancied, when they saw me home returning,
That all my soul to meet with them was yearning,
That every wave I'de bless which bore me hither;
They thought my spring of life could never wither,
That in the dry the green leaf I could keep,   300
As pliable as youth to laugh or weep;
They did not think how oft my eyesight turned
Toward the skies where Indian sunshine burned,
That I had perhaps left an associate band,
That I had farewells even for that wild Land;   305
They did not think my head and heart were older,
My strength more broken, and my feelings colder,
That spring was hastning into autumn sere--
And leafless trees make loveliest prospects drear--
That sixteen years the same ground travel oer   310
Till each wears out the mark which each has left
     before.

     "So--old affection is an empty name
When nothing that we loved remains the same,
But while we gaze upon the vapour gay,
The light that gave it glory, fades away.   315
And--Home Affection--where have we a home?--
For ever doomed in thought or deed to roam,
To lay our parents in their narrow rest
Or leave their hearthstones when we love them best,
Nay--sometimes scarce to know we love at all   320
Till oer loves object death has spread his pall!--
I feel tis sad to live without a Heart,

But sadder still to feel dart after dart
Rankling within it--sad to see the dead,
But worse to see the sickmans tortured bed.   325
   "Well I have talked of change--But, oh how
         changed
Am I from him who oer those dim hills ranged
With trusty Dog--poor Rover!--where art thou?--
I seem to see thee looking upward now
To thy young Masters face, with honest eye   330
Shining all over with no selfish joy.
Ah Rover!--wert thou here and couldst thou feel
The utter change this spirit would reveal,
Thou'dst rather keep thy long neglected grave
Than kiss again the hand which would not have   335
One welcoming stroke to give--My Dog--they say
That when I left thou pinedst fast away
Till death restored thee to thy humble clay,
And there forgot at last to think of me
Who then afar was fast forgetting thee!   340
Yes--twas forgetting--Memory lingered yet
But--lost affection makes the word <u>forget</u>!"

He paused with heavy eye, and, round the room
Looked, through the shadows of descending gloom,
Like one heart sick for twas a bitter task   345
The hollowness of spirit to unmask
And shew the wreck of year's--To change his mind
He took a book lying by in which to find
Some other course for thought--and, turning oer
Its leaves, He thought he'd known that book before; 350
And on one page some hand had lightly traced
These lines by time's dim finger half effaced--

   "My Father and my childhood's guide,
      If oft I've wandered far from Thee,
   Even though Thine only Son has died   355
      To save from death a child like me,

   Oh! still, to Thee when turns my heart
      In hours of sadness--frequent now!--
   Be still the God that once Thou wert
      And calm my breast and clear my brow.   360

   I am now no more a guileless child
      Oershadowed by Thine angel wing,
   For even my dreams are far more wild
      Than those my slumbers used to bring;

   I Farther see--I deeper feel,   365
      With hopes more warm but heart less mild,

481

And ancient things new Forms reveal
      All strangely brightened or despoiled;

I am entering on life's open tide,
      So--Fare ye well--lost shore's divine!--   370
And--Oh My Father!--deign to guide
      Through its wild waters--CAROLINE!"

Long oer that darkening page Sir Henry pondered,
Nor from its time worn words his eye sight wandered,
Yet scarce he comprehended what they were   375
For other words were sounding in his ear--
Sent to him from the grave--far off and dim,
As if from Heaven a spirit spoke to him,
That bade the shadows of past time glide by
Till present times were hidden from his eye   380
By their strange pictured vail--scene after scene
Sailing around him of what once had been--
He saw a Drawingroom revealed in light
From the red fireside of a winter night,
With two fair beings seated side by side,   385
The one arrayed in all a Soldiers pride,
The other sadly pale, with angel eyes,
Oer whose fair orbs a gushing gleam would rise
Whenever--tremblingly she strove to speak,
Though scarce a sound the voiceless calm would
            break,   390
So silent seemed despair--He took her hand
And told her something of a distant land
Soon to be won with fame, and soon again,
Of his return victorious oer the main.
      "Oh no!"--at last She said--"I feel too well   395
The hollow vanity of all you tell--
You'll go you'll join the ranks by Ganges flood,
You'll perhaps survive through many a feild of
            blood,
You'll perhaps gain fames rewards--but never more
Those far off climes My Henry shall restore   400
To Englands hills again--another mind--
Another heart than that he left behind--
And other hopes he'll bring--if hope at all
Can outlive fancy's flight and feeling's fall
To flourish on an iron hardened brow--   405
The Soldier may return--but never Thou!
And, farther, know, Our meeting must not be
For even thyself wilt not be changed like me.
I shall be changed--my Love, to change no more,
I shall be landed on a farther shore   410
Than Indian Isles--a wider sea shall sever
My Form from thine--a longer time--For ever!
      Oh! when I am dead and mouldering in my grave,
Of me, at least some dim remembrance have,

Saved from the sunken wrecks of ancient time   415
Even if to float oer thoughts of strife and crime:
Then--on the grave of Her who died for thee
Cast one short look--And, Oh! Remember Me!"

    Alas lost Shade! why should I look upon
The mouldring letters of thy burial stone?   420
Why should I strive thine image to recall,
And love thy beauty's flower and weep its fall?
It cannot be--For far too well I know
The narrow house where thou art laid below,
I know its lifeless chill--its rayless gloom,   425
Its voiceless silence, and--its changeless doom--
I know that if from weeds I cleared thy name
And gazed till memories crowding round me came
Of all that made the Sunshine of my home,
Twould be of no avail--Thou couldst not come   430
That I might almost think I saw thee stand
Beside me--almost feel thy fairy hand,
Still would that form be pressed neath earth and
    stones,
And still that hand would rest in dust and bones.
    No, Caroline--The hours are long gone by   435
When I could call a shade, reality,
Or make a world of dreams, or think that one
Was present with me who, I knew, was gone.
No--if the sapling bends to every breeze,
Their force shall rather break the full grown
    trees.   440
If Infancy will catch at every toy
Pursuits more solid must the Man employ.
He feels what is and nought can charm away
The rough realities of present day.
    Thou art dead--I am living--my world is not
    thine   445
So, keep thy sleep--and, Farewell, Caroline!

    "Yet--while I think so, while I speak farewell
Tis not in words the dreariness to tell
Which sweeps across my spirit--for my soul
Feels such a midnight oer its musings roll   450
At losing--though it be a vapour vain,--
What once was rest to toil and ease to pain.
I knew not, while afar, how utterly
These memories of youth were past from me,
It seemed as if, though buisness warped my mind,   455
I could assume them when I felt inclined;
That though like dreams they fled my wakened brain
I, if I liked, could dream them oer again.
I did not think I could be seated here,
After the lapse of many a toilsome year   460

Once more returning to accustomed places
Amid the smiles of "old familiar faces,"
Yet--shrinking from them--hiding in the gloom
Of this dull evening and secluded room,
Not to recall the spirit of the boy,   465
But all my world worn energies to employ
In pondering oer some artifice to gain
A seat in council--or command in Spain.

        "Well--world, oh world!--as I have bowed to thee
I must consent to suffer thy decree;   470
I asked--Thou'st given me my destiny;
I asked--when gazing on that pictured wall,
Like Englands Hero to command or fall;
I asked when wandering over mountains lone,
Some day to wander over lands unknown;   475
I asked for gain and glory--place and power,
Thou gavest them all--I have them all this hour;
But--I forgot to ask for youthful blood,
The thrill divine of feelings unsubdued,
The nerves that quivered to the sound of fame,   480
The tongue that trembled oer a lovers name,
The eye that glistened with delightful tears,
The Hope that gladdened past and gilded future
        years;
So--I have rigid nerves and ready tongue
Fit to subdue the weak and serve the strong,   485
And eyes that look on all things as the same
And Hope--No, callousness that thinks all things a
        name!
        So, Caroline--I'll bid farewell once more,
Nor mourn, lost shade, for though thou'rt gone
        before
Gone is thy Henry too--and didst not thou--   490
While just departing from this world below
Say, thou no longer wert a guileless child,
That all old things were altered or despoiled?--
And--hadst thou lived--thine angel heart, like
        mine,
Would soon have hardened with thy youths decline-- 495
Cold, perhaps, to me, if beating, as when laid
Beneath its grave stone neath the church yard shade.
        It rests--mine labours--there the difference
        lies
For mine will change but little when it dies.

        "I home returned for rest--but feel to day   500
Home is no rest--and long to be away,
To play life's game out where my soldiers are,
Returned from India to a wilder war
Upon the hills of Spain--again to ride

Before their bayonets at Wellesley's side,   505
Again to sleep with horses trampling round,
In watch cloak wrapped and on a battle ground,
To waken with the loud commencing gun,
And feed life's failing flame and drive the moments
    on--
There is our aim--to that our labours tend--   510
Strange--we should love to hurry on our end!
But, so it is--and no where can I speed
So swift through life as on my battle steed!"--

He ceased--unconsciously declined his head,
And stealingly the sense of waking fled,   515
Wafting his spirit into weeping Spain:
Till--starting momently--he gazed again,
But all looked strange to his beclouded brain:
And all was strange--for though the scenes were
        known
The thoughts that should have cherished them were
        gone   520
Gone like the Sunshine--and none others came
To shake the encroaching slumbers from his frame--
So while he lay there, twilight deopened fast,
And, silent, but resistless, hours swept past,
Till chairs and pictures lost themselves in gloom,   525
And but a window glimmered through the room,
With one pale star above the sombre trees
Listening from Heaven to Earths repining breeze.
    That Star looked down with cold and quiet eye,
While all else darkened, brightening up the sky,   530
And though his eye scarce saw it, yet, his mind
As, half awake and half to dreams resigned,
Could scarce help feeilng in its holy shine
The solemn look of Sainted Caroline
With mute reproachfulness reminding him   535
That faith and fondness were not all a dream,
That Form, not feeling, should be changed by clime,
That looks, not love, should suffer hurt by time,
That oer lifes waters, guiding us from far,
And brightening with lifes night, should glisten   540
    Memory's Star.

P. B. B
Broughton in Furness
April 15. 1840.

red Assaye: a village in Hyderabad where the English under
               Wellesley (later Duke of Wellington) won a re-
               sounding victory against tremendous odds over
               the Mahratta forces in September 1803.

485

1. 186:   the line is probably an adaptation of l. 376 of
          Byron's **English Bards and Scotch Reviewers.**
11. 234-36: the painting referred to is West's "The Death of
          Wolfe," 1771 (Gérin BB, p. 25). Nelson (see the
          next poem) was fond of paintings of the death of
          General Wolfe.

127

The text is again the last of three versions, and again a
fair copy, suggesting it too was to be submitted for
publication. While there is no evidence that it actually
was, this is likely the version Banwell sent to F. H. Grundy:
"He wrote a poem called 'Brontë,' illustrative of the life
of Nelson, which, at his special request, I submitted for
criticism to Leigh Hunt, Miss Martineau, and others. All
spoke in high terms of it" (**Pictures of the Past,** London,
1879, p. 79).

> Mosquito shore: the eastern shore of Central America;
> Nelson was given the command to pro-
> tect the area against privateers in
> 1778-79.
>
> San Juan: in 1780 Nelson commanded a naval force that
> sailed up the San Juan River in Nicaragua
> to the Spanish stronghold of San Juan.
>
> Teneriffe: in the Battle of the Canary Islands
> (1797), Nelson lost his right arm leading
> an attack on Teneriffe.
>
> Copenhagen's shore: in April 1801, Nelson sailed into
> Copenhagen harbour and destroyed
> all seventeen Danish Navy vessels
> anchored there in a bloody
> battle, but sent a flag of truce
> to the King of Denmark to prevent
> further bloodshed.
>
> L'Orient and Aboukir: on August 1, 1798, Nelson dis-
> covered Napoleon's fleet in
> Aboukir Bay at the mouth of the
> Nile and annihilated it, thus
> re-establishing British control
> of the Mediterranean.
> L'Orient, the largest ship of
> the French fleet, caught fire
> and exploded.
>
> A vessel: Nelson's flagship, Victory.
>
> Trafalgar: in October 1805, the British defeated the
> French off Cape Trafalgar, but Nelson was
> killed by a sniper's bullet.

wise Cornelius: a magician who could conjure up past
and future in his mirror.

ll. 157-198: these lines refer to the mortally wounded Nelson at the Battle of Trafalgar.
Vice-Admiral Collingwood, Nelson's
life-long friend, took command after
Nelson died; Rear-Admiral Troubridge,
also a life-long friend, participated in
many of Nelson's campaigns, as did
Vice-Admiral Hardy.

l. 245: a reference to Christ's parable of the ten
talents (Matthew 25: 14-30).

Branwell's earliest version (see p. 212) is in Notebook D,
scattered over twelve pages, with two other poems intervening
(see p. liv n. 26). Although mostly written in 1841 (l. 114
refers to Nelson's death in 1805 as occurring 36 years ago),
it was not completed until after he left Luddenden Foot;
ll. 238-68 follow No. **116** dated April 25, 1842.

LORD NELSON
NELSONI MORS. H. K. White

Man thinks too often that the ills of Life
Its fruitless labours and its causeless strife
Its fell disease grim want and cankering care
Must wage gainst Spirit a succesful war
That faint and feeble proves the st[r]uggling soul   5
Mid the dark waves that ever round it roll
That it can never triumph or feel free
While pain its body holds or poverty
    No words of mine have power to rouse the brain
Distressed with grief. the body bowed with pain   10
They will not hear me if I prove how high
Mans Soul can soar oer bodys misery
But where orations long and deep and loud
Are weak as air to move the listening crowd
A single word, just then, if timely spoken   15
The mass inort has roused, their silence broken
And driven them shouting for revenge or fame
Trampling on fear or death Led by a <u>single</u> <u>Name</u>
So now to him whose worn out Soul decays
Neath nights of sleepless pain or toilsome days   20
Who thinks his feeble frame must vainly long
To tread the footsteps of the bold and strong
Who thinks that born beneath a lowly Star
He cannot climb those heights he sees from far
To him I name one word (it needs but one)   25
NELSON a worlds defence a Kingdoms noblest son

Ah! little child torn early from thy home
Over a desolate waste of waves to Roam
I see thy fair hair streaming in the wind
Wafted from green hills left so far behind   30
A farewell given to thy English Home
And hot tears dimming all thy views of fame to come!

Thou then perhaps wert clinging to the mast
Rocked high above the northern Oceans waste
Stern accents only shouted from beneath,   35
Above, the keen winds bitter biting breath,
And thy yong eyes attentive to descry
The Ice blink gleaming neath a Greenland sky
All round the presages of strife and storm
Engirdling thy young heart and feeble form   40
    Each change thy frame endured were fit to be
        (grave)
The total rond of common destiny
For next upon the wild Mosquito shore
San Juans guns their deadly thunders pour
Though deadlier far that pestilential sky   45
Whose hot wind only whispered who should die
Yet, while--forgotten--all their honours won
Strong frames lay rotting neath a tropic sun
And mighty breasts heaved in deaths agony
Death only left the wind worn Nelson free   50
Left him to dare his darts through many a year
Of storm tossed life--unbowed by pain or fear

    Death saw him laid on Rocky Tenereiffe,
Where sailors bore away their bleeding cheif
Struck down by shot and beaten back by fate   55
Yet keeping Iron front and soul elate

    Death saw him--calm off Copenhagens shore
Amid a thousand Guns death dealing roar.
Triumphant riding oer a fallen foe
With hand prepared to strike and heart to spare the
        blow   60

    Death touched but left him when a tide of blood
Stained the dark waves of Egypts Ancient flood
When mighty L'Orient fired the midnight sky
And the clouds first dimmed Napoleons destiny
When neath that blaze flashed flashed redly sea &
        shore   65
When far Aboukir shook beneath its roar
Then fell on all one mighty pause of dread
As if wide heaven were shattered over head
Then from the pallet where the Hero lay
With forehead laced with blood and pale as clay   70

488

He rose revived by that resounding call
Forgot the blow that latly made him fall
And bade the affrighted battle hurry on
Nor thought of rest or pain till victory was won

    I see him sit--his Coffin by his chair   75
With pain worn cheeks and wind dishevelled hair
A little shattered wreck from many a day
Of ocean storm and battle passed away
Prepared at any hour God bade to die
But not to rest or stop or strike or fly   80
While like a burning brand his spirits flame
Brightened as it consumed its mortal frame
He heard Death tapping at his cabin door
He knew his lightning course must soon be oer
That he must meet the grim yet welcome guest   85
Not on a palace bed of downy rest
But where the stormy waters rolled below
And pealed above the thunders of the foe
That no calm sleep must smooth a slow decay
Till scarce the watchers knew life past away   90
But stifling agony, and gushing gore
Must tell the moments of his parting hour
He knew but smiled--for, as that Polar Star
For thousand years as then had shone from far
While all had changed beneath its changeless sky   95
So what to earth belongs on earth must die
While he all soul should only take his flight
Like yon through time a soft and steady light
Like yon to England's Sailors given to be
The guardian of their fleets the pole star of the free 100

    A vessel lies in England's proudest port
Where venerating thousands oft resort
And though ships round her anchor bold and gay
They seek her only in her grim decay
They tread her decks all tenantless with eyes   105
Of musing awe not vulgar vain suprise
They enter in a cabin dark and low
And oer its time stained floor in reverence bow
Theres nought to see but rafters worn and old
No mirrored walls no cornice bright with gold   110
Yon packet steaming through the smoky haze
Seems fitter far to suit the wanderers gaze
But--tis not present times they look on now
They gaze on six and thirty years ago
They see where fell the "Thunder bolt of war"   115
On the storm swollen waves of Trafalgar
They see the spot where fell a star of glory
The Finis to one page of Englands story

They read a tale to wake their pain and pride
In that brass plate engraved "HERE NELSON DIED"   120

     As "wise Cornelius" from his mirror bade
A veil of formless cloudiness to fade*
Till gleamed before the awestruck gazers eye
Scenes still to come or passed for ever by
So let me standing in this darksome room   125
Roll back its shapelessness of mourning gloom
And show the morn and evening of a Sun
The memory of whose light still cheers Old England on

     Where ceasless showers obscure the misty vale
And winter winds through leafless Osiers wail   130
Beside yon swollen torrent rushing wild
Sits calm, amid the storm that fair haired child
He cannot cross--so full the waters flow--
So bold his little heart--he will not go
He has been absent wandering many an hour   135
As wild waves toss a solitary flower
While from the old Rectory his distant home
'All hands' to seek their missing darling roam
And one--his Mother--with instinctive love
Like that which guides aright the timid dove   140
     Finds her dear child his cheeks all rain bedewed
The unconscious victim of those tempests rude
And panting, asks him, why he tarries there--
Did he not dread his fate? his danger fear?
That child replies--all smiling mid the storm   145
"Mother--what is this fear? I never saw his form"
Oft since, he saw the waters howling round
Oft heard unmoved as then the tempest sound
Oft unshaken stood with death and danger near--
150 But knew no more than then the phantom Fear   150

     Now wave the wand again--let England's shore
Be lost amid a distant oceans roar
Return again this cabin dark and grim
Beheld through smoke wreaths indistinct and dim
"Where is my child" methinks the Mother cries!   155
No--far away that mothers grave stone lies!
Where is her child? he is not surely here
Where reign mid storm and darkness Death & FEAR
     A prostrate form lies neath a double shade
By stifling smoke and blackened rafters made   160
With head that backward rolls wheneer it tries
From its hard thundershaken bed to rise
Methought I saw a brightness on its breast
As if in royal orders decked and dressed
But that wan face those grey locks crimson died   165
Have nought to do with human power or pride

Where Death his mandate writes on that white brow
"Thy earthly course is done--come with me now"
Stern faces oer this figure weeping bend
As they had lost a father and a freind   170
And all unnoticed burst yon conquering cheer
Since HE their glorious cheif is dying here
They heed it not but with rekindling eye
As he even Death would conquer ere he die
Asks--"What was't? What deed had England done?   175
What ships had struck, was victory nobly won?"
Did Collingwood--did Trowbridge face the foe?
Whose ship was first in fight, who dealt the
        sternest blow
I could not hear the answer lost and drowned
In that tremendous crash of earthquake sound   180
But I could see the dying hero smile
For pain and sickness vanquished humbly bowed the
        while
To SOUL, that soared prophetic, o'er their sway
And saw beyond deaths night Fames glorious day
That deemed no bed so easy as the tomb   185
In old Westminsters hero sheltering gloom
That knew the laurel round his dying brow
Must bloom for ever as it flourished now
That felt this pain he paid was cheaply given
For endless fame on earth, and joy in heaven   190
It was a smile as sweet as ever shone
On that wan face in childhood long since gone
A smile that asked as plainly "What is fear"
As then unnoticed though as then so near!
4   That spirit cared not that his wornout form   195
4   Was soon to be a comrade of the worm
4   Nor shuddered at the Icy hand of Death
6   So soon--so painfully to stop his breath
        The guns were thundering fainter on his ear
More fading fast from sight that cabin drear   200
The place the Hour became less clearly known
He only felt that his great work was done
That one brave Heart was kneeling at his side
So murmuring "Kiss me Hardy Nelson smiling died

But when I think upon that awful day   205
When all I know or love must fade away
When, after weeks, perhaps, of agony,
237 Without a hope of aught to succor me
I must lie back and close my eyes upon
The parting glories of Gods holy Sun   210
And feel his warmth I never more must know
Mocking my wretched frame of pain and Woe
Yes--feel his light is brightning up the sky
As shining clouds and summer airs pass by

491

While I a shrouded corpse this bed must leave   215
To lie forgotten in my dreary grave
The world all smiles above my covering clay
I silent--senseless--festering fast away!

    And if my children mongst the church yard
        stones
Years hence should see a few brown mouldering
        bones   220
Perhaps a scull that seems with hideous grin
To mock at all this world takes pleasure in
They'd only from the unsightly relics turn
Or into ranker grass the fragments spurn
Nor know that those were the remains of him   225
Whom they remember like a happy dream.
Who kissed and danced them on a fathers knee
In long departed hours of happy Infancy!

    O Mighty being give me strength to dare
The certain fate--the dreadful hour to bear   230
As thou didst Nelson mid that awful roar
Lying pale with mortal sickness--choked with gore
Yet thinking of thine ENGLAND saved that hour
From her great Foemans empire crushing power
Of thy poor frame so gladly given to free   235
Her thousand happy homes from Slavery
Of stainless name for her--of endless fame for thee!

    Give me Great God. give all beneath thy sway
Soul to command and body to obey
When dangers threat a heart to beat more high   240
When doubts confuse a more observant eye
When fate would crush us down a steadier arm
A firmer front as stronger beats the storm
We are thy likeness--give us on to go
Through lifes long march of chance and change &
        woe   245
Resolved Thine Image shall be sanctified
By humble confidence not foolish pride
We have our task set let us do it well
Nor barter ease on earth with pain in Hell
We have our Talents from thy treasury given   250
Let us return thee good account in heaven
    I see thy world--this age--is marching on
Each year more wondrous than its parent gone
And shall my own drag heavily and slow
With wish to rise yet grovelling far below   255
Forbid it God who madst what I am
Nor made to honour let me bow to shame
But as yon moon that <u>seems</u> through clouds to glide
Whose dark breasts ever strive her beams to hide

Shines <u>really</u> heedless of that earthly sway   260
In her <u>own</u> Heaven of glory far away!

     So may my soul that seems involved below
In lifes conflicting mists of care and woe
Far far remote from its own heaven look down
On clouds of shining fleece or stormy frown   265
And while--so oft eclipsed--men pity me
Gaze steadfast at their lifes inconstancy
And feel myself like her at home with heaven and thee

Text: Title: Nelsoni Mors: the title of a poem by Henry
        Kirk White.
        l. 46:   "air" and "wind," both uncanceled, written
        above "breeze," canceled
        l. 81:   "brand" written above "reed"; neither is
        canceled
        l. 92:   "parting" written above "dying"; neither is
        canceled
        ll. 101-04: There are six trial lines for this pass-
        age on the facing page. The first four are identical
        to ll. 101-04; the next two read:
            That vessel once bore Thunder oer the sea
            Her Chief was Englands sword her name was VICTORY
        ("sword" written above "arm"; neither is canceled)
        l. 122: the asterisk is Branwell's
        l. 141:   "all" written above "by"; neither is
        canceled
        l. 145: "replies" written above "looks up"; neither
        is canceled
        l. 149: "Oft unshaken stood" written above "stood
        unshaken"; neither is canceled
        l. 186: "Westminsters": Nelson is buried in the
        crypt of St. Paul's
        ll. 199-204 originally followed l. 237 with a note at
        the end: "Should this come after 'So soon so pain-
        fully" and then 'But when I think!'"
        l. 259: "strive" written above "seek"; neither is
        canceled
        l. 268: "with" written above "in"; "and" written
        above "with"; none are canceled
        The numbers in the right margin are Branwell's

A partially completed second draft, probably done in the
summer of 1842 (see p. 228), appears in Notebook C; it is not
included in Branwell's table of contents for the Notebook--
see pp. xii-xiv.

     Man thinks too often that the ills of life--
Its fruitless labour--Its unceasing strife--
With all its train of want disease and care

493

Must wage 'gainst spirit a successful war:
That faint indeed must prove the shackled soul   5
Struggling with waves that ever round it roll--
That it can never triumph or feel free
While pain its body binds, or poverty
Nor will Man hear me if I prove how high
His soul may soar oer bodys misery   10
For if I bid him rise and point the way
He points in answer to his bonds of clay
But--where orations, eloquent and loud
Prove weak as air to move the listening crowd
A single word just then if timely spoken   15
The Mass inert has roused--their silence broken
And driven them shouting for revenge or Fame
Trampling on fear and death led by a single name
          So now--To him whose worn out soul decays
Neath nights of sleepless pain and toilsome days   20
Who thinks his feeble frame in vain may long
To tread the footsteps of the bold and strong
Who thinks that--born beneath a lowly star
He cannot climb those heights he sees from far
To him I speak one word--it needs but one--   25
NELSON--a worlds defence--a Kingdoms noblest son!

     Ah! Little Child, torn early from thy home
Over a desolate waste of waves to roam
I see thy fair hair streaming in the wind
Wafted from green hills left so far behind   30
Like one lamb seen upon a gloomy moor
Or one flower floating leagues away from shore
Thou hast given thy farewell to thine English home
And hot tears dim thy views of fame to come
     Thou then, perhaps, wert clinging to the mast   35
Rocked high above the Northern Oceans waste
Stern accents only shouted from beneath--
Above--the keen winds bitter biting breath
While thy young eyes were straining to descry
The ice blink gleaming neath a Greenland sky   40

     Each change thy frame endured might meetly be
The Total round of common destiny
For next upon the wild Mosquito shore
San Juan's guns their deadly vollies pour
Though deadlier far that pestilential sky   45
Whose hot wind only whispered who should die
And while--forgotten all their honours won
Strong frames lay rotting neath a tropic sun
While mighty breasts heaved in deaths agony
Death only left the feeble Nelson free   50
Left him--to dare his darts through many a year
Of storm tossed life unbowed by pain or fear

Death saw him laid on rocky Tenereiffe
Where sailors bore away their bleeding cheif
Struck down by shot and beaten back by fate   55
Yet keeping front unblenched and soul elate
    Death saw him--calm, off Copenhagens shore
Amid a thousand guns heaven-shaking roar
Triumphant riding oer a fallen foe
With arm prepared to strike but heart to spare the
    blow   60
    Death saw him, conquerer, where a tide of blood
Stained the swollen waves of Egypts ancient flood
Where clouds first dimmed Napoleons destiny
When mighty L'Orient fired the midnight sky
When in its blaze flashed redly sea and shore   65
And sudden silence stilled the battles roar
As fell on all one mighty pause of dread
As though wide heaven were shattered overhead
But--from his pallet--where the Hero <u>lay</u>
His forehead laced with blood and <u>pale</u> as clay   70
He rose--revived by that tremendous call--
Forgot the blow which latly made him fall
And bade the affrighted battle hurry on
Nor thought of pain or rest till he the victory won

    I see him sit--his coffin by his chair--   75
With pain worn cheek and wind dishevelled hair
A little shattered wreck from many a day
Of Ocean storm and battle passed away
Prepared at any hour God bade to die
But not to stop or rest or strike or fly   80
While like a burning reed his spirits flame
Brightened while it consumed his mortal frame

He knew his lightening course would soon be oer
That Death was tapping at his cabin door
That he must meet the grim yet welcome guest   85
Not on a palace bed of downy rest
But where the stormy waters rolled below
While pealed above the thunders of the foe
That no calm sleep should sooth a slow decay
Till scarce the watchers knew life passed away   90
But stifling agony and gushing gore
Should fill the moments of his parting hour
He knew--but smiled--for, as that polar star
A thousand years as then had shone from far
While all had changed beneath its changeless sky--   95
So--what to earth belonged--on earth should die
While he--all soul--should only take his flight
Like yon--through time a still an steady light
Like yon--to Englands sailors given to be

The guardian of their fleets--the pole star of the
    free   100

    A Vessel lies in Englands proudest port
    Where venerating Britons oft resort
    And though ships round her anchor bold and gay
    They seek her only in her grim decay
    They tread her decks all tenantless, with eyes   105
    Of awe struck musing not of vague suprise
    They enter neath a cabin dark and low
    And oer its time stained floor in reverence bow
    Theres nought to see but rafters worn and old--
    No mirrored walls--no cornice bright with gold   110
    Yon packet steaming through its smoky haze
    Seems fitter far to suit the wonderers gaze
    But--Tis not present times they look on now--
    They look on six and thirty years ago
    They look where fell the "thunderbolt of war"   115
    On the storm swollen waves of Trafalgar!
    They see the spot where sank a star of glory:
    The 'finis' to one page of Englands story
    They read a tale to wake their pain and pride
In that brass plate engraved--"HERE NELSON DIED."!   120

Text: 1. 84 originally read "He heard Death tapping at his
       cabin door"; neither reading is canceled

128

In Notebook D, written shortly after Branwell took up his
post as tutor at Thorp Green in January 1843.

129

Grafton Hill, near Thorp Green, commands a panoramic view
across much of Yorkshire, and as Flintoff has pointed out (p.
243), Branwell's description is quite accurate. "Caledonia,
stern and wild" (l. 13) is taken from Scott's **Lay of the
Last Minstrel** (Canto 6, stanza 2). According to Hatfield,
and corroborated by Sotheby's Sale Catalogue of Mrs.
Nicholls' effects, June 1914, item 187, the verso of the
manuscript leaf contained a continuation of the minutes of
the Haworth Operative Conservative Society Branwell began at
the back of Notebook C in January 1837, suggesting that he
took the notebook with him to Thorp Green. The text provided
is Hatfield's.

130

This poem, undated and unsigned, is scrawled in pencil with many corrections on both sides of a single leaf of the same size as Nos. **125-127** and **129**. The poem obviously refers to Lydia Robinson and has traditionally been assigned to the early post Thorp Green period. However, Flintoff (p. 243) makes a very convincing argument for the poem having been written at Thorp Green; hence my tentative date of 1844/45.

131 and 132

The manuscript for the second of these companion poems is untraceable, but Leyland ascribes both, under the title **The Emigrant**, to May 1845, shortly before Branwell's dismissal at Thorp Green. The text for No. **132** is from Leyland.

133

The similarity of the distinctive cursive hand, on the same size paper, in Nos. **125-27**, **129-31**, **133**, and **134** suggests that Branwell carried out the unfinished revisions in **133** and **134** just before or just after his departure from Thorp Green. The manuscript for No. **133**, a single sheet folded, has two stitch holes, suggesting it was at one time part of a manuscript volume. An earlier version (see p. 133) in Notebook B (pp. 29-30), spoken by Percy, reads:

Jan 13. 1837

Sleep Mourner sleep!--I cannot sleep
   My weary mind still wanders on
Then silent weep--I cannot weep
   For eyes and tears seem turned to stone

Oh might my footsteps find a rest!   5
   Oh might my eyes with tears run oer!
Oh could the World but leave my breast
   To lapse in days that are no more!

And if I could in silence mourn
   Apart from lying sympathy   10
And Mans remarks or sighs or scorn
   I should be where I wish to be

For nothing nearer Paradise
   Ought for a moment to be mine

I've far outlived such real joys   15
   I could not bear so bright a shine

For I've been consecrate to greif
   I should not be if that were gone
And all my prospect of releif
   On earth, would be--To Greive Alone!   20

To live in sunshine would be now
   To live in Lethe every thought
Of what I have seen and been below
   <u>Must</u> first be utterly forgot

And I can not forget the years   25
   Gone by as if they'd never been
Yet if I will remember Tears
   Must always dim the dreary scene

So theres no choice--However bright
   May beam the blaze of July's sun   30
Twill only yeild another sight
   Of scenes and times forever gone

However young and lovely round
   Fair forms may meet my cheerless eye
They'll only hover oer the ground   35
   Where fairer forms in darkness lye

And voices tuned to Music's thrill
   And laughter light as marriage strain
Will only wake a ghostly chill
   As if the buried spoke again   40

All all is over freind or Lover
   Cannot awaken gladdness here
Though sweep the strings their music over
   No sound will rouse the stirless air

I am dying away in dull decay   45
   I feel and know the sands are down
And Evenings latest lingering ray
   At last from my wild heaven is flown

Not now I speak of things whose forms
   Are hid by intervening years   50
Not now I peirce departed storms
   For bygone greifs and dried up tears

I cannot weep as once I wept
   Over my Western Beauty's grave

Nor wake the woes that long have slept   55
By Gambia's towers and trees and wave

I am speaking of a later stroke
A death--the doom of yesterday
I am thinking of my latest shock
A Noble freindship torn away   60

I feel and say that I am cast
From Hope and peace and power and pride
A withered leaf on Autumns blast
A shattered wreck on Oceans tide

Without a voice to speak to me   65
Save that deep tone which told my doom
And made my dread futurity
Look darker than my vanished gloom

Without companion save the sight
For ever present to my eye   70
Of that tempestuous winter night
That saw my Angel Mary die [unfinished]

134

This unfinished revision of a poem written in May/June 1837,
borrowing heavily from No. **60**, is on the same paper and
in the same hand as No. **133**, suggesting that it may have
belonged to the same manuscript volume. Although only ll.
1-24 of the revision, on a half-leaf, are extant, Branwell
sent the completed revision to Joseph Leyland (probably in
1846), and asked for its return in January 1848 (SHB LL, II,
177). Apparently Leyland did not return it and Francis Leyland printed it in 1886, noting that it was intended to be
the first canto of a long poem (I, 213), although he may have
been thinking of **Morley Hall**. The text provided is Leyland's except for the opening twenty-four lines, which are
based on the manuscript. "Agrippa's wand"--line 73--probably
refers to Cornelius Agrippa, author of **The Vanity and
Uncertainty of Arts and Sciences**, who was supposed to have
the power of calling up the shades of the dead. The 1837
version in Notebook C (see p. 186) reads:

A Fragment.
Rough Draft

=====

1814.

==

On one sweet afternoon, when the Summer was mellowing into
Autumn, and the Sun declined toward his setting, She sat at
her open window with the curtains all drawn back, giving
herself up to the softened glories of the scene.--She had
cast the encroaching curls from her forhead, she had smoothed
it to a harmony with that clear blue heaven, and then, with
clasped hands resting on her knee, and eyes that wandered
through the cloudland in the sky, she let her spirit stray
from anxious thought into those day dreams with which fancy
can sometimes fill the mind.

Beyond the groves which skirted that sunny lawn rose the
Tower of the Aged Church and at that hour the only sound
audible from earth or Heaven tolled slowly from it in the
melancholy music of the Funeral bell.--To Her it spoke like
the very voice of that Afternoon, so sweet and yet so
mournful, so calm and measured too and withal so much in
accordance with the associations which were gathering on her
mind--I cannot give the feeling of those thoughts but by
poetry for as that was the impulse from which they had
utterance it ought now to be the Language in which they are
read.

She said then within her heart:

        The Clouds are rolled away--the light
    Breaks suddenly upon my sight
    And feelings that no words can tell
    Have utterance in that funeral bell!

    My Heart, my Soul, was full of feeling   5
    Yet nothing clear to me revealing
    Sensations strong but undefined
    The Eolian music of the mind!

    Then; strikes that Chord--and all subsides
    Into a harmony that glides   10
    Tuneful but solemn like the dream
    Of some remembered burial Hymn

    This scene was that Mysterious glass
    Which bore upon its changing face
    Strange shadows that deceived the eye   15
    With form's defined uncertainly

    That bell the Enchanters stern command
    Which parts the clouds on either hand
    And shews the pictured forms of doom
    One moment brightning through the gloom   20

500

It shews a scene of bygone years
It opes a fount of sealed up tears
It wakens in my memory
An hour by time born far from me

A Day like this--a summer's day   25
Shining its hours in peace away
With Hills as blue and groves as green
Clouds piled as bright skies as serene!

    Oh! well I recollect the Hour!
    Seated alone as I sit now   30
And gazing toward that very Tower
    Oer these wild flowers which wave below!

No--not these flowers!--They're long since dead
    And flowers have come and flowers have
            gone
Since those which wither round the Head   35
    Laid low beneath that churchyard stone!

I stretched to pluck a rose that grew
    Close by this window waving then
But back again my hand withdrew
    With a strange sense of inward pain   40

For she who loved it was not there
    To check me with her dove like eye
And something bid my heart forbear
    Her favoured floweret to destroy

Was it the bell--the funeral bell   45
    So sudden sounding on the wind?
Yes--twas that melancholy knell,
    Which woke to woe my infant mind.

I looked upon my mourning dress
    Till my heart beat with childish fear   50
When--startled at my loneliness
    I bent, some distant sound to hear

But all without was silent, in
    The sunny hush of afternoon
And only muffled steps, within,   55
    Paced slow afar and soon were gone!

Well do I recollect the awe
    With which I hasted to depart
    And--hurrying from the room--the start
With which my Mothers form I saw   60
All robed in black with pallid face

And hood, and kerchief wet with tears,
Who stooped to kiss my infant face
And hush my childish fears!

She led me on with muffled sound   65
Through galleries vast to one high room
Neath whose black hangings crowded round
With funeral dress and looks of gloom
Stood Lords and Ladies--And with head
Bent sadly oer that gilded bed   70
My awful Father dropt a tear
In the dark coffin rested there

My Mother raised me to survey
What twas which in that coffin lay
But--To this moment I can feel   75
The voiceless gasp the shuddering chill
Wherwith I hid my whitening face
Within the folds of her embrace--!
I dared not even turn my head
Lest it should glance toward that bed!   80
    "But--will you not my child"--said she--
"Your Sisters form one moment see?
One moment--ere that form be hid
For ever neath its coffin lid!"
    I Heard the appeal and answered too   85
I turned to look that last adieu
And hushed at once my aimless fright
Into a trance of calm delight!

There lay she then--as now she lies
For not a limb has moved since then   90
In dreamless slumber closed those eyes
That never more should wake again

She lay as I had seen her lie
On many a moonlight night before
When I perhaps was kneeling by   95
The Almighty to adore

Oh! Just as when by her I prayed
While she was listening to my prayer
She lay--with wild flowers round her head
And lillies in her hair   100

Still did her lips their smile retain--
The smile with which she died--
Still was her brow as smooth from pain
As in its beauty's pride

Though strange and narrow looked her bed   105
    In slumber sweet she seemed
And as I bent above her head
    I thought on Heaven she dreamed

And yet I felt--I knew not how
    A sudden chilld come oer me   110
When my hand touched the marble brow
    Of that fair form before me

In fright I called on--"Caroline!"
    And bid her wake and rise
But--answered not her voice to mine   115
    Or oped her sleeping eyes

I turned toward my Mother then
    And prayed of her to call
But though she strove to hide her pain
    Full fast her tears did fall   120

She pressed me to her aching breast
    As if her heart would break
And silent hung above the rest
    Which she could never wake

The rest of her whose Infant years   125
    So long she'd watched in vain
The end of all a mothers fears
    That neer need brood again!

They came--they pressed the coffin lid
    Above my Caroline   130
And--then I felt--for ever hid
    My sisters face from mine!

There was one moments wildered start
    One pang--remembered well!--
And--from the fountain of the heart   135
    My tears of anguish fell!

Seems all a blank the Mourning March
    The proud parade of woe
The passage neath the churchyard arch
    The crowd that met the shew.   140

My place--my thoughts amid the train

And filled with thousand thoughts of greif
    And sick with ghastly fear
And longing--for a last relief--
    That day would re appear   145

And even praying that I might die--
     But thus the thought would come
How--if I died--my corpse would lie
     In yonder awful Tomb!

It seemed as though I saw its stone   150
     By moonlight dim and drear
While oer it keeping watch alone
     Her spirit lingered there

All white with Angel Wings she seemed
     And weeping ceaslessly   155
Yet--while her tears in silence streamed
     She beckoned still to me

And faded beckoning--while the wind
     Around that midnight wall
To me--Thus lingering long behind--   160
     Seemed her departing call!

And thus it brought me back the hours
     When we would lie together
Listening in silence to the showers
     Of Wild November's weather   165

And sometimes as they woke in her
     The chords of inward feeling
She'd imagine on the midnight air
     Scenes thick and fast revealing

Or she would talk of distant Isles--   170
     Our Fathers far of shore--
Where seldom summers sunshine smiles
     And ever Oceans roar

And tell me of its moonlight lakes
     And fairy peopled bowers   175
Or of that Benshee whose ghastly shreiks
     Rung round the castle towers

When--clasped within our Mothers arms
     She left that Ancient home
To join across Atlantic storms   180
     A rising world to come

Oh! for a while, methought again
     I heard her silver tongue
Rehearsing some remembered strain
     Of Ages vanished long   185

And, somehow, flashed across my sight
    What she had often told me
When, laid awake on Christmas night
    Her sheltering arms would fold me

That midnight noon that darksome day   190
    Whose gloom oer Calvary thrown
Shewed trembling Natures deep dismay
    At what her sons had done,
When all around, the murky air
    Was riven with one hoarse cry   195
That told how wretched Mortals dare
    Their Saviour crucify
When those who sorrowing sat afar
    With dimmed and frighted eye
Saw on his cross extended there   200
    That Great Redeemer die
When Mortal vigour fell and fled
When thirst and faintness bowed his head
When his pale limbs all darkning oer
With deathly dews and dropping gore   205
Quivered as that last sickness came
Across his chill and stiffning frame
When upward gazed his dying eyes
To the tremendous blackning skies
When burst one cry of agony   210
'My God My God hast Thou forgotten Me!'
    I heard amid the darkness then
The mighty Temple rend in twain
Horribly pealing on the ear
With a deep Thunder note of fear   215
And wrapping all the world in gloom
As it were Natures general Tomb
While sheeted ghosts before my gaze
Flitted across the murky maze
Called from their graves on that dread day   220
When Death an hour oer heaven had sway
    In glistning charnel damps arrayed
They came and gibbered round my head
All pointing through the dark to me
Toward still and shrouded Calvary   225
Where gleamed the Cross with steady shine
Around that thorn crowned head divine
A Fiery Cross! a Beacon light
To this world's universal night!
    Still, still, it shoen with glorious glow   230
Into my spirit searching so
That panting first, I strove to cry
For help to Her who slumbered by
And hid my face from that dread shine
In the embrace of Caroline   235

505

Awakening with the attempt--
                              --Twas day
The Troubled vision passed away--
Twas day--and I alone was laid
In that great room and statly bed   240
No Caroline beside me!--
                              Wide
And deep and darksome rolled the tide
Of Life Twixt her and me!

She stopped--The day Dream was over--For with the readiness
wherewith persons musing in silence can catch the slightest
sound or motion, she she heard approaching wheels and looked
up to behold glancing in the level light a Barouche driving
rapidly up the walk, and from which on its drawing up
alighted a Gentleman young and of statly height who hasted
across the lawn to her window whereat she rose agitatedly to
welcome him.

P B Brontë

written from May 4th
To June 15th 1837.
Transcribed June 16 1837.
316 lines

Seventy-two lines are missing between 11. 141 and 142.
Because 1. 141 is at the bottom of a manuscript page and the
page beginning with 1. 142 has thirty-six lines, two pages of
the manuscript have probably been removed and lost.   See also
No. 103.

135

These lines appear in the first volume of Branwell's proposed
three-volume novel **And the Weary are at Rest**, completed,
according to a letter to Leyland, by September 10, 1845
(Leyland Letters, p. 19).   Percy, as Rev. Alexander Percy, in
the Sanctification Chapel (Primitive Methodists) on the first
day of the Ardmore Fair, carrying out a parody of a Methodist
revival meeting, says to his congregation, "Let us miserable
worms send up our cry as if from Tophet in the following
words and adapted to the tune of 'Widdops 100th.'"   In
describing the meeting, the narrator says:

'I speak not in anger but in sorrow' reader for though I
could point out many an illustrious exception I have
seen enough of what were once called 'conventicals' to
feel aware that the slight sketch I have just drawn or
the more finished picture that I mean to paint give no

exaggerated idea of the follies into which man can
plunge when he wishes to appear more holy than he is."

For other similar parodies, see Nos. **45** and **46**.

In the earliest version (see p. 114), written on or before
May 4, 1836 as part of a manuscript dealing with the history
of Angria, and bound by Wise with leaves from various
manuscripts, the preacher is Ashworth, who says, "Let us sing
to the praise and glory of God--Long metre. four eights":

Milton!

<pre>
"I   Before Jehovahs awful throne
          Now let us trembling kneel in prayer
       And Justice ask and justice own
          For we must pray that he may hear
 2   An   eep O Lord be our despair   5
       And clear our consciousness of sin
       Lest from thine eyes our outside fair
          Should strive to hide the crimes within
 3   We know that we are formed in crime
          And through our lives that crimes we form 10
       Yet maddly dreaminq all the time
          That mercy sheilds us from the strom
 4   Or as long since in Shinars plain
          Rebellious men their tower of pride
       Raised up, in hope, by labours vain   15
          That thus thy power might be defyed
 5   So we by impious moral code
          And creeds of ever changing faith
       Think we may climb the heavenly road
          And shun thy power and vanquish death   20
 6   But oh when once we reach the gate
          In hopes the eternal crown to win
       Long must we knock and lingering wait
          Ere yon bright spirit lets us in
 7   "Hast thou repented from thy sin"   25
          And who oh who can answer then!
       "Go back thy path again begin
          And weep and watch and wait again"
 8   But if returning be denied
          By Deaths grim portal closed behind   30
       Where flies our Heaven and hope and pride
          Vanished like chaff before the wind
 9   Lord may we know our treacherous mind
          And feel the feirceness of despair
       Since grovelling thus accursed and blind   35
          We must not hope that thou wilt hear"
</pre>

The first line is the first line of a hymn by Isaac Watts, but the rest is Branwell's.

On May 26, 1837, Branwell transcribed the poem in Notebook C (see p. 175) as follows:

Ashworths Hymn
composed by Percy.

Before Jehovah's awful throne
   Now let us trembling kneel in prayer
And mercy ask and Justice own
   For we must pray that he may hear

And deep O Lord be our despair   5
   And clear our consciousness of sin
Lest from thine eyes our outside fair
   Should strive to hide the crimes within

We know that we are formed in crime
   And through our lives that crimes we form   10
Yet madly dreaming all the time
   Thy Mercy sheilds us from the storm

Or as long since in Shinar's plain
   Rebellious men their Tower of pride
Raised up in hopes by labours vain   15
   That thus thy power might be defied

So we by impious moral code
   And ever changing creeds of faith
Think we may climb the heavenly road
   And shun thine arm and vanquish death   20

But Oh when once we reach thy gate
   In hopes the eternal crown to win
Long must we knock and lingering wait
   Ere yon bright spirit lets us in

"Hast thou repented of thy sin?"   25
   And who Oh God can answer then
"Go back thy path again begin
   And weep and watch and wait again"

But if returning be denied
   By Deaths grim portal closed behind   30
Where flies our Heaven and hope and pride?
   Vanished like chaff before the wind!

Lord may we know our treacherous mind
Even though that knowledge bring despair
Since wandering thus accursed and blind   35
We cannot hope that Thou wilt hear!

                P B Brontë
                    written May 4th 1836
                    Transcribed May 26 1837.
                    36 lines

136

The manuscript is untraceable; the text is from the **Halifax
Guardian**, November 8, 1845. Line 35 seems to refer to Mrs.
Robinson. The opening description of the corpse in the water
has some fascinating similarities with the early version of
Charlotte's poem **Gilbert** probably written in early 1845
(see Neufeldt PCB, pp. 438-44).

137

According to Hatfield's transcription (the text provided) and
partially corroborated by the 1914 Sotheby's Sale Catalogue
of Mrs. Nicholls' effects, the title, which is Mrs. Robinson's maiden name, appeared in Greek letters, and the manuscript, in pencil, contained a sketch of some hills, with the
right-hand one labeled "Penmaenmawr," suggesting that the
poem was written shortly after Branwell's trip to North Wales
between 29 July and 3 August 1845. He wrote to Leyland the
day after his return, "I found during my absence that wherever I went a certain woman robed in black, and calling herself "MISERY" walked by my side, and leant on my arm as
affectionately as if she were my legal wife" (Leyland
Letters, p. 17). In his letter to Leyland of 28 April 1846,
which also contained his questions about **Morley Hall** (No.
147) and a draft of No. **144**, Branwell included a
slightly revised version of the last stanza, prefaced with
the comment, "The Quietude of home, and the inability to make
my family aware of the nature of most of my sufferings makes
me write" (Leyland Letters, p. 25):

                "Home thoughts are not, with me
                    Bright, as of yore;
                Joys are forgot by me,
                    Taught to deplore!
                My home has taken rest   5
                In an afflicted breast
                Which I have often pressed
                    But--may no more!"

The text is that in the **Halifax Guardian**, December 20,
1845. Branwell sent a copy of the poem to Leyland in a
letter dated 25 November 1845, in which he wrote:

I send through yourself the enclosed scrap for the
Halifax Guardian--and I ought to tell you why I wish
anything of so personal a nature to appear in print.
I have no other way, not pregnant with danger, of
communicating with one whom I cannot help loving.
Printed lines with my usual signature "Northangerland"
would excite no suspicion--as my late employer shrunk
from the bare idea of my being able to write anything,
and had a day's sickness after hearing that Macaulay had
sent me a complimentary letter . . . .
These lines have only one merit--that of really
expressing my feelings while sailing under the Welsh
mountains, when the band on board the steamer struck up
'Ye banks and braes'--and God knows that, for many
different reasons, these feelings were far enough from
pleasure (Leyland Letters, p. 23).

The second paragraph suggests that Lydia Robinson would have
recognized Branwell's pseudonym. In Mary Pearson's Commonplace Book, on the page opposite the one containing a clip-
ping of the poem from the **Halifax Guardian**, Branwell
sketched a bust of "ALEXANDER PERCY. EsQ^R M.P." and underneath quoted from Byron's **Don Juan** I, CCXIV:

No more--no more--oh never more on me
    The freshness of the heart shall fall like dew,
Which, out of all the lovely things we see
    Extracts emotions beautiful and new!

Underneath he sketched a recumbent marble effigy on a tomb.
He quoted these lines again in a letter to Leyland in January
1847 (Leyland Letters, p. 40). Hatfield's transcription at
the BPM of the penciled first draft reads:

PENMAENMAWR.

This wind, these clouds, that chill November
        storm,
Bring back again thy tempest beaten form
To eyes that gaze upon yon dreary sky
As late they gazed on thy sublimity;
When I, more troubled than the restless sea,   5
Upon its waters made a friend of thee.
'Mid mists thou frownedst o'er "dreary Arvon's
        shore"--

'Mid tears I watched thee o'er old Ocean's roar;
And thy blue front by thousand storms laid bare
Seemed kindred to a heart worn down with care.   10
No smile hadst thou, o'er smiling fields aspiring,
And none had I, from smiling scenes retiring.
Blackness, 'mid sunshine, cloud thy stately brow;
I, 'mid sweet music, looked as dark as thou.
Old Scotland's song, o'er murmuring surges borne,   15
Of "times departed, never to return",
Was echoed back in mournful tones from thee,
And found an echo quite as sad in me.
Waves, clouds, and shadows, moved in restless
          change
Around, above, and on thy rocky range,   20
But seldom saw that sovereign front of thine
More frequent ones than those which passed o'er
          mine.
And as wild blasts and human hands at length
Have changed to scattered stones the mighty
          strength
Of that old fort whose belts of boulders grey   25
Roman or Saxon legions held at bay,
So had--methought--the young unshaken nerve
That, when WILL <u>wished</u>, no doubts could cause to
          swerve
That on its vigour ever held reliance,
And to its sorrows sometimes bade defiance,   30
Now ruined, left me, like thyself, old hill,
With head defenceless against mortal ill!
And as thou ever looked upon the wave
That takes but gives not, like a churchyard grave,
And like life's course--through ether's weary
          range,   35
Offers no rest from ceaseless noise and change.
    But, Pen-maen-mawr, a better fate was thine,
Through all thy shades, than that which darkened
          mine.
No quick thoughts thrilled through thy gigantic
          mass
Of woe for what may be, or is, or was.   40
Thou hadst no memory of the glorious hour
When Britain rested on thy giant power.
Thou hadst no feeling for the verdured slope
That leant on thee as man's heart leans on hope.
The pastures chequered o'er with cot and tree,   45
Though thou wert guardian, got no smile from thee.
Old ocean's wrath their charms might overwhelm,
Still thou couldst keep thy own cliff-girdled
          realm--
But I felt flashes of an inward feeling
As fierce as those thy craggy form revealing   50

511

In nights, when blinding gleam and deafening roar,
Hurls back thy echoes to old Mona's shore.
I knew a flower whose leaves were meant to bloom
Till Death should snatch it to adorn his tomb
Now blanching 'neath the blast of hopeless grief   55
With never blooming, yet still living leaf;
A flower on which my soul would wish to shine,
If but one beam could break from mind like mine!
I had an ear that could on accents dwell
That might as well say "perish" as "farewell"--   60
An eye that saw far off a tender form
But unprotected by affliction's storm.
                    a lip that trembled to embrace
My Angel's gentle breast and smiling face
A mind that clung to Ouse's fertile side,   65
While tossing--objectless--on Menai's tide!
    Oh Soul that drawst yon mighty hill and me
Into communion of vague amity,
Tell me--can I obtain the stony brow
That fronts the storms as much unshaken now   70
As when it once upheld the fortress proud,
Now gone, like its own morn o'ercapping cloud?
Its breast is stone--can I have one of steel
To endure--inflict--defend--yet never feel?
It stood as firm when haughty Edward's word   75
Gave hill and vale to England's fire and sword,
As when white sails and steam-smoke tracked the
    sea,
And all the world breathed peace save waves and me.
    Let me, like it, arise o'er mortal care,
All evils bear, yet never know despair   80
And rise o'er storm or shine like moveless
    Penmaenmawr.

Text: 1. 63:   partially blank in the manuscript
        1. 81 of the printed text is missing in the
        manuscript
        On the verso of sheet one appear the words, in
        capitals, "ACTON" and OUSEBURN
        dreary   Arvon's   shore: Carnaervon   in   the
        Mabinogion is "Kaer seint yn Arvon"
        times departed, never to return: from Burns' "Ye
        banks and braes"
        Mona's shore: Roman name for the island of Anglesey
        Ouse's fertile tide: River Ouse near Thorp Green
        Menai's tide: the Menai Straits separate Carnaervon-
        shire from Anglesey

139

Although undated, these lines thematically belong with Branwell's poems in the latter part of 1845 that still express some hope of acceptance in his presumed relationship with Mrs. Robinson. The reference to December in l. 7 suggests a late 1845/early 1846 date.

140

The text provided is based on a photograph of the manuscript at the BPM. Although the 1914 Sotheby's Sale Catalogue of Mrs. Nicholls' effects and Hatfield's transcription at the BPM both list the first two and the last two stanzas as separate items, the similarity of stanza form, rhyme scheme, meter and subject matter, especially the presence of Sir Henry Hardinge in both, suggest one poem. Sir Robert Sale was Quartermaster General of the British Army during the First Sikh War in India, where Hardinge was Governor-General, but was killed at the battle of Mudki in December 1845. On February 28, 1846 the **Leeds Mercury** reprinted from the **Morning Chronicle** the poem, **On the Death of Sir Robert Sale Killed in Action Against the Sikhs.** Hardinge, who had played a crucial role in the British victory over the French under Marshal Soult at Albuera in Spain in 1811, played an equally crucial role in the defeat of the Sikh army in December 1845 and January 1846. For his efforts he received the thanks of Parliament and a peerage. The **Halifax Guardian** stated on 7 March 1846, "Never did the Houses of Parliament more truly represent the unanimous voice of the country than when voting on Monday last the thanks of the country to the brave heroes with whose achievements on the Sutlej the nation is still ringing. And though for a time some doubt appeared to be cast on the wisdom of the commanders on that occasion, we rejoice to find it vindicated as clearly, and as undeniably, as the heroism of the troops they led to victory. The only exception to the unanimity of this national tribute of thanks were the petition presented by Quaker Bright and the remarks made by the Duke of Richmond". For a more detailed discussion of the background, see Flintoff, p. 246. As with No. **119**, Branwell quite possibly hoped that the national interest in the subject would lead to publication.

141

The manuscript is untraceable; the text is that in the **Halifax Guardian,** April 18, 1846. Leyland states that the manuscript was dated April 3, 1846.

In the Sotheby's 1914 sale of Mrs. Nicholls' effects this
poem was one of three constituting lot 183. For the other
two see Nos. **137** and **138**. The text is based on Hatfield's transcription at the BPM. The suggested date, admittedly speculative, is based on the similarity of the subject
matter to Branwell's other poems in spring and summer 1846.

143

As in the case of No. **137**, the title is again in Greek
letters. Both Hatfield and the 1914 Sotheby's Sale Catalogue
indicate the date of June 1, 1846 on the manuscript. The
text provided is Hatfield's transcription at the BPM.
Accompanying the sonnet was a sketch of a man looking across
a river toward flat countryside and the setting sun. In the
bottom left-hand corner was a stone with "Memoria" engraved
upon it. On the verso of the manuscript leaf are the lines
for No. **152 (c)**.

144

Branwell inscribed these lines in Mary Pearson's Commonplace
Book in the autumn of 1846 (see comment for No. **118**);
below them he sketched a cemetery containing a tombstone
inscribed with "I IMPLORE FOR REST" and a skull and cross-
bones. He enclosed an earlier version in the letter to Leyland noted in No. **137**, prefaced with, "I enclose a hor-
rible ill drawn daub done to wile away the time this morning.
I meant it to represent a very rough figure in stone." The
sketch, containing a female figure with clasped hands,
streaming hair and averted face, and a tombstone inscribed
"Nuestra Senor de la Pena--Our Lady of Grief" refers to Mrs.
Robinson--Leyland comments, "We need not entertain a doubt as
to whom it is intended to represent" (Leyland Letters, p.
26).

> When all our cheerful hours seem gone for ever;
>   And lost that caused the body or the mind
>   To nourish love or friendship for our kind,
> And Charon's boat, prepared--oer Lethe's river--
> Our souls to waft, and all our thoughts to sever   5
>   From what was once lifes light, still there may
>   be
>   Some well loved bosom to whose pillow we
> Could heartily our utter self deliver:
> And, if--toward her grave--Death's dreary road

Our darling's feet should tread, each step by
       her   10
Would draw our own steps to the same abode,
And make a festival of sepulture;
For, what gave joy, and joy to us had owed,
Should Death affright us from, when he would her
    restore?

145

Branwell inscribed these lines in Mary Pearson's Commonplace
Book under a pen-and-ink profile of himself. Because Leyland
(II, 208) quotes these lines, Branwell must also have sent
Joseph a copy.

146

These lines accompany a set of sketches Branwell sent to
Joseph Leyland in late 1846 or January 1847 (Leyland Letters,
p. 37). Above the lines is a sketch of Branwell as a recumbent statue, resting on a slab. Below the lines is a tombstone inscribed "HIC JACET," under which appears: "'MARTINI
LIUGI IMPLORA ETERNA QUIETE!': 'Martin Luke implores for
eternal rest!' (Italian Epitaph.)"

147

Because of the similarity of page size, paper, and handwriting, Nos. **147-49** seem to have been written at roughly
the same time. Branwell likely began No. **147** in April
1846 when he wrote to Joseph Leyland asking for details of
the history of Morley Hall (Leyland Letters, p. 25). His
intention, according to Leyland, was to write an epic "in
several cantos, dealing with a succession of romantic epi-
sodes, of which an elopement that actually took place . . .
was the chief feature" (II, 242). In various subsequent
letters (June 1846, 2 July 1846, October 1846--"'Morley Hall'
is in the eighth month of her pregnancy and expects ere long
to be delivered of a fine thumping boy whom its father means
to christen Homer at the least . . . .") Branwell suggests he
is working at his epic, but he seems (despite the claim in
the October letter) never to have got beyond this portion of
the introductory canto. According to legend, Anne Leyland,
after her father forbade the connection, eloped with Edward
Tyldesley; she tied a rope around her waist and threw the
loose end across the moat to Tyldesley, who pulled her
across. The reference in the final line is to Sir Thomas

Tyldesley, a Major-General in the Royalist army, killed at
Wigan in August 1651.

148

<blockquote>

stern Marius: the Roman general, known as the saviour
of his country after protecting Rome from
the northern Barbarians, who then fought
with and was defeated by a fellow
general, Sulla, who ordered his
execution. However Marius was allowed to
flee by the soldier sent to execute him.
When he was not allowed to land at
Carthage, he sent the Governor a message
saying he had seen himself amidst the
ruins of Carthage.

Falkland: Viscount Falkland, a Royalist and close
friend of the Earl of Clarendon, tried to
exercise a moderating influence in the
struggles preceding the Civil War. As a
member of the Long Parliament he opposed
Charles I's policies and supported the
impeachment of the Earl of Stafford.
However, he opposed the bill for the aboli-
tion of the episcopacy, and became Charles'
Secretary of State after the Puritans gained
control of Parliament. Disillusioned by the
Civil War, he was killed at the Battle of
Newbury in 1643.

Hucknall Thorkard: a town three miles from Newstead
Abbey, Byron's family home. The
tomb of Byron is in the church of
St. Mary Magdalene in the town.

</blockquote>

149

The references to Anson in **148** and **149** suggest that
Branwell had read the two volumes of Anson's **Voyages** in
the Robinson's library (Gérin BB, p. 260). The word "Lydia"
in Greek in the left-hand margin opposite ll. 129-30, and a
tombstone sketched in the right margin opposite the last
three lines of No. **149**, suggest that in ll. 110ff. Branwell is again expressing his agony and despair over his
"loss" of Mrs. Robinson. Opposite ll. 21-26 he wrote in the
margin "What have I to do with him--Trace the real parallel."
George Anson commanded a poorly manned and equipped squadron
of six ships sent to the Pacific to harass Spanish shipping.
He lost three ships in the storms off Cape Horn, and finally
arrived at Juan Fernandez Island, off the coast of Chile, in

June 1741, with his remaining three ships badly damaged and only 335 out of the 961 men he had left England with. He eventually continued on in one ship (the Centurion), captured a Spanish treasure ship off Manilla, and returned to London with his prize, having sailed around the world. The island's most famous resident was Alexander Selkirk, on whose adventures Defoe based **Robinson Crusoe.**

150

The manuscript consists of four pages (one leaf folded over), but contains only the first sixteen lines on part of the first page (the remaining pages are blank). Thus these lines seem to be an earlier version of the text Branwell sent to Joseph Leyland, with the comment: "I enclose the accompanying fragment, which is so soiled that I would have transcribed it, if I had the heart to exert myself only to get from you an opinion as to whether, when finished, it would be worth sending to some respectable periodical like Blackwood's Magazine" (Leyland Letters, p. 42). The text provided is that in Leyland; the earlier version of ll. 1-16 reads:

> The westering sunshine smiled on Percy Hall
> And gilt the ivy on its aged wall
> Where Mary sat to feel the fanning breeze
> And hear it's music murmering 'mid the trees
>   She had reclined in that secluded bower   5
> Throughout the afternoon while hour on hour
> Stole softly past her, shining till the shades
> Stretched--slowly length[en]ing in the grassy
>   glades
> Yet she reclined as if she scarce knew how
> The time wore on with heaven directed brow   10
> And closing eyes which only oped wheneer
> Her face was fanned by summer's evening air
>   She seemed that day a weariness to feel
> As if upon her sleep might almost steal
> And scarce could rouse her failing thoughts to care   15
> For day or hour or what she was or where

Mary is presumably Maria Henrietta, Percy's second wife. See also No. **154.**

151

These lines occur on one side of a half page, with the other side blank; they seem to be the beginning of a poem Branwell did not develop further, or if he did, the continuation has been lost. The poem refers to the encounter between Beresford and Soult, May 16, 1811, during the Peninsular War, which in terms of the percentage of men lost was one of the bloodiest on record. Branwell may have been inspired by the reference to the battle in Scott's **The Vision of Don Roderick** (Conclusion, st. xiv) or in Byron's **Childe Harold**, I, xliii. See also No. **140**.

152

In terms of hand and content, these undated fragments seem to be related to the revisions of Angrian materials in Nos. **150, 153, 154.** Fragments (a) and (b) occur on two sides of a half page with the top half missing. Therefore (b) is a continuation of (a) with a half page missing. The third fragment occurs on the verso of No. **143;** the text is taken from Hatfield's transcription at the BPM. These fragments may be part of a continuation of No. **150,** but I have been unable to discover who Amelia is.

153 and 154

Thematically, both poems are a continuation of No. **150,** though the verse form is different. See also No. **87,** ll. 270-97. No. **153** is a fragment on a half page. The manuscript for No. **154** is untraceable; the text provided is that in the **Halifax Guardian,** June 5, 1847. An earlier version (see p. 199), originally part of Notebook C but now detached from it and bound separately, reads:

Upon that dreary winters night
   Before my angel Mary died,
I, by the fires declining light
   Sat, comfortless, and silent, sighed,
   While burst unchecked the bitter tide   5
In thoughts how I, when she was gone,
   Through many an hour like that must bide
To wake and watch and weep alone.

All earthly Hope had passed away,
   And every hour brought death more nigh   10
To the still chamber where she lay
   With looks and thoughts composed to die.
But--mine was not her heavenward eye,
But--mine was not her heavenward eye,
Whose hot tears gathered oer her doom,
   While my sick Heart throbbed heavily   15
To give impatient anguish room.

Oh now,--I thought,--A little while,
    And that great House should hold no more
Her, whose fond love the gloom could wile
    Of many a long night gone before!   20
    Oh! all those happy hours were oer
When, seated by our own fire side,
    I smiled to hear the loud wind's roar
And turned to clasp my beauteous Bride!

I could not bear the thoughts that rose   25
    Of what had been and was to be,
But, still, the darkness would disclose
    Its sorrow pictured prophecy,
    Still saw I miserable me
Long, long years hence, in lonley gloom,   30
    With time bleached locks and trembling knee,
Go, freindless, mourning to my tomb.

Still--Still--the graves eternal shade
    Oppressed my Heart with sickning fear
When I beheld its darkness spread   35
    Over each desolate coming year
    Whose long vale's filled me with despair
Till, with the sweat drops on my brow
    I wildly raised my hands in prayer
That Death would come and take me now!   40

And stopped--to hear an answer given--
    So much had madness wraped my mind--
When sudden through the midnight Heaven
    With long howl rose the winter wind
    And woke at once--all undefined--   45
A gushing thought like tumbling seas
    Whose wide waves wandering unconfined
Afar off surging, whispered--peace!--

I cannot speak the feeling strange
    Which shewed that vast and storm swept sea   50
Nor tell whence came such sudden change
    From aidless hopeless misery
    But somehow--it revealed to me
A life when all I loved was gone
    Whose solitary liberty   55
Should suit me wandering tombward on

Twas not that I forgot my love
    That night departing evermore;
Twas Hopeless greif for Her that drove
    My Soul from all it prized before   60
    Till that blast called it to explore
A new born life whose lonely joy

519

Might calm the pangs of sorrow oer
Might shrine its memory--not destroy!

I rose and drew my curtains back   65
    To gaze upon the starless waste
And image on that midnight wrack
    The path oer which I longed to haste
    from storm to storm continual cast
And not a moment given to view   70
    Oer the far winds the memories past
Of Hearts I loved and scenes I knew

My mind anticipated all
    The things these eyes have seen since then
I heard the Trumpets battle call   75
    I rode oer ranks of bleeding men
    I swept the waves of Norway's main
I tracked the sands of Syria's shore
    I felt such dangers strife and pain
Might me from living death restore   80

Ambition I would make my bride
    And joy to see her robed in red
For none through blood so wildly ride
    As those whose hearts before have bled
    Yes! even though Thou shouldst long have laid   85
All coldly pressed by churchyard clay
    Though I knew thee thus decayed
I might smile, to be away!

Might lull from greif my aching breast
    Might dream--But oh! that heart wrung groan   90
Forced from me with the thought confessed
    That all would go if she were gone!
    I turned and wept and wandered on
All restlessly from room to room
    To the still chamber where alone   95
A sick light glimmered through the gloom

There all unnoticed time flew oer me
    While I knelt beside the bed
And the life which loomed before me
    Choked my voice and bowed my head   100
    Many a word to me she said
Of that bright Heaven which shone so near
    And oft and fervently she prayed
That I might sometime meet her there

But Oh! how soon all words were over   105
    When Earth passed and paradise
Through mortal darkness seemed to hover

```
      Oer her smiling Angel eyes
      One last look she gives her lover
      One embrace before she dies                          110
      Then--while He is bowed above Her--
      She beholds him from the Skies

                      P. B. B.
                   December 15th 1837.
                      112 lines
```

Text: l. 88: "to be away" originally read "so far away";
        neither is canceled
        l. 112: originally read: "Cold her Corpse beneath
        him lies!"; neither is canceled

See also No. **150.**

155

These lines constitute pp. 5-7 of a partial notebook, with
the two sections separated by unrelated prose on the lower
half of p. 5. Pages 8 and 9 also contain verse, so badly
rubbed as to be virtually undecipher able, but p. 8 and the
top half of p. 9 seem to contain ten four-line stanzas, signed "Northangerland," with "I shall remember Thee!" as the
final line of each stanza. The lower half of p. 9 contains
thirteen lines of couplets, which may well be a continuation
of the lines on Wheelhouse, the doctor who attended Branwell
in his final illnesses. Page 10 contains two adaptations of
Burns' lines from "Had I a Cave":

```
      Falsest of womankind, canst thou declare
      All thy fond plighted vows--fleeting as air?
         To thy new lover hie,
         Laugh o'er thy perjury,
         Then in thy bosom try                             5
            What peace is there.
```


Appendix A

Branwell sent these translations to Hartley Coleridge accompanied by a letter, dated 27 June 1840, in which he
stated:

      During the delightful day which I had the honour of
      spending with you at Ambleside, [1 May] I received
      permission to transmit to you, as soon as finished, the
      first book of a translation of Horace, in order

that, after a glance over it, you might tell me whether
it was worth further notice or better fit for the fire.

I have--I fear most negligently, and amid other very
different employments--striven to translate 2 books, the
first of which I have presumed to send to you, and will
you, sir, stretch your past kindness by telling whether
I should amend and pursue the work or let it rest in
peace?

Great corrections I feel it wants, but till I feel
that the work might benefit me, I have no heart to make
them; yet if your judgment prove in any way favourable,
I will re-write the whole, without sparing labour to
reach perfection.

I dared not have attempted Horace but that I saw the
utter worthlessness of all former translations . . .
(SHB LL, I, 210).

There is some evidence to suggest that Branwell had begun
work on Book II: in Mr. Brontë's **Horace** at the BPM,
Branwell has noted at the beginning of Ode X "March 5th
1839," and at the end of Book II "P B B March 9th 1839."

Although there is no evidence that Coleridge ever
replied to Branwell's request, an incomplete draft of a
letter at the HRC indicates that he intended to do so:

Dear Bronte

I fear you have thought me unkind or forgetful in
neglecting so long to notice your letter and the enclosed
translations. Believe me, I would not be the one, and could
not be the other--but I am a sad Procrastinator. I run in
debt to Time--and debts of that nature bear compound
interest. The longer unpaid--the more difficult to pay. I
have however been wiping out a few old scores--this evening--
and though I know not whether it be today--or tomorrow--
whether Nov 30th or December 1st, I will make an
instalment to you forthwith. You are by no means the first
or the only person who has applied to me for judgement upon
their writings. I smile to think that so small an asteroid
as myself should have satellites. But you have heard the
distich--

Fleas that bite little dogs have lesser fleas that bite
    em--
The lesser fleas--have fleas still less--so on--ad
    infinitum.

Howbeit, you are--with one exception--the only young Poet in
whom I could find merit enough to comment without flattery--
on stuff enough to be worth finding fault with. I think, I

told you how much I was struck with the power and energy of
the lines you sent before I had the pleasure of seeing you.
Your translation of Horace is a work of much greater promise,
and though I do not counsel a publication of the whole--I
think many odes might appear with very little alteration.
Your versification is often masterly--and you have shown
skill in great variety of measures--There is a racy english
in your language which is rarely to be found even in the
original--that is to say--untranslated, and certainly un-
translateable effusions of many of our juveniles, which con-
sidering how thorough[ly] Latin Horace is in his turns of
phrase, and collocation of words--is a proof of sound
scholarship--and command of both languages--But we will--if
you please examine a few odes--rather critically--and
analytically.

The first is not one of Horace's best, and I must say
that it is your worst. Whatever merit it has in the
original, is in the precise word, and juncture--for which our
language cannot ever compensate. That Mecaenas, atavis edite
regibus--Had Horace set about of malice prepense to cast the
infirmities of our old mother lingo in her teeth--I could not
have done it more provokingly. For what is the English of
Atavus? Great-great-great grandfather! There is no language
which I know the least of--that is so miserably off for terms
of lineage as ours. Pater-- Avus--Proavus--Abavus--Atavus
Tritavus, is a line of Plautus which it would be impossible
to render into any modern language. I do not know whether
Horace meant to compliment Mecaenas with that precise degree
of descent from the Etruscan Monarchy but your--Sprung of
kingly line--is far too weak and vague. The feeling is much
the same as if you were to address a welsh squire as a des-
cendant of Caractacus or Howel Dha.

        Oh Davy Dean, sprung from the blood
        That was true Welsh before the flood
        And royally from sire to son
        Descended ere the world begun--

I once essayed to imitate the Ode in an irregular metre--
somewhat after this fashion

        Mecaenus--sprung of kings renownd in story--
        At once my sure defence, and pleasant glory--
        Here we that have a mighty past
        For trophies of olympic dust
        When the glowing wheels have nicely turned
        The <goal>, and the palm is nobly earnd
        Nobly earned and justly given
        It lifts the Lords of Earth to Heaven--

523

But your four lines
    Whom dust clouds drifting oer the throng

Although Branwell clearly put much effort into these
translations while he was employed as a tutor by the Postlethwaite family at Broughton-in-Furness from January to June
1, 1840 and after his return home, he had begun work on them
by Spring 1838 or earlier. Notebook C contains the following
version of the last sixteen lines of Ode XIV.

Even God--Lost Ship--in thy despair+
Will deign no answer to thy prayer
Oh! Though thou claimst a race divine
As fashioned from the pontic pine
The Noblest Daughter of the wood   5
The oldest floater on the flood--
All vain thy boast!--for Sailors now
Trust nothing to a painted prow.
Beware!--unless thou long'st to be
A Mockery to the howling sea!   10
And though of late thy very name
In me has waked no thought save shame
Yet when thy danger draws so near
My sorrow tells me--still thou'rt dear!
Oh shun the rocky Cyclades   15
That stud thy pathway through the seas!

P.B.B.   written April 30th
    Transcribed May 12th 1838.
     24 lines

+no literal translation of "Non Dii, quos iterum pressa voces
malo:" but more conformable to a modern interpretation.
P.B.B.--

Some time later (perhaps 1840) Branwell made several changes
in pencil. Above the first line he wrote "Where are thy
cords and canvas where/ Thy Gods to hearken to thy prayer,"
which he then changed to "Thou hast not one unriven sail/ Nor
God to trust when man may fail." Line 2 he changed to "To
give an answer to . . ."; l. 7 to "In vain thy boasting!--
sailors now"; in l. 9 "Beware" to "So stay"; and in l. 15
"Oh" to "So."

Notebook C also contains the following version of Ode XV.

    Twas when the Traitorous Shepherd bore
        His Royal prize away

524

In Phrygian ships to Ilions shore
    Across the Western sea

That Nereus raised his awful brow   5
    And hushed each favouring breeze
Till not a ship her path could plough
    Upon the slumbering seas

And thus did that old Sea God sing
    His prophecy of doom--   10
"Vain Man! Ill omens dost thou bring
    To thy forefather's Home

Which Greece shall seek with Armed Host
    All sworn to overwhelm
Thy pleasure stoln at such a cost   15
    And thy Ancestral Realm

Alas! what strife round Xanthus wave
    Thy Treacherous crime shall bring!
What fiery funerals oer the grave
    Of Ilion and her king!   20

See!--Pallas lays her Olive by,
    And grasps her sheild and spear,
And mounts her chariot in the sky,
    And wakes her rage for war!

In vain thy patron Godess' care   25
    Thy spirits may inspire
In vain thou combst thy curling hair
    Or wakest thy wanton lyre!

In vain mayst thou the lances thrust
    Or Ajax, following, fly;   30
For, soon,--Thy long locks trailed in dust--
    Adulterer!--Thou shalt die!

Even now, Beholdst thou Nestor grave
    And old Laertes son
And Sthenelus and Teucer brave   35
    Rush to thy downfall on

Tis Sthenelus the reins can guide
    While Noble Diomede
Greater than Tydeus at his side
    Hunts for the Adulterers head   40

Whom thou shalt fly as flies the Hind
    In vale or woodland lone

525

From the deep death bark heard behind
Of wild wolf hasting on.

Pelidean ships Pelides Arm   45
    Oer yonder fated shore
For her he loved the avenging storm
    Resistlessly shall pour

And years of ceaseless wars
    Thy deed shall wrap in flam[e]   50
Unquenched by all her blood and te[ars]
    Even Ilions very name!"

            P.B.B.   written May 1st
                      Transcribed May 12th 1838.
                      52 lines

Again Branwell made changes and additions in pencil at a
later date:

l. 1: "Treacherous" written above "traitorous"
l. 3: "Ilian" written above "Phrygian"
l. 4: "Ionnian" written below "Western"
l. 11: in the right margin: "he brings her with ill omens";
        "The <Adultress>" written above "Ill omens"
l. 12: above the line: "ill omened to thy"
l. 13: above "Which Greece," "whom Helen"
l. 14: above "All sworn," "Conjured"
l. 30: "or" changed to "of"
l. 33: above the line: "Ulysses see and Nestor"
l. 34: above the line: "Thy hapless peoples scourge"
l. 36: below the line: "Thy flying footsteps urge"
Between ll. 44 and 45, the following stanza in the margin:
    With beating heart and bated breath
        Oer Mountain stream and grove
    Was this the glory this the death
        Thy promisedst thy love
l. 47: "he loved" canceled in ink but no alternative
        offered
l. 49: "ceaseless" canceled in ink but no alternative
        offered

In all likelihood, Branwell was also, in the Spring of 1838,
working on the translations of the five odes (**IX, XI, XV,
XIX, XXXI**) he sent, along with the manuscript of **Sir
Henry Tunstall** (No. **126**), to Thomas De Quincey in April
1840 (see comment on p. 479 and De Quincey, II, 208-33).
According to Alexander Japp, however, "it is certain that
they reached De Quincey at a time of sickness and great
prostration, which may account for their having been swallow-

ed up in his vast piles of papers and never recovered till his death" (p. 212). A comparison of the versions sent to De Quincey and those sent to Coleridge indicates that Branwell made significant revisions before he sent the manuscript to Coleridge. The odes sent to De Quincey read as follows:

Horace

Ode XV Book 1.st

Twas when the treacherous shepherd bore
   His Royal prize away,
In Phrygian Ship--from Spartan Shore--
   Across the Aegean sea,

That Nereus raised his awful brow   5
   And hushed each favouring breeze,
Till not a ship its path could plough
   Upon the slumbering seas;

And thus did that Old Sea God sing
   His prophecy of doom--   10
"Vain Man! ill omened thou dost bring
   Thine hostess to thy home,

Whom Greece shall seek with mighty host
   Conjured to overwhelm
Thy pleasures, bought at such a cost,   15
   And thy Ancestral realm.

Alas! what strife round Xanthus wave
   Thy treachery shall bring!
What fiery funerals oer the grave
   Of Ilion and her King!   20

Now--Pallas lays her olive by
   And grasps her sheild and spear,
And mounts her chariot in the sky
   And wakes her rage for war.

In vain thy guardian Godess' care   25
   Thy spirits may inspire,
In vain thou combst thy curling hair,
   Or wakest thy wanton lyre;

In vain the shouts--the Lances thrust--
   Or Ajax--thou mayst fly,   30
For, with thy long locks trailed in dust,
   Adulter[er]! Thou shalt die!

Ulysses see; and Nestor grave--
    Thy hapless peoples scourge;
And Sthenelus, and Teucer brave   35
    Thy flying footsteps urge:

Tis Sthenelus the reins can guide,
    While noble Diomede
Greater than Tydeus--at his side
    Hunts for the adulterers head;   40

Whom thou shalt fly as flies the hind
    In vale or woodland lone,
From the deep death bark, heard behind,
    Of wild wolf hastening on;

With beating heart, and bated breath,   45
    Oer mountain and through grove--
Was this the victory--this the death
    Thou promisedst thy love?

Pelides' ships; Pelides' arm
    Oer Phrygia's fated shore   50
For these thy deeds, the avenging storm
    Resistlessly shall pour;

And after years of weary wars,
    Shall wrap in funeral flame,
Unquenched by all her blood and tears,   55
    Thy Ilions very name.

Book 1st. Ode XI

    Leuconoe, seek no more
    By magic arts 't explore
How long a life our God has given to thee or me:
    If we've winters yet in store;
    Of if this whose tempests roar   5
Across the Tyrrhene deep, is the <u>last</u> that we shall
    see.

    Be cheerful wisdom thine;
    Thy Goblet fill with wine;
And shape thy hopes to suit the hour that hastes
    away:
    For while we speak, that hour   10
    Is past beyond our power;
So do not trust to morrow, <u>but</u> <u>seize</u> <u>upon</u> <u>to</u> <u>day</u>.

B I. Ode IX

See'st thou not amid the skies
White with snow, Soracte rise;
While the forests on the plain
Scaroe their hoary weight sustain;
And congealed the waters stand   5
Neath the frosts arresting hand.
   Drive away the winter wild;
On the hearth be fuel piled;
And from out its sacred cell--
Kept in Sabine vase so well--   10
Generous--bring thy four years wine;
Wakener of the song divine.
   Wisely leave the rest to heaven;
Who, when warring winds have striven
With the forests, or the main,   15
Bids their raging rest again.
   Be not ever pondering
Over what the morn may bring.
Whether it be joy or pain
Wisely count it all as gain.   20
And, while age upon thy brow
Shall forbear to shed his snow;
Do not shun the dancers feet;
Nor thy loved one's dear retreat.
Hasten to the plain or square;   25
List the whisper, telling where
When the calm night rules above,
Thou mayst meet thy dearest love:
When the laugh round corner sly
Shall instruct thee where to spy: 30
When the wanton's feigned retreating
Still shall leave some pledge of meeting:
Perhaps a ring or bracelet bright,
Snatched from arm or finger white.

D Ist Ode [XXXI]

For what does the poet to Phoebus pray--
   With new wine from his vessels flowing?
Not for the flocks oer Calabria that stray;
   Nor for corn in Sardinia growing;

Nor prays he for ivory, or gold, or land   5
   Which the Liris, gently gliding,
Would crumble away into fugitive sand
   Down its silent waters sliding.

Let him gather the grapes who has planted the vine;
   Let the Merchant, whom Jupiter favours,   10
His Syrian treasures exchange for wine
   Which a golden goblet flavours:

Thrice in a season oer passing the sea;
   Nor by waters or winds prevented;
While olives and mallows shall satisfy me,   15
   With the lot fortune gives me contented.

Son of Latona! Oh grant me to taste
   The goods thou hast placed before me.
And a spirit undimmed; and an age undisgraced;
   And a Harp with whose strains to adore thee!   20

Book Ist Ode XIX

The Mother of Love and the father of wine
   And passion resuming its throne
Backward command me my mind to incline
   And kindle the flame that seemed gone
      For Glycera warms   5
      My heart with her charms
      Whiter than parian stone

Her sweet arts inflame me her countenance beams
   Too bright to be gazed upon
Till Venus departing from Cyprus seems   10
   To rush upon me alone
      And no longer my verse
      The deeds can rehearse
      By Scythian or Parthian done

Raise me an altar of living sod   15
   And crown it with garlands and bear
Wine undiluted a drink for a God
   That Glycera hearing my prayer
      May know I adore
      And be cruel no more   20
      But an answering passion declare

There are doubtless many mistakes of sense and language--
except the first--I had not when I translated them, a Horace
at hand, so was forced to rely on memory. P B Brontë

530

Index of Titles and First Lines